The Broadview Guide to Writing
revised sixth Canadian edition

A Note on the Cover

For thousands of years humans have been likening the process of writing to the ways in which we interact with the land—ploughing and digging, sowing and reaping. In the early seventh century CE Isadore of Seville tells of how the Romans for their writing used styluses that were at first made of iron, later of bone, and quotes from a now-lost Roman play by the now-unknown playwright Atta: "we shall turn the ploughshare upon wax, and plough with a bone point." Around 1400 the German poet Johannes von Tepl begins his long poem *The Ploughman of Bohemia* with a reference to what he refers to as a well-known maxim of scribes: "the quill is my plough." In some sense the quill or pen is of course like a plough in that it digs into the writing surface. But the digging can also be likened more broadly to what writing does—as Seamus Heaney famously likens it in a 1964 poem about his father's digging and what Heaney himself will do with his "squat pen."

An image of ploughing, then, connects with the substance of this book as a metaphorical image of writing. But this particular image of ploughing connects in a more specific fashion to this particular writing guide: an extended discussion of *Landscape with the Fall of Icarus* features prominently in a chapter that is new to this edition, "Seeing and Meaning: Reading (and Writing About) Visual Images." The cover image is in this case also a reminder that writing is a matter of content as well as process.

The Broadview Guide to Writing
revised sixth Canadian edition

Doug Babington, Don LePan,
Maureen Okun, and Nora Ruddock

Contributing Editor: Laura Buzzard

broadview press

BROADVIEW PRESS – www.broadviewpress.com
Peterborough, Ontario, Canada

Founded in 1985, Broadview Press remains a wholly independent publishing house. Broadview's focus is on academic publishing; our titles are accessible to university and college students as well as scholars and general readers. With over 600 titles in print, Broadview has become a leading international publisher in the humanities, with world-wide distribution. Broadview is committed to environmentally responsible publishing and fair business practices.

© 2017 Doug Babington, Don LePan, Maureen Okun, and Nora Ruddock
Reprinted with corrections 2017.

Library and Archives Canada Cataloguing in Publication

Babington, Doug, author
    The Broadview guide to writing / Doug Babington, Don LePan, Maureen Okun, and Nora Ruddock ; contributing editor: Laura Buzzard. — Revised 6th Canadian edition.

Includes bibliographical references and index.
ISBN 978-1-55481-335-3 (paperback)

    1. English language—Rhetoric—Textbooks. 2. English language—Grammar—Textbooks. 3. Report writing—Textbooks. 4. Bibliographical citations—Standards—Textbooks. I. LePan, Don, 1954-, author II. Okun, Maureen, 1961-, author III. Ruddock, Nora, author IV. Buzzard, Laura, editor V. Title. VI. Title: Guide to writing.

LB2369.B23 2016   808'.042   C2016-906252-X

Broadview Press handles its own distribution in North America
PO Box 1243, Peterborough, Ontario K9J 7H5, Canada
555 Riverwalk Parkway, Tonawanda, NY 14150, USA
Tel: (705) 743-8990; Fax: (705) 743-8353
email: customerservice@broadviewpress.com

Distribution is handled by Eurospan Group in the UK, Europe, Central Asia, Middle East, Africa, India, Southeast Asia, Central America, South America, and the Caribbean. Distribution is handled by Footprint Books in Australia and New Zealand.

Broadview Press acknowledges the financial support of the Government of Canada through the Canada Book Fund for our publishing activities.

Canada

Cover Design: Lisa Brawn
Design and Typesetting: Eileen Eckert

PRINTED IN CANADA

◎ CONTENTS

◎ HOW TO USE THIS BOOK AND ITS COMPANION WEBSITE

The goal of *The Broadview Guide* is to provide a comprehensive yet concise writing reference that is easy to use in every respect. We've made the book easy to carry around, and easy to use lying flat on a desk. We've also built in several features that we hope will make the book easy for you to find your way around in:

section dividers: Flip to the section you want using the tabs on the section dividers. Here you'll find the contents of that section.

page headers: Flip through the book with your eye on the page headers; these list section headings on the left, chapter headings on the right.

index: Go to the index at the back of the book to find the location in the book for any topic, large or small.

table of contents: The detailed table of contents at the beginning of the book sets out the sections, chapters, and topics within chapters.

The book opens with a substantial discussion of the writing process, focusing in particular on what is involved in writing essays at the university level. Like the rest of the book, this part has headers provided for ready reference, but we recommend reading it in its entirety.

If you are using this book as a reference for essay writing, you may wish to pay particular attention to the sample essays provided:

- the sample essay in MLA format reproduced on pages 605–32 is an example of essay style and structure, as well as format and referencing style; the essay is continually referred to as an example during the discussion of the essay-writing process (pages 17–94).
- the sample essay in APA format reproduced on pages 659–76 will also be helpful for all who are required to use APA style in any of their courses.

The purchase price of this book includes free access to *The Broadview Guide to Writing* website, where you will find various sorts of

11

material related to this book. (If you have purchased a used rather than a new copy, you may purchase a passcode online through the main Broadview Press website.) Perhaps most importantly, the companion website includes a wide range of exercises relating to almost every aspect of grammar and usage. Many of these are interactive; you can check immediately if you have answered correctly, and—if you haven't—find an explanation. (Instructors may of course ask that you complete particular exercises and hand in your score sheet to them, but we encourage you to try the exercises on your own as well—especially in areas that the Diagnostic and Review Exercises suggest may not be areas of strength for you.)

You will also find several other sorts of material on *The Broadview Guide to Writing* companion website:

- a selection of expository essays, ranging from Montaigne to the present day, each accompanied by questions and topics for discussion.
- links to a variety of other helpful sites.
- complete sample essays in Chicago and CSE formats, as well as additional complete essays in MLA and APA formats.

This book does *not* provide certain features that you will find in most other writing guides and handbooks: glossy paper that is both expensive and environmentally unfriendly, and highlighting in many different colours throughout the book. We have added one accent colour, but we have no desire to add more—or to move away from our long-standing policy of using plain (and, as much as possible, recycled) paper stock. That's a choice that's good for the environment—and also one that helps us keep the price of this book at a level little more than half that of most other writing guides or handbooks.

If you have questions or comments about *The Broadview Guide* (or suggestions as to what else we should consider including for future editions, whether on the website or in the bound book), we'd like to hear from you. Just email customerservice@broadviewpress.com. Thank you!

◎ PREFACE TO THE REVISED SIXTH CANADIAN EDITION

As with every new edition, the revised sixth edition of *The Broadview Guide to Writing* has been fully updated throughout, with many small changes made. But there are also large changes; indeed, this edition has been revised and rewritten more fully than has been the case for any previous new edition. These are some of the changes:

- The revised sixth edition has been fully updated to reflect the 2016 changes to the MLA style of documentation.

- The material on research has been fully rewritten so as to give students practical advice that reflects the realities of the digital age.

- The material on argument has been expanded and revised. More attention is now paid both to the rhetoric of academic arguments and to paragraphing and essay structure.

- Coverage of MLA, APA, Chicago, and CSE styles of referencing has been substantially expanded, with material covering electronic sources now fully integrated with material covering print sources. Complete sample papers in both MLA and APA style are included.

- Coverage of how to cite sources and how to integrate quotations into a research paper has also been expanded.

- The reference guide to basic grammar (formerly an appendix) has been brought into the body of the book.

- Far more material on the conventions of writing in different academic disciplines is now included, with full chapters on Writing about Literature/Writing about Texts and on Writing About Science.

- The coverage of language and issues relating to gender, race, religion, sexual orientation and so on has been substantially expanded, and now forms a separate chapter ("How to Be Good with Words").

- A new chapter, "Seeing and Meaning: Reading (and Writing about) Visual Images" provides wide-ranging coverage of a topic now widely taught at the introductory level.

As with every edition, the authors are indebted to a great many academics who have used *The Broadview Guide* with their students and have taken the time to comment and to offer suggestions. Our thanks to all of you! We encourage you to be in touch as well if you would like to suggest ways in which we might further improve the book in the future.

◎ INTRODUCTION

Selecting symbols and arranging them (in the case of English, left to right, top to bottom) so that they communicate sensibly is every writer's occupation. Nothing more, in the end. But at the beginning, and at every step along the way, the experiences of writers can be very frustrating and uncertain, whether they work in journalism, business, the performing arts, advertising, sports, politics, or—where so many really get their start—at a university or college, writing essays.

Because it deals with writing, *The Broadview Guide* looks at ways of handling frustration and uncertainty. But a grim primer on pain-survival it certainly is not. Satisfaction, discovery—and even playfulness—are all part of the demanding and worthwhile experience shared by capable writers in every field of professional endeavour; we hope we have succeeded in reflecting at least something of all of these.

If it is true that a wide range of feelings can be part of the writing process, it is also true that writing itself can be a wide range of things. It would be impossible to provide complete guidance in a single book to all the sorts of writing that are commonly found in academic environments—let alone to creative writing, journalism, and the rest. Of necessity, some degree of focus is required. Part One of *The Broadview Guide* discusses the process of writing an academic essay, with a particular focus on the sorts of discourse and argumentation that are common to many academic disciplines in the humanities and social sciences. Frequent reference is made throughout this part of the text to the sample essay in MLA style ("What Limits to Freedom?") that is included later in the book. But a recognition that the style adopted for an essay in a humanities or social science discipline is not the only discursive or argumentative style in the academic world is fundamental to *The Broadview Guide*'s approach. So too is a recognition that, even within the humanities and social sciences, students will find many different sets of conventions regarding such matters as style of writing and structure of argument. We thus include an extended (and, for this edition, substantially expanded) treatment of Writing Across the Disciplines, providing in that section of the book far more information on the conventions of writing in a variety of different disciplines than is the norm in guides of this sort. Also new to this edition is a full chapter on Writing about Science, as well as a full-length research paper in APA style—the latter provided in the same spirit as the sample MLA research paper, as a model of a particular style of discourse as well as a sample of citation practice. And, just as we present two full sample essays, we offer dual coverage of such matters as how to integrate quotations into an argument. Certain principles are of course common to essays in many different disciplines (have a clear structure, focus in each paragraph on a clearly defined topic, don't make unsupported claims, and so on). But there are also important differences; so it is that in our treatment of MLA and APA styles, for example, we draw attention to ways in which the styles differ from each other in matters that go beyond the placing of commas and parentheses.

As do other handbooks, *The Broadview Guide* devotes considerable space to grammar, usage, and a range of other mechanical and stylistic issues. We aim for a common-sense approach; the emphasis throughout is on showing through example. In presenting the examples, we use a "needs checking" and "revised" structure that is designed to encourage students to focus on the process of revising and improving their writing. And, by choosing examples from highly respected writers as well as from student writing, we attempt to underscore the point that *everyone's* writing can benefit from careful checking and revision; no student should be demoralized by the presence of imperfections in a final draft—let alone a first one. The process of working towards better writing is always ongoing; it may never be easy, but it can be tremendously rewarding.

◎ THE WRITING PROCESS

⊙ Voice Work

Academic writing is easy to spot, even when it appears well beyond the academic world. Take, for instance, "The Brain of Brawn," a baseball article written by the late Stephen Jay Gould of Harvard University. Gould presents a thoughtful analysis of second baseman Chuck Knoblauch's difficulty in making accurate throws to his New York Yankee teammate over at first base. The writer asserts that "one of the most intriguing, and undeniable, properties of great athletic performance lies in the impossibility of regulating certain central skills by overt mental deliberation: the required action simply doesn't grant sufficient time for the sequential processing of conscious decisions" (17). He goes on to point out that "one form of unwanted, conscious mentality may be intruding upon a different and required style of unconscious cognition."

Knoblauch's manager and coaches wouldn't have expressed themselves in quite the same manner, even if they agreed with Gould. Their voices would probably be much less formal, less abstract, less rigorous in distinguishing between, say, *mentality* and *cognition*. In other words, their voices would be less academic.

Formal phrasing, abstract language, and logical rigour certainly contribute to a recognizably academic *voice*. In writing university essays, however, it is tempting to rely excessively on these characteristics: you may end up using plenty of fancy words without presenting a clear argument; or you may create a magnificent deductive path that carries the reader far, far away from the announced topic.

Another challenge in establishing an appropriate voice is, of course, the fact that reading and writing are predominantly silent endeavours. A speaking voice has little in common with a writing voice, as Louis Menand explains:

> In fact, speech is characterized by all the things writing teachers
> tell students to eliminate from their prose in the interest of clar-
> ity: repetition, contradiction, exaggeration, run-ons, fragments,

and clichés, plus an array of tonal and physical inflections—drawls, grunts, shrugs, winks, hand gestures—unreproducible in written form. People talk for hours without uttering a single topic sentence. (94)

By contrast, essay-writers must always deal with the necessity of topic sentences, not to mention the impossibility of winking or grunting in the middle of a paragraph.

Such pressure can drain the voice of a good writer, just as pressure drains the throw of a good second baseman: "Knoblauch's problem takes the same form as many excruciating impediments in purely mental enterprises with writer's block as the most obvious example, when obsession with learned rules of style and grammar impedes the flow of good prose." Gould is a successful writer who knows better than to become obsessed by learned rules of style and grammar. Important as those rules are, it is far better—at the outset of the writing process—to approach your essay as an opportunity for clear and fluent expression of independent, informed thinking. In other words, concentrate on developing a *voice* that will enhance your own ideas, acknowledge the needs of your readers, and make clear the main reason for the essay's existence.

O Attitude

One key to successfully putting forward your own ideas in writing is a mental *attitude* of self-confidence. A competent writer's voice is born from a position of power over the assignment at hand, the resources at hand, and the deadline that looms ahead. If no real power is felt to exist, then it's worth trying to manufacture it:

> "Three-thousand words in five days? Not a problem."
> "There are definitely ways in which Milton's verse disappoints me."
> "This professor of mine is about to really learn something."

Of course, establishing full control at the outset of the writing process is impossible. "How do I know what I think," wrote E.M. Forster, "until I see what I have to say?" The point is that writers see what they have to say—they start writing—only by believing in themselves. Some manufactured power at the outset will lead to real power along the way.

Weak writing, then, can often be traced to an attitude problem. The passive writer-in-waiting views his or her blank pages like some ominous battlefield whose land mines will commence exploding with the first timid step forward. Passiveness and timidity combine to abort the writer's fledgling voice. But **active** confrontation with an assignment, however tough that assignment may first appear, allows the voice to grow. As one sociology professor advises (in notes distributed to all her students),

> In writing the work, do not be afraid to give your own views. It is of considerable interest to the tutor to know what students think about the material, and especially what they think they have learned from the exercise. If you find material obscure or unconvincing say so, but always give the reasons.

O *Audience*

Attention to attitude, which gives birth to a writer's voice, is often followed by attention to audience, which modifies that voice. Competent writers realize the danger of locking themselves in to any set formulas of style or organization—because these things often change, depending upon the demands or expectations of a given audience. Different academic disciplines have different conventions for writing, and for structuring academic work. Beyond that, different instructors within a single academic discipline may favour quite different aproaches to writing. What's a writer to do? Listen carefully, for one thing, and ask questions. Look over past essays written for similar audiences. Conformity to reasonable audience expectations does not mean slavish imitation. Ideas can be strong and original, and evidence can be compelling, even as a writer writes to please, say, the grammatical or bibliographical preferences of his or her reader-to-be.

Two examples from the world of academic publishing illustrate the sort of concessions good writers make to their audiences—and point up something important about the matter of writing introductions to essays. Here are introductory paragraphs from two articles, both of which appeared in publications that are aimed at a general academic audience. The first appeared in the Canadian journal *Queen's Quarterly*, the second in *The New York Review of Books*. First, from Susan P.C. Cole's "The Legacy of Terry Fox":

> More than nine years have elapsed since Terry Fox began his run across Canada to raise money for cancer research and eight years have passed since his death from the disease he sought to conquer. The events of the early 1980s surrounding Terry's Marathon of Hope can now be viewed with some perspective, and one might begin to answer a number of questions. Could the medical profession do more for Terry if he were alive today than they were able to do when he was first stricken with cancer? How has the money raised been spent? What has been the impact of his run on the efforts of the cancer research community in Canada? Has Terry's dream been kept alive? This article will address these questions and discuss the influence of Terry Fox and his Marathon of Hope on cancer research in Canada. (253)

Second, from Garry Wills's "The Negro President" (an article summarizing for a wider readership the argument of his own book on the same topic):

> I have admired Jefferson all my life, and still do.... But I have now devoted an entire book to one deadly part of his legacy— the protection and extension of slavery through the three-fifths clause in the Constitution. That work depends on the general and growing labour of modern historians to grasp the pervasiveness of slavery's effects on early American history. I don't mean to join an unfortunate recent trend toward Jefferson-bashing. I disagree with those who would diminish his great achievement, the Declaration of Independence (Maier 1997). Or those who call him more a friend to despotism than to freedom (Cruise O'Brien 1996). Or those who would reduce his whole life to an affair with a slave. My Jefferson is a giant, but a giant trammeled in a net, and obliged, he thought, to keep repairing and strengthening the coils of that net. (45)

Cole is a pharmacologist, used to writing for other scientists, while Wills is a historian, used to writing for other humanists. Not surprisingly, given this background, their approaches to writing introductory paragraphs differ. After clearly announcing her topic, the scientist poses a series of relevant questions and then confirms for her readers what the article will accomplish. (She would be in trouble with the English professor who instructs his students to "avoid telling the reader about your writing; stick to your topic instead. Cut phrases such as *We will examine* and *This paper will show that*.") The humanist also begins with a clear announcement of his topic, but that is where the similarity ends. He immediately carves out the argumentative territory of his essay, stating his topic in his second sentence, and then summarizing a range of opposing views before presenting his own thesis statement (20) in the final sentence of the paragraph. (Wills would find more favour with the English professor: "I consider it conventional, and therefore essential, that your thesis be stated in the last sentence of paragraph one.")

Like most scientific writers, Susan Cole saves her argumentative assertions—the answers to questions posed in the introductory paragraph—for the "Conclusion" of her article. Again, this bottom-heavy approach, which contrasts with the top-heavy approach of Wills, is related to the discipline the writer works in. Yet neither Cole nor Wills ignores the wider profile of the *Queen's Quarterly* and *New York Review of Books* readership; both publications are intended to appeal to a broad, interdisciplinary readership.

Certainly, the more diverse the audience, the more freedom a writer may enjoy in decisions of organization and style. Many university essay-writers tend to err, however, in the other direction: by envisioning an audience of one—namely, the professor responsible for the assignment. Even if she may, in fact, be the only one who will read the paper, it is better to write not only for the professor but also for one's peers, for the other people in the lecture hall or classroom, so as to avoid unnaturally stilted language and overly grandiose assertions. In writers' worlds, the most successful voices are the least strained.

O *Purpose: From Topic to Thesis Statement*

Each writer requires a purpose, one that is more than the mere desire to earn this month's salary or this term's B+ in history.

The stated assignment is an obvious place to begin. "Discuss the rise to power of Francisco Franco." Or "Thoroughly explain the advances in medical imaging since the beginning of this century." Or "Analyse the connections between Margaret Atwood's poetry and her novels." Very few writers are absolutely free to devise their own purposes. Most receive orders or commands (*Discuss, Explain, Analyse*), either from some external figure of authority or from inside their own writerly consciences. Such commands are usually quite vague and open-ended, though. It's enough to make an honest writer quiver and squirm:

> How am I supposed to discuss the rise to power of Francisco Franco? That could take years! And what is "Discuss" supposed to mean? Do I tell the story of the Spanish Civil War? Do I try to ascertain Franco's psychological makeup, or to analyse socio-economic influences at work at the time? How does my professor feel; what exactly is she expecting with this paper, anyway?

If she's a professor who really cares about writing, she's expecting some tension to be located and resolved. Purpose in writing comes from tension, from the writer's personal sense of things out of kilter, in conflict:

> This clash engenders puzzlement, curiosity, a sense of enigma, sometimes of wonder, a pressure to restore equilibrium. While some people suppress such tension, the inquirer, the learner, strives to resolve it by searching for new understanding, by going beyond the known. (Lauer 90)

What Janice Lauer is actually recommending here is an attitude of risk; "the inquirer, the learner" confronts the essay topic in much the same way that King Lear confronts his stormy heath or Alice confronts her Wonderland. Worthy purposes are often a little off-beat, a little idiosyncratic. They turn otherwise formulaic, encyclopedia-entry essays into essays of personally distinct intellect.

Competent writers can write personally without being subjective and intellectually without being pretentious or false.

What if (returning to Francisco Franco) a prospective writer is bothered by the whole notion of "power" in the world of Spanish politics and warfare? Ignoring that abstract and difficult word might very well short-circuit her ability to handle the assignment—whereas grappling with its definition (see page 51) might be sufficient purpose to set her writing in gear. Rather than half-heartedly narrate a string of events from the 1930s or merely list the political parties of that era, she would be motivated to write by the tension and ambiguity surrounding a single word in the assignment. Focusing on the nature of power might lead the writer to her thesis statement:

- Like most fascists, Franco saw power as an end in itself, not merely as a means to achieving other ends.

Unlike the topic, the **thesis statement** expresses an argumentative purpose and a point of view. It should be meaningful, clear, and concise—typically, according to most authorities, no more than a sentence or two. In certain contexts, however (such as when complex and subtle arguments are being expressed), it may be helpful to extend the "thesis statement" over a full paragraph, setting out a series of claims.

A thesis statement need not declare anything earth-shattering, but it should not be trivial or self-evident. Effective thesis statements are moulded to fit both the length of the essay and the expertise of its writer. There is no logical sense in asserting, at the outset of a 3,000-word history paper, that *every military leader since Attila the Hun has repeated his mistakes*. The vocabulary of absolutes (*every, all, best, only*, etc.) commits a writer to universal coverage—and authoritative knowledge—of the topic. Strength in argumentative writing often comes from a willingness to qualify assertions and to acknowledge that contrary points of view are, if not convincing, at least intelligent and comprehensible. Words such as *often, usually,* and *largely,* and phrases such as *for the most part,* and *to a great extent* are not necessarily signs that the writer lacks the courage of her convictions; more frequently they are indications that she is careful.

All of the above rests on one important presupposition—that the writing assignment is clear to the student. What if you are uncertain not only about what the professor wants, but also about what she means? After all, the language of assignments, like academic language generally, is often difficult. Here, for example, is the gloss to an assignment provided by a sociology professor:

> The assignment involves learning to think sociologically and to present a sociological argument. The process involved is analogous to "inductive" reasoning (or what some sociologists refer to as "grounded theory") in that the object is to start from where you are and refine your thinking such that you develop general statements that represent the character of human social activity and that are capable of being treated with reference to empirical reality.

No student should be ashamed of asking for clarification here. In fact, it would be far worse to plunge blindly ahead, hoping against hope that your professor might not notice how much your sentences squirm. The language of intellectual discourse involves concepts, all of which are made up of abstract nouns—words representing things that cannot be seen or heard or appreciated by any physical sense. Consequently, concepts are difficult to grasp, especially when the abstract noun is preceded by an equally abstract adjective: *empirical reality*, for example, or *sociological argument*, or (turning to this very paragraph) *intellectual discourse*. Grappling independently with difficult concepts is central to anyone's higher education. Nevertheless, uncertainty and confusion may strike even the most experienced of writers. So always keep your lines of communication open. Talk over the assignment with fellow students, writing tutors, and teaching assistants, as well as with professors.

⊙ Before the Writing Starts: Essential Activities

Something's been bothering Melissa Davis, ever since she received her "Effective Writing" essay assignment: "Discuss and examine a case that raises issues of social or cultural importance in North America. Include in your essay references to both popular and scholarly discussions of the issue." Selecting a general topic wasn't a problem; she had always been interested in the issue of censorship and freedom of expression. But what specific case should she focus

Thesis Statements: Some Examples

needs checking   Art is important to society in many ways, and I will talk about them in this essay. One of the artists I will focus on is Robert Mapplethorpe, the subject of much controversy over many years.

(Yawn. The statement is too general and too vague to have significance.)

revised   The art of Robert Mapplethorpe deserves to be exhibited—and at public expense—even if most people find it abhorrent.

(This statement is more precise, more limited, more interesting.)

needs checking   In this paper I will examine various reasons for launching the war in Kosovo in 1999.

(This is a statement of topic rather than of thesis. It's also wordy.)

revised   The moral case for the US and its allies to wage a bombing-only war against Yugoslavia in 1999 was stronger than the strategic one; air attacks alone had never before been enough to win a war.

(Suddenly an argument is being made.)

needs checking   The purpose of this essay is to explore the interplay between poetry and the novel. I will demonstrate that good poets don't usually write good novels and vice versa.

(Full points for ambition, but it's the subject for a book, not a term paper. At most, a short paper might justifiably speculate about such a large question in its conclusion; the main focus should be much narrower. Also, the statement is far too bold in its generalization. "What about Thomas Hardy?" the professor will ask. "What about Boris Pasternak?")

revised   Ondaatje's characters seem thin and unreal to the reader—alternately brittle and transparent. Paradoxically, however, it may be precisely these qualities that allow the poetic power of his prose—at once brutal and fragile—to strike the reader with full force.

(A much narrower but still controversial thesis exploring the connections between poetry and prose.)

on? She had been extraordinarily interested in the 2013 case of an art student in Calgary who, as part of a project on the art of protest, had killed and eviscerated a chicken in front of other students in the college cafeteria. It was a case that had aroused intense debate over freedom of expression, but Melissa finally decided against making it the central subject of her essay. She had strong feelings about a range of issues to do with the food humans consume and with cruelty towards non-human animals—issues that, in the 2013 Calgary case, were powerfully entangled with the issue of freedom of expression. She realized that she would be better off to keep her focus clearly on freedom of expression; with that in mind she started googling, looking for a classic case that might make a good focus for discussion. She found a number of references to a highly controversial episode involving a painting of the Virgin Mary by Chris Ofili which had incorporated feces into the artwork; this had been part of a notorious 1999 exhibition at the Brooklyn Museum, entitled simply "Sensation." Much as Melissa believed in freedom of speech and of expression, the more she tried to imagine a "painting" of this sort the more unsettled she felt. Others had clearly shared that feeling; the issue had inspired heated debate, with spirited defences of free speech on one side, and on the other side heated condemnations of art galleries "feeding from the public trough to finance ... hate art targeting Christians" (Schlafly). Melissa didn't find the idea of this sort of art to be very appealing, but nor did she find the polemical attacks on it convincing. She began, then, with a desire to sort out her own gut reaction. In other words, Melissa Davis had a purpose in writing. Exactly how she would sort out either her own feelings or the various arguments was initially far from clear.

The final draft of Melissa's essay on freedom of expression (pages 605–32) is exactly that: the *final* residue of an intense thinking process, during which the purpose in her gut found articulate expression in a thesis and in the material supporting it. This mental refinement—from purpose to ideas—is usually the most mysterious and satisfying phase of the writing process: "The initial delight is in the discovery of something I didn't know I knew," the poet Robert Frost once said, realizing from long experience how completely writing and thinking grow together—mutually supportive and absolutely bound.

○ Reading and Note-taking

First among activities that assist writers in discovering their own thoughts is *reading*. According to another celebrated American poet, Walt Whitman, it requires no less self-confidence and self-assertion than writing itself:

> Books are to be call'd for, and supplied, on the assumption that the process of reading is not a half-sleep, but, in the highest sense, an exercise, a gymnast's struggle; that the reader is to do something for himself, must be on the alert, must himself or herself construct indeed the poem, argument, history, metaphysical essay—the text furnishing the hints, the clue, the start or framework. Not the book needs so much to be the complete thing, but the reader of the book does. (par. 129)

The question of *what* to read is discussed below under "Collaboration and Research." Just as important is *how* to read. As Whitman's remarks imply, it is essential to be able to read actively rather than passively—to be prepared to make connections, be able to extend the ideas you are presented with, and to be able to question those ideas. In the case of Melissa Davis's research, it was important to be able to discern the underlying assumptions both of those who called Ofili's work an "assault on religion" and of those who condemned any limits to government funding for the arts as censorship. It was important as well, of course, to weigh the arguments presented by all sides against the evidence. Through this sort of reading it becomes clear that there is no such thing as a frozen, immutable text whose message can be unlocked only by a single, privileged reading. Rather, each reader has the opportunity to construct the text anew, provided that he or she is paying close attention to the words on the page. Even when faced with assigned chapters by renowned scholars, the reader must be ready to respond independently. Whitman is right: reading is valuable because it provides "the hints, the clue, the start or framework" of the reader's own understanding of the text.

In practice, this means taking notes. As work begins for many a writer, paper and pencil are nearby. Or paper and pen, or laptop computer. Thoughts and insights can strike at any time, but they also have a way of evaporating quickly—so it's wise to be prepared. From the word "*Go!*", writing things down is central to the writing process. Some reading writers favour the pencil-in-the-margin approach, which yields brief and pointed reactions (such as "Bad logic" or "?" or "!" or "Yes!" or "Ho hum"). Others keep sheets of paper handy, to work up some preliminary sentences—or even paragraphs. Either way, the objective is to use reading as a catalyst in the discovery of one's own ideas. (Another important function of note-taking—namely, as a research tool—will be discussed later in the book, on pages 554–55.)

For many people who are reading to survive at universities, though, note-taking seems like a utopian luxury enjoyed in some distant time warp. There are simply too many pages of too many books and articles to plough through. Among such burdened readers, the most fortunate and effective are those who hang on to their pens by forfeiting some text: they *do* take notes, but they read selectively. Before ploughing through anything in an assigned reading, they skim over the introduction, the lead sentences of paragraphs, and the conclusion. In other words, they conduct a reconnaissance mission, based on strategic knowledge of most essays' terrains. The likely result is an accurate sense of the essay's thesis, key terminology, range of evidence, and logical organization. Such readers will then select passages for sustained and thorough surveillance, according to their own purposes.

O *Mapping*

In the beginning, when the task at hand is choosing a topic or developing material for a thesis, an essay-writer's thinking may be quite unstructured. Indeed, it's beneficial to play with ideas, to think freely, and to take rough notes based on whatever comes to mind. Rather than sit for hours mulling over an assignment sheet, better to see what can be discovered by putting pen to paper—or fingers to keyboard.

As the topic comes into focus, though, a bit more structure is needed; the writer begins working on the details of his argument. Of course, those very details may change as the writing process moves

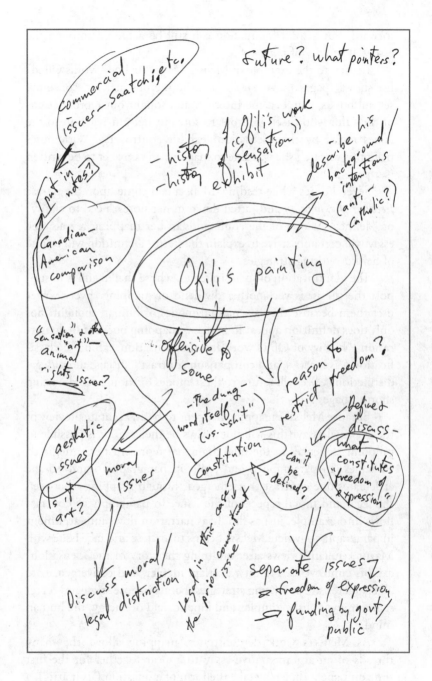

forward, but a solid foundation can still be achieved through the essential activity of *mapping*.

Return to the example of Melissa Davis. As her "Works Cited" list shows (pages 628–32), she read numerous articles, consulted several books, searched the Internet, and sought out reproductions of the Ofili work itself in order to sort out her gut reaction to the issues raised by the "Sensation" exhibit controversy. With notes from this research she was able to map out an essay yet to be written (see page 29).

Several times while reading, Melissa had come upon the phrase *freedom of expression* and jotted down in her notes "need to clarify" or "define." As one of the commands in her mapping reveals, the essay will certainly strive to explain that term. Definition will be one of her key writing strategies.

The identification of such strategies, whose shared aim is to support the thesis, is yet another dividend of mapping. Every writer uses them because they are natural modes of human thought: not only does **definition** appear in Melissa's mapping out, but so do **narration** ("history of Ofili's work and the 'Sensation' exhibit"), **classification** ("is it art?"), and **comparison contrast** ("discuss moral/legal distinction"). We will return to these modes of thought and writing shortly (pages 49–57).

Because Melissa's mapping happens to be an accurate preview of the eventual essay (this will not always be the case), it is possible to pinpoint sentences in the final draft that represent her anticipated strategies. In paragraph 6 and again in paragraphs 9 and 10 she articulates one **contrast** that emerged through mapping—between the legal and moral aspects of the issue. In paragraph 10 **contrast** flows into example, just as fluidly as **narration** flows into **argument** in paragraph 5—where Melissa begins to analyse and take issue with Mayor Giuliani's views after outlining the story of the "Sensation" exhibit controversy. Fluidity, overlap, merger, and convergence are all characteristic of writing strategies, because those strategies represent a miraculously complex and kinetic field of energy: the human mind.

As Melissa's work demonstrates, mapping allows the many threads of an argumentative essay to appear together for the first time on paper. They may take the form of a question ("is it art?"), a key image (the dung itself), or a sub-topic (the issue of prior commitment). All of them, however, connect ultimately to the biggest idea of all—Melissa's thesis concerning freedom of expression. Its two-pronged appearance on the map carries over to the final draft (at the end of paragraph one): *Along the way cultural conservatives have raised legitimate concerns about the obligation of any society to provide funding for activities of which it disapproves; a greater concern, however, is that a free society continue to provide opportunities for the free expression both of artistic vision and controversial thought.* This sentence constitutes the thesis statement.

O Writer's Block

Of course, not even the most thorough of essay-maps can guarantee a smooth journey; always lurking on the horizon are the frustrations of writer's block. Almost all of us know the experience of sitting down to write, notes and outlines and books close at hand. Then uncertainty strikes: "Perhaps my plan needs a bit more tinkering. What was it again that Smith and Sapsucker said about all this? Maybe I should go back and reread that passage. Maybe I should get a new pen to write with—or take a few minutes to find some motivating music to listen to while I write this essay. Actually, a coffee might help." Students aren't the only ones susceptible to writer's block. Many's the time that a professor will say, "I'm working on a paper dealing with such and such. It's pretty much done; all I have to do is write it up." The prof knows as well as the student that this is a convenient fiction—that the writing is the main business, not merely an afterthought. Sometimes, though, the task just seems too daunting.

How can the affliction of writer's block be avoided? As mentioned at the outset of this section, the free play of ideas is one antidote. Just force that pen to move across the paper (or those keyboard keys to start clicking), quite literally writing anything that comes to mind, whether coherent or not, whether on or off topic. After ten or fifteen minutes, usable material will have turned up. The writing won't, of course, display perfect grammar, spelling, or punctuation—nor will it be organized into coherent paragraphs. But at this stage none of that matters.

Once a writer has begun writing fluidly on the topic, it does *not* pay to pause when she hits a point in the argument that requires an example or a reference that's not handy. Instead, she should jot down a note in the margin ("find example—Taylor's book?" or "support this with quotation—gravediggers' scene?") and keep on going. There will be plenty of time later to check for the required item, and chances are that doing so now will mean losing the flow of the argument.

Eventually the moment comes to set down the pen for a few minutes and take stock of the words on the page or the screen: to decide how much fits in, and where, what needs fleshing out, what should be scrapped. It may be the time to start revising the map in the light of what's been discovered while writing. For, as every experienced writer knows, writing is *not* simply a process of putting down on paper what is already known in the writer's mind. The very act of writing forces the writer, inevitably (but often quite unexpectedly), to see things differently, to combine ideas in unanticipated ways.

O *Dialogue*

Reading and mapping are two essential activities for the essay writer; dialogue with others is a third. Its importance is continually demonstrated these days by the success and rapid growth of writing centres at universities throughout North America. Here are a few impressions from Queen's University students, following one-to-one sessions with writing tutors:

- "I had a chance to explain what I wanted to convey. My tutor had a chance to look at my essay and then together we made progress based on her suggestions."

- "I liked the fact that I wasn't told what to do—it was more a discussion about possibilities. But I was also given excellent suggestions and advice on things that I was concerned about, such as my paragraph transitions."

- "I appreciate having someone new look over my work to give me a fresh perspective. Her helpful, clear comments will really aid me when I go back to revise my work."

Such dialogue is immediately encouraging for a serious essay-writer, who can step away from his solitary turbulence and benefit from an attentive eye and sympathetic heart (writing centre tutors tend to be writers themselves!). As the Queen's students express, a conversation about your essay can be a truly collaborative exercise, one that places your work in a new light. Sometimes the simplest of gestures—such as hearing your paper read aloud by another person—will lead to revisions that might never have occurred otherwise.

Certainly a writing tutor may clarify the proper use of the semi-colon or answer some other question of English usage (such as those discussed elsewhere in this book). But productive dialogue goes far beyond the details of proofreading; its real value lies in the mutual encouragement of two writers' minds. Together they can travel further than either one alone.

Often, though, it may not be possible to see someone at a writing centre about each essay. One should also be ready and willing to show one's writing to friends, classmates—and of course instructors—at any stage. Too often we look at our work as sacrosanct; we are embarrassed by its weaknesses, shy of showing it to others before it's what we like to think of as perfect. And if at that late stage others see imperfections, we are too easily hurt. Ironically, the more experienced and confident a writer is, the more she is usually willing and eager to seek out dialogue—and criticism—from others. She has developed even within herself a critical stance towards her work; she knows it is not and will never be perfect, but she knows as well that dialogue with others is always a way to improvement, and is in itself a stimulating and enjoyable activity.

⊙ Logical Fluency: The Nature of Argument

Smooth, easy flow. Effortless movement. In a word, fluency—something that we aim for in any finished piece of writing. As all experienced writers know, however, the appearance of effortlessness and ease is superficial; the final draft of an essay is an opaque surface, showing readers none of the turbulence that is so much a part of the writing process.

We tend to think of fluency in writing as purely a matter of writing *style*—of diction, syntax, rhythm, of the way in which the words flow together on a sentence by sentence basis. But it is just as important that the ideas of an essay flow smoothly from one to the other as that the sentences do so. Assertions need to be clearly supported by reasons, and those reasons need to be convincing. "Try to be more clear, convincing, and logical in future papers," advises many a well-meaning professor. Easier said than done.

The flow of one's argument and the flow of one's writing, then, are intimately connected. How can a written argument be structured so that it flows smoothly and logically from one point to the next? One fruitful approach to answering that question is to look at the nature of argument and the nature of the paragraph side by side.

What precisely is an argument, anyway? How is it different from just saying what you feel, or what you believe?

When people use the noun *argument* in everyday speech, of course, they tend to use it in this sense: *a heated exchange of opposing views.* This type of argument tends to be angry and loud and not very well reasoned. To speak of the argument of an essay, however, or of an argument presented in a debate, is to use the noun *argument* in a different sense: *a reason or set of reasons presented in order to persuade others.*

Here is the beginning of an argument in the first sense:

> "I can't believe marijuana is still illegal; our government is really stupid!"
> "You're stupid to smoke it! You just want everyone to be as stupid as you are."
> "You're stupid if you think marijuana makes a person stupid."
> "Oh, go ahead: smoke your brain out. See if I care."

Notice that neither person here is advancing arguments in the second sense of that word. They are making assertions, they are hurling insults at each other, and they are ascribing motivations for the views the other person is asserting. But they are not providing reasons for what they believe—let alone putting a series of reasons together into a coherent whole.

For the sort of argument that is a reason or set of reasons presented in order to persuade others, then, it is not enough simply to assert what you feel. An argument in this sense may be passionately advanced, or even scathing, but it is not angry; it aims to bring light, not heat. An argument explains; draws distinctions; considers possible exceptions to generalizations; provides evidence; asks questions, suggests answers—and responds to objections. An argument is alert for ambiguities and contradictions. An argument tries to consider a range of different possibilities—often including hypothetical possibilities that may help to clarify the ideas involved. But an argument in this sense is never open-ended: it must always lead to a conclusion.

How does one construct this sort of argument in writing? There are many ways in which that question can be answered; a little further on we will discuss at some length various modes of thought that may be involved in constructing arguments (*cause and effect, classification, generalization*, and so on). But in another sense there is a one-word answer to the question *How does one construct an argument?*—with paragraphs.

○ *Argument Structure, Paragraphing, and Topic Sentences*

On what basis is writing divided into paragraphs? We should be careful to note that different principles apply to narrative, descriptive, and persuasive writing (see pages 49–57, 263–64). But most essay writing for undergraduates is persuasive writing—writing that aims to present an argument. As it happens, it's with persuasive writing that the structuring of paragraphs is both most difficult and most important. The paragraph is the structural unit of argument in an essay of this sort. And in such essays paragraphs come in three basic types: body paragraphs, which comprise the bulk of the essay; introductory paragraphs; and concluding paragraphs. In order to keep things clear both in the mind of the writer (as the essay is being composed) and in the mind of the reader (as the essay is being read), each of the paper's significant points should have its own body paragraph. But how many significant points should an essay include? In practice, that depends less on the subject of the essay than on the length of the essay. Let's say you have been asked to write a paper of 1,000 to 1,500 words arguing either for or against legalizing marijuana in your state or province. That's a topic on which it's possible to make a case very concisely in a sentence or two, and just as possible to make a book-length case of 100,000 words or more. How many significant points should you try to make in an essay of 1,000 to 1,500 words?

The short answer in most cases is four or five. As writers, we are often told that in the interests of variety and freshness it's good to vary the lengths of paragraphs—as it is to vary the lengths of sentences. That's absolutely true, but it's also true that extremely short or extremely long paragraphs should generally be avoided in academic essay writing. It's all too easy for writers to lose their focus in writing an extremely long paragraph—and for readers to lose their focus as they try to wade through it. At the other extreme, the one-sentence paragraph is only rarely appropriate to academic writing. It is a punchy form that may have the force of an exclamation mark in certain styles of journalistic writing; like the exclamation mark itself, though, it very rarely serves to further the flow of an argument in academic writing.

The *average* length of a paragraph, then, tends to be in the range of 150 to 250 words. Some significant points can be made in a couple of sentences, and some may require a full page or more to elaborate properly, but in most cases 150–250 words will be an appropriate amount of space to devote to introducing, clarifying, and dealing with a significant point in the paper.

Let's take the marijuana topic as an example. Say you decide to argue in favour of legalization. An essay of between 1,000 and 1,500 words has room for six or seven paragraphs—an introductory paragraph, a concluding paragraph, and four or five paragraphs that make significant points. Here's what a simple paragraph plan for an essay of between 1,000 and 1,500 words might look like:

First paragraph: Introduction: sketch of the historical and contemporary background; thesis statement

Second paragraph: Illegal marijuana sales help to finance organized crime

Third paragraph: Enforcing marijuana laws is too expensive

Fourth paragraph: Taxes on marijuana as potential revenue source

Fifth paragraph: Marijuana use is not that harmful; compare with other legal substances

Sixth paragraph: Rebut counter argument that legalization will lead to an increase in hard drug use

Seventh paragraph: Conclusion

As everyone knows, there is more than one side to every argument. Let's say you'd prefer to argue against legalization. Then your plan might look like this:

First paragraph: Introduction: sketch of the historical and contemporary background; thesis statement

Second paragraph: Rebut counter argument that marijuana is less harmful than other legal substances

Third paragraph: Legalization could lead to increase in drug use

Fourth paragraph: Specific harms from smoking and from eating

Fifth paragraph: Marijuana is a gateway drug

Sixth paragraph: Rebut counter argument that marijuana should be treated the same way as alcohol

Seventh paragraph: Conclusion

The above outlines give a sense of how an argument might be formed on two directly opposing viewpoints. Often, of course, there are more than two possibilities. One important lesson in developing thesis statements for arguments of your own is to try to resist habits of binary thinking—of thinking that there can be two and only two possibilities. On a topic such as this one, one might also, for example, argue one of the following:

Where there are good arguments from opposing sides of an issue, searching for a middle way is often the best course; marijuana should be decriminalized, but not legalized.

It is almost as bad where harmful substances are concerned to let corporate interests play a leading role as it is to let organized crime play a leading role; our goal should be to make marijuana legal, safe, and not very popular. The best way to accomplish that goal is for the government to take full control—for government rather than for-profit corporations to grow and process the plants, to operate non-glamorous retail outlets in out-of-the-way locations, to package the drug in plain wrappings, and to allow no advertising.

With some North American jurisdictions now experimenting
with different approaches to legalization, the safe course for other
jurisdictions to follow is to wait until conclusive results are in
from those experiments—which may take a decade or more.

O ORGANIZING PARAGRAPHS IN LONGER ESSAYS

The paragraph structure of longer essays tends to be more complex
than in the two examples provided above. It is often helpful to think
of such structures in terms of paragraph clusters as well as individual
paragraphs. The structure of Melissa Davis's essay, for example,
might fruitfully be broken down into the paragraph clusters shown
in the essay outline on page 39 (see box).

Paragraph Clusters: Notice here that not all the paragraphs directly
advance the argument. Paragraphs 2 and 3 form a cluster providing background information; the writing here is primarily narrative and descriptive rather than argumentative. The same is true of
paragraphs 11 and 12, which provide background information on
Ofili's art and the theorizing behind it. Once that information has
been put forward, it is a straightforward matter to argue (in paragraph 13) that the artist's work has to be classified as art, regardless
of whether or not the viewer likes it or dislikes it. The same is true
as well of much of paragraphs 14 through 17, which form a cluster discussing how the legal issue was resolved (paragraph 14), how
cultural conservatives continued to use the "Sensation" exhibit as
a focal point for attack (paragraph 15), and how the controversy
continues to affect other galleries (paragraphs 16 and 17).

The paragraph-by-paragraph outline on page 39 follows exactly
the paragraphs in Melissa Davis's paper. It's important to be aware,
though, that any paragraph outline you develop during the planning
and writing process should be regarded as subject to change as you
move forward. Such a document is a much more detailed and formal
outline than the rough plan that appears on page 59 (let alone than
the *very* rough mapping document that appears on page 29). It's an
important step in the process—but even at later stages you may well
find that you need to make structural adjustments. You may decide
that a paragraph is really expressing two important ideas instead of
one, and should be split in two. You may decide that a couple of

Paragraph-by-Paragraph Essay Outline

Introduction
1. Introduction to topic and the example of the "Sensation" exhibit; thesis statement

Background
2. Background information—the "Sensation" exhibition
3. Background information—criticisms of the "Sensation" exhibition

Main body of the general argument
4. Summary of the Giuliani argument
5. Importance of government subsidies for work that may offend
6. Distinction between overt censorship and expenditure of public funds
7. The narrow issue: reneging on prior commitments
8. The broader issue: the obligation of government to support free expression
9. Obligation of government to support free expression is not unlimited (a caution to liberals and civil libertarians)
10. Government should not concern itself too much with issues of "decency" in art (a caution to cultural conservatives)
11. A culture of free expression not only a matter of the law and the government—also a matter of social attitudes

Specifics regarding Chris Ofili's work
12. Ofili's work: background, praise, awards
13. Ofili's work: the artist's ideas—African heritage and artistic tensions
14. Ofili's work: unreasonable not to classify it as art, even if one doesn't like it

Follow-up to the controversy
15. How things turned out (1): legal victory
16. How things turned out (2): continued attacks by cultural conservatives
17. How things turned out (3): continued controversy with public galleries to 2008
18. How things turned out (4): since 2008—public galleries scared of controversy?

Conclusion
19. Conclusion: the importance of encouraging freedom of expression

paragraphs represent an unnecessary digression, and should simply be cut. Or you may decide that one or more paragraphs would be more effective if they were moved to a different position in the essay. Like so many other things, it's virtually impossible to get all this right in your first draft; paragraphing should be something you pay almost as much attention to in the revision process as you do during the planning process.

Subordination: As the outline shows, these paragraph clusters form the large units in this long essay. In this light, the individual paragraphs may be seen as subordinate categories within the clusters. In one case, the essay outline indicates a further level of subordination. Paragraphs 8 and 9 provide additional nuance on each side of the main point made in paragraph 7 ("We value a society in which a wide range of free expression is supported, and we rightly have come to expect that governments will provide a good deal of that support"). Those paragraphs have been indented in the outline, so as to show that they have a subordinate status, clarifying and expanding on the larger point made in paragraph 7.

In much the same way, you will see that the table of contents of this book is structured according to a hierarchy, with headings, sub-headings, and sub-sub-headings to indicate which topics are subordinate categories within larger, more general ones.

Topic Sentences: Each paragraph should not only have a topic; it should have a point to make. To make sure it does, you may find it helpful to compose a *topic sentence* for each paragraph—a sentence in which you set out clearly what you intend the paragraph to show. (Sentences of this sort might well be called thesis statements at the paragraph level; by convention, though, the term thesis statement is reserved for the statement of the argument of the full essay.)

Many writers find it helpful to draft topic sentences when they make outlines for their papers. This takes a little bit more time up front, but often saves quite a lot of time later; when you go to write the first draft, you can use them as the first or second sentence of each paragraph, and they will help you—and, later, your reader— keep track of the structure of your argument. To return to the essay in favour of marijuana legalization we outlined above, an outline that uses topic sentences would look something like this:

First paragraph: Introduction leading to thesis statement: In both financial and social terms, the costs to society of enforcing the current marijuana laws far outweigh the benefits.

Second paragraph: Making marijuana illegal has the effect of encouraging more serious crime; the activities of organized crime are often largely financed with revenues from the sale of marijuana.

Third paragraph: Enforcing the marijuana laws is a poor way to spend taxpayers' money; huge unnecessary costs are incurred on police resources, the courts, and the correctional system.

Fourth paragraph: In addition, making marijuana legal and taxing its sale (as we do with alcohol) would provide substantial funding for all sorts of good purposes.

Fifth paragraph: The harm caused by marijuana smoking is far, far less than that caused by substances which are already legal—notably alcohol.

Sixth paragraph: Those who claim that legalizing marijuana would lead to greater use of more dangerous drugs are committing the slippery slope fallacy.

Seventh paragraph: Conclusion: On balance, the benefits of legalizing marijuana far outweigh the risks....

A similar outline for the essay against legalization would look something like this:

First paragraph: Introduction leading to thesis statement: The risks to society of legalizing marijuana far outweigh the potential benefits.

Second paragraph: Much as it is often argued that marijuana isn't *very* harmful, or isn't *as* harmful as alcohol or *as* harmful as heroin, no one has ever suggested that marijuana is not to some degree a harmful drug.

Third paragraph: If marijuana is legalized and thereby made more widely available, it stands to reason that this harmful drug will become more widely used than it is today.

Fourth paragraph: If marijuana is smoked, it causes harm to the lungs (in addition to the chemical changes brought about by the action of THC in the brain); if it is eaten, there is a severe danger of overdose when those who do not fully appreciate its effects fully consume more than the recommended maximum dose.

Fifth paragraph: There is abundant evidence that many users of marijuana move on to other, more dangerous, "hard" drugs; if society were to give marijuana use its blessing, that drug will likely become a stepping stone to hard drug use for more and more people.

Sixth paragraph: The most common argument in favour of legalizing marijuana is that it's less dangerous than alcohol and alcohol is already legal. But if both are harmful, why should we add to the harmful temptations that people are already exposed to?

Seventh paragraph: Conclusion: From all the angles discussed, the risks to society of legalizing marijuana far outweigh the potential benefits....

Implied Topic Sentences: Just as beginners do, many experienced writers try to include in almost every paragraph a topic sentence to make it clear just what that paragraph is arguing. They don't *always* do that, though; indeed, some highly accomplished writers only rarely include explicit statements in each paragraph of the paragraph's purpose. But that doesn't mean the underlying structure isn't there. One interesting exercise is to go through an essay by an experienced writer and for each paragraph either identify the topic sentence or—where the topic is implied rather than expressly stated in a topic sentence—compose the "missing" topic sentence.

Let's again look to Melissa Davis's essay as an example. Davis appears to be an accomplished writer at the advanced undergraduate level; though the progression of her argument is usually quite clear to the reader, the main idea of many of her paragraphs is implied rather than expressly stated. But it is not difficult to construct a topic sentence for each paragraph.

First paragraph: Introduction leading to thesis statement: In the course of the Ofili controversy cultural conservatives raised legitimate concerns about the obligation of any society to provide funding for activities of which it disapproves. This essay will argue, however, that the greater concern is in the other direction; a free society must continue to provide opportunities for the free expression both of artistic vision and of controversial thought.

Second paragraph: This paragraph will provide background information about the "Sensation" Exhibit.

Third paragraph: The show in general and the Ofili piece in particular provoked a number of angry reactions.

Fourth paragraph: In Mayor Guiliani's view, the issue was not censorship but whether the government should provide funding for activities that some people find deeply offensive.

You might find it helpful to continue this exercise yourself and identify or construct topic sentences for the rest of the paragraphs in Davis's essay.

For more on using paragraphs to structure arguments, we recommend Ian Johnston's *Essays and Arguments: A Handbook on Writing* (3rd edition 2015); it's a text that has a proven track record of improving students' skills in formulating written arguments.

Additional Material Online

Exercises on paragraphing may be found at **sites.broadviewpress.com/writing**. Click on **Exercises** and go to **"Putting Ideas Together."**

O *Your Arguments, Others' Arguments*

Another way to look at the organization of arguments is in terms of one's own ideas and those of others. When the concepts of plagiarism and of "original work" are discussed, it is rightly emphasized that any essay (or article, or web posting, or full-length book) should present one's own ideas, not simply regurgitate the ideas of others. But does that mean one's own work has to be written without reference to that of others? No—far from it. Nor does "original" in the context of academic writing mean that an essay or academic book has to present ideas no one has thought of before. It simply means that the ideas put forward should be thought through and synthesized by you as an individual—that you should not simply borrow someone else's thinking.

That process of thinking-through, synthesizing, and developing an argument cannot and should not be done in a vacuum. An essay in which Melissa Davis tried to think through a response to the Ofili artwork entirely on her own, without reference to the arguments others had made either about that specific exhibition or about the larger issues involved, would be far less interesting than the essay she produced—an essay that draws on others' arguments for support, but also that engages directly with opposing arguments. The importance of engaging in this way with the arguments of others is the central point of one of the past generation's most influential books about the nature of academic argument, Gerald Graff and Cathy Birkenstein's *They Say / I Say*. As they point out,

> the underlying structure of effective academic writing—and of responsible public discourse—resides not just in stating your own ideas, but in listening closely to others around us, summarizing their views in a way they will recognize, and responding with our own ideas in kind.… [T]o argue well you need to do more than assert your own ideas. You need to enter a conversation, using what others say (or might say) as a launching pad or sounding board for your own ideas. (3)

Engaging with the arguments of others is important as a means of helping your reader to locate what you are saying in a broader context. But it is also important in helping you to formulate your own arguments for the reader. Obviously it can be helpful to draw on the arguments of others to support the views you are trying to convince your reader to adopt. By citing the arguments others have made—and, where appropriate, by summarizing or quoting from those arguments in support of your own—you can often make the points in your argument more persuasive.

Even more important is to come to grips with what those who oppose the arguments you wish to make have said. Crafting strong arguments often entails pointing out weaknesses in the arguments of those who argue opposing positions—but it also entails seeking out the strongest points that have been made against the position you have adopted. If you're arguing in favour of legalizing marijuana, you might well want to refer to (or quote from) the substantial series of articles and editorials that the *New York Times* ran in favour of legalization in late July and early August of 2014, but you would also be well advised to look at some of the strongest arguments made on the other side—by the American Medical Association, for example. If you are arguing against legalization, of course you may want to cite the AMA in support of your argument—but it may also be advisable to try to counter some of those *New York Times* arguments.

Let's look at how Melissa Davis's essay incorporates the arguments of others. She doesn't spend time arguing against the more extreme and ill thought-out positions of those who claimed at the time that Ofili's artwork constituted an attack on religion and should be flat-out banned. Instead she focuses (in paragraphs 4–11) on the stronger position advanced by Giuliani and others who argued not that the work should be banned, but rather that it should not be supported by public funds or exhibited in a publicly funded institution.

What if you aren't able to find strong arguments that challenge the points you wish to make? That may be a sign of several things. First of all, you should ask yourself if you have chosen a sufficiently interesting and challenging topic. If you are thinking of writing an essay arguing that men and women should receive equal pay for equal work, or that racism is bad, you're not likely to find strong and interesting opposing views to come to grips with. (For a discussion of how to formulate appropriate topics and thesis statements, see the section above headed "Purpose: From Topic to Thesis Statement.")

But what if you are thinking of writing an essay arguing a particular position about a newly published short story, or about a very recent political development, or about a philosophical position that has recently been advanced for the first time? You may not be able to find strong and interesting opposing views to come to grips with in those sorts of cases either—but that doesn't mean you've chosen a poor topic. So what should you do—just state your own views and not worry about opposing arguments? Here's a better way: invent as strong a set of opposing arguments as you can. You should try to anticipate the strongest possible argument you can imagine might be made by someone taking an opposing position. If you can persuasively counter any such arguments, you will have surmounted an important test—and written a first-rate essay.

In this connection it is worth drawing attention to the phrase in parentheses in the passage from Graff and Birkenstein quoted above: "You need to enter a conversation, using what others say (or might say) as a launching pad or sounding board for your own ideas." There are many ways in which writers introduce what others might say into their arguments. Sometimes these will merely be straw figure arguments, but in many cases they represent a genuine effort on the part of the writer to imagine and to counter the strongest possible case that might be made against one's own position. Here are some ways in which ideas of this sort can be introduced:

> An opponent might argue that.... But that would be to....

> On the other side, it could be suggested that.... But in that case....

> We may well imagine the counter argument to this—that.... But this counter argument does not hold up to close scrutiny....

A much larger catalogue of words and expressions commonly used in structuring arguments appears below, in the chapter "Putting Ideas Together." The discussion of integrating quotations and using signal phrases (pages 564–66) may also be helpful.

⊙ Logical Fluency: Modes of Writing, Modes of Thought

Another angle from which to approach the writing process is through looking at mental processes, and the patterns they lead to in writing. One first step towards logical fluency is to be aware of the premises that guide your thought process. Most writing starts with certain conscious premises: Melissa Davis, for example, begins mapping out her essay by assuming that freedom of expression is a fundamental good. With this premise in mind she seeks to build a logical argument concerning the Ofili piece—why it has created controversy, and to what extent the objections to it may be justified. Along the way she also works from the premise that "moral obligations may often exceed legal ones." Consciously held premises such as these are useful and indeed necessary steps in building an argument.

Watch out, though, for the power of unconscious premises—general beliefs and automatic assumptions that may covertly direct your critical thinking. *I cannot possibly have anything worthwhile to say on this topic* is an example; if allowed to lurk in the back of the mind, this premise—this crisis of attitude (pages 18–19)—will paralyse an essay's development. *Children over five years of age are just miniature adults* is a premise that could lead an editorialist to call for a return to corporal punishment in our schools. *Capitalism is in all circumstances the best system* is a premise that would certainly cloud a writer's judgement and reduce her capacity for understanding if she were writing an essay on the economic system of medieval Europe, or that of traditional Inuit society. *Something I find offensive could never be a work of art* is perhaps another premise capable of clouding a writer's judgement. Premises, be they strong or weak, do not always appear in the text of an essay. All the·more reason, then, for every writer to examine hers attentively, so that the essay's logic will be intentional, not inadvertent.

O *Elaboration and Repetition*

Even a clear and manageable thesis will be ineffective unless every one of its parts is clearly elaborated. When moving from paragraph to paragraph, it is all too easy to omit steps in the argument that you, the writer, feel are obvious. The problem is that readers may not feel the same way. Deliberate writers always ask themselves one key question: "Am I making everything clear for someone who has not done the research I have and who does not know anything of my argument beyond what I've told him?" In conversation, it's easy enough for the other person to interrupt by saying, "I can't follow your reasoning there." Readers don't have the same luxury. In Melissa Davis's essay paragraphs 4 through 7 include a good deal of elaboration, as the writer clearly lays out the legal limitations to freedom of expression, and the principles behind government support of the arts.

The amount of space that is devoted to the ideas that appear is of as much importance as the order in which they appear. For this reason it is important to avoid long discussions of matters you consider to be of less importance—or else to relegate them to a note outside the main body of the text. (Notice how Melissa Davis has relegated several interesting points to the notes of her essay.) Similarly, it is wise to provide enough elaboration of your main idea, whether through extending the argument itself or through providing numerous examples, to signal your sense of the relative importance of the various ideas you are presenting. A good essay typically gives the most space to the ideas that the writer considers most important. (Obviously you may also signal this through the use of words and phrases such as *most important, crucially*, and so on.)

The amount of space devoted to an idea is one way of signalling its importance; another is to return more than once to an essay's most important points. Mere repetitiveness is obviously off-putting to the reader—but continually drawing attention to the way paragraphs connect to key points over the course of an essay can greatly

---

Elsewhere in this book

The focus of this first section of *The Broadview Guide to Writing* is on the process of writing. A good deal more on how to shape written arguments effectively appears elsewhere in this book:

- The chapter "Putting Ideas Together" includes
  - additional material on **paragraphing**;
  - a substantial discussion of argument from a **critical thinking** point of view (including a catalogue of fallacies);
  - a comprehensive overview of **how particular words and expressions may be used to join ideas together**;
  - an extended treatment of **sentence combining** as a means of developing facility in using varied sorts of grammatical structures in constructing an extended piece of writing.

- The sections on **Writing about Literature** and **Writing about Science** have a good deal to say on shaping those particular sorts of written argument.

- The long chapter **"Across the Disciplines"** includes material on the conventions of presenting written arguments in a wide range of academic disciplines.

enhance its argumentative focus. At the end of Melissa's seventh paragraph, for example, she reiterates her thesis from her essay's introduction: *We value a society in which a wide range of free expression is supported—and we have come to expect that governments will provide a good deal of that support.* This statement not only repeats her position but also places it clearly in the context of public funding obligations. Similarly, in the essay's final paragraph, Melissa reiterates the central point of her thesis. The essay's concluding sentences provide an expanded statement of that central point.

O *Modes of Thought / Modes of Writing*

Traditionally, essays tend to be grouped into categories such as descriptive, narrative, expository, or argumentative. In practice, such distinctions are overly simplistic; very few papers are written purely in one mode. Since college and university essays are usually organized around thesis statements, they tend to be primarily argumentative: the writer's paramount concern is the presentation of an informed point of view on her topic. Along the way, however, most argumentative essays employ several other modes of thought.

Melissa Davis's essay "What Limits to Freedom?", for example, is typical of university essays in the Humanities or Social Sciences in that it is primarily argumentative. But at two significant points Davis employs a narrative mode—first in Paragraph 2 (in summarizing the background of the exhibition coming to Brooklyn) and then again in Paragraph 14 (in summarizing the story of the court verdict and its aftermath). Narration is the first of four modes of writing whose academic purposes deserve detailed consideration.

O NARRATION

The basic mode of thought involved in narration is a very simple one: one thing happens, and then another thing happens, and then another thing happens. For example, the "Methods" section of a scientific lab report is usually organized around a narrative sequence of events:

> A sugar maple leaf was collected from an area close to the trunk.
> This leaf was cut so as to cover the surface area of a leaf chamber,

which was attached to a sensor. Carbon dioxide was flushed into the chamber and the oxygen production per minute was measured using a serial interface and computer. The average per cent oxygen output per minute was then calculated, as was the standard deviation.

Considering its linkage of events through time, narration is the most straightforward mode of thinking and of writing. Nevertheless, it should be used sparingly in academic essays. Professors of literature often warn students to "assume your reader has read the work," realizing that if an argumentative essay merely retells a novelist's story, it's not much of an argumentative essay. Remember that any plot summary included in your paper must support a point—not substitute for one. You should always ask yourself the question your marker is sure to ask: "Why is this important?" If a writer is discussing the violence that broke out in the Sudanese region of Darfur in 2003, the narrative mode may well be the best one to adopt, at least for portions of the paper; the sequence of events is a complex one, and getting it straight is crucial to any argument as to the guilt or innocence of those involved. But in most academic arguments narration should be introduced only in support of the writer's own argument; it should not be allowed to take the place of that argument.

O CLASSIFICATION

Classification is the process of sorting into groups. The mental act of classifying can be enormously complex, but it can also be enormously satisfying to our sense of order. And how well we learn to do it will make a real difference to the logical fluency of our writing.

Classification is particularly important to argumentative essays that make comparisons or draw contrasts. If the writer is comparing the Canadian economy with that of the United States, for example, she will sort the data or other evidence she has assembled into various classes: sizes of the two economies; strengths of particular economic sectors (manufacturing, services, government, etc.); trade; banking and interest rates; geographical and climatic inputs; and so on. In doing so she will need to make a number of choices. The boundary lines between groups are often fragile or give trouble; what should be grouped with what? What will go in and what will be left out? In large part this will be dictated by the thrust of her argument. (Essays of comparison and contrast, like other essays, must have a purpose; they should never be mere lists.) She must be careful, certainly, not to make the selection on a random or arbitrary basis.

Then there are questions of where given topics should appear in the paper. Should the essay deal with all aspects of one country's economy first, and then turn to the economy of the other country? Usually this approach weakens structural unity; it would be better to compare Canadian manufacturing with American manufacturing, Canadian banking with American banking, et cetera.

Classification is of equal importance if the essayist is writing in a descriptive mode: telling what something looks like or how it works. (This mode of writing is particularly common in the sciences.) If the writer is describing the behaviour patterns of the beaver, for example, he may decide to group them into headings such as feeding, dam- and lodge-building, and breeding habits. He will probably also want to discuss how the anatomy of the animal and its behaviours are adapted to each other—perhaps pausing after each category of behaviour has been described to relate it to particular anatomical features.

Classification is also vital to another mode of writing—definition. Sometimes an entire essay may have a question of definition as its focus:

- Definitions of "Liberalism" from the Nineteenth to the Twenty-first Century
- The Concept of Metonymy in Sixteenth-century Rhetoric and in Deconstructionist Criticism
- "Making Love" from the 1950s to the 2000s

In such cases the writer describes or analyses the ways in which a term or concept has been understood differently in different eras. How did the term *liberal*, which in the nineteenth century implied firm opposition to government intervention in the economy, come to imply the very opposite a hundred years later? How did *making love*, once understood to refer to acts of courtship that stopped short of the overtly sexual acts, come in the 1960s to refer to nothing but such acts? And how do such changes in definition reflect or even cause broader changes in social attitudes?

Definition can also be an important part of other sorts of essays, as Melissa Davis's writing illustrates. In establishing her position Melissa is careful to inquire into what constitutes *freedom of expression*, and to define it with reference both to legal rights as set out constitutionally, and to the reality of social practice. Notice that she does not rely here on a dictionary as her source; she is aware that dictionary definitions are usually inadequate to the needs of academic writing. (Indeed, if a term has a meaning particular to an academic discipline, dictionary definitions can be downright misleading.)

○ GENERALIZATION AND ABSTRACTION

Generalization is the process of moving from an observation or conclusion about a single thing or a small number of things to a conclusion about all or most of that group. Abstraction, on the other hand, is at its most basic level the isolation of some particular quality of a thing from the rest of its properties—the consideration of the colour of a particular object, for example.

Many people are a bit hazy on the difference between abstraction and generalization—not surprisingly, since the two are related activities that we often perform simultaneously. Perhaps the best way of keeping them straight is to remember (as C.R. Hallpike puts it) that "while the opposite of *general* is *particular*, the opposite of *abstract* is *concrete*" (171). *Emotions* is a broad general category; love and hate are particular emotions. (*Neither* is a concrete thing.) The redness of the Canadian flag is an abstraction; the flag itself is a concrete thing. (We may also, of course, speak of one particular Canadian flag or of the Canadian flag in general, or of all flags in general; there can be numerous levels of both abstraction and generalization.)

Melissa Davis's essay is continually involved with the abstract (concepts such as *decency* and *freedom of expression*) and with the concrete (perhaps most memorably, the materials used in Ofili's piece). It is intensely involved, as well, with various generalizations—about the "Sensation" exhibit, for example, and about the appropriate role of government in a democratic society.

Most essays involve shifts not only from the general to the particular and back again, but also from one level of generalization to another:

- An art history essay on Chippendale chairs would probably refer to particular examples from the eighteenth-century studio of Thomas Chippendale himself, generalize about all chairs of that type, generalize further about the furniture of the period, and perhaps generalize at one higher level about how and why such designs suited the overall sensibilities of eighteenth-century England.

- An English literature essay might make a general claim about Jane Austen's use of irony. It might then descend one level of generality to discuss the differences in the degree to which the generalization applies in the various novels. It might then move to a lower level of generality, distinguishing between the scenes in *Northanger Abbey* that are suffused with the characteristic Austen sense of irony and those (apparently remaining from the first draft of the novel) that are almost pure melodrama with no irony to them whatsoever. Finally, the essay would doubtless give particular examples—quote sentences or paragraphs that exemplify an ironic tone and a melodramatic one.

Both abstraction and generalization are important mental processes for any writer; they help us, as Janet Giltrow puts it, to "name and manage otherwise unruly details" (141). But writers have to learn to use them with care. As a rule, generalizations must be supported by evidence. (Generalizations that are commonplace may be made without support; one does not need to provide evidence in support of the generalization that dogs have four legs or that war is a terrible thing, or cite sources to back up a claim that Jane Austen has been widely admired for her use of irony.) If an essay makes any claim that is not generally accepted (and if it is an interesting essay it usually will make several such claims), the claim must be supported. And if generalizations are made, the writer must be particularly careful to show that she is aware that her generalizations may not apply in all cases. She should make clear if she is writing about the way beaver build lodges that not all beaver do so; river beaver have quite different quarters, and behave differently in other ways as well.

And she should be precise. *Most Canadians voted against the Free Trade Agreement in the 1988 election* is an imprecise generalization. *In the 1988 election most Canadians voted for parties that opposed the Free Trade Agreement* is more accurate. Such concern for precision may seem like pedantry; is there any difference between the two state-ments? Yes, there is. In that election many Canadians who opposed Free Trade nevertheless voted for the Progressive Conservatives, just as many Canadians who supported Free Trade voted for the Liberals or New Democrats. Free Trade was the most contentious issue in the campaign, but not the only one; it was an election, not a referen-dum. Being careful about such distinctions is an important part of what is involved in a college or university education.

○ CAUSES, REASONS, EXPLANATIONS

A great deal of university and college writing involves discerning and analysing causes and effects. Whereas the natural connectives in narrative writing are *and* and *then*, the natural connectives when discussing causes and effects, or giving reasons, or providing expla-nations, are words such as *because* and *therefore*. The ways in which these connectives relate to causes and effects are treated more fully below (pages 54–56). Here we touch on a few general points.

Events often have more than one cause, and often claims must be justified by more than one reason. This sounds straightforward enough, but it is easy to forget, as the following examples show. Many of the arguments against military intervention in the Persian Gulf (both before the 1991 Gulf War and in 2003) took this form:

> Americans are willing to fight Saddam Hussein because they believe the oil reserves of the Gulf region are of strategic and eco-nomic importance to them. This is not a good moral justification for going to war. Therefore we should not fight.

To begin with, this sort of argument confuses explanation with justification. To ask what American motives were is to ask why the country went to war—a very different thing from asking if the country should have gone to war. Quite possibly America may have done "the right deed for the wrong reason."

Beyond this, however, the argument assumes that if one expla-nation can safely be advanced for an action, it is also safe to conclude that it is the only explanation. Surely it is entirely possible for the US and its allies to have been willing to go to war *both* out of a self-interested desire to protect oil reserves *and* out of unselfish desires to resist aggression or potential aggression, to prevent the development or deployment of chemical and biological weapons, and so on.

Reasoning used by many on the opposite side of such debates may be equally flawed. The gist of the argument of the American, British, and Canadian political leaders in 1991 was this:

> In an act of brutal aggression, Iraq invaded and annexed Kuwait, killing many of its citizens in the process. Aggression must be resisted. Therefore we should be willing to go to war.

And in 2003:

> In contravention of UN resolutions, Iraq has refused to allow monitoring of strategic sites on which it may have been developing chemical and biological weapons. Contempt for international law must be resisted. Therefore we should be willing to go to war.

As with the anti-war arguments above, the pro-war arguments here suffer from incomplete reasoning—reasoning that fails to allow for any multiplicity of causes, reasons, and effects. Did Iraq in 1991 have a legitimate historical claim on the territory of Kuwait (which, like Iraq, was carved out of what had been a part of the Ottoman Empire by the British)? What are the casualties likely to be in the event of war? Should aggression be resisted in all circumstances, and at all costs? These are some of the questions left unanswered.

And similarly in 2003: should defiance or partial defiance of UN resolutions be punished at any cost? Who is likely to suffer, and how much? Does military intervention in the Persian Gulf carry with it the risk of sparking a larger conflict? Have other means short of military action been exhausted? Depending on the answers one gives to such questions, the appropriate course of action may seem far less clear.

A useful distinction in sorting out the relative importance of multiple causes, effects, and reasons is that between necessary and sufficient conditions. The presence of oxygen is a necessary condition for there to be fire; there can be no fire without oxygen. But it is not a sufficient condition; everything in the presence of oxygen does not automatically catch fire.

Similarly (in the argument discussed above), the 1991 political leaders were in effect arguing that the fact of Iraq having invaded and annexed another sovereign country was in itself a sufficient condition to justify going to war. Someone arguing against going to war in the same circumstances might claim that the invasion of one country by another was a necessary condition for going to war, but not a sufficient one—that other, additional justification was required. And a third person might say that the invasion constituted neither a necessary nor a sufficient condition; that we should stay out of such affairs in any circumstances.

Another useful distinction—particularly in the sciences and social sciences—is between cause and correlation. Again, this may be made clear by example. A recent study has shown that the rate of breast cancer in women has increased markedly over the past twenty years. Over the same period, the average child-bearing age has also increased dramatically. Now, it is possible that the connection between those two occurrences may be causal in nature—that, for example, waiting until later in life to have children increases one's risk of breast cancer. But researchers caution that we should not assume this to be the case; more research needs to be done. As it stands, the connection is merely a correlation: an interrelationship of variable qualities. In this case, over the same period and under the same conditions, both variables increased.

When a correlation between two things exists:

- there may be a common cause or common causes for both
- one may cause the other (or help to cause the other; again, more than one cause may be involved)
- the two may happen coincidentally as a result of quite separate causes

○ COMBINING MODES OF THOUGHT

A detailed look at Melissa Davis's essay will show how different modes of thought combine to produce logical fluency. Her introduction (paragraph 1) moves quickly from a general topic—public galleries as forums for presenting new and controversial material—to the particular example of Ofili's work in the "Sensation" exhibit. She briefly describes the sequence of events involving the presentation of the "Sensation" exhibit and the flurry of discussion that ensued. This sets the stage for the statement of the thesis at the end of the paragraph.

Both narrative and classification are important to the paragraphs in which Melissa narrates the background of the "Sensation" exhibit and the controversy surrounding it. Notice here how she classifies different aspects of the controversy. She refers to the disagreements about Marcus Harvey's work—disagreements involving the issues of decency and freedom of expression that are her central concern—in the body of her essay. The controversy over the financing of the "Sensation" exhibit, on the other hand, she relegates to a note; it is not directly relevant to her topic.

Paragraph 3 is linked to paragraph 2 as an extension of the narrative of the controversy; it uses quotation judiciously to express the flavour of the debate. Paragraph 4 uses quotation much more extensively. Here Melissa is presenting the core argument of those opposed to the exhibit—and, in paragraph 5, in analysing the thrust of their argument is beginning to elaborate her own. She moves beyond responding to Giuliani's argument, and begins to draw the distinctions between moral and legal obligations that will be central to her conclusion. From here through paragraph 11 is the core of her general argument.

Paragraphs 12–14 shift focus to discuss the issue not in generalities or from first principles but through a detailed consideration of the specific artwork at issue. Here Melissa relies on quotation of the artist himself, on quotation of a recognized authority in the field, and on her own arguments. She again touches on definition here—in this case not treating at length the question of "what is art?" but noting that even a conservative definition of art would have to allow Ofili's work to qualify. Paragraphs 15 through 18 turn again to narrative, recounting the resolution of the case in the courts and the repercussions since. Notice in these paragraphs how cause-and-effect analysis is intertwined with the narrative.

The essay's conclusion is signalled at the outset of paragraph 19 by two statements of generalization. The topic of the essay is reiterated without being merely repeated. In other words, Melissa Davis makes the effort to find other words. She returns not only to the general topic of the essay but also to its all-important thesis, and she does so without simply cutting and pasting the introduction from paragraph 1. Melissa then punctuates her argument by recognizing the profound changes wrought by the 9/11 attacks—and by holding to her own position on freedom of expression. Her position is clearly elaborated. The essay is complete.

O *Reasoning*

Nothing sinks an essay more quickly than an illogical argument. Readers expect a writer's assertions to be supported by solid evidence. None of the modes of thought discussed in this book will succeed unless employed along a clear path of reasoning.

Consider once again Melissa Davis's essay. Her use of the various modes of thought—such as classification or narration—is complemented by a strong linkage between the essay's main points and the reasons supporting them. Chief among her main points is, of course, the essay's thesis at the end of paragraph 1: the thesis statement commits Melissa to the logical task of demonstrating (a) that the case against Ofili's work, as it was advanced in the context of the "Sensation" show, rests on an insufficiently strong foundation and (b) that, more generally, artistic and intellectual activity deserves government support in the interest of preserving and promoting freedom of expression.

In arguing (a) effectively, Melissa first demonstrates her understanding of the defects in Giuliani's arguments and then later defends the Ofili piece directly. Melissa advances two lines of argument for (b), both presenting the historical justifications for such support and arguing the case from general principles.

In structuring her essay, Melissa signals that she wishes to put more emphasis on (b) than on (a). She devotes far more space to arguing (b) than she does to arguing (a), and she returns in the essay's final paragraph to her general points regarding freedom of expression. Such decisions concerning an essay's structure, as well as the weight to be placed on its various points, are often as important as the essay's internal logic—which brings us to our next topic.

For much more on reasoning and argumentation, see the chapter **"Putting Ideas Together."**

Introduction
— frame in historical context (galleries & freedom of expression)
— very brief summary of "Sensation" case
— touch on the issues — offence vs. decency
                        — free expression
                        — public funding
[THESIS] — opponents have some legitimate concerns
BUT free expression a core principle

Body
① extended presentation of issues
    — history of exhibit
    — reactions — politicians
                — press
② analyse/examine Giuliani's argument
    — the issue of prior commitment in this case
③ Ofili's work itself — aesthetic considerations (legitimate artistic activity?)
④ broader issues re, gov't. support for arts & intellectual activity obligation? Probably not — but fabric of society would suffer if support withdrawn

Conclusion
① Since "Sensation" (change in climate?) — and looking forward
touch on thesis again → ② return to issue of principle — and not only a legal issue. Freedom of expression will always need to be defended.

Melissa Davis's planning and prewriting moves from mapping to an informal outline, which helps her to arrange the sequence of points in her argument. Notice the three-part skeleton (introduction/body/conclusion), with the essay's thesis as the focus of the introduction.

O *Subordination*

We have already discussed ways of structuring your argument through paragraphing (see pages 35–42), but in the most successful essays even individual sentences are structured in a way that mirrors the logic underlying the argument and the relative importance of the ideas being discussed. At the grammatical level, the principle of subordination helps writers to emphasize one idea while drawing attention away from another. Look, for example, at the topic sentence that appears as the conclusion to Melissa Davis's thirteenth paragraph, which opens with a subordinate clause introduced by the phrase "even if…":

> Even if some find this art offensive, it is hard not to think that on its merits Ofili's work deserves to be widely exhibited.

Now imagine the parts of the sentence without the structure of subordination—set out as two independent sentences:

> Some find this art offensive. On its merits Ofili's work deserves to be widely exhibited.

Because the first clause is subordinated in Davis's version, the second clause is given prominence. Grammatically, the second half is stronger; it could stand on its own as a complete sentence. And that grammatical structuring exactly mirrors the structuring of Davis's argument.

Thus, the grammar of subordination mirrors the logic of the ways in which an essay makes transitions from one idea to the next. It allows the acknowledgement in one paragraph or sentence of a preceding paragraph or sentence's material, while still introducing (and grammatically asserting) its own. This sort of signalling can greatly enhance logical fluency.

O *Connectives*

If the paragraphs and the sentences in an essay are to convey a sense of logical fluency to the reader, connectives are of vital importance. *Even if* … and *despite* … in the above examples are connectives.

So is the word *however*, used in the last sentence of Melissa's first paragraph: ... *a greater concern, however, is* .... Like others of this kind (*moreover, consequently, therefore, furthermore, admittedly*), connectives such as *however* and *even if* are a writer's road signs, indicating to readers where the logical structure of the essay has come from, and where it is headed. (See pages 276–301 for a full treatment of the ways in which such words can be used.) Melissa's use of *however* conveys a clear message: the "greater concern" that is being introduced will be one that stands in contrast to the concerns just referred to. (If, on the other hand, she were to write ... *a greater concern, moreover, is* ... the reader would be led to expect an extension of the ideas presented previously.)

Additional Material Online
Exercises on connectives may be found at
sites.broadviewpress.com/writing.
Click on **Exercises** and go to **"Putting Ideas Together."**

Sometimes connectives may be made up of more than one word; such is the case not only with *even if* but also with the phrases *by contrast, in addition, for example, to summarize,* and *all in all*. Whether through phrases such as these or through one-word connectives, an essay's logical fluency often depends on choosing the right way to connect your ideas.

⊙Stylistic Fluency

Unfortunately, the achievement of logical fluency does not guarantee the achievement of its necessary other, stylistic fluency. Consider, for example, these meticulously thought-out instructions for patrons of the Bank of Nova Scotia:

> The annual rental fee for the lease of the box is subject to change from time to time by the Bank either giving notice in writing to the lessee by mailing the notice to the lessee at the address given

hereunder (or such address as the lessee may from time to time in writing instruct the Bank to substitute thereof) and any such notice shall be deemed to have been duly given when mailed, or by posting a notice in a readily accessible place in the branch of the Bank.

Or this paragraph from a university student's critique of an assigned reading:

Rembar simply uses refutation to make a greater distinction between impeachment and the judiciary system. Refutation, in this instance, clarifies the distinction. The natural confusion which exists initially is suppressed as Rembar offers explanation. The effect has tremendous influence and we progressively take stance with Rembar's viewpoint.

Neither writer is thoughtless or incompetent, but each has developed a case of what James Thurber once called "inflammation of the sentence structure." Fortunately, this stylistic disease is curable, provided the patient is willing to rehabilitate his diction (choice of words) and syntax (arrangement of words).

O Diction

As George Orwell warned repeatedly, the great danger of English is its insidious power over the human thought process. Words come in familiar, formulaic packages that often leap from a writer's pen or keyboard before she's had a chance to really think. Worse yet, the familiar and formulaic tends to be hypnotic; writers are often unaware that Language is leading Thought on its leash:

Ready-made phrases come crowding in. They will construct your sentences for you—even think your thoughts for you, to a certain extent—and at need they will perform the important service of partially concealing your meaning even from yourself.... This invasion of one's mind by ready-made phrases ... can only be prevented if one is constantly on guard against them. (362)

Four eyes are better than two when it comes to sighting an invasion force. In dialogue with another person, any university essay-writer will resist more strongly the temptations of ready-made academic prose (what Northrop Frye calls "verbal cotton wool" [107]). Such temptations are very real. It is easy for any experienced consumer of university writing to summon a lifeless introductory sentence from her general memory-bank:

Certain	definite	elements	can be	identified
Several	key	components		illuminated
Three	crucial	factors		underlined
		aspects		isolated
		facets		
		areas		

... when discussing the topic of the "Sensation" show controversy.

Even the most attentive writers can inadvertently slip into this passive game of fill-in-the-blanks, dulling their topics (and their minds!) with phrases like *Certain crucial facets* or *Three key elements* or *Several definite components* or (even worse) *Certain crucial facets and several definite components*. Usually there is nothing at all "definite" or "certain" about such writing. Rather, its anesthetized perpetrator conjures up vague categories—factors, areas, components, etc.—without having any specific material to fill them in. "What is above all needed," as Orwell insists, "is to let the meaning choose the word, and not the other way about" (366).

Many people believe that their writing will be made more impressive if they use long, unusual words and long, complicated sentences. About one per cent of us are capable of impressing in this way; the rest of us only end up making more mistakes than we would have otherwise, and looking rather foolish. Of course, academic writing depends upon the use of jargon—namely, the specialized language of any scholarly field. But the best writers always aim to express their ideas in the most straightforward manner possible. The goal is a varied and flexible style, one that uses simple words wherever possible without becoming simplistic.

Because they are involved in intellectual discourse, academic and professional writers must rigorously monitor their use of abstract and conceptual nouns. Too dense a concentration will sap an essay's clarity; the ideas will be—as the overused idiom has it—too difficult to grasp. But the metaphor is apt: readers can't put their hands on something that is too airy. They require, and deserve, a balance between abstraction and solidity. Competent writers choose from several techniques—including example, definition, reference to data, and quotation—in order to keep their abstract diction out of the rhetorical clouds.

Many who have written on style have advised against using too many adjectives or adverbs—though it is rare to find "too many" quantified. No doubt the widespread prejudice against adjectives and adverbs is in part a reaction against two unfortunate tendencies that many of us share. The first is to be repetitive in our use of adjectives; *tiny little* and *great big* are common conversational combinations that sometimes find their way onto the page as well. The second is to use adverbs as largely meaningless intensifiers; we don't usually need the *very* in *very important* or the *extremely* in *extremely tragic*. But in fact most good writers use adjectives and adverbs freely, and with great effect. Look, for example, at the following description by Charles Simic, a Pulitzer Prize–winning poet as well as a superb essayist:

> In Clarksdale, the former capital of the Cotton Kingdom which President Clinton visited during his 1999 tour focusing on the nation's poorest communities, I saw in a parking lot of a closed supermarket two ancient cars parked side by side with their four doors wide open. Over their hoods, roofs, and doors, spread out and draped, someone's once-pretty dresses and worn children's clothes were covering every available space. Two black women sat on low stools, one on each side, waiting for a customer. (45)

Notice in particular here that of the many adjectives used, none is at all rare, and none is used in a particularly striking or original fashion. *Ancient, once-pretty, worn, low*; these are everyday adjectives, carefully chosen. Writers can certainly create an effect with references to the *elaborate casualness* of a hostess or the *cerulean intensity* of an actor's blue eyes. But well-chosen adjectives and adverbs do not need to be unusual or showy; they simply need to fit the context, and help the writer convey to the reader the desired sense.

As mentioned earlier, word-choosing can also be perilous whenever a writer's topic involves jargon—that is, technical or specialized language. "In order to ensure that a truly regional renal care delivery structure will be optimally functional, there must be patient accessibility to a number of interdigitated modalities of care," writes the medical essayist, forgetting simplicity in his pursuit of kidney doctors' respect. Chances are he has misconstrued his audience, anyway; even professionals at ease with the jargon of their own specialty would prefer *work well* to *be optimally functional*; and *several interconnected clinics* to *a number of interdigitated modalities of care*. Who really wants to read *the plan is more philosophical than operational in terms of framework*, rather than *the plan is still an idea; it has not been tested yet*?

In addition to technical or specialized language, the word *jargon* also ·refers to unnecessarily vague and unfocused vocabulary. This second connotation—a very negative one—points more to a problem of psychology than to a problem of grammar and usage. It comes from people being more concerned with making themselves sound knowledgeable and intellectual than with acquiring knowledge or developing their intelligence; more concerned with making their ideas sound important than with thinking them through and expressing them clearly. Unfortunately, most students are sufficiently impressionable to be taken in by the pretence that some jargon puts forward. Even more sadly, many working adults who should know better are just as easily taken in. The best way to safeguard against jargon is to embrace simplicity of expression. Writers who are always willing to revise their choices, who realize that no word in any draft of an essay is inevitable, will best resist being hypnotized by jargon.

> ### Additional Material Online
> Exercises on jargon and on word choice may be found at
> **sites.broadviewpress.com/writing**.
> Click on **Exercises** and go to **"Style."**

O *Figures of Speech*

Yet another ingredient of stylistic fluency is figurative language, the persuasive use of images from beyond the realm of the essay's primary topic—most commonly in the form of metaphors or similes. By appealing to readers' senses, such images give life and clarity to abstract diction. An excellent example appears in George Orwell's famous essay on politics and language, where the writer complains about people who believe that "any struggle against the abuse of language is a sentimental archaism, like preferring candles to electric light or hansom cabs to aeroplanes" (353). His introduction of an abstract and difficult concept (*sentimental archaism*) is followed by two vivid figures of speech, which aid readers in understanding the point being made.

Orwell's use of the word *like* is enough to classify his figures of speech as similes, which are distinct from metaphors: *My love is a red, red rose* is a metaphor; *My love is like a red, red rose* is a simile. The difference is simply that similes make comparisons explicit through the use of words such as *like* or *as if*, whereas metaphors fuse the objects of comparison.

Of course, as Orwell himself warns, dull or overly familiar figures of speech can undermine not only stylistic but also logical fluency. Most writers drink from the well of stale imagery more often than they realize. When they do, what ends up on the page has little life to it: *that will be the acid test; the United States is a melting pot; he's barking up the wrong tree; I threw caution to the wind; we were told that we would have to bite the bullet; put that on the back burner; this university is a hotbed of unrest.*

For the most part these are what are known as dead metaphors—metaphors that have been used so frequently that they no longer conjure up any physical image in the minds of those who hear or read them. When we hear the phrase *miss the boat* we do not think of a boat, any more than we think of pavement when we hear the expression *paved the way for*. In similar fashion a phrase such as *the lifeblood of democratic society* has been used so often that the blood has been drained out of it. Melissa Davis realized exactly that on re-reading the second draft of her essay—and changed *that are the lifeblood of democratic society* to *that continually replenish the red blood cells of democratic society*. It is a moot point whether a dead metaphor is better than no metaphor at all, but certainly a fresh metaphor is far better than either. Instead of *paved the way*, for example, what about *opened a new channel*? Instead of a *hotbed*, try a *cauldron*. Instead of *nipping something in the bud*, try *digging up the seedlings*. It may take a little longer, but the improvement in style will be worth it.

Of course, so many people have been using metaphors for so long that it is extremely difficult to find a fresh one for every situation. One useful compromise is to try to bring dead metaphors to life by using them in new ways. For example, no one thinks of a wave in this sentence:

- The Prime Minister of Britain has been riding a wave of popular support since his election.

Mention the wave again in a slightly different way, however, and it becomes water again to the reader:

- The Prime Minister of Britain has been riding a wave of popular support since the election. The question now is when that wave will crest.

Similarly, few people think of plants when they read of something having been *nipped in the bud*—unless the writer has made an effort to bring the dead metaphor back to life:

- The company wanted to nip the spreading unrest among its employees in the bud.

- The company wanted to nip the spreading unrest among its employees in the bud before it became a tangled, snake-infested jungle.

Writers who use dead metaphors are also more likely to mix their metaphors. A mixed metaphor occurs when we are not really thinking of the meaning of the words we use:

- If we bite the bullet we have to be careful not to throw the baby out with the bath-water.

As soon as one really thinks about such sentences one realizes that the bullet is really better off out of the baby's bath-water:

needs checking   Now the president is out on a limb and some of his colleagues are trying to pull the rug out from under him.

revised   Now the president is out on a limb and some of his colleagues are preparing to saw it off.

> **Additional Material Online**
> Exercises on mixed metaphors may be found at
> **sites.broadviewpress.com/writing**.
> Click on **Exercises** and go to **"Style."**

O *Syntax*

Syntax is simply the order in which words appear. As the following examples show, poor syntax can quite thoroughly disrupt stylistic fluency:

- Trapped in a 101-foot mine shaft abandoned for almost fifty years, two injured men were rescued over the weekend after they lit a fire to attract the attention of passers-by.

- The macadamia was named for Dr. John MacAdam, an enthusiastic scientist who promoted the nut in its native Australia, and was dubbed "the perfect nut" by Luther Burbank.

At times, words and phrases seem to have wills of their own, teaming up unexpectedly to completely undermine writers' intended meanings. Like some subversive magnet, the word *trapped* (in the first sentence) lures the prepositional phrase *for almost fifty years* to its side. And, in sentence 2, the verbal phrase *was dubbed* ignores the macadamia and aligns itself instead with poor Doctor MacAdam.

Writers must, however, shoulder the blame for such syntactical insurrections. They may not know the grammatical jargon—may not know that "a past participle preceding the object of a preposition will surrender control of a subsequent prepositional phrase to a second past participle that precedes either of the two prepositional phrases in question." But they must know that the phrase *for almost fifty years* in the first example is controlled by the word *abandoned*—not the word *trapped*. They may not know that "the second of two past-tense verbs in the passive voice, instead of aligning itself to the subject word of the sentence, will align itself to the relative pronoun that introduces an adjective subordinate clause, when that clause modifies a noun in apposition to the object of a prepositional phrase syntactically adjacent to the first past-tense verb in the passive voice."

But they must know that in the second example the verb *was dubbed* refers to *the macadamia*—not the scientist.

Rare is the writer who always thinks in grammatical terms as she writes. Nevertheless, successful writers develop an eye for the syntax of English grammar by allowing time between successive drafts of an essay. A good night's sleep enhances objectivity, so that the person who wrote the sentences can respond more as their eventual readers will respond.

O *Rhythm*

A writer's pursuit of stylistic fluency is not complete without attention to the music created by words and sentences—to the rhythm of language. The most predictable syntax in the grammar of English is SUBJECT-VERB-PREDICATE, as in the sentence, *The response of the mayor was more vehement.* Upend that predictability, and a writer such as Melissa Davis is on her way (in paragraph 3 of the essay) to rhythmical distinctiveness: *Even more vehement was the response of....*

An important element in rhythmical distinctiveness is balance. Sometimes a pleasing balance is achieved simply by deliberately repeating phrases or grammatical forms:

- We may not wish to deny academics the right to publish such research. But nor can we deny the harm that it causes.

Sometimes balance may be achieved by placing words or phrases in apposition:[1]

- Haldeman was Nixon's closest confidant, his most influential advisor.

- The generality of the images here has the effect of opening up the scene to the reader, of allowing her to graft her own archetypes of *river* and *hill* and *woods* onto the story.

Often paired connectives *(if ... then, either ... or, not only ... but also)* can help in achieving balance. But here, as always, the writer must be careful that the words are in the right places; otherwise the fragile element of balance is lost:

---

1 I.e., where successive words or phrases fulfill the same grammatical function in a sentence, with the second helping to elaborate on or explain the first.

needs checking   Hardy was not only a prolific novelist but wrote poetry too, and also several plays.

revised   Hardy was not only a prolific novelist but also a distinguished poet and a dramatist.

(Here the noun *novelist* is balanced by the later nouns *poet* and *dramatist*.)

needs checking   The experiment can either be performed with hydrogen or with oxygen.

revised   The experiment can be performed with either hydrogen or oxygen.

(Here the choice is between the two gases, not between performing and some other thing.)

needs checking   To subdue Iraq through sanctions, the United Nations felt, was better than using military force.

revised   To subdue Iraq through sanctions, the United Nations felt, was better than to use military force.

or   Subduing Iraq through sanctions, the United Nations felt, was better than using military force.

(Here infinitive balances infinitive; participle balances participle.)

needs checking   In 1984 there was a female Vice-Presidential candidate for a major American political party, and in 2008 too.

revised   In both 1984 and 2008 a major American political party chose a female Vice-Presidential candidate.

Repetition of some grammatical phrase allows readers to sense a pattern in the writing. If parallel structure has been used to balance the parts of a sentence, even long sentences can be made easily digestible to the reader. Let's look again to Melissa Davis's essay for an example:

> The resulting uproar led both to a widely publicized court case and to an ongoing campaign to support "decency" in artistic expression. Should such art be banned? Should it be exhibited at public expense?

Notice here the balancing of *both to* ... with *and to* ..., as well as the common structure of the two sentences that follow.

But even careful balancing cannot make a steady diet of long sentences palatable; a rich source of rhythm in any well-written essay is the short sentence, a highly visible minority in the academic world of long, drawn-out sentences. No writer naturally thinks, as she is drafting an essay, "Now I must remember to vary the length of my sentences." But when she comes to revise her work—particularly if she has allowed a day or two to elapse after completing the rough draft—she is better able to notice if and when the writing becomes too dominated either by very long sentences or by very short ones. She is able too to notice such things as a preponderance of *it is* ..., *there is* ..., and *there are* sentences:

> *needs checking*   It is important to remember that there are cultural as well as economic effects of Free Trade. There are many people who argue that over the long term these are just as significant.
>
> *revised*   Free Trade has cultural as well as economic effects. Indeed, many argue that over the long term these are just as significant.

By making such changes as these, even when there are no actual errors in her rough draft, the careful writer is able—with very little effort expended—to make her prose clearer, crisper, and more concise. And by doing so she makes things considerably easier for her reader.

> **Additional Material Online**
> Exercises on balance and parallelism may be found at
> **sites.broadviewpress.com/writing**.
> Click on **Exercises** and go to **"Style."**

O *Voice*

As many authorities have pointed out, in most cases writers can make their sentences less wordy and more effective by using the active voice rather than the passive:

needs checking   The election was lost by the premier. (Passive—7 words)
revised   The premier lost the election. (Active—5 words)

needs checking   Union power was seen by them to have constrained the possibilities for full investment, and for achieving full employment.

revised   The shareholders thought that union power had constrained the possibilities for full investment, and for achieving full employment.

It is too extreme, however, to conclude that the passive should be avoided wherever possible. Writers often want—for perfectly good reasons—to keep the focus of their writing on the recipient of an action rather than its agent. In such cases they are quite right to use the passive voice:

passive   John Paul Getty III was released in Italy after a 2.8-million-dollar ransom had been paid.

active   His kidnappers released John Paul Getty III in Italy after they had been paid a 2.8-million-dollar ransom.

If John Paul Getty III is the focus, it may be more appropriate to keep him as the subject of the sentence than to shift the focus to his kidnappers.

The passive is also sometimes useful as a means of dealing with issues of gender and usage. Compare, for example, the following sentences:

- If a writer uses vivid adjectives, his or her descriptive writing will carry greater force.

- If vivid adjectives are used, descriptive writing will carry greater force.

Additional Material
Further discussion of
active and passive voice
may be found on
pages 136–38.

The passive-voice version allows the wordy *his or her* to disappear. Altering syntax in this sort of way can help writers to write bias-free prose without resorting to awkward phrasing. (For a full discussion of this issue see below, pages 355–56.)

The vice associated with the passive voice, then, is not the passive *per se*, but the wordiness it sometimes gives rise to.

Additional Material Online
Exercises on active and passive voice may be found at
sites.broadviewpress.com/writing.
Click on **Exercises** and go to **"Verbs."**

O *Tone*

The voice of logical fluency is not supposed to gush or cajole or insult or amuse or exclaim. After all, most academic essays are formal pieces of writing, and should be approached as such. Your readers expect a calm and disinterested tone, free of extreme emotion or conversational touches (for advice on avoiding slang expressions and contractions, turn to page 327). Thinking rigorously about a topic does not, however, preclude feeling strongly about it. As Susan Cole demonstrates in her essay on Terry Fox, sentences that are both logically and stylistically fluent will convey emotion without the need for fanfare:

> Terry's Marathon of Hope was a tremendous athletic accomplishment, and the physical punishment to which he subjected himself is almost beyond imagining. It is not a well-known fact that he was advised before his run that he had a heart condition.... As he approached Thunder Bay in late August, he experienced a persistent intense pain in his upper chest and he was unable to go any further. Terry's run was finished on the first of September, 114 days and 3,339 miles after it had begun. (255)

Cole's style is personal without being subjective. Like many a practiced writer, she maintains objectivity while relying on diction and syntax to express an earnestness of tone that complements her subject matter.

Notice in particular how Cole manages to personalize the tone of her writing without employing the first-person singular pronoun; indeed, most academic writers use *I* or *me* infrequently, if at all. The objective of most formal essays is to present a clear argument; writers succeed by letting the evidence speak for itself. Thus many instructors advise their students to avoid using first-person pronouns.

As with all stylistic guidelines, though, this one should not be regarded as written in stone. As the other introductory passage quoted earlier demonstrates, the acclaimed historian Garry Wills uses *I* and *me* frequently. So does George Orwell, often praised as the finest essayist of the past century.

⊙ Revision and Proofreading

Perhaps the greatest failing among those learning to write well is a reluctance to spend sufficient time reworking and reorganizing their prose. Far too many students—not to mention people working in business and government—assume that completing a first draft means, essentially, finishing the job. Feeling the pressure of a deadline, they're inclined to ask the same rhetorical question that Louis Menand asks himself:

> Why burn through limited time and brain cells trying to coax coherence out of a ramshackle string of half-baked ideas embedded in badly written sentences when you could be forging your verbal chain one exquisite and unbreakable link at a time? (94)

Menand himself is a truly extraordinary writer, who is indeed capable of forging marvellous essays one exquisite and unbreakable link at a time, but for most of us, exquisite first drafts are few and far between. As Ian Cameron puts it in *For All Practical Purposes*:

> A few students feel that they are as likely to make more mistakes in checking and correcting their work as they are to correct the mistakes they have already made, but in fact almost every student is able to improve his or her work at least 15% by checking it slowly and carefully. Remember, you are not checking simply for details such as spelling; you should be trying to replace words, to re-arrange paragraphs, to cut entire sections, to alter almost every sentence. (276)

By its very nature revising is likely to lead to more cuts than additions. Might this not cause damage? "Aren't I more likely to do well," some students may ask themselves, "if I've written more than the prof asked for?" If the instructor has asked for 1,000 words, they feel they should write 1,500; if 2,500 words are requested, they are sure to top 3,000. Experienced writers have learnt that quantity matters much less than quality; unless an essay is well below the requested number of words the only thing that matters is what it says, and how well it says it.

What, then, should you be looking for as you read over your first draft (or your second, or your third)? Are your points clear? Have you given appropriate emphasis to your most important points—and, conversely, signaled where you are providing supporting material or briefly digressing? More generally, do the ideas hang together? Does the argument make sense, and do the ideas of each paragraph seem to flow naturally from the preceding paragraph? Is the same true on a sentence-by-sentence basis; does each sentence flow naturally from the preceding sentence?

If not, what can you do to make the sentences and/or the paragraphs flow together better? Perhaps some paragraphs would work better at a different point in the essay. Perhaps some sentences would also work better if they appeared a little earlier or a little later in the argument. If you decide to move paragraphs or sentences, of course, you should be very careful about words and phrases that are designed to link them to the surrounding paragraphs; when you move a sentence from near the beginning to near the end of a paragraph, for example, you may need to introduce it with "Moreover, …" rather than "To begin with,…" And you may similarly need to change the connective tissue of adjacent sentences; the sentence that used to start "A second point here is that…" may now need to begin, "For one thing,…."

In revising your early draft(s), you should also be alert to what you *haven't* written. It may well be that you have omitted to mention one or more connections that seem to you to be obvious, but may well be anything but obvious to the reader. (This is one of the many areas in which having a friend read over what you have written may be immensely valuable.)

One other thing to watch for: have you made any overly broad generalizations or overly bold statements? Much as it is important to exhibit a strong point of view, it is also important to be careful in the observations you make and the conclusions you draw. Here's an example:

> For all these reasons, then, the threat of climate change deserves to be seen as the most important issue of our time.

This is a perfectly well-constructed sentence, but it unnecessarily overstates the conclusion. Unless your essay really has compared the threat posed by climate change with that of every single other issue of our time (worldwide poverty, inequality, disease, all other threats to the environment, conventional war, nuclear war, etc.) you are making a claim far stronger than you need to when you describe it as "***the*** most important issue of our time." Happily, the matter is easily addressed through the addition of a word or two to qualify your conclusion:

> For all these reasons, then, the threat of climate change deserves to be seen as **among the most important issues** of our time.
>
>> (or "…deserves to be seen as one of the most important issues…" or "…deserves to be rated high among the most important issues…")

Students sometimes feel they will weaken their arguments if they use qualifying phrases in this sort of way. In fact, making sure the assertions you make in an essay are not overstated will always strengthen the essay's arguments, not weaken them.

Here's a slightly more complicated example of the same sort of thing:

> As I have demonstrated in this essay, it was Dorothy Richardson—not James Joyce or Virginia Woolf—who pioneered stream of consciousness techniques in English literature. Joyce and Woolf have received all the credit for the innovations of stream of consciousness fiction, when that credit should really go to Richardson.

Dorothy Richardson did indeed pioneer stream of consciousness techniques years before Joyce or Woolf. But is *who came first* the only thing that matters? Should the pioneer receive all the credit for a literary innovation? Christopher Marlowe is responsible for certain innovations in dramatic writing that Shakespeare then took full advantage of and extended, but no one suggests that all the credit should go to Marlowe. And is it really true that Joyce and Woolf have received *all* the credit, and Richardson absolutely none? The writer here has engaged in a bit of hyperbole that spoils what would otherwise be an excellent conclusion. Again, the problem is easily remedied:

> As I have demonstrated in this essay, it was Dorothy Richardson—not James Joyce or Virginia Woolf—who pioneered stream of consciousness techniques in English literature. Joyce and Woolf have received virtually all the credit for the innovations of stream of consciousness fiction, when much of that credit should really go to Richardson.

Overstating your case, then, is one important thing to watch for when you are working on the second draft of your essay.

There are also some things you *shouldn't* be looking for during this sort of revision—among them typos or other spelling mistakes, mistakes in capitalization, errors in spacing, poor formatting of notes, and so on. If you happen to notice issues of this sort that you can easily address as you are working on the larger revisions, by all means do so. But for most of us the work of checking all these sorts of things engages a different part of the brain; if you're pre-occupied with checking format issues you will be less likely to realize it if your argument does not flow well from one paragraph to the next. Our advice is to focus first on revision—and to focus on proofreading only once you have a solid second draft in hand.

What, then, does proofreading entail? It's your last chance to notice issues of logical or stylistic fluency, of course, but at this stage that shouldn't be your primary focus. You should be looking for commas out of place—or places that need commas. You should be checking that every open quotation mark is followed a little further on by a closed quotation mark. You should be checking for words repeated—or missing words. You should be checking that all appropriate titles are italicized, that all appropriate words are capitalized, that all the notes and references are formatted correctly. These and many other similar matters are often termed "mechanical," but if you are sloppy over them, that sloppiness will certainly take away from the effect of the essay as a whole. Proofreading is often thought of as a boring job, yet it can be one that brings real satisfaction: no writer is able to proofread an essay without finding things to fix, things to improve.

One final suggestion about proofing: try reading the essay aloud. Many writers feel silly reading aloud to themselves, but inevitably they find they catch things—a missing word, an extra letter—that even the most diligent silent proofing will have missed. For the few minutes it takes, it is always worth giving voice, in an entirely literal sense, to the written text.

⊙ Collaboration and Research

Stop and think for a moment about the experiences of writers described in this book: developing a voice; working out the argumentative structure for an essay; refining the stylistic fluency of phrases, sentences, and paragraphs. Some of those experiences are collaborative by nature, involving—for instance—the one-to-one dialogue of writing tutorials. There is simply no such thing as a hermetically sealed, totally isolated writer of utterly personal beliefs and insights. As long as he is acquiring new knowledge, a competent writer relies on collaboration—and research is a meaningful and productive way for writers to collaborate with other writers.

O *Approaches to Research*

Regrettably, some university students approach research as an endeavour entailing nothing more than the finding and collating of old material on their assigned subject. The more imaginative and independent, however, will set out to use others' work as a stepping stone to new insights, seeking to arrange and examine what exists in order to present that which has never existed. Their essays' arguments are thereby strengthened through collaborative exposure to the work of others.

Consider the research presented by Melissa Davis—and, in particular, the authority she quotes in paragraph 8, Peter Levine. She quotes Levine only once (at a point where he makes a significant historical point succinctly and effectively), and she never paraphrases any of Levine's arguments; indeed, the article she quotes reaches a substantially different conclusion than she does herself. Nevertheless, the Levine article was of considerable help to Davis: a strong, collaborative voice providing information and arguments that helped her to sort out a number of facts, and to clarify her own views—and (through its own Works Cited list) pointing her in the direction of significant other voices.

How does an industrious student locate strong, collaborative voices of this sort—voices that she can be confident are responsible ones, regardless of whether or not she may in the end agree with their conclusions? Search engines such as Google will turn up vast amounts of material on almost any topic—more than could possibly be taken account of in a single essay, perhaps more than could be read in an entire academic year. How do you choose? And how do you judge what is likely to be reliable, and what isn't?

One important research principle is to give consideration to material that has been refereed. The term "refereed journal" (or "refereed monograph," where a book-length academic study is concerned) refers to the publishers' practice of sending all submissions to respected academic authorities to be vetted before the material is published. (Another term often used for the same process is "peer-review"—the research of one scholar is reviewed by his or her peers before it is accepted for publication.) The process of refereeing or peer review is far from foolproof, and it's often the case that refereed journal articles or monographs will come to very different conclusions. But it is one important filtering device that can help separate responsible sources from irresponsible ones.

You should be aware that most refereed journals (and the electronic copies of most academic monographs) are not accessible to anyone who goes online. It is often the case that the article will be listed by your search engine but protected by a paywall, such that only a brief abstract (or the first page of the article) will be publicly accessible, and nothing more. It is also often the case that outstanding academic material will be given such a low score by the search engine's algorithm that you are never likely to find it in an ordinary Google search; like other search engines, Google tends to put frequently consulted material at the head of lists—a practice that may place pieces by popular astrologers or political cranks far ahead of the less flamboyant but more reliable work of reputable scholars. For academic research, Google Scholar (scholar.google.com) is often a far better choice than the main Google search engine. But like Google, Google Scholar will give you no more than an abstract or the first page of a scholarly article—just as Google Books (or Amazon's "Look Inside" feature) will typically provide only selected pages of monographs. It's worth making a note of anything that looks interesting from your initial search process on Google and Google Scholar—but to fully explore many of the articles and books that look to be interesting and relevant to your research, you'll need to be inside the paywall that protects them.

Getting inside that paywall, then, is a vitally important first step in academic research. The way to do that, of course, is through your institution's library. If you are a college or university student in good standing, you will have been given an identification number and passcode to access the library's collection. Almost all university libraries today include a vast array of electronic material: newspapers, magazines, scholarly journals, and academic monographs that cannot be accessed by anyone without a passcode.

Let's follow some of the details of Melissa's research process. An initial Google search for "Sensation Exhibit Brooklyn" returns something close to half a million results. Many of these are for newspaper reports—which are likely to be good sources for a research paper of this sort that concerns the reaction of the public and of city officials to a public event. Given that the event occurred in a borough of New York City and that *The New York Times* has a reputation as among the most reliable of the world's newspapers, she will naturally want to check out the numerous articles in that paper on the controversy and its aftermath. She will be able to find all the articles listed on Google—but she will only be able to access half a dozen before the paywall takes effect and she will be invited to become a *New York Times* subscriber on a trial basis. Instead, of course, she can find unlimited access to *The New York Times* through her university's library, once she has logged in using her passcode.

Several articles from *The New York Times* and other reputable newspapers reporting on the events as they happened show up on the first few pages of returns to that Google Search. But what about scholarly articles? Especially, what about recent scholarly articles? When Melissa turns to Google Scholar as a search engine, and restricts her search to material from 2010 onwards, Peter Cramer's 2013 article "Sick Stuff: A Case Study of Controversy in a Constitutive Attitude" from the academic journal *Rhetoric Society Quarterly* immediately pops up at the top of the list. When she tries to access the article directly, though, it turns out to be protected by a paywall; *Rhetoric Society Quarterly* is made available electronically through Taylor & Francis Online, one of many online aggregators that sell access to different bundles of scholarly journals. When she tries to access the article through Google or Google Scholar, Melissa can see only the abstract and the rest of the first page. The Taylor & Francis Online site tells her this:

> Sorry, you do not have access to this article.
> How to gain access:
>> Recommend to your librarian that your institution purchase access to this publication.
>> If you already have an individual subscription, please log in using your Taylor & Francis Online ID to gain access.

The Taylor & Francis Online site also informs her of "purchase options"; she can purchase the article for $39, or the full issue in which it appears for $86.

There's nothing here to indicate that, if she is attending a good-sized institution, chances are the library will *already* have purchased access to this publication, and *Rhetoric Society Quarterly* will be accessible to her at no charge through her university's library.

Fortunately, Melissa is familiar with search engines and online aggregators, and knows that paying $39 for this article without checking out her university library would be most unwise. She realizes that what she needs to do is search for that article and that journal on her university library's search engine. She'll need to log in using her library passcode, but then she'll find the entire article fully accessible.

The same is true of David Darts's article from *Studies in Art Education*, "The Art of Culture War: (Un)Popular Culture, Freedom of Expression, and Art Education." Melissa can find out that the article exists easily enough using Google Scholar, and the search engine lets her know that the article mentions the "Sensation" Exhibit at the Brooklyn Museum—but she can't check out anything beyond the article's first page. The online aggregator in this case is JSTOR ("a not-for-profit, founded to help academic libraries and publishers"); unlike Taylor & Francis Online, they do raise the possibility that Melissa "might have access to this item" already via her library—though only after suggesting that she "register for a MyJSTOR account."

Just as was the case with *Rhetoric Society Quarterly*, it turns out that *Studies in Art Education* (and, specifically, this David Darts article) is available through her university library. Melissa finds the journal, and that article, using her university library's search engine. This time, though, the article isn't quite so easy to find; searching for the article title produces no results, so she has to find the journal in the library's alphabetical listings, then find the article in the table of contents for the winter 2008 volume. Fortunately, again, Melissa has been informed both by a couple of her professors and by one of the university librarians that her library's search engine isn't the greatest. The best way to use it is in conjunction with Google, Google Scholar, and other search engines—and it's never a good idea to give up easily if the first indication from the university library search engine is that the library doesn't provide access to a particular scholarly journal or academic monograph. (This is one area where libraries vary quite significantly; some university libraries seem to have search engines just as good as those of Google Scholar, whereas others are clunky and unpredictable.)

Whatever combination of search engines you are using, chances are high that you will find far more material than you can easily deal with. How can you avoid spending a large amount of time merely amassing a large quantity of material, much of which may be unreliable or not relevant for your purposes?

There is no one easy answer to this question. Part of the answer is often psychological; it can be important for many writers to start actually writing even before they are sure they have all the information they will want; the very process of writing often helps them to realize what sorts of information they still need. But much of the answer is also in what priority you give to different sorts of material. Whether or not material has been reviewed is one criterion. Another is how often you find it cited. Many good researchers like to start by making a very brief list of materials to consult, working purely on

Searching through Old Newspapers

Here's one small example of how difficult it can be for a novice to navigate the world of electronic research. Imagine you are doing an essay on some aspect of nineteenth-century British history or literature and you would like to check out what the newspapers of that era had to say about a particular figure—the poet Augusta Webster, say, or the activist and inventor Lewis Gompertz. So far as newspapers go, you might well think of *The Times* of London, and no doubt you would try to google their archives. You would quickly find that, as with most newspaper archives nowadays, they are protected by a paywall.

Luckily for you, almost every university library has a subscription to the *Times* archive. If you check your university library's website you are likely to find "The Times of London Digital Archive" quite readily—listed under "newspapers," as one would expect. It's protected by a paywall, but so long as you have your university ID and passcode you'll be able to access it easily—and utilize its very good search engine to quickly find electronic facsimiles of all articles mentioning Webster or Gompertz.

But what about other British newspapers of the nineteenth century? Chances are you won't find nineteenth-century archives for any other British newspapers listed in the same section of your library's website. Don't give up! If you root about a bit using Google or another search engine outside the library site, you are likely to find pointers to what you're looking for. Googling "Victorian newspapers" or "British Newspapers 1800–1900" will likely bring up "19th Century British Library Newspapers"—a database that brings together four dozen different British newspapers covering the years 1800 to 1913. Back on your university's library site you'll find it under "databases," not "newspapers." Like the *Times* site, it has an excellent search engine; once you are on the site you will quickly and easily be able to search those 48 newspapers and check out all the articles in any of them that mentioned Webster or Gompertz at any time during the nineteenth century.

If Google fails you in such situations, you still need not give up; you can always ask your instructor, or your university librarian. Chances are they will either be able to point you in the direction of what you want—or, at the very least, save you from hours of fruitless searching by letting you know that there is no convenient way to find what you'd like to find!

the basis of what seems most relevant to the topic they are tackling. Then, as they are scanning those, they will pay attention to which other books or articles are referred to most often by the authors. If a work is frequently cited by others, it will be one that you should take into account.

Where articles are concerned, the researcher should pay attention to the journal or newspaper in which the piece was originally published. Often she will be able to pick up on clues as to whether or not it is a publication with a good reputation. As Melissa Davis was following up a lead that Levine had mentioned, for example—an article by Arthur C. Danto in *The Nation*—she noticed on the masthead that *The Nation* had been published "since 1865," and that Danto had been for many years "Columbia University's Johnsonian Professor of Philosophy." At the other end of the spectrum, she found a vast amount of material on the Web the reliability of which seemed difficult to vouch for. An article on the Bush Watch website, for example, discussing George W. Bush's stance towards the "Sensation" exhibit, was by an unnamed author and referred to Bush as "Dubya." Unsurprisingly, the article in *The Nation* seemed both far better informed and far better written than the commentary on the Bush Watch site.

Where newspapers are concerned it is also helpful to acquire some sense of the reputation of the publication. *The New York Times*, *The Washington Post*, *Los Angeles Times*, and *The Wall Street Journal* are all American newspapers with strong reputations; in Canada the equivalents are *The Globe and Mail* and *National Post*; in the UK *The Times*, *The Telegraph*, *The Independent*, *The Guardian*, and *The Economist* (the latter now published weekly in a magazine format, but still resolutely styling itself as a "newspaper"). Though all these are reputable publications, it is also helpful to know that some (e.g., *The Wall Street Journal*, *National Post*, *The Telegraph*) tend to be ideologically very conservative, while others (e.g., *The Washington Post*, *The Guardian*) tend to be ideologically somewhat to the left.

If you are uncertain about how reputable a source may be, it is a good idea to consult your instructor. She will be able to tell you, for example, that *The American Historical Review* and *The Journal of American History* are both highly reputable, that *The Journal of Philosophy* is a much more reputable publication than is *Animus: A Philosophical Journal for Our Time*, and so on. That should not lead you to agree with everything you find in *The Journal of Philosophy*, of course—but it should save you some time.

It's also worth thinking of the credentials of the publisher. Whether in bound or electronic form, a book from one of the world's most prestigious university presses (among them Oxford and Cambridge in Britain; California, Chicago, Duke, Harvard, Princeton, Stanford, and Yale in the US; Toronto and McGill-Queen's in Canada) is more likely to provide reliable information than one from Pelican Publishing (a non-scholarly Louisiana publisher of books on politics, cooking, and various other topics) or from Sentinel Press (an imprint within the Penguin Group that dedicates itself to the promotion of right-wing causes). The experienced researcher will thus take account of the publisher of any book or article. But at the same time, one should never take a book's reliability for granted based on the reputation of the publisher. The university presses of Oxford and Harvard may be highly reputable, but even the most prestigious presses have published some real duds in their time. And, because librarians often have standing orders for all books from such prestigious presses as these, the chances of a real dud from such a press finding its way onto the library's shelves or databases are far greater than the chances of an inferior book from a lesser known publisher being included in the library's offerings.

With the growth of the Open Access movement in recent years, it is becoming more and more common for leading scholars and other reputable writers to bypass the traditional "gatekeepers" and post material online without it having been vetted beforehand by any process of peer review or assessment by publishers. There may often be significant advantages to this approach for both authors and readers; open access publishing makes up-to-date research available more quickly; makes available not only a larger volume of material, but also a wider range of viewpoints; and reduces the undue influence that a handful of academic journal publishers have for many years exerted over the dissemination of research. But when you are checking out material published through an open-access publisher, you should be aware that not every publisher is alike. Open access publishers such as PLOS and SSRN were founded by academics and are highly reputable. Even where there may be no formal process of peer review for self-archived pieces, basic vetting has been carried out with material published on these sites, such that articles by cranks and crackpots are few and far between. Some other open access publishers, on the other hand, operate primarily through unsupervised self-archiving, where authors of any sort post their own work. Outstanding work may certainly sometimes be found on such a site, but it is likely to constitute a much smaller percentage of the total than it does on PLOS or SSRN. Outstanding work may also be found on websites or blogs unaffiliated with any institution or aggregating site—but as a general principle, material on a site with the domain name of an accredited university is more likely to be more reliable. (In some countries accredited institutions may be identified by the style of their domain names; in the US, for example, accredited universities and colleges have .edu domain names, whereas in Britain they have .ac.uk domain names.)

Think too of the credentials of the author. Is he or she an academic at a respected institution, and has he or she published widely on the topic? And think of how recent the material is; for certain sorts of research there is an obvious premium to be placed on more recent material. But the most recent is not always the best, of course. Ask too if the work provides sources to back up the arguments made. And is it possible readily to check the accuracy of those sources?

Another important criterion for certain sorts of research is point of view. If you are conducting research on a controversial topic, it's important to make sure that you consult a range of different viewpoints. You should not feel obligated, though, to give equal weight to all points of view. Particularly where material on the Web is concerned, it will sometimes be the case that implausible or downright irresponsible points of view will be more widely represented than views that deserve greater respect. Such is obviously the case with websites promulgating racist, homophobic, or otherwise bigoted views, but it may also be the case with certain scientific matters. By the late 1990s, for example, the vast majority of reputable scientific opinion was in broad agreement as to the dangers of global climate change. Dissenting scientific voices comprised only a small minority among the community of reputable scientists—but for years their views received disproportionate space on the Web, where numerous sites were largely devoted to casting doubt on the consensus scientific view on climate change (and, not by coincidence, to preserving the status quo for the coal industry, the oil and gas industry, and so on). Where such ideologically charged issues as these are concerned, it is worth paying particularly close attention to accounts that run counter to the normal ideological stance of the publication. When the right-wing magazine *The Economist* accepted several years ago that the weight of evidence overwhelmingly supported the argument that global warming posed a real danger, or when the left-of-centre British newspaper *The Guardian* concluded that despite its socialist rhetoric the Mugabe government in Zimbabwe was denying its people both economic justice and basic human rights, such views deserve special respect.

Finally, the experienced researcher is willing to trust her own judgement: to glance at the table of contents and skim quickly through two or three dozen works on a subject and in each case make a snap decision as to its likely usefulness. These decisions are not, of course, irreversible; she may well find that one of the books initially set aside with barely a moment's notice is generally regarded as among the most important works in the field (in which case she will, of course, return to it with more care). But she must in the first instance have some way of making the mass of material manageable.

What of the opposite problem? What if there seems to be little or nothing published on the subject? Perhaps it's an area on the border with one or more other territories; in that case, surveying those territories may be necessary. Perhaps it's a relatively new subject; in that case—as indeed for any research—it's always helpful to check the relevant indices of journal articles. Some of the most important of these for work in the arts and social sciences are as follows:

- *Humanities Index:* covers articles published from 1974 onwards in such disciplines as English, history, and philosophy.
- *MLA Bibliography:* offers articles on the English language and literature as well as on French, German, Italian, Spanish, and so on.
- *Philosopher's Index:* the most comprehensive listing of articles on philosophy.
- *Social Sciences Index:* covers articles published from 1974 onwards in such areas as anthropology, economics, political science, psychology, and sociology.

These days, virtually all indices appear in electronic form;[1] keyword searches are indispensable for researchers. The idea is to use a

---

1   For listings by academic discipline see pages 420–70.

single word—or a combination of words—that you consider to be the "key" or main focus of your topic. The computer system will look through every author, title, and subject heading that includes the keywords (in any order). Queen's University provides its students with the following "Basic Search Tips":

Title or journal article
- Omit initial article (*a, the, le*)
- Type just the first few words
- Use journal title for magazines, journals, newspapers

Author
- Type last name first: *einstein, a*
- Add first initial if known
- For organizations use normal word order

Keyword
- Results can include any of your words
- Must use + to indicate essential terms
- Use ? to truncate; use quotes for phrases: "*meech lake*"

Call number
- Include punctuation and spaces

One further note about academic research in the second decade of the twenty-first century: it's worth remembering that your academic library doesn't exist only in electronic form. It still has a physical location, where you will be sure to find a number of helpful librarians. Their job is to help you understand how to do research and do it well; they really can help. And the library also provides a great deal of material that you can touch and turn the pages of. It's worth doing that for at least two reasons. One is the process of browsing in the stacks of the library can lead you to make connections and generate ideas in ways that don't always happen when you are searching and reading online. The second may surprise you: some important material is simply not available electronically. That's not only true of certain books and articles from decades or centuries ago; it's also true of some very recent material. The respected academic journal *Studies in Canadian Literature*, for example, is available only in bound volumes for the first three years after publication; you can access an article that's three years old electronically, but for a recent article you'll need to check out your library in person—unless you subscribe to the journal yourself.

Whether the information comes from bound volumes of printed material or articles in an electronic database, when it comes time to use research in an essay it is essential to strike an appropriate balance between one's own ideas and those of others. The assertive attitude developed during the writer's voice work is crucial at this point, since quotations from experts can easily obscure or overwhelm an essay's thesis. Peter Levine or Arthur C. Danto are more qualified than is Melissa Davis. She is the writer, though, and must therefore remain in full control of the essay's argumentative force, while drawing on others' writing for much of her raw material.

O *Citation*

Note that, after the quoted phrase from MacRitchie in paragraph 12, Davis has included a parenthetical reference to cite the quotation's source. Here as in the rest of her essay, she is following a system currently recommended by the *MLA Handbook* (an authoritative guide, published by the Modern Language Association of America). The parenthetical reference may be followed up by readers under "Works Cited" at the end of Davis's essay:

> MacRitchie, Lynn. "Ofili's Glittering Icons." *Art in America*, Jan. 2000, pp. 96–101.

Under the MLA system, which dispenses with the traditional footnote still used in some other citation systems, the parenthetical reference should include the author's last name unless that name is clearly linked to the cited material in the actual text of the essay. Thus, when Davis provides Arthur Danto's name in the body of her text, the parenthetical reference accompanying the quotation includes only the relevant page number:

> As Arthur C. Danto has pointed out, "since it is unlikely that as a black Anglo-African Ofili would have used dung to besmirch the slaves [in the picture "Afrobluff"], there is no reason to suppose

he was bent on besmirching the Holy Virgin through its presence there either" (2).

Notice here that when Davis feels it appropriate to add a few words of explanation in the midst of Danto's words, she puts them in square brackets to indicate that these are not part of the quotation.

Melissa's list of "Works Cited" also demonstrates the format for arrangement of titles (alphabetical, according to the authors' last names), for indentation of successive lines, and for listing differ-ent sorts of sources. Notice the sequence of information for a cita-tion from a website: after the source's publication date comes the website's URL or DOI. After this, in MLA style it is optional, but recommended, to give the researcher's date of access.

The MLA system of citation is the most commonly employed system in many humanities disciplines; in this book, Davis's essay is preceded by a full summary of how to use "MLA style"—along with full summaries of other leading systems of citation.

All university professors, like all book publishers and all jour-nal editors, are primarily concerned with two things when it comes to citing and documenting material: accuracy and consistency. Whatever system is recommended, a research writer must take the responsibility of following it closely—by consulting a manual or a style sheet (some professors compose their own) or, if accessible, exemplary essays. Just as audiences vary from discipline to disci-pline, so do systems of documentation; those provided by the MLA and the APA are certainly not the only ones. While their differences may at times seem trivial (professors have been known to penal-ize essays whose citations exhibit misplaced commas), accuracy and consistency should nevertheless be sought. This is the one facet of essay-writing that calls on a good writer to suspend his independent attitude in favour of slavish obedience and conformity.

Most systems currently in use have done away with citations at the bottoms of the pages (footnotes), but they have preserved a means for writers to offer marginal explanations to their read-ers. Called endnotes, or simply "notes," these explanations appear immediately after the text of an essay but before the list of "Works Cited." Endnotes have one of two purposes. The first is to direct readers towards additional sources of information on the topic, as does Melissa Davis's note 4. The second is to digress responsibly from a topic, as Davis does, for example, in her notes 1 and 3. The effect of such brief explanatory paragraphs is to enhance—from a peripheral position—the strength of the essay.

For an extended treatment of these matters, see the chapter "Documentation and Research."

O Criticism

The ultimate, and often most volatile, collaboration occurs when a writer faces the criticism and responses of a reader. For journalists, such collaboration is fairly routine, since both editors and subscribers are only too eager to correct and modify articles. The university writer also expects regular doses of criticism and advice. Professorial zeal can, however, prove to be a shock, as one student explains:

> My problem is that my essays are perfect only up until the moment I hand them in to be marked. Suddenly, the paper undergoes a drastic transformation. Red marks appear scattered across the page. Words like *NO!* or *EXPLAIN!* appear, linked by arrows to the short forms *AWK* and *SP*. Then there's the ultimate in humiliation—a red line scribbling out my sentence, and a better one written in its place.

Warding off humiliation very often depends on active response to criticism. Collaboration is, after all, a two-sided affair; no red-penned advice or correction has the power to improve a writer's skills unless that writer evaluates it independently. Questions are bound to arise ("Sure, this passage is awkward, but how can I improve it?" "What's wrong with this?!"); finding satisfactory answers depends on continued dialogue and revision. When all is said and done, when all is written and submitted, competent assessors of essays— while experienced and qualified—are far from dictatorial. They look for logical coherence, not for reflections of their own beliefs; and for stylistic clarity, not for imitations of their own writing. Writers who take advantage of actually collaborating with their most demanding readers are the ones who progress most steadily.

O *Examinations and In-class Essays*

The discussion of essay-writing in these pages has presumed that the process is likely to extend over several days, or even several weeks. How does the situation change when the student is asked to write an essay in a much more limited time, as part of an in-class assignment or an examination? Many students have a natural—and understandable—tendency to assume that entirely different principles must apply to this second category of essay-writing.

There are differences, of course, but the basic similarities must also be kept in mind. Success in either situation depends upon clearly understanding the task at hand. By zeroing in on the command words (*explain, analyze, argue, compare, summarize*, etc.), an exam-writer will know precisely what kind of response (explanatory, argumentative, etc.) the professor wants. Reading the questions carefully and with an attitude of self-confidence; assessing the relative value of each question, so as to better apportion the time available; remembering (as the essay-writer must) that quantity matters much less than quality: these are the means to the mastery of examinations. Here too are a few additional pointers:

- Examination questions never ask the student to write down all he has in his head on the given topic. If the student is asked to write on Austen's use of irony in *Emma*, he will not do well by recounting the full story of the book, or discussing Emma's character at great length. If asked to comment on the claim that "the Treaty of Versailles caused World War II," he will not do well by simply reciting a list of the main historical developments between the two world wars.

- As in writing essays, the use of a map or plan is an asset. It won't, of course, be as well thought-out; indeed, it may well be just a frenzied clutter of words. But it's important to have some sense of structure, and some place to jot down ideas that come to mind unexpectedly. A rough sheet for notes and plans kept always at hand can help.

- Another similarity between essays and essay answers on exams is the importance of checking written work. Make sure nothing important has been left out; make sure the points are expressed concisely and clearly. And avoid writing madly right up to the end of the time allotted. Again, a well-written short answer will be better received than a sloppy and long-winded one.

Note: An excellent guide to the peculiarities of exam-writing is the University of Reading's "Answering Exam Questions."

O *Works Cited*

"Answering Exam Questions." *University of Reading Study Advice*, www. libguides.reading.ac.uk/exams/answering. Accessed 26 Aug. 2016.

Cameron, Ian. *For All Practical Purposes*. Broadview Press, 1988.

Cole, Susan. "The Legacy of Terry Fox." *Queen's Quarterly*, vol. 97, no. 2, 1990, pp. 253–76.

Frye, Northrop. "Humanities in a New World." *Divisions on a Ground*, edited by James Polk, House of Anansi Press, 1982, pp. 102–17.

Giltrow, Janet. *Academic Writing*. 3rd ed., Broadview Press, 2002.

Gould, Stephen Jay. "The Brain of Brawn." *New York Times*, 25 June 2000, p. 17.

Graff, Gerald, and Cathy Birkenstein. *They Say / I Say: The Moves That Matter in Academic Writing*. 3rd ed., W.W. Norton & Co., 2014.

Hallpike, C.R. *The Principles of Social Evolution*. Clarendon Press, 1984.

Johnston, Ian. *Essays and Arguments: A Handbook for Writing Essays*. Rev. ed., Broadview Press, 2015.

Lauer, Janice. "Writing as Enquiry: Some Questions for Teachers." *College Composition and Communication*, vol. 33, no. 1, 1982, pp. 89–93.

Menand, Louis. "Comp Time." *New Yorker*, 11 Sept. 2000, pp. 124–29.

Orwell, George. "Politics and the English Language." *Collected Essays*, Secker Press, 1961, pp. 353–67.

Ross, Alex. "Shostakovich and Stalin." *New Yorker*, 20 March 2000, pp. 124–29.

Simic, Charles. "Down there on a Visit." *Memory Piano*, U of Michigan P, 2006, pp. 165–78.

Whitman, Walt. "Democratic Vistas." *Prose Works 1892: The Collected Writings of Walt Whitman*, edited by Floyd Stovall, vol. 2, New York UP, 1964, pp. 361–426.

Wills, Garry. "The Negro President." *The New York Review of Books*, 6 Nov. 2003, pp. 45–51.

◎ BASIC GRAMMAR: *An Outline*

⊙ Parts of Speech

● *Nouns*

Nouns are words that name people, things, places, or qualities. Some examples follow:

- names of people: *boy, John, parent*
- names of things: *hat, spaghetti, fish*
- names of places: *Saskatoon, Zambia, New York*
- names of qualities: *silence, intelligence, anger*

Nouns can be used to fill the gaps in sentences like these:

- I saw _____ at the market yesterday.
- He dropped the _____ into the gutter.
- Has learning Italian taken a lot of _____ ?
- Hamilton is a _____ with several hundred thousand people living in it.
- _____ is my favourite ski resort.

Some nouns (e.g., *sugar, milk, confusion*) are uncountable—that is, we cannot say *a sugar, two sugars,* or *three sugars.*

● *Pronouns*

Pronouns replace or stand for nouns. For example, instead of saying, *The man slipped on a banana peel* or *George slipped on a banana peel,* we can replace the noun *man* (or the noun *George*) with the pronoun *he* and say *He slipped on a banana peel.*

personal and indefinite pronouns: Whereas a personal pronoun such as *he* or *she* refers to a definite person, the words *each, every, either, neither, one, another,* and *much* are indefinite. They may be used as pronouns or as adjectives; in either case, a singular verb is needed.

- Each player wants to do her best.
  (Here the word *each* is an adjective, describing the noun *player*.)

95

- Each wants to do her best.
    (Here the word *each* is a pronoun, acting as the subject of
    the sentence.)
- Each of the players wants to do her best.
    (The word *each* is still a pronoun, this time followed by the
    phrase *of the players*. But it is the pronoun *each* that is the
    subject of the sentence; the verb must be the singular *wants*.)

possessive pronouns and adjectives: See under "Adjectives" below.

relative pronouns: These pronouns relate back to a noun that has
been used earlier in the same sentence. Consider how repetitious
these sentences sound:

- I talked to the man. The man wore a red hat.

We could of course replace the second *man* with *he*. Even better,
though, is to relate or connect the second idea to the first by using
a relative pronoun:

- I talked to the man who wore a red hat.
- I found the pencil. I had lost the pencil.
- I found the pencil that I had lost.

The following are all relative pronouns:

- who whose (has other uses too)
- which that (has other uses too)
- whom

Try replacing the second noun in these pairs of sentences with a
relative pronoun, so as to make only one sentence out of each pair:

- I polished the table. I had built the table.
- Premier Wall is vacationing this week in Quebec's Eastern
    Townships. The premier cancelled a planned holiday last fall.
- The word *other* is often used by literary theorists when speak-
    ing of a sense of strangeness in the presence of cultural differ-
    ence. *Other* is usually preceded by the definite article when so
    used.

pronouns acting as subject and as object: We use different forms of some pronouns depending on whether we are using them as subjects or objects and whether they are singular or plural.

	singular	*plural*
Subject	I	we
Pronouns	you	you
	he/she/it	they
	who, what, which	who, what, which

	singular	*plural*
Object	me	us
Pronouns	you	you
	him/her/it	them
	whom, what, which	whom, what, which

- She loves Frankie.

  (Here the pronoun *she* is the subject of the sentence.)
- Frankie loves her.

  (Here the word *her* is the object; *Frankie* is the subject.)
- That's the woman who loves Frankie.

  (Here the pronoun *who* is the subject of the clause *who loves Frankie*.)
- That's the woman whom Frankie loves.

  (Here the pronoun *whom* is the object of the verb *love*; *Frankie* is the subject of the clause *whom Frankie loves*.)

The distinctions between *I* and *me* and between *who* and *whom* are treated more fully under Pronouns, pages 180–86.

● *Articles*

Articles (determiners often classed as a form of adjective) are words used to introduce nouns. There are only three of them: *a*, *an*, and *the*. Articles show whether or not one is drawing attention to a particular person or thing.

For example, we would say *I stood beside a house* if we did not want to draw attention to that particular house, but *I stood beside the house that the Taylors used to live in* if we did want to draw attention to the particular house. *A* (or *an* if the noun following begins with a vowel sound) is an indefinite article—used when you do not wish to be definite or specific about which thing or person you are referring to. *The* is a definite article, used when you do wish to call attention to the particular thing or person, and when a noun is followed by a specifying phrase or clause (such as *used to live in*, which follows the noun *Taylors*). Remember that if you use *the*, you are suggesting that there can be only one or one group of what you are referring to.

Choose the appropriate article (*a*, *an*, or *the*):
- _____ moon shone brightly last night.
- She had _____ long conversation with _____ friend.
- Have you ever driven _____ car?
- Have you driven _____ car that your wife bought on Monday?

● *Adjectives*

Adjectives are words used to tell us more about (describe or modify) nouns or pronouns. Here are some examples of adjectives:

big	good	heavy
small	bad	expensive
pretty	careful	healthy
quick	slow	unexpected

- The small boy lifted the heavy table.
    (Here the adjective *small* describes or tells us more about the noun *boy*, and the adjective *heavy* describes the noun *table*.)
- The fast runner finished ahead of the slow one.
    (*Fast* describes *runner* and *slow* describes *one*.)

Notice that adjectives usually come before the nouns that they describe. This is not always the case, however; when the verb *to be* is used, adjectives often come after the noun or pronoun, and after the verb:

- That woman is particularly careful about her finances.
    (*Careful* describes *woman*.)
- It is too difficult for me to do.
    (*Difficult* describes *it*.)

Adjectives can be used to fill the gaps in sentences like these:

- This _____ sweater was knitted by hand.
- As soon as we entered the _____ house we heard a clap of _____thunder.
- Those shoes are very _____.
- Derrida's argument could fairly be described as _____.

Some words can be either adjectives or pronouns, depending on how they are used. That is the case with the indefinite pronouns (see above), and also with certain possessives (words that show possession):

	singular	*plural*
Possessive	my	our
Adjectives	your	your
	his/her	their
	whose	whose

	singular	*plural*
Possessive	mine	ours
Pronouns	yours	yours
	his/hers	theirs
	whose	whose

- I have my cup, and he has his.
    - (Here the word *his* is a pronoun, used in place of the noun *cup*.)
- He has his cup.
    - (Here the word *his* is an adjective, describing the noun *cup*.)
- Whose book is this?
    - (Here the word *whose* is an adjective, describing the noun *book*.)
- Whose is this?
    - (Here the word *whose* is a pronoun, acting as the subject of the sentence.)

● *Verbs*

Verbs are words that express actions or states of affairs. Most verbs can be conveniently thought of as "doing" words (e.g., *open, feel, do, carry, see, think, combine, send*), but several verbs do not fit into this category. Indeed, the most common verb of all—*be*—expresses a state of affairs, not a particular action that is done. Verbs are used to fill gaps in sentences like these:

- I _____ very quickly, but I _____ not _____ up with my brother.
- She usually _____ to sleep at 9:30.
- Stephen _____ his breakfast very quickly.
- They _____ a large farm near Chicago.
- There _____ many different languages that people _____ in India.

One thing that makes verbs different from other parts of speech is that verbs have tenses; in other words, they change their form depending on the time you are talking about. For example, some present tense forms of the verb *to be* are as follows: *I am, you are, he is,* etc.; these are some past tense forms: *I was, you were, he was,* etc. If you are unsure whether or not a particular word is a verb, one way to check is to ask if it has different tenses. For example, if you thought that perhaps the word *football* might be a verb, you need only ask yourself if it would be correct to say, *I footballed, I am footballing, I will football,* and so on. Obviously it would not be, so you know that *football* is the noun that names the game, not a verb that expresses an action. See the next chapter in this book for a discussion of verb tenses.

● *Adverbs*

These words are usually used to tell us more about (describe or modify) verbs, although they can also be used to tell us more about adjectives or about other adverbs. They answer questions such as *How ...?, When ...?,* and *To what extent ...?,* and often they end with the letters *ly*. Here are a few examples, with some adjectives also listed for comparison:

Adjective	*Adverb*
careful	carefully
beautiful	beautifully
thorough	thoroughly
sudden	suddenly
slow	slowly
easy	easily
good	well

- He walked carefully.
    - (The adverb *carefully* tells us how he walked; it describes the verb *walked*.)
- He is a careful boy.
    - (The adjective *careful* describes the noun *boy*.)
- My grandfather died suddenly last week.
    - (The adverb *suddenly* tells how he died; it describes the verb *died*.)
- We were upset by the sudden death of my grandfather.
    - (The adjective *sudden* describes the noun *death*.)
- She plays the game very well.
    - (The adverb *well* tells us how she plays; it describes the verb *plays*. The adverb *very* describes the adverb *well*.)
- She played a good game this afternoon.
    - (The adjective *good* describes the noun *game*.)
- She played a very good game.
    - (The adverb *very* describes the adjective *good*, telling us how good it was.)
- Our friends will meet the new baby soon.
    - (The adverb *soon* describes the verb *will meet*, telling when the action will happen.)

Choose adverbs to fill the gaps in these sentences:

- Ralph writes very _____.
- The judge spoke _____ to her after she had been convicted on six counts of stock manipulation and fraud.
- They were _____ late for the meeting this morning.

● *Prepositions*

Prepositions are joining words, normally used before nouns or pronouns. Some of the most common prepositions are as follows:

about	across	after
at	before	for
from	in	into
of	off	on
over	to	until
with		

Choose prepositions to fill the gaps in these sentences:

- I will tell you _____ it _____ the morning.
- Please try to arrive _____ eight o'clock.
- He did not come back _____ Toronto _____ yesterday.
- I received a letter _____ my sister.

● *Conjunctions and Conjunctive Adverbs*

Conjunctions and conjunctive adverbs are normally used to join groups of words together, and in particular to join clauses together. Conjunctions can be divided into three types: coordinating, subordinating, and correlative.

coordinating conjunctions: Coordinating conjunctions join parallel groupings of words. Since there are only seven such conjunctions in English, they can be memorized easily. Some people use the acronym *FANBOYS* as a memory aid:

> **F**or
> **A**nd
> **N**or
> **B**ut
> **O**r
> **Y**et
> **S**o

- Carmen thought the movie was silly, but we really liked it.
    (The coordinating conjunction *but* joins the main clauses *Carmen thought the movie was silly* and *we really liked it.* Note that a comma precedes a coordinating conjunction used in this way.)

- His anxiety about public performance made him uncomfortable yet improved his playing.
    (The coordinating conjunction *yet* joins the verb phrases *made him uncomfortable* and *improved his playing.*)

- The novel was short, dense, and gripping.
    (The coordinating conjunction *and* joins the adjectives *short*, *dense*, and *gripping*—as it does in this sentence! When joining more than two words or phrases, a coordinating conjunction may be preceded either by a comma or not, as long as the choice is consistent in a single piece of writing.)

subordinating conjunctions: Subordinating conjunctions join subordinate clauses to main clauses. Any clause beginning with a subordinating conjunction is a subordinate clause. English has many subordinating conjunctions; here is a partial list of commonly used ones (note that some are groups of words):

after	although	as	as long as
as though	because	before	even though
if	in order that	since	so that
unless	until	whereas	while

- They stopped playing because they were tired.
    (The subordinating conjunction *because* joins the clauses *They stopped playing* and *they were tired*, making the second of these subordinate.)

- I will give her your message if I see her.
    (The subordinating conjunction *if* joins the clauses *I will give her your message* and *I see her*, making the second of these subordinate.)

conjunctive adverbs: Conjunctive adverbs, as their name suggests, are adverbs that join word groups as well as modifying them. Conjunctive adverbs can join main clauses together or join a stand-alone main clause to a previous sentence; either way, and unlike other types of conjunctions, conjunctive adverbs need not appear exactly at the beginning of the word groups they join. Wherever it appears, a conjunctive adverb must be set off with commas or preceded by a semicolon if (and only if) it joins two clauses in one sentence. Here are some common conjunctive adverbs (note that some of them are phrases):

alternatively	certainly	furthermore
however	indeed	in fact
in other words	likewise	meanwhile
moreover	nonetheless	on the other hand
otherwise	similarly	that is
therefore	thus	unfortunately

- Miss Polly was busy hiding the silverware. Meanwhile, the Foley brothers arrived at the ranch.
  (*Meanwhile* links the two sentences by indicating the time relationship between them.)

- That new tablet is fantastic. No one, however, will want to pay such a high a price for it.
  (*However* signals a contrast between the two points made by the two sentences, and so is a transition joining them. Because it is embedded in its sentence, *however* is set apart with commas.)

- I have excellent reasons for abandoning this project; unfortunately, the others on my team disagree with me.
  (*Unfortunately* joins the two main clauses of one sentence, and so is preceded by a semicolon and followed by a comma.)

correlative conjunctions: Correlative conjunctions come in pairs and can join single words or word groups. Here are some examples:

both ... and	either ... or
neither ... nor	not only ... but also
so ... that	such ... as

Whatever is joined by correlative conjunctions must have the same grammatical structure, as in the examples below:

- That dishcloth is both smelly and unsanitary.

    (*Both* and *and* join the adjectives *smelly* and *unsanitary*.)

- Neither the dollar nor the economy will fare well if oil prices drop any lower.

    (*Neither* and *nor* join the noun phrases *the dollar* and *the economy*.)

- Not only is our candidate well educated but she is also personable.

    (*Not only* and *but also* join the clauses *our candidate is well educated* and *she is personable*. Note that when joining clauses, *not only* requires that the usual order of subject and verb in the following clause be reversed—and *but also* is split by the following clause's subject and verb.)

Many conjunctions can also act as other parts of speech, depending on how they are used. Notice the difference in each of these pairs of sentences:

- He will not do anything about it until the morning.

    (Here *until* is a preposition joining the noun *morning* to the rest of the sentence.)

- He will not do anything about it until he has discussed it with his wife.

    (Here *until* is a subordinating conjunction introducing the clause *he has discussed it with his wife*.)

- I slept for half an hour after dinner.

    (Here *after* is a preposition joining the noun *dinner* to the rest of the sentence.)

- I slept for half an hour after they had gone home.

    (Here *after* is a subordinating conjunction introducing the clause *they had gone home*.)

- She wants to buy that dress.

    (Here *that* is an adjective describing the noun *dress*: "*Which dress?*" "*That dress!*")

- George said that he was unhappy.

    (Here *that* is a subordinating conjunction introducing the clause *he was unhappy*.)

Choose conjunctions to fill the gaps in the following sentences:

- We believed _____ we would win.
- They sat down in the shade _____ it was hot.
- My father did not speak to me _____ he left.

⊙ Parts of Sentences

● Subject

The subject is the thing, person, or quality about which something is said in a clause. The subject is usually a noun or pronoun.

- The man went to town.
  (The sentence is about the man, not about the town; thus, the noun *man* is the subject.)
- Groundnuts are an important crop in Nigeria.
  (The sentence is about groundnuts, not about crops or about Nigeria; thus, the noun *groundnuts* is the subject.)
- Nigeria is the most populous country in Africa.
  (The sentence is about Nigeria, not about countries or about Africa; thus, the noun *Nigeria* is the subject.)
- He followed me up the stairs.
  (The pronoun *He* is the subject.)

core subject: The core subject is the single noun or pronoun that forms the subject.

complete subject: The complete subject is the subject together with any adjectives or adjectival phrases modifying it:

- The woman in the huge hat went to the market to buy groceries.
  (The core subject is the noun *woman* and the complete subject is *the woman in the huge hat*.)

● Object

An object is something or someone towards which an action or feeling is directed. In grammar an object is the thing, person, or quality affected by the action of the verb. (To put it another way, it receives the action of the verb.) Like a subject, an object normally is made up of a noun or pronoun.

direct object: The direct object is the thing, person, or quality directly affected by the action of the verb. A direct object usually answers the question *What?* or *Who?* Notice that direct objects are not introduced by prepositions.

indirect object: The indirect object is the thing, person, or quality that is indirectly affected by the action of the verb. All indirect objects could be expressed differently by making them the objects of the prepositions *to* or *for*. Instead, the prepositions have been omitted. Indirect objects answer the questions *To whom?* and *For whom?*

- McGriff hit the ball a long way.
  (What did he hit? The ball. *The ball* is the direct object of the verb *hit*.)
- She threw me her hat.
  (What did she throw? Her hat. *Her hat* is the direct object. To whom did she throw it? To me. *Me* is the indirect object. Note that the sentence could be rephrased: *She threw her hat to me*.)
- They gave their father a watch for Christmas.
  (The direct object is *watch*, and the indirect object is *father*.)

● Predicate

The predicate is everything that is said about the subject. In the example under "Subject," *The woman in the huge hat went to the market to buy groceries, went to the market to buy groceries* is the predicate. A predicate always includes a verb.

● Clause

A distinct group of words that includes both a subject and a predicate. Thus a clause always includes a verb.

● Phrase

A distinct group of words that does not include both a subject and a verb. Examples:

Clauses	Phrases
because he is strong	because of his strength (no verb)
before she comes home	before the meeting (no verb)
the professor likes me	from Halifax
a tree fell down	at lunch
who came to dinner	in the evening

● Types of Clauses

main clause (or **independent clause**): A main clause is a group of words that is, or could be, a sentence on its own.

subordinate clause (or **dependent clause**): A subordinate clause is a clause that could not form a complete sentence on its own.

Except for the coordinating conjunctions (*and, but, or, nor, for, yet,* and *so*), conjunctions do not introduce main clauses, so if a clause begins with a word such as *because, although,* or *if,* you can be confident it is a subordinate clause. Similarly, relative pronouns introduce subordinate clauses—never main clauses.

- She lives near Victoria.
   (One main clause forming a complete sentence. The pronoun *She* is the subject, *lives* is the verb, and the preposition *near* and the noun *Victoria* together form a phrase.)
- He danced in the street because he was feeling happy.
   main clause: He danced in the street
   subject: _____
   predicate: _____
   subordinate clause: because he was feeling happy
   subject: _____
   predicate: _____
- Mavis has a cat who likes to drink from the kitchen faucet.
   main clause: Mavis has a cat
   subject: _____
   predicate: _____
   subordinate clause: who likes to drink from the kitchen faucet
   subject: _____
   predicate: _____

● *Types of Subordinate Clauses (or "Dependent Clauses")*

adjectival subordinate clause: a subordinate clause that tells us more about a noun or pronoun. Adjectival clauses begin with relative pronouns such as *who, whom, whose, which*, and *that*.

adverbial subordinate clause: a subordinate clause that tells us more about the action of the verb—telling *how, when, why*, or *where* the action occurred.

noun subordinate clause: a clause that acts like a noun to form the subject or object of a sentence.

Examples:

- He talked at length to his cousin, who quickly became bored.
  (*Who quickly became bored* is an adjectival subordinate clause, telling us more about the noun *cousin*.)
  subject of subordinate clause: the pronoun *who*
  verb in subordinate clause: _____
  subject of main clause: the pronoun *He*
  verb in main clause: _____
- My husband did not like the gift that I gave him.
  (*That I gave him* is an adjectival subordinate clause telling us more about the noun *gift*.)
  subject of subordinate clause: the pronoun *I*
  verb in subordinate clause: _____
  subject of main clause: _____
  verb in main clause: _____
- The boy whom she wants to marry is very poor.
  (*Whom she wants to marry* is an adjectival subordinate clause telling us more about the noun *boy*. Notice that here the subordinate clause appears in the middle of the main clause, *The boy is very poor*.)
  subject of subordinate clause: _____
  verb in subordinate clause: _____
  subject of main clause: _____
  verb in main clause: _____

- I felt worse after I had been to the doctor.
  (*After I had been to the doctor* is an adverbial subordinate clause telling us when I felt worse.)
- He could not attend because he had broken his leg.
  (*Because he had broken his leg* is an adverbial subordinate clause telling us why he could not attend.)
- She jumped as if an alarm had sounded.
  (*As if an alarm had sounded* is an adverbial subordinate clause telling us how she jumped.)
- What he said was very interesting.
  (*What he said* is a noun clause acting as the subject of the sentence, in the same way that the noun *conversation* acts as the subject in *The conversation was very interesting.*)
- Sue-Ellen told me that she wanted to become a lawyer.
  (*That she wanted to become a lawyer* is a noun clause acting as the object, in the same way that the noun *plans* acts as the object in *Sue-Ellen told me her plans.*)

● Types of Phrases

adjectival phrase: a phrase that tells us more about a noun or pronoun.

adverbial phrase: a phrase that tells us more about the action of a verb, answering questions such as *When ...?, Where ...?, How ...?,* and *Why ...?*

- The boy in the new jacket got into the car.
  (*In the new jacket* is an adjectival phrase telling us more about the noun *boy.*)
- I drank from the cup with a broken handle.
  (*With a broken handle* is a phrase telling us more about the noun *cup.*)
- We went to the park.
  (*To the park* is an adverbial phrase telling where we went.)
- They arrived after breakfast.
  (*After breakfast* is an adverbial phrase telling when they arrived.)

● *Distinguishing Phrases and Clauses*

- They were late because of the weather.
    (*Because of the weather* is an adverbial phrase telling us why they were late. It has no verb.)
- They were late because the weather was bad.
    (*Because the weather was bad* is an adverbial clause telling us why they were late.)
    subject: _____
    verb: _____
- The man at the corner appeared to be upset.
    (*At the corner* is an adjectival phrase telling us more about the noun *man*.)
- The man who stood at the corner appeared to be upset.
    (*Who stood at the corner* is an adjectival clause telling us more about the noun *man*.)
    subject: _____
    verb: _____

● *Parts of Speech and Parts of the Sentence*

- After the generous man with the big ears has bought presents, he will quickly give them to his friends.

Parts of speech:

after: *conjunction*   the: *article*

generous: _____   man: _____

with: _____   the: _____

big: _____   ears: _____

has bought: _____   presents: _____

he: _____   will give: _____

quickly: _____   them: _____

to: _____   his: _____

friends: _____

Parts of the sentence:

main clause: He will quickly give them to his friends.

subject: _____

predicate: _____

verb: _____

direct object: _____

indirect object: _____

subordinate clause: After the generous man with the big ears has bought presents,

> Is this an adjectival or an adverbial subordinate clause?
> core subject: the noun _____
> complete subject: _____
> adjectival phrase: with the big ears
> this phrase tells us more about the noun: _____
> predicate: _____
> direct object: _____

Additional Material
A discussion of run-on sentences
("comma splices") and sentence fragments
("incomplete sentences") may be found on **pages 509–13.**
For exercises on grammar go to
sites.broadviewpress.com/writing.
Click on **Exercises.**

(A1 – A211)

(A1 – A211)

◎ WRITING GRAMMATICALLY

⊙ Right and Wrong in Writing

In what sense are errors in grammar and usage wrong? *Are* they in fact wrong in any meaningful sense? Should "wrong" in this context be read as always having quotation marks around it?

Too often this sort of question becomes so infused with assumed political content that it is not taken seriously. On the one hand the conservative is likely to regard the question of whether *you* is a formation inherently superior to the vulgar *y'all* or *youse* as unworthy of debate. Of course the form established as correct is superior; of course the colloquialism is debased. On the other side are those who regard it as an article of faith that there are no universal or objectively verifiable truths, and that consequently there can be no rational justification for preferring *you* to *youse* or *y'all.*

Is *Would you like anything else?* correct and *Would youse like anything else?* incorrect in the same way that *12 x 3 = 36* is correct and *12 x 3 = 35* incorrect? Or in the same way that *The capital of Maharashtra is Mumbai* is correct and *The capital of Maharashtra is Delhi* is false? No. It is not wrong in either of those sorts of ways; one pointer is that it would seem distinctly odd to describe *Would youse like anything else?* as false. In what sense, then, is it wrong? The problem is not that it fails to map onto a structure of reality. In fact, as the cognitive scientist Steven Pinker points out, it makes such a connection with a greater degree of precision than does currently correct usage:

> The mavens lament the loss of conjugal distinction in *he don't* and *we was.* But this has been the trend in standard English for centuries. No one minds that we have abandoned the second-person singular form of verbs, as in *thou sayest.* And by this criterion it is the non-standard dialects that are superior, because they provide their speakers with second-person plural pronouns such as *y'all* and *youse.* (23)

Returning for a moment to Mumbai may help us to sense the way in which *youse* and *y'all* may fairly if in a limited sense be thought of as wrong. The sentence *The capital of Maharashtra is*

Bombay is wrong in something like the same sense that *Would youse like anything else?* is wrong. Both use the symbolic system of language to correspond to an understood reality. But in both cases the signs used are not those used under currently accepted conventions; though a few may still cling to the old usage, almost everyone has now adopted the late 1995 change of name (from Bombay to Mumbai) for India's largest city. "Bombay" certainly still corresponds to reality; it is not false. But nor is it right.

Online

A fascinating discussion of the ways in which issues of correctness are often confused with issues of style, tone, and voice in writing may be found in Louis Menand's review of *Eats, Shoots & Leaves: The Zero Tolerance Approach to Punctuation*. The review is entitled "Bad Comma: Lynne Truss's Strange Grammar"; it first appeared in the 28 June 2004 issue of *The New Yorker*, and may be found online at www.newyorker.com/2004/06/bad-comma.

Similarly, if one were to transplant from Alberta to Massachusetts one of the Alberta highway signs that reads "Speed Limit 110," it would not be in any way false. Given that the convention in all Canadian provinces is to measure speed in kilometres and the convention in the United States is to measure it in miles, however, the sign would in an important sense be wrong (much more wrong, indeed, than would be the use of *youse*, even in the most formal of essays).

But why stick to the conventional where the essay or the business report is concerned? Is there any legitimate argument in favour of the conventions of standard English? One such argument may fairly be grounded in pedagogy; the acquiring of a knowledge of English grammar and syntax is an enormously helpful way of strengthening habits of abstract thought. But that speaks to the value of a byproduct, not of the thing itself. There may be only two *essential* justifications for standard English: ease of communication, and elegance of expression. The first of these is to a large extent obvious, but it is worth stressing that the ease of communication which standard forms or conventions of usage make possible extends not only from individual to individual but also from one culture to another, and over very long periods of time. It has been often noted that the ordinarily literate person in our own time is able to respond to the language of Shakespeare in a way that the ordinarily literate person in Shakespeare's day was quite unable to respond to *Beowulf*, simply because the conventional codification of grammar and usage that print made possible has drastically slowed down the rate of linguistic change. (Cullen Murphy has interestingly suggested that the development beginning in the late nineteenth century of electric and then of electronic methods of reproducing sound has given the sloppy and unruly nature of the spoken word a much greater influence on the shaping of the language and on the speed of change than it had in the sixteenth through nineteenth centuries.)

The second legitimate argument in favour of standard English is by far the weaker, and it should be readily conceded that elegance of expression is often achievable outside the confines of standard English. But complex syntactical and grammatical pathways will inevitably tend to have been worn smoother in a greater variety of ways in long-established conventions of formal expression. Colloquial or non-standard usages may have a freshness to them or in other syntactical ways may appeal strongly in ways that standard English cannot compete with. But they are unlikely to consistently lend themselves to long and elegantly balanced combinations of clauses and phrases in the way that the mainstream of our culture has been training standard English to do for centuries.

◎ ◎ ◎

If this book is prescriptive, then, it should be understood that it is prescriptive only in a context that recognizes correct English as a matter of convention, not as one in which one form is understood to be necessarily or absolutely better than another. Sentences such as *use "aggravate" to mean "make worse," not to mean "annoy" or "irritate"* should always be taken as a convenient short form for "in formal written English, if you wish to conform to the most commonly accepted conventions of usage, use...." And, to return to the example with which this chapter began, *y'all* and *youse* are alternative, arguably superior forms, that we may legitimately reject only on the grounds of convention.

On other specific issues, though, the case for standard usage is sometimes considerably stronger. The confusion of *uninterested* and *disinterested*, for example, will if *disinterested* is driven from the field represent a measurable loss of the communicative capacity of the English language. If we lose *disinterested* it will be more difficult and more cumbersome to express a variety of meanings. Yet there can be no question that many who are unperturbed by *disinterested* having largely been swamped by *uninterested*—indeed, many who do not even recognize the distinction—cringe at the supposed abomination of *youse* or *y'all*. What such cases drive home to us is the degree to which the ways in which we use standard English (and the assumptions we make about standard English) may be linked to irrational sentiments such as social snobbery, or class or gender-based prejudice. (How many there still are who ludicrously claim *fisher* and *chair* to be "more awkward" than the longer and cumbersome forms *fisherman* and *chairman*.) There are good reasons for not abandoning standard English—but good reasons as well to keep questioning our own assumptions about it.

One of the ways in which this book differs from many other guides to grammar and usage is in its approach to change in language, and in the degree to which it attempts to resist the assumption that where the English language is concerned, change implies debasement. Thus in the chapter on part-of-speech conversions such previous entries as *liaise* and *mandate* have been dropped. The back formation of a verb from the noun *liaison* might not be a pretty thing. But a bias against it might not reflect anything more than habit; certainly it can be difficult in many cases to choose more economical replacements. The prejudice against such words might not be any better grounded than was the bias a generation or two ago against using *contact* as a verb. *Finalize* still grates slightly on some ears, too. But sometimes *finish* just does not capture the sense, and *finalize* is more concise than *make final* or *put into final form*. A comparison of the current state of attitudes today towards the word *finalize* with attitudes of the mid-twentieth century may be instructive as to whether or not there are any good grounds today for objecting to *finalize*:

> *Finalize* is not standard: it is special, and it is a peculiarly fuzzy and silly word. Does it mean *terminate*, or does it mean *put into*

final form? One can't be sure, really, what it means, and one gets the impression that the person using it doesn't know, either, and doesn't want to know. (Strunk and White, *The Elements of Style*, [New York, Macmillan: 2/e, 1972] 75–76)

That may have been true in 1957, when the first edition of *The Elements of Style* appeared, or even in 1972, when the second edition was published. But no one today uses *finalize* to mean *terminate*; that denotation has dropped away, and the word's meaning has stabilized as *put into final form*.

If Strunk and White are out of date on the particulars, this remains a good example of the wisdom of their advice to writers that one danger of "adopting new coinages too quickly is that they will bedevil one by insinuating themselves where they do not belong" (75–76). What was a fuzzy coinage in the 1950s has found a clearly defined place in the language of today. And even conservative arbiters such as Strunk and White recognize that language must change, and that this is no bad thing. In the end guides such as this one should continually strive for a balance between the value of continuity in language and in usage, and the value of language as a living thing; without change there can be no life.

⊙   ⊙   ⊙

In one area in particular this guide is not only unresistant to change but embraces change: the move towards bias-free language. In this one area a different sort of *correctness* than the correctness spoken of elsewhere in these pages is involved. Call it political correctness if you will,[1] but however it is referred to, it concerns things that are right and wrong in a sense that goes far beyond questions of what

---

1   When the pejorative term "political correctness" is fairly and carefully used—as it is, for example, by Pinker when he discusses taboos and dissent—it refers to a lamentable tendency to restrict free discussion of controversial topics. Sadly, it is more common to find the term used in shrill polemical discourse that itself seems more interested in closing down free discussion than opening it up. (See, for example, John Harmon McElroy's rant that, "since the 1960s, a 'correct' political language has been imposed on Americans." What evidence does McElroy provide that the terms he dislikes (among them *African-American*, *environmentalism*, *Native American*, and *human being* as a substitute for *man*) are being "imposed"? Simply the fact that they are now listed in the dictionary.

is conventional or convenient. The point involved here is that language can have an important part to play in helping us to do the right thing. To treat men and women on an equal footing, to avoid discrimination on the basis of religion, or race, or class—language can be used to help accomplish all of these goals.

David Foster Wallace is not alone in claiming that the "central fallacy" of the so-called politically correct is "that a society's mode of expression is productive of its attitudes rather than a product of those attitudes" (55). In fact, the fallacy is to assume that it need be either/or; research has suggested *both* that changes in attitudes produce changes in modes of expression *and* that modes of expression help shape attitudes. Of course it is not possible to eliminate elitism and unfairness simply by ceasing to use "vocabulary that is historically associated with elitism and unfairness" (55). But equally clear is that the perpetuation of such vocabulary can only help to perpetuate elitism and unfairness; precisely how much difference language makes may be open to dispute, but it *does* make a difference.

See the section "How to Be Good with Words" for guidance on the avoidance of bias in writing.

O *Works Cited*

Lukianoff, Greg, interviewer. "Steven Pinker on Taboos, Political Correctness, and Dissent." 13 Sept. 2012. *YouTube*, 6 Jan. 2016, www.youtube.com/watch?v= hAMTPBspcfs. Accessed 2 Sept. 2016.

McElroy, John Harmon. "Leftists' Politically Correct Dictionary." *The Washington Times*, 15 Oct. 2012, www.washingtontimes.com/news/2012/oct/15/leftists-politically-correct-dictionary-activists-/. Accessed 5 July 2016.

Murphy, Cullen. "The Lay of the Language: The Decline of Semantic Distinction, and What It Suggests about Linguistic Evolution." *The Atlantic Monthly*, May 1995, pp. 20–22.

Pinker, Steven. "Grammar Puss: The Fallacies of the Language Mavens." *New Republic*, 31 Jan. 1994, pp. 19–24.

Strunk, William Jr., and E.B. White. *The Elements of Style*. 2nd ed., Macmillan, 1972.

Wallace, David Foster. "Tense Present: Democracy, English, and the Wars over Usage." *Harper's Magazine*, Apr. 2001, pp. 39–58.

⊙ Verb Problems

○ *Verbs and Verb Tense Difficulties*
○ THE INFINITIVE

Although not properly speaking a verb tense, the infinitive is the starting point for building a knowledge of verb tenses; the infinitive is the most basic form of the verb. Some examples of infinitives are *to go, to be, to do, to begin, to come, to investigate*. The infinitive form remains the same, of course, whether the action referred to happens in the past, the present, or the future.

EAL
For particular problems with verbs faced by those whose native language is not English, see the EAL section later in the book (pages 499–508).

A1. **split infinitives:** The most commonly made mistake involving infinitives is undoubtedly the slang substitution of *and* for *to*, especially in the expression *try and do it* for *try to do it* (see pages 260–61 for a fuller treatment). The great issue in this area among grammarians, however, is the split infinitive—the infinitive which has another word or words inserted between *to* and the verb:

> *needs checking*   The time has come to once again go to the polls. Economic conditions are likely to greatly influence the outcome, and the prime minister has promised to forcefully speak out in defense of the government's fiscal record.

With re-united infinitives, the same passage looks like this:

> *revised*   The time has come to go once again to the polls. Economic conditions are likely to influence greatly the outcome, and the prime minister has promised to speak out forcefully in defense of the government's fiscal record.

On what grounds can the second passage be considered better? It comes down to a matter of sound and rhythm. To most ears *to go once again* and *to speak out forcefully* are preferable to the split alternatives, but *to influence greatly* seems more awkward than *to greatly influence*. Happily, most authorities are now agreed that it is not a grievous sin to split an infinitive; Philip Howard, former editor of *The Times* of London, calls the split infinitive "the great shibboleth of English syntax," and even the traditionalist H.W. Fowler allows that while "the split infinitive is an ugly thing, we must warn the novice against the curious superstition that splitting or not splitting makes the difference between a good and a bad writer."

This is not to say that the splitting of infinitives should be encouraged. In many cases a split infinitive is a sign of wordiness; in cases such as the following it is better to drop the adverb entirely:

poor The chair said it was important to really investigate the matter thoroughly.

better The chair said it was important to investigate the matter thoroughly.

Like all verb forms, most infinitives have both an *active* and a *passive* voice. The active, which is more common, is used when the subject of the verb is doing the action, whereas the passive is used when the subject of the verb is receiving the action, or being acted on. *To do, to hit, to write* are examples of infinitives in the active voice, while *to be done, to be hit, to be written* are examples of infinitives in the passive voice.

Additional Material Online

Exercises on split infinitives may be found at **sites.broadviewpress.com/writing**. Click on **Exercises** and go to **"Verbs."**

○ THE SIMPLE PRESENT TENSE

	singular	*plural*
1st person	I say	we say
2nd person	you say	you say
3rd person	he, she, it says	they say

A2. **subject-verb agreement**: The simple present tense seems entirely straightforward, and usually it is. Most of us have no difficulty with the first person or the second person. But almost all of us occasionally have problems in writing the third person correctly. All too often the letter *s* at the end of the third person singular is left out. The simple rule to remember is that whenever you use a verb in the third person singular of the simple present tense, it must end in *s*:

needs checking   He go to Seattle at least once a month.
revised   He goes to Seattle at least once a month.
needs checking   The litmus paper change immediately when the solution is poured into the beaker.
revised   The litmus paper changes immediately when the solution is poured into the beaker.
(*Paper*, which is the subject, is an *it* and therefore third person singular.)

It is not particularly difficult to ensure that the subject agrees with the verb in the above examples, but even professional writers often have trouble with more complex sentences. Here are two common causes of subject-verb agreement errors:

(a) The subject and verb are separated by a long phrase or clause.

needs checking   The state of Afghanistan's roads reflect the chaotic situation.
revised   The state of Afghanistan's roads reflects the chaotic situation.

Here the writer has made the mental error of thinking of *roads* as the subject of the verb *reflect*, whereas in fact the subject is the singular noun *state*. *The state reflect ...* would immediately strike most people as wrong, but the intervening words have in this case caused grammatical confusion.

needs checking   As the statement by Belgium's prime minister about his country's deficit and unemployment problems indicate, many nations are in the same shape, or worse.
revised   As the statement by Belgium's prime minister about his country's deficit and unemployment problems indicates, many nations are in the same shape, or worse.
(The subject is the singular noun *statement*, so the verb must be *indicates* rather than *indicate*.)

needs checking Courses offered range from the history of the Greek and Roman world to the twenty-first century, and covers Britain, Europe, North America, Africa, and the Far East. (History Dept. Prospectus, Birkbeck College, University of London)

revised Courses offered range from the history of the Greek and Roman world to the twenty-first century, and cover Britain, Europe, North America, Africa, and the Far East.

Sometimes a long sentence can in itself throw off a writer's sense of subject-verb agreement, even if subject and verb are close together. In the following example the close proximity of the subject *simplifications* to the verb has not prevented error:

needs checking The decline in the quality of leadership is mirrored in the crude simplifications which characterizes the average person's view of the world.

revised The decline in the quality of leadership is mirrored in the crude simplifications which characterize the average person's view of the world.

(b) The error of using *there is* instead of *there are* when the subject is plural has become more and more frequent in writing as well as in speech. When these two expressions are used, remember that the subject comes after the verb; use *is* or *are* depending on whether the subject is singular or plural:

needs checking There's many more opportunities of that sort than there used to be.

revised There are many more opportunities of that sort than there used to be.

Additional Material Online
Exercises on subject-verb agreement may be found at **sites.broadviewpress.com/writing**. Click on **Exercises** and go to **"Verbs."**

A3. **historical present**: To use the "historical present" is to use the present tense in a narrative set in the past. In many medieval histo-

ries the narrative alternates frequently between the present tense and
the past tense, but from the sixteenth century until the late twentieth century most narratives of past action were recounted using the
past tense. The historical present was used on a very selective basis
by some historians and journalists (and by a few writers of fiction),
the purpose being to lend a sense of immediacy to particular scenes
that the writer wanted to express with memorable vividness. Here is
an example, from Pierre Berton's 1980 work of popular history, *The
Invasion of Canada*:

> [The British] are encouraged to strengthen their defences in Can-
> ada against possible invasion. This is Isaac Brock's doing.... The
> young lieutenant-colonel ... goes on to press for a better trained
> and expanded militia and for repairs to the fortress of Quebec.
> He does not easily get his way, but from this time on the pros-
> pect of an American invasion is never far from that determined
> and agile mind. When and if the Americans come, Isaac Brock
> intends to be ready. (38–39)

In the twenty-first century the historical present has become much
more commonly used in a wide variety of contexts. Many works of
fiction are now written entirely in the present tense. Many works of
history shift back and forth continually between the past tense and
the historical present. Even newscasts now use the historical present frequently. As in earlier eras, the aim is presumably to impart a
greater sense of immediacy and interest to what is being recounted.
It is all too easy in such circumstances, however, to create a sense of
confusion rather than a sense of immediacy in the reader's mind—
particularly given that the present tense is often also used idiomati-
cally to refer to future events (e.g., *We arrive at 9:00 in the morning*
rather than *We will arrive at 9:00 in the morning*). It is essential,
then, to pay careful attention to what tenses are being used.

needs checking   Throughout the day, shells fall on the city. Dozens are
killed. The President, however, refused to authorize a
ceasefire. The Cabinet holds an emergency meeting
tonight.

> (The passage begins in the historical present,
> but then switches to the past tense. The fourth
> sentence shifts back to present tense—but it is
> not clear what time is being referred to. Is the

emergency meeting also in the past (and the report being filed late at night)? If so, what was the outcome of the meeting? Or is the report being filed before "tonight"—in which case the emergency meeting is still in the future.)

revised Throughout the day, shells fell on the city. Dozens were killed. The President, however, refused to authorize a ceasefire. The Cabinet will hold an emergency meeting tonight.

or Throughout the day, shells fall on the city. Dozens are killed. The President, however, refuses to authorize a ceasefire. The Cabinet will hold an emergency meeting tonight.

○ THE PRESENT PROGRESSIVE (OR CONTINUOUS) TENSE

	singular	*plural*
1st person	I am saying	we are saying
2nd person	you are saying	you are saying
3rd person	he, she, it is saying	they are saying

A4. **verbs not normally used in the continuous tenses:** In English the continuous tenses are not normally used with many verbs which have to do with feelings, emotions, or senses. Some of these verbs are *to see, to hear, to understand, to believe, to hope, to know, to think* (meaning *believe*), *to trust, to comprehend, to mean, to doubt, to suppose, to wish, to want, to love, to desire, to prefer, to dislike, to hate.*

needs checking He is not understanding what I meant.
revised He does not understand what I meant.

○ THE SIMPLE PAST TENSE

	singular	*plural*
1st person	I finished	we finished
2nd person	you finished	you finished
3rd person	he, she, it finished	they finished

A5. **irregular verbs:** The occasional problems that crop up with the simple past tense usually involve irregular verbs—that is to say, verbs that do not follow a regular pattern in the formation of the simple past and other tenses. (See page 146 for a fuller discussion and list.) The use of *may, might* is a good example:

needs checking	Bands such as U2 and Simple Minds gained a foothold in North America through campus radio; without it they may not have broken through.
revised	Bands such as U2 and Simple Minds gained a foothold in North America through campus radio; without it they might not have broken through.

Two other verbs that often cause problems with the simple past tense are *lie* and *lay* (see also page 150). The difficulty many people have in keeping these straight is often ascribed to other factors, but is in part also attributable simply to the forms of the tenses; the past tense of *lie* is the same as the present tense of *lay*. Also, the past participle of *lie* is *lain*, not *laid*:

needs checking	Many in our party have just laid down and rolled over; they cannot get over the fact that we have lost control of the House of Representatives.
revised	Many in our party have just lain down and rolled over; they cannot get over the fact that we have lost control of the House of Representatives.

Given the difficulty of getting one's tongue round *lain down* rather than *laid down*, and the fact that almost anyone will know what meaning is intended with these words, many now feel that the distinctions are not worth troubling over in formal contexts. They remain important, however, in formal, written English.

A6. habitual action: The simple past tense is often mistakenly used to express what is called habitual action—the way an action ordinarily, or habitually, occurs. The simple present tense should be used to name such action even if the main verb of the sentence is in the past or future tense:

needs checking	The professor told us that Jupiter was the largest planet.
revised	The professor told us that Jupiter is the largest planet.
	(Jupiter has not stopped being the largest since he spoke.)

○ THE PAST PROGRESSIVE (OR CONTINUOUS) TENSE

	singular	*plural*
1st person	I was leaving	we were leaving
2nd person	you were leaving	you were leaving
3rd person	he, she, it was leaving	they were leaving

The problems that sometimes occur with the past continuous tense are the same as those that occur with the present continuous (see above, number A4). Remember to avoid these tenses when using verbs having to do with feelings, emotions, or senses (e.g., *see, hear, understand, believe, hope, know, think, trust, comprehend*) and when using the verb *to have* to mean *own, possess,* or *suffer from*:

needs checking	At that time he was believing that everything on earth was created within one week.
revised	At that time he believed that everything on earth was created within one week.

○ THE SIMPLE FUTURE TENSE

	singular	*plural*
1st person	I will arrive	we will arrive
2nd person	you will arrive	you will arrive
3rd person	he, she, it will arrive	they will arrive

○ THE FUTURE PROGRESSIVE (OR CONTINUOUS) TENSE

	singular	*plural*
1st person	I will be finding	we will be finding
2nd person	you will be finding	you will be finding
3rd person	he, she, it will be finding	they will be finding

○ THE PERFECT TENSES

As used to refer to the perfect tenses, the word *perfect* means *completed*; as you might expect, then, the perfect tenses are often (though not always) used to express actions that have been completed. They are formed by combining some form of the verb *to have* with a past participle (e.g., *opened, finished, believed, done*).

○ THE PRESENT PERFECT TENSE

	singular	*plural*
1st person	I have worked	we have worked
2nd person	you have worked	you have worked
3rd person	he, she, it has worked	they have worked

A7. **continuing past actions:** One way in which this tense is used is to speak of past actions which may continue into the present, or be repeated in the present or future. In the sentence *Anne Carson has written a number of books,* for example, the form of the verb shows that she will probably write more; she has neither died nor given up writing.

Understanding this sort of thing is a simple enough practice in normal usage, but in the long sentences that often occur in academic writing, it is easy to become confused:

> *needs checking* Since it called the First World Food Congress in 1963, the Food and Agriculture Organization has said clearly that the world, with the science and technology then known, had enough knowledge to ensure man's freedom from hunger. Successive world congresses and conferences have repeated this contention. (from a paper given by a distinguished professor at an academic conference)

Here the writer has evidently chosen the present perfect, thinking that he is referring to a situation which has continued on into the present. But when he refers to the science and technology then known and to successive world congresses and conferences, he has cut off the 1963 conference from any grammatical connection with the present. This is the sort of mistake that most writers can catch only during the revision process.

> *revised* When it called the First World Food Congress in 1963, the Food and Agriculture Organization said clearly that the world, with the science and technology then known, had enough knowledge to ensure man's freedom from hunger. Successive world congresses and conferences have repeated this contention.

○ THE PAST PERFECT TENSE

	singular	*plural*
1st person	I had believed	we had believed
2nd person	you had believed	you had believed
3rd person	he, she, it had believed	they had believed

Since the verb remains unchanged in all these forms, the past perfect is one of the easiest tenses to remember. What is difficult is learning how and when to use it. In English, however, there are quite definite rules about when the past perfect tense should be used. Its chief use is to show that one action in the past was completed before another action in the past began. Here are some examples:

- I told my parents what had happened.
  (The happening occurred before the telling.)
- By the time the group of tourists left Mozambique, they had formed a very favourable impression of the country.
  (The forming occurred before the leaving.)
- When he had gone I thought very seriously about what he had said.
  (Both the going and the saying occurred before the thinking.)

The usefulness of the past perfect tense can be clearly seen in passages in which the writer wishes to flashback, or move backwards in time. If you compare the following passages, you will see that the use of the past perfect tense in the second passage removes any confusion about the order in which the events happened. In the example below, when only the simple past tense is used, it sounds as if the dead snake is able to crawl:

needs checking   The tail was still moving, but the snake itself was quite dead. It crawled out from under a rock and slowly moved towards me as I was lowering the canoe at the end of the portage.

revised   The tail was still moving, but the snake itself was quite dead. It had crawled out from under a rock and had moved slowly towards me as I had been lowering the canoe at the end of the portage.

> (In the second passage it is clear that the snake approached this person *before* it died, and not afterwards.)

Perhaps the most common occasions in which we use the past perfect tense are when we are using indirect speech:

- She said that she had knocked on my door in the morning, but that there had been no answer.
  (The knocking happened before the saying.)
- The chair of the committee repeatedly asked the witness when the president had known of the diversion of funds.
  (The knowing happened before the asking.)

In a few cases it is possible to speak correctly of two actions which happened one after the other in the past by using the simple past tense for both actions. The use of the word *after*, for example, often makes it clear that the first action was completed before the other began.

A8. past actions at different times, or over a prolonged period: Writers often neglect to use the past perfect to name the earlier action when they are speaking of two (or more) actions that happened at different times in the past:

needs checking	He asked me if I talked to his secretary before coming to him.
revised	He asked me if I had talked to his secretary before coming to him.
needs checking	By the time the Allies decided to resist Hitler, the Nazis built up a huge military machine.
revised	By the time the Allies decided to resist Hitler, the Nazis had built up a huge military machine.
needs checking	Johnson's girlfriend, Marsha Dianne Blaylock, said she knew Williams since October 2013, when she and Johnson began their relationship.
revised	Johnson's girlfriend, Marsha Dianne Blaylock, said she had known Williams since October 2013, when she and Johnson began their relationship.

(Note that like the present perfect, the past perfect is very fre-quently required with *since* or *for*.)

The past perfect is also used to indicate that a past action occurred over a prolonged period:

- In the early 1960s Sonny Bono was a dishevelled pop singer and songwriter with hippie tendencies; by the time of his death in 1998 he had become a conservative Republican member of the House of Representatives.

needs checking   In 1980, 10 per cent of Chile's families did not have sufficient income to satisfy the minimum food require-ments recommended by international organizations; in 2000 the figure grew to 32 per cent.

revised   In 1980, 10 per cent of Chile's families did not have sufficient income to satisfy the minimum food require-ments recommended by international organizations; by 2000 the figure had grown to 32 per cent.

or   ... in 2000 the figure was 32 per cent.

(The original suggests that the figure had re-mained at 10 per cent in every year from 1980 to 2000, and then jumped in the course of one year to 32 per cent.)

○ THE FUTURE PERFECT TENSE

	singular	*plural*
1st person	I will have gone	we will have gone
2nd person	you will have gone	you will have gone
3rd person	he, she, it will have gone	they will have gone

○ OTHER TENSES

The present perfect continuous tense—*I have been running, you have been working*, etc.

The past perfect continuous tense—*I had been looking, you had been following*, etc.

The future perfect continuous tense—*I will have been sleeping, they will have been studying*, etc.

The conditional continuous tense—*I would be bringing, she would be starting*, etc.

The past conditional continuous tense—*I would have been working, he would have been driving*, etc.

O *Mood: Indicative, Imperative, and Subjunctive*

The tenses discussed above are all in the **indicative mood**; that is the way we express ourselves most of the time as we name real or possible actions. The **imperative mood** is used for commands and instructions:

- Follow the path to the right.
- Come here immediately!

The mood that even many native English speakers find difficult to use correctly is the **subjunctive mood**. The subjunctive is used to denote actions that are wished for or imagined, or contrary to fact or expectation. In common English usage the indicative mood is now often employed where once the subjunctive was mandatory, but the subjunctive has by no means disappeared—and, particularly where conditional constructions are concerned, it is a frequent source of difficulty for writers. Here are a few examples of sentences that use the subjunctive:

- If I were you, I would do what she says.
  (not *if I was you*)
- The doctor advises that he stop smoking immediately.
  (not *that he stops*)
- If we can't even get this much done, God help us.
  (not *God helps us*)
- Suffice it to say that the subject is a controversial one.
- Be that as it may, the central assertion of Smith's book is irrefutable.
- If you went to Iceland, would you visit a volcano?
  (not *if you go*)

In the last of these examples one may use as a subjunctive form either *if you went* or *if you were to go*. Until the second half of the twentieth century it was far more common than it is today to form subjunctive constructions such as this only by using "were." Over the past fifty years it has become much more acceptable in formal writing as well as in conversation to use as a subjunctive a verb in the same form as that of the simple past tense in the indicative mood. Where people used to say *If I were to send her something...* (when they were not in fact planning to send anything), they would now typically say *If I sent her something....* Where they used to say *If the Cubs were to win...* when they believed a Cubs win to be extremely unlikely, they would now typically say *If the Cubs won....* In such sentences the simple past form (*sent, won*) has replaced the old subjunctive form (*were to send, were to win*).

Much as subjunctive forms are less widely used in these sorts of conditional constructions, there still are important rules as to the correct combinations in grammatical constructions dealing with conditions. Given the difficulties involved, it may be worth spending some time on these.

○ THE CONDITIONAL

	singular	*plural*
1st person	I would go	we would go
2nd person	you would go	you would go
3rd person	he, she, it would go	they would go

The above forms are used when we are speaking of actions which would or might happen if certain conditions were fulfilled. Here are some further examples:

- If I wanted to go to Australia, I would have to fly.
- If I drank a lot of gin, I would be very sick.
- I would lend Joe the money he wants if I trusted him.
- I might enjoy basketball more if I were taller.

Each of these sentences is made up of a main clause, in which a modal auxiliary verb (*would, might*) is used, and a subordinate clause beginning with *if,* with a verb in the same form as the simple past tense (*wanted, drank, trusted,* etc.). In all cases the action named in the *if* clause is considered by the speaker to be unlikely to happen, or quite impossible. The speaker does not really want to go to Australia; she is just speculating about what she would have to do if she did. Similarly the second speaker does not expect to drink a lot of gin; if he did, he would be sick, but he does not plan to. In the same way, the speaker of the third sentence does not trust Joe; he is speaking about what the situation would be if he did trust Joe. Situations like these which are not happening and which we do not expect to happen are called *hypothetical situations*: we speculate on what *would* or *might* happen *if* ... but we do not expect the *if* ... to come true.

If we think the *if* ... is likely to come true, then we use the future tense instead of the conditional in the main clause, and the present tense in the subordinate *if* clause, as in these examples:

- If I drink a lot of gin, I will be very sick.
  (Here the speaker thinks that it is very possible or likely that he will drink a lot of gin.)
- If I want to go to Australia, I will have to fly.
  (Here the speaker thinks that she may really want to go.)

Notice the difference between the following two sentences:

- If a socialist government is re-elected in Venezuela, the American administration will not be pleased.
  (Here the writer thinks that it is quite possible or likely that the socialists will be re-elected.)
- If a socialist government were elected in Venezuela, the American administration would not be pleased.
  (Here the writer is assuming that the socialists probably will not be re-elected.)

Following are listed the most commonly experienced difficulties in forming conditional constructions.

A9. **forming the subjunctive**: Although it is now acceptable with most verbs to form a verb in the subjunctive mood by using the same form as that of the simple past tense (see above), this is not the case with the verb *to be*. In formal writing *were* remains the only accepted subjunctive formation of the verb *to be*:

needs checking   If a bank was willing to lend new businesses very large amounts without proper guarantees, it would go bankrupt very quickly.

revised   If a bank were willing to lend new businesses very large amounts without proper guarantees, it would go bankrupt very quickly.

needs checking   If I was an NHL player, I would be happy to play for less than $500,000 per year.

revised   If I were an NHL player, I would be happy to play for less than $500,000 per year.

Additional Material Online

Exercises on conditional sentences may be found at **sites.broadviewpress.com/writing**. Click on **Exercises** and go to **"Conditional Constructions."**

A10. **choosing the right verb when writing about conditions**: Some writers mistakenly use the auxiliary verb *would* in the *if...* clause when they are also using *would* in the main clause. Others use the present tense (instead of the past tense) in the *if...* clause when they are using *would* in the main clause. Both are incorrect.

needs checking   If television networks would produce fewer series about violent crime, parents would allow their children to watch even more television than they do now.

revised   If television networks produced fewer series about violent crime, parents would allow their children to watch even more television than they do now.

or   If television networks were to produce fewer series about violent crime, parents would allow their children to watch even more television than they do now.

needs checking   If I want to buy a car, I would look carefully at all the models available.

revised   If I wanted to buy a car, I would look carefully at all the models available.

(The speaker does not want to buy a car.)

or   If I want to buy a car, I will look carefully at all the models available.

(The speaker may really want to buy a car.)

Remember that the subjunctive (typically, identical in form to that of the simple past tense) is used in the conditional *if...* clause whenever one is referring in the main clause to present or future situations that are imagined, wished for, or in some other way contrary to fact.

○ THE PAST CONDITIONAL

	singular	*plural*
1st person	I would have gone	we would have gone
2nd person	you would have gone	you would have gone
3rd person	he, she, it would have gone	they would have gone

This verb form is used in conditional sentences in which we are speaking of actions which never happened. It is used in the main clause, with the past tense in the subjunctive mood being used in the *if...* clause. Notice in the examples below that these past tense subjunctive forms are identical in form to the past perfect tense formations in the indicative mood.

- If I had studied harder, I would have passed.
  (meaning that in fact I did not study very hard, and did not pass)
- If Kitchener had arrived at Khartoum a day earlier, he would have saved Gordon and the rest of the British garrison force.
  (meaning that Kitchener did not come early enough, and was not able to prevent the 1885 massacre at Khartoum)

Here again the subjunctive used to be formed with a *were to...* construction much more commonly than is the norm today. Instead of saying *if I had studied harder ...* or *if Kitchener had arrived a day earlier ...* it was once common to say *if I were to have studied harder ..., if Kitchener were to have arrived a day earlier ...,* and so on. It is easy to understand why these more cumbersome formulations are now relatively rare.

A11. **choosing the right verbs when writing about past conditions:** Some people mistakenly use the past conditional in both clauses of sentences such as these; remember that the past conditional should be used only in the main clause:

needs checking   If the Titanic would have carried more lifeboats, hundreds of lives would have been saved.

revised   If the Titanic had carried more lifeboats, hundreds of lives would have been saved.

needs checking   If the Yes campaign in Quebec would have won 200,000 more votes, the course of Canadian politics in the mid-1990s would have been very different.

revised   If the Yes campaign in Quebec had won 200,000 more votes, the course of Canadian politics in the mid-1990s would have been very different.

○ Active and Passive Voice

As touched on above (pages 71–73), discussions of the active and passive in writing are often the site of considerable controversy—and considerable confusion. The most frequent reference point in such discussions is George Orwell's "Politics and the English Language," in which Orwell made "never use the passive where you can use the active" one of his six elementary rules of writing. In his essay Orwell persuasively suggests links between verbal subterfuge and political duplicity. Given this background, it is perhaps unsurprising that many have tended to conflate the use of a passive voice (in itself a matter purely of grammar and sentence construction) with the use in general of words to disguise agency—something that may be effected through a variety of verbal means. For example, the sentence *the police officer killed the protestor with a single baton blow to the head* is a simple sentence using the verb *to kill* in the active voice. One way to disguise agency here is to make *the protestor* the subject of the sentence and use the same verb in the passive voice. Such a construction readily allows for the omission of any mention of who wielded the baton: *the protestor was killed by a single baton blow to the head.* But one could also disguise agency with a sentence such as the following: *a blow to the head from a baton was the cause of the protestor's death.* In that case the change is not a matter of shifting from the active to the passive voice but of choosing a different verb.

As background here, it is essential to appreciate that the distinction between active and passive voice is not relevant to all verbs, but only to transitive verbs. You can hit someone or something, and someone or something can be hit by you; the active voice/passive voice distinction is certainly relevant to the verb *to hit*. But you cannot sleep someone or something, or be slept by someone or something; the active voice/passive voice distinction is not relevant to an intransitive verb such as *to sleep*. Nor is it relevant to that most common of verbs, the verb *to be*. In some cases agency may be disguised by using either the active voice or the passive voice of a verb. Such, for example, is the case with the verb *to violate*, which may be used with the agent as the subject but may also be used with the action itself as the grammatical subject:

> The detention of the suspect without any charges violates her constitutional rights.

> The suspect's constitutional rights are violated by her detention without any charges.

> The prosecutor violated the defendant's constitutional rights by detaining her without laying any charges.

Agency is as much disguised in the first of these sentences as in the second, though the first is in the active voice, the second in the passive voice.

Let us look at another example of disguised agency. The sentence *I knocked that vase off the shelf* uses the past tense *knocked* in the active voice. Switching to the passive voice gives us *that vase was knocked off the shelf*, and of course allows for the option of omitting *by me*; this is one way of disguising agency. But if I wanted to disguise agency in such a situation I would be more likely to choose a different verb entirely, perhaps an intransitive verb such as *to fall* for which the active voice / passive voice distinction is not relevant: *that vase fell off the shelf*.

Many verbal stratagems that disguise agency use the pronoun *it* as the grammatical subject. If someone has just dumped a girlfriend or boyfriend, for example, the "dumper" is not always keen to say *I dumped her* or *I dumped him*. But nor is it likely that the speaker will shift to the passive voice and say *she was dumped by me/he was dumped by me*. Much more likely would be a shift to the use of *it* as the subject, together with intransitive verbs such as *to be* or *to work*: *it is over between us*, for example, or *it just didn't work out*.

It is important to recognize that there is nothing pernicious *in itself* in the passive voice. In many cases, indeed, one may wish to use the passive voice in making political points of the sort that Orwell himself would approve of. Orwell does precisely this when he wishes to place appropriate emphasis on the recipient of an action—as in the following example, where he is emphasizing the experience of victims as well as the duplicity of language used to describe their suffering: "People are imprisoned for years without trial, or are shot in the back of the neck, or are sent to die of scurvy in Arctic lumber camps: this is called *elimination of unreliable elements.*"

A12. **awkwardness or wordiness arising from inappropriate use of the passive voice:** The passive voice, then, is one means that *may* be used to disguise agency, and it is also a verbal construction that *may* involve awkwardness or unnecessary wordiness. If either is the case, it is often better to rephrase by using the active voice:

needs checking   The ceremonial first pitch was thrown by the president. (Passive—9 words)

revised   The president threw the ceremonial first pitch. (Active—7 words)

But again, the passive voice *per se* is not the problem. For more on this issue see the discussion of style in the first section of this text, and the section on writing in scientific disciplines such as biology (page 428).

O *Dangling Constructions*

The error that is made most frequently by writers at all levels of ability—including holders of graduate degrees in English—is that of allowing large chunks of their sentences to "dangle," unrelated grammatically to the core of the sentence. For that reason several pages are devoted here to that problem.

Additional Material Online

In *The Broadview Guide* we group together under
the heading *dangling constructions* types of error that in
many other texts are treated as separate categories.
Information on the complex taxonomy of *dangling modifiers*,
misplaced modifiers, and *squinting modifiers* is provided
alongside a range of relevant exercises at
sites.broadviewpress.com/writing.
Click on **Exercises** and go to **"Verbs."**

● *Dangling Participles and Infinitives*

A present participle is an *-ing* word (*going, thinking*, etc.). When
combined with a form of the verb *to be*, participles form part of a
complete verb. They can also be used in a number of ways on their
own, however:

- The president felt that visiting China would be unwise at that
  time.
  (Here *visiting China* acts as a noun phrase.)
- Having taken into account the various reports, the committee
  decided to delay the project for a year.
  (Here *having taken into account the various reports* acts as an
  adjectival phrase modifying the noun *committee*.)

A13. **dangling present participles or participial phrases**: The danger
of dangling occurs with sentences such as the second example above.
If the writer does not take care that the participial phrase refers to
the subject of the main clause, some absurd sentences can result:

needs checking	Waiting for a bus, a brick fell on my head.
	(Bricks do not normally wait for buses.)
revised	While I was waiting for a bus, a brick fell on my head.
needs checking	Leaving the room, the lights must be turned off.
	(Lights do not normally leave the room.)
revised	When you leave the room you must turn off the lights.

In sentences such as these the amusing error is relatively easy to
notice; it can be much more difficult with longer and more complex
sentences. Even seasoned writers and public speakers can easily find
themselves using dangling constructions. Here, for example, is what
Peter Kent (at the time Canada's Environment Minister) said in July

of 2013 as he contemplated the prospect of leaving the federal cabinet: "Although still hypothetical, I would be able to better devote myself to my Thornhill constituents, to their issues, and to the issues of the Greater Toronto Area." What he meant to say, of course, is that the prospect of his retirement from cabinet was hypothetical—not that *he* was hypothetical.

Experienced writers are especially alert to this pitfall if they begin a sentence with a participle or participial phrase that describes a mental operation; they are wary of beginning by *considering, believing, taking into account, remembering, turning for a moment,* or *regarding*:

needs checking	Believing that he had done no wrong, the fact of being accused of dishonesty infuriated the company's CEO.
revised	Believing that he had done no wrong, the company's CEO was infuriated at being accused of dishonesty.
or	The company's CEO was infuriated at being accused of dishonesty; he believed he had done no wrong.
needs checking	Considering all the above-mentioned studies, the evidence shows conclusively that smoking can cause cancer.
revised	Considering all the above-mentioned studies, we conclude that smoking causes cancer.
better	These studies show conclusively that smoking can cause cancer.
needs checking	Turning for a moment to the thorny question of Joyce's style, the stream of consciousness technique realistically depicts the workings of the human mind.
revised	Turning for a moment to the thorny question of Joyce's style, we may observe that his stream of consciousness technique realistically depicts the workings of the human mind.
better	Joyce's style does not make *Ulysses* easy to read, but his stream of consciousness technique realistically depicts the workings of the human mind.
needs checking	Taking into account the uncertainty as to the initial temperature of the beaker, the results are not conclusive.
revised	Taking into account the uncertainty as to the initial temperature of the beaker necessitates that the results be deemed inconclusive.

> *better*   Since the initial temperature of the beaker was not recorded, the results are inconclusive.

Notice that in each case the best way to eliminate the problem is to dispense with the participial phrase entirely. More often than not one's writing is improved by using active verbs rather than participial phrases. Many people seem to feel that writing which is filled with participial phrases somehow sounds more important; in fact, such phrases tend to obscure the writer's meaning under unnecessary padding. This is true even when the participles are not dangling:

> *needs checking*   Another characteristic having a significant impact on animal populations is the extreme diurnal temperature range on the desert surface.
>
> (Can a characteristic have an impact? A small point is here buried in a morass of meaningless abstraction.)
>
> *better*   The extreme diurnal temperature range on the desert surface also affects animal populations.
>
> *needs checking*   Referring generally to the social stratification systems of the city as a whole, we can see clearly that types of accommodation, varying throughout in accordance with income levels and other socio-economic factors, display an extraordinary diversity.
>
> (Is there anything either clear or extraordinary about this?)
>
> *better*   In this city rich people and poor people live in different neighbourhoods, and rich people live in larger houses than poor people.

By cutting out the padding in this way the writer may occasionally find to his surprise that instead of saying something rather weighty and important as he had thought he was doing, he is in fact saying little or nothing. But he should not be discouraged if this happens; the same is true for all writers. The best response is simply to chuckle and scratch out the sentence!

A14. **dangling past participles** (e.g., *considered, developed, regarded*): The same sorts of problems that occur with present participles occur frequently with past participles as well:

needs checking   Considered from a cost point of view, Combarp Capital Corporation could not really afford to purchase Skinflint Securities.

> (Combarp is not being considered; the purchase is.)

poor   Considered from the point of view of cost, the purchase of Skinflint Securities was not a wise move by Combarp Capital Corporation.

better   Combarp Capital Corporation could not really afford to buy Skinflint Securities.

needs checking   Once regarded as daringly modern in its portrayal of fashionable *fin de siècle* decadence, Wilde draws on traditional patterns to create a powerful new Gothic tale. (*The Cambridge Guide to Literature in English*)

> (The novel is an *it*; Oscar Wilde was a *he*.)

revised   *The Picture of Dorian Gray* was once regarded as daringly modern in its portrayal of fashionable *fin de siècle* decadence. In the novel Wilde draws on traditional patterns to create a powerful new Gothic tale.

needs checking   Used with frequency, a man will feel refreshed and rejuvenated. (aftershave advertisement)

revised   Used with frequency, this product will help a man feel refreshed and rejuvenated.

A15. dangling infinitive phrases:

needs checking   To conclude this essay, the French Revolution was a product of many interacting causes.

> (The French Revolution concluded no essays.)

poor   To conclude this essay, I would like to say that the French Revolution was a product of many causes.

better   The explanations given for the French Revolution, then, are not mutually exclusive; it was a product of many interacting causes.

> (A good writer does not normally need to tell her readers that she is concluding an essay; they can see the space at the bottom of the page. A little word such as *then*, set off by commas, is more than enough to signal that this is a summing-up.)

needs checking	To receive a complimentary copy, the business reply card should be returned before June 30.
	(The card will not receive anything.)
revised	To receive a complimentary copy, you should return the business reply card before June 30.
needs checking	To appreciate the full significance of the Camp David Accords, a range of factors needs to be considered.
	(A factor cannot appreciate.)
poor	To appreciate the full significance of the Camp David Accords, we need to consider many things.
better	The Camp David Accords were important in many ways.

A16. dangling gerund or prepositional phrases:

needs checking	In reviewing the evidence, one point stands out plainly.
	(A point cannot review evidence.)
poor	In reviewing the evidence, we can see one point standing out plainly.
better	One point stands out plainly from this evidence.
needs checking	When analyzing the figures, ways to achieve substantial savings can be discerned.
	(The ways cannot analyze.)
poor	When we analyze the figures we can see ways to achieve substantial savings.
better	The figures suggest that we can greatly reduce our expenses.

Other sorts of phrases can be caught dangling too. But almost all writers are capable of attaching them properly if they re-read and revise their work carefully.

needs checking	On behalf of city council and the people of Windsor, it gives me great pleasure to welcome you to our city. (from an announcement by the mayor)
	(The mayor, not a faceless *it*, is acting on behalf of the others.)
revised	On behalf of city council and the people of Windsor, I am pleased to welcome you to our city.
needs checking	By adding more component parts to the prototype, this would cause an increase in the price of the product.

> *revised*   By adding more component parts to the prototype, we force an increase in the price of the product.
>
> *or*   Adding more component parts to the prototype makes it necessary to increase the price of the product.

○ *Sequence of Tenses*

If the main verb of a sentence is in the past tense, other verbs must also express a past viewpoint (except when a general truth is being expressed). Some writers have trouble keeping the verb tenses they use in agreement, particularly when indirect speech is involved, or when a quotation is incorporated into a sentence.

A17. agreement of tenses in indirect speech—past plus subjunctive:

> *needs checking*   He said that he will fix the engine before the end of the year.
>
> *revised*   He said that he would fix the engine before the end of the year.
>
> > (*He said that he will fix the engine* implies that the fixing has not yet occurred but may still occur.)

A18. agreement of tenses in indirect speech—past plus past perfect:

> *needs checking*   He claimed that he smoked drugs many years earlier, but that he never inhaled.
>
> *revised*   He claimed that he had smoked drugs many years earlier, but that he had never inhaled.

A19. agreement of tenses—quoted material:

> *needs checking*   Prime Minister Rudd admitted that "such a policy is not without its drawbacks."
>
> > (The past tense *admitted* and the present tense *is* do not agree.)

There are two ways of dealing with a difficulty such as this:

    (a) Change the sentence so as to set off the quotation without using the connecting word *that*. Usually this can be done with a colon. In this case the tense you use does not have to agree with the tense used in the quotation. The words before the colon, though, must be able to act as a complete sentence in themselves.

(b) Use only that part of the quotation that can be used in agreement with the tense of the main verb:

revised   Prime Minister Rudd did not claim perfection: "such a policy is not without its drawbacks," he admitted.

or   Prime Minister Rudd admitted that such a policy was "not without its drawbacks."

Here are some other examples:

needs checking   Churchill promised that "we shall fight on the beaches, ... we shall fight in the fields and in the streets, we shall fight in the hills; we shall never surrender."

(This suggests that you, the writer, will be among those fighting.)

revised   Churchill made the following promise: "We shall fight on the beaches, ... we shall fight in the fields and in the streets, we shall fight in the hills; we shall never surrender."

(Notice that the word *that* is now removed.)

or   Churchill promised that the British people would "fight on the beaches, ... in the fields and in the streets, ... in the hills," and that they would "never surrender."

needs checking   In the 1974 election campaign the Liberals claimed that "the Land is strong."

revised   In the 1974 election campaign the Liberals' slogan was "The Land is Strong."

or   In the 1974 election campaign the Liberals asserted that the Land was strong.

Additional Material Online

Exercises on sequence of tenses may be found at **sites.broadviewpress.com/writing**.

Click on **Exercises** and go to **"Verbs."**

○ *Irregular or Difficult Verbs*

The majority of verbs in English follow a regular pattern—*I open* in the simple present tense, *I opened* in the simple past tense, *I have opened* in the present perfect tense, and so forth. However, most of the more frequently used verbs are in some way or another irregular. To pick an obvious example, we say *I went* instead of *I goed*, and *I have gone* instead of *I have goed*. What follows is a list of the main irregular or difficult verbs in English. The past participle (column 3) is used in tenses such as the present perfect (e.g., *I have grown, he has found*) and the past perfect (*I had grown, I had found*).

The verbs that most frequently cause problems are given special treatment in the following list:

(Note: In both regular and irregular verbs, the present tense is formed by using the infinitive without the preposition *to*.)

	Present & *Infinitive*	*Simple* *Past*	*Past* *Participle*
A20.	arise	arose	arisen

check	A problem had arose even before the discussion began.
revised	A problem had arisen even before the discussion began.

	Present & *Infinitive*	*Simple* *Past*	*Past* *Participle*
	awake	awoke	awoken/woken
		(passive: *was awakened*)	
	be	was/were	been
A21.	bear	bore	borne

check	It was heartbreaking for her to lose the child after having bore it for so long.
revised	It was heartbreaking for her to lose the child after having borne it for so long.

A22.	beat	beat	beaten

check	The Yankees were badly beat by the Blue Jays.
revised	The Yankees were badly beaten by the Blue Jays.

	become	became	become

	Present & Infinitive	Simple Past	Past Participle
A23.	begin	began	begun

check   He had already began treatment when I met him.
revised   He had already begun treatment when I met him.

	Present & Infinitive	Simple Past	Past Participle
	bend	bent	bent
	bite	bit	bitten
	bleed	bled	bled
	blow	blew	blown
	break	broke	broken
	bring	brought	brought
	build	built	built
	burn	burned/burnt	burned/burnt
A24.	burst	burst	burst

check   The pipes bursted while we were on holiday.
revised   The pipes burst while we were on holiday.

	Present & Infinitive	Simple Past	Past Participle
	buy	bought	bought
	can	could	been able
	catch	caught	caught
A25.	choose	chose	chosen

check   In 1999 East Timor choose to become a nation.
revised   In 1999 East Timor chose to become a nation.

	Present & Infinitive	Simple Past	Past Participle
	cling	clung	clung
	come	came	come
	cost	cost	cost
	dig	dug	dug
A26.	dive	dived/dove	dived

less accepted   He dove into the shallow water.
more formal   He dived into the shallow water.

	Present & Infinitive	Simple Past	Past Participle
	do	did	done

	Present & Infinitive	Simple Past	Past Participle
A27.	drag	dragged	dragged

check The newspapers drug up a lot of scandal about her.
revised The newspapers dragged up a lot of scandal about her.

	draw	drew	drawn
	dream	dreamed/dreamt	dreamed/dreamt
A28.	drink	drank	drunk

check He has drank more than is good for him.
revised He has drunk more than is good for him.

	drive	drove	driven
	eat	ate	eaten
	fall	fell	fallen
	feel	felt	felt
	fight	fought	fought
	find	found	found
	fit	fit (US) fitted (UK)	fitted
	flee	fled	fled
A29.	fling	flung	flung

check George flinged his plate across the room.
revised George flung his plate across the room.

	fly	flew	flown
A30.	forbid	forbade	forbidden

check Yesterday he forbid us to climb the fence.
revised Yesterday he forbade us to climb the fence.

Additional Material Online
Exercises on irregular or difficult verbs may be found at
sites.broadviewpress.com/writing.
Click on **Exercises** and go to **"Verbs."**

	Present & *Infinitive*	*Simple* *Past*	*Past* *Participle*
A31.	forecast	forecast	forecast

check   The weather office has forecasted more rain.
revised   The weather office has forecast more rain.

	Present & *Infinitive*	*Simple* *Past*	*Past* *Participle*
	forget	forgot	forgotten
	forgive	forgave	forgiven
	freeze	froze	frozen
	get	got	got
	give	gave	given
	go	went	gone
	grind	ground	ground
	(e.g., *I have ground the coffee.*)		
	grow	grew	grown
A32.	hang	hanged/hung	hanged/hung

Note: *Hanged* is used only when referring to a person being killed by hanging. Say *The criminal has been hanged*, but *We have hung the picture on the wall*:

check   No one has been hung in Canada since 1962.
revised   No one has been hanged in Canada since 1962.

	Present & *Infinitive*	*Simple* *Past*	*Past* *Participle*
	have	had	had
	hear	heard	heard
	hide	hid	hidden
	hit	hit	hit
	hold	held	held
	hurt	hurt	hurt
	keep	kept	kept
	kneel	knelt	knelt
	know	knew	known
A33.	lay	laid	laid

(Note: Although many authorities feel that the distinction is not worth troubling over in informal English, formal English still distinguishes between *lay* and *lie*; you *lay* something on a table, and a hen *lays* eggs, but you *lie* down to sleep. In other words, *lie* is an intransitive verb; it should not be followed by a direct object. *Lay*, by contrast, is transitive.)

check   That old thing has been laying around for years.
revised   That old thing has been lying around for years.

Present & Infinitive	Simple Past	Past Participle
lead	led	led
lean	leaned/leant	leaned/leant
leap	leaped/leapt	leaped/leapt
learn	learned/learnt	learned/learnt
leave	left	left
lend	lent	lent
let	let	let

A34.   lie   lay   lain

check   He asked if I would like to lay down and rest.
revised   He asked if I would like to lie down and rest.

See also above, number A5.

light	lighted/lit	lighted/lit
lose	lost	lost
make	made	made
may	might	
mean	meant	meant
meet	met	met
must	had to	had to
pay	paid	paid

A35.   plead   pleaded/pled   pleaded/pled

(Note: The growing use of *pled* rather than *pleaded* irks some traditionalists, but it is difficult to see why *pleaded* should not follow *leaded* to the grave where the latter was long ago led. If you are trying to please a traditionalist professor, it is probably still best to avoid *pled*. Otherwise, use consistently whichever of the two you prefer.)

| *accepted* | He had pled guilty to the same offense previously. |
| *accepted* | He had pleaded guilty to the same offense previously. |

	Present & Infinitive	Simple Past	Past Participle
A36.	prove	proved	proven

| *check* | We have proved the hypothesis to be correct. |
| *revised* | We have proven the hypothesis to be correct. |

	put	put	put
	read	read	read
A37.	ride	rode	ridden

| *check* | The actor had never rode a horse before. |
| *revised* | The actor had never ridden a horse before. |

A38.	ring	rang	rung

| *check* | I rung the bell three times, but no one answered. |
| *revised* | I rang the bell three times, but no one answered. |

	rise	rose	risen
	run	ran	run
	saw	sawed	sawed/sawn
	say	said	said
	see	saw	seen
	seek	sought	sought
	sell	sold	sold
	sew	sewed	sewed/sewn
	shake	shook	shaken
	shall	should	
A39.	shine	shone	shone

| *check* | The moon shined almost as brightly as the sun. |
| *revised* | The moon shone almost as brightly as the sun. |

(Note: *Shined* is the accepted formation of the simple past tense where the verb is transitive. Thus we say *she shined her shoes*.)

Present & Infinitive	Simple Past	Past Participle
shoot	shot	shot
show	showed	showed/shown

A40. shrink | shrank | shrunk

check The government's majority shrunk in the election.
revised The government's majority shrank in the election.

shut	shut	shut
sing	sang	sung

A41. sink | sank | sunk

check The *Edmund Fitzgerald* sunk on Lake Superior.
revised The *Edmund Fitzgerald* sank on Lake Superior.

sit	sat	sat
sleep	slept	slept
slide	slid	slid
smell	smelled/smelt	smelled/smelt
sow	sowed	sowed/sown
speak	spoke	spoken
speed	speeded/sped	speeded/sped
spell	spelled/spelt	spelled/spelt
spend	spent	spent
spill	spilled/spilt	spilled/spilt
spin	spun	spun
spit	spat	spat
split	split	split
spread	spread	spread

A42. spring | sprang | sprung

check The soldiers hurriedly sprung to their feet.
revised The soldiers hurriedly sprang to their feet.

stand	stood	stood
steal	stole	stolen
stick	stuck	stuck
sting	stung	stung

Present & Infinitive	Simple Past	Past Participle
strike	struck	struck
swear	swore	sworn
sweep	swept	swept

A43.

stick	stuck	stuck

A44.

swim	swam	swum

check   Pictures were taken while the royal couple swum in what they thought was a private cove.

revised   Pictures were taken while the royal couple swam in what they had thought was a private cove.

swing	swung	swung
take	took	taken
teach	taught	taught
tear	tore	torn
tell	told	told
think	thought	thought
throw	threw	thrown
tread	trod	trodden/trod
understand	understood	understood
wake	woke	woken
wear	wore	worn
weep	wept	wept
win	won	won
wind	wound	wound
wring	wrung	wrung

(e.g., *She wrings out her clothes if they are wet.*)

write	wrote	written

O *Infinitives, Gerunds, Objects: "To Be or Not To Be?"*

gerunds and prepositions: Gerunds have the form of verbs but act as nouns, and as such they do not necessarily require any preposition to introduce them. In particular, when a gerund does not relate to a preceding verb, it should not be accompanied by a preposition. Nor does it require a pronoun to stand in for it as the subject of a verb:

> *needs checking* With using coal-fired generators, it is bad for the environment.
>
> *revised* Using coal-fired generators is bad for the environment.

When a gerund follows a verb, however, it often must be introduced by a preposition—and unfortunately, there are no rules governing when this happens, or which preposition should be used. More broadly, there are no rules in English to explain why some words must be followed by an infinitive (*to go, to do, to be,* etc.), while others must be followed by a preposition plus a gerund (*of going, in doing,* etc.), and still others by a direct object. Following are some of the words with which difficulties of this sort most often arise:

A45. **accept something** (not *accept to do something*): It needs a direct object.

> *needs checking* The committee accepted to try to improve the quality of the postal service.
>
> *revised* The committee accepted the task of trying to improve the postal service.
>
> *or* The committee agreed to try to improve the postal service.

A46. **accuse someone of doing something** (not *to do*)

> *needs checking* Klaus Barbie was accused to have killed thousands of innocent civilians in WW II.
>
> *revised* Klaus Barbie was accused of having killed thousands of innocent civilians in WW II.

A47. **appreciate something**: When used to mean *be grateful,* this verb requires a direct object.

> *needs checking* I would appreciate if you could respond quickly.

  revised I would appreciate it if you could respond quickly.
  or I would appreciate a quick response.
    (The verb *appreciate* without an object means *increase in value*.)

A48. assist in doing something (not *to do*)

needs checking He assisted me to solve the problem.
revised He assisted me in solving the problem.
or He helped me to solve the problem.

A49. capable of doing something (not *to do*)

needs checking He is capable to run 1500 metres in under four minutes.
revised He is capable of running 1500 metres in under four minutes.
or He is able to run 1500 metres in under four minutes.

A50. confident of doing something (not *to do*)

needs checking She is confident to be able to finish the job before dusk.
revised She is confident of being able to finish the job before dusk.
or She is confident that she will finish the job before dusk.

A51. consider something or someone to be something or consider it something (not *as something*)

needs checking According to a recent policy paper, the party now considers a guaranteed annual income as a good idea.
revised According to a recent policy paper, the party now considers a guaranteed annual income to be a good idea.
or According to a recent policy paper, the party now regards a guaranteed annual income as a good idea.

A52. discourage someone from doing something (not *to do*)

needs checking The new Immigration Act is intended to discourage people to enter the country illegally.
revised The new Immigration Act is intended to discourage people from entering the country illegally.

A53. forbid someone to do something (not *from doing*)

needs checking   The witnesses were forbidden from leaving the scene of the crime until the police had completed their preliminary investigation.

revised   The witnesses were forbidden to leave the scene of the crime until the police had completed their preliminary investigation.

EAL

For particular problems with infinitives, gerunds, and objects faced by those whose native language is not English, see the EAL section later in this book.

A54. insist on doing something or **insist that something be done** (but not *insist to do*)

needs checking   The customer has insisted to wait in the front office until she receives a refund.

revised   The customer has insisted on waiting in the front office until she receives a refund.

A55. intention: *Have an intention of doing something* but *someone's intention is/was to do something*

needs checking   Hitler had no intention to keep his word.

revised   Hitler had no intention of keeping his word.

or   Hitler did not intend to keep his word.

or   Hitler's intention was to break the treaty.

A56. justified in doing something (not *to do something*)

needs checking   He is not justified to make these allegations.

revised   He is not justified in making these allegations.

A57. look forward to doing something (not *to do something*)

needs checking   I am looking forward to receive your reply.

revised   I am looking forward to receiving your reply.

A58. opposed to doing something (not *to do something*)

needs checking   He was opposed to set up a dictatorship.
revised   He was opposed to setting up a dictatorship.
or   He was opposed to the idea of setting up a dictatorship.

A59. organize something (not *to do something*)

needs checking   We organized to meet at ten the next morning.
revised   We organized a meeting for ten the next morning.
or   We arranged to meet at ten the next morning.

A60. persist in doing something (not *to do something*)

needs checking   Despite international disapproval, the Reagan administration persisted to help the rebels in Nicaragua.
revised   Despite international disapproval, the Reagan administration persisted in helping the rebels in Nicaragua.

A61. plan to do (not *on doing*)

needs checking   They planned on closing the factory in Windsor.
revised   They planned to close the factory in Windsor.

A62. prohibit someone from doing something (not *to do*)

needs checking   Members of the public were prohibited to feed the animals.
revised   Members of the public were prohibited from feeding the animals.

A63. regarded as (not *regarded to be*)

needs checking   He is commonly regarded to be one of the country's best musicians.
revised   He is commonly regarded as one of the country's best musicians.
or   He is commonly thought to be one of the country's best musicians.

A64. responsible for doing (not *to do*)

needs checking   Mr. Dumphy is responsible to market the full line of the company's pharmaceutical products.
revised   Mr. Dumphy is responsible for marketing the full line of the company's pharmaceutical products.

A65. sacrifice something (not *to do*): The use of *sacrifice* without a direct object may have crept into the language through the use of the verb as a baseball term (*Delgado sacrificed in the ninth to bring home Chavez*):

needs checking   He sacrificed to work in an isolated community with no electricity or running water.

revised   He sacrificed himself to work in an isolated community with no electricity or running water.

or   He sacrificed a good deal; the isolated community he now works in has no electricity or running water.

A66. seem to be (not *as if*)

needs checking   The patient seemed as if he was in shock.

revised   The patient seemed to be in shock.

(Exception: When the subject is *it*, *seem* can be followed by *as*. [e.g., *It seemed as if he was sick, so we called the doctor.*])

A67. suspect someone of doing something (not *to do*)

needs checking   She suspected him to have committed adultery.

revised   She suspected him of committing adultery.

or   She suspected that he had committed adultery.

A68. tendency to do something (not *of doing*)

needs checking   Some Buick engines have a tendency of over-revving.

revised   Some Buick engines have a tendency to over-rev.

or   Some Buick engines have a habit of over-revving.

⊙ Preposition Problems: *"Up With Which I Will Not Put"*

The prepositions used in English often make little or no sense. What good reason is there for saying *inferior to* but *worse than*? None whatsoever, but over the centuries certain prepositions have come to be accepted as going together with certain verbs, nouns, etc. There are no rules to help one learn the combinations; here are some of the ones that most commonly cause difficulty:

A69. agree with someone, with what someone says; agree to do something, to something; agree on a plan, proposal, etc.

needs checking	The union representatives did not agree with the proposed wage increase.
revised	The union representatives did not agree to the proposed wage increase.
or	The union representatives did not agree with management about the proposed wage increase.

A70. angry with someone; angry at or about something

needs checking	He was angry at me for failing to keep our appointment.
revised	He was angry with me for failing to keep our appointment.

A71. annoyed with someone; annoyed by something

needs checking	The professor is often annoyed with the attitude of the class.
revised	The professor is often annoyed by the attitude of the class.
or	The professor is often annoyed with the class.

A72. appeal to someone for something

needs checking	The premier appealed for the residents to help.
revised	The premier appealed to the residents for help.

A73. approve; approve of: When the verb *approve* is used with *of* (and without a direct object), it means *have a good opinion of.* In this sense the verb is frequently used where issues of right and wrong are concerned (e.g., *I don't approve of allowing children to run wild like that*). When the verb *approve* is used with a direct object (e.g., *approve a proposal, approve the application*), it typically refers to formal administrative or bureaucratic procedures.

needs checking	The issue of new shares was formally approved of by the Board of Directors at their August 28 meeting.
revised	The issue of new shares was formally approved by the Board of Directors at their August 28 meeting.

A74. argue with someone about something

needs checking   They argued against each other for half an hour.
revised   They argued with each other about the merit of exams.

A75. arrive in a place, at a place (not *arrive a place*, except *arrive home*).

Airlines have led the way in using both *arrive* and *depart* without prepositions. In formal writing one should still say *arrive in* or *arrive at*, and *depart from*.

needs checking   He won't join the team until tomorrow night when they arrive Milwaukee.
revised   He won't join the team until tomorrow night when they arrive in Milwaukee.

A76. attach two or more things (not *attach together*)

needs checking   The Siamese twins were attached together at the hip.
revised   The Siamese twins were attached at the hip.

A77. borrow something from someone

needs checking   I borrowed him a pair of trousers.
revised   I borrowed a pair of trousers from him.

A78. cancel something (not *cancel out*, except when the verb is used to mean *counterbalance* or *neutralize*)

needs checking   She cancelled out all her appointments.
revised   She cancelled all her appointments.
or   After playing hockey, he ate a huge snack that canceled out the calorie loss of the exercise.

A79. care about something (meaning *to think it worthwhile or important to you*)

needs checking   George does not care for what happens to his sister.
revised   George does not care what happens to his sister.
or   George does not care about what happens to his sister.

A80. centre: centred on something (not *around something*; for one thing to be centred around another is physically impossible)

needs checking   The novel is centred around the conflict between British imperialism and Native aspirations.

revised   The novel centres on the conflict between British imperialism and Native aspirations.

> ## Additional Material Online
> Exercises on preposition problems may be found at
> **sites.broadviewpress.com/writing**.
> Click on **Exercises** and
> go to **"Parts of Speech."**

A81. **chase someone or something away for doing something**:
Despite the way the word is used in baseball slang, in formal writing
the verb *chase* with no preposition means *run after*, not *send away*.

informal   Starting pitcher José Fernandez was chased in the fifth
inning.

more formal   Starting pitcher José Fernandez was pulled from the
game in the fifth inning.

A82. **collide with something** (not *against something*)

needs checking   The bus left the road and collided against a tree.

revised   The bus left the road and collided with a tree.

A83. **compare to, compare with**: To compare something *to* something else is to liken it, especially when speaking metaphorically
(e.g., *Shall I compare thee to a summer's day?*). To compare something
with something else is to judge how the two are similar or different
(*If you compare one brand with another you will notice little difference*).
Use *compare with* when noting differences:

needs checking   The First World War was a small conflict compared to
the Second World War, but it changed humanity even
more profoundly.

revised   The First World War was a small conflict compared with
the Second World War, but it changed humanity even
more profoundly.

A84. **concerned with something** (meaning *having some connection
with it, having something to do with it*) **and concerned about something** (meaning *being interested in it or worried about it*)

needs checking	The inspector is very concerned with the level of pollution in this river.
revised	The inspector is very concerned about the level of pollution in this river.

A85. conform to (not *with*)

needs checking	The building does not conform with current standards.
revised	The building does not conform to current standards.
or	The contractors did not comply with current standards.

A86. connect two things, connect one thing with another (not *connect up with*)

needs checking	As soon as he connects up these wires, the system should work.
revised	As soon as he connects these wires, the system should work.

A87. conscious of something (not *that*)

needs checking	He was not conscious that he had done anything wrong.
revised	He was not conscious of having done anything wrong.
	(Note: Unlike *conscious*, *aware* can be used with *of* or with a *that* clause.)

A88. consist in/consist of: *Consist in means to exist in, to have as the essential feature; consist of means to be made up of.*

needs checking	Success consists of hard work.
	(i.e., *The essence of success is hard work.*)
revised	Success consists in hard work.
needs checking	The US Congress consists in two houses—the House of Representatives and the Senate.
revised	The US Congress consists of two houses—the House of Representatives and the Senate.

A89. consult someone (not *consult with someone*). Unlike the verbs *talk* and *speak*, the verb *consult* does not need *to* or *with*.

needs checking	She will have to consult with the board of directors before giving us an answer.
revised	She will have to consult the board of directors before giving us an answer.

> *or* She will have to talk to the board of directors before giving us an answer.

A90. continue something, with something, to a place (not *continue on*)

needs checking We were told to continue on with our work.
revised We were told to continue with our work.

A91. convenient for someone, for a purpose; convenient to a place

needs checking This house is very convenient to me; it is only a short walk to work.
revised This house is very convenient for me; it is only a short walk to work.

A92. cooperate with someone (not *cooperate together*)

needs checking Countries should cooperate together to break down trade barriers.
revised Countries should cooperate with one another to break down trade barriers.

A93. correspond to (*be in agreement with*); **correspond with** (*exchange letters with*)

needs checking The fingerprints at the scene of the crime corresponded with those of the suspect.
revised The fingerprints at the scene of the crime corresponded to those of the suspect.

A94. couple of things, times, people, etc.

needs checking The body had been partially hidden under a pier on Lake Union, a couple hundred feet from the Aurora Avenue Bridge.
revised The body had been partially hidden under a pier on Lake Union, a couple of hundred feet from the Aurora Avenue Bridge.
or The body had been partially hidden under a pier on Lake Union, approximately two hundred feet from the Aurora Avenue Bridge.
(In formal writing it is better to use *two* than *a couple of*.)

A95. criticism of something or somebody (not *against*)

needs checking His criticisms against her were completely unfounded.
revised His criticisms of her were completely unfounded.

A96. depart from a place: See also **arrive** (A75).

needs checking One woman was heard saying to a friend as they departed Wrigley Field....
revised One woman was heard saying to a friend as they departed from Wrigley Field....
or One woman was heard saying to a friend as they left Wrigley Field....

A97. die of a disease, of old age; die from injuries, wounds

needs checking My grandfather died from cancer when he was only forty-two years old.
revised My grandfather died of cancer when he was only forty-two years old.

A98. different from, to, than: *Different to* and *different from* are both accepted British usage; *different from* is the preferred form in Canada and the US. (*Different than* is a common alternative in certain contexts in the United States, but in formal writing *different from* is the more widely accepted of the two.)

UK These results are different to those we obtained when we did the same experiment yesterday.
North America These results are different from those we obtained when we did the same experiment yesterday.

A99. discuss something (not *discuss about something*; no preposition is needed)

needs checking They discussed about what to do to ease tensions in the Middle East.
revised They discussed what to do to ease tensions in the Middle East.

A100. divide something (no preposition necessary)

needs checking Lear wants to divide up his kingdom among his three daughters.

> revised   Lear wants to divide his kingdom among his three daughters.

A101. do something for someone (meaning *something that will help*); **do something to someone** (meaning *something that will hurt*)

> needs checking   Norman Bethune did a lot to the people of China.
> revised   Norman Bethune did a lot for the people of China.

A102. end: at the end of something; in the end: *In the end* is used when the writer does not say which end he means, but leaves this to be understood by the reader. *At the end of* is used when the writer mentions the end he is referring to.

> needs checking   In the end of *Things Fall Apart*, we both admire and pity Okonkwo.
> revised   At the end of *Things Fall Apart*, we both admire and pity Okonkwo.
> or   In the end, we both admire and pity Okonkwo.

A103. end at a place (not *end up at*)

> needs checking   We do not want to end up at the same place we started from.
> revised   We do not want to end at the same place we started from.

A104. fight someone or with someone (not *against*; *fight* means *struggle against*, so to add *against* is redundant)

> needs checking   They fought against each other for almost an hour.
> revised   They fought with each other for almost an hour.
> or   They fought each other for almost an hour.

A105. frightened by something (when it has just frightened you); **frightened of something** (when talking about a constant condition)

> needs checking   He was suddenly frightened of the sound of a door slamming.
> revised   He was suddenly frightened by the sound of a door slamming.

A106. graduate from a school

> needs checking   He graduated McGill in 2014.

revised   He graduated from McGill in 2014.

A107. help doing, as in *be unable to refrain from doing* (not *help from doing*)

needs checking   She could not help from agreeing to his suggestion.
revised   She could not help agreeing to his suggestion.

A108. hurry (not *hurry up*)

needs checking   She told me to hurry up if I didn't want to miss the train.
revised   She told me to hurry if I didn't want to miss the train.

A109. identical to (not *with*)

needs checking   This hotel is identical with the Holiday Inn we stayed in last week.
revised   This hotel is identical to the Holiday Inn we stayed in last week.

A110. in/into/throughout/within: Whereas *in* typically indicates a particular location, *into* implies motion, and *throughout* implies omnipresence. *Within* and *in* are not interchangeable; *within* should be used only in certain contexts involving extent, duration, or enclosure.

needs checking   Within the prologue to the play, the chorus addresses the audience directly.
revised   In the prologue to the play, the chorus addresses the audience directly.

Note as well that *in to* should not always be converted to *into*; often the word *in* goes together with a previous verb rather than with *to*.

needs checking   The authorities keep giving into her demands.
revised   The authorities keep giving in to her demands.

A111. independent of something or someone (not *from*)

needs checking   I would like to live entirely independent from my parents.
revised   I would like to live entirely independent of my parents.

A112. inferior to someone or something (not *than*)

needs checking   Most people think that margarine is inferior than butter.

      revised   Most people think that margarine is inferior to butter. (*Inferior* and *superior* are the only two comparative adjectives which are not followed by *than*.)

A113. **inside or outside something** (not *of something*)

  needs checking   Within thirty minutes a green scum had formed inside of the beaker.

      revised   Within thirty minutes a green scum had formed inside the beaker.

A114. **interested in something, in doing something** (not *to*)

  needs checking   She is very interested to find out more about plant genetics.

      revised   She is very interested in finding out more about plant genetics.

A115. **investigate something** (not *investigate about or into something*)

  needs checking   The police are investigating into the murder in London last week.

      revised   The police are investigating the murder in London last week.

A116. **join someone** (not *join up with*)

  needs checking   Conrad Black joined up with his brother Montagu in making the proposal to buy the company.

      revised   Conrad Black joined his brother Montagu in making the proposal to buy the company.

A117. **jump** (not *jump up*)

  needs checking   Unemployment has jumped up to record levels recently.

      revised   Unemployment has jumped to record levels recently.

A118. **lift something** (not *lift up*)

  needs checking   I twisted my back as I was lifting up the box.

      revised   I twisted my back as I was lifting the box.

A119. **lower something** (not *lower down something*)

  needs checking   They lowered the coffin down into the grave.

      revised   They lowered the coffin into the grave.

A120. meet/meet with: *Meet with* in the sense of *attend a meeting with* is a recent addition to the language. If one is referring to a less formal or less prolonged encounter, however, there is no need for the preposition.

needs checking	Stanley finally met with Livingstone near the shores of Lake Tanganyika.
revised	Stanley finally met Livingstone near the shores of Lake Tanganyika.
	(The meaning here is *came face to face with for the first time.*)

A121. mercy: have mercy on someone; show mercy to or towards someone

needs checking	We should all have mercy for anyone who is suffering.
revised	We should all have mercy on anyone who is suffering.

A122. near something (not *near to something*)

needs checking	The village of Battle is very near to the place where the Battle of Hastings was fought in 1066.
revised	The village of Battle is very near the place where the Battle of Hastings was fought in 1066.

A123. object to something (not *against*)

needs checking	Some people have objected against being required to wear a seat belt.
revised	Some people have objected to being required to wear a seat belt.

A124. off something (not *off of*)

needs checking	The man stepped off of the platform into the path of the moving train.
revised	The man stepped off the platform into the path of the moving train.

A125. opposite: When used as a noun, *opposite* is followed by *of*; when used as an adjective, it is followed by *to* or *from*, or by no preposition.

needs checking	His conclusion was the opposite to mine.
	(Here, *opposite* is a noun.)

> *revised*   His conclusion was the opposite of mine.
> *or*   His conclusion was opposite to mine.
>   (Here, *opposite* is an adjective.)

A126. partake of something; participate in something

needs checking   They have refused to partake in a new round of talks on the subject of free trade.

revised   They have refused to participate in a new round of talks on the subject of free trade.

or   They have refused to partake of a new round of talks on the subject of free trade.

A127. prefer one thing or person to another (not *more than another*)

needs checking   They both prefer tennis more than golf.

revised   They both prefer tennis to golf.

A128. protest something (not *protest against*). *To protest* means *to argue against*; the preposition is redundant.

needs checking   The demonstrators were protesting against the government's decision to allow missile testing.

revised   The demonstrators were protesting the government's decision to allow missile testing.

A129. refer to something (not *refer back to something*)

needs checking   If you are confused, refer back to the diagram on page 24.

revised   If you are confused, refer to the diagram on page 24.

A130. regard/regards: With regard to something; as regards something

needs checking   I am writing in regards to the balance owing on your account.

fair   I am writing with regard to the balance owing on your account.

better   I am writing about the balance owing on your account.

(Note that *in regard to, with regard to,* and *as regards* may often be used interchangeably [*in regard to the issue you have raised, with regard to the issue you have raised, as regards the issue you have raised*]. All tend towards wordiness, however; usually there is a better way.)

A131. rejoice at something (not *for something*)

needs checking   He rejoiced for his good fortune when he won the lottery.

revised   He rejoiced at his good fortune when he won the lottery.

A132. repeat something (not *repeat again*)

needs checking   If you miss an answer you must repeat the whole exercise again.

revised   If you miss an answer you must repeat the whole exercise.

A133. request something or request that something be done (but not *request for something* unless one is using the noun—*a request for something*)

needs checking   He has requested for two more men to help him.

revised   He has requested two more men to help him.

or   He has put in a request for two more men to help him.

A134. retroactive to a date (not *from*)

needs checking   The tax changes are retroactive from July 1.

revised   The tax changes are retroactive to July 1.

A135. return to a place (not *return back*)

needs checking   He wanted to return back to the city as soon as possible.

revised   He wanted to return to the city as soon as possible.

A136. seek something or someone (not *seek for something*)

needs checking   She suggested that we seek for help from the police.

revised   She suggested that we seek help from the police.

A137. sight: in sight (*near enough to be seen*); **out of sight** (*too far away to be seen*); **on sight** (*immediately after being seen*)

needs checking   The general ordered that deserters be shot in sight.

revised   The general ordered that deserters be shot on sight.

A138. speak to someone (when one speaker is giving information to a listener); **speak with someone** (when the two are having a discussion)

needs checking	She spoke harshly with the secretary about his spelling mistakes.
revised	She spoke harshly to the secretary about his spelling mistakes.

A139. **suffer from something** (not *with*)

needs checking	He told me that he was suffering with the flu.
revised	He told me that he was suffering from the flu.

A140. **superior to someone or something** (not *than someone or something*)

needs checking	The advertisements claim that this detergent is superior than the others.
revised	The advertisements claim that this detergent is superior to the others.

A141. **surprised at or by something**: *At* is used to suggest that the person is disappointed or scandalized; unless one wishes to suggest this, *by* is the appropriate preposition.

needs checking	I was surprised at the arrival of my sister.
revised	I was surprised by the arrival of my sister.

A142. **type of person or thing**

needs checking	This type carburetor is no longer produced.
revised	This type of carburetor is no longer produced.

A143. **underneath something** (not *underneath of*)

needs checking	When we looked underneath of the table, we found what we had been looking for.
revised	When we looked underneath the table, we found what we had been looking for.

A144. **until a time or an event** (not *up until*)

needs checking	From 1942 up until 1967 the National Hockey League was made up of only six teams.
revised	From 1942 until 1967 the National Hockey League was made up of only six teams.

A145. warn someone of a danger, against doing something (*not about something or to do something*)

needs checking She warned me about the danger involved in the expedition.

revised She warned me of the danger involved in the expedition.

A146. worry about something (not *at something or for something*)

needs checking He is always worried at what will happen if he loses his job.

revised He is always worried about what will happen if he loses his job.

A147. prepositions in pairs or lists: If a sentence includes two or more nouns or verbs that take different prepositions, make sure to include all the necessary words:

needs checking The fire was widely reported in the newspapers and television.

revised The fire was widely reported in the newspapers and on television.

A148. ending a sentence with a preposition: Some authorities have argued that it is poor English to end a sentence with a preposition. The best answer to them is Winston Churchill's famous remark upon being accused of ending with a preposition: "This is the sort of pedantic nonsense up with which I will not put." Obviously such awkwardness as this can be avoided only by ending with a preposition. It is surely true that in many other cases ending sentences with prepositions is awkward. In practice, however, these are situations that we are already likely to avoid. The following dialogue (a version of which was passed on to me by Prof. A. Levey of the University of Calgary) provides in dramatic form another demonstration of the absurdity of strictures against ending with prepositions:

> "Where do you come from?"
> "From a place where we don't end sentences with prepositions."
> "Let me rephrase. Where do you come from, you stupid pedant?"

⊙ Nouns and Pronouns: *Singular Difficulties*

A149. unusual nouns: A number of nouns are unusual in the way that either the singular or the plural is formed. Here is a list of some that frequently cause mistakes. The most troublesome—as well as a few pronouns that cause similar difficulties—are also given individual entries below:

appendix	appendices
attorney general	attorneys general
bacterium	bacteria
basis	bases
court martial	courts martial
crisis	crises
criterion	criteria
curriculum	curricula
datum	data
daylight-saving time	[no plural]
ellipsis	ellipses
emphasis	emphases
erratum	errata
father-in-law	fathers-in-law
focus	foci
index	indexes or indices
matrix	matrixes or matrices
medium	media
millennium	millennia
nucleus	nuclei
parenthesis	parentheses
referendum	referenda or referendums
runner-up	runners-up
stratum	strata
symposium	symposia
synthesis	syntheses
thesis	theses

A150. accommodation: The plural form is not normally used:

needs checking   My family and my friend's family were both unable to find accommodations downtown.

revised   My family and my friend's family were both unable to find accommodation downtown.

A151. anyone/anybody/each/every/no one/nobody/someone/some-body: All are singular. It is often necessary to spend a few moments puzzling over how to phrase one's ideas before one finds a way to get all the verbs and subjects to agree, and at the same time avoid awkwardness. Ironically, however, the correct solution may in this case not be the best one. (See pages 356–57.)

not in agreement	Anyone may visit when they like.
in agreement	Anyone may visit when he or she likes.
in agreement	Anyone may visit at any time.
not in agreement	No one likes to leave a place that they have grown fond of.
in agreement	No one likes to leave a place that he or she has grown fond of.
in agreement	No one likes to leave a place that has fond memories attached to it.
not in agreement	Each person applying for the job must fill out this form before they will be granted an interview.
in agreement	Each person applying for the job must fill out this form before he or she will be granted an interview.
in agreement	Each person applying for the job must fill out this form before being granted an interview.

Be careful with sentences involving one of these pronouns and the pronoun *they*; getting the phrasing right is not always easy:

needs checking	Someone has forgotten to turn off the stove; they should be more careful.
revised	Someone has forgotten to turn off the stove; he or she should be more careful.
or	Some careless person has forgotten to turn off the stove.

Following is a list of common indefinite pronouns:

always plural: *both, many*

always singular: *another, anybody, anyone, anything, each, either, every, everybody, everyone, everything, neither, nobody, no one, nothing, one, somebody, someone, something*

singular or plural, depending on the context: *all, any, more, most, none, some*.

A152. **bacteria**: A plural word; the singular is *bacterium.*

> *needs checking*   There were many bacterias in the moldy bread.
> *revised*   There were a lot of bacteria in the moldy bread.

A153. **behaviour**: Although social scientists speak of *a behaviour* or of *behaviours* in technical writing, in other disciplines and in conversational English the word is uncountable (i.e., it cannot form a plural or be used with the indefinite article). Say *types of behaviour,* not *behaviours*:

> *needs checking*   He has a good behaviour.
> *revised*   His behaviour is good.
> *or*   He behaves well.

A154. **between/among**: It is often supposed that *between* should always be used for two, *among* for more than two. As the *Oxford English Dictionary* points out, however, "in all senses *between* has been, from its earliest appearance, extended to more than two." Perhaps the most important difference is that *between* suggests a relationship of things or people to each other as individuals, whereas *among* suggests a relationship that is collective and vague. Thus we say *the ball fell among the hollyhocks* where we are expressing the relationship of the ball to many flowers collectively, and where the precise location of the ball is unspecified. But we should not say, as we watch a baseball game, *the ball fell among the three fielders*; here we know the precise location of the ball and are expressing the relationship between it and the three individuals.

A155. **both/all**: Use *both* to refer to two, and *all* to refer to more than two.

> *needs checking*   Harris and Waluchow were the chief speakers in the debate yesterday. They all spoke very well.
> *revised*   Harris and Waluchow were the chief speakers in the debate yesterday. They both spoke very well.

A156. **brain**: One person can have only one brain. The use of the plural to refer to the brain of one person (e.g., *He blew his brains out*) is slang, and should not be used in formal written work.

needs checking   He used his brains to solve the problem.
    revised   He used his brain to solve the problem.

A157. **children:** Be careful when forming the possessive; the apostrophe should come before the *s*.

needs checking   All the childrens' toys had been put away.
    revised   All the children's toys had been put away.

A158. **confusion:** Uncountable—we do not normally speak of *a confusion* or of *confusions*:

needs checking   The misunderstanding about his time of arrival caused a confusion.
    revised   The misunderstanding about his time of arrival caused confusion.

A159. **criteria:** Plural; the singular is *criterion*.

needs checking   The chief criteria on which an essay should be judged is whether or not it communicates clearly.
    revised   The chief criterion on which an essay should be judged is whether or not it communicates clearly.

EAL

For particular problems with nouns faced by those whose native language is not English, see the EAL section later in this book.

A160. **damage:** In its usual meaning, this noun has no plural, since it is uncountable. We speak of *damage*, not *a damage*, and of *a lot of damage*, not *many damages*. The word *damages* means *money paid to cover the cost of any damage one has caused*:

needs checking   The crash caused many damages to his car, but he was unhurt.
    revised   The crash caused a lot of damage to his car, but he was unhurt.

A161. data: Like *bacteria, media,* and *phenomena,* the noun *data* is plural. The singular form, which is rarely used, is *datum*:

needs checking   This data proves that the lake is badly polluted.

revised   These data prove that the lake is badly polluted.

A162. each other/one another: Use *each other* for two, *one another* for more than two:

needs checking   The three brothers always tell stories to each other before going to sleep.

revised   The three brothers always tell stories to one another before going to sleep.

needs checking   The two men had long since begun to get on one another's nerves. (Alan Moorehead, *The White Nile*)

revised   The two men had long since begun to get on each other's nerves.

A163. either/neither: *Either* and *neither* are both singular. This can create considerable awkwardness in structuring sentences. (See also pages 556–57 on this point.)

needs checking   Somehow, neither Sally nor Great Uncle Magnus were as tidy as they had been when they set out. (Margaret Mahy, *Ultra-Violet Catastrophe*)

Trying to correct the error here by simply changing *were* to *was* creates a new problem with the word *they* in the second half of the sentence; a further change is also necessary:

revised   Somehow, neither Sally nor Great Uncle Magnus was as tidy as both had been when they set out.

needs checking   So far neither the party rank and file nor the electorate seem satisfied with the leader's performance.

revised   So far neither the party rank and file nor the electorate seems satisfied with the leader's performance.

A164. either/any; neither/none: Use *either* and *neither* for two, *any* and *none* for more than two:

needs checking   Shirley has six sisters, but she hasn't seen either of them since Christmas.

revised   Shirley has six sisters, but she hasn't seen any of them since Christmas.

A165. government: A singular noun:

needs checking The government are intending to build a new terminal at this airport before 2015.

revised The government is intending to build a new terminal at this airport before 2015.

A166. graffiti: A plural noun; the singular form is *graffito*:

needs checking Graffiti covers most of the subway cars in the city.

revised Graffiti cover most of the subway cars in the city.

A167. media: Plural; the singular is *medium*:

needs checking The media usually assumes that the audience has a very short attention span.

revised The media usually assume that the audience has a very short attention span.

A168. money: Some people seem to think that *monies* has a more official ring to it than *money* when they are talking of business affairs, but there is no sound reason for using this plural form in good English:

needs checking The mayor has promised to provide some monies for this project.

revised The mayor has promised to provide some money for this project.

A169. news: Despite the *s*, this is a singular collective noun. Make sure to use a singular verb with it:

needs checking Today's news of troubles in the Middle East are very disturbing.

revised Today's news of troubles in the Middle East is very disturbing.

A170. none: Although *no one* and *not one* are always singular, common usage allows *none* to be either singular or plural depending on the context. In a sentence such as *Of all European cities, none is more beautiful than Prague* the pronoun *none* is clearly singular—just as *not one* would be if used in its place. In the sentence *None of the field is dry* the pronoun *none* refers to the singular noun *field*—though here, we notice, it would not be possible to substitute *not one*. In the sentence *None of the girls want to leave* the word *none* refers to the plural noun *girls*, and may thus take a plural verb. In the same way the pronouns *all, any, more, most*, and *some* may be either singular or plural depending on whether they refer to a singular or a plural referent. *Most of the sugar is gone*, but *most of the people are happy*. Some argue, however, that *none* should be treated grammatically as *no one* and *not one* are treated, and should always take a singular verb (i.e., that we should say *none of the girls* **wants** *to leave, none of the things she wants* **is** *available*, and so on). If in doubt (or in fear of a grammatical traditionalist) treat *none* as always singular; otherwise, make it agree with its referent.

widely accepted	None of the issues concerning indefinite pronouns are of earth-shattering importance.
universally accepted	None of the issues concerning indefinite pronouns is of earth-shattering importance.

A171. **phenomena:** Plural; the singular is *phenomenon*:

needs checking	The great popularity of disco music was a short-lived phenomena.
revised	The great popularity of disco music was a short-lived phenomenon.

A172. **police:** A plural noun. Be sure to use a plural verb with it:

needs checking	The police is investigating the case, and hope to make an arrest soon.
revised	The police are investigating the case, and hope to make an arrest soon.

Additional Material Online
Exercises on singular and plural nouns and pronouns may be found at **sites.broadviewpress.com/writing**. Click on **Exercises** and go to **"Parts of Speech."**

⊙ Pronouns: *Who Cares about Whom?*

Those unfamiliar with the territory may wish to refer to the section on pronouns in "Basic Grammar: An Outline" (pages 95–112). Readers may also wish to refer to the discussion of *y'all* and *youse* on pages 113–14 above.

A173. **extra pronoun:** It is easy to add an extra pronoun, particularly if the subject of the sentence is separated from the verb by a long adjectival clause:

needs checking	The countries which Hitler wanted to conquer in the late 1930s they were too weak to resist him.
revised	The countries which Hitler wanted to conquer in the late 1930s were too weak to resist him.
needs checking	The line that is longest in a right-angled triangle it is called the hypotenuse.
revised	The line that is longest in a right-angled triangle is called the hypotenuse.

A174. **first person:** In formal writing it is customary to use *I* and *me* infrequently or not at all. The object of a formal piece of writing is normally to present an argument, and writers realize that they can best argue their case by presenting evidence rather than by stating that such and such is what they think. Thus many teachers advise their students always to avoid using the first person singular (*I* and *me*) in their writing.

This guideline should not be regarded as a firm and fast rule. George Orwell, often praised as the finest essayist of the last century, uses *I* and *me* frequently. As the following example illustrates, however, he employs the first person to guide the reader through his argument, not to make the points in the argument:

If one gets rid of these habits one can think more clearly, and to think more clearly is a necessary first step towards political regeneration: so that the fight against bad English is not frivolous and is not the exclusive concern of professional writers. I will come back to this presently, and I hope that by that time the meaning of what I have said will become clearer. (*Politics and the English Language*)

Phrases such as *I think* and *I feel,* on the other hand, will not help you convince the reader of the strength of your main points.

needs checking Many authorities assume inflation to be a cause of high interest rates, but I think that high interest rates are a cause of inflation. This essay will prove my argument through numerous examples.

revised Many authorities assume inflation to be a cause of high interest rates; in fact, high interest rates are often a cause of inflation. Let us take the years 1978 to 1983 in the US as an example.

A175. I/me/myself: Perhaps as a result of slang use of *me* as a subject pronoun (*Me and him got together for a few beer last night*), the impression seems to have lodged in many minds that the distinction between *I* and *me* is one of degree of politeness or formality. It's not; the distinction is simply between subject pronoun (*I*) and object pronoun (*me*).

needs checking There is no disagreement between you and I.

revised There is no disagreement between you and me.

(Both *you* and *I* are here objects of a preposition—*between. Between you and I* is no more correct than is *I threw the ball at he.*)

Many are also sometimes uncertain as to how *myself* should be used. One way is as a reflexive pronoun used as a direct or indirect object (*I hurt myself; I talk to myself*). Another is as an intensifier, to point up a contrast or add emphasis (*Someone from our company will attend, but I won't be there myself*). Note that *myself* is used in conjunction with another first person pronoun, however, not in place of *I* or *me.*

needs checking There was no need to consult Carol and myself about this.

revised There was no need to consult Carol and me about this.

Additional Material Online
Exercises on pronoun problems may be found at
sites.broadviewpress.com/writing.
Click on **Exercises** and go to **"Parts of Speech."**

A176. non-human and human animals: Is a non-human animal an *it*? Or a he or *she*?

Over the past two generations the ways in which humans treat other animals have become the subject of widespread discussion. But there has been scant attention paid to how changing attitudes should be reflected in English usage. In particular, the issue of what pronouns to use has until recently been little discussed—but it is arguably of considerable importance.

No one nowadays thinks it odd to refer to a pet as *he* or *she*, but beyond that there is a great deal of inconsistency. At issue is not only *it* versus *he* or *she*, but also *who* and *whom* versus *that* and *which*. Should we say *the dog that lives next door* or *the dog who lives next door*? Should we say *the pig that plays a central role in* Charlotte's Web? Or *the pig who plays a central role in* Charlotte's Web? Should we say *the pig that they ate for dinner* or *the pig who they ate for dinner*?

In contexts where non-human animals are portrayed as pets or as friendly and lovable, "who" seems to be quite accepted. "The cat who..." and "The dog who..." are commonly used, as are "the pig who..." and "the cow who" in contexts such as children's stories. With dogs and cats *who* seems the more widely accepted alternative, even in negative contexts; Google shows "dogs who bite" occurring more than twice as frequently as "dogs that bite." Wild animals too we seem comfortable referring to as living creatures rather than things. In the case of the non-human animals many humans make a practice of eating, though, *it*, *that*, and *which* are used far more frequently. Should they be? Is a cow any more a thing than is a tail-wagging Labrador? Is a calf or a piglet any more a thing than is a kitten or a puppy? What about a shrimp? Or a clam? Where does one draw a line? For many people there may be no easy answers to such questions, but they are surely worth asking; as has often been the case in human history, debates over appropriate linguistic usage provide some of the most interesting windows into large ethical, political, and epistemological issues.

What should you do if you are writing of non-human animals? Treat them grammatically as things? Or treat them in the way we do fellow creatures? To some extent the answer may be necessarily context-dependent. If you cannot tell whether the bird you see flashing by in the sky or the fish you see flashing by in the water is male or female, you are surely not likely to refer to the creature as *he or she*. But if you do know whether what you are looking at is male or female, is there any good reason to refer to that animal as *it* rather than *he* or *she*? Or to say *that* rather than *who*?

Try as we might, we can't see any. We have to acknowledge that the state of our language is still some distance away from any point where it would be frowned upon to refer to non-human animals as things—calves or chimpanzees, bears or bonobos, dogs or ducklings, hens or hippopotamuses. But we'd like to try to bring all of us, as human beings—human animals—closer to that point.

worth checking	The cow that's pictured on that carton of milk looks a lot happier than the real cows that produce the milk.
revised	The cow who's pictured on that carton of milk looks a lot happier than the real cows who produce the milk.

Much as it may seem new-fangled or odd to refer to non-human animals in this way, English usage of this sort in fact represents a return to linguistic practice that was once well established. In 1865, for example, one Dr. Kidd recounted in the *Times* of London how he had saved a cow during the cattle plague of that year: "The men thought her dying...," "Determined not to give her up..." "little by little she revived." With "intensive" farming practices having become near universal in North America, most of us now have little or no contact with living cows and pigs and sheep and hens; no doubt it is not by coincidence that the growth of factory farming has been accompanied by a shift in the English language towards usages that encourage us to think of non-human animals as things rather than living creatures.

One point of English usage not in dispute is that human animals should be referred to using *he, she, who*, and *whom*—not *it* or *that* or *which*. The use of *that* to refer to humans, however, has become increasingly widespread, usually in linguistic contexts where *that* is slightly easier to say than *who*.

> *needs checking*   The woman that wanders aimlessly round the park every morning is an Alzheimer's patient.
>
> *revised*   The woman who wanders aimlessly round the park every morning is an Alzheimer's patient.

A177. **than**: Does *than* take a subject or an object pronoun? Purists argue that we should say *She's brighter than I* [*am*], and *He's louder than she* [*is*]—that the verb is always understood in such sentences, even when we do not say it or write it, and that the unspoken verb requires a subject. It's hard to argue, however, that the increasingly widespread use of object pronouns after *than* is either ugly or confusing.

> *less formal*   She always sleeps later than him.
>
> *more formal*   She always sleeps later than he [does].

A178. **unreferenced or wrongly referenced pronoun**: Normally a pronoun must refer to a noun in the previous sentence or clause. In the following sentence, for example, the pronoun *she* clearly refers to the noun *Charity*, which is the subject of the first clause in the sentence:

- Charity told Alfred that she would start work at nine.

Notice how confusing the sentence becomes, however, if there are two possible *shes* in the first part of the sentence:

- Charity told Mavis that she would start work at nine.

Does this mean that Charity will start work at nine, or that Mavis will? From the sentence it is impossible to tell. In cases like this, where it is not absolutely clear whom or what a pronoun refers to, use the noun again instead:

> *clear*   Charity told Mavis that she (Charity) would start work at nine.

In the following case the writer has gone astray by mentioning two things—one singular, one plural—and then matching only one of the two with a pronoun. In this instance the best remedy is to substitute a noun for the pronoun:

needs checking   Shields's characters are so exquisitely crafted and her plot so artfully conceived that it keeps the reader riveted until the final page.

revised   Shields's characters are so exquisitely crafted and her plot so artfully conceived that the book keeps the reader riveted until the final page.

Similar mistakes are often made in writing about a general class of people, such as police officers, or doctors, or football players. When writing in this way one can use either the third person singular (e.g., *A doctor helps patients. She* ....) or the third person plural (*Doctors help patients. They* ....). Mixing the two in such situations often leads people to write unreferenced pronouns:

needs checking   A herbalist knows a lot about plants. They can often cure you by giving you medicine.

    (Here the pronoun *they* is presumably meant to refer to the plural noun *herbalists*, but the writer has referred only to *a herbalist*.)

revised   A herbalist knows a lot about plants. He can often cure you by giving you medicine.

or   Herbalists know a lot about plants. They can often cure you by giving you medicine.

It may also not be clear what or whom a pronoun refers to if it is placed too far away from the noun:

needs checking   The finance minister increased corporate taxes by an average of 43 per cent. Other measures in the budget included $100 million in student assistance and new funding for the ombudsman. He also introduced a variety of measures to help small businesses.

revised   The finance minister increased corporate taxes by an average of 43 per cent. Other measures in the budget included $100 million in student assistance and new funding for the ombudsman. The minister also introduced a variety of measures to help small businesses.

Be particularly careful when using *this* as a pronoun; if the preceding sentence is a long one, it may not be at all clear what *this* refers to:

needs checking   The deficit was forecast to be $800 million, but turned out to be over $6 billion. This reflected the government's failure to predict the increase in interest rates and the onset of a recession.
                    (*This what?*)
revised   The deficit was forecast to be $800 million, but turned out to be over $6 billion. This vast discrepancy reflected the government's failure to predict the increase in interest rates and the onset of a recession.

Sometimes the meaning may be clear, but the omission of a pronoun may create unintended and humorous ambiguity:

needs checking   She visited a doctor with a bad case of the flu.
                    (Did the doctor have the flu?)
revised   She visited a doctor when she had a bad case of the flu.
needs checking   The Cougar was a sporty car aimed at the youthful-feeling who wanted luxury in their automobiles. Its buyers were similar to Mustangs, but more affluent.
revised   The Cougar was a sporty car aimed at the youthful-feeling who wanted luxury in their automobiles. Its buyers were similar to those who bought Mustangs, but more affluent.

A179. **who/whom:** The subject pronoun and the object pronoun, but it's not as simple as that. Nor is the distinction merely a matter of stuffiness or pedantry on the part of grammar purists. Sound has a great deal to do with it. Even purists must sometimes find themselves saying, *I didn't know who I was talking to*, even though the rules say it should be *whom* (subject—*I*; object—*whom*). In similar fashion the enemies of *whom* must surely be tempted to sacrifice principle rather than attempt such an owlish mouthful as *To who was he talking?* They would do so not on the grammatical grounds of *whom*, the object pronoun, being correct since it is acting as the object of the preposition *to*, but on the grounds of *whom*, the word with an *m* on the end, being in that sentence a lot easier to say. In such circumstances convenience of pronunciation occasionally overrides arguments either for or against formality.

less formal   Scott Fitzgerald never cared who he irritated.
more formal   Scott Fitzgerald never cared whom he irritated.

⊙ Part-of-speech Conversions:
A Question of Principle?

A well-known Calvin and Hobbes cartoon strip nicely conveys the amusement that part-of-speech conversions may engender:

Calvin: "I like to verb words."
Hobbes: "What?"
Calvin: "I take nouns and adjectives and use them as verbs. Remember when *access* was a thing? Now it's something you do. It got verbed....Verbing weirds language."
Hobbes: "Maybe we can eventually make language a complete impediment to understanding."

In fact, however, there is no good reason why a word that has become established as one part of speech should not be used as another; the language has always been changing and growing in this way. As Tom Shippey asks:

What can be the matter with using nouns as adjectives? Everyone does it; how about *stonewall*? It has been built into the language since before English settlers found Ireland, let alone America.... As for converting nouns to verbs, what about *water*? *Watering the horses* is recorded from before the Conquest. (*Times Literary Supplement*, 19–25 October 1990)

For that matter, what about *chair, table, paper, shelf, bottle, cup, knife, fork, eye, mouth, finger*? The list of nouns that have also become verbs or other parts of speech is a very long one, and it includes many of the most basic words in the language. (Ironically enough, the adjective *weird*, used humorously in the cartoon as a verb, began life as a noun; in Old English a weird was the personification of a powerful but unpredictable natural force.) The point in being aware of the conversion of one part of speech to another, then, is not that the practice is always a bad one. Rather it is to keep oneself aware of whether or not one is saying something in the best possible way. If the new creation fills a need, saying something more clearly and concisely than it is possible to do otherwise, then it deserves to survive. But if it fulfills no useful purpose—if clearer and more concise ways of saying the same thing already exist—then it's better to avoid it.

A180. **access**: For many years authorities felt, except in the vocabulary of computers, *access* should be used as a noun, not a verb. The use of *access* as a verb is now much more widely accepted, but some purists still argue that alternatives such as *enter* and *reach* are usually more precise:

less widely accepted	The cafeteria may be accessed from the warehouse or the accounts department.
more widely accepted	The cafeteria may be reached through the warehouse or the accounts department.

A181. **adjective for adverb**: If a word is modifying a verb, it should as a general rule be an adverb rather than an adjective. This is normally the case when the descriptive word comes directly after the verb. We say *The boy laughed quietly*, for example (rather than *The boy laughed quiet*), because the descriptive word *quietly* refers to the verb *laughed*, not the noun *boy*. Similarly, in the sentence *The quiet boy laughed* we use the adjective *quiet* to refer to the noun *boy*.

In most cases a descriptive word following a verb will apply to that verb, and should take the form of an adverb:

needs checking	She asked us not to talk so loud.
revised	She asked us not to talk so loudly.
needs checking	According to Mr. Adams, "most books will go heavier into evolution, which is a good thing."
revised	According to Mr. Adams, "most books will go more heavily into evolution, which is a good thing."
needs checking	He performs bad whenever he is under pressure.
revised	He performs badly whenever he is under pressure.

In some cases, however, a descriptive word following a verb may refer not to the verb, but to the subject. This happens most frequently with the verb *to be*, which of course does not name an action in the way that other verbs do. Thus we say *The boy is quiet*, not *The boy is quietly*; we use the adjective rather than the adverb because we are describing the boy, not the action of being. Verbs such as *taste*, *smell,* and *feel* resemble *be* in this respect; it is correct to say *I feel good* rather than *I feel well,* since the descriptive word is clearly intended to describe your condition, and not the act of feeling. Similarly, we say *it tastes good,* not *it tastes well,* and *it smells sweet,* not *it smells sweetly.* In some other cases, too, an adjective rather than an adverb will be appropriate after a verb. It makes perfect sense, for example, to write that *someone sliced the bread thin* (rather than *sliced the bread thinly*), since the descriptive word is intended to refer to the resulting slices, and not to the action of slicing.

The principles outlined above also apply to the comparative and superlative forms of adjectives and adverbs:

needs checking	They both ran quicker in the final than they had in the semi-final.
revised	They both ran more quickly in the final than they had in the semi-final.
needs checking	He performs worse under pressure than he does when he is relaxed.
revised	He performs less well under pressure than he does when he is relaxed.
needs checking	Of all the contestants, Hawkins ran the quickest.
revised	Of all the contestants, Hawkins ran the most quickly.

Given that comparative and superlative adverbs are often more long-winded compound formations, it is not surprising that in everyday speech the shorter adjectival equivalents are often used in their stead. And such usages are becoming more and more common as well in written English. Should the *Financial Post* editor have corrected the headline that read "Northern Miners Breathe Easier"? Certainly it's easier to use the adjective here in place of the two-part adverb *more easily.* Whether or not it's better is less clear; certainly many purists are not pleased by the practice.

less widely accepted	The purpose of desktop publishing is to do the same old thing cheaper, easier, and quicker.
more widely accepted	The purpose of desktop publishing is to do the same old thing more cheaply, more easily, and more quickly.

A182. **advice/advise:** *Advice* is the noun; *advise* is the verb.

needs checking	They refused to take our advise.
revised	They refused to take our advice.

A183. affect/effect: *Effect* is normally used as a noun meaning *result*. (It can also be used as a verb meaning *put into effect*, as in *The changes were effected by the committee*.) *Affect* is a verb meaning *cause a result*. (It can also be used as a noun meaning *emotion* or *mental state*, as in *affect theory*.)

needs checking	When the acid is added to the solution, there is no visible affect.
revised	When the acid is added to the solution, there is no visible effect.
needs checking	"The issues that effect us here on the reserve are the same issues that effect the whole constituency," Mr. Littlechild said. (*The Globe and Mail*)
revised	"The issues that affect us here on the reserve are the same issues that affect the whole constituency," Mr. Littlechild said.

A184. author: A noun, not a verb. If you wish to suggest that someone's name appears on the cover as the author but that in fact the book has been ghost-written, "authored" may be a good choice. Otherwise, there is no need to find a substitute for *write*.

needs checking	Smith is a member of the Appeals Court, and has authored two books on the judicial system.
revised	Smith is a member of the Appeals Court, and has written two books on the judicial system.

A185. bear/birth/give birth to: Twenty years ago a woman would *bear children* or *give birth to children*, but there was no single word to describe the process of giving birth. The word *birthing* was coined to fill the linguistic gap, and from there the use of *birth* as a transitive verb quickly became common. The new coinage *birth a child* is certainly more concise than *give birth to a child*, and is widely felt to better reflect the active nature of the process.

A186. breath/breathe: *Breath* is the noun, *breathe* the verb.

needs checking	When you breath, your lungs take in oxygen.
revised	When you breathe, your lungs take in oxygen.

A187. dependent/dependant: *Dependent* is the adjective, *dependant* the noun. You are dependent on someone or something, and your young children are your dependants; they are dependent on you.

> *needs checking*   Emily is still dependant on her parents for financial support.
>
> *revised*   Emily is still dependent on her parents for financial support.

A188. dialogue: As a verb, *talk* serves perfectly well, even after all these years.

> *awkward*   The two department heads should dialogue with each other more frequently.
>
> *better*   The two department heads should talk to each other more frequently.

A189. enthuse/enthusiastic: The verb *enthuse* is a relatively recent back formation from the adjective *enthusiastic*; *enthused* is its simple past tense form. Confusion between the two forms is now common.

> *needs checking*   In 2014 millions were enthused about Norway's Olympic performance.
>
> *revised*   In 2014 millions were enthusiastic about Norway's Olympic performance.
>
> *or*   In 2014 millions enthused over Norway's Olympic performance.

A190. first/firstly: *Firstly* is now generally thought of as archaic, though it is not incorrect. Be sure to be consistent, though, in the use of *first, second*, etc., in lists.

> *needs checking*   There were several reasons for France's reluctance to commit more resources to the New World. First, she was consumed with the battle for supremacy in Europe. Secondly, the returns on previous investments had been minimal.
>
> *revised*   There were several reasons for France's reluctance to commit more resources to the New World. First, she was consumed with the battle for supremacy in Europe. Second, the returns on previous investments had been minimal.

A191. **give/gift**: Until relatively recently it was universally understood that *give* is a verb and *gift* is a noun. The use of *gift* as a verb seems to have arisen in the context of institutional fundraising; it is difficult to see any reason to say "thank you" for this *gift*.

needs checking	Mr. Dench has generously gifted the university with funding for a new library.
revised	Mr. Dench has generously given the university funding for a new library.

A192. **good/well**: The most common of the adjective-for-adverb mistakes.

needs checking	As the manager put it, "He pitched good, but not real good."
fair	He pitched well, but not really well.
better	He did not pitch very well.

A193. **impact**: The use of *impact* as a verb has become widespread even in formal English, but *affect* remains an attractive option.

awkward	The government's decision will impact upon wholesalers in all areas of the country.
better	The government's decision will affect wholesalers in all areas of the country.

A194. **like/as**: *Like* is a preposition, not a conjunction; it introduces a noun or pronoun in a phrase. If introducing a clause, which always includes a verb, use *as* in formal writing.

- He looks like his father.
  (*Like* introduces the noun *father*.)
- He looks as his father did at his age.
  (*As* introduces the clause *as his father did at his age*.)
- He is acting like a drunkard.
  (*Like* introduces the noun *drunkard*.)
- He is acting as if he were drunk.
  (*As* introduces the clause *as if he were drunk*.)

needs checking	Like I said before, smoking is forbidden.
revised	As I said before, smoking is forbidden.

needs checking	He runs like I do—with short, choppy strides.
revised	He runs as I do—with short, choppy strides.
or	He runs like me. We both take short, choppy strides.

needs checking	Duvalier ran Haiti like his father had done.
revised	Duvalier ran Haiti the way his father had.

The attempt is also sometimes made to use *like what* in place of *as.*

needs checking	Bush Sr. wanted to appear tough, like what Reagan had when he ordered the invasion of Grenada.
revised	Bush Sr. wanted to appear tough, as Reagan had when he ordered the invasion of Grenada.

A195. its/it's: *Its* is an adjective meaning *belonging to it. It's* is a contraction of *it is*—a pronoun plus a verb. (Similarly, *whose* is an adjective meaning *belonging to whom*, whereas *who's* is a contraction of *who is.* See A211.)

needs checking	Its important to remember that the population of North America in this period was less than 10 million.
revised (*less formal*)	It's important to remember that the population of North America in this period was less than 10 million.
revised (*more formal*)	It is important to remember that the population of North America in this period was less than 10 million.
needs checking	A coniferous tree continually sheds it's leaves.
revised	A coniferous tree continually sheds its leaves.

A196. lend/loan: In formal English *loan* should be used only as a noun; *lend* is the verb.

needs checking	He was unwilling to loan his sister any money.
revised	He was unwilling to lend his sister any money.

Additional Material Online

Exercises on part-of-speech conversions may be found at **sites.broadviewpress.com/writing**. Click on **Exercises** and go to **"Parts of Speech."**

A197. **loath/loathe:** *Loath* is the adjective; *loathe* is the verb.

needs checking He told me he is beginning to loath his job.
revised He told me he is beginning to loathe his job.
or He is loath to return to his old job.

A198. **loose/lose:** *Loose* is normally used as an adjective meaning *not tight*; as a verb it means to *make loose* (e.g., *He loosed the reins*). *Lose* is, of course, always a verb.

needs checking As soon as it became dark she began to loose control of herself.
revised As soon as it became dark she began to lose control of herself.

needs checking If this movie doesn't bring the song back to the hit parade, then you know it's flopped—and that Spielberg is loosing his touch.
revised If this movie doesn't bring the song back to the hit parade, then you know it's flopped—and that Spielberg is losing his touch.

A199. **maybe/may be:** *Maybe* is an adverb that should be replaced by *perhaps* in formal writing. *May be* is a compound verb.

needs checking May be he will come, but I doubt it.
revised Maybe he will come, but I doubt it.
or Perhaps he will come, but I doubt it.

needs checking The prototype maybe ready by 2020.
revised The prototype may be ready by 2020.

A200. **meantime/meanwhile:** *Meantime* is a noun, used most frequently in the phrase *in the meantime*. *Meanwhile* is an adverb.

needs checking The Germans were preparing for an attack near Calais. Meantime, the Allies were readying themselves for the invasion of Normandy.
revised The Germans were preparing for an attack near Calais. Meanwhile, the Allies were readying themselves for the invasion of Normandy.

A201. **medal/win a medal:** Until quite recently English lacked a one-word verb meaning *win a medal*. The verb *to medal* now fills that function, but many feel the new coinage has the feel of a counterfeit. In formal writing it is probably still best to use the more widely accepted currency.

less widely accepted	She medalled twice at the 2008 Olympics.
more widely accepted	She twice won medals at the 2008 Olympics.
or	She won two medals at the 2008 Olympics.

A202. **orgasm/have an orgasm:** Until recently the only one-word synonyms for *have an orgasm* or *achieve orgasm* were vulgar terms that clearly had no place in formal writing. In recent years *orgasm* itself has begun to be used as a verb as well as a noun. The new usage has as yet not excited much attention, and it is too early to say if it will come to be accepted in formal English; for the moment it is probably best to use more established constructions.

less widely accepted	Twenty per cent of the respondents reported that on average they had orgasmed fewer than three times per month.
more widely accepted	Twenty per cent of the respondents reported that on average they had experienced orgasm fewer than three times per month.
or	Twenty per cent of the respondents reported that on average they had had fewer than three orgasms per month.

A203. **practice/practise:** In the US *practice* serves as both noun and verb. In Canada and Britain *practise* (verb) and *practice* (noun) should be distinguished.

| *US* | The team will practice on Thursday. |
| *UK/CDA* | The team will practise on Thursday. |

A204. **predominate/predominant:** *Predominate* is the verb, *predominant* the adjective. (Either *predominately* or *predominantly* may be used as adverbs.)

| *needs checking* | The Social Credit movement was predominate only in Alberta and British Columbia. |

revised   The Social Credit movement was predominant only in
              Alberta and British Columbia.

or   The Social Credit movement predominated only in
              Alberta and British Columbia.

A205. principal/principle: *Principal* can be either a noun or an
adjective. As a noun it means *the person in the highest position of
authority in an organization* (e.g., *a school principal*) or *an amount
of money*, as distinguished from the interest on it. As an adjective it
means *first in rank or importance* (*The principal city of northern Nigeria is Kano*). *Principle* is always a noun, and is never used to describe
a person; *a principle* is *a basic truth or doctrine, a code of conduct*, or
a law describing how something works.

needs checking   We feel this is a matter of principal.
revised   We feel this is a matter of principle.

needs checking   Up went the shares of the two principle companies in
                     this emerging field.
revised   Up went the shares of the two principal companies in
                     this emerging field.

A206. prophecy/prophesy: *Prophecy* is the noun, *prophesy* the verb.

needs checking   His comment should be regarded as a prediction, not a
                     prophesy.
revised   His comment should be regarded as a prediction, not a
                     prophecy.

A207. quality: Although in colloquial English *quality* is frequently
used as a replacement for *good* or *worthwhile*, in formal writing it
should be used as a noun, not an adjective. It is useful to remember
that something may as easily be of poor quality as of good quality.

needs checking   The salesperson claims that this is a quality product.
revised   The salesperson claims that this is a product of high
                     quality.
or   The salesperson claims that this is a good product.

needs checking   "It was Mother's Day. I was trying to spend some quality
                     time with my wife." (An NHL vice-president explaining
                     why he had not attended an important playoff game, as
                     quoted in *The Toronto Star*)

> *revised* "It was Mother's Day. I was trying to spend some time with my wife."

A208. quote/quotation: In formal English *quote* is the verb, *quotation* the noun.

> *needs checking* The following quote shows just how determined she is to change the constitution.
>
> *revised* The following quotation shows just how determined she is to change the constitution.

A209. real/really: One of the most commonly made adjective-for-adverb mistakes.

> *needs checking* Some of the fish we caught were real big.
>
> *fair* Some of the fish we caught were really big.
>
> *better* Some of the fish we caught were very big.

A210. verb-noun confusion: Where verbs and nouns have similar forms, be careful not to confuse them. Some of the most common examples are: *advice* (noun) and *advise* (verb); *extent* (noun) and *extend* (verb); *device* (noun) and *devise* (verb); *revenge* (noun) and *avenge* (verb); *loan* (noun) and *lend* (verb).

> *needs checking* Gerald Ford, president from 1974 to 1976, has now to a large extend been forgotten.
>
> *revised* Gerald Ford, president from 1974 to 1976, has now to a large extent been forgotten.

> *needs checking* She wanted to revenge the harm he had caused her.
>
> *revised* She wanted to avenge the harm he had caused her.

A211. whose/who's: *Whose* means *belonging to whom*; *who's* is a contraction of *who is*.

> *needs checking* Kennedy is not normally remembered as the president who's policies embroiled the US in the Vietnam conflict, but several scholars have suggested that he was as much responsible as was Johnson.
>
> *revised* Kennedy is not normally remembered as the president whose policies embroiled the US in the Vietnam conflict, but several scholars have suggested that he was as much responsible as was Johnson.

Red Tape Holds Up New Bridge

The following are all examples of ambiguity in newspaper headlines. In some cases it may take several moments to decipher the intended meaning.

Two pedestrians struck by bridge
Man held over giant L.A. brush fire
Illegal aliens cut in half by new law
Passerby injured by post office
Red tape holds up new bridge
Village water holds up well
Jerk injures neck, wins award
Bishop thanks god for calling

(The above examples come courtesy of columnist Bob Swift of Knight-Ridder Newspapers, and Prof. A. Levey of the University of Calgary.)

Here are two gems provided by editor Beth Humphries:

The fossils were found by scientists
embedded in red sandstone.
She walked into the bathroom tiled in
sea-green marble.

And, from a Global News weather telecast, the following prediction:

"Out west tomorrow, they're going to see the sun,
as well as Atlantic Canada."

⊚ WORDS

⊙ Word Order Problems

Word order problems are of many sorts. See also, for example, the discussions elsewhere in this book of syntax; of ambiguity; of split infinitives; of indefinite pronouns such as *each*, *every*, and *anyone*; and of *not only ... but also*.

B1. **ambiguity/confusion**: Inappropriate word order is one of the most common sources of ambiguity and confusion. Often a change in punctuation may also be required to correct the problem.

> *needs checking* The liner tilted dramatically after fire broke out in the engine room, 50 miles south of Cyprus.
>
> *revised* The liner tilted dramatically after fire broke out in the engine room. At the time the ship was 50 miles south of Cyprus.

> *needs checking* He has not come under any pressure to make way for a new leader, despite the failure of any tangible benefits from his government's economic policies.
>
> *revised* He has not come under any pressure to make way for a new leader, despite the failure of his government's economic policies to bring any tangible benefits.

> *needs checking* Proportion of overweight people between 18 and 64 years trying to lose weight by sex in Alberta, 1990. (Heading on chart, Alberta Heart Health Survey, reprinted in *The Calgary Herald*)
>
> *revised* Proportion in Alberta, Canada, of overweight people between 18 and 64 years, by sex, who were trying to lose weight, 1990.

B2. **amounts**: For no good reason, adjectives having to do with amounts or quantities (e.g., *much*, *few*, *many*) normally precede the noun or pronoun to which they refer, even when the verb *to be* is used. In this way such adjectives differ from other adjectives. For example, we can talk about a happy man, putting the adjective *happy* before the noun *man*, or we can use the present tense of the verb *to be* and say, *The man is happy*, in which case the adjective *happy* comes after the noun *man*. In contrast, it is considered awkward to say, *We were many at the meeting*, or *The people here are few*. Instead the sentence should be changed around, and the adjectives put before the nouns. The easiest way to do this is by using *there* and the verb *to be*. The revised versions of the above sentences are as follows:

> *revised*   There were many of us at the meeting.
> *revised*   There are few people here.

A further example:

> *needs checking*   The students at the football game were many.
> *revised*   There were many students at the football game.

EAL

For particular problems with word order faced by those whose native language is not English, see the EAL section later in this book.

B3. **balance and parallelism**: As discussed earlier (61), paired connectives (*if ... then, either ... or* [given a separate entry below], *not only ... but also, both ... and*) can help in achieving balance. But difficulties in getting all the words in the right order can easily arise.

> *needs checking*   As a critic she is both fully aware of the tricks used by popular novelists to score easy successes with readers through stylized depictions of sex and violence, as well as realizing that "serious" novelists are sometimes not above resorting to the very same tricks.
> *revised*   As a critic she is fully aware both of the tricks used by popular novelists to score easy successes with readers through stylized depictions of sex and violence, and of the fact that "serious" novelists are sometimes not above resorting to the very same tricks.

needs checking   The argument that Hellman puts forward not only fails to rebut the strongest arguments of Singer and Regan, but he also does not even directly engage with those arguments.

revised   Hellman not only fails to rebut the strongest arguments of Singer and Regan; he does not even directly engage with those arguments.

We tend to think of constructions involving words such as *both … and* and *not only … but also* when we think of balance and parallelism in written work. But the principles involved extend far more widely. Finding the right order for the words in a long sentence can be surprisingly challenging, even for experienced writers. Keeping words, phrases, and clauses grammatically balanced is less difficult where a pairing of two is concerned—though even here it is easy enough to go astray if you're not careful:

needs checking   This holiday we plan on keeping healthy and we'll get lots of rest.

revised   This holiday we plan on keeping healthy and getting lots of rest.

needs checking   The new government aims to reduce conflict with its neighbours and increasing the rate of economic growth.

revised   The new government aims to reduce conflict with its neighbours and to increase the rate of economic growth.

needs checking   The study concludes that Facebook use is associated with declines in subjective measures of well-being, and the more people use Facebook, the worse they tend to feel.

revised   The study concludes that Facebook use is associated with declines in subjective measures of well-being, and that the more people use Facebook, the worse they tend to feel.

Repetition of the function word *that* makes clear to the reader how the second part of the sentence is connected to the first; the sentence's second part reports another of the same study's conclusions.

When it is a matter of keeping three or more elements parallel or in balance, everything becomes more difficult.

needs checking   His accomplishments included a succession of strategic successes during World War II, helping to revive Europe after the war, and he founded an important new international organization.

revised   His accomplishments included a succession of strategic successes during WWII, a plan to revive Europe after the war, and the foundation of an important new international organization.

or   He is remembered for his strategic successes during WWII, for his plan to revive Europe after the war, and for the foundation of an important new international organization.

> [These are only two of many ways in which the sentence might be revised so as to make its three parts grammatically parallel.]

needs checking   A plant-based, whole foods diet is associated with improvements in heart condition, greater life expectancy, diabetes is reduced, lowering of cancer rates, less chance of Alzheimer's, and also there are other health benefits.

revised   A plant-based, whole foods diet is associated with improvements in heart condition, greater life expectancy, lower rates of diabetes, lower incidence of cancer, lower incidence of Alzheimer's, and many other health benefits.

or   A plant-based, whole foods diet typically improves heart condition; increases one's life expectancy; significantly lowers one's chances of being afflicted with diabetes, heart disease, cancer, or Alzheimer's; and is associated with many other health benefits as well.

> [Again, these are only two of many ways in which the problem of the sentence's faulty parallelism may be corrected.]

In the above examples parallelism is a matter of grammatical structure first and foremost. But (as we touched on the first section of this book) the importance of balance and parallelism to writing is not only a matter of grammar. Sentences that are balanced and that include parallel structures tend to be both more comprehensible and more pleasing to the reader. In the following examples the initial sentence is not grammatically incorrect; the revisions are a matter of style rather than of correctness. You may judge for yourself as to how they compare in terms of the reader's experience.

worth checking Teams with very low payrolls are unlikely to achieve much success, even in the regular season, and very unlikely to be able to win in the postseason against teams who are able to afford the best-paid stars. The Oakland As are often cited as an exception to the rule that low budget teams are unlikely to succeed in baseball, and it's true that they have enjoyed a surprising degree of success in the regular season. Perhaps inevitably, however, they have not enjoyed much success in the postseason.

revised Teams with very low payrolls are likely to struggle in the regular season, and to struggle even more if they reach the playoffs and face teams who can afford the best-paid stars. If the Oakland As's low payroll makes their regular season success seem surprising, it also makes their postseason failures seem inevitable.

Additional Material Online

Exercises on balance and Parallelism may be found at **sites.broadviewpress.com/writing**. Click on **Exercises** and go to **"Style."**

worth checking What Marianne and her mother conjectured one moment as perhaps being possible, the next moment they believed to be probable. Anything they wished might happen they soon found themselves hoping

	for, and soon after that the hope would become an expectation.
revised	What Marianne and her mother conjectured one moment, they believed the next; with them, to wish was to hope, and to hope was to expect.
	(Jane Austen, *Sense and Sensibility*)

worth checking	Our nation is made up of people of all sorts of religious beliefs. Many Americans are Christians but we also have Jews, Muslims, and Hindus among us, and there are also many American nonbelievers. America has also been shaped by many languages and cultures, from all over the world.
revised	We are a nation of Christians and Muslims, Jews and Hindus, and nonbelievers. We are shaped by every language and culture, drawn from every end of this earth.
	(Barack Obama, First Inaugural Address)

In most cases, revising to strengthen parallel structures in your writing will have the happy byproduct of making it more concise. But that's not always the case; the second sentence from the Obama passage quoted above is longer than it need be, but a pleasing instance of parallelism nonetheless.

B4. **direct object position:** The normal position for direct objects is after the verb. When the direct object is put at the beginning of a sentence it sounds awkward, and the word order may lead writers to include an extra, unwanted pronoun later in the sentence. It is usually best to keep the direct object after the verb.

needs checking	Some of the money I put it in the bank.
	(Notice the extra pronoun *it*.)
revised	I put some of the money in the bank.
	(*I* is the subject; *some of the money* is the direct object of *put*.)

B5. **either ... or:** These words should directly precede the pair of things to which they refer. The same applies to *neither ... nor*.

needs checking	I will either pick an apple or a banana.
revised	I will pick either an apple or a banana.
	(*Either* and *or* refer to *apple* and *banana*. Therefore they must come immediately before those words.)
needs checking	He will go either to New York for the holiday or remain here.
revised	He will either go to New York for the holiday or remain here.
	(The choice is between *going* and *remaining*.)
needs checking	We will either buy a poodle or a spaniel.
revised	We will buy either a poodle or a spaniel.
	(The choice is between breeds of dogs, not between *buying* and a dog breed.)

B6. **except:** A phrase beginning with *except* should appear directly after the noun or pronoun to which *except* refers.

needs checking	We all had to wait except for those who had bought tickets in advance.
revised	All except those who had bought tickets in advance had to wait.

B7. **first person last:** When speaking about both yourself and another person (or other people), always mention the other person first. The first person pronoun (*I, me*) should come last.

needs checking	I and my brother decided to go shopping.
revised	My brother and I decided to go shopping.

Additional Material Online

Word order mistakes involving words such as *only* are often classed as one variety of misplaced modifier error; a full discussion of the category **misplaced modifier** (including how it relates to the category **dangling modifier**) is provided alongside a range of relevant exercises at **sites.broadviewpress.com/writing**. Click on **Exercises** and go to **"Verbs, Subjects, Modifiers."**

B8. **only:** The adverb *only* should come directly before the word or words it refers to. *She could only see him* implies that she could not hear, smell, or touch him; *She could see only him* implies that she had eyes for no one else.

> *needs checking*   She only asked six people to the party.
> *revised*   She asked only six people to the party.

B9. **questions in indirect speech**: In a question we normally reverse the order of the subject and the verb. For example, to change the statement *She was sad* to a question, we reverse the order of *she* and *was* and ask, *Was she sad?* The same rule does not apply, however, to questions in indirect speech. These are considered to be part of a statement and, as in any other statement, the entire verb should come after the subject. For example, to turn the above sentence into indirect speech we would say, *I asked her if she was sad* (not *I asked her was she sad*).

> *needs checking*   I asked him how was he.
> *revised*   I asked him how he was.
> *needs checking*   She asked her brother where was he going.
> *revised*   She asked her brother where he was going.

Notice as well that these sentences are statements, not questions. They therefore do not end with a question mark.

B10. **relative pronouns**: Relative pronouns (*who, which, whom, whose*, etc.) normally refer to the word that has come immediately before them. This may sometimes turn out to be difficult, in which case the word order may have to be changed.

> *needs checking*   He purchased his friend's shop, whom he had known for many years.
>   (The relative pronoun *whom* refers to *friend*, not *shop*. Change the word order to put *whom* directly after *friend*.)
> *revised*   He purchased the shop from his friend, whom he had known for many years.

needs checking	On Saturday I went to my brother's wedding, whose new wife is a senior government official.
revised	On Saturday I went to the wedding of my brother, whose new wife is a senior government official.

⊙ One Word or Two?

A number of very commonly used English words have over many years become accepted as one word because they are combined so often. Other similar combinations, however, should still be written as two words. In a few cases one can see English usage changing on this point right now. A generation ago, for example, *alright* as one word could not have been found in any dictionary. Now numerous authorities regard *alright* as acceptable, and perhaps in another generation or two it will have completely replaced *all right*. For the moment, though, it is best to stick with *all right* rather than the more colloquial *alright*.

B11. **one word preferred**: What has been written as two words should be one. Here are some common examples:

already:	one word when used as an adverb (*He has finished already.*)
altogether:	one word when used as an adverb to mean *completely* or *entirely* (*He is not altogether happy with the result.*)
another	
anybody	
anyone:	one word unless it is followed by *of*
anytime:	one word when used as an adverb (*You can come over anytime*)
awhile:	one word when used as an adverb
bathroom	
bloodshed	
businessman	(but see "Bias-free Vocabulary" on page 384)
cannot:	*can not* is less common, but still acceptable
everybody	

everyday: one word when used as an adjective (*Brushing your teeth should be part of your everyday routine*—here *everyday* is an adjective modifying the noun *routine*.)

needs checking   Doctors perform procedures of this sort everyday.

revised   Doctors perform procedures of this sort every day.

needs checking   Doctors perform procedures of this sort as part of their every day routine.

revised   Doctors perform procedures of this sort as part of their everyday routine.

everyone: one word unless it is followed by *of*
everything
forever
furthermore
indeed
intact
into: one word except in the relatively few cases where the senses of *in* and *to* are clearly separate (*She brought the craft in to land.*)

maybe: when used as an adverb meaning *perhaps* (*Maybe I will join you later*—here the verb is *will join* and *maybe* is an adverb.)

nearby
nobody
onto: see *into*
ourselves
somebody
someone
sometime: one word when used as an adverb (*I would love to see you sometime.*)

straightforward
themselves
wartime
whatever
whenever

B12. **two words preferred**: What has been written as one word should be two words. Here are some common examples:

a lot

all ready: two words when not used as an adverb (*We are all ready to go.*)

all right

all together: two words when not used as an adverb (*They were all together when I left them.*)

any time: two words when used in a sentence as noun preceded by modifier (*Is there any time next week when we could meet?*)

every day: two words when not used as an adjective (*We see each other every day.*)

every time

in fact

in front

in order

in spite of

may be: two words when used as a verb (*He may be here later tonight—may be* is the verb in the sentence.)

no one

some time: two words when used in a sentence as noun preceded by modifier (*Will you be ale to take some time to study this?*)

Additional Material Online
An exercise on word order and on one-word/two-word problems may be found at
sites.broadviewpress.com/writing.
Click on **Exercises** and go to
"Words and Usage."

⊙ Word Meanings: *Are Cars Ever Stationery?*

B13. **accept/except:** These two words are often confused because of their similar sounds. *Accept* is a verb meaning *to receive something favourably* (or at least without complaining). Examples:

- We accepted the invitation to his party.
- We will have to accept the decision of the judge.

Except, on the other hand, is a conjunction (or sometimes a preposition) which means *not including* or *but.*

> *needs checking*   All the permanent members of the Security Council accept China voted to authorize the use of force.
> *revised*   All the permanent members of the Security Council except China voted to authorize the use of force.

B14. **adapt/adopt/adept:** *To adapt something* is *to alter or modify it*; *to adopt something* is *to approve it* or *accept responsibility for it*; *adept* is an adjective meaning *skillful.*

> *needs checking*   The board adapted the resolution unanimously.
> *revised*   The board adopted the resolution unanimously.

B15. **adverse/averse:** *Adverse* means *unfavourable*; *averse* means *reluctant* or *unwilling.*

> *needs checking*   The plane was forced to land because of averse weather conditions.
> *revised*   The plane was forced to land because of adverse weather conditions.
> *or*   The pilot was averse to the idea of landing in the fog.

B16. **afflict/inflict:** A person *inflicts* pain or hardship on someone else, who is *afflicted* by the pain and hardship.

> *needs checking*   The Mugabe government began as early as 1983 to afflict terrible suffering on large numbers of Zimbabweans living in Matabeleland.
> *revised*   The Mugabe government began as early as 1983 to inflict terrible suffering on large numbers of Zimbabweans living in Matabeleland.

B17. **aggravate/annoy/irritate:** *Aggravate* means *make worse.* Here is an example:

- The injury was aggravated by the bumpy ride in the ambulance.

In formal English *aggravate* should not be used to mean *annoy* or *irritate.*

needs checking She found his constant complaints very aggravating.
revised She found his constant complaints very irritating.

B18. **alliterate/illiterate:** *Alliterate* is a verb meaning *to use consecutively two or more words that begin with the same sound.*

- The big, burly brute was frighteningly fat.

Illiterate is an adjective meaning either *unable to read* or *unable to read and write well.* Those who confuse the two are sometimes, if unfairly, accused of being illiterate.

needs checking Over forty per cent of the population of Zambia is functionally alliterate.
revised Over forty per cent of the population of Zambia is functionally illiterate.

B19. **alternately/alternatively:** *Alternately* means *happening in turn, first one and then the other*; alternatively means *instead of.* Be careful as well with the adjectives *alternate* and *alternative.*

needs checking An alternate method of arriving at this theoretical value would be to divide the difference between the two prices by the number of warrants.
revised An alternative method of arriving at this theoretical value would be to divide the difference between the two prices by the number of warrants. (or Another method of ...)
needs checking Professor Beit-Hallahmi seems to have trouble alternatively in reading his own book accurately and in reading my review of it correctly.
revised Professor Beit-Hallahmi seems to have trouble alternately in reading his own book accurately and in reading my review of it correctly.

B20. **ambiguity**: There are many types of ambiguity; for other references see the chapters on "Pronouns" and "Word Order Problems," and the entries below for such words as *flammable*. Also see the box on page 198.

B21. **amiable/amicable**: *Amiable* is used to describe someone's personality; *amicable* describes the state of relations between people.

> *needs checking*   Navratilova said that the split with her former tennis partner had been an amiable one.
>
>   *revised*   Navratilova said that the split with her former tennis partner had been an amicable one.

B22. **amoral/immoral**: An *amoral* act is one to which moral standards do not apply; an *immoral* act, on the other hand, is one that goes against a moral standard.

> *needs checking*   The reader is unlikely to share Austen's views as to what constitutes amoral behaviour.
>
>   *revised*   The reader is unlikely to share Austen's views as to what constitutes immoral behaviour.

B23. **anti/ante**: If you remember that *anti* means *against* and *ante* means *before* you are less likely to misspell the many words that have one or the other as a prefix.

> *needs checking*   The UN had many anticedents—most notably the League of Nations formed after World War I.
>
>   *revised*   The UN had many antecedents—most notably the League of Nations formed after World War I.

B24. **antonym/homonym/synonym**: Antonyms are opposites—two words with opposite meanings (e.g., *hot* and *cold*, *good* and *bad*). Homonyms have different meanings but the same spelling or sound. There are thus two types of homonyms; homophones (e.g., *sight* and *site*) have the same sound but different spellings, while homographs (e.g., *slough* meaning *swampy area*, pronounced *sloo*, and *slough* meaning *shed tissue*, pronounced *sluff*) have the same spelling, though they may be pronounced differently. *Pole* meaning *long stick* and *pole* meaning *extremity of a planet* are homonyms that are both homophones and homographs. Synonyms (e.g., the verbs *shut* and *close*) are words with the same meaning.

B25. **anxious/eager:** The adjective *anxious* means *uneasy, nervous, worried*; it should not be used in formal writing to mean *eager.*

needs checking   He was anxious to help in any way he could.
revised   He was eager to help in any way he could.

B26. **appraise/apprise:** *To appraise something* is *to estimate its value*; *to apprise someone of something* is *to inform him or her of it.*

needs checking   The house has been apprised at $160,000.
revised   The house has been appraised at $160,000.
or   He apprised her of the house's jump in value.

B27. **assure/ensure/insure:** *To assure someone of something* is *to tell her with confidence or certainty*; *to insure* (or *ensure,* in common Canadian, UK, and Australian usage) *that something will happen* is *to make sure that it does*; *to insure something* is *to purchase insurance on it so as to protect yourself in case of loss.*

needs checking   Our inventory is ensured for $10,000,000.
revised   Our inventory is insured for $10,000,000.
needs checking   I will insure you that this will not happen again.
revised   I assure you that it will not happen again.
or (US)   I will insure that it does not happen again.
or (CDA, UK, AUS)   I will ensure that it does not happen again.

B28. **be/become:** The difference between the two is that *to be* simply indicates existence, while *to become* indicates a process of change. Whenever you are talking about a change, use *become* instead of *be.*

needs checking   I had been quite contented, but as time went by I was unhappy.
revised   I had been quite contented, but as time went by I became unhappy.
needs checking   After years of struggle, East Timor finally was independent in 2002.
revised   After years of struggle, East Timor finally became independent in 2002.

B29. **beg the question:** The original meaning of *beg the question* is *take for granted the very thing to be argued about*—not *invite the question.* In the words of philosopher Thomas Hurka, "'begging the question' is not what Alex Trebek does on Jeopardy." The extension of the phrase to mean *invite the question* or *prompt the question* has become so widespread in recent years that it may be vain to think of the tide being reversed, but the original concept of question begging is a useful one, and we should be reluctant to allow it to disappear.

needs checking   This sort of sexual abuse case begs the question as to how such behaviour could be hidden for so many years.

revised   This sort of sexual abuse case makes us wonder how such behaviour could be hidden for so many years.

Note: For more on *begging the question* see C8 below.

B30. beside/besides: *Besides* can mean *in addition to, moreover* (as in the sentence *Besides, he deserved to lose*), *other than,* or *except* (as in *no one was there besides me*). *Beside* may mean *at the side of* (as in *no one was there beside me*) or *irrelevant to* (as in the common phrase *beside the point*); in this latter meaning confusion with *besides* sometimes arises.

needs checking   Much of Dawkins's argument is besides the point.

revised   Much of Dawkins's argument is beside the point.

B31. bored/boring: *Bored* is the opposite of *interested* and *boring* is the opposite of *interesting*. In other words, one is quite likely to be bored when someone reads out what one has already read in the newspaper, or when one is watching a football game when the score is 38–0, or when one is doing an uninteresting job. To be bored, however, is not the same as to be sad, or depressed, or irritated, or angry.

needs checking   She was so bored with her husband that she tried to kill him.

revised   She was so angry with her husband that she tried to kill him.

B32. breach/breech: *To breach a wall or a contract* is *to break or break through it,* and *the breach* is *the breaking. Breech* refers to a part of a cannon or rifle—or to *the buttocks* (hence a *breech birth*, in which the buttocks or feet emerge before the head).

needs checking   The lawyers claimed that her actions constituted a breech of contract.

revised The lawyers claimed that her actions constituted a breach of contract.

B33. brusque/brisk: *To be brusque is to be abrupt or slightly rude in speech or manner; brisk means quick or lively.*

needs checking He didn't say anything rude to me, but his manner was rather brisk.

revised He didn't say anything rude to me, but his manner was rather brusque.

B34. can/may: In formal writing *can* should be used to refer to *ability*, *may* to refer to *permission*.

needs checking Can I leave the room?
(This makes literal sense only if you are an injured person conversing with your doctor.)

revised May I leave the room?

B35. capital/capitol: As a noun, *capital* can refer to *wealth*, to *the city from which the government operates*, to *an upper case letter*, or to *the top of a pillar*. It can also be used as an adjective to mean *most important* or *principal*. *Capitol* is much more restricted in its meaning—*a specific American legislative building or Roman temple*.

needs checking The prosecution alleged that he had committed a capitol offense.

revised The prosecution alleged that he had committed a capital offense.

B36. career/careen: As a verb, *career* means *to swerve wildly*. *Careen* originally meant *tilt or lean*, but now in North America especially is often treated as a synonym for *career*. Since *careen* has other specifically nautical meanings, some authorities resist the conflation of the two verbs—but the fact that *career* carries unintended echoes of the noun meaning *profession* leads many, not unreasonably, to prefer *careen*.

B37. careless/uncaring: *Careless* means *negligent* or *thoughtless*; you can be careless about your work, for example, or careless about your appearance. Do not use *careless*, however, when you want to talk about *not caring enough about other people*.

needs checking	He acted in a very careless way towards his mother when she was sick.
revised	He acted in an uncaring way towards his mother when she was sick.

B38. censor/censure: *To censor something* is *to prevent it, or those parts of it that are considered objectionable, from being available to the public.* *To censure someone* is *to express strong criticism or condemnation.*

needs checking	The Senate censored the attorney general for his part in the scandal.
revised	The Senate censured the attorney general for his part in the scandal.

B39. childish/childlike: The first is a term of abuse, the second a term of praise.

needs checking	Her writing expresses a childish innocence.
revised	Her writing expresses a childlike innocence.

B40. classic/classical: As an adjective *classic* means *of such a high quality that it has lasted or is likely to last for a very long time. Classical* is used to refer to *ancient Greece and Rome,* or, particularly when speaking of music, to refer to *a traditional style.*

needs checking	Sophocles was one of the greatest classic authors; his plays are classical.
revised	Sophocles was one of the greatest classical authors; his plays are acknowledged classics.

B41. climatic/climactic: Weather is not necessarily the high point of life.

needs checking	Difficulties in predicting long-term trends are inherent in any climactic projections.
revised	Difficulties in predicting long-term trends are inherent in any climatic projections.

B42. collaborate/corroborate: *To collaborate* is *to work together,* whereas *to corroborate* is *to give supporting evidence.*

needs checking	He collaborated her claim that the Americans had corroborated with the Nazi colonel Klaus Barbie.

revised   He corroborated her claim that the Americans had col-
laborated with the Nazi colonel Klaus Barbie.

B43. **compliment/complement:** *To compliment someone is to praise
him,* and a *compliment is the praise; to complement something is to add
to it to make it better or complete,* and a *complement is the number or
amount needed to make it complete.*

needs checking   None of the divisions had its full compliment of troops.
revised   None of the divisions had its full complement of troops.
needs checking   Prince Fielder's mission in Detroit was to compliment
Miguel Cabrera, who was at that time the best hitter in
baseball.

(Literally, this would mean that Fielder's job
was to keep saying, "Nice work, Miguel," and
so on.)

revised   Prince Fielder's mission in Detroit was to complement
Miguel Cabrera, who was at that time the best hitter in
baseball.

Additional Material Online
Exercises on word meanings may be found at
sites.broadviewpress.com/writing.
Click on **Exercises** and go to **"Words and
Usage."**

B44. **comprise/compose/constitute:** The whole *comprises* or includes
the various parts; the parts *compose* the whole. The verb *constitute,*
similar in meaning to *compose,* is commonly used to refer to abstract
concepts (e.g., *The point you make does not constitute an argument,
The case you refer to constitutes a legal precedent*).

needs checking   The British government is comprised of far fewer ministries than is the Canadian government.
revised   The British government comprises far fewer ministries
than does the Canadian government.
or   The British government is composed of far fewer ministries than is the Canadian government.

B45. **conscience/conscious/consciousness:** *To be conscious is to be* *awake and aware of what is happening,* whereas *conscience* is *the part of our mind that tells us it is right to do some things and wrong to do other things (such as steal or murder).* Conscience and *consciousness* are both nouns; the adjectives are *conscientious (aware of what is right and wrong)* and *conscious (aware).*

> *needs checking*   She was tempted to steal the chocolate bar, but her conscious told her not to.
>
> *revised*   She was tempted to steal the chocolate bar, but her conscience told her not to.

B46. **contemptuous/contemptible**: We are *contemptuous* of anyone or anything we find *contemptible.*

> *needs checking*   The judge called the delinquent's behaviour utterly contemptuous.
>
> *revised*   The judge called the delinquent's behaviour utterly contemptible.

B47. **continual/continuous**: If something is *continuous* it *never stops*; something *continual* is *frequently repeated but not unceasing.* The same distinction holds for the adverbs *continually* and *continuously.*

> *needs checking*   He has been phoning me continuously for the past two weeks.
>
>   (Surely he stopped for a bite to eat or a short nap.)

B48. **decimate**: Most etymologists agree that originally this word meant *kill one of every ten.* It has come to be used more loosely to mean *destroy a considerable number of,* and sometimes *kill nine of every ten,* but it is best not to use it in a way that some authorities feel, as H.W. Fowler puts it, "expressly contradicts the proper sense."

> *needs checking*   The regiment was decimated; fewer than 40 per cent of the troops survived.
>
> *revised*   The regiment suffered extreme losses; fewer than 40 per cent of the troops survived.

B49. **deduce/deduct**: *Deduction* is the noun stemming from both these verbs, which is perhaps why they are sometimes confused. *To deduce* is *to draw a conclusion,* whereas *to deduct* is *to subtract.*

> *needs checking* Sherlock Holmes deducted that Moriarty had committed the crime.
>
> *revised* Sherlock Holmes deduced that Moriarty had committed the crime.

B50. **definite/definitive**: If something is *definite* then there is *no uncertainty about it*; a *definitive* version of something *fixes it in its final or permanent form*—just as a dictionary definition attempts to fix the meaning of a word. Often a sentence is better with neither of these words.

> *needs checking* Glenn Gould's recording of Bach's Goldberg Variations is often thought of as the definite modern version.
>
> *revised* Glenn Gould's recording of Bach's Goldberg Variations is often thought of as the definitive modern version.
>
> *needs checking* Once we have completed our caucus discussion I will be making a very definitive statement.
>
> *revised* Once we have completed our caucus discussion I will be making a statement.
>
> *or* Once we have completed our caucus discussion I will have something definite to say.

B51. **degradation/decline**: *Degradation* carries the connotation of *shame and disgrace*. To degrade something is not *to reduce it*, or *downgrade it*, or *destroy it*.

> *needs checking* Among those units in which women played a combat role there was no degradation in operational effectiveness.
>
> *revised* Among those units in which women played a combat role there was no decline in operational effectiveness.
>
> *or* ... there was no reduction in operational effectiveness.
>
> *needs checking* According to some authorities, the Iraqi threat has now been significantly degraded.
>
> *revised* According to some authorities, the Iraqi threat has now been significantly reduced.

B52. **deny/rebut/refute**: *To deny something is to assert that it is not true; to rebut an argument is to oppose it; to refute it is to prove conclusively that it is not true.*

needs checking During yesterday's press conference the president angrily refuted the allegations: "There has been no improper relationship," he said.

revised During yesterday's press conference, the president angrily denied the allegations: "There has been no improper relationship," he said.

B53. **deprecate/depreciate**: *To deprecate something* is *to suggest that it is not valuable or worthy of praise*; something that *depreciates* loses its value.

needs checking Leonard Cohen was very self-depreciating throughout the interview.

revised Leonard Cohen was very self-deprecating throughout the interview.

B54. **discrete/discreet**: *Discrete* means *separate* or *distinct,* whereas *discreet* means *prudent* and *tactful; unwilling to give away secrets.*

needs checking Anthony Weiner is not renowned for being discrete.

revised Anthony Weiner is not renowned for being discreet.

B55. **disinterested/uninterested**: A *disinterested* person is *unbiased; uninfluenced by self-interest, especially of a monetary sort.* It is thus quite possible for a person who is entirely disinterested in a particular matter to be completely fascinated by it. If one is *uninterested in* something, on the other hand, one is *bored by* it.

needs checking He was so disinterested in the game that he left after the fifth inning with the score at 2–2.

revised He was so uninterested in the game that he left after the fifth inning with the score at 2–2.

needs checking The controlling shareholders had grown tired of the CEO's futuristic strategies and disinterest in day-to-day operations.

revised The controlling shareholders had grown tired of the CEO's futuristic strategies and lack of interest in day-to-day operations.

B56. **disorient/disorientate**: Both are considered correct by many authorities, but the extra syllable of the second grates on the ear.

needs checking I was entirely disorientated in the darkness.

    revised   I was entirely disoriented in the darkness.

B57. dissemble/disassemble: *To dissemble* is *to disguise your feelings*—a mild form of lying (e.g., *Some still claim that Bill Clinton was guilty of little more than dissembling*). *To disassemble* is *to take apart.*

    needs checking   For the test we are required to first assemble and then dissemble a six-cylinder engine.

    revised   For the test we are required to first assemble and then disassemble a six-cylinder engine.

B58. dissociate/disassociate: There is no need for the extra syllable.

    needs checking   T.S. Eliot speaks of a disassociation of sensibility that began in the seventeenth century.

    revised   T.S. Eliot speaks of a dissociation of sensibility that began in the seventeenth century.

B59. distinct/distinctive: *Distinct* means *able to be seen or perceived clearly; easily distinguishable from those around it. Distinctive* means *unusual; not commonly found.* There is a similar contrast between the adverbs *distinctly* and *distinctively*, and the nouns *distinction* and *distinctiveness*.

    needs checking   I distinctively heard the sound of a car engine.

    revised   I distinctly heard the sound of a car engine.

B60. economic/economical: *Economic* means *pertaining to economics,* or *sufficient to allow a reasonable return for the amount of money or effort put in. Economical* is a word applied to people, which means *thrifty.* The difference applies as well to *uneconomic* and *uneconomical.*

    needs checking   Controversy over whether it would be economical to develop the vast Hibernia oilfield continued for many years.

    revised   Controversy over whether it would be economic to develop the vast Hibernia oilfield continued for many years.

B61. effective/efficacious/effectual/efficient: *Effective, efficacious,* and *effectual* all mean *sufficient to produce the desired effect. Efficacious,* however, applies only to *strategies* or *things* (though it strikes many as a rather pompous word in any application). A person, then, cannot be efficacious. *Effectual* was once applied only to actions, but is now sometimes applied to people as well. *Effective* can apply to actions or people. *Efficient* has an added connotation: *producing results with little waste of money or effort*. Thus a promotional campaign to persuade people to buy a product by giving away free samples to every man, woman, and child in the country might be effective, but it would certainly not be efficient; a good deal of waste would be involved. The same difference applies to the nouns *effectiveness* and *efficiency*. (*Efficacy* is a rather pretentious noun that is usually best avoided.)

needs checking	The board wants to increase the efficacy of the machinery we use.
revised	The board wants to increase the efficiency of the machinery we use.
needs checking	He is the most efficacious worker in the office.
revised	He is the most effective worker in the office.

B62. **e.g./i.e.**: The abbreviation *e.g.* is short for *exemplum gratia* ("example given"; or, in the plural *exempli gratia*, "examples given"). It is sometimes confused with the abbreviation *i.e.*, which is short for *id est* ("that is to say").

needs checking	Those citizens of India who speak Hindi (e.g., over 500 million people) are being encouraged to learn a second language.
revised	Those citizens of India who speak Hindi (i.e., over 500 million people) are being encouraged to learn a second language.

B63. **elemental/elementary**: A thing is *elemental* if it forms *an important or essential element of the whole*; it is *elementary* if it is *easy to understand*, or *at a relatively simple level*.

needs checking	He lacked even the most elemental understanding of the problem.
revised	He lacked even the most elementary understanding of the problem.

B64. **elicit/illicit**: *Elicit* is a verb; one elicits information about something. *Illicit* is an adjective meaning *illegal* or *not approved*.

needs checking	She has been dealing in elicit drugs for some time.
revised	She has been dealing in illicit drugs for some time.
or	The police elicited details about her drug use.

B65. eligible/illegible: One is *eligible* for a job or for membership in an organization if one *meets the standard* set for applicants. One of the requirements might be that one's handwriting not be *illegible*.

needs checking	He regretted that I was not illegible to join his club.
revised	He regretted that I was not eligible to join his club.

B66. emigrant/immigrant: *To migrate* is *to move from one place to another.* The prefix *ex*, shortened to *e*, means *out of,* so an *emigrant* from a country is *someone who is moving out of it.* The prefix *in* or *im* means *in* or *into,* so an *immigrant* to a country is *someone moving into it.* Similarly, *emigration* is *the movement of people out of a country,* while *immigration* is *the movement of people into a country.* Notice the spelling in both cases: *e-migrant* (one *m*), *im-migrant* (two *ms*).

needs checking	More than 100,000 emigrants entered America last year.
revised	More than 100,000 immigrants entered America last year.

B67. eminent/imminent/immanent: A person is *eminent* if she is *well-known and well-respected*; an event is *imminent* if it is *about to happen*; a quality (or a god) is *immanent* if it *pervades* everything.

needs checking	Even those working for the party in the campaign did not believe that a majority victory was immanent.
revised	Even those working for the party in the campaign did not believe that a majority victory was imminent.

B68. enervate/invigorate: Because of the similarity in sound between *enervate* and *energy*, *enervate* is often thought to mean *make more energetic.* In fact *enervate* means just the opposite—*to lessen the strength of.* If something makes you more *energetic* it *invigorates* you.

needs checking	She found the fresh air quite enervating; I haven't seen her so lively in months.
revised	She found the fresh air quite invigorating; I haven't seen her so lively in months.

B69. enormity/enormousness: Originally the adjective *enormous* simply meant *deviating from the norm,* but by the early nineteenth century it had also come to mean *abnormal, monstrous,* or *extraordinarily wicked.* Today the only meaning is of course *vast in size or quantity,* but the connotation of wickedness is preserved in the noun *enormity.* We may speak of the enormity of a person's crime, but if we want a noun to express vast size we should use *enormousness* or *vastness.*

needs checking	What most impresses visitors to the Grand Canyon is its sheer enormity.
revised	What most impresses visitors to the Grand Canyon is its sheer enormousness.
better	What most impresses visitors to the Grand Canyon is its vastness.

B70. **epithet/epigraph/epitaph/epigram:** four words often confused. Here are their meanings:

- Epithet—an adjective or short phrase describing someone (*"The Legion of Boom"—an epithet first used in 2012 to describe the secondary defence of the Seattle Seahawks—invovles an allusion to another epithet, "Legion of Doom," which has been used by teams both in ice hockey and in professional wrestling*).
- Epigraph—an inscription, especially one placed upon a building, tomb, or statue to indicate its name or purpose; or a motto or quotation appearing at the beginning of a book (or the beginning of a chapter in a book).
- Epitaph—words describing a dead person, often the words inscribed on the tomb.
- Epigram—a short, witty, or pointed saying.

needs checking	His epigram will read, "A good man lies here."
revised	His epitaph will read, "A good man lies here."

B71. **equal/equitable/equable:** Things that are *equal* have the *same value.* Arrangements that are *equitable* are *fair and just.* An *equable* person is one who is *moderate and even-tempered.*

needs checking	The distribution of seats in the American Senate is not an equable one; Rhode Island, with its one million people, is allocated two senators, while California, with its forty million people, is also allocated two senators.

revised   The distribution of seats in the American Senate is not an equitable one; Rhode Island, with its one million people, is allocated two senators, while California, with its forty million people, is also allocated two senators.

B72. explicit/implicit: If something is *explicit* it is *unfolded—stated in precise terms, not merely suggested or implied.* Something that is *implicit* is *folded in—not stated overtly.* By extension *implicit* has also come to mean *complete or absolute* in expressions such as *implicit trust* (i.e., trust so complete that it does not have to be put into words).

needs checking   I told you implicitly to have the report on my desk first thing this morning.

revised   I told you explicitly to have the report on my desk first thing this morning.

B73. financial/fiscal/monetary/economic: The terms used in personal, business, and government finance are not always the same. Here are four that are often not clearly understood:

- Financial—having to do with finance or the handling of money.
- Fiscal—having to do with public revenue.
- Monetary—having to do with the currency of a country. (Only in very limited circumstances, such as the expression *monetary value*, can *monetary* have the more general meaning of *having to do with money.*)
- Economic—having to do with the economy. Thus a government's economic program embraces both fiscal and monetary policies.

needs checking   My brother is a nice person, but he has no monetary ability.

revised   My brother is a nice person, but he has no financial ability.

B74. finish/be finished/have finished: In slang usage *to be finished* means *to be at the end of one's life or career* (*If that player's knee is seriously injured again, he will be finished*). This special use should not be extended to the verb *finish* in its normal meaning.

needs checking   Are you finished your work?

revised Have you finished your work?

B75. flammable/inflammable: The two words share the same meaning; *flammable* may have originated because of the possibility for confusion with the word *inflammable*, which looks like a negative but isn't. *Non-flammable* should be used to mean *difficult or impossible to burn*.

needs checking Asbestos is an inflammable material.
revised Asbestos is a non-flammable material.

B76. flout/flaunt: *To flout is to disobey or show disrespect for; to flaunt is to display very openly.*

needs checking Aggressive policing seems to have had no effect on the number of people flaunting the law.
revised Aggressive policing seems to have had no effect on the number of people flouting the law.

B77. formerly/formally: The similarity of sound often leads to confusion.

needs checking In August Mr. Laurel formerly broke with Mrs. Aquino.
revised In August Mr. Laurel formally broke with Mrs. Aquino.

B78. fortunate/fortuitous: *Fortunate* means *lucky* and can refer to people as well as occurrences; *fortuitous* means *happening by chance*, and can refer only to occurrences or situations, not people.

needs checking This combination of circumstances is not a fortuitous one for our company; we shall have to expect reduced sales in the coming year.
revised This combination of circumstances is not a fortunate one for our company; we shall have to expect reduced sales in the coming year.

B79. forward/foreword: You find a *foreword* before the other words in a book (and an *afterword* after the other words).

needs checking The author admits in the forward to her book that the research was not comprehensive.
revised The author admits in the foreword to her book that the research was not comprehensive.

B80. **founder/flounder**: As a verb, *founder* means *to get into difficulty, to stumble or fall, to sink* (when speaking of a ship), or *to fail* (when speaking of a plan). *To flounder* is *to move clumsily or with difficulty*, or *to become confused in an effort to do something*.

> *needs checking* He foundered about in a hopeless attempt to solve the problem.
>
> *revised* He floundered about in a hopeless attempt to solve the problem.

B81. **fulsome/effusive**: *Fulsome* means *insincere* or *excessively flattering*; fulsome praise is not the sort one wants to receive. But we all like to receive *effusive* (or *enthusiastic*) praise.

> *needs checking* He was pleased to be showered with fulsome compliments.
>
> *revised* He was pleased to be showered with effusive compliments.

B82. **further/farther**: *Farther* refers only to *physical distance*.

> *needs checking* Eisenhower argued that the plan should receive farther study.
>
> *revised* Eisenhower argued that the plan should receive further study.

B83. **historic/historical**: *Historic* means *of sufficient importance that it is likely to become famous in history*; *historical* means *having to do with history* (*historical research, historical scholarship*, etc.).

> *needs checking* We are gathered here for a historical occasion—the opening of the city's first sewage treatment plant.
>
> *revised* We are gathered here for a historic occasion—the opening of the city's first sewage treatment plant.

B84. **hopefully**: one of the greatest causes of disagreement among grammarians. Traditionalists argue that the correct meaning of the adverb *hopefully* is *filled with hope*, and that the use of the word to mean *it is to be hoped that* is therefore incorrect. On the other side it is plausibly argued that many adverbs can function as independent comments at the beginning of a sentence. (*Finally, let me point out that* ... ; *Clearly, we have much to do if we are to* ... ; *Obviously, it will* *not be possible to ...*). Why should *hopefully* be treated differently? Why indeed? Using *hopefully* for this purpose might not make for beautiful English, but it should not be regarded as a grievous error.

needs checking   Hopefully, it will be possible to finish before tomorrow.
                 (As usually happens, *hopefully* is here used with the passive, making for a wordy sentence.)

revised   We hope we can finish before tomorrow.

needs checking   Hopefully, we will arrive before dusk.
                 (This sentence should be rewritten in order to ensure that the sentence does not suggest the meaning, *we will arrive filled with hope before dusk.*)

revised   I hope we will arrive before dusk.

B85. human/humane: Until the eighteenth century there was no distinction made between the two in either meaning or pronunciation; they were simply alternative ways of spelling the same word. In recent centuries *humane* has come to be used to refer exclusively to the more attractive human qualities—kindness, compassion, and so forth.

needs checking   Their group is campaigning for the human treatment of whales and dolphins.

revised   Their group is campaigning for the humane treatment of whales and dolphins.

B86. idioms: Similarity in sound and meaning between words often leads to the mixing-up of idioms.

needs checking   Authorities termed it a democratic transition, but for all intensive purposes it was a coup d'état.

revised   Authorities termed it a democratic transition, but for all intents and purposes it was a coup d'état.

needs checking   The new recruits were reminded that they would have to tow the line.

revised   The new recruits were reminded that they would have to toe the line.

B87. illusion/allusion: An *allusion* is *an indirect reference to something*; an *illusion* is *something falsely supposed to exist.*

needs checking   Joyce is making an illusion in this passage to a Shake-
                    spearean sonnet.
    revised   Joyce is making an allusion in this passage to a Shake-
                    spearean sonnet.

B88. **imply/infer:** *To imply something* is *to suggest it without stating it
directly*; the other person will have to *infer* your meaning. It may be
a comfort to the many who have confused the two to know that the
mistake goes back at least as far as Milton:

needs checking   Great or Bright infers not Excellence. (*Paradise Lost* viii,
                    91)
    revised   Great or Bright implies not Excellence.
                    (The fact that a thing is great or bright does
                    not imply that it is also excellent.)
needs checking   I implied from his tone that he disliked our plan.
    revised   I inferred from his tone that he disliked our plan.

B89. **in to/into:** The difference is that *into* is used to indicate movement from outside to inside.

needs checking   Writers in Britain generally expressed sympathy for
                    Rushdie's decision, although some said he was caving
                    into pressure.
    revised   Writers in Britain generally expressed sympathy for
                    Rushdie's decision, although some said he was caving in
                    to pressure.

Note: See also pages 166, 208.

B90. **incidents/incidence:** *Incidents* is the plural of *incident* (*happening*), whereas *incidence* is a singular noun meaning *the rate at which
something occurs.*

needs checking   The incidents of lung cancer is much lower in Zambia
                    than it is in North America.
    revised   The incidence of lung cancer is much lower in Zambia
                    than it is in North America.

B91. **ingenious/ingenuous:** *Ingenious* means *clever*; *ingenuous* means
pleasantly open and unsophisticated.

needs checking   Her manner was completely ingenious; I cannot imagine she was trying to deceive us.

revised   Her manner was completely ingenuous; I cannot imagine she was trying to deceive us.

B92. **innumerable**: *so numerous that it is impossible to count*; do not use this word as a synonym for *many*.

needs checking   Scholars have advanced innumerable explanations for the dinosaurs' disappearance.

revised   Scholars have advanced many explanations for the dinosaurs' disappearance.

B93. **insist/persist**: To *insist* (that something be done, or on doing something) is to *express yourself very forcefully*. To *persist in doing something* is to *keep on doing it, usually despite some difficulty or opposition*.

needs checking   Even after he had been convicted of the crime, he persisted that he was innocent.

revised   Even after he had been convicted of the crime, he insisted that he was innocent.

B94. **instinctive/instinctual**: There is no difference in meaning; it is thus better to stay with the older (and more pleasant sounding) *instinctive*.

needs checking   Biologists disagree as to what constitutes instinctual behaviour.

revised   Biologists disagree as to what constitutes instinctive behaviour.

B95. **judicial/judicious**: *Judicial* means *having to do with law courts and the administration of justice*. *Judicious* means *having good judgement*.

needs checking   He made one or two judicial comments about the quality of the production.

revised   He made one or two judicious comments about the quality of the production.

B96. **know**: When one *knows* something, that piece of knowledge has been in one's mind for some time. The process of gathering or acquiring knowledge is called *discovering*.

needs checking	Although I noticed the new employee on Monday, I did not know her name until today.
revised	Although I noticed the new employee on Monday, I did not discover her name until today.

B97. **later/latter:** *Later* means *afterwards in time,* whereas the *latter* is the *last mentioned (of two things).*

needs checking	I looked up the battle of Stalingrad in both the *Encyclopedia Britannica* and Wikipedia. The later provided much more information.
revised	I looked up the battle of Stalingrad in both the *Encyclopedia Britannica* and Wikipedia. The latter provided much more information.

B98. **laudable/laudatory:** *Laudable* means *worthy of praise;* *laudatory* means *expressing praise.*

needs checking	His efforts to combat poverty are very laudatory.
revised	His efforts to combat poverty are very laudable.

B99. **liable/likely:** *Liable* means *obliged by law* or *responsible under the law (You will be liable for any damage caused when you are driving the vehicle);* or *in danger of doing or suffering from something undesirable (That chimney is liable to fall).* Since in the latter meaning *likely* can often be used in place of *liable,* it is often assumed that there is really no distinction between the two. Careful writers, however, do not use *liable* unless they are referring to possible consequences of an undesirable nature.

needs checking	Last Sunday Singh won the Colonial Open. He's liable to win again before the end of the year.
revised	Last Sunday Singh won the Colonial Open. He's likely to win again before the end of the year.

B100. **libel/slander:** *Libel* is written (and published); *slander* is oral.

needs checking	He was careful in his speech to avoid making any libellous remarks.
revised	He was careful in his speech to avoid making any slanderous remarks.

B101. **lightning/lightening**: One is not likely to see the sky *lightening* until after the thunder and *lightning* are over.

needs checking   Three of the men were severely injured by the lightening.
revised   Three of the men were severely injured by the lightning.

B102. **like/such as**: Whereas *like* is used to draw comparisons, *such as* is used when you want to provide examples. *We need someone like Michael Jordan on this team* means *We need someone who resembles Michael Jordan*—a superb all-round basketball player. If you say *The Chicago Bulls teams of the 1990s featured stars like Michael Jordan and Scottie Pippen*, the literal meaning of the sentence is that those teams featured stars who *resembled* Michael Jordan and Scottie Pippen—which presumably is not what you mean to say, since these players didn't resemble the leading stars; they were the two leading stars. In a case such as this the words you want are *such as*: *The Chicago Bulls teams of the 1990s featured stars such as Michael Jordan and Scottie Pippen*.

needs checking   In the early twentieth century, writers like T.S. Eliot, Ezra Pound, and Virginia Woolf were leading figures in the movement we now call modernism.

revised   In the early twentieth century, writers such as T.S. Eliot, Ezra Pound, and Virginia Woolf were leading figures in the movement we now call modernism.

or   T.S. Eliot, Ezra Pound, and Virginia Woolf were leading figures in the early twentieth-century movement we now call modernism.
[It was not writers similar to Eliot, Pound, and Woolf who led the literary movement; it was Eliot, Pound and Woolf themselves.]

See also A194 above (pages 192–93)—**like/as**.

B103. **literally**: *Literal* means *by the letter—in exact agreement with what is said or written*. A literal meaning is thus the opposite of a figurative or metaphorical meaning. Do not use the adverb *literally* simply to emphasize something.

needs checking   As silviculturalists, we are—literally—babes in the woods. (Ken Drushka, *Stumped: The Forest Industry in Transition*)

> (Silviculturalists may be literally in the woods, but they are not literally babes.)

revised   As silviculturalists, we are babes in the woods.

B104. make/allow/make possible: *To make someone do something* is *to force them to do it (often against their wishes)*; *to allow someone to do something* is *to permit them or make it possible for them to do something that they want to do.*

needs checking   A new hospital wing is being built; this will make many more people come for treatment.

revised   A new hospital wing is being built; this will allow many more people to come for treatment.

or   A new hospital wing is being built; this will make it possible for many more people to come for treatment.

B105. masterful/masterly: *Masterful* means *domineering*; *masterly* means *exhibiting mastery or great skill.*

needs checking   Once again last night, Liona Boyd gave the audience a masterful performance.

revised   Once again last night, Liona Boyd gave the audience a masterly performance.

B106. mitigate/militate: To *mitigate something* is to *make it less harsh or severe*; thus, mitigating circumstances are those that make a criminal offense less serious. *To militate against something* is *to act as a strong influence against it.*

needs checking   The natural history orientation of early anthropology also mitigated against studies of change. (Bruce G. Trigger in *Natives and Newcomers*)

revised   The natural history orientation of early anthropology also militated against studies of change.

B107. momentarily: *Momentarily* means *lasting only a moment (He was momentarily confused).* Common usage also allows the word to mean *in a moment* or *soon*; in formal writing it is best to avoid this use.

needs checking   Ms. Billings has informed me that she will join us momentarily.

revised   Ms. Billings told me that she will join us soon.

B108. **moot/mute:** A *moot court* discusses a hypothetical case; a *moot point* is one that may be argued from either side. *Mute* means *silent* or *incapable of speech.*

needs checking   In her recent article Nussbaum suggests that Williams's point is mute.

revised   In her recent article Nussbaum suggests that Williams's point is moot.

B109. **need/want:** The verb *need* conveys the idea that it would be difficult or impossible for you to do without the needed thing. If you are talking about acquiring something that is not necessary or essential, use *want* instead; everyone *needs* water and food, but no one really *needs* a new smartphone. Be careful too not to commit to paper the slang use of *need to* for *should.*

needs checking   I need to marry someone who is very beautiful, very intelligent, very kind, and very rich.

revised   I want to marry someone who is very beautiful, very intelligent, very kind, and very rich.

needs checking   The government needs to improve the roads in this area.

revised   The government should improve the roads in this area.

B110. **non sequitur:** A *non sequitur* is a *statement that has no clear relationship with what has preceded it.* There may be some connection within the mind of the speaker or writer, but it has not been expressed in words.

needs checking   It's time our government did more to help southern Africa. Besides, consumers appreciate inexpensive clothes.

revised   It's time our government did more to help southern Africa. Lowering the current barriers against importing cheap food and textiles would be an important step in that direction. Such a move would benefit our own citizens too; consumers appreciate inexpensive food and clothing.

B111. **numbers and things:** In any sentence about things and numbers associated with those things, it can be easy enough to become grammatically tangled up between the things and the measure of number. Always have this question in the back of your mind: what is the subject of the verb? Here's an example:

needs checking   Delays in new product launches have hammered the company's share price, which started the year at about $60 and now trades at less than $30.

That may seem fine at first glance, but look again. What is the subject of the verb *trades*? It's the noun *price*. But is it in fact the price that trades at under $30? No; it's the shares that trade at less than $30.

revised   Delays in new product launches have hammered the company's share price, which started the year at about $60 and is now less than $30.

or   Delays in new product launches have hammered the company's shares, which started the year at about $60; now the stock trades at less than $30.

Here are other examples of the same sort of problem:

needs checking   Many people have said that the price of the Tesla is too expensive.

revised   Many people have said that the price of the Tesla is too high.

or   Many people have said that the Tesla is too expensive.

needs checking   The height of the Shanghai Tower rises more than 2,000 feet.

revised   The Shanghai Tower rises more than 2,000 feet.

or   The height of the Shanghai Tower is more than 2,000 feet.

needs checking   The speed of the Sopwith Camel flew at just over 100 miles per hour during WWI.

revised   The Sopwith Camel flew at just over 100 miles per hour during WWI.

or   The maximum speed of the WWI Sopwith Camel was just over 100 miles per hour.

Additional Material Online
Exercises on word meanings may be found at
sites.broadviewpress.com/writing.
Click on **Exercises** and go to **"Words and Usage."**

B112. **of/have:** The difference in meaning is obvious, but the similarity in sound consistently leads people to write sentences involving such meaningless expressions as *should of, would of, could of, may of, might of,* and *must of.*

needs checking   The experiment would of succeeded if the solution had been prepared correctly.

revised   The experiment would have succeeded if the solution had been prepared correctly.

needs checking   Hitler believed that Rommel should of been able to defeat Montgomery at El Alamein.

revised   Hitler believed that Rommel should have been able to defeat Montgomery at El Alamein.

B113. **other:** If one uses the words *the other* it suggests that the thing or person one is about to mention is the only other one is going to write about. If there are several others to be mentioned, *another* is the word to choose.

needs checking   One reason Germany lost the Second World War was that Hitler underestimated the importance of keeping the United States out of the conflict. The other reason was that the German intelligence network was inferior to that of the Allies. Moreover, Hitler's decision to invade Russia was a disastrous mistake.

(Here the use of *the other* in the second sentence leads the reader to believe this is the only other reason. When a third reason is mentioned in the next sentence, the reader is taken by surprise.)

revised   One reason Germany lost the Second World War was that Hitler underestimated the importance of keeping the United States out of the conflict. Another reason was that the German intelligence network was inferior to that of the Allies. Moreover, Hitler's decision to invade Russia was a disastrous mistake.

B114. **our/are:** Like the substitution of *of* for *have*, the confusion of *our* and *are* should never survive the rough draft stage.

needs checking   Almost all are time is spent together.
revised   Almost all our time is spent together.

B115. **palate/palette/pallet:** Your *palate* is in your mouth. An artist uses a *palette* to mix paint on. (By extension people often refer to the range of colours typically used by a painter as her *palette*.) Finally, a *pallet* (or skid) is a *wooden frame designed for transporting goods.*

needs checking   In his later work Matisse's pallet was more limited; much of his work was in unmodulated, primary colours.
revised   In his later work Matisse's palette was more limited; much of his work was in unmodulated, primary colours.

B116. **partake/participate:** *Partake* refers to *things* (especially food and drink), *participate* to *activities.*

needs checking   The mayor made a brief appearance, but did not partake in the festivities.
revised   The mayor made a brief appearance, but did not participate in the festivities.

B117. **persecute/prosecute:** *To persecute someone is to treat them in a harsh and unfair manner, especially because of their political or religious beliefs. To prosecute someone is to take legal action against them in the belief that they have committed a crime.*

needs checking   Catholics began to be prosecuted in England in the sixteenth century.
revised   Catholics began to be persecuted in England in the sixteenth century.

B118. **persuade:** *To persuade someone of something is to make that person believe that it is true. To persuade someone to do something is to lead that person, through what one says, to do the desired thing.* If one does not succeed in making people believe or do what one wants, then one has not persuaded or convinced them, but only tried to persuade them. (The confusion of *refute* with *deny* [page 219] is a parallel mistake.)

> *needs checking* After all Portia's persuasion Shylock still refuses to change his mind.
>
> *revised* After all Portia's attempts to persuade him, Shylock still refuses to change his mind.

B119. **pore/pour**: As *The Globe and Mail Style Book* puts it, one should "not write of someone pouring over a book unless the tome in question is getting wet."

> *needs checking* After pouring over the evidence, the committee could find no evidence of wrongdoing.
>
> *revised* After poring over the evidence, the committee could find no evidence of wrongdoing.

B120. **practical/practicable**: *Practical* means *suitable for use,* or *involving activity rather than theory. Practicable* means *able to be done.* Changing the railway system back to steam locomotives would be practicable but extremely impractical. In most cases *practical* is the word the writer wants; excessive use of *practicable* will make writing sound pretentious rather than important.

> *needs checking* We do not feel that the construction of a new facility would be practicable at this time.
>
> *revised* It would not be practical to construct a new facility now.

B121. **prescribe/proscribe**: *To prescribe something* is *to recommend or order its use; to proscribe something* is *to forbid its use.*

> *needs checking* One local physician has already proscribed this new drug for a dozen of her patients, and in every case their condition has improved after they take it.
>
> *revised* One local physician has already prescribed this new drug for a dozen of her patients, and in every case their condition has improved after they take it.

B122. **presently**: The subject of much disagreement among grammarians; should *presently* be restricted to its original meaning of *soon,* or should common usage of the word to mean *now* be allowed to spread unopposed? Traditionalists argue that the acceptance of both meanings encourages ambiguity, but in fact the verb tense usually makes clear whether the speaker means *soon* or *now* (*I will be there presently, I am presently working on a large project,* etc.). Perhaps the best solution is to avoid the rather pompous *presently* altogether, and stick to those fine Anglo-Saxon words *soon* and *now.*

needs checking	I am seeing Mr. Jones presently.
revised	I am seeing Mr. Jones now.
or	I will be seeing Mr. Jones soon.

B123. **proposition/proposal:** The only formally correct meaning of *proposition* is *a statement that expresses an idea,* as in *This country is dedicated to the proposition that all humans are created equal.* It is better not to use it to mean *proposal.*

needs checking	The department has put forward a proposition for increasing sales.
revised	The department has put forward a proposal for increasing sales.

B124. **prove:** *To prove something* is *to eliminate any doubt whatsoever as to its truth.* Outside of mathematic or philosophical logic, proof is rarely possible; what one is doing when writing about history or political science or literature is presenting an argument, not a proof. Be cautious in the claims you make in formal writing.

needs checking	The following passage proves that T.S. Eliot was anti-Semitic.
revised	The following passage strongly suggests that T.S. Eliot was anti-Semitic.
or	Anti-Semitic feeling is clearly present in the following passage.

B125. **raise/rise:** As a verb, *raise* means *to lift*; *rise* means *to come up.*

needs checking	They rose the curtain at 8 o'clock.
revised	They raised the curtain at 8 o'clock.
or	The curtain rose at 8 o'clock.
	(Note: Both words are also used as nouns; in North America a *raise* is an *increase in salary*; the UK equivalent is a *rise* in salary.)

B126. **rational/rationale:** *Rational* is an adjective meaning *logical* or *sensible.* A *rationale* is *an explanation for something.*

needs checking The underlying rational for the proliferation of soaps and detergents is not to make our skin or clothes any cleaner, but to increase the profits of the manufacturers.

revised The underlying rationale for the proliferation of soaps and detergents is not to make our skin or clothes any cleaner, but to increase the profits of the manufacturers.

B127. **ravish/ravage:** *Ravish* has two quite unrelated meanings—*to rape,* or *to fill with delight. To ravage* is *to damage or destroy.*

needs checking The tree had been ravished by insects.

revised The tree had been ravaged by insects.

B128. **real/genuine:** The basic meaning of *real* is *existing*; the opposite of *fake* or *forged* is *genuine.*

needs checking The buyer had thought the painting was a Cezanne, but he soon discovered it was not real.

revised The buyer had thought the painting was a Cezanne, but he soon discovered it was not genuine.

B129. **regime/regimen/regiment:** A *regime* is either a *system of government* or a *period in which a particular government is in power* (e.g., *military regime, democratic regime*). A *regimen* is a *precisely fixed course of activity* (e.g., a *program of daily exercise and dieting,* a *schedule according to which medication must be taken*). A *regiment* is an *army unit.* Sometimes medical authorities use *regime* and *regimen* interchangeably; there is some benefit to keeping all three clearly separate.

needs checking A regiment of exercise and heavy medication kept Kennedy performing into his third year as president. (*The National Post,* 7 June 2003)

revised A regimen of exercise and heavy medication kept Kennedy performing into his third year as president.

B130. **reign/rein:** A monarch *reigns* over a territory; to control a horse you *rein* it in (using the reins). A new manager takes up the *reins* of an organization.

> *needs checking* The new leader has so far shown no signs of reigning in the armed forces.
>
> *revised* The new leader has so far shown no signs of reining in the armed forces.

B131. **respectively/respectfully**: *Respectively* means *in the order mentioned*; *respectfully* means *done with respect.*

> *needs checking* Seattle, Denver, and New England were, respectfully, the three best teams in the NFL last season.
>
> *revised* Seattle, Denver, and New England were, respectively, the three best teams in the NFL last season.

B132. **reticent/reluctant**: *Reticent* means *reluctant to speak*; *reserved about speaking*. A country may be *reluctant* to go to war; it cannot be *reticent* to go to war. And to say *reticent to speak* is to repeat oneself.

> *needs checking* She was reticent to speak up, even when her family's reputation had been attacked.
>
> *revised* She was reluctant to speak up, even when her family's reputation had been attacked.
>
> *or* She remained reticent, even when her family's reputation had been attacked.

B133. **rite/right**: A *rite* is a *ceremonial or ritualistic act*; the word is most frequently used to denote formal acts, such as those of religious ceremonies (e.g., *marriage rites*). Many cultures have formal ceremonies to mark a new stage in a person's life—ceremonies referred to by social scientists as *rites of passage*. That phrase has come to be used informally to refer to any event marking a significant life change. Perhaps because rights and privileges are sometimes conferred during a ceremonial *rite*, the two words are sometimes confused and two *right*s end up making a wrong.

> *needs checking* For many students, deconstruction was a right of passage into the world of rebellious intellect. (*New York Times*, 10 October 2004)
>
> *revised* For many students, deconstruction was a rite of passage into the world of rebellious intellect.

B134. **sensory/sensuous/sensual**: Advertising and pornography have dulled the distinction among these three adjectives. The meanings of *sensory* and *sensuous* are similar—*sensual* is the sexy one:

- Sensory—having to do with the senses.
- Sensuous—having to do with the senses, or appealing to the senses.
- Sensual—offering physical pleasure, especially of a sexual sort.

needs checking Boswell suggested they go to a house of ill repute, but Johnson had no desire for sensuous pleasures.

revised Boswell suggested they go to a house of ill repute, but Johnson had no desire for sensual pleasures.

B135. **set/sit**: *To set* means *to place something somewhere.*

needs checking I could remember everything, but I had difficulty sitting it down on paper.

revised I could remember everything, but I had difficulty setting it down on paper.

needs checking He asked me to set down on the couch.

revised He asked me to sit down on the couch.

B136. **shall/will**: Historically *shall* was used primarily for simple statements or questions in the first person—both singular (*I*) and plural (*we*)—and *will* primarily for simple statements or questions in the second person and third person. When *shall* was used in the second or third person it implied control or authority, expressing promises, commands, or a sense of determination. The old "distinctions" are still maintained in questions (*shall I eat a peach?, will you have some tea?*) but in other respects the distinctions long ago weakened. A sense of control is expressed with just as much force in the second person using *will* (*you'll do as I say*) and expressions of determination in the first person often use *shall* (*we shall overcome*). At most, then, a slight difference in tone lingers. In legal documents, for example, *shall* is often used rather than *will*, but either wording carries with it the same meaning—and confers the same legal obligation.

correct The undersigned shall fulfill the said requirements on or before December 31, 2020.

also correct The undersigned will fulfill the said requirements on or before December 31, 2020.

B137. **simple/simplistic**: *Simplistic* is a derogatory word meaning *too simple* or *excessively simplified.*

> *needs checking* The questions were so simplistic that I was able to answer all but one correctly.
> *revised* The questions were so simple that I was able to answer all but one correctly.

B138. somehow: *Somehow means by some method (Somehow I must repair my car so that I can arrive in time for my appointment).* It does not mean *in some ways, to some extent,* or *somewhat.*

> *needs checking* His brother is somehow mentally disturbed.
> *revised* His brother is mentally disturbed in some way.
> *or* His brother is somewhat disturbed mentally.

B139. specially/especially: *Specially means for a particular purpose (These utensils are specially designed for left-handed people). Especially* means *particularly* or *more than in other cases.*

> *needs checking* The entire system pleased her, but she was specially happy to see that the computer program had been especially created for small business users.
> *revised* The entire system pleased her, but she was especially happy to see that the computer program had been specially created for small business users.

B140. stationary/stationery: *Stationary means not moving; stationery* is *what you write on.*

> *needs checking* As Mr. Blakeney remembered it, Lord Taylor "would always park his car in the no-parking zone outside the Bessborough Hotel, leaving House of Lords stationary on the windshield."
> *revised* As Mr. Blakeney remembered it, Lord Taylor "would always park his car in the no-parking zone outside the Bessborough Hotel, leaving House of Lords stationery on the windshield."

B141. stimulant/stimulus: *Stimulus* (plural *stimuli*) is the more general word for *anything that produces a reaction; stimulant* normally refers to *a drink or drug that has a stimulating effect.*

> *needs checking* The shocks were intended to act as stimulants to the rats that we used as subjects for the experiment.
> *revised* The shocks were intended to act as stimuli to the rats that we used as subjects for the experiment.

B142. **tack/tact**: *Tack* is a sailing term; *a different tack* means *a different direction relative to the wind*. *Tact* is *skill in saying or doing the right or polite thing.*

needs checking   We will have to exercise all our tack in the coming negotiations.

revised   We will have to exercise all our tact in the coming negotiations.

B143. **then/than/that**: The difference in meaning is obvious, but slips of the pen or keyboard too often allow the error to make it to the final draft. Spell-check won't help, of course.

needs checking   It turns out that the company needs more money that we had expected.

revised   It turns out that the company needs more money than we had expected.

needs checking   There were fewer people in attendance then had been predicted.

revised   There were fewer people in attendance than had been predicted.

B144. **they/their/there/they're**: Four words that are confused perhaps more frequently than any others. *They* is a pronoun used to replace any plural noun (e.g., books, people, numbers). *There* can be used to mean *in* (or *at*) *that place*, or can be used as an introductory word before various forms of the verb *to be* (*there is, there had been*, etc.). *Their* is a possessive adjective meaning *belonging to them*. *They're* is a contraction of *They are*. Beware in particular of substituting *they* for *there*:

needs checking   They were many people in the crowd.

revised   There were many people in the crowd.

The easiest way to check whether one is making this mistake is to ask if it would make sense to replace *they* with a noun. In the above sentence, for example, it would obviously be absurd to say, *The people were many people in the crowd.*

The confusion of *they*, *there*, and *their* is the sort of mistake that all writers are able to catch if they proofread carefully—particularly if they do so out loud.

needs checking	Defenceman Zdeno Chára was considered to be there toughest player.
revised	Defenceman Zdeno Chára was considered to be their toughest player.
needs checking	There all going to the dance this Saturday.
revised	They're all going to the dance this Saturday.
or	They are all going to the dance this Saturday.

B145. **tiring/tiresome:** Something that is *tiring makes you feel tired,* though you may have enjoyed it very much. Something that is *tiresome* is *tedious and unpleasant.*

needs checking	Although it is tiresome for him, my father likes to play tennis at least twice a week.
revised	Although it is tiring for him, my father likes to play tennis at least twice a week.

B146. **to/too/two:** Too can mean *also* or be used to indicate *excess* (*too many, too heavy*); *two* is of course the number.

needs checking	She seemed to feel that there was to much to do.
revised	She seemed to feel that there was too much to do.

B147. **to/towards:** *To* indicates *direction*; *towards* indicates *motion.*

(Note that *toward* and *towards* may be used interchangeably.)

needs checking	The deer moved slowly to me through the tall grass.
revised	The deer moved slowly towards me through the tall grass.

B148. **unexceptional/unexceptionable:** *Unexceptional* means *ordinary, not an exception*; *unexceptionable* is used when you do not object (or take exception) to the thing or person in question.

needs checking	A great deal of confusion and controversy surrounded the unexceptional White House plan to reflag 11 Kuwaiti tankers with the Stars and Stripes. It was a modest proposal that in itself should not have caused the handwringing it did on Capitol Hill.
	(The plan to reflag Kuwaiti tankers as American ships clearly was an exception; the US had not done anything similar for years. What the writer means to say is that the plan was

unexceptionable—that no one should have any objection to it.)

revised A great deal of confusion and controversy surrounded the unexceptionable White House plan to reflag 11 Kuwaiti tankers with the Stars and Stripes. It was a modest proposal that in itself should not have caused the handwringing it did on Capitol Hill.

B149. **unique/universal/perfect/complete/correct:** Many authorities insist that none of these terms can be a matter of degree. According to this line of thought, something must be either *unique* or *not unique*, *perfect* or *imperfect*, and so on; it is thought to be wrong to speak of something as being *very unique* or *largely correct*, or as being *more complete* than something else. Instead, we are instructed to use phrases such as *almost unique* and *more nearly complete*. It's worth noting that not all authorities agree as to the importance of drawing a clear line in this way between adjectives and adverbs which admit of comparison and adjectives and adverbs which do not. Not a few have pointed out that the phrase "more perfect union" has been lent authority through its inclusion in the preamble to the American constitution. Nevertheless, students are well advised to pay attention to this issue in formal writing.

needs checking Frida Kahlo made a rather unique contribution to twentieth-century art.

revised Frida Kahlo made a unique contribution to twentieth-century art.

or It is arguable that Frida Kahlo made a unique contribution to twentieth-century art.

B150. **valid/true/accurate:** An *accurate* statement is one that is *factually correct*. A combination of accurate facts may not always give a true picture, however. For example, the statement *former Canadian Prime Minister Mackenzie King often visited prostitutes* is entirely accurate, but gives a false impression; in fact King visited prostitutes not to use their services but rather to try to convince them to give up their profession. *Valid* is often used carelessly and as a consequence might seem fuzzy in its meaning. Properly used it can mean *legally acceptable*, or *sound in reasoning*; do not use it to mean *accurate, reasonable, true*, or *well-founded*.

needs checking Churchill's fear that the Nazis would become a threat to all of Europe turned out to be valid.

revised Churchill's fear that the Nazis would become a threat to all of Europe turned out to be well-founded.

B151. **vein/vain:** *Veins* run through your body; *to be vain* is *to be conceited*; an effort that fails to bring any of the desired results has been *in vain*.

needs checking Shakespeare portrays Sir John Oldcastle—or Falstaff, as he is usually known—as vein and irresponsible but immensely amusing and likeable.

revised Shakespeare portrays Sir John Oldcastle—or Falstaff, as he is usually known—as vain and irresponsible but immensely amusing and likeable.

B152. **verbal/oral:** *Oral* means *spoken* rather than written, whereas *verbal* means *having to do with words*. A person who is unable to speak may have a high level of verbal skill.

needs checking I can write well enough, but I have difficulty in expressing ideas verbally.

revised I can write well enough, but I have difficulty in expressing ideas orally.

B153. **were/where:** *Were* is of course a past tense form of the verb *to be*, while *where* refers to a place. Spell-check will not tell you if you have used the correct word.

needs checking This is the place were Dante met Beatrice.
revised This is the place where Dante met Beatrice.

Some other words over which issues of meaning often cause confusion:

amused/bemused: If you are *bemused*, you are a bit puzzled about something—though not in any troubled fashion, and perhaps even in a somewhat amused one. From that slight point of connection (as well as the similarity in sound) has arisen the erroneous belief that the two words are synonymous.

demur/demure: To *demur* is to raise an objection; to be *demure* is to be modest and shy in an appealing way.

ecology/environment: *Ecology* is the study of some aspects of the environment; you cannot "harm the ecology."

empathy/sympathy: To *sympathize* with another person is to feel for that person; to *empathize* is to do so in a way that identifies oneself with that person.

envious/jealous: One is envious of someone else's good fortune, jealous of one's own possessions. In common parlance *jealous* is often used as a synonym for *envious*, but arguably the distinction between the two words is worth preserving.

fleshing/flushing: The expression *flesh out* means add to—just as flesh is added to a growing animal. The similarity in sounds often leads people to write *flush* instead of *flesh*, but if you suggest someone *flush out* their argument, you are surely not suggesting they expand it.

gender/sex: The word *gender* is used to refer to characteristics that are associated with one's sex but that have been formed through social influences. When we refer to the *female sex* or the *male sex*, on the other hand, we are speaking of biological difference.

herbs/spices: The difference lies in the origin; *herbs* come from the stems, leaves, or flowers of plants, while *spices* come from the roots, the bark, the seeds, or the buds.

moral/morale: The *morale* of a group is their level of confidence, optimism, shared positive feeling—not to be confused with the *moral* of a story, or with *moral* issues.

nauseous/nauseated: Something that is *nauseous* makes you feel *nauseated*. Informally many people speak of feeling *nauseous*; in the context of formal writing they should feel *nauseated* instead.

obsolescent/obsolete: Something *obsolescent* is becoming out of date; something *obsolete* is completely outmoded.

obtuse/abstruse: *Obtuse* means *rounded* or *blunt* (as opposed to sharp)—and by extension, when used about humans, *dull* or *dim-witted* (sometimes with the implication that the person is wilfully refusing to see the truth). *Abstruse* refers to ideas, not people, and means *obscure, difficult to understand* (sometimes with the implication that the material is of considerable weight or importance).

penultimate/ultimate: The *penultimate* one comes just before the last one; the *ultimate* one is the last one. A widespread misconception is that *penultimate* carries the implication of being higher than or better than or beyond the *ultimate*; not so.

tortuous/torturous: *Tortuous* means *full of twists and turns*; *torturous* means *having to do with torture.*

⊙ Usage: *Word Conventions*

B154. **according to:** This expression normally is used only when one is referring to a person or to a group of people (e.g., *According to his lawyer, the accused was nowhere near the scene when the crime was committed*; *According to Shakespeare, Richard III was a murderer*).

needs checking	According to geography, Congo is larger than all of Western Europe.
revised	As we learn in geography, Congo is larger than all of Western Europe.
needs checking	According to the story of *Cry, the Beloved Country*, Stephen Kumalo has a quick temper.
revised	The events of the story show that Stephen Kumalo has a quick temper.

B155. **age/aged:** Do not use the noun *age* as a participle.

needs checking	A woman age 35 was struck and killed by the car.
revised	A woman aged 35 was struck and killed by the car.

B156. **all of:** Many authorities advise that the expression *all of* should be avoided in the interests of economy. Perhaps so, but there is certainly no error involved, and in many cases the addition of the word *of* improves the rhythm of the sentence; Lincoln's famous maxim "You can not fool all the people all of the time" would not be improved by dropping the *of.*

B157. **amount:** This word should be used only with things that are uncountable (sugar, goodwill, etc.).

needs checking	A large amount of books were stolen from the library last night.

    revised   A large number of books were stolen from the library last night.

B158. and: In most cases *or* rather than *and* should be used as a connective if the statement is negative.

    needs checking   Moose are not found in South America, Africa, and Australia.

    revised   Moose are not found in South America, Africa, or Australia.

B159. anyways/anywheres: There is never a need for the *s*.

    needs checking   We were unable to find him anywheres.

    revised   We were unable to find him anywhere.

B160. as: When this word is used to relate the times at which two actions happened, the actions must have happened at the same time (e.g., *As I got out of bed, I heard the sound of gunfire*, where the hearing happens during the action of getting out; *As he was walking to work, he remembered that he had left the stove on*, where the remembering happens during the walking). *As* should not be used in this way if the two actions happened at different times. If one action is completed before the other begins, always use *when*.

    needs checking   As I had finished my geography assignment, I started my history essay.

    revised   When I had finished my geography assignment, I started my history essay.

        (The finishing happens before the starting.)

    needs checking   As she discovered that the engine was overheating, she stopped the car immediately.

    revised   When she discovered that the engine was overheating, she stopped the car immediately.

        (The discovering happens before the stopping.)

Note: Since *when* can be used both when actions happen simultaneously and when they happen at different times, anyone who is at all uncertain about this point is wise to avoid using *as* to refer to time, and always stick to *when*. This has the added advantage of avoiding the possible ambiguity as to whether *as* is being used to mean *because* or to mean *when*.

B161. **as/that/whether**: Do not use *as* to mean *that* or *whether*.

> *needs checking* I don't know as how I can do the job in time.
> *revised* I don't know whether I can do the job in time.

B162. **back formations**: A back formation is the formation of a word from what one would expect to be its derivative. The verb *laze*, for example, is a back formation from the adjective *lazy*; a more recent (and similar-sounding) back formation is the verb *liaise* from the noun *liaison*. Many back formations may be created from negatives that lack a positive form (*kempt, gruntled, ruthful, solent,* etc.). These may constitute amusing colloquialisms, but should be avoided in formal written English except where the writer is striving for a humorous effect.

> *informal* Toronto is a pretty ruly place to watch a game. (Baseball manager Lou Piniella, as quoted by Robertson Cochrane in *The Globe and Mail*, 29 Oct. 1994)
> *more formal* Toronto is a pretty civilized place to watch a game.

B163. **because of the following reasons/some reasons/many reasons**: The word *because* makes it clear that a cause or reason is being introduced. The addition of a phrase such as *of the following reasons* is redundant. Either use *because* on its own, or use *for the following reasons/many reasons*, etc.

> *needs checking* During her first few years in New York, Susanna was unhappy because of several reasons.
> *revised* During her first few years in New York, Susanna was unhappy for several reasons.

B164. **both**: The expressions *both alike, both equal*, and *both together* all tend to involve repetition.

> *needs checking* Macdonald and Cartier both arrived together at about eight o'clock.
> *revised* Macdonald and Cartier arrived together at about eight o'clock.

B165. **can be able**: *I can do it* and *I am able to do it* mean the same thing. Using the verbs together is redundant.

> *needs checking* He thinks Minnesota can be able to win the Cup.

> *revised*   He thinks Minnesota can win the Cup.
> *or*   He thinks Minnesota will be able to win the Cup.

B166. **cannot help but**: One too many negatives; use *can but* or *cannot help*.

> *needs checking*   He couldn't help but think he had made a mistake.
> *revised*   He couldn't help thinking he had made a mistake.
> *or*   He could but think he had made a mistake.

B167. **change**: You *make a change* (not *do a change*).

> *needs checking*   The manager did several changes to the roster before the match with Russia.
> *revised*   The manager made several changes to the roster before the match with Russia.

Additional Material Online

Exercises on the conventions of English usage may be found at **sites.broadviewpress.com/writing**. Click on **Exercises** and go to **"Words and Usage."**

B168. **comment**: We *make comments* (not *say* or *do them*).

> *needs checking*   Anyone who wishes to say any comments will have a chance to speak after the lecture.
> *revised*   Anyone who wishes to make any comments will have a chance to speak after the lecture.

B169. **compared to/than**: The use of *compared to* as a participial phrase often leads to ambiguity and error. Unless one is speaking of one person comparing something to something else, it is usually better to use *than*.

> *needs checking*   There were far fewer frogs in the area in 2008 compared to previous years.
> *revised*   There were far fewer frogs in the area in 2008 than there had been in previous years.

B170. **convince**: You *convince* people that they should do something, or *persuade* them to do it.

needs checking	Reagan's advisers convinced him to approve the arms-for-hostages deal with Iran.
revised	Reagan's advisers persuaded him to approve the arms-for-hostages deal with Iran.

B171. **elder/older:** *Elder* can act as an adjective (*my elder son*) or a noun (*the elder of the two*). *Older* can act only as an adjective. If using *than*, use *older*.

needs checking	She is four years elder than her sister.
revised	She is four years older than her sister.

B172. **for:** One use of this preposition is to show purpose. Normally, however, *for* can be used in this way only when the purpose can be expressed in one word (e.g., *for safety, for security*). It is not usually correct to try to express purpose by combining *for* with a pronoun and an infinitive: expressions such as *for him to be happy, for us to arrive safely* are awkward and should be avoided. Instead, one can express purpose either by beginning with *in order to* (e.g., *in order to make life easier, in order to increase yield per hectare*), or by using *so that* (e.g., *so that life will be made easier, so that yield per hectare will be increased*).

needs checking	Please speak slowly for me to understand what you say.
revised	Please speak slowly so that I can understand what you say.
needs checking	The team must work hard for it to have a chance at the Stanley Cup.
revised	The team must work hard if it is to have a chance at the Stanley Cup.

B173. **forget:** *To forget something* is *to fail to remember it*, not *to leave it somewhere*.

needs checking	I forgot my textbook at home.
revised	I left my textbook at home.
or	I forgot to bring my textbook from home.

B174. **had ought/hadn't ought:** Use *ought* or *ought not* instead.

needs checking	He hadn't ought to have risked everything at once.
revised	He ought not to have risked everything at once.
or	He should not have risked everything at once.

B175. **hardly**: *Hardly* acts as a negative; there is thus no need to add a second negative.

> *needs checking*   The advertisers claim that you can't hardly tell the difference.
>
> *revised*   The advertisers claim that you can hardly tell the difference.

B176. **how/what**: One may talk about *how something* (*or someone*) is, or *what something* (*or someone*) is like, but not *how they are like*.

> *needs checking*   Tell me how it looks like from where you are.
>
> *revised*   Tell me how it looks from where you are.
>
> *or*   Tell me what it looks like from where you are.
>
> *needs checking*   I do not know how the roads are like between St. John's and Corner Brook.
>
> *revised*   I do not know what the roads are like between St. John's and Corner Brook.
>
> *or*   I do not know how the roads are between St. John's and Corner Brook.

B177. **increase**: Numbers can be *increased* or *decreased*, as can such things as production and population (nouns which refer to certain types of numbers or quantities). Things such as houses, however, or books (nouns which do not refer to numbers or quantities) cannot be increased; only the number of houses, books, etc. can be increased or decreased, raised or lowered. (See also pages 234–35.)

> *needs checking*   The government has greatly increased low-rent houses in the suburbs of Seattle.
>
> *revised*   The government has greatly increased the number of low-rent houses in the suburbs of Seattle.

B178. **information**: One *gives information* (not *tells it*).

> *needs checking*   He told me all the information I wanted about how to apply.
>
> *revised*   He gave me all the information I wanted about how to apply.

B179. **investigation**: We *make, carry out,* or *hold an investigation* (not *do one*).

> *needs checking* The manager did a thorough investigation into the disappearance of funds from his department.
>
> *revised* The manager made a thorough investigation into the disappearance of funds from his department.

B180. **irregardless:** The result of confusion between *regardless* and *irrespective.* Use *regardless.*

> *needs checking* She told us to come for a picnic, irregardless of whether it is rainy or sunny.
>
> *revised* She told us to come for a picnic, regardless of whether it is rainy or sunny.

B181. **is when/is where:** Many people use these phrases when attempting to define something. There is always a better way.

> *needs checking* Osmosis is when a fluid moves through a porous partition into another fluid.
>
> *revised* Osmosis occurs when a fluid moves through a porous partition into another fluid.
>
> *or* Osmosis is the movement of a fluid through a porous partition into another fluid.

B182. **journey:** You *make a journey* (not *do one*).

> *needs checking* If we do not stop along the way, we can do the journey in an hour.
>
> *revised* If we do not stop along the way, we can make the journey in an hour.

B183. **law:** A law is *passed, made,* or *put into effect* by the government, and *enforced* by the police. Laws are not *put* or *done.*

> *needs checking* I think the government should put a law increasing the penalty for drunk driving.
>
> *revised* I think the government should pass a law increasing the penalty for drunk driving.

B184. **less/fewer:** When something can be counted (e.g., people, books, trees), use *fewer.* Use *less* only with uncountable nouns (e.g., *sugar, meat, equipment*).

needs checking As the modern economy spreads through the country-side, less people will die of tropical diseases or infected wounds. (*The New York Times*, 12 May 1997)

revised As the modern economy spreads through the country-side, fewer people will die of tropical diseases or infected wounds.

needs checking There are less steps, and that means there is more room for error.

revised There are fewer steps, and that means there is more room for error.

B185. **lie** (meaning *speak falsely*): You *lie about something*, not *that something*.

needs checking He lied that he was eighteen years old.

revised He lied about his age, stating that he was eighteen.

or He lied when he said he was eighteen years old.

B186. **mistake**: Mistakes are *made* (not *done*).

needs checking He did seven mistakes in that short spelling exercise.

revised He made seven mistakes in that short spelling exercise.

B187. **more/most**: Most adjectives and adverbs have comparative and superlative forms; the comparative is used when comparing two things, the superlative when comparing three or more.

needs checking Smith was the most accomplished of the two.

revised Smith was the more accomplished of the two.

To use *more* with a comparative adjective, or *most* with a superlative adjective is to repeat oneself.

needs checking The bride looked like the most happiest person in the world.

revised The bride looked like the happiest person in the world.

or The bride looked like the most happy person in the world.

needs checking Gandalf is much more wiser than Frodo.

revised Gandalf is much wiser than Frodo.

B188. **nor**: This word is usually used with *neither*. Do not use it with *not*; when using *not*, use *or* instead of *nor*.

needs checking	She does not drink nor smoke.
revised	She does not drink or smoke.
or	She neither drinks nor smokes.
needs checking	Graham does not have the money nor the organizational skills to succeed in business.
revised	Graham does not have the money or the organizational skills to succeed in business.
or	Graham has neither the money nor the organizational skills to succeed in business.

B189. **nothing/nobody/nowhere:** These words should not be used with another negative word such as *not*. If one uses *not*, then one should use *anything* instead of *nothing, anybody* instead of *nobody, anywhere* instead of *nowhere*.

needs checking	He could not do nothing while he was in prison.
revised	He could not do anything while he was in prison.

B190. **old-fashioned:** Be sure not to leave off the *-ed* in this adjectival expression.

needs checking	Let's do it the old-fashion way.
revised	Let's do it the old-fashioned way.

B191. **opposed:** You are opposed *to* something or someone (not *with* or *against*)

needs checking	Charles Darwin was opposed against the literal interpretation of the story of Creation, as found in Genesis.
revised	Charles Darwin was opposed to the literal interpretation of the story of Creation, as found in Genesis.

B192. **per cent/percentage:** If you use *per cent*, you must give the number. Otherwise, use *percentage*.

needs checking	The per cent of people surveyed who reported any change of opinion was very small.
revised	The percentage of people surveyed who reported any change of opinion was very small.
or	Only six per cent of the people surveyed reported any change of opinion.

Note: *Percentage* is always one word; authorities differ as to whether *per cent* should always be written as two words, or whether it also may be written as one word (*percent*).

B193. **preclude**: *To preclude something* is *to exclude any possibility of it happening*; people cannot be precluded.

needs checking	Our cash flow problems preclude us from entering into any new commitments before 2020.
revised	Our cash flow problems preclude any new commitments before 2020.
or	We do not have enough money to make a commitment to you now.

B194. **position/theory**: Positions and theories *are held* or *are argued*; they do not hold or argue themselves.

needs checking	Devlin's position holds that a shared public morality is essential to the existence of society.
revised	Devlin's position is that a shared public morality is essential to the existence of society.
or	Devlin holds that a shared public morality is essential to the existence of society.

B195. **reason**: The phrase *the reason is because* involves repetition; use *that* instead of *because*, or eliminate the phrase completely.

needs checking	The reason ice floats is because it is lighter than water.
revised	The reason ice floats is that it is lighter than water.
or	Ice floats because it is lighter than water.
needs checking	The reason I have come is because I want to apply for a job.
revised	I have come to apply for a job.

B196. **short/scarce**: If a person is *short of something*, that thing is *scarce*.

needs checking	Food is now desperately short throughout the country.
revised	Food is now extremely scarce throughout the country.
or	The country is now desperately short of food.

B197. **since/for**: Both these words can be used to indicate length (or duration) of time, but they are used in slightly different ways. *Since* is used to mention the point at which a period of time began (*since 6 o'clock, since the beginning of 2015, since last Christmas*, etc.). *For* is used to mention the amount of time that has passed (*for two years, for six months, for centuries*, etc.).

needs checking	She has been staying with us since three weeks.
revised	She has been staying with us for three weeks.
or	She has been staying with us since three weeks ago.

B198. **so:** When used to show degree or extent, *so* is normally used with *that*: *so big that ...* , *so hungry that ...* , etc. *So* should not be used as an intensifier in the way that *very* is used.

needs checking	When George stepped out of the church he looked so handsome.
revised	When George stepped out of the church he looked very handsome.
or	When George stepped out of the church he looked so handsome that it was hard to believe he had once been thought of as unattractive.

B199. **some/any/someone/anyone:** With negatives (*not, never*, etc.) *any* is used in place of *some*.

needs checking	He never gives me some help with my work.
revised	He never gives me any help with my work.

B200. **speech:** You *make a speech* or *give a speech* (not *do a speech*).

needs checking	The dean was asked to do a speech at the convocation.
revised	The dean was asked to give a speech at the convocation.

B201. **start:** If both the time at which an event begins and the time that it finishes are mentioned, it is not enough to use only the verb *start*.

needs checking	The dance started from 9 p.m. till midnight.
revised	The dance started at 9 p.m. and finished at midnight.
or	The dance continued from 9 p.m. until midnight.
or	The dance lasted from 9 p.m. until midnight.

B202. **suppose/supposed:** Be sure to add the *d* in the expression *supposed to*.

> *needs checking* We are suppose to be there by eight.
> *revised* We are supposed to be there by eight.

B203. supposed to/should: These two are very similar in meaning, and may often be used interchangeably; if a person is *supposed to* do something, then that is what she *should* do. In the past tense, however, the question of when and when not to use *supposed to* is quite tricky. You may use it when you are clearly talking about a fixed plan that has not been carried out (e.g., *He was supposed to arrive before two o'clock, but he is still not here*). You should not use it to apply to any action that you think was wrong, or you feel should not have been carried out. The safe solution to this problem is always to use *should* instead of *supposed to*.

> *needs checking* What she said was impolite, but he was not supposed to hit her for saying it.
> *revised* What she said was impolite, but he should not have hit her for saying it.

> *needs checking* The National Party government was not supposed to keep Nelson Mandela in jail for so many years.
> *revised* The National Party government should not have kept Nelson Mandela in jail for so many years.

B204. thankful/grateful: We are *thankful* that something has happened, and *grateful* for something we have received.

> *needs checking* I am very thankful for the kind thoughts expressed in your letter.
> *revised* I am very grateful for the kind thoughts expressed in your letter.

B205. too: The word *too* suggests that something is *more than necessary*, or *more than desired*. Do not use it indiscriminately to lend emphasis.

> *needs checking* He looked too handsome in his new suit.
> *revised* He looked very handsome in his new suit.

B206. try/sure: Perhaps the most common error of all, in published books and articles as well as in less formal writing, is the use of *and* rather than *to* after *try* and *sure*.

needs checking	No one stepped in to try and save the poor animal.
revised	No one stepped in to try to save the poor animal.
needs checking	Burton had agreed with the Sultan not to try and convert the Africans to Christianity. (Alan Moorehead, *The White Nile*)
revised	Burton had agreed with the Sultan not to try to convert the Africans to Christianity.
needs checking	Be sure and take out the garbage before you go to bed.
revised	Be sure to take out the garbage before you go to bed.

B207. use/used: Be sure to add the *d* in the expression *used to*.

needs checking	He use to be much more reckless than he is now.
revised	He used to be much more reckless than he is now.

B208. where: Do not use *where* for *that*.

needs checking	I read in the paper where the parties are now tied in popularity.
revised	I read in the paper that the parties are now tied in popularity.

For a discussion of how to use
paragraphs to structure arguments, see pages **35–43**.
Exercises on paragraphing may be found at
sites.broadviewpress.com/writing.
Click on **Exercises** and go to
"Putting Ideas Together."

◎ PUTTING IDEAS TOGETHER

⊙ Paragraphing

C1. There is a degree of flexibility when it comes to the matter of where and how often to start new paragraphs. Sometimes a subtle point in an argument will require a paragraph of almost an entire page to elaborate; occasionally a single sentence can form an effective paragraph. Yet separating ideas into paragraphs remains an important aid to the processes of both reading and writing. Here are some guidelines as to when it is appropriate to begin a new paragraph:

O *In Narration:*

- whenever the story changes direction.
  (*This was the moment Stephen Harper had been waiting for ...,
  When Napoleon left Elba he....*)
- when there is a gap in time in the story.
  (*Two weeks later the issue was raised again in cabinet....*)

O *In Description:*

- whenever you switch from describing one place, person, or thing to describing another.
  (*Even such a brief description as this is enough to give some sense of the city and its pretensions. Much more interesting in many ways are some of the province's smaller cities and towns....*)

O *In Persuasion or Argument:*

- when a new topic is introduced.
  (*There can be little doubt that Austen's asides on the literary conventions of her time provide an amusing counterpoint to her story. But does this running commentary detract from the primary imaginative experience of* Northanger Abbey?)

- when there is a change in direction of the argument.
  (*To this point we have been looking only at the advantages of a guaranteed annual income. We should also ask, however, whether or not it would be practical to implement.*)

Description, narration, and argument are commonly blended together in writing, and it is usually also advisable to start a new paragraph when changing from one mode to another. If, for example, a text moves from describing an experiment to analyzing its significance, it's a good time to start a new paragraph. If it moves from telling where Napoleon went and what he did to discussing why events unravelled in this way, the same holds true.

There are many ways of putting ideas together. Much of this chapter is concerned with the particulars of joining words and how to use them. It may be useful, however, to begin with a look at some of the mental processes involved in putting ideas together into strong and coherent arguments.

N.B. For more on paragraphing see pages 35–43 of "The Writing Process" at the beginning of this book.

⊙ Argument

It is widely accepted that problems with writing are often closely intertwined with a lack of training in thinking critically; for that reason coverage of some basic concepts in critical thinking is included here. Of course thousands of books have been written on critical thinking and logical argument—and on the subtleties of logical argument in English. In a book of this sort it is not possible to do more than touch on a few key distinctions.

C2. **deductive and inductive arguments**: We should distinguish first of all between "argument" in the everyday sense (a confrontation in which people become angry with each other) and argument in an academic context. The latter sort of argument has nothing to do with being angry; it is a way of putting facts and ideas together in a reasoned way in an effort to convince others of the truth of something. Arguments in this sense may be described as having formal parts—chief among them their **premises** and their **conclusion**. The premises are statements that are made in order to provide logical support for another statement—the argument's conclusion. Here's an example:

- When the economy is strong the ruling party always wins elections in this country. The economy as we approach the next election is extremely strong. Therefore the ruling party will win.

The first two statements in the example are the premises; the third is the conclusion.

Notice here that if each of the premises are true, the conclusion here *must* follow logically from the premises—must be true. Arguments such as these, in which the truth of the conclusion is guaranteed by the truth of the argument's premises, are known as **deductive** arguments. The classic examples of deductive arguments are syllogisms—logical structures such as the one above, in which a conclusion is drawn from two premises. Here is the classic example of a deductive argument in the form of a syllogism:

- Socrates is a human. All humans are mortal. Therefore Socrates is mortal.

Since most of us are more likely to put forward arguments about matters other than whether or not a particular human is mortal, it may be helpful to provide a further example:

- A successful baseball team must have good starting pitchers. This year's White Sox team does not have good starting pitchers. Therefore, this year's White Sox team will not be successful.

In this example there are two premises. The first is that *a successful baseball team must have good starting pitchers*; the second is that *this year's White Sox team does not have good starting pitchers*. The conclusion is drawn by putting together the ideas advanced in the two premises: *this year's White Sox team will not be successful.*

Note that the reasoning of a deductive argument may be **valid** even if one or more of its premises is false. For example, the above syllogism is a valid argument regardless of whether or not it is in fact true that to be successful a team must have good starting pitchers.

In a valid deductive argument, the conclusion must be true if the premises are true. If the premises of the above argument are true, then the argument is sound as well as valid: we know *with certainty* that the White Sox will not be successful.

The conclusion of an **inductive** argument, on the other hand, is not guaranteed by the truth of the argument's premises. Inductive arguments often generalize from particular instances to a general conclusion. Here is an example:

- Since the creation of the National League, every World Series winner has had at least three outstanding starting pitchers on its roster. It seems reasonable to conclude from this that a team with fewer than three outstanding starting pitchers has an extremely slight chance of winning the World Series.

Notice that inductive arguments are often based on numbers, percentages, and estimates of probabilities.

In practice, arguments very frequently combine inductive and deductive elements; let's look at a couple of examples.

- Every poodle I've met has been friendly, so I suppose that all poodles must be friendly. Since all poodles are friendly, Maggie the poodle must be friendly.

The initial inference here is inductive; the general friendliness of poodles is inferred from particular observations of friendly poodles. The general claim is not established with certainty and might in fact be false, but lack of certainty doesn't necessarily mean that the inductive inference is unreasonable.

If the general claim about the friendliness of poodles is true, then we can be certain that Maggie is friendly, given that she is a poodle. This second inference is deductive because the conclusion must be true if the premises are true.

- I looked at the stats beforehand. Almost no one ever dies from this sort of operation; there seemed to be no chance Frank would die. And yet he *did die* during the operation. It must be a case of malpractice on the part of the surgeons!

This is an argument that draws on both inductive and deductive reasoning—and that has multiple problems. The fact that very few people die during a particular procedure, of course, creates a probability for anyone about to undergo that procedure themselves—not a certainty. A further problem with this argument is that it relies on an unstated premise which happens to be false. The unstated premise here is that the small percentage of people undergoing this operation in the past who have *not* survived have all died as a result of malpractice. As soon as we state it, we realise how improbable that is.

C3. **some/all**: Regardless of whether one's arguments are inductive or deductive, it is vitally important to be sensitive to the difference between *some* and *all*. This may seem an obvious point, but it is one that it is easy to lose track of in the twists and turns of an argument—or, indeed, in making off-hand observations about things that seem self-evident:

• I asked some female hockey players if they wanted to play in the men's league and they said 'no.' Why should we open up the league to women if they don't even want to play?

The fact that *some* women wouldn't like to play in the men's league doesn't imply that *no* women would like to play in the men's league. The inductive inference from *some* to *all* would require additional evidence in this case.

The distinction between *some* and *all* should also be kept in mind when it comes to arguments with several interconnected strands. Does what one is saying apply to all the facts of the argument, or only to some of them? Here is an example:

• What on earth is wrong with *spinster, chairman, mankind*, or, for that matter, adjectives such as *blind* and *deaf*, to name just a few? These are perfectly legitimate and serviceable terms, yet an arbitrary, malevolent connotation has been assigned them. In their place we are asked to draw from a silly artificial glossary of convoluted euphemisms to describe people and events, a glossary replete with all manner of adverbs with the word *challenged* suffixed leech-like to them.

The writer here is arguing against bias-free language. The core of the argument is that the new terms we are asked to use are silly, artificial, and convoluted. That may well be true of a term such as *mentally challenged*. But notice how difficult it is to make such claims stick with all or even most of the examples here. The non-sexist alternatives for *chairman* and *mankind*—*chair, humanity*, and the like—are hardly silly, artificial, or convoluted. And are we in fact asked to replace the word *deaf* with *aurally-challenged*? Not at all. Those working in the field do indeed use *aurally-challenged* as a blanket term to refer to all those who have any hearing impairment, ranging from mild loss of hearing to complete deafness, but they do not shy away from using terms such as *deaf* and *partially deaf.* In short, the objection raised by this writer to "politically correct" language in general turns out to apply only to a very few instances.

C4. **trends**: In matters of any complexity involving numbers and trends, it is easy to lose sight of the big picture—and many verbal arguments are constructed in a way that encourages those listening to the arguments to lose sight of the big picture. Here is an example:

- Even many of those who support the proposed climate change treaty say that it will cost jobs in industries ranging from oil and gas to mining to automobile manufacturing—perhaps hundreds of thousands of jobs. We cannot afford to let our economy shrink; it is essential that we oppose ratification of this treaty.

An unstated premise in this argument is that if jobs are lost in the stated sectors, the economy shrinks. But no estimate is given of the number of jobs that would in this sort of situation be created (in industries such as solar and wind power) or jobs that would be saved (for example at ski resorts) if strong action were taken against climate change. Some have suggested that the economy in general would grow just as fast if such action were taken. Others have estimated it would grow more slowly, but few have suggested it would actually shrink. Here, as in many other cases, it is important to be aware of distinctions between a decline, a decline in the rate of increase, and so on.

C5. **relevance**: It is often much more difficult than one would think to judge what is relevant or irrelevant to a given argument. Here is an example:

- I don't agree with the arguments of those who are promoting foreign aid spending by countries such as the United States and Canada. Before we worry about troubles people halfway round the world may have, we should take care of the problems people have here at home.

The concluding statement here may seem at first glance a quite powerful argument against foreign aid. But is it? The subtle suggestion here is that those who support foreign aid want us to help those who are far away *rather than* helping those close to home—something that in fact no supporter of foreign aid would argue. How relevant is the statement quoted above to the core arguments of those who support foreign aid? In fact, the claims being made here are entirely irrelevant to all but one of the arguments that are put forward by supporters of foreign aid activists. Nothing is said in the quoted statement concerning the degree of hardship endured by many people elsewhere in the world, about their need for help, or about the efficacy of foreign aid spending in helping them. Nor does it address the more fundamental argument that we have some level of obligation to other humans who are enduring extreme suffering. There are a variety of important points that could be made as to the efficacy of foreign aid as it has been structured, but those points are not touched on here. Much as the quoted statement may seem to be taking issue with the position that we should try to help those far away instead of helping those closer to home, in fact it takes issue only with the far less extreme suggestion that we should pay *some* attention to the plight of those far away, even while we are also attempting to address problems closer to home. If we are to accept the position of this opponent of foreign aid, then, we are saying that we should *never* provide any help to those far away, no matter how extreme their suffering, so long as there is *any* problem at all closer to home, however modest in extent it may be. Suddenly the quoted statement seems a lot weaker as an argument—and largely irrelevant to most of "the arguments of those who are promoting foreign aid."

"We Are Omnivores": A Case Study in Argument

Here's a little case study in argument, on the topic of human and non-human animals. The context is a complaint from Christof Koch that, in a December 19, 2013 *New York Review of Books* article discussing extreme eating ("Food Tips for Christmas"), Jason Epstein made no mention of the suffering of the non-human animals. Koch put it in this way in his letter ("The Pain of Animals," February 6, 2014):

> the penises, brains, hearts, and whole embryos that are now de rigueur to consume by our haute cuisine establishment derive from sentient creatures. These animals are all capable of sophisticated behaviors that, when they occur in people, are associated with empathy, attachment, curiosity, metacognition, and conscious awareness. Maybe even food writers and their critics can acknowledge this uncomfortable truth and face up to their ethical blindness.

The New York Review of Books also printed a response to this letter by the writer of the article. Epstein *might* have responded to Koch's letter simply by saying that food writers reviewing steakhouses or sushi restaurants are not expected to discuss the fact that much of the food consumed in such establishments comes from sentient creatures. Why should an article discussing the human consumption of less-frequently eaten parts of the same animals be any different? Would that have been a fair response, focused on questions of relevance?

Instead, Epstein responded in this way:

> We are omnivores. We eat anything edible, including ourselves. I deeply regret the suffering of animals but there are not enough vegetarians to solve the problem. Even Adolf Hitler, a vegetarian himself according to his intimates, with absolute power over those in his net, could do nothing to prevent this pain. I wish it were different but we are what we are.

There are several questions that may fairly be asked about the lines of argument Epstein uses here.

- Are humans necessarily omnivores (as cats are necessarily carnivores, as a matter of the capacity of the digestive system)? The good health of most vegans, and the fact that in a great deal of the world (most of India, for example), most people are vegetarian suggests otherwise. How would you assess the strength of the appeal to nature that Epstein is making?

- Does the mention of humans being capable of eating other humans support Epstein's case? Does it weaken it? Is it in any way relevant?

- Does the mention of Hitler strengthen Epstein's case? (Hitler did not in fact make any effort to impose his own vegetarianism on others.)

- How many forms of argument can you identify in Epstein's five sentences? Can you describe how his argument goes wrong? How common are the sorts of mistakes he makes?

O *Fallacies and Faulty Arguments*

A fallacious argument is one that suffers from faulty reasoning. Many forms of faulty reasoning have been identified; following is a list of some of the most common forms of fallacy.

C6. **ad hominem**: The Latin *ad hominem* means *directed at the person*; an attempt to persuade through ad hominem comments entails attacking the person making the claim rather than attacking the claim itself. In both the following examples the pieces of information supplied may be of interest, but do not constitute good arguments:

- Nothing that former President George W. Bush has ever said about energy policy makes any sense. Remember, he made a fortune in the oil industry.

- Any arguments John McCain makes about the beer industry cannot be taken seriously; he is married to a beer distributor heir.

C7. **straw figure argument**: A common practice in argument is to ascribe to one's opponent an extreme view that in fact one's opponent has never put forward, and then suggest that in knocking down the extreme "straw figure" argument you have won. Here are two examples:

- I fully support capital punishment. How can anyone claim that the life of a convicted murderer is more valuable than the life of the innocent person he has killed?

- I oppose capital punishment. How can anyone claim that there is no chance of a criminal reforming, and no intrinsic value in human life itself?

Of course, neither the opponents nor the supporters of capital punishment make the suggested claims—but often people are able to get away with this sort of sleight of hand in the midst of an argument.

C8. **begging the question**: An argument begs the question if it assumes the truth of what it sets out to prove. Here is an example:

- The Bible tells us that God exists. The Bible is the Word of God, and God doesn't make mistakes. Therefore, God exists.

If the premises of this argument are all true, then it seems that the conclusion must be true. Nevertheless, we can't be certain of the truth of the premises unless we are already certain of the truth of the conclusion. The problem is that the argument assumes what it sets out to prove.

[Note that "beg the question" is often misunderstood to mean "raise the question."]

C9. **formally invalid arguments**: If the formal structure of a deductive argument is not valid, then the argument is fallacious.

Two common sorts of formally invalid arguments are those which *deny the antecedent*, and those which *affirm the consequent*. Here is an example of the former:

- If water starts dripping from this ceiling during a rainstorm, then you can be sure there is a problem with your roof. No water has dripped from the ceiling during a rainstorm. There-fore, there is no problem with the roof.

In this case it is certainly true that water dripping from the ceiling is a reliable sign of there being some problem with the roof. But of course there can be a problem with the roof even without there being such a visible sign; very frequently, roof leaks result in water saturating rafters and seeping down inside walls without there being any drips from the ceiling. The first sentence of the example tells us what we know about the roof if there *is* water dripping from the ceiling, but it doesn't tell us anything about the state of the roof if there *isn't* water dripping from the ceiling. (Like so many elements of reasoning, the ability to recognize this fallacy connects to the ability to be sensitive to the distinction between *some* and *all*; some roof leaks result in dripping ceilings, but others don't.) The *if...* part of an argument such as this is known as the *antecedent*. And, as the example shows, denying the antecedent has no argumentative force.

- If a lake is very seriously affected by acid rain, no fish can sur-vive in it. This lake has no fish living in it whatsoever. This lake must be seriously affected by acid rain.

It is entirely true that lakes seriously affected by acid rain cannot support any aquatic life. But that is not the only possible cause for the disappearance of aquatic life from a lake. If, for example, a com-pany had been using the lake as a toxic waste dump, that would also have the effect of killing all the fish. The first sentence of the exam-ple tells us that no fish can survive in a lake if that lake is affected by acid rain; it doesn't tell us that the lake must be affected by acid rain if it doesn't contain any fish. (Again, the distinction between *some* and *all* is crucial; some lifeless lakes got that way because of acid rain, but not all). The *then ...* part of an argument is called the *consequent*. As the example shows, affirming the consequent does nothing to prove the antecedent.

C10. **slippery slope arguments**: The fallacy of the slippery slope argument is the suggestion that one development in a certain direction will inevitably lead to further developments in the same direction or *down the same slope*. Here is an example:

- The idea of people being required to carry identity cards may seem innocuous enough, but in fact it should be resolutely opposed. If we allow the government to force us to carry identity cards, pretty soon they'll be keeping track of all our movements with video cameras, and placing all sorts of restrictions on our privacy. We have to stop these government intrusions into our lives!

This argument says nothing about the issue of identity cards per se. It is entirely based on the premise of one move by the government being followed by other, more drastic moves. Sometimes, of course, developments are part of long-term trends, but sometimes they are not part of any trend—or may represent the furthest extent of a particular trend. Certainly there is no inevitability about any particular move in one direction being followed by subsequent moves in the same direction.

C11. **false dichotomy**: A *dichotomy* occurs when *things or ideas are split into two distinct alternatives*. An argument that tries to insist on two and only two alternatives when in fact three or more possibilities exist (or gradations among possibilities exist) is one that poses a false dichotomy. Here is an example:

A. There should be laws prohibiting people from inciting hate against those of other races or religions.
B. So you're against freedom of speech? Without freedom of speech we wouldn't have a democracy!
A. No, I support freedom of speech—but with certain limits to prevent the most harmful extreme views from being promulgated. It sounds to me as if you are not willing to do anything to combat bigotry and racism.
B. Not at all. But I believe that people speaking out freely against freely expressed bigoted or racist opinions will combat them more effectively than government attempts to prohibit them.

In this case both arguers pose false dichotomies in their characterizations of the other's viewpoint—whereas in fact both hold nuanced views.

C12. **false premises**: Even a formally valid argument may be flawed if it depends on premises that are not true. Often, it is the unstated premises of an argument that are false or inadequately supported.

- Many have suggested that the presence of extreme poverty and oppression in the world makes it more likely that terrorism will take root. But that just doesn't square with the facts; the vast majority of the September 11th terrorists and the Al Qaeda leadership did not come from backgrounds of extreme hardship. Some, including Osama bin Laden, were among the most privileged members of Saudi Arabian society.

The missing or unacknowledged premise in this argument is that people will always struggle only on behalf of those from their own nationality or social class. In fact, however, history is filled with examples of individuals from one nation or social class who became so involved with the plight of another that they devoted all their energies to fighting for change.

An example like this illustrates just how readily our perceptions of argument are influenced by emotion and ideology. In this case, an entirely appropriate sense of anger and revulsion at the terrorist acts makes it difficult for us to imagine that the terrorists might consider themselves as acting altruistically on behalf of the poor and the oppressed. And maybe most of them do not in fact think of themselves in this way. The only point here is that the fact of someone coming from a privileged background does not in itself preclude the possibility that such a person will act in a way he or she perceives as benefiting the less privileged.

C13. **appeals to nature**: Many arguments implicitly or explicitly make an appeal to nature—the assumption being that if something it is "natural" it is good, and if it is "unnatural" it is bad. But let us reflect on some of the things that have in the past been widely accepted as good on the basis that they represented the natural state for humans. The enslavement of members of one race by the members of another was until the late eighteenth century presumed to be natural. So too (until well into the twentieth century in our society, and in many societies even today) has the subjection of women by men been taken to be natural, and therefore right. Looking further back, anthropologists tell us that unrestricted warfare came naturally to many early members of our species; no doubt we would find it came naturally to us as well were it not for all the unnatural restrictions our society places on activity of that sort.

C14: **post hoc, propter hoc**: The fallacy here is to imagine that if one thing happens after the other, then it will have happened because of the other. (The Latin *post hoc, propter hoc* translates as *after this, because of this*). Here is an example:

- The decline of frog populations throughout the world started to happen just after the thinning of the ozone layer; there has to be a connection!

But there doesn't have to be a connection—as becomes plain if we substitute a different event in the same logical structure:

- The decline of frog populations throughout the world started to happen just after the Montreal Canadiens stopped winning the Stanley Cup with any degree of frequency; there has to be a connection!

In the first case damage from ultraviolet radiation is indeed one possible cause for the decline of frog populations—but scientists are still weighing the evidence, and are far from certain if it is one of several contributing causes, the primary cause, or simply an unrelated event.

⊙ Joining Words

The art of combining correct clauses and sentences logically and coherently is as much dependent on taking the time to think through what we are writing—and how the reader will respond to what we write—as it is on knowledge of correct usage. It is all too easy for most of us to assume that the flow of our thoughts will be as clear to the reader as it is to us. In practical terms this leads to the omission of links in the argument or of joining words that help the reader to see those links. Almost as common is the tendency to give too many or contradictory cues to the reader—a tendency that is often an indication that ideas have not yet been thoroughly thought out. That in itself is nothing to be ashamed of; the key is to be willing to take the time to re-read and revise the work. Every good writer makes at least two and sometimes as many as five or six drafts of any piece of writing before considering it finished. Here are two examples, both taken from early drafts of books published by Broadview Press:

- At the end of World War II there was substantial optimism that the application of Keynesian analysis would lead to economic stability and security. Over the post-war period optimistic rationalism weakened in the face of reality.

- A short report in which you request an increase in your department's budget should be written in the persuasive mode. Most reports, however, do not have persuasion as their main objective. Persuasion, though, will often be one of their secondary objectives.

C15. **too few or too many cues** (see also "Non Sequitur"): The first of these passages gives the reader too few cues. What is the connection between the idea of the first sentence and that of the second? One can figure it out without too much difficulty, but the flow of the argument is briefly interrupted while one does so. The problem is easily solved by the addition of one word to the second sentence:

> *revised*   At the end of World War II there was substantial optimism that the application of Keynesian analysis would lead to economic stability and security. Over the post-war period, however, optimistic rationalism weakened in the face of reality.

The second passage suffers from the opposite problem; the use of *however* and *though* in consecutive sentences gives the reader the sense of twisting back on himself without any clear sense of direction. This sort of difficulty can be removed by rewording or re-arranging the ideas:

> *revised*   A short report in which you request an increase in your department's budget should be written in the persuasive mode. Most reports, however, do not have persuasion as

their main objective. Persuasion will thus be at most a secondary objective.

The following pages list the chief words and expressions used in English to join ideas together, and discuss problems that are often experienced with them.

O Words to Connect Ideas Opposed to Each Other

All these words are used to indicate that the writer is saying two things which seem to go against each other, or are different from each other. For example, in the sentence, *He is very rich, but he is not very happy*, the fact that he is not happy is the reverse of what we might expect of a rich man. The word *but* indicates this opposition of ideas to the reader.

although	nevertheless
but	though
despite	whereas
even if	while
however	yet
in spite of	

● *Although, though*

These words are used to indicate that, within the same sentence, two things that seem to go against each other are being said. *Although* is usually used to introduce subordinate clauses, not phrases.

- Although he has short legs, he can run very quickly.
- Hume and Dr. Johnson, indeed, have a good deal in common, although Hume's attitude towards religion earned him Johnson's scorn.

C16. **although/but**: Be careful not to use both *although* and *but* in the same sentence; one is enough:

needs checking   Although in many African countries the government is not elected by the people, but in Botswana the government is democratically elected.

revised   Although in many African countries the government is not elected by the people, in Botswana the government is democratically elected.

or   In most African countries the government is not elected by the people, but in Botswana the government is democratically elected.

● *But*

This word is usually used in the middle of a sentence to show that the two ideas in the sentence oppose or seem to oppose each other. It is also quite correct, however, to use *but* at the beginning of a sentence, if what one is saying in the sentence forms a complete clause and if the idea of the sentence seems to oppose the idea of the previous sentence. Examples:

- The civilization of ancient Greece produced some of the world's greatest works of art and gave birth to the idea of democracy, but the Greeks also believed in slavery.
- The civilization of Greece produced some of the world's greatest works of art and gave birth to the idea of democracy. But the Greeks also believed in slavery.

C17. **opposing or supporting ideas**: When one is dealing with complex combinations of ideas it is sometimes easy to forget which ideas are in fact in opposition and which in support.

needs checking   Brandy and bourbon, with the most "congenors," have the highest hangover ratings. Red wine is a close second, followed by dark rum, sherry, scotch, rye, beer, white wine, gin, and vodka. Vintage red wines have 15 times as much histamine (it triggers allergic reactions) as white wine, but vintage whites have fewer congenors.

   (The use of *but* is inappropriate here; that whites have both less histamine and fewer congenors is as one would expect; the two facts are both instances of white wines having fewer side effects than reds.)

revised   Brandy and bourbon, with the most "congenors," have the highest hangover ratings. Red wine is a close second, followed by dark rum, sherry, scotch, rye, beer, white wine, gin, and vodka. Vintage red wines also have 15 times as much histamine (it triggers allergic reactions) as white wine does.

C18. **but**: Experienced writers are careful not to use *but* more than once in a single sentence, or in consecutive sentences; they realize that doing so tends to confuse the reader. (It is also unwise to use any combination of *but* and *however* in this way.)

needs checking   Detective Smith said that Ryan had been legally in possession of three handguns and two rifles, but he thought it "incredible" that someone should be allowed to keep ammunition at his home. But he said any change in the firearms law was something which would not be discussed by him.

revised   Detective Smith said that Ryan had been legally in possession of three handguns and two rifles. Smith said he thought it "incredible" that someone should be allowed to keep ammunition at his home, but he would not comment directly on whether there should be a change in the firearms law.

● *Despite*

This word means the same as *although*, but it is used to introduce phrases, not clauses.

- Despite his old age, his mind is active and alert.
  (*Despite his old age* is a phrase; it has no verb.)
- Although he is very old, his mind is active and alert.
  (*Although he is very old* is a clause, with *he* as a subject and *is* as a verb.)
- Despite the rain, she wanted to go out to the park.
- Although it was raining, she wanted to go to the park.

C19. **despite**: Remember not to introduce clauses with *despite*.

needs checking   Despite that the drink tasted very strong, there was very little alcohol in it.

revised   Despite its strong taste, there was very little alcohol in the drink.

or   Although the drink tasted very strong, there was very little alcohol in it.

● *Even if*

This expression is used when one is introducing a clause giving a condition. The word *even* emphasizes that the condition is surprising or unusual. Examples:

- Even if I have to stay up all night, I am determined to finish the job.
  (Staying up all night would be very unusual.)
- Even if Bangladesh doubled its food production, some of its people would still be hungry.
  (Doubling its food production would be very surprising.)

● *However*

When used as a joining word, *however* usually indicates that what one is saying seems to go against what one has said in the previous sentence. It should normally be set off by commas when used in this way:

- The country suffered greatly during the three-year drought. This year, however, the rains have been heavy.

C20. **however:** *However* should not be used to combine ideas within one sentence, unless a semicolon is used.

needs checking	Hitler attempted to conquer the Soviet Union however he was defeated.
revised	Hitler attempted to conquer the Soviet Union; however, he was defeated.
or	Hitler attempted to conquer the Soviet Union. However, he was defeated.
or	Hitler attempted to conquer the Soviet Union but he was defeated.
needs checking	There will not be regular mail pick-up from boxes this Friday, however regular mail pick-up will resume Monday.
revised	There will not be regular mail pick-up from boxes this Friday, but regular mail pick-up will resume Monday.
or	There will not be regular mail pick-up from boxes this Friday. However, regular mail pick-up will resume Monday.

(Note that *however* in the sense of *to whatever
extent* is an adverb, and does not need to be set
off by commas. *However tired we are, we must
finish the job tonight.*)

● *Nevertheless*

C21. Like *however*, *nevertheless* is normally used to show that the
idea of one sentence seems to go against the idea of the previous sentence. It should not be used to join two clauses into one sentence.
Example:

- According to the known laws of physics it is not possible to
  walk on water. Nevertheless, this is what the Bible claims Jesus
  did.

Additional Material Online
Exercises on joining words may be found at
sites.broadviewpress.com/writing.
Click on **Exercises** and go to
"Putting Ideas Together."

● *Whereas*

This word is commonly used when one is comparing two things and
showing how they differ. Like *although*, it must begin a subordinate
clause, and may be used either at the beginning or in the middle of
a sentence. Examples:

- Whereas the stereotypical American is usually thought of as
  being loud and confident, Canadians are typically characterized as being quieter and less sure of themselves.
- The stereotypical American is usually thought of as being loud
  and confident, whereas Canadians are typically characterized
  as being quieter and less sure of themselves.

C22. **whereas**: Any sentence that uses *whereas* must have at least two
clauses—a subordinate clause beginning with *whereas* and a main
clause.

needs checking In "The Rain Horse" a young person feels unhappy when he returns to his old home. Whereas in "The Ice Palace" a young person feels unhappy when she leaves home for the first time.

revised In "The Rain Horse" a young person feels unhappy when he returns to his old home, whereas in "The Ice Palace" a young person feels unhappy when she leaves home for the first time.

● *While*

C23. **while:** *While* can be used in the same way as *although*. If there is any chance of confusion with the other meanings of *while*, however, it is better to use *although* in such circumstances.

needs checking While I support free trade in principle, I think it hurts this industry.

revised Although I support free trade in principle, I think it hurts this industry.

● *Yet*

This word can be used either to refer to time (e.g., *He is not yet here*), or to connect ideas in opposition to each other. When used in this second way, it may introduce another word or a phrase, or a completely new sentence.

- His spear was firm, yet flexible.
- Barthes decries the language of "realism"—the pretense that one can represent on the page life as it really is. Yet it is difficult to see how following his prescriptions for an art of signs that "draw attention to their own arbitrariness" can entirely escape a tendency towards art that calls too much attention to its own surface, even art that is self-indulgent.

C24. **yet:** *Yet*, like the other words in this group, should not be paired with another conjunction in such a way as to create too many twists and turns in the argument.

needs checking Varying the pace, altering the tone, director Joseph Rubens keeps us off balance. Ultimately, though, the pedestrian script catches up with him, yet not before *Sleeping with the Enemy* has made its point.

> (The combination of *yet* and *though* is confusing for the reader.)

revised   Varying the pace, altering the tone, director Joseph Rubens keeps us off balance. Ultimately, the pedestrian script catches up with him, yet not before *Sleeping with the Enemy* has made its point.

O *Words to Join Linked or Supporting Ideas*

also	indeed
and	in fact
as well	moreover
besides	plus
further	similarly
furthermore	so too
in addition	: [colon]
not only ... but also	; [semicolon]

● *Also, as well*

These two are very similar both in meaning and in the way that they are used. It is best not to use *also* to start sentences or paragraphs. Examples:

- He put forward his simplistic credo with enormous conviction. "To do well at school," he assured us, "you must be willing to study. It is also important to eat the right foods, exercise regularly, and get plenty of sleep." All the while, the one thing we all wanted, and none of us had managed to get, was plenty of sex.
- He put forward his simplistic credo with enormous conviction. "To do well at school," he assured us, "you must be willing to study. It is important as well to eat the right foods, exercise regularly, and get plenty of sleep." All the while, the one thing we all wanted, and none of us had managed to get, was plenty of sex.

C25. **also:** *Also* should not be used in the way that we often use *and*—to join two clauses together into one sentence.

needs checking	We performed the experiment with the beaker half full also we repeated it with the beaker empty.
revised	We performed the experiment with the beaker half full, and we repeated it with the beaker empty.
or	We performed the experiment with the beaker half full. We also repeated it with the beaker empty.

● *And*

C26. **and:** If this word appears more than once in the same sentence, it's worth stopping to ask if it would not be better to start a new sentence. Usually the answer will be yes.

needs checking	All my family attended the celebration and most of my friends were there and we enjoyed ourselves thoroughly.
revised	All my family attended the celebration, and most of my friends were there, too. We enjoyed ourselves thoroughly.

C27. **as ... as:** When making comparisons one may use the *as ... as* combination or use a comparative adjective with *than*. But the two should not be combined.

needs checking	Recent studies indicate that the average smoker is three times as likely to develop cancer than his non-smoking counterpart.
revised	Recent studies indicate that the average smoker is three times more likely to develop cancer than is his non-smoking counterpart.

C28. **as well:** To avoid repetition, do not use *as well* in combination with *both*.

needs checking	This method should be rejected, both because it is very expensive as well as because it is inefficient.
revised	This method should be rejected, both because it is very expensive and because it is inefficient.

● *In addition, further, furthermore, moreover*

All of these are commonly used to show that what the writer is saying gives additional support to an earlier statement she has made. An example:

- It was easy to see why many countries, despite their intense dislike of apartheid, still traded with South Africa. For one thing, it was the richest country in Africa. Many of its resources, moreover, were of strategic importance.

Notice that all four expressions are often used after sentences that begin with words such as *for one thing* or *first.*

● *Indeed, in fact*

Both of these are used to indicate that what the writer is saying is a restatement or elaboration of the idea he has expressed in the previous sentence. Notice that a colon or semicolon may also be used to show this. Examples:

- Asia is the world's most populous continent. In fact, more people live there than on all the other continents combined.
- Asia is the world's most populous continent: more people live there than on all the other continents combined.

● *Not only ... but also*

C29. **not only ... but also:** This combination is used to join two pieces of supporting evidence in an argument. The combination can help to create balanced, rhythmic writing, but if it is to do so it must be used carefully. Notice that it is not necessary to use *but also* in all cases, but that if the phrase is omitted a semicolon is normally required in order to avoid a run-on sentence.

needs checking	Not only was Nirvana a commercial success, it was also among the first grunge bands to achieve musical respectability.
revised	Not only was Nirvana a commercial success; it was also among the first grunge bands to achieve musical respectability.

or   Nirvana was not only a commercial success, but also a critical one; it was among the first grunge bands to achieve musical respectability.

● *Plus*

C30. **plus:** Do not use this word in the same way as *and* or *as well.*

needs checking   For one thing, the council did not much like the design for the proposed new City Hall. Plus, there was not enough money available to build it that year.

revised   For one thing, the council did not much like the design for the proposed new City Hall. As well, there was not enough money available to build it that year.

O *Words Used to Introduce Causes or Reasons*

Relationships of cause and effect are at the heart of many arguments. It is common to experience some difficulty at first in understanding such relationships clearly. The discussion below of the word *because* may be helpful in this respect. To begin with, though, here is a list of words that are used to introduce causes or reasons:

as
as a result of
because
due to
for
on account of
since

● *As*

This word can be used either to show the relationship between two events in time, or to indicate that one event is the cause of another. This sometimes leaves room for confusion about meaning (ambiguity). The following sentence is a good example:

• As he was riding on the wrong side of the road, he was hit by a car.

This can mean either *When he was riding on the wrong side of the road* ... or *Because he was riding on the wrong side of the road* ....

Unless the writer is absolutely certain that the meaning is clear, it may be better to use *while* or *when* instead of *as* to indicate relationships in time, and *because* instead of *as* to indicate relationships of cause and effect.

● *Because*

This word creates many problems for writers. The first thing to remember is that any group of words introduced with *because* must state a cause or reason. It must not state a result or an example.

C31. **because:** In the following sentences, *because* has been wrongly used:

needs checking   The wind was blowing because the leaves were moving to and fro.

needs checking   He had been struck by a car because he lay bleeding in the road.

A moment's reflection leads to the realization that both of these sentences are the wrong way round. The movement of the leaves is the result of the blowing of the wind, and the man's bleeding is the result of his having been hit. When the sentences are turned around, they become correct:

revised   The leaves were moving to and fro because the wind was blowing.

revised   He lay bleeding on the road because he had been struck by a car.

What leads many people to make mistakes like these is the sort of question that begins, *How do you know that...* or *Prove that...* or *Show that....* The person who is asked, "How do you know that the wind is blowing?" is likely to answer wrongly, "The wind is blowing because the leaves are moving to and fro." What he really means is, "I know the wind is blowing because I see the leaves moving to and fro." That answer is quite correct, since here the seeing is the cause of the knowing. Similarly, someone who is asked to show that the man in a newspaper story had been hit by a car might answer wrongly, "He had been struck by a car because he lay bleeding in the road." What he really means is, "I know that he had been struck by a car because I read that he lay bleeding in the road." It is of course awkward to use a lot of phrases such as *I know that* and *I see that*. Here are some easier and better ways of answering such questions:

- The movement of the trees shows that the wind is blowing.
- The fact that the leaves are moving proves that the wind is blowing.
- Since the man lay bleeding in the road, it seems likely that he had been hit by a car.

C32. **because**: *Because* is also often used incorrectly to introduce examples.

Look carefully at the following sentences:

needs checking   The Suharto regime detained people in jail for long periods without ever bringing them to trial because it had little respect for the law.

needs checking   In the story "The Hero," Dora feels sorry for Julius because she sheds tears when he is expelled from school.

In these sentences the source of confusion might not be immediately clear. If we ask ourselves whether the regime's actions caused it to have little respect for the law, however, we realize that the answer is no. Are Dora's tears a cause of her feeling sorry for Julius? Again, no. It might be a result of her feeling sorry, or an example chosen to show that she feels sorry, but it is certainly not a cause. Again, it is possible to correct these sentences as we did the ones above—by reversing the order of the ideas. But this might not always be an appropriate solution to the problem, particularly if what the writer is trying to show is an example or an illustration rather than a relationship of cause and effect. If, for example, one had been asked, "How do you know that Dora feels sorry for Julius?" or told to "Show that the Suharto regime had little respect for the law," one would not normally want to answer using *because*. Here are various ways of dealing with such difficulties:

- Dora feels sorry for Julius when he is expelled; that is made clear when she sheds tears for him.
- It is clear that Dora feels sorry for Julius, since she sheds tears for him.
- We can see from the fact that Dora sheds tears for Julius that she feels sorry for him.

- The fact that the Suharto regime in Indonesia detained people for long periods without ever bringing them to trial shows that it had little respect for the law.
- The Suharto regime in Indonesia showed little respect for the law. It detained people for long periods, for example, without ever bringing them to trial.
- The Suharto regime in Indonesia had little respect for the law; it detained people for long periods without ever bringing them to trial.

Of all these examples the last is perhaps the best, since it is the most succinct.

C33. **because**: It is best not to use *because* when listing several reasons for something; otherwise the writer gives the reader the impression that the first reason given is to be the only reason. The reader will then be surprised when others are mentioned.

needs checking He was happy because it was Friday. He was also happy because his team had won the game that morning and he had scored the winning goal. Finally, he was happy because he had done well on his exams.

revised He was happy for several reasons: it was Friday, he had scored the winning goal for his team that morning, and he had done well on his exams.

needs checking Frederick was able to enjoy such success because he was adroit at waiting for the right opportunity, and seizing it when it was handed him. He was also successful because he created a military machine that had no equal.

revised One reason Frederick was able to enjoy such success was that he was adroit at waiting for the right opportunity, and seizing it when it was handed him. But none of this would have been possible had he not also created a military machine that had no equal.

C34. **because**: Some people like to answer *How ...?* questions by using *because*. Instead, the word *by* should be used.

needs checking How did she help him? She helped him because she lent him some money.

revised How did she help him? She helped him by lending him some money.

● *Due to*

C35. **due to:** *Due* is an adjective and therefore should always modify a noun (as in the common phrase *with all due respect*). When followed by *to* it can suggest a causal relationship, but the word *due* must in that case refer to the previous noun:

- The team's success is due to hard work.
  (*Due* refers to the noun *success.*)

It is not a good idea to begin a sentence with a phrase such as *Due to unexpected circumstances ...* or *Due to the fact that....* To avoid such difficulties it is best to use *because.*

needs checking	Due to the sudden resignation of our sales manager, the marketing director will take on additional responsibility for a short time.
revised	Because our sales manager has resigned suddenly, the marketing director will take on additional responsibility for a short time.

● *Since*

When used to introduce causes or reasons (rather than as a time word) *since* is used in essentially the same way as *because.*

O *Words Used to Introduce Results or Conclusions*

accordingly	therefore
as a result	thus
consequently	to sum up
hence	to summarize
in conclusion	in consequence
in sum	so
it follows that ...	

● *As a result, hence*

Both of these are used to show that the idea being talked about in one sentence follows from, or is the result of, what was spoken of in the previous sentence.

- His car ran out of gas. As a result, he was late for his appointment.
- His car ran out of gas. Hence, he was late for his appointment.

Notice the difference between these two and words such as *because* and *since*; we would say *Because* (or *since*) *his car ran out of gas, he was late for the appointment.*

C36. **hence:** Hence should not be used to join two clauses into one sentence, or to join words or phrases.

needs checking	Her phone is out of order hence it will be impossible to contact her.
revised	Her phone is out of order. Hence, it will be impossible to contact her.
needs checking	It is not the film but the advertising that is exploitative, hence pornographic.
revised	It is not the film but the advertising that is exploitative, and hence pornographic.

● So

This word may be used to introduce results when one wants to mention both cause and result in the same sentence (e.g., *Her phone is out of order, so it will be impossible to contact her*). It is usually best not to use *so* to begin a sentence, in order to avoid writing sentence fragments.

C37. **so:** If *so* is used, *because* is not needed, and vice versa. One of the two is enough.

needs checking	Because he was tired, so he went to bed early.
revised	Because he was tired, he went to bed early.
or	He was tired, so he went to bed early.

● Therefore

C38. **therefore:** *Therefore* should not be used to join two clauses into one sentence.

needs checking	Training is perceived as good, therefore the payment of a $30 million subsidy to McDonald's can be made to look like a benign act.

revised	Training is perceived as good; therefore the payment of a $30 million subsidy to McDonald's can be made to look like a benign act.

O *Words Used to Express Purpose*

in order to	so that
in such a way as to	so as to

● *So that*

C39. **so that:** When used beside each other (see also *so ... that* below) these two words show purpose; they indicate that we will be told why an action was taken. Examples:

- He sent the parcel early so that it would arrive before Christmas.
- She wants to see you so that she can ask you a question.

The words *such that* should never be used in this way to indicate purpose.

needs checking	The doctor will give you some medicine such that you will be cured.
revised	The doctor will give you some medicine so that you will be cured.
needs checking	Fold the paper such that it forms a triangle.
revised	Fold the paper so that it forms a triangle.
or	Fold the paper in such a way that it forms a triangle.

O *Words Used to Introduce Examples*

for example	such as
for instance	: [colon]
in that	

● *For example, for instance, such as*

The three expressions are used differently, even though they all introduce examples. *Such as* is used to introduce a single word or short phrase. It always relates to a plural noun that has appeared just before it.

- Crops such as tea and rice require a great deal of water.
  (Here *such as* relates to the noun *crops*.)
- Several African peoples, such as the Yoruba of Nigeria and the
  Makonde of Tanzania, attach a special ceremonial importance
  to masks.
  (*Such as* relates to *peoples*.)

For example and *for instance*, on the other hand, are complete phrases in themselves, and are normally set off by commas. Each is used to show that the entire sentence in which it appears gives an example of a statement made in the previous sentence. Examples:

- Some crops require a great deal of water. Tea, for example, requires an annual rainfall of at least 1500 mm.
- Several African peoples attach a special ceremonial importance to masks. The Yoruba and the Makonde, for example, both believe that spirits enter the bodies of those who wear certain masks.
- Tornadoes are not only a Midwestern United States phenomenon. In 1983, for instance, more than 30 people were injured by a tornado in Los Angeles, California.

C40. **for example, for instance:** *For example* and *for instance* should not be used to introduce phrases that give examples. In such situations use *such as* instead.

needs checking   In certain months of the year, for example July and August, El Paso, Texas, receives most of its rainfall.

revised   In certain months of the year, such as July and August, El Paso, Texas, receives most of its rainfall.

or   In certain months of the year El Paso, Texas, receives most of its rainfall.

● *In that*

C41. **in that:** Do not confuse with *in the way that*.

needs checking   He is cruel in the way that he treats his wife harshly.
revised   He is cruel in that he treats his wife harshly.
or   He is cruel in the way that he treats his wife.

● *Such as*

C42. **such as**: The addition of *and others* at the end of a phrase beginning with *such as* is redundant.

needs checking   In contrast to this perspective, sociological studies of ethnicity written from the "class" perspective (such as Benarez and Lee's 2014 paper, Chang's 2012 monograph, and others) have argued that ethnic inequality is only a special class of inequality in general.

revised   In contrast to this perspective, sociological studies of ethnicity written from the "class" perspective (such as Benarez and Lee's 2014 paper, and Chang's 2012 monograph) have argued that ethnic inequality is only a special class of inequality in general.

O *Words Used to Indicate Alternatives*

either ... or	otherwise
if only	rather than
instead, instead of	unless
in that case	whether ... or
neither ... nor	

● *If only*

This expression is normally used when we wish that something would happen, or were true, but it clearly will not happen, or is not true.

- If only he were here, he would know what to do.
  (This indicates that he is not here.)
- "If only there were thirty hours in a day ...," she kept saying.

● *In that case*

This expression is used when we wish to explain what will happen if the thing spoken of in the previous sentence happens, or turns out to be true. Examples:

- He may arrive before six o'clock. In that case we can all go out to dinner.
- It is quite possible that many people will dislike the new law. In that case the government may decide to change it.

Do not confuse *in that case* with *otherwise*, which is used in the reverse situation (i.e., when one wishes to explain what will happen if the thing spoken of in the previous sentence does not happen, or turns out to be false).

● *Otherwise*

This word has two meanings. The first is *in other ways* (e.g., *I have a slight toothache. Otherwise I am healthy*). The second meaning can sometimes cause confusion: *otherwise* used to mean *if not*. Here the word is used when we want to talk about what will or might happen if the thing spoken of in the previous sentence does not happen. Examples:

- I will have to start immediately. Otherwise, I will not finish in time.
  (This is the same as saying, *If I do not start now, I will not finish in time.*)
- The general decided to retreat. Otherwise, he believed, all his troops would be killed.
  (This is the same as saying, *The general believed that if he decided not to retreat, all his troops would be killed.*)
- You must pay me for the car before Friday. Otherwise, I will offer it to someone else.
  (i.e., *If you do not pay me for the car before Friday, I will offer it to someone else.*)

C43. **otherwise**: When used to mean *if not*, *otherwise* should normally be used to start a new sentence. It should not be used in the middle of a sentence to join two clauses.

needs checking   I may meet you at the party tonight, otherwise I will see you tomorrow.

revised   I may meet you at the party tonight. Otherwise, I will see you tomorrow.

O *Words Used to Show Degree or Extent*

for the most part	to some extent
so ... that	too ... for ... to
such ... that	to some degree
to a certain extent	

● *So ... that*

C44. **so ... that**: When separated from each other by an adjective or adverb, these two words express degree or extent, answering questions such as *How far ...?*, *How big ...?*, *How much ...?* (Grammatically, *so* in these contexts introduces adjectives.) Examples:

- How fat is he? He is so fat that he cannot see his feet.
- How large is Texas? It is so large that you need several days to drive across it.

So ... that is the only combination of words that can be used in this way; it is wrong to say *very fat that ...* or *too large that*, just as it is wrong to leave out the word *so* and simply use *that* in such sentences.

needs checking	She was very late for dinner that there was no food left for her.
revised	She was so late for dinner that there was no food left for her.
needs checking	Dominic speaks quickly that it is often difficult to understand him.
revised	Dominic speaks so quickly that it is often difficult to understand him.

● *Such ... that*

C45. **such ... that**: Like *so ... that*, the expression *such ... that* is used to express degree or extent, answering questions such as, *How big ...?*, *How long ...?*, *How fast ...?* Grammatically, *such* in these contexts introduces noun phrases. Notice the difference in the way *so ... that* and *such ... that* are used.

- How far is it? It is such a long way that you would never be able to get there walking.

- It is so far that you would never be able to reach there walking.
- How fat is he? He is such a fat man that his trousers need to be made specially for him.
- He is so fat that his trousers need to be made specially for him.

The difference between the two is of course that only one word is normally used between *so* and *that*, whereas two or three words (usually an article, an adjective, and a noun) are used between *such* and *that*. Be careful not to confuse the two, or to leave out *such*.

needs checking   It was a hot day that nobody could stay outside for long.
revised   It was such a hot day that nobody could stay outside for long.

O *That* and *Which*

To understand when to use *that* and when to use *which* (according to traditional grammatical principles), one must first understand the difference between a restrictive clause and a non-restrictive clause (see also pages 516–18). A restrictive clause restricts the application of the noun it modifies. Here is an example:

- The horse that was injured yesterday should recover.

Here the clause *that was injured yesterday* restricts the meaning of the subject of the sentence—*horse*—to a particular horse. The clause helps to define the subject more narrowly. A non-restrictive clause does not restrict the application of the noun it modifies; instead it tells us more about the subject. Again, here is an example:

- The injured horse, which was the favourite to win today's race, should recover in time for the Derby.

Here the clause *which was the favourite to win today's race* tells us more about the horse but is not necessary to its definition. Notice that the non-restrictive clause is set off by commas, while the restrictive clause follows on directly after the noun it describes, with no intervening comma. As these examples illustrate, *that* is typically used with restrictive clauses, *which* with non-restrictive clauses.

C46. **that/which**: Students have long been taught that it is correct to use *that* in restrictive clauses and *which* in non-restrictive clauses.

needs checking   The only store which sells this brand is now closed.

revised   The only store that sells this brand is now closed.

needs checking   The position which Marx adopted owed much to the philosophy of Hegel.

revised   The position that Marx adopted owed much to the philosophy of Hegel.

Although the use of the word *which* in any restrictive clause provokes a violent reaction among some English instructors, there are clearly instances in which one is quite justified in using *which* in this way. Such is the case when the writer is already using at least one *that* in the sentence:

needs checking   He told me that the radio that he had bought was defective.

revised   He told me that the radio which he had bought was defective.

Better yet, in many cases, is to avoid the use of a second relative pronoun by rephrasing:

revised   He told me that the radio he had bought was defective.

Indeed, instructors who object to *which* point out that rephrasing can often make the sentence shorter and crisper:

needs checking   The ending, which comes as a surprise to most readers, is profoundly unsettling.

revised   The ending is both surprising and unsettling.

needs checking   The 2008 campaign, which had been carefully planned, was an enormous success.

revised   The carefully planned 2008 campaign was an enormous success.

But *which* is not a special case in this regard. *That*, *who*, and *whose* can often be fruitfully removed in the same way:

needs checking   The surplus that we now project for 2017 will probably be exceeded in 2018.

revised   The projected 2017 surplus will probably be exceeded in 2018.

needs checking   Eisenhower hired as his personal driver a woman who
turned into a long-term friend.

revised   Eisenhower and his driver became close friends.

The vice, then, is not *which* per se, but wordiness in general.
Those who focus their attention on the one word and rail that
"witches ride on broomsticks" might do better to treat the excessive
use of *which* as a symptom of a much broader disease.

Interestingly, the rule about *that* and *which* seems to be a relatively recent invention, dreamt up by Henry and Francis Fowler and
first propounded in their book *The King's English* in 1906. In the
words of Joseph M. Williams, they felt

> the random variation between *that* and *which* in restrictive
> clauses [to be] messy, so they simply asserted that henceforth
> writers should (with some exceptions) limit *which* to non-
> restrictive clauses. (*Style: Ten Lessons in Clarity and Grace*, New York,
> Longman, 2000, 24–25)

Many instructors today are as anxious as were the Fowlers to
limit the messiness in English. But, as Robert M. Martin fairly
observes, it is "hard to imagine real contexts in which observation
of the *that/which* distinction would result in better communication"
(*Dalhousie Review*, Spring 2003, 19). Again, the better reason for
observing the distinction is that doing so may help to reduce wordiness—not that the distinction itself rests on a particularly strong
foundation.

O Words Used to Make Comparisons

along the same lines	likewise
by comparison	on the one hand ...
in contrast	... on the other hand
in the same way	similarly

O *Other Joining Words and Expressions*

as illustrated above/below	in other words
as mentioned above/below	in the event of
as we can see/we can see that	in light of
assuming that	in this respect/in some respects
as shown in the diagram	above/below
in that	firstly/in the first place
these findings indicate that	secondly/in the second place
to begin with	for one thing
whereby	

⊙ Sentence Combining

As they become more and more skilled, writers become more adept at manipulating and varying the structures of their sentences. Such flexibility is a goal all serious writers should aspire to reach, and one of the best ways to achieve it is to engage in a process called sentence combining. As a means of helping students develop facility with more mature sentence structures, this technique goes back to the writing classrooms of the nineteenth century. But it wasn't until the 1960s that sentence combining gained a substantial following among writing teachers, largely because Noam Chomsky's new, highly influential linguistic theory, transformational-generative grammar, appeared to provide a theoretical rationale for this writing exercise. Subsequent research into the effectiveness of sentence combining in improving the fluency and maturity of developing writers' sentence structures gave the technique firm support (Connors 103–07). Since then, newer alternatives to and further development of Chomsky's grammar may also give some insight into the basis for the efficacy of sentence combining (Myers 611–12). But since it works, many are content to leave theoretical discussion to the specialists and simply take advantage of this useful practice.

In its most elementary practice, writers join two or more simple sentences, called "kernels," into a longer sentence or group of sentences. Kernels can be kept as they are and joined with conjunctions or conjunctive adverbs, or they can be embedded into other kernels, a process that often involves shortening the inserted structures. The corollary to combining short sentences is taking apart long sentences in order to examine how they were put together in the first place. Writers can analyze their own sentences in this way as well as those of other, admired authors, becoming conversant with the many options present whenever a writer considers how to express and even create a thought with words. Together, these combining and analyzing procedures are simple but effective. Mastering them confers an important component of the stylistic fluency described in the "Writing Process" chapter of this guide; writers gain greater conscious control over and facility with their sentence structures and sentence variety, become better able to avoid problems like wordiness and repetition, and find elegance and strategic emphasis easier to achieve. Research into writing practices has shown that when unskilled writers revise a draft, they tend to focus exclusively on deleting and changing single words and phrases (Sommers 381–82). What these basic writers often fail to do is reorder and add to their initial material (386); experienced writers, on the other hand, use all of these revision techniques, especially the latter two. Rewriting for them is an entire reworking and rethinking of their arguments (see pages 74–78 of this book for more advice in this regard). At the level of sentence style, then, inexperienced writers would do well to include in their studies practice in the reordering of sentences. The work of sentence combining, "de-combining," and recombining affords just such practice.

For many students, another plus of sentence combining and its offshoots is that they don't require an extensive knowledge of grammatical terminology. The exercises work on writers' intuitive understanding of language structures and help practitioners build an increased "feel" for them, which translates into yet another benefit: the ability to avoid certain kinds of grammatical sentence errors. For example, because some sentence combining exercises require kernels to be shortened and embedded as modifiers into other sentences, practice makes it easier to spot dangling constructions and other modifier errors (see as well the discussion on dangling constructions starting on page 138). Working with kernels, which are always short but full sentences, helps students internalize what constitutes a full sentence or main clause and so avoid sentence fragments, run-ons, and comma splices (see also pages 507–08). Developing writers are also better able to recognize and write balanced, parallel structures (see pages 69–71 and 200–04) after gaining greater awareness of sentence constituents.

A key ability of more experienced writers is reading well. Writers who are also good readers are able to see their own work as a reader would see it and allow that crucial insight to guide their revisions. Combining kernels and reconfiguring the results a few times gives writers more practice in reading at the level of the sentence, and because the process generates a variety of arrangements of the same words, students have an opportunity to compare them and decide which of the structures are most effective and why. It's important to note, though, that sentence combining alone cannot confer the ability to judge such matters well. Enthusiastic combining sessions can produce all manner of unfortunate sentences; an important complementary exercise is analysis both of sentences that work well and of ones that work less well. Those that work well may of course be used as models. Practice in analyzing the work of others also yields another benefit: greater ease in reading more sophisticated and difficult texts. Along the way, students can also examine the elements that make up an individual author's style. All told, diligent sentence "de-combining" and recombining leads to better reading skills, and better reading leads to better writing.

These exercises in sentence manipulation and analysis have been shown to be particularly useful for students who are learning to write in English as an additional language. The kernels and guidelines for combining them in various ways contain both explicit and implicit instructions on how English sentences are structured and on which words can combine with others in which ways (Myers 615–17). All of this information provides EAL students with useful models for their own writing.

For a closer look at sentence combining in action, see the books by William Strong and the articles by Sharon A. Myers, and Glenn J. Broadhead and James A. Berlin, and Charles R. Cooper listed in Works Cited at the end of this chapter; these works inform what follows.

O *Combining*

● *Joining Kernels*

One of the simplest ways to combine kernel sentences is to join them with a connecting word or phrase. Deciding on the best connector, of course, depends on the relationship among the kernels' ideas; see the section on joining words (276–301) for advice on appropriate choices.

Consider the following kernels:

1) My ruse was sloppy.
2) My ruse deceived everyone.

Two noticeable features of a list of kernels are their choppiness of style and their tendency towards unnecessary repetition of words and phrases. Two of the tasks of sentence combining, consequently, are to create more fluent structures out of the kernel lists and to avoid wordiness. An obvious strategy in the case of the kernels above is to use a pronoun to replace one of the "my ruse" phrases. Joining the kernels will take care of the choppiness. Because the second kernel reverses the expectations raised by the first, a helpful joining word may be used to signal the contrast between the two. Here are some options for joining them.

A coordinating conjunction:

My ruse was sloppy, but it deceived everyone.

A subordinating conjunction (note that this conjunction does join the kernels despite its position before one of the kernels rather than between the two):

Even though my ruse was sloppy, it deceived everyone.

A conjunctive adverb:

My ruse was sloppy; nevertheless, it deceived everyone.

In some cases, word order can be rearranged somewhat, as in the following example that joins the kernels with the subordinating conjunction "though":

Sloppy though my ruse was, it deceived everyone.

If a pair of kernels consists of linked or supporting ideas, several connecting words would be suitable (see, for examples, those listed on pages 284–87), but it might also be stylistically effective to join the kernels with only a mark of punctuation. This option makes for a punchier sentence that emphasizes the closeness of relationship between the joined ideas. Consider the following kernels:

1) My ruse was brilliant.
2) My ruse deceived everyone.

Joined with a conjunction, the kernels make a sentence that is satisfactory:

My ruse was brilliant, and it deceived everyone.

Using only a semicolon as a connector, however, makes a more dramatic alternative:

My ruse was brilliant; it deceived everyone.

Using a dash instead heightens the drama even further:

My ruse was brilliant—it deceived everyone.

If one kernel illustrates, specifies, or provides an explanation for the other, a colon is an appropriate connector:

1) She had only one thing to say.
2) Don't touch the chocolate.

She had only one thing to say: don't touch the chocolate.

● *Embedding Kernels*

Structurally more complex sentences can be built by embedding one kernel within another. The embedded kernel can stay whole or substantially so, or parts of it can be deleted to create phrases and even single words for insertion into what then becomes the sentence's main kernel.

○ WHOLE CLAUSES EMBEDDED WITH PUNCTUATION

Certain marks of punctuation—paired dashes and parentheses, for example—allow for an entire kernel to be embedded in another unchanged.

1) The secret to Edith's success is her stubbornness.
2) The secret cannot be denied.

The secret to Edith's success—it cannot be denied—is her stubbornness.

1) She hung on to the bitter end.
2) She is so very stubborn.

She hung on (she is so very stubborn) to the bitter end.

O RELATIVE CLAUSES

An embedded kernel left whole can also take the form of a relative clause, that is, an adjective clause introduced by a relative pronoun (see page 96). Like other pronouns, relative pronouns eliminate some repetition of words or phrases by substituting for them. Below are examples of embedded relative clauses using the relative pronouns *that, who, which, where,* and *when.*

1) The music is the best music of all.
2) The music plays only in Chester's head.

The music that plays only in Chester's head is the best music of all.

Note that in the next two examples, which involve the relative pronoun *who,* the kernel that will become the relative clause in the combined sentence indicates which form, *who* or *whom,* the pronoun should take. In the first example, the pronoun takes the place of the kernel's subject and so takes the subject form, *who.* In the second, the pronoun takes the place of the kernel's object and so takes the object form *whom.* Here is one instance of the ways in which sentence combining practice can help writers master some grammatical rules.

1) Lewis writes the best books.
2) Lewis is despicable.

Lewis, who is despicable, writes the best books.

1) Lewis writes the best books.
2) I despise Lewis.

Lewis, whom I despise, writes the best books.

1) Lewis is despised by all.
2) Lewis's books are the best.

Lewis, whose books are the best, is despised by all.

1) That book is everyone's favourite.
2) No one can understand that book.

That book, which no one can understand, is everyone's favourite.

1) Frieda's thoughts turned to evil at a precise moment.
2) No one knows the precise moment.

No one knows the precise moment when Frieda's thoughts turned to evil.

1) She left him in the attic.
2) No one ever goes to the attic.

She left him in the attic, where no one ever goes.

● *Abbreviated Kernels Joined as Absolute Phrases*

Absolute phrases are shortened kernels that contain nouns and modifiers but no main verb (see page 100 for a definition of verbs). Absolutes often modify entire sentences and attach to them with commas.

1) Willard is an impatient man.
2) The experiment went badly.

Willard being an impatient man, the experiment went badly.

1) No one waited for the banana flambé.
2) The party was already wrecked by Shirley's antics.

The party already wrecked by Shirley's antics, no one waited for the banana flambé.

● *Abbreviated Kernels Embedded as Verb and Noun Phrases*

Kernels can be abbreviated to phrases or even single words before being inserted into other kernels. When the ideas of paired kernels have an equal, independent status, they can be shortened to phrases and joined with coordinating conjunctions.

○ NOUN PHRASE

    1) Dolores always cries at *Casablanca*.

    2) Stan always cries at *Casablanca*.

    Dolores and Stan always cry at *Casablanca*.

○ VERB PHRASE

    1) Morton sang "Danny Boy."

    2) Morton expected our applause.

    Morton sang "Danny Boy" and expected our applause.

● *Abbreviated Kernels Embedded as Modifiers*

Shortened kernels can also serve as various kinds of modifiers, including adjectives, adverbs, prepositional phrases, past and present participles, infinitive phrases, and appositives.

○ KERNELS EMBEDDED AS SINGLE-WORD ADJECTIVES

    1) Herman's handshake was floppy.

    2) Herman's handshake irritated his in-laws.

    Herman's floppy handshake irritated his in-laws.

○ KERNELS EMBEDDED AS SINGLE-WORD ADVERBS

    1) Estelle was doubtful.

    2) Estelle frowned at the chocolate mousse bombe.

    Estelle frowned doubtfully at the chocolate mousse bombe.

○ KERNELS EMBEDDED AS PREPOSITIONAL PHRASES

    1) The glove looked suspiciously familiar.

    2) The glove was in the hallway.

    The glove in the hallway looked suspiciously familiar.

    1) Terrence threw Mabel's letter.

    2) Mabel's letter landed on the fire.

    Terrence threw Mabel's letter on the fire.

○ KERNELS EMBEDDED AS PRESENT PARTICIPLES

    1) Walter paddled doggedly.
    2) Walter finished another lap of the pool.

    Paddling doggedly, Walter finished another lap of the pool.

○ KERNELS EMBEDDED AS PAST PARTICIPLES

    1) Rita's insight was wrapped in obscurity.
    2) Rita's insight went unnoticed.

    Rita's insight, wrapped in obscurity, went unnoticed.

○ KERNELS EMBEDDED AS INFINITIVE PHRASES

    1) They went home.
    2) They reflected on their bad behaviour.

    They went home to reflect on their bad behaviour.

○ KERNELS EMBEDDED AS APPOSITIVES

    1) Carl is a wily tactician.
    2) Carl always wins at checkers.

    A wily tactician, Carl always wins at checkers.

○ *Combining and Recombining*

For building effective revision practices, exercises in recombining kernels work very well. The idea is to combine the same list of kernels into several combinations and compare the results. An important decision in any combination is which kernel will form the main clause or clauses of the sentence. The rule of thumb is that the main idea should rest in the main clause. Varying the way the kernels are combined can change the emphasis or even the fundamental idea of a sentence. Consider the following kernels:

    1) I love ice cream.
    2) I don't eat ice cream often.

The two could be given equivalent status and joined by a coordinating conjunction or conjunctive adverb into a sentence with two main clauses:

> I love ice cream, but I don't eat it often.

> I love ice cream; however, I don't eat it often.

In combinations such as this, notice that *but* must stay where it is, while *however* is able to move to a variety of spots in the sentence:

> I love ice cream; I don't, however, eat it often.

> I love ice cream; I don't eat it often, however.

Each option is subtly different from the others. Placed at the beginning of its clause, *however* signals an upcoming contrast right away, so readers anticipate some sort of reversal of the first idea. Placed after *I don't*, the transition word interrupts its clause and so emphasizes the idea of not doing something; the shift from the first clause's affirmative statement to the second's negative one is thus immediately more specific than the first sentence's broader signal of contrast. The third sentence delays the transition word until the very end, confronting the readers with a starker contrast between the affirmative and negative statements as their expectations after reading the first clause are suddenly reversed without notice.

Coordinating main clauses is not the only option for these kernels; one clause can be subordinated to the other for still different effects.

> Although I love ice cream, I don't eat it often.

> Although I don't eat it often, I love ice cream.

Each kernel becomes the sole main clause in each of the variations above. In the first, the emphasis is on not eating ice cream, while in the second, the focus is on loving it.

Embedding each kernel as a relative clause achieves a similar effect, but again, there are subtle differences:

> I love ice cream, which I don't eat often.

> I don't often eat ice cream, which I love.

There, the relative clauses feel more like wistful afterthoughts and less like blunt statements of fact (as in the sentences using *although*). Here are still more variations with still different effects:

> I love but don't often eat ice cream.

> I don't often eat my beloved ice cream.

Despite loving ice cream, I don't often eat it.

Despite not often eating it, I love ice cream.

Depending on a writer's rhetorical purposes, any of these sentences would work well in a larger context. Sentence recombining helps writers see what options are available to them so that they can consider which would be preferable.

● *Combining Several Kernels into a Single Sentence*

The next step after the simple combining of pairs of kernels is to work on joining three, four, and even more kernels. Consider the following list of kernels:

1) Clutter is far from causing certain things.
2) Clutter does not make the mind disorganized.
3) Clutter does not make the mind distracted.
4) Clutter does not make the mind distressed.
5) Clutter can foster thinking.
6) The thinking is creative.
7) Clutter can contain order.
8) The order is of a high degree.
9) The order is not visible to observation.
10) The observation is initial.
11) The observation is casual.

The more kernels in a list, the more options there are for combining them, and the more choices a writer must make. Not all possibilities are equally felicitous, however. It is very possible for an excited sentence combiner to produce questionable sentences. Here is one example:

You might say that clutter makes the mind disorganized, that it makes the mind distracted, and that it makes the mind distressed, but clutter is far from having these effects; instead, it can foster thinking in a creative manner, and it can also contain a kind of order that is of a high degree but that is not visible to the first glance of the casual observer.

The sentence above is grammatically correct and makes some interesting substitutions and additions to the original list of kernels, but it is unnecessarily wordy and needn't be so long. The goal of sentence combining is never to write the longest, most complex sentence possible. Good writers vary their sentence lengths and recognize the rhetorical value of short, simple sentences for emphasis. For combining exercises involving more than two kernels, leaving one or more kernels uncombined is always an option. Other stylistic choices that such exercises call for are whether kernels should be joined or embedded, where embedded kernels should be placed within the finished sentence, whether transitions or conjunctions would be effective and which ones would work best, and, importantly, which kernel should become the main clause of a combined sentence. The section on stylistic fluency in this book, starting on page 61, gives some guidance on how to make such choices well. Some writers also find reading sentences out loud helpful, and many solicit the opinions of other readers. But particularly beneficial is taking the time to configure and then reconfigure a list of kernels, and then compare the results. Here are two more arrangements of the kernel list above:

> Clutter, far from making the mind disorganized, distracted, and distressed, can foster creative thinking and, moreover, contain a high degree of order not at first visible to casual observation.

> Clutter seems sure to make the mind disorganized, distracted, and distressed. Not so, however—it can actually foster creative thinking. Even more surprising, it can contain a high degree of order, which casual observation may not at first reveal.

Both of the recombinations above are less wordy than the first try and seem better for that reason. Which of the last two you prefer, however, will likely depend on what context you imagine the passages belonging to. The final combination includes more transitional words and so directs readers more strongly toward conclusions to be drawn from the claims it makes. It is also more casual in tone, largely because of phrases like *seems sure to*, and *not so*, and the use of a dash rather than, say, a semicolon. The middle combination is leaner and gives the impression of a less familiar, perhaps more professional voice behind the words.

● *"De-Combining" and Recombining*

While combining kernels improves a writer's understanding of sentence structure, analyzing a complete sentence into its possible constituent kernels yields even more insights. The practice can clarify certain grammar problems (as in the relative clause examples above that use *who* and *whom*), helping writers to avoid them and, in the process, become better readers of their own work, an important skill that sets experienced writers apart from the less skilled. "De-combining" sentences can also help students become better able to read even difficult texts and more adept at grasping the components that make up the styles of a variety of writers and types of writing.

○ *Help with Some Grammatical Errors: Two More Examples*

● *Dangling Modifiers*

Inexperienced writers sometimes dangle modifiers (see the section beginning on page 138 for more information on dangling constructions). Sentence combining can help writers recognize and so better avoid this common problem. Consider the following sentence:

> While watching an abominable film, even the popcorn tasted vile.

Dividing the sentence into kernels gives the following result:

1) The popcorn tasted vile.
2) _____ watched a film.
3) The film was abominable.

There is an obvious problem with kernel 2; it has no subject. That's what causes it to dangle when combined with the others. Embedded as a modifier, it attaches to the closest noun, *popcorn*, and creates the unintentionally amusing image of popcorn watching a film. Once the problem is clearly laid out in a kernel list, it's easy to see and to fix:

1) The popcorn tasted vile.
2) We watched a film.
3) The film was abominable.

Because we were watching an abominable film, even the popcorn tasted vile.
We were watching an abominable film; even the popcorn
tasted vile.

● Syntactic Ambiguity

Sometimes, unwanted ambiguity in a sentence comes from its syntax, or the arrangement of its words. The following is the title of an
anthology of key philosophical texts:

Enduring Issues in Philosophy

The title is not an entire sentence, but there are nonetheless abbreviated kernels underlying it. Analyzing the title shows that it has two
possible underlying groups of kernels:

1) Philosophy has issues.
2) The issues have endured.

1) Philosophy has issues.
2) People can endure the issues.

It's doubtful that the publisher of that book intends us to read the
second possible meaning of the title, but that reading is nonetheless available. An unambiguous title would combine one of the
pairs of kernels above, presumably the first. Here are two possible
reconfigurations:

Some Enduring Issues in Philosophy
Philosophy's Enduring Issues.

O Help with Reading Challenging Texts

Often, students have difficulty reading the work of authors from
earlier eras simply because the language has changed considerably in
the interval. Some of the challenge comes from changes in vocabulary, of course, for which the best remedy is to consult a good dictionary or glossary of words from the period. But some confusion
can result from unfamiliar sentence structure, too; careful analysis
of some sample sentences into their constituent kernels will, with
practice, help students raise their literacy skills to the point where

such texts no longer pose a problem. Look, for example, at the following passage from Thomas Hobbes's *Leviathan* (16):

> A LAW OF NATURE (*lex naturalis*) is a precept or general rule, found out by reason, by which a man is forbidden to do that which is destructive of his life, or taketh away the means of preserving the same, and to omit that by which he thinketh it may be best preserved. (98)

Here is a possible division of this sentence into kernels:

1) The Latin for "law of nature" is *lex naturalis*.
2) A law of nature is a precept.
3) A law of nature is a general rule.
4) A law of nature is found out by reason.
5) A law of nature forbids a man to do certain things.
6) Some things are destructive of the man's life.
7) Some things take away means.
8) The means are for preserving his life.
9) A law of nature forbids the man to omit certain things.
10) Some things preserve the man's life.
11) The man thinks this.

Recombining these kernels into more contemporary language and, for better understanding, expanding them somewhat can help elucidate Hobbes's meaning.

> A law of nature, which in Latin is called a *lex naturalis*, is a precept or general rule. This kind of law can be discovered by reasoning; that is, the law does not need to be revealed to us by any other agent. A law of nature forbids a person[1] to do anything that would destroy his life or that would take away the means by which he preserves his life. A law of nature also obliges a person to follow any course of action that he thinks will help preserve his life.

The result is perhaps a little more cumbersome than it need be, but it is clear, and the point of this exercise in any case is to understand a challenging passage rather than offer a rewrite of it to a reader.

---

1   In working through the meaning of a passage such as this, we may also need to ask whether the writer intended words such as man to apply only to males, or to all humans. In this case context makes clear that Hobbes intended the latter.

Here is another example, this time a passage from Sonnet 116 by William Shakespeare.

> Let me not to the marriage of true minds
> Admit impediments. Love is not love
> Which alters when it alteration finds,
> Or bends with the remover to remove.
> O, no, it is an ever-fixèd mark
> That looks on tempests and is never shaken;
> It is the star to every wandering bark,
> Whose worth's unknown, although his height be taken.

Part of our potential puzzlement on reading this passage comes again from unfamiliar vocabulary (for example, *remove* means *leave*, not *take away*, and *bark* is a noun meaning *ship*), but the glosses that are now almost always published with Shakespeare's work can help with that. Beyond gaining experience with his words and terms, readers of Shakespeare must gain skill interpreting the structures of his lines of verse. An important first step is to realize that a line does not necessarily constitute a sentence; the periods in the passage above show that it consists of three sentences divided over eight lines. Here is a list of kernels generated from the passage above, with more modern expressions substituted as needed. For ease of analysis, the kernels are grouped according to the sentences they make up, and the kernel that underlies each sentence's main clause or clauses are underlined:

Sentence One

1) <u>Do not let me allow certain things</u>.
2) The things are impediments.
3) The impediments interfere with a marriage.
4) The marriage is between minds.
5) The minds are true.

Sentence Two

1) Certain things can seem like love.
2) <u>These things are not love</u>.
3) One thing changes under a certain circumstance.
4) This thing finds a change (in the one loved).
5) Another thing changes (*bends*) under a certain circumstance.

6) The loved one (*the remover*) goes away.
7) This thing departs (*removes*).

Sentence Three

1) Love is not this thing.
2) <u>Love is a landmark that never moves or changes</u>.
3) The landmark looks at tempests.
4) The landmark is not shaken.
5) <u>Love is a star</u>.
6) The star guides ships.
7) The ships are off course.
8) The star has a worth.
9) The worth is unknown.
10) The star has a height (above the horizon).
11) The height has been measured.

Note that some of the kernels include understood elements that don't appear in the original but that must nonetheless be included in the kernels in order to make them complete. Consider the clause *when it alteration finds*; in order to understand the point of this clause, we need to answer the question *alteration in what*? The line does not directly say what it is that alters, but the context of the rest of the poem, with its focus on the properties of true love, strongly suggests that this hypothetical alteration is in the object of such love.

Once the kernels are carefully written, recombining them yields a paraphrase of the passage. The meaning of much poetic language lies condensed in the structures of its words; the rendering below of the ideas of this sonnet includes an interpretive expansion of the metaphors used in the poem.

> Do not let me allow impediments to the marriage of minds that are true to one another. Some things can seem like love, but they are not love. For example, if a supposed lover changes his or her attitude when there is a change in the loved one, it is not love. Similarly, when a supposed lover stops loving if the beloved is gone, it is not love. Love is like an unchanging landmark at sea. Such a landmark is witness to tempests, but storms cannot move or change it. Likewise, love does not change or fall if there is any upheaval in its circumstances. Love is like a guiding star that

helps every ship that's gone off course find its way. Such a star has a worth so great that it cannot be known, even if its physical height above the horizon has been measured. Likewise, the worth of love is too great to know, even if love's more mundane details can be described.

The process of analysis again helps to clarify the original meaning and points to the places where material must be added to or expanded on in order to facilitate this illumination. The subsequent recombination of the kernels is thus an exercise in careful interpretation of what rests within the poetic language. The paraphrase is again ungraceful, and because it provides a single reading with little possibility of variation in its own interpretation, it paints a unidimensional picture of a deeply textured original. But all that just serves to highlight the beauty and mastery of the sonnet, in which multiple meanings are folded into musical lines.

O Gaining Awareness of Writing Style

A particular benefit of sentence "de-combining" comes from analyzing the work of admired writers. A close look at their sentences reveals sentence strategies that less experienced writers can use as models for their own writing. It may also serve to illuminate the characteristics of a given writer's style or the characteristics of a particular genre of writing.

Below is a passage by Lewis Thomas, a non-fiction writer justly praised for his prose style:

> I am a member of a fragile species, still new to the earth, the youngest creatures of any scale, here only a few moments as evolutionary time is measured, a juvenile species, a child of a species. We are only tentatively set in place, error-prone, at risk of fumbling, in real danger at the moment of leaving behind only a thin layer of our fossils, radioactive at that. (25)

Here is a list of kernels generated from the passage by Thomas. Again, the kernels are grouped according to the sentences they are part of, with the main clause kernels underlined:

Sentence One

1) <u>I am a member of a species.</u>
2) The species is fragile.
3) The species is new to the earth.
4) The species consists of creatures.
5) The creatures are the youngest.
6) All creatures are ranked on many scales.
7) The creatures are here over moments.
8) The moments are few.
9) The moments are measured.
10) The measurement is of evolutionary time.
11) The species is juvenile.
12) The species is a child.

Sentence Two

1) <u>We are set in place.</u>
2) The setting is temporary.
3) We are error-prone.
4) We are at risk.
5) The risk is of fumbling.
6) We are in danger.
7) The danger is real.
8) The danger is now.
9) The danger is of leaving a residue.
10) The residue is the only one.
11) The residue is a layer.
12) The layer is of fossils.
13) The layer is thin.
14) The fossils are radioactive.

The list of kernels makes some aspects of Thomas's style jump out. Both of the two sentences that make up the passage start with a main clause made up of a whole kernel without any kind of transition leading in to it. Each of the sentence-opening kernels has another kernel embedded in it as a single-word modifier: *fragile* and *tentatively*. A series of abbreviated kernels acting as modifiers then follows each main clause. In the first sentence, if we consider the first three phrases following the main clause, *still new to the earth, the youngest creatures of any scale,* and *here only a few moments as evolutionary time is measured,* we can see that they are progressively more complex—each contains more embedded kernels than the last. The final two phrases of sentence one, *a juvenile species* and *a child of a species,* are then again made up of simple abbreviated kernels.

The pattern of the second sentence is similar, though not exactly the same. Set off by commas after the main clause are three phrases that are again progressively more complex: *error-prone, at risk of fumbling,* and *in real danger at the moment of leaving behind only a thin layer of our fossils.* The sentence then ends with one simple abbreviated kernel: *radioactive.* The two sentences together, then, create a pleasing symmetry that is varied just enough to keep it from being rigid. Another graceful touch is the pairing of a whole kernel with a list of abbreviated kernels in each sentence. Within the lists themselves, the movement in the modifying phrases toward greater complexity gives each sentence a momentum that is softly slowed with the simple closing kernels. In all, these structural elements contribute to the elegance of the passage.

Here, from Ursula K. Le Guin's novel *Lavinia,* is a passage of fictional prose that reveals the author's skill in crafting language. The speaker is Lavinia, a young woman. Her future husband, Aeneas, is looking with his people for a new homeland and has just arrived in her country.

> And in the twilight of morning of the next day, alone, kneeling in the mud by Tiber, I saw the great ships turn from the sea and come into the river. I saw my husband stand on the high stern of the first ship, though he did not see me. He gazed up the dark river, praying, dreaming. He did not see the deaths that lay before him, all along the river, all the way to Rome. (95)

This passage can be "de-combined" into kernels as follows (the italicized kernel of sentence two is a full but subordinate clause):

Sentence One

1) It was twilight.
2) It was morning.
3) It was the next day.
4) I was alone.
5) I was kneeling in the mud.

6) The mud was by the Tiber.
7) <u>I saw ships</u>.
8) The ships were great.
9) The ships turned from the sea.
10) The ships came into the river.

Sentence Two

1) <u>I saw my husband</u>.
2) My husband stood on the stern.
3) The stern was of the first ship.
4) The stern was high.
5) *My husband did not see me.*

Sentence Three

1) <u>My husband gazed up the river</u>.
2) The river was dark.
3) My husband was praying.
4) My husband was dreaming.

Sentence Four

1) <u>My husband did not see the deaths</u>.
2) The deaths lay before him.
3) The deaths lay all along the river.
4) The deaths lay all the way to Rome.

Kernel analysis shows that Le Guin's passage also has an overall symmetry, though again it is not strict. The passage pulls the reader along from sentence to sentence with a pattern in which structures are mirrored by what follows next across sentence boundaries. After opening with six abbreviated kernels, the first sentence consists of one main clause, *I saw the great ships*, with three kernels embedded in it. The very next clause at the start of sentence two, *I saw my husband stand*, also contains three shortened kernels serving as modifiers. In structure (as well as wording), it closely repeats the pattern of the first sentence's main clause: *I saw the great ships turn* and *I saw my husband stand* echo one another substantially, and both are similarly followed by a short series of abbreviated kernels.

The next full clause is the second, subordinate clause of the second sentence, *he did not see me*. This clause, again a whole kernel,
is itself echoed, though again not rigidly, by the next clause, which
opens sentence three: *He gazed up the dark river*. This clause also
consists of an unshortened kernel, though it has one embedded
modifier. Attached to the end of this clause are two kernels abbreviated into a pair of present participles, *praying* and *dreaming*. That
structure is loosely repeated in the next sentence, which features a
whole kernel, *He did not see the deaths*, with one embedment (the
relative clause *that lay before him*), to which are attached a pair of
kernels shortened into two prepositional phrases, *all along the river*
and *all the way to Rome*.

All of these echoed structures are contained within a whole that
has its own mirror symmetry: the passage begins with six abbreviated kernels leading into a main clause, and ends with a main clause
leading to three abbreviated kernels. These strings of shortened kernels slow the reader's progress, creating a heightened anticipation
at the start of the passage and a sense of ending and inevitability at
the close. In addition, the four kernels that are left whole are similar
in wording and thematically linked; *I saw*, *I saw*, *He gazed*, and *He
did not see* are all about seeing and not seeing, key themes in the
novel as a whole. That these clauses have little or nothing embedded
directly within them makes them stand out, startling and grave; the
important themes they embody are thus highlighted and reinforced.

As the structure of such samples suggests, an almost but not
quite exact symmetry is a common feature of powerful prose—both
fictional and non-fictional.

Finally, consider the opening to the play *Glengarry Glen Ross* by
David Mamet. The speaker is Shelly Levene, a real estate salesman
in imminent danger of losing his job; he is addressing John Williamson, his supervisor:

> **Levene:** John ... John ... John. Okay. John. John. Look: *(Pause.)*
> The Glengarry Highland's leads, you're sending Roma out. Fine.
> He's a good man. We know what he is. He's fine. All I'm say-
> ing, you look at the *board*, he's throwing ... wait, wait, wait, he's
> throwing them *away*, he's throwing the leads away. All that I'm
> saying, that you're wasting leads. I don't want to tell you your
> *job*. All that I'm saying, things get *set*, I know they do, you get a

certain *mindset*.... A guy gets a reputation. We know how this ...
all I'm saying, put a *closer* on the job. There's more than one man
for the ... Put a ... wait a second, put a *proven man out* ... (15)

A possible breakdown of the passage into kernels is as follows:

1) John, listen. (uttered four times)
2) John, look.
3) You are sending Roma out.
4) Roma (is to do something).
5) Roma (will close) the Glengarry Highland leads.
6) That is fine.
7) Roma is a good man.
8) We know Roma.
9) Roma is (a certain kind of salesman).
10) Roma is fine.
11) I am saying only one thing.
12) Look at the board.
13) Roma is throwing the leads away. (uttered three times)
14) John, wait. (uttered three times)
15) I am saying only one thing.
16) You are wasting leads.
17) I don't want to tell you something.
18) Your job (is a certain thing).
19) I am saying only one thing.
20) Things get set.
21) I know they do.
22) You get a mindset.
23) The mindset is a certain kind.
24) A guy gets a reputation.
25) We know something.
26) This happens (in a certain way).
27) I am only saying one thing.
28) Put a closer on the job.
29) More than one man is suitable.
30) The suitability is for the (job).
31) Put a (closer on the job).
32) John, wait a second.
33) Put a man out.
34) The man is proven.

The kernel list makes several remarkable features of the passage immediately apparent. Four kernels (1, 11, 13, and 14) are repeated several times, with three of the repetitions (all but kernel 11) occurring in sequence. Other kernels are close but not exact repetitions: *Roma is a good man* and *Roma is fine*, and *put a closer on the job* and *put a proven man out*, for example. Very few kernels are embedded into others; in fact, almost all of the passage's sentences either consist of single, unembellished kernels or are a string of simple kernels. Some of the kernels as represented in the passage are incomplete: for example, *John* for *John, listen to me*; *all I'm saying* for *I'm only saying one thing*; and *The Glengarry Highland's leads, you're sending Roma out*, with the connection between the two elements left unspoken. Several of the kernels are also conceptually incomplete: how do things get set, and what are those things? What sort of mindset does one get about what? What kind of reputation does a guy get, and how?

These arresting features create some important effects. With its many broken and repeated kernels, the passage closely mimics spontaneous speech and implies non-verbal responses by Williamson to which Levene subsequently reacts. Both stylistic effects are common to drama, particularly modern drama. The choppy strings of simple and incomplete kernels also help establish Levene's emotional agitation. But the structure of the passage has thematic significance, as well. Throughout the play, salesmen use words to manipulate one another and their clients ruthlessly; what is implied by and left out of the utterances creates a subtext that has a crucial importance to the circumstances of each man. Unspoken completions to fragmented kernels imply a shared understanding and friendly intimacy, neither of which may actually exist. But their apparent existence is all that matters. Levene is clearly trying hard to play this game well, to manoeuvre Williamson into giving him a break. The gradual deterioration of the speech graphically illustrates Levene's growing desperation as he feels his skill at closing a "sale" slip away.

With great skill, Mamet has built word structures that fulfill a writing purpose quite different from Le Guin's.

O *Works Cited*

Broadhead, Glenn J., and James A. Berlin. "Twelve Steps to Using Generative Sentences and Sentence Combining in the Composition Classroom." *College Composition and Communication*, vol. 32, no. 3, 1981, pp. 295–307. *JSTOR*, doi: 10.2307/356192. Accessed 20 June 2016.

Connors, Robert J. "The Erasure of the Sentence." *College Composition and Communication*, vol. 52, no. 1, 2000, pp. 96–108. *JSTOR*, doi: 10.2307/358546. Accessed 18 July 2016.

Cooper, Charles R. "An Outline for Writing Sentence-Combining Problems." *The English Journal*, vol. 62, no. 1, 1973, pp. 96–108. *JSTOR*, doi: 10.2307/814087. Accessed 14 July 2016.

Eichhoefer, Gerald W., editor. *Enduring Issues in Philosophy*. Greenhaven Press, 1995.

Hobbes, Thomas. *Leviathan*. 1651. Edited by A.P. Martinich, Broadview Press, 2002.

Le Guin, Ursula K. *Lavinia*. Harcourt, 2008.

Mamet, David. *Glengarry Glen Ross*. Grove, 1982.

Myers, Sharon A. "ReMembering the Sentence." *College Composition and Communication*, vol. 54, no. 4., 2003, pp. 610–28. *JSTOR*, doi: 10.2307/3594187. Accessed 15 Feb. 2016.

Shakespeare, William. Sonnet 116. *The Longman Anthology of British Literature*, edited by David Damrosch, vol. 1, Longman-Addison, 1999.

Sommers, Nancy. "Revision Strategies of Student Writers and Experienced Adult Writers." *College Composition and Communication*, vol. 31, no. 4, 1980, pp. 378–88. *JSTOR*, doi: 10.2307/356588. Accessed 10 Mar. 2016.

Strong, William. *Sentence Combining: A Composing Book*. 3rd ed., McGraw Hill, 1994.

——. *Writer's Toolbox: A Sentence-Combining Workshop*. McGraw-Hill, 1996.

Thomas, Lewis. "The Art and Craft of Memoir." *The Fragile Species*, Touchstone Press, 1992, pp. 16–27.

Additional Material Online

Exercises on Slang and Informal English may be found at
sites.broadviewpress.com/writing.
Click on **Exercises** and go to
"Words and Usage."

⊚ STYLE

⊙ Slang and Informal English

D1. **slang/informal English**: The column to the left below lists words and expressions often used in conversation, but not in formal English. The corresponding formal words are listed to the right. The most frequently troublesome entries are given a separate number.

anyways	anyway
anywheres, anyplace	anywhere
awful	poor, miserable, sick
awfully	very, extremely

Some authorities continue to hold that *awful* should retain its original meaning of *filled with or inspiring awe*. In any case, a better replacement can always be found. The same is even more true of the use of the adverb *awfully* as an intensifier to mean *very* (*awfully good*, *awfully small*, etc.).

boss	manager, supervisor
bunch	group
(except for grapes, bananas, etc.)	
buy	bargain
(as a noun—*a good buy*, etc.)	
go (to mean "say")	say
have got	have, own
kid	child, girl, boy
kind of, sort of	rather, in some respects
let's us	let us
lots of	a great deal of
mad	angry
(unless the meaning is *insane*)	

All contractions (*it's, he's, there's, we're*, etc.) should be avoided in formal writing, as should conversational markers such as *Well*, ...

D2. **attitude**: In colloquial English in recent years *attitude* has undergone a considerable transformation, becoming first a synonym for *bad attitude* and then a word that (depending on context)

327

may denote an air of superiority or suggest the audacity and forceful irreverence of an "in-your-face" personality. In formal written English such colloquial usages as *she's got attitude* should be avoided.

D3. could care less/couldn't care less: In the early 1990s people started to say sarcastically *I could care less* to mean the opposite—that they couldn't care less. For some time *I could care less* seemed to be taking over, regardless of the tone of voice used, and the meaning of the words themselves seemed in danger of being lost. In recent years *couldn't care less* has made something of a comeback.

> *needs checking* Most of the time most people could care less about what their elected representatives are doing.
> *revised* Most of the time most people couldn't care less about what their elected representatives are doing.

D4. get: should not be used to mean *come, go, be,* or *become.* Such expressions as *get a hold of* are also inappropriate in formal writing.

> *needs checking* Henry and Jane Seymour got married in 1536, only ten days after the death of Anne Boleyn.
> *revised* Henry and Jane Seymour were married in 1536, only ten days after the death of Anne Boleyn.

D5. go (to mean *say*)

> *needs checking* He goes, "What do you mean?"
> *revised* He says, "What do you mean?"

D6. have got (to mean *have*)

> *needs checking* He has got two houses and three cars.
> *revised* He has two houses and three cars.

In conversational English *got* has become widely used as an auxiliary verb, probably because of the awkwardness of pronouncing certain combinations involving common contractions. Thus we would never shorten *I have you covered* to *I've you covered*; instead we would say, *I've got you covered. Have got* is also an informal synonym for *have* in the sense of *possess.* Both these uses of *got* are usually to be avoided in formal writing.

D7. let's say: This expression should be omitted entirely from writing.

> *needs checking*   Let's say for example a relative dies, a poor family will
> have to deal with financial worries as well as with grief.
>
> *revised*   If, for example, a relative dies, a poor family will have to
> deal with financial worries as well as with grief.

D8. like (to mean *say* or *indicate through gesture*): An expressive idiom, but one to be avoided in writing.

> *conversational*   She's like, "Why do we have to be here?" and I'm like,
> "Duh!"
>
> *formal*   She wondered why we had to be there; to me it was
> obvious.

D9. look to: In formal writing one may speak of *looking to the future*, but the informal use of *look to* to mean *attempt* or *intend* should be avoided.

> *needs checking*   From the moment he took power in France, Napoleon
> was looking to conquer Europe.
>
> *revised*   From the moment he took power in France, Napoleon
> intended to conquer Europe.

D10. off (to mean *from*)

> *needs checking*   I got it off him for two dollars.
> *revised*   I bought it from him for two dollars.

D11. put across, get across (one's point): *Express, convince.*

> *needs checking*   He could not get his point across.
> *revised*   He could not persuade us he was right.

D12. till/until: In conversation or in literature *till* is a perfectly acceptable informal substitute for *until*. In formal written English, however, *until* should be used.

> *needs checking*   They waited till dawn to launch the attack.
> *revised*   They waited until dawn to launch the attack.

D13. well: In conversation *well* is often added to sentences while you are thinking of what to say. Do not do this in writing.

> *needs checking*   Well, at the end of the meeting there was some doubt
> within the cabinet as to which course to take.
>
> *revised*   At the end of the meeting there was some doubt within
> the cabinet as to which course to take.

D14. **when you get right down to it**: usually best omitted; use *otherwise, indeed,* or *in fact.*

⊙ Wordiness

Wordiness is perhaps the most persistent disease afflicting modern writing; references to it permeate this book. Its opposite—the mistake of including too few words in a sentence—is also discussed in this section.

D15. **actual/actually**: Usually redundant.

> *needs checking*   Many people assume that Switzerland is made up entirely of bankers and watchmakers. In actual fact, the Swiss economy is very diversified.
>
> *revised*   Many people assume that Switzerland is made up entirely of bankers and watchmakers. In fact, the Swiss economy is very diversified.

D16. **as regards**: Use *about*, or rephrase.

> *needs checking*   As regards your request for additional funding, we have taken the matter under advisement.
>
> *revised*   We are considering your request for more money.

D17. **as stated earlier**: If so, why state it again?

> *needs checking*   The Venus flytrap, which as stated earlier is an insectivorous plant, grows only in a restricted area of New Jersey.
>
> *revised*   The Venus flytrap grows only in a restricted area of New Jersey.

D18. **as you know, as we all know**: Usually better omitted.

> *needs checking*   As we all know, Barack Obama won in convincing fashion over Mitt Romney in 2012.
>
> *revised*   Barack Obama won in convincing fashion over Mitt Romney in 2012.

D19. **aspect**: Often a pointer to an entire phrase or clause that can be cut.

needs checking   The logging industry is a troubled one at the present
time. One of the aspects of this industry that is a cause
for concern is the increased production of cheaper timber in South America.

revised   The logging industry is now a troubled one. Increased
production of cheaper timber in South America has
reduced the market for North American wood.

D20. at a later date: *Later*.

needs checking   We can decide this at a later date.
revised   We can decide this later.

D21. at the present time: *Now*, or nothing.

needs checking   At the present time the company has ten employees.
revised   The company has ten employees.

D22. attention: *It has come to my attention* that this expression is almost always unnecessarily wordy.

needs checking   It has come to my attention that shipments last month
were 15 per cent below targeted levels.

revised   Shipments last month were 15 per cent below targeted
levels.

D23. basis/basically: Both are often pointers to wordiness.

needs checking   On the basis of the information we now possess it is
possible to see that William Bligh was not the ogre he
was once thought to be. Basically, he was no harsher
than most captains of the time.

revised   Recent research suggests that William Bligh was not the
ogre he was once thought to be. He was no harsher than
most captains of the time.

D24. cause: Sentences using *cause* as a verb can often be rephrased more concisely; try to think of other verbs.

needs checking   The increased sales tax caused the people to react with
fury.
revised   The increase in sales tax infuriated the people.

needs checking   The change in temperature caused the liquid to freeze within seventeen minutes.

revised   The liquid froze within seventeen minutes of the temperature change.

D25. close proximity to: *Near.*

needs checking   The office is situated in close proximity to shops and transportation facilities.

revised   The office is near a shopping centre and a bus stop.

D26. e.g. ... etc.: If you begin by saying *for example*, it is redundant to add *and others* at the end of your list. See *also* and *such as* in "Joining Words."

needs checking   In several African nations (e.g., Rwanda, Malawi, Democratic Republic of the Congo, etc.) tyrannical or murderous regimes were overthrown in the 1990s.

revised   In several African nations (e.g., Rwanda, Malawi, Democratic Republic of the Congo) tyrannical or murderous regimes were overthrown in the 1990s.

D27. etc.: The Latin *et cetera*, or *etc.* for short, means *and the rest* or *and others.* To say *and etc.* is really to say *and and others.* Beware as well of combining *etc.* with expressions such as *such as.*

needs checking   During recent years several countries (Greece, Argentina, and etc.) have amassed huge debts, which they are now unable to pay.

revised   During recent years several countries (Greece, Argentina, etc.) have amassed huge debts, which they are now unable to pay.

needs checking   Plants such as Venus flytraps, pitcher plants, etc. feed on insects.

revised   Plants such as Venus flytraps and pitcher plants feed on insects.

or   Some plants (Venus flytraps, pitcher plants, etc.) feed on insects.

D28. exists: Often a pointer to wordiness.

needs checking	A situation now exists in which voters suspect the government's motives, regardless of whether or not they approve of its actions.
revised	Voters now suspect the government's motives even if they approve of its actions.

D29. **fact:** Be wary of *the fact that* (as well as *in point of fact* and *actual fact*).

needs checking	Due to the fact that we have discontinued this product, we are unable to provide spare parts.
revised	Because we have discontinued this product, we are unable to provide spare parts.
needs checking	The fact that every member nation has one vote in the General Assembly does not give each one equal influence.
revised	Each member nation has one vote in the General Assembly, but some have more influence than others.
needs checking	Despite the fact that virtually no one in those days could foresee the end of American surpluses, Jones could.
revised	Jones was one of the few to foresee the end of American surpluses.

D30. **factor:** Heavily overused, and a frequent cause of wordiness.

needs checking	An important factor contributing to the French Revolution was the poverty of the peasantry.
revised	The poverty of the peasantry was a major cause of the French Revolution.

D31. **from my point of view, according to my point of view, in my opinion:** All three expressions are usually redundant.

needs checking	From my point of view, basic health care is more important than esoteric and expensive machines or procedures that benefit few.
fair	I think that basic health care is more important than esoteric and expensive machines or procedures that benefit few.
better	Basic health care is more important than esoteric and expensive machines or procedures that benefit few.

D32. **I myself:** In almost all cases the addition of *myself* is needlessly repetitive.

needs checking   I myself believe in freedom of speech.
      revised   I believe in freedom of speech.

(Note: For more on *myself* see page 184.)

D33. **in all probability:** *Probably.*

needs checking   In all probability we will be finished tomorrow.
      revised   We will probably be finished tomorrow.

D34. **include:** Often a needed word or two is omitted after this verb. The best solution may be to rephrase or find another verb.

needs checking   The report includes both secondary and post-secondary education.
      revised   The report includes material on both secondary and post-secondary education.
      or   The report deals with both secondary and post-secondary education.
needs checking   The Thirty Years War included most countries in Europe.
      revised   The list of countries that fought in the Thirty Years War includes almost every European nation.
      revised   Almost every European country fought in the Thirty Years War.

D35. **interesting:** In most cases the writer should not have to tell the reader that what he is saying is interesting.

needs checking   It is interesting to observe that illiteracy affects almost as high a proportion of native-born Americans as it does immigrants.
      revised   Illiteracy affects almost as high a proportion of native-born Americans as it does immigrants.

D36. **mean for:** The preposition is unnecessary.

needs checking   I did not mean for him to do it all himself.
      revised   I did not want him to do it all himself.

D37. **nature:** Often contributes to wordiness.

needs checking	The nature of the brain is to process information incredibly swiftly.
revised	The brain processes information extremely swiftly.

D38. **personally**: As a way of distinguishing views expressed by the same person acting in different capacities, *personally* serves a very useful function (e.g., *As a member of the cabinet he is obliged to support the measure, but personally he has doubts as to its appropriateness*). If you are not making this sort of distinction, though, it is safe to let your reader take it for granted that you are speaking for yourself rather than on behalf of others.

needs checking	Personally, I feel that the Supreme Court has usually exercised its constitutional authority wisely in recent years.
revised	I feel the Supreme Court has usually exercised its constitutional authority wisely in recent years.

D39. **point in time**: *Now* or *then*.

needs checking	At that point in time central Africa was very sparsely populated.
revised	Central Africa was then very sparsely populated.

D40. **really**: The adverb *really* has a place in formal writing when used to mean *in reality, truly* (*Vervoerd said he would change the regulations, but really he had no intention of doing so*). If you want to use an intensifier, however, *very* is preferable.

needs checking	It is really important that this be done today.
revised	It is very important that this be done today.
or	This must be done today.

Often in such cases your point may be made more effectively without using intensifiers—and even without using adjectives:

needs checking	Like any other animal raised in a modern factory farm, a factory-farmed pig leads a very appalling life. It spends its entire life in really hideous pens that do not permit it to turn around, let alone to walk or run. Such incredibly barbaric cruelty is justified on the grounds that without it, humans would be forced to pay somewhat more for bacon and ham.

> *revised* Like any other animal raised in a modern factory farm, a factory-farmed pig leads an appalling life. It spends its entire life in pens that do not permit it to turn around, let alone to walk or run. Such cruelty is justified on the grounds that without it, humans would be forced to pay somewhat more for bacon and ham.

D41. **regard, with regard to, as regards**: Try *about* or *over*, or rephrase.

> *needs checking* I am writing with regard to your proposal to centralize production.
>
> *revised* I am writing about your proposal to centralize production.
>
> *needs checking* As regards the trend in interest rates, it is likely to continue to be upward.
>
> *revised* Interest rates are likely to continue to increase.
>
> *needs checking* This Act gave the government powers with regard to the readjustment of industry.
>
> *revised* This Act gave the government powers over the readjustment of industry.

D42. **redundancy**: *Redundancies* are words or expressions that repeat in different words a meaning already expressed. Commonly used expressions that involve redundancy include *ATM machine, NDP party, end result, plans for the future, general public, nod your head, optimistic about the future, a personal friend of mine,* and *mutual cooperation.* Sometimes a case may be made for using a phrase of this sort in order to emphasize a point. What is to be avoided is thoughtless and purposeless wordiness.

> *needs checking* This property will appreciate greatly in value.
>
> *revised* This property will appreciate greatly.
>
> *needs checking* The house is very large in size.
>
> *revised* The house is very large.
>
> *needs checking* It was decided it would be mutually beneficial to both of us if he left.
>
> *revised* It was decided it would be mutually beneficial if he left.
>
> *or* We agreed it would be better for both of us if he left.

D43. **situation**: By avoiding this word you will usually make your sentence shorter and better.

needs checking   This treaty created a situation in which European countries gave up a degree of autonomy in return for greater
security.

revised   Through this treaty European countries gave up a degree
of autonomy in return for greater security.

D44. there is/are/was/were: These constructions often produce sentences that are needlessly long.

needs checking   There were many factors which undermined the government's popularity in this period.

revised   Many things undermined the government's popularity
in this period.

needs checking   There are many historians who accept this thesis.

revised   Many historians accept this thesis.

Additional Material Online
Exercises on wordiness may be found at
sites.broadviewpress.com/writing.
Click on **Exercises** and go to **"Words and
Usage."**

D45. too few words: This mistake can happen anywhere in a sentence. One of the best tests of whether or not a writer has checked
her work is whether or not there are missing words. In almost all
cases, such omissions will be noticed through careful proofreading.

needs checking   She rushed home to tell my family and about the
accident.

revised   She rushed home to tell my family and me about the
accident.

needs checking   Gandhi reminded the Conference that just one intercontinental ballistic missile could plant 200 million
trees, irrigate one million hectares of land, or build
6,500 health care centres.

revised   Gandhi reminded the Conference that the money spent
on just one intercontinental ballistic missile could be
used to plant 200 million trees, irrigate one million hectares of land, or build 6,500 health care centres.

D46. **too many words**: Many of the causes of this problem have been given separate entries.

needs checking	So far as the purpose of this essay is concerned, it will concentrate on the expansion of Chinese influence.
revised	This essay will concentrate on the expansion of Chinese influence.
needs checking	Although the author does not claim to be writing a social study, the question arises whether the social implications of his analysis can be ignored.
revised	Although the author does not claim to be writing a social study, his analysis does have social implications.

D47. **tragic/tragically**: Unnecessary use of either the adjective or the adverb constitutes overkill.

needs checking	Her husband, her child, and more than two hundred others died in a tragic plane crash in 2014.
revised	Her husband, her child, and more than two hundred others died in a plane crash in 2014.

D48. **would like to take this opportunity to**: *Would like.*

needs checking	I would like to take this opportunity to thank my cousin in Peoria.
revised	I am very grateful to my cousin in Peoria.
or	I would like to thank my cousin in Peoria.

⊙ Writing by Computer

No one born later than, say, 1950 needs to be convinced of the advantages of computers for writing. But many of us need to remind ourselves periodically of some of the pitfalls. Some problems are readily avoided if one retains the habit of careful proofreading. It is all too easy to come to rely on the computer a little too heavily in such contexts—as you would find if you instructed your computer to replace all occurrences of *author* with the word *senior editor* in a book contract. Suddenly, you would find the absurdities *senior editorization* and *senior editority*. The computer would have no way of knowing where to stop searching and replacing.

Proofreading may check some of the bad cognitive habits that computers breed in many writers who work only on screen; it certainly will not eliminate them all. For some of us, computers can be wonderful facilitators of flow; many people find it easier to get a lot of ideas out of their heads and "on paper" by using a computer than by using a pen and paper. But the same habits of scrolling that can facilitate flow in writing and in reading can distort our ability to arrange ideas in an ordered fashion so as to best present an argument. Though researchers are far from understanding why, they have now assembled a considerable body of evidence suggesting that seeing a succession of printed pages enables one to combine and connect ideas in ways that are not always evident if one restricts oneself to scrolling on the screen. This is why it is helpful for most writers to work with paper as well as on screen. It is ironic that the very means by which the re-ordering of blocks of text has become a matter of effortlessly keyboarding (rather than of laboriously retyping) also acts to dull the cognitive processes that are required for humans to re-order those blocks most effectively. But for most writers that is the reality.

O *Spell-check and Grammar-check*

Today's spell-checkers and grammar checkers have many virtues. If you confuse *its* and *it's* or *there* and *their*, Microsoft Word will often draw your attention to your mistake. It will even silently correct the mistake for you if you type, "Its a lovely day." But it will also often suggest there is something wrong with your writing when nothing whatsoever is wrong. (Not infrequently, for example, it will suggest you change from the subjunctive mood to the indicative when the subjunctive is in fact entirely correct.) And it will do nothing to alert you to any problem if you write either of the following sentences:

- The company's literary wing compliments its academic publishing program.
- The book includes a forward as well as a preface and an introduction.

No computer software, in short, can provide a reliable substitute for careful proofreading.

What is true for spelling and grammar is even more true for matters of style. Grammar checkers also offer advice on matters such as the length of sentences and the degree to which the passive voice is used. Such issues are by their nature not readily subject to precise formulations, and one should thus take advice of this sort from software programs with more than a grain of salt.

Online

There are several good grammar sites on the Internet; one of the best is Purdue University's Online Writing Lab (OWL), which may be accessed at **https://owl.english.purdue.edu/.**

O *Observing Online Etiquette*

The word *netiquette* is a clever little pun that neatly encapsulates the notion that standards of courtesy and consideration are as important in cyberspace as they are in other areas of human existence—and that the Internet is sufficiently different from other forms of communication as to make some special guidelines advisable.

Anyone who has used e-mail has probably sensed that the medium lends itself to a higher degree of informality (for both sender and recipient) than does the sending of a letter printed on corporate or departmental letterhead. The combination of distance, informality, and invisibility that electronic communication embodies seems to encourage the spontaneous expression of emotion in ways that might otherwise not feel appropriate. It often seems to foster a breeziness that is as friendly as it is efficient. But it also seems to lend itself to the venting of certain sorts of anger, in ways that other means of communication do not. And sometimes it leads people to divulge personal information that on reflection they might rather have kept to themselves. These tendencies of e-mail—to foster sometimes unexpected degrees of intimacy, and to facilitate the unbridled expression of anger—argue for the wisdom of taking the time to edit and proof any electronic message, checking its tone quite as much as its grammar.

The ever-increasing use of electronic communication in a wide variety of contexts continues to raise issues of appropriate tone and of level of formality. For the most part, no one expects e-mails to conform to all the conventions of more formal communications; it would be foolish to worry about a typo or two in an e-mail dashed off to a friend—let alone in a text message! But any e-mail should be clear, unambiguous, and written in an appropriate tone; again, it is wise to edit and proofread carefully any message you send. And if you are using e-mail as a convenient way to convey a more formal document, that document should indeed conform to the conventions of standard usage. A proposal submitted electronically or a memo circulated electronically should be phrased, proofread, and presented as carefully as you would the same document in hard copy form. As with writing, faxing, or phoning, then, the context and the expectations of your audience are always important.

Privacy issues are at least as important with electronic communications as they are with other forms of communication. As a recipient, consider the feelings of the sender; unless it is obviously appropriate to forward a message, for example, ask the permission of the sender before you pass it on. And as a sender, it is worth remembering that electronic communication can often end up being less private than regular mail, since recipients are not always as considerate as one might wish. And, particularly given that e-mails are often forwarded or copied by mistake to unintended recipients, it is wise to consider whether the potential recipients of a message may be a much larger group than intended—and word the message accordingly.

O *Point-form Online Etiquette*

- Keep messages clear and brief.
- Edit/proof all messages before sending—for tone as well as form.
- Use clear subject headings.

- Make the text as easy to read as possible; leave a line between paragraphs (rather than indent); use italics—or place an underscore mark before and after the relevant word(s) as a substitute for italics; use only well-known abbreviations.
- When quoting from a previous message, quote only the necessary passage(s).
- Address the message carefully.
- Attachments: be aware that some recipients may have difficulty downloading attachments, and be prepared to use alternative means in such circumstances.
- Social media: be careful of sharing too much information through social media such as Facebook and Twitter—and, as with e-mail, think twice of who might read your messages if you're thinking of writing something intimate or rude. In any social forum, be very careful of airing grievances online. On Twitter, don't tweet too frequently—and be sure to have something to say when you say something.
- In all communication, be sensitive to the demands you may be making on the time of others. If, for example, you are sending an "information-only" e-mail to a department head who may deal with a hundred e-mails a day, make it clear in the heading or at the beginning of the message that this is for information only, and that no reply is required.
- The overriding principle: always show consideration for your reader(s).

O Copyright and the Web

Copyright rules for written materials apply to the Internet just as they do to books or articles; written work is under copyright protection for many years after it is published. Indeed, copyright restrictions have been extended in recent years in many jurisdictions. In the United States the 1998 Sonny Bono Copyright Amendment Act extended copyright protection by an additional twenty years; most written material published in 1923 or later will remain in copyright until at least 2019. In the UK and other European countries copyright restrictions were extended in the 1990s, such that work is now in copyright for seventy years after the death of the author (or translator); similar restrictions were imposed as of January 2005 in

Australia. In Canada copyright restrictions are somewhat less severe; copyright protection extends for fifty years after the death of the author or translator.

There is now considerable feeling in many countries that, in extending copyright restrictions as far as they have been, governments have tilted the balance that such laws attempt to find (between the interests of authors and their heirs, and the interests of the general public) too much away from the public interest. Nevertheless, unless and until such laws are changed, a text such as E.M. Forster's *A Passage to India*, first published in 1924, will be in copyright in the United States until 2020, and in Europe (including Great Britain) and in Australia until 2051 (Forster died in 1970). In Canada it will remain in copyright until 2021.

Except for quoting brief passages (with the proper acknowledgement), you may not reproduce copyright material, whether you have found it in a written publication or on the Web, without the permission of the copyright holder. Nor may you post copyrighted materials on the Web without permission from the copyright holders.

Online

The Canadian Intellectual Property Office posts "A Guide to Copyright" on its site. For the United States, information may be found at **www.copyright.gov**.

⊙ Business Writing

Tone may be the most important aspect of business writing. The adjective *businesslike* conjures up images of efficiency and professional distance, and certainly it is appropriate to convey those qualities in most business reports, memos, and correspondence. In a great deal of business writing, however, it is also desirable to convey a warm personal tone; striking the right balance between the personal and the professionally distanced is at the heart of the art of business writing. A few guidelines are offered here.

Perhaps the best guard against significant errors in tone is to consult your colleagues whenever you are uncertain. Circulate a draft of any important document to others and ask their opinion. Is the tone too cold and formal? Is it too gushy and enthusiastic? Is it too direct? Or not direct enough?

needs checking   Do you think it's fair to ask the accounts department to handle the extra work that would be entailed in moving to your new system? Get serious!

revised   If we adopted the proposed new plan, there would be questions of fairness involved that I think would need to be addressed. The accounts staff is seriously concerned that the proposed new plan would entail significantly more work for them, while there appear to be no provisions for additional staff or compensation in the accounts area.

Perhaps because a direct and forceful style is often highly valued in business writing, it's easy to be *too* forceful. Bald statements are often not the most appropriate; it is better to qualify any generalizations you are making so as to be certain they are accurate. Be particularly careful about suggesting you are speaking for your entire organization; unless you are sure, you are well advised to qualify any extreme statements.

needs checking   Our organization always underprices every competitor.

revised   Our organization always tries to keep its prices lower than those of major competitors.

needs checking   There is no way our organization would ever cut back on research and development.

revised   As an organization we have a strong commitment to research and development.

D49. courtesy and consideration: Given that business communication usually operates within a hierarchical power structure, it is particularly important to foreground consideration in business, memos, letters, and e-mails. Avoid direct commands wherever possible; give credit to others when things go right; and take responsibility and apologize when things go wrong.

needs checking   Here is the material we spoke of. Send the report in by the end of the month to my attention.

revised   I enclose the material we spoke of. If you could send in the report by the end of the month to my attention, I'd be very grateful.

needs checking   I am writing in response to your complaint. We carry a large number of products with similar titles, and sometimes errors in shipping occur. Please in future specify the ISBN of the item you are ordering, as that will help keep errors to a minimum.

revised   Thank you for your letter—and my sincere apologies on behalf of our company for our mistake. As you may know, we carry a large number of products with similar titles, and (particularly in cases where our customer service department is not able to double-check against an ISBN) errors do sometimes occur. But that is an explanation rather than an excuse; I do apologize, and I have asked that the correct item be shipped to you immediately. Again, my sincere apologies—and my thanks to you for drawing this matter to my attention.

needs checking   It has come to my attention that you have not been filling in your expense forms in the proper fashion, or submitting them promptly. I refer you to Section C in the Staff Manual for instructions on how these forms are to be filled out, and I would remind you that all employees are to submit expense forms within one week of the end of the month in which the expenses were incurred. Thank you for your attention to this matter.

revised   Harry, you've been doing a great job these past few months—which is something I probably haven't mentioned enough! There is a small thing I want to draw to your attention, though, which I think can make things go even better. I know it makes a real difference to Carol and the others in accounts if they get the expense forms submitted promptly so that they can keep proper records month to month. If they have to keep going back into the records to make adjustments it can end up consuming an awful lot of their time. I know it can be a pain at the end of the month to fill in these forms, but it really does make a difference. Again, I appreciate the effort you've been putting in—as I know Carol does too.

D50. **memos:** The memo is a standard form of communication within an organization. In order to retain the attention of readers, memos are usually kept brief. (If a large volume of material is to be dealt with, it may be better to present the material in the form of a report, with a covering memo summarizing the key points or recommendations for action.)

Memos should follow a conventional format, whether on paper or in electronic form. See sites.broadviewpress.com/writing for a sample memo.

D51. **business letters:** It is now considered to be appropriate to send out business letters electronically. The advantage in speed is obvious; just as important is the time saved in printing, stuffing and addressing an envelope, stamping, and mailing.

Some business communication is still generally sent by mail. A personal thank-you to a business colleague is best sent by mail, as are contracts and any letters or other documents accompanying them. Remember that all letters sent by mail should be signed by hand above the sender's printed name.

As with letters, a conventional format should be followed with business letters. There should be room for considerable flexibility as to the details of format. Some prefer to use commas after the salutation, for example, while others don't. The main thing is to be consistent. See page 350 for a sample letter.

D52. **résumés and application letters:** A résumé is also sometimes referred as a CV—short for the Latin *curriculum vitae*, or, roughly, *the outline of a life*. In most circumstances these should be kept short—one or two pages (one exception is an application for an academic job, which would require you to list publications or other academic achievements). The cover letter should also be kept brief, businesslike, and free of puffery. Résumés may be organized chronologically (in reverse order, so that the most recent accomplishments or occupations are listed first), thematically (Education; Employment; etc.), or by skills (Research Skills; Management Skills; etc.). See page 348 for a sample cover letter and page 349 for a sample résumé.

business reports, plans, and proposals: Documents such as these often begin with an *executive summary*—a concise summary prepared for the benefit of executives or others who do not have time to read the full document. In any business report, plan, or proposal, it is recommended practice to keep sentences and paragraphs brief, and to come directly to the point. Frequent headings are common—again, as a means of helping busy readers to navigate the document quickly and easily. For the same reason it is sometimes recommended practice to highlight the topic sentence in each paragraph, and it's common to present material in bulleted point form. The inclusion of visual material—charts, graphs, and diagrams that can often convey a point more quickly than words—is generally encouraged. See sites.broadviewpress.com/writing for a sample opening of a business report.

Note: Sometimes reports, plans, and proposals are presented in the form of memoranda (see above).

Additional Material Online

Sample memos and business reports may be found at **sites.broadviewpress.com/writing**. Click on **Exercises** and go to **"Writing Samples."**

Joseph Alvarez
316 7th St. NW
Calgary, AB T2N 1N3
joseph.alvarez@hotmail.com

Ms. Dorothy Rosenberg
Personnel Dept.
Golden Mountain Resort
1212 James St.
Golden, BC V2R 4K5

April 3, 2016

Dear Ms. Rosenberg

I am writing to apply for employment at the Golden Mountain Resort this coming summer.

A résumé is enclosed; as you see, I have previous experience working outdoors as a guide, and I would certainly be interested in something similar this summer. I am also nearing completion of a university degree in English, and I would be particularly interested in any work there that might involve written communication.

My university classes are on Mondays, Wednesdays, and Fridays; I could come to Golden for an interview on any Tuesday or Thursday, and could probably make arrangements for another day if that were more convenient for you.

I can be reached either at the above address and e-mail address or by phone at (403) 283-8550; I will hope to hear from you. With best wishes,

Yours sincerely

Joseph Alvarez
encl.

Résumé
Joseph Alvarez • 316 7th St. NW
Calgary AB T2N 1N3 • (403) 283-8550
joseph.alvarez@hotmail.com

Education:

University of Calgary (2012–present)
• Two years completed towards a BA (Hons), English Literature
• Irene Stitt Scholarship, 2012–13

John A. Macdonald Secondary School
• Graduation Diploma, 2013

Employment:

Larry's Books (2012–2014)
Employer: Lawrence McPage
Position: Bookstore Clerk
• Maintained a well-stocked, organized book department
• Assisted customers with questions and special request
• Used computer system to update inventory, place orders, and
  perform returns

Infinity Research (2011-2012)
Employer: Jane Rich
Position: Survey Assistant
• Conducted surveys by phone and email in a friendly and efficient
  manner
• Reorganized and updated office records

Other Activities:

• Sports Editor, UC News Campus Newspaper, 2012–13
• Captain, Senior Basketball Team, John A. Macdonald Secondary
  School, 2013
• Member, Debating Team, John A. Macdonald Secondary School,
  2012

References available upon request.

Prof. Elizabeth Jones
Department of English
Faculty of Arts & Social Sciences
Loyola University
Ames, Iowa 64223

March 22, 2016

Dear Prof. Jones

Many thanks indeed for the proposal from you and Gary Collins for a new annotated edition of selected poems by Emily Dickinson.

As with all proposals for our Broadview Editions series, this one will go to outside reviewers before being brought to a meeting of our Humanities Editorial Board; the process typically takes two to three months before a formal decision is reached. I gather, however, that you are planning in the near future to apply for a grant to assist in research connected to this project. With that in mind I would like to say that we at Broadview have read through the proposal and find it extremely impressive. Certainly we are convinced that a market exists for a good edition of this sort, and I find it almost unimaginable that outside reviewers and Editorial Board members will not feel (as I do) that this is a very good proposal indeed. I fully expect as well as hope that it will move forward to publication with Broadview! With all best wishes,

Yours sincerely,

Don LePan
Director, Special Projects

⊙ How to Be Good with Words:
Styles of Writing When Considering
Gender, Race and Ethnicity, Class,
Religion, Sexual Orientation, and Disability

In at least one important respect the issues discussed in this section of *The Broadview Guide to Writing* differ from every other issue
discussed in this book. Throughout, our focus has been on formal
writing, and it has frequently been emphasized that many informal
and colloquial usages that are inappropriate to formal writing may
be quite unexceptional in other forms of writing, or in speech. The
same cannot be said of the difference between offensive language
and considerate habits of English usage. It is no less damaging to
use sexist, racist, or homophobic language in speech than it is in
writing; indeed, it may even be more so.

For authors of writing guides, the question of how to approach
issues such as sexist language and cultural bias has often been a
vexed one. The most popular writing handbook (*A Writer's Reference*, by Diana Hacker and Nancy Sommers, 5e 2012), includes
a section entitled "Avoid sexist language," followed by a section
entitled "Revise language that may offend groups of people." The
first of these headings is surely unproblematic (we will come in a
moment to the issue of gender and language). But what of the second? Should we really avoid all language that "may offend groups of
people"? If so, George Orwell and Simone de Beauvoir and Martin
Luther King and Nelson Mandela should certainly not have spoken out as plainly as they did. If so, we should never use a phrase
such as "the cruelties of factory farming," for it is surely offensive to
most managers of what they would prefer to call "intensive farming
operations" or "concentrated animal feeding operations." If so, we
would have to be quite inventive in referring to the bitumen extrac-
tion industry in northern Alberta, since one group is offended if the
phrase "tar sands" is used, while an equally large group is offended
if the alternative term, "oil sands," is used. The point about non-
sexist language and culturally sensitive language, then, is not that
you should never be willing to use language that might offend. It is
that you should try never to use language that stereotypes particular
groups, or that presumes other groups to be inferior.

Another leading writing handbook—Andrea Lunsford's *The Everyday Writer* (5e, 2012) introduces this topic by referencing the so-called "golden rule"—*Do unto others as you would have them do unto you*—a Christian concept that has parallels in numerous other religions. "The golden rule of language," writes Lunsford, "might be 'Speak to others the way you want them to speak to you.'" But surely this is precisely what we should *not* always do if we are truly to be considerate of others. A young person in the habit of using crude language might well prefer others to respond to him in the same way—to tell him that anything he has accomplished is "f---ing fantastic," for example. But in most cases it would be both inconsiderate and unwise of him to use the same language to his grandparents. Another young person might be pleased to hear from a friend that she looks really sexy in her new outfit. But it would in most cases be both inconsiderate and unwise of her to speak in the same way to a young woman wearing a nun's habit. The point, then, is not that we should do or say to others exactly what we would like them to do or say to us, but that we should be considerate of them, just as we would want them to be considerate to us. Rather than presuming others to be like us, we should try to think of how they might like to be treated, and how that in many cases might be different from our own preferences.

The heading of this section in previous editions of *The Broadview Guide to Writing* was "Bias-free Writing." That was a title we adopted in large part to get away from negatively focused headings such as "sexist language" or "biased language," or "the language of prejudice." But "bias-free" is a term that can perhaps too easily take on a self-congratulatory ring. We should surely all keep trying to find and use bias-free language, but we should also always try to remember that none of us will ever be entirely free of bias or prejudice—and that the struggle against it is not only an ongoing one in society as a whole, but also a lifelong one within each one of us.

Most writing guides and handbooks inform the reader that certain usages "are considered" inappropriate (and provide a short list), but do not devote much space to explaining why. Our intent in this section of *The Broadview Guide* is both to provide wider coverage of inappropriate usages than is the norm in guides of this sort, and to go into greater detail as to why they are considered inappropriate. A substantial discussion of issues relating to gender is followed by an expanded section on issues relating to race, class, religion, sexual orientation, and disability.

D53. **Gender:** The healthy revolution in attitudes towards gender roles in recent generations has created some awkwardness in English usage—though not nearly so much as some have claimed. *Chair* is a simple non-sexist replacement for *chairman*, as is *business people* for *businessmen*. Nor is one forced into *garbageperson* or *policeperson*; *police officer* and *garbage collector* are entirely unobjectionable even to the linguistic purist. Nor can the purist complain if *fisher* replaces *fisherman*; far from being a new or artificial coinage, *fisher* was linguistic currency when the King James version of the Bible was written in the early seventeenth century. Here again, there is no need for the *-person* suffix.

The use of *mankind* to mean *humanity*, and of *man* to mean *human being*, have for some years been rightly frowned upon. Ironically enough, *man* originally had *human being* as its only meaning; in Old English a *werman* was a male adult human being, a *wifman* a female. It was not until after the Norman Conquest in 1066 that the word *man* began to do double duty—to be used both to mean *human being* and to mean *male human being*. No doubt inevitably, that lopsided pattern of usage fostered a bias towards the masculine in the word *man*. That male bias became powerfully reinforced over the centuries—until finally, in the twentieth century, the use of *man* to mean *human being* or *humankind* came to be broadly recognized as biased towards the male—sexist, in other words. Broadly recognized, but not universally: a remarkable number of adults still cling to these sexist usages. A few openly prefer to use a word that is biased towards male people, while others manage to persuade themselves that it remains possible to use *man* in a gender-neutral fashion.

Among them are the editors of at least one of the world's leading magazines. More than a decade and a half into the twenty-first century, the majority of reputable English-language newspapers and magazines use words like *people* or *humanity* when they are referring to everyone. *The Economist* and a few others, though, still stick to the old ways. Back in their September 14, 1996, issue, the magazine's editors posed the question "What is Man?" in their lead article. "To what extent are men's actions determined by their genes?" the article asked, and clearly did not intend the answer to apply to only one-half the human race.

Well, why can't *man* be gender neutral? To start with, because of the historical baggage such usage carries with it. Here, for example, is what the best-selling novelist Grant Allen had to say on the topic in a magazine called *Forum* in 1889:

> In man, I would confidently assert, as biological fact, the males are the race; the females are merely the sex told off to recruit and reproduce it. All that is distinctly human is man—the field, the ship, the mine, the workshop; all that is truly woman is merely reproductive—the home, the nursery, the schoolroom.

But the baggage is not merely historical; much of the problem remains embedded in the language today. A useful litmus test is how sex and gender differences are approached. Look, for example, at this sentence from that September 14, 1996 issue of *The Economist*:

- One of the most basic distinctions in human experience—that between men and women—is getting blurrier and blurrier.

Now let's try the same sentence using *man's* instead of *human*:

- One of the most basic distinctions in man's experience—that between men and women—is getting blurrier and blurrier.

In this sort of context we are all forced to sense that something is amiss. We have to realize when we see such examples that *man* and *he* and even *mankind* inevitably carry with them some whiff of maleness; they can never fully and fairly represent all of humanity. (If they didn't carry with them some scent of maleness it wouldn't be possible to make a joke about the difficulty of turning men into human beings.) Most contexts are of course more subtle than this, and it is thus often easy for humans—but especially for men—not to notice that the male terms always carry with them connotations that are not gender-neutral. *Humanity, humans, people*—these words are not in any way awkward or jargon-ridden; let's use them.

inappropriate	Mankind cannot bear too much reality.
gender neutral	Humankind cannot bear too much reality.

> [T.S. Eliot, *Murder in the Cathedral*, and also *Four Quartets*]

On the same grounds, it of course makes sense to say *police officers* instead of *policemen*, and *salespeople* (or *sales clerks* or *sales representatives*) instead of *salesmen*. But what of less obvious words that have *man* or *men* embedded within them? What of *man*ual, or *man*ipulate, or *Man*itoba? If we are to find substitutes for *policeman* and *salesman*, should we not also find replacements for these words? Should we not, as more than a few wags have sarcastically suggested, start saying *personipulate* and *Personitoba*? "But wait!" the satirist is likely to continue. "Look at the *-son* in *person*. We mustn't have male bias of that sort! Surely we had better say *peroffspringulate* and *Peroffspringitoba*. Shouldn't we?"

The short answer to that, of course, is no. And not only because of the awkwardness of such words. Constructions of this sort are "solutions" to a problem that never existed. In any meaningful sense, there is no maleness embedded in the noun *Manitoba*, for *Manitoba* does not mean "place of man" or anything of that sort. It derives from words in a First Nations language (probably the Cree words *manito-wapau*, meaning *strait of the Spirit*). The word *manual* stems from the Latin *manus*, meaning hand, rather than from any word having to do with gender—and there should thus be no suggestion of manual work being for males only. And the word *person*? It stems not from anything having to do with a male child but rather from the Latin *persona*, meaning *human being*. In any meaningful sense, there is not in fact a son in *person*.

The same sort of etymological confusion lies at the heart of any suggestion that we should regard it as problematic that there is a *-man* in *human*, and a *-man* in *woman*, and a *-male* in *female*. The word *human* derives from the Latin words *humanus* and *humana*, meaning "of or relating to the human." The word *female* comes to us not from anything to do with masculinity but from the Latin *femella*, meaning *girl*. The word *male*, on the other hand, comes from the Old French *masle*, which in turn comes from the Latin *masculus*—both meaning masculine. (Along the way we may as well point out that the word for *bad* in French is *mal*, but that there is no *mal* in *male*, any more than there is any *ale* in *male*—or in *female*, for that matter.)

To replace *man* with *humanity* is not inherently awkward to even a slight degree. But the pronouns are more difficult. Clearly the consistent use of *he* to represent both sexes is unacceptable. Yet *he/she*, *s/he*, and *he or she* are undeniably awkward. *S/he* is quite functional on the printed page, but defies translation into oral English. Another solution is to avoid the singular pronoun as much as possible either by repeating nouns (*An architect should be aware of the architect's clients' budgets as well as the architect's grand schemes*) or by switching to the plural (*Architects should be aware of their clients' budgets as well as of their own grand schemes*). Of these two the second is obviously preferable. In longer works some prefer a third strategy that eliminates awkwardness entirely: to alternate between the masculine pronoun *he* and the feminine pronoun *she* when referring to a single, generic member of a group. Using *she* to refer to, say, an architect, or a professor, or a sports star, or a prime minister can have the salutary effect of reminding readers or listeners that there is nothing inherently male in these occupations. In a short piece of writing, however, it can be distracting to the reader if there are several bounces back and forth between female and male in the same paragraph. And a cautionary note should accompany this strategy even when it may conveniently be employed: be very careful not to assign *he* to all the professors, executives, or doctors; and *she* to all the students, secretaries, or nurses.

pronouns: Undoubtedly the most troublesome questions for those who are concerned both about gender equality and about good English arise over situations involving singular pronouns such as *everyone, anyone, anybody, somebody, someone, no one, each, either, neither*. It can be difficult enough to re-cast sentences involving such words so that everything agrees, even before the issue of gender enters the picture.

- Everybody felt that the film was better than any other they had seen that year.

According to the rules most of us have been taught, that sentence is wrong; *everybody* is singular, and *they* must therefore be changed:

- Everybody felt that the film was better than any other she had seen that year.
- Everybody felt that the film was better than any other he had seen that year.

- Everybody felt that the film was better than any other she or he had seen that year.

But, as many have pointed out, the insistence on the singularity of such pronouns is a relatively recent phenomenon, dating from the codification of English grammar that took root in the eighteenth century. Before that time Chaucer, Shakespeare, Swift, and the rest had no qualms about using *they* or *their* to refer to *anyone* and *everyone*. When alternatives are either awkward or sexist, it may be best to return to the ways of Chaucer and Shakespeare:

awkward Everyone will have a chance to express his or her views before the meeting is over.

gender neutral Everyone will have a chance to express their views before the meeting is over.

Questions relating to pronouns and to gender issues are not restricted to pronouns such as *everyone* and *everybody*; they are also a matter of when to choose *we* and *us* or *they* and *them*. It is always good to think about the first or third person pronouns one is using, and who they may include or exclude. In some cases it may be better to repeat a noun than to replace it with a pronoun.

worth checking The twentieth century brought a revolution in the roles that women play in North American society; in 1900 they still were not allowed to vote in any North American jurisdiction.

  [If the writer is male and addressing an audience of both women and men, it is more inclusive to avoid using the third person "they."]

revised The twentieth century brought a revolution in the roles that women play in North American society; in 1900 women still were not allowed to vote in any North American jurisdiction.

or The twentieth century brought a revolution in gender roles in North American society; in 1900 women still were not allowed to vote in any North American jurisdiction.

Of course issues of gender are not confined to the right word choice. Consider the following descriptions of political candidates with essentially the same backgrounds:

- Carla Jenkins, a lawyer and a school board trustee, is also the mother of three lovely daughters.
- George Kaplan, a lawyer and a school board trustee, has a long record of public service in the region.
- George Kaplan, a lawyer and a school board trustee, is also the father of three lovely daughters.
- Carla Jenkins, a lawyer and a school board trustee, has a long record of public service in the region.

The impression left in many minds by such phrasings is that the person described as having a long record of public service is well suited to public office, while the person whose parenting is emphasized may be better suited to staying at home.

Some may feel that parenthood is relevant in such cases; if you do, be sure to mention it both for women and for men. The general rule should be that, when describing a person, you should mention only the qualities you feel are relevant. And be sure to describe women and men with the same lens: if you feel it necessary to refer to relationship status or physical appearance, be sure to do so for men as well as women; if you mention degree qualifications or career achievements, be sure to do so for women as well as men.

Here's another example, from the October 17, 2012 issue of *The Globe and Mail*: "A female Canadian border guard was shot at one of the country's busiest crossings Tuesday." Is there any reason to foreground the sex of the border guard in this way? If the guard had been a man, the writer would surely not have written "A male Canadian border guard was...." Whereas using gender-neutral terms helps to reinforce our acceptance of the idea that occupations are not inherently male or female, terms such as "female border guard" (or "female electrician," or "male nurse," or "woman doctor") work in the opposite direction, reinforcing old stereotypes.

Before leaving the issue of gender and language, it may be worth raising the issue of the attitude we bring with us when we read or write. It is often claimed that "political correctness" goes to ridiculous lengths to avoid giving offense—and that does indeed sometimes happen. In a great many cases, however, the complaints that are made as to the supposed excesses of political correctness are entirely spurious. Some writers seem to *prefer* to think of gender-neutral language as inherently awkward or absurd. Here's an example, taken from a widely adopted textbook:

Maintaining Objectivity

Avoiding discriminating language is important. Just as important, however, is avoiding a witch hunt. Taken to extremes, political correctness will weaken your writing. *Middleman*, for example, is a perfectly legitimate term, widely understood. There is no point in confusing readers by substituting *distributional intermediary* merely to avoid the suffix *-man*. Little is gained by referring to a stripper as an *ecdysiast* when most readers will not recognize the euphemism. And no one is going to take seriously a writer who calls short people *vertically challenged*. Remember, the point of considerate language is to be fair and polite, not to be obscure or silly. (Bonnie Carter & Craig Skates, *The Rinehart Guide to Grammar and Style*, Fort Worth: Rinehart, 4/e 1996)

Think about this for only a moment, and it may seem quite unexceptionable—entirely reasonable, even. Think again. The tip-off here is the way that the question of the word *middleman* has been approached: not as the occasion for an interesting, if possibly difficult, search for ways of expressing ourselves that will avoid both awkwardness and bias, but rather as a matter that will inevitably involve a choice between the two. The authors here seem more interested in finding reasons to ridicule the struggle for fairness than in joining in the effort to improve things.

Let's approach the word *middleman* in a different frame of mind. To start with, the fair comparison is not between *distributional intermediary* and *middleman* but between *intermediary* and *middleman*. Perhaps the former is more awkward, but it is not obviously so:

- One of the reasons for high prices in this industry is that there are too many middlemen.
- One of the reasons for high prices in this industry is that there are too many intermediaries.

Alternatives in different circumstances may include *wholesalers*, *distributors*, *go-betweens*—none of them obscure, confusing, or laughable. *Ecdysiast* is indeed a laughable euphemism, but not one that is needed to circumvent biased usages. (*He's a male stripper* suffers from the same defect as *He's a male nurse*, but *stripper* in itself is gender-neutral.) And, though there is indeed a societal bias against short people, no one seriously suggests euphemism as a solution.

For many years now "politically correct" has been used with quotation marks around it to mean esthetically distasteful and ethically wrong-headed—and we are often meant to be left with the suggestion that those who criticize the "politically correct" do not themselves have a political agenda; they are "maintaining objectivity." It is telling in this connection that the authors of *The Rinehart Guide* couch the matter as an issue of etiquette rather than one of equity: "the point of considerate language is to be fair and polite." To be sure, it is a virtue to be polite and considerate. But unquestioning politeness to those in positions of power and privilege may sometimes entail an acceptance of terms of reference that are anything but fair. Sometimes one may have to choose between being fair and being polite. And the point of searching for bias-free ways of expressing oneself is in fact not to be polite, but to be fair. Sometimes it comes to a choice; language can be an instrument of positive change, or an instrument of repression. In that context we can probably never avoid being biased in one direction or the other, and we are wise to remember that complete objectivity is impossible.

Regrettably, the attitudes evident in the Carter and Skates passage quoted above are not disappearing quickly. And the prevailing tack taken by those fighting against bias-free language remains mockery rather than argument. Thus, for example, columnist Ron Haggart mocks efforts to replace the term *manhole cover* by suggesting as an alternative *circular utility access alternative facilitative infrastructure* (*The Globe and Mail*, "That Covers It," 19 March 2004). The most commonly proposed alternative to *manhole*, of course, is nothing so awkward or absurd. Moreover, *sewer hole* more accurately describes the object in question; someone new to English would surely never be able to guess the meaning of *manhole* from its component parts.

None of this should be taken to suggest that there are not awkwardnesses to struggle with in the search for bias-free coinages. (*Statesman* and *manned spaceflight*, for example, resist easy substitutions.) But these are surprisingly few. *Chair* and *flight attendant* felt a little odd at first (in language as in the rest of life it may take a while to get used to new things), but few are bothered by them now. *First-year student* still feels odd to many Americans, but not in Canada, where it has always been used. And the process continues. *Snowbody* (rhymes with nobody) is a wonderful word, but it will be years before *snowman* begins to sound as clunky as *stewardess*. Try it, though—and try to smile in fun rather than in derision. This one may never catch on, but it's worth noting that there are few things more gender-neutral than a body made up of three spheres of snow.

transgender people and language: Given the extent of the prejudice that transgender people continue to face in the twenty-first century, it is important to choose words that don't reinforce that prejudice. Slang terms such as *tranny* and *shemale* are obviously offensive and should never be used by *cisgender* (that is, non-transgender) people. Other terms are more subtly disrespectful; common mistakes include referring to all transgender people as *transsexuals* (to some, *transsexual* has a medical connotation many transgender people don't identify with), using *transgender* as a noun (i.e., calling people *transgenders* instead of *transgender people*), and using quotation marks around terms relating to a transgender person's gender:

needs checking   In her autobiographical essay, "Leanne" writes about "her" personal experience coming out as a "woman."

revised   In her autobiographical essay, Leanne writes about her personal experience coming out as a woman.

The general rule is to use the pronouns and other language that match a transgender person's gender identity, and never to imply through your language that any transgender person is not "really" his or her identified gender.

needs checking   Jamie was born a woman, but she identifies as a man.

revised   Jamie was assigned female at birth, but he identifies as a man.

Where possible, when addressing or referring to specific individuals, it is best to follow their own preferences regarding terminology and pronouns; while one transgender person might want to be called a *trans woman*, a *transsexual woman*, or simply a *woman* and prefer *she/her* pronouns, another person might identify as *genderqueer* and prefer gender-neutral pronouns such as *they/them* or *ze/hir*. Always use an individual's preferred pronouns, but, as with gender in general, there is no need to mention someone's transgender status unless it is relevant to the subject being discussed.

D54. **Race and ethnicity, class, religion, sexual orientation, disability, etc.:** Although gender has long been the most contentious and many-sided issue in the struggle for bias-free language, it is very far from being the only one. Relatively few people in North American society are overtly bigoted in the style that was routine a little over a century ago—though any visit to a news website's comments section will demonstrate how far there is still to go. But the context in which such language is used has changed; well into the twentieth century it was still common to hear in respectable North American society language that was overtly racist, or anti-Jewish, or anti-Catholic, or anti-Polish, or anti-Italian, or contemptuous of "the lower classes." The sorts of crude slur that were routine then have very largely disappeared from accepted usage, but many of the old prejudices persist in subtler forms, and not a few new ones have taken root as well. If they are not always visible or audible in polite company, they nevertheless can have devastating effects. Experiments in which large numbers of identical résumés are sent out, for example, indicate that a person with an African American name is far less likely to be granted an interview—much less be hired—than is a white American with exactly the same credentials. Similarly, in France someone with a Muslim-sounding name is vastly less likely to be considered for a job than someone with a traditional French name. (Similar studies have found that a woman is far less likely to be considered for a science-related position at Yale University than is a male with identical credentials.)

Often, of course, prejudices are held silently—and often they are held in our subconscious rather than our conscious mind. Often too a style that is considerate to others is not simply a matter of avoiding prejudiced words. The issues discussed above regarding when to use *we* and *us* or *they* and *them* apply just as much where matters of race or religion or sexual orientation are concerned as they do to matters of gender:

worth checking   In the late twentieth and early twenty-first centuries several rulings by the Supreme Court altered the landscape considerably where Canada's aboriginal peoples are concerned. They now have much greater leverage when it comes to natural resource issues than they did before the Court's Delgamuukw and Tsilhqot'in decisions.

[If the writer is not Aboriginal and is addressing an Aboriginal audience or an audience of both Aboriginal and non-Aboriginal people, it is more inclusive to avoid using the third-person "they" and "them."]

revised　In the late twentieth and early twenty-first centuries several rulings by the Supreme Court altered the landscape considerably where Canada's Aboriginal peoples are concerned. First Peoples now have much greater leverage when it comes to natural resource issues than was the case before the Court's Delgamuukw and Tsilhqot'in decisions.

worth checking　I would like to conclude my remarks with a prayer that has meant a great deal to me. We all know how God can bring light into our lives; certainly He has done so for me.

[appropriate if the speaker is addressing a crowd that she knows is entirely made up of fellow believers—but inappropriate if the speaker is addressing a mixed crowd of believers, agnostics, and atheists.]

revised　I would like to conclude my remarks with a prayer that has meant a great deal to me. Many of you may have experienced the feeling of God bringing light into your life; certainly He has done that for me.

[appropriate if the speaker is addressing a mixed crowd of believers, agnostics, and atheists.]

A related issue often arises in student essays dealing with political and cultural issues. It is all too easy to slip into language that presumes the norm in one's own area to be the norm throughout the entire country, or the norm in one's own society to be the norm worldwide. In such situations it is worth taking the time to find wording that is more precise.

worth checking　In the world we live in today, most people learn to drive before they reach their late twenties.

[This is no doubt true in North America and much of Europe—but it is certainly not true

of "most people" in India, or Nigeria, or Papua
New Guinea. Overall, far fewer than half the
world's population learn to drive at any age.]

revised   In the United States and Canada today, most people
learn to drive before they reach their late twenties.

Another unconsciously biased habit to avoid is the use of
unnecessary racial or religious identifiers. As with gender, mentioning a person's race, religion, or sexual orientation in connection
with occupation is a common habit, but one that reinforces stereotypes as to what sort of person one would naturally expect to be a
lawyer or a doctor or a nurse. Unless race or gender or religion is in
some way relevant to the conversation, it is inappropriate to refer
to someone as a male nurse, or a Jewish doctor, or a Native lawyer.
Nor is it generally appropriate to stereotype members of particular
groups even in ways that one considers positive; by doing so one
may fail to give credit for individual achievement, while leaving the
harmful impression of the group possessing qualities that are essential to it.

needs checking   Of course she gets straight As in all her subjects; she's
from Hong Kong.

revised   It's no wonder she gets straight As in all her subjects; her
parents have given her a great deal of encouragement,
and she works very hard.

Many other issues of bias in language are specific to particular categories; the discussion below is of course far from comprehensive.

race: As with gender or disability or sexual orientation, one should
not foreground racial or cultural background unless it is clearly relevant to what is being discussed. The more we foreground a person's
race or gender when it is *not* a characteristic relevant to the discussion, the more we encourage people to emphasize race or gender
rather than focusing on other human attributes.

worth checking   I was given a ticket for speeding last week; a black police
officer pulled me over just after I'd crossed the Port
Mann bridge. So I had to pay the bridge toll *and* an
eighty dollar fine!

revised I was given a ticket for speeding last week; a police officer pulled me over just after I'd crossed the Port Mann bridge. So I had to pay the bridge toll *and* an eighty dollar fine!

worth checking I've heard that Professor Andover's course in Canadian literature is very interesting. She's of Asian background from the look of her; she just joined the department this year. Apparently she's an expert on Leonard Cohen and the connections between literature and music.

> [It may not be immediately apparent to some readers that there is anything odd or problematic about this example. Substitute "She's white—of Caucasian racial background from the look of her" and the point may become more clear; the racial or cultural background of Professor Andover is not relevant here.]

revised I've heard that Professor Andover's course in Canadian literature is very interesting. She just joined the department this year; apparently she's an expert on Leonard Cohen and the connections between literature and music.

Race and Inequality in North America: When Joe Biden entered the race to become the Democratic Party's nominee for the American presidency in 2007, he put his foot in his mouth right away by praising fellow-candidate Barack Obama; for the first time in American history, he suggested, a presidential race included a "mainstream" African-American who was "articulate and bright and clean and a nice-looking guy." Biden quickly apologized for the remark and was forgiven by Obama, who made an effort to minimize the significance of Biden's gaffe ("We have got more important things to worry about. We have got Iraq. We have got health care. We have got energy. This is low on the list."). But he and millions of others nevertheless recognized the inappropriateness of what Biden had said. To understand why such comments are inappropriate, one has to explore what is implied as well as what is stated. "Articulate" is a long way from "eloquent"; it's a weak term of praise used particularly in situations where one doesn't expect someone to be able to speak well at all. If someone who looks as if they are very drunk starts to speak in perfect sentences, one might describe them as "surprisingly articulate." If one praises a candidate as an "articulate African American," one is thus implying that, among African Americans, the norm is to be inarticulate. And if one praises an African American for being "clean and nice-looking," one is again implying that such is not the norm. The depth of racial baggage that such phrasings carry may perhaps be better sensed if we imagine how they would sound applied to other people, or other groups. Imagine if Biden had said how good it was to have Hillary Clinton in the race because she was a mainstream white American who was articulate and bright and nice looking. Imagine if Barack Obama had described Hillary Clinton in that way.

Obama, of course, recognized that Joe Biden was no out-and-out racist—that while he may have had a few prejudices embedded in his habits of thought and of language, they were habits he was trying to change, and he was a person of fundamentally good character; less than a year and a half after Biden's unfortunate remarks, a victorious Obama chose Biden to be his Vice Presidential running mate. And the rest is history, so far as American presidential politics is concerned.

Unfortunately, vast and persistent inequality is also part of history—in Canada as elsewhere. Inequality in Canada is of course not only a matter of racial inequality; overall, as of 2014, the richest 10% of Canadians own almost 48% of everything there is to own in the country, and wealth inequality is on the rise. But inequality is particularly pronounced when it comes to race: black, Aboriginal, Asian, and Latin American Canadians are paid significantly less than white Canadians, and are much more likely to be unemployed regardless of education level. These effects are even more pronounced for women than for men. For example, in Ontario, while a white Canadian man makes on average $50,250 per year, the average salary of a Korean Canadian man is $32,825—and a Korean Canadian woman's is more than $10,000 less than that. But inequality is not felt only in economic terms: a particularly alarming example is the incarceration level of Aboriginal Canadians, who are ten times more likely to be imprisoned than other Canadians are. Extreme levels of inequality also persist, of course, in the United States and in many other countries as well.

Why is it important to know some of that background when you are thinking about language? Think of the case of a white student who is not accepted to Harvard Medical School, even though some Hispanic and African American applicants with somewhat lower marks were accepted; not infrequently you'll hear it claimed that this sort of result amounts to "racism" or "reverse racism" against whites and in favour of members of these or other minority groups. Is that in fact the case? Emphatically not. By definition, *racist* opinions or actions are founded on the core belief that the members of each race possess qualities that are characteristic of the race, and that on the basis of these characteristics some races can be classed as superior, others as inferior. Whatever the rights or wrongs of the policies followed by institutions such as the Harvard Medical School that do not base admission solely on marks, they are surely not policies founded on a belief that one race is superior to another. They may be intended to create a campus environment more representative of society as a whole; they may be intended to take account of inequality of opportunity; they may be intended in some measure to redress other inequities. Whether such policies are appropriate or not, whether they are effective or not—these are legitimate questions to debate. But such policies are surely not based on a belief that whites are inferior and should be classed as such—and it is thus wrong to describe them as racist.

nigga/nigger: Almost everyone knows that *nigger* is a highly derogatory term that was once very widely used in North America; that the term conveyed a presumption that black people were inferior to whites—and that the term was frequently employed as an expression of blatant hatred and contempt. In the mid twentieth century the word *nigger* began to be acknowledged as racist and hence utterly unacceptable, and it disappeared from respectable publications and from polite conversation. But it never went away: the forbidden term continued to be used in certain less polite circles as an expression of racism—and it still continues to be so used today.

In the late twentieth century, as a gesture of resistance in the face of the continuing oppression of black people in the United States, some groups of young African Americans began to "reclaim" the term *nigger* (or *nigga*) as their own, using it defiantly among themselves to refer to one another. That remains common practice today—and as a result, some young people of other backgrounds now sometimes wonder why they too shouldn't be allowed to use the "forbidden" term. The reason is simple: it remains tainted by the history of oppression with which it is associated. It is one thing for members of a group that has been on the receiving end of oppression to embrace such a term as an expression of solidarity among themselves. It is quite another for those belonging to other groups to presume to do the same.

Indian/First Nations/Aboriginal: In Canada the word *Indian* has become tainted by centuries of history in which those who had taken the land from the indigenous peoples used the word *Indian* to denigrate those peoples. It's not uncommon for some First Nations people to refer to one another informally or ironically as *Indians*. If you hear an Aboriginal person calling another Aboriginal person *Indian*, does that mean it's all right for every Canadian to do that? Emphatically not: given that many First Nations people consider the term offensive, other Canadians should avoid using it. (One exception is discussions of individuals or groups who embrace the term because of the political rights it connotes; the word *Indian* is still used by the Canadian government to indicate *Indian status*.)

The most widely accepted terms used to refer to indigenous Canadians are *Aboriginal people* and, less often, *First Peoples*. Canada's Aboriginal peoples can be divided into three large groups—*First Nations, Inuit,* and *Métis*—and these terms should be used when you are referring to one group specifically, but be careful not to make the common mistake of using *First Nations* when you really mean *Aboriginal people* more generally:

needs checking In the past decade, government policies have reflected a change in attitude toward First Nations rights in Canada, from the Far North to the Great Lakes.

revised In the past decade, government policies have reflected a change in attitude toward Aboriginal rights in Canada, from the Far North to the Great Lakes.

Whenever you can, the best thing to do is refer to a specific tribe or Nation:

worth checking Neal McLeod is a First Nations painter, poet, and Indigenous Studies teacher.

revised   Neal McLeod is a Cree painter, poet, and Indigenous
Studies teacher.

African American/black: For the past two or three generations *black*
and (in the United States) *African American* have both been widely
considered appropriate terms. The latter, of course, is only appropriate if one is referring to an American:

needs checking   Nelson Mandela is widely considered to have been the
greatest leader of his generation—not just the greatest
African-American leader, but the greatest leader, period.

revised   Nelson Mandela is widely considered to have been the
greatest leader of his generation—not just the greatest
black leader, or the greatest African leader, but the greatest leader, period.

Orientalism and Occidentalism: Readers will find "Oriental" on the
list at the end of this chapter of terms to avoid. Why? "The Orient"
was for centuries an acceptable short form combining geographical
areas that are now referred to as "the Far East" and "the Middle
East"—or by more specific names. Why the problem with the old
name? In a now-famous book called *Orientalism* (1978), the literary
and political scholar Edward Said set out to answer that question.
As Said demonstrated conclusively, the term had come to embody
a great many deeply rooted stereotypes. "Orientals" were regarded
as exotic, inscrutable, less fully human than white Europeans, and
mentally unsuited to the job of governing themselves; they were better off under the colonial rule of a Western power. Such views have
underlain a great many of the actions of Western powers over several
centuries—from the exertion of British colonial power in India and
the Middle East in the nineteenth century to the approach taken
by the American government of George W. Bush to Iraq. The term
"Oriental" also, of course, had the effect of flattening difference. Use
of the term reinforced the human tendency to see individuals from
other groups as indistinguishable—and, in this case,[1] thereby rein-

---

1   "Don't they all look the same?" There is a seemingly universal human tendency
to perceive the individual members of racial or ethnic groups one is unfamiliar
with as all looking very similar. When I was working for some years as a teacher
in rural Zimbabwe, I was for an extended period one of only two white men for

forced racist views of those groups. If one uses a single patronizing umbrella term to group together a vast and diverse body of different cultures, one is spared the effort of learning about how those groups may differ one from another.

As Said and others have argued, the political dominance of the West has made Western prejudices disproportionately damaging—but the process by which humans form biases and prejudices of this sort is not, of course, one that happens only in the minds of Westerners. Ian Buruma and Avishai Margalit pointed out in 2002 that many critics of "the West" in Asia and elsewhere have conflated the United States with all of Western culture, have stereotyped this culture as coldly mechanistic and entirely oriented towards money, and, in extreme cases such as various jihadis, have come to regard the West and Westerners as "less than human, to be destroyed, as though ... a cancer." Buruma and Margalit suggest that these extreme views may have originally taken root as the flip side of the attitudes that were being directed towards Asians by Westerners, and there is no doubt some truth to that. But regardless of how these prejudices originated, there can be no doubt that they are terribly damaging, that they operate in more than one direction, that they are often embedded in language—and that it is vitally important to do everything we can to counteract them.

Arguably "Africa" and "African" have taken on some of the same qualities that "the Orient" and "Oriental" once held for Westerners.

---

miles around—the other being Bernard Uters, a German doctor. I was thirty-ish, slight of build, dark haired and clean shaven; Bernard was fortyish, muscular, blond, and bearded. We could hardly have looked more different—to anyone used to looking at white people and interacting with them. But many in the local community were not—and so it was that I would very frequently be accosted in the marketplace by people calling me "Doctor" and hoping I would be able to help them.

In itself, then, the tendency to perceive the members of unfamiliar groups as all appearing similar is not necessarily racist; those who called me "Doctor" clearly were not stereotyping all white people in any racist way. But it is nevertheless a tendency to be wary of (and to try actively to counteract as one becomes more familiar with members of other groups), for it can have truly pernicious effects if combined with various sorts of negative feeling. Such combinations are indeed a recipe for full-blown racism. [DL]

Victorian writers such as the famous journalist and explorer Henry Morton Stanley (author of *In Darkest Africa*) helped to spread outrageous stereotypes about Africa, many of which are still with us in one form or another—as is the tendency to flatten distinctions between the many different parts of the continent and its many different cultures, reducing the continent to one amorphous mass. In reality, how much do the peoples of Morocco and Nigeria and the Sudan and Botswana have in common with each other? Certainly far less than do the people of the United States and Canada, or the people of France and Belgium. But we do not flatten Europeans in the same way as we do Africans; North Americans might speak of a vacation in Amsterdam or in Italy, but if they go on a vacation to Kenya they are likely to say they are going "to Africa."

Terms with offensive history: A few racial and cultural terms are so deeply encoded in the language that people may use them without being aware of their underlying meaning.

> *needs checking*   I'm convinced that the shopkeeper tried to gyp me.
> (*Gyp* originated in the prejudice that Roma were congenital cheats.)
> *revised*   I'm convinced that the shopkeeper tried to cheat me.

class: Another example of a widely used expression that is strongly coloured with bias is the expression *white trash*. The implications of the expression are brought forward in the following passage:

> The [Jerry Lee] Lewis and [Jimmy] Swaggart clans were, in the harsh modern parlance, white trash. They lived in the black part of town, and had close relations with blacks. Mr. Swaggart's preaching and Mr. Lewis's music were strongly influenced by black culture. "Jimmy Swaggart was as black as a white man can be," said black elders in Ferriday. (*The Economist*, April 15, 2000)

This passage brings out the implication of the expression; the 'trashiness' that is the exception for white people is implicitly regarded as the norm for black people.

The expression "that's so ghetto" brings together class and race in a similar way. Used to describe something that is makeshift or shoddily put together, the expression carries the implication that such is the norm for African Americans living in poor neighbourhoods. It's an expression that's derogatory both towards poor people and towards black people, and it should be avoided.

The inappropriateness of expressions such as "white trash" and "that's so ghetto" is often acknowledged. Less widely understood is the degree to which various expressions that are often used to describe wealthy people carry class baggage. Think, for example, of expressions such as these:

- She comes from a good family.
- He's making a good income now.
- By some definitions the couple may not be rich, but they are certainly well-off.

A centuries-old tradition among the rich and the middle class in North American and European culture holds that it is vulgar to refer to oneself or to friends and acquaintances as rich. For generations it has been accepted among the wealthy (and among many who aspire to wealth) that in most situations one should use euphemisms when referring to wealth and income. Many euphemisms do no harm, of course. But when one uses phrases such as *good family* to mean *rich family*, one is subtly colouring the financial with the moral. By implication, such phrasings further disadvantage those already disadvantaged by poverty, lending it a taint of a moral as well as a financial shortfall. Of course a phrase such as *good family* can also be used in contexts where wealth is not implied; the phrase can be and is often applied to families that are not rich. All who believe that it's preferable to make one's meaning clear (and who believe that poverty is not evidence of any moral failing) should consider avoiding such euphemisms, and using more precise wording:

- She comes from a family that has long been regarded as wealthy and respectable.

    [if one means to convey that the family is wealthy]

- She comes from a poor family that is very well regarded in the community.

    [if one is using the phrase without any connotation of wealth]

- He's making a large amount of money now.

- By some definitions the couple may not be rich, but they own a summer place as well as a large house in town, and most years they manage a vacation in Europe.

worth checking   The novel focuses on a woman who comes from a good family in New York; when the family falls on hard times, she faces difficult choices.

revised   The novel focuses on a woman who has moved in high society in New York; when her family falls on hard times, she faces difficult choices.

Even when you are using accepted terminology to discuss class, it is good to keep in mind the effects your word choice might have. *Lower class*, for example, is a widely used term that suggests a negative value judgement; descriptors such as *working class* (where appropriate) and *low-income* may be preferable.

religion: Given the generally high level of awareness in Western society of the evils of anti-Semitism it is extraordinary that *Jew* is still sometimes used in casual conversation as a verb in the same way that *gyp* is used—and that *Jewish* can still sometimes be encountered as a synonym for *stingy*. These are usages that have their roots in a long tradition of anti-Jewish prejudice—in the many centuries during which most Christian societies prohibited Jews from entering most respectable occupations, leaving Jews little choice but to provide services such as moneylending that Christians needed but for various reasons did not want to provide themselves. Moneylending then became part of the vicious stereotyping that surrounded Jews. Like other extremely offensive terms discussed in this book, terms that preserve old anti-Semitic prejudices should never be allowed to go unchallenged. When they are challenged, speakers will often realize they have been unthinkingly using a coinage learnt in childhood—and will change.

A difficult issue is how to refer to extremists affiliated with a particular religion. Should those who profess faith in Islam but believe it is acceptable for them to kill and maim vast numbers of civilians who are associated with organizations they despise (Osama bin Laden's followers killing 2,996 people on September 11, 2001, followers of the Islamic State movement killing thousands in Iraq and Syria in 2014) be called Islamic fundamentalists, or Islamists, or jihadis, or terrorists, or simply mass killers? If someone claims to be following the Islamic faith and commits extreme acts of horrendous violence against unarmed civilians in the name of his faith, many argue that it's entirely fair to describe that person as an Islamic extremist. But fair to whom? When the two words are brought together, inevitably something of the one rubs off on the other, leaving some suggestion in the minds of those reading or hearing the term that extremism comes naturally to Muslims. Many North Americans may appreciate this point more clearly if we think of the phrase *Christian extremist*. Would it seem appropriate to use that term to describe one of the murderers of a dozen or more workers in abortion clinics in North America in the 1980s and 1990s (most of whom professed to be inspired by their Christian faith)?[1] Probably not: a strong argument can be made that no religion deserves to be identified through the actions of its most violent and unprincipled adherents.

The best way to approach such questions may be to be as specific as possible—and to try to use language that cannot be taken to equate the beliefs of an entire religion with those of extremists on the fringes of that religion.

worth checking   Hindu terrorists killed over a thousand Muslims in the violence in India's Gujarat state in 2002.

revised   Extremists believed to be associated with the Vishva Hindu Parishadm (VHP) killed over a thousand Muslims in the violence in India's Gujarat state in 2002.

Much as one should be careful in choosing one's words in such cases,

---

1   Tragically, further examples abound for virtually all religions. Timothy McVeigh professed his faith in Christianity but killed 168 innocent people in Oklahoma City in 1995, just as Anders Behring Breivik professed his faith in Christianity but killed 77 innocent people (many of them children) in Norway in 2011; should they be called Christian extremists, or right-wing extremists, or terrorists, or simply shooters and bombers? Baruch Kopel Goldstein professed his faith in Judaism but killed 29 innocent people at prayer in 1994; should he be called a Jewish extremist, or a Zionist extremist, or a terrorist, or simply a shooter? Various people professing faith in Hinduism killed over 1,000 innocent Muslims in the Indian state of Gujarat in 2002; should they be called Hindu radicals, or Hindu extremists, or terrorists, or simply mass killers?

one should also strive to be direct where the facts are plain, or where the weight of probability points clearly to a particular conclusion.

worth checking   Extremists believed to be associated with the Vishva Hindu Parishadm (VHP) killed over a thousand Muslims in the "communal violence" in India's Gujarat state in 2002. Some have claimed that the state police and the Gujarat state government were complicit in the violence; it has been alleged that the police and the Gujarat state government (led by Narenda Modi, now Prime Minister of all of India) did little or nothing to stop the massacres or to prosecute the perpetrators, and some have suggested that Modi's government helped to plan the targeted attacks on Muslims.

[Though Modi and others deny it, Human Rights Watch and other impartial organizations have all concluded that the police and Gujarat state government facilitated the killings. What remains to some degree uncertain is whether or not they helped plan the attacks. In such cases responsible writers give their readers a sense of the weight of probability, rather than retreat into a "he said / she said" form of obfuscation.]

revised   Extremists believed to be associated with the Vishva Hindu Parishadm (VHP) killed over a thousand Muslims in the "communal violence" in India's Gujarat state in 2002. A strong body of evidence suggests that the state police and the Gujarat state government were complicit in the violence; the police and the Gujarat state government (led by Narenda Modi, now Prime Minister of all of India) did little or nothing to stop the massacres or to prosecute the perpetrators, and reputable sources have claimed that Modi's government helped to plan the targeted attacks on Muslims.

sexual orientation: There remains a great deal of confusion in North America over what constitutes acceptable language regarding sexual orientation. We can start with those very words—*sexual orientation*. That term has for the most part now replaced *sexual* *preference* when it comes to describing gay, lesbian, bisexual, heterosexual, and other sexualities—and for a good reason. The word "preference" carries with it a connotation of choice—the notion that one *chooses* whether or not to be gay. It was on that sort of presumption that past generations tried to "cure" people of same-sex desires. It's on that presumption too that some still refer to a "gay lifestyle," as if sexual orientation were akin to deciding either to settle down in a quiet, leafy suburb or travel round the world as a backpacker. In fact, of course, gay, lesbian, and bisexual people choose from among just as many lifestyles as do heterosexual people. And, as a great many scientific studies have shown, most gays and lesbians no more "choose" to be attracted to members of the same sex than most heterosexuals "choose" to be attracted to members of the opposite sex. Nor do bisexuals typically choose to be bisexual; they simply find themselves being attracted to individuals of either sex.

gay/homosexual: The term *gay* is now preferred to the term *homosexual*; why is that? Because of its history, is the short answer. The term *homosexual* was for so many generations used as a term of abuse—and, in the medical profession, as a term naming a form of mental illness—that it has now become tainted. That said, there are still a variety of contexts in which the word may (and should) still be used.

> *needs checking* Wilde was said to have had a gay relationship with Lord Douglas.
>
>> [A term such as "gay relationship" is anachronistic when applied to events in other historical eras—such as the famous trial of Oscar Wilde in the 1890s—and "homosexual" may better reflect the terminology and cultural categories of the time.]
>
> *revised* Wilde was said to have had a homosexual affair with Lord Douglas.
>
>> [However, in some contexts, it may be possible or even preferable to avoid using homosexual while still reflecting historical realities:]
>
> *or* Following his romantic affair with Lord Douglas, Wilde was charged with the crime of "gross indecency."

needs checking Male bonobos typically engage in a wide variety of gay sex.

["Gay" is generally used only where human sexuality is concerned; "homosexual" remains the prevalent term when one is writing of non-human species.]

revised Male bonobos typically engage in a wide variety of homosexual activity.

"That's so gay": Soon after the word *gay* came to be recommended in the late twentieth century as the preferred non-pejorative term for same-sex sexual orientation, the expression "that's so gay" began to be widely used in conversation by young people. Its meaning? "That's really stupid," or "That's weak and ineffectual," or "…" But inevitably such usages connect at some level with other meanings; it's impossible if you use such a term to avoid a broader association of what is gay with what is stupid, weak, and ineffectual. (Imagine if people started to use the expression "that's so white" or "that's so black" or "that's so Christian" to mean "that's really stupid.") Much as many have protested that "that's so gay" is an "innocent expression," it's not. The cumulative repetition of this and similar colloquial expressions does a great deal to reinforce human prejudice against gays, lesbians, and bisexuals, and to make it more difficult for those who are gay to be open about it, and proud of it.

queer: What of the term *queer*? For much of the twentieth century *queer* and *faggot* were the most common terms of abuse hurled at gays and lesbians. In the last quarter of the last century, however, many gays began to defiantly claim the term as their own—in the process declaring their difference from what was felt (with good reason) to be the straightjacket of straight society. "We're queer and we're here—get used to it"[1] became a familiar chant at gay rallies and protests.

As with other terms of abuse that have been reclaimed by members of the group that has been on the receiving end of the abuse, use of the term *queer* should not be taken lightly by those who are

---

1 · A variant has long been used in cities such as Vancouver during the annual Pride parade as marchers move through the downtown retail district, or demonstrate at malls: "We're here; we're queer; we're not going shopping!"

not members of the victimized group. But while with cases such as *nigga* the right approach is straightforward—those not part of the group the word is used to denigrate should simply never use the word—the case of *queer* is more complicated. While many gay, lesbian, bisexual, and transgender people feel that the word is inherently and extremely offensive, the word has also been taken up by others in ways that call upon people outside the community to use it. In the humanities, *queer theory* (a branch of critical theory) attaches specific meanings to the word *queer*, and the word can and should be used as an academic term in that context. Many activists also use phrases such as *queer community* to refer to all people whose sexual orientation or gender identity challenges cultural norms; the commonly used alternative, *LGBT* (an acronym meaning *lesbian/ gay/bisexual/transgender*),[1] is seen by some as less inclusive because it does not—and could not possibly—name all of the incredibly diverse identity markers that fall under the umbrella of *queer*. And some people with whom the radical tone or the open-ended meaning of *queer* resonates prefer to identify themselves as *queer* in addition to—or even instead of—*gay*, *lesbian*, or anything else. The bottom line is that some audiences will find the use of *queer* alienating and offensive while others will find it inclusive and celebratory, so it is important to take care when deciding whether or not to use the word in a given context.

disability: There has long been uncertainty about how best to speak of disabilities in general, as well as about how best to speak of individual people who have particular disabilities. Terms such as *cripple* and *mentally retarded* had by the late twentieth century come to be universally regarded as derogatory, but there is a great deal of ongoing discussion as to the specific terms that have been put forward as replacements. It is rightly believed that we should use terms that do not suggest a person's disability to be greater than is in fact the case; we should use terminology that avoids reducing individuals or groups of people to their disabilities. If someone is described as *a disabled person*, it is easy to see how the assumption

---

1   Sometimes a *Q* for *queer* and/or *questioning* is added to the end of the acronym; some organizations use longer acronyms to acknowledge other identity markers, such as *asexual*, *intersex*, and *pansexual*; the shorter acronym *LGB* is used to refer exclusively to sexual orientation as distinct from gender identity.

may take root that the person is *entirely* disabled—unable to function in human society or contribute usefully in the world. But in the other direction, terms such as *differently abled, physically challenged,* and *mentally challenged* strike many as euphemisms devoid of any content suggesting the nature or extent of what are often very serious issues faced by people with disabilities. No two people have precisely the same abilities, and everyone faces challenges in life, both mental and physical; what's so special about having different abilities, or facing challenges? One common approach is to use phrasing that begins with *person* or *people*; consider the phrase *people with disabilities,* and how it differs from *the disabled.* So too with individuals: whereas saying "she is disabled" might be taken to suggest the person you are speaking of is incapable of making a significant contribution, saying "she has a disability" suggests nothing of the sort.[1]

As with gender and race or cultural background, there is no need to mention a disability unless it is relevant to the topic of discussion.

needs checking   Professor Caswell joined the History Department in 2006. A distinguished scholar, he is the author of several books on early American society. He's confined to a wheelchair, though.

[If you are outlining Professor Caswell's credentials and accomplishments, his physical disability is not something you need to mention.]

revised   Professor Caswell joined the History Department in 2006. A distinguished scholar, he is the author of several books on early American society.

Notice also how the reference to the wheelchair is worded in the above example. Phrases such as "confined to a wheelchair" can subtly colour people's judgements as to whether or not someone will be an asset to a community, or a burden on it.

---

1   There are some exceptions to this approach; many members of the Deaf community, for example, embrace this identity and prefer to be described simply as Deaf.

needs checking	The members of the interviewing committee noticed that Professor Caswell is confined to a wheelchair.
revised	The members of the interviewing committee noticed that Professor Caswell gets around in a wheelchair.

Seriousness and humour, euphemism and plain speaking: It's often felt that all the issues we are asked to take account of in speaking and writing about gender, race, religion, sexual orientation, and disability create, in aggregate, something of an oppressive atmosphere—that we are forced to tread on our toes all the time in the name of "political correctness," that we can't speak plainly, and that we're being asked to give up our sense of humour. It's true that there are serious issues involved, and that trying not to denigrate people different from ourselves can take a fair bit of thought and a fair bit of effort. In that respect it's not a lot different from the rest of life. It can take a fair bit of thought and a fair bit of effort to be courteous and tactful to our relatives, or to people in our school or at our place of work who are from backgrounds quite similar to our own. And yet we manage—and we manage to express our sense of humour, too.

We do have to acknowledge that there are restrictions in what it's appropriate to say or do—just as we have to acknowledge that the conventions of acceptable behaviour impose restrictions when it comes to what we can say to our parents and grandparents, and how we refer to them. Not least of all, we are obliged to accept some restrictions on certain forms of humour. It's often suggested by well-meaning opponents of racism, sexism, and so on that racist and sexist jokes are never truly funny. But that's just not true; if it were not possible for humans to find humour in racist and sexist jokes and comments, no one would ever have laughed at them. One of the saddest things about the human species is that our sense of humour is far from an unqualified good; we are all too easily amused by jokes about those who are less powerful than we are, or who are simply different from us.

We should, then, be prepared *not* to make some jokes, even if they really are funny, and *not* to comment in certain ways, even if we know that the comment is sure to get a laugh. We should, as we grow up (and for some of us this takes longer than for others[1]), be

---

1   One of the authors wishes to take this opportunity to acknowledge that he was well into his twenties before he started to realize that jokes about "Personitoba"

prepared to put other values ahead of *getting a laugh*. But does that mean we have to give up our sense of humour? Not at all. We don't even have to give up humour that's about gender or race or religion or sexual orientation. What we should be prepared to give up is humour that's based on contempt and superciliousness, humour that comes at the expense of those less privileged than ourselves, humour that comes at the expense of those who have done nothing to deserve it. Let's look at a comparative example:

> Three religious leaders are comparing notes on how they deal with the funds that have been donated to their institutions during services.
>
> "Well, I have a system that seems to work pretty well," says one. Of course my institution is a place of God, and when people donate money they expect that it will be for God's work. But I have various expenses, and I could not do God's work myself without receiving some recompense. This is the system that I have found works best: I draw a line on the floor, and from a point on that line I throw the entire amount donated that week into the air. What lands on one side of the line is for God's work; what lands on the other side of the line is my own compensation."
>
> "How funny!" says the second religious leader. "I have a very similar system. I draw a circle on the floor, and from any point on the circumference of that circle I throw the entire amount donated that week into the air. What lands inside the circle is for God; what lands outside is my own compensation."
>
> "This is truly extraordinary!" says the third religious leader. "We all three of us have very similar systems. The way I do things is almost precisely the same. Of course everyone takes a somewhat different approach when it comes to the specifics. My own approach this: I throw the entire amount donated that week into the air—and what God wants, he keeps."

This is a joke that has been told in slightly different ways for decades, almost always with the three leaders identified as belonging to a particular religious group—Catholics, Scottish Presbyterians, Muslims, Jews, whoever. Told that way, it becomes a joke that is in part at least

---

(see above) were neither as pointed nor as funny as he had previously thought. [DL]

against a particular religion; however funny it may be, it is surely an example of humour that is objectionable. Told in the way it is set out above, on the other hand, with no religions specified, it becomes a joke about selfishness and greed, and about how humans are all too often able to rationalize their selfishness and greed.

What about race? Again, let's look at a case in point:

> Just a few years before Barack Obama's ascent to the White House, few people imagined that in 2008 America would be ready to elect as their president someone who was sort-of African American.

Is this one liner a case of appropriate humour on the subject of race? Surely the answer is yes. It's perhaps in part a joke about Obama's unusual background. But more importantly, it's a joke about the *degree* to which America was ready in 2008 to elect a black President; as was widely discussed at the time, many Americans who would have been reluctant to vote for someone as black as Obama's father were quite prepared to vote for someone whose parentage was half black, half white.

We should perhaps not leave the subject of humour without acknowledging that efforts to insist on bias-free language can legitimately be the butt of humour too. Here's a dialogue among three characters with unusual names:

> *Unthinking* That's really gay!
> *Thinking* Could you could put that in a different way? "That's so gay" is an expression that really is hurtful to gay people.
> *Unthinking* What I mean is, that's really stupid.
> *Overthinking* I'm afraid that what you've just said could be regarded as offensive by anyone who's ever done anything stupid.

If humour is consistent with doing one's best to take ethical considerations into account in one's speaking and writing, so too is plain speaking. The view of Bonnie Carter and Craig Skates quoted above is widely shared; a great many people feel that striving to make the language we use free of bias is likely to result in euphemism and silliness—and that, for that reason, it's not worth the effort. Absurd examples such as "vertically challenged" are put forward again and again as if they were the typical products of any striving for bias-free language; in fact, such euphemisms are seriously recommended by almost no one. That's not to say that ongoing efforts to speak and write fairly about other groups have not resulted in some absurdity, and some euphemistic language. To be sure, they have—and in some of those cases the euphemisms may have been unfortunate. But anyone who wishes to take issue with the use of a euphemism such as *mentally challenged* should on the same grounds take issue with other forms of euphemism—most certainly including euphemisms of a truly horrific sort that are sometimes used by some who style themselves as opponents of "political correctness." Former American Vice President Dick Cheney, who oversaw the American government's use of interrogation techniques during the administration of George W. Bush, is an example of just such a person. Cheney has attacked others for using euphemisms rather than speaking plainly. But how does he refer to the practice of repeatedly subjecting prisoners to extreme pain? He calls it "enhanced interrogation of high-value detainees." A wide range of impartial authorities have concluded that the "waterboarding" and other techniques practised by the American military under Cheney's oversight were, quite simply, forms of torture. Republican Senator John McCain, who underwent torture himself during the Vietnam war, has said exactly that quite unequivocally—and not just about waterboarding: "you can't claim that tying someone to the floor and having them freeze to death is not torture.... What [Americans] need to do is come clean, move forward, and vow never to do it again." Dick Cheney will have none of that; he continues to insist on euphemism. Asked when he appeared on December 14, 2014 on NBC's *Meet the Press*, he was adamant about "what we did with respect to enhanced interrogation."

Like many others, some politicians will doubtless never learn how to be good with words.

Additional Material Online

Exercises on bias-free language may be found at
sites.broadviewpress.com/writing.
Click on **Exercises** and go to **"Style."**

O *Bias-free Vocabulary: A Short List*

actress	actor
alderman	councillor
anchorman	anchor/news anchor
Asiatic	Asian
bad guy	villain
bellboy	bellhop
bogeyman	bogey monster
brotherhood	fellowship, community

(when not speaking of all-male situations)

businessman	businessperson, entrepreneur
caveman	cave-dweller
chairman	chair
cleaning lady	cleaner
clergyman	minister, member of the clergy
common man	common person, average person, ordinary person
congressman	representative
con-man	con-artist
draftsman	drafter
Eskimo	Inuit

(Note: Some Alaskan groups still prefer *Eskimo*.)

farmer's wife	farmer
fireman	firefighter
fisherman	fisher
forefathers	ancestors
foreman	manager, supervisor
freshman	first-year student
frontman	figurehead, front
garbageman	garbage collector
grandfather	grandparent

(Note: As in "Those currently covered by the old provisions will be grandfathered in.")

gunman	shooter
gyp	cheat, con

Gypsies   Roma

(Note: When a nomadic people from India began to appear in Britain in the late medieval period, they were thought to have come from Egypt and were termed *'gypcian*. Over the centuries, however, *Gypsies* was very frequently used in a derogatory way; the term *Roma* has now come to be generally accepted as the best term for those outside the culture to use. (*Gypsy* may still be a useful term of self-description for some of Roma background.)

Indian   Aboriginal, First Nations,

                              First Peoples

(Note: As with *Eskimo/Inuit* and *African American/black*, the key consideration is sensitivity to audience. If you do not belong to the group but you know that the people you are writing about prefer a particular designation, that is the one to use. The above references current Canadian usage; in the United States, *American Indian* and *Native American* remain commonly used.)

infantryman	footsoldier
insurance man	insurance agent
layman	layperson
longshoreman	shiploader, stevedore
maid	housekeeper
mailman	letter carrier, mail carrier
male nurse	nurse
man	humanity
man (an exhibit)	staff
man (a barricade)	fortify, occupy
man (a ship)	crew
manhandle	rough-up, maul
manhole	sewer hole, access hole
manhole cover	sewer cover
man enough	strong enough
man hours	staff time, work time
mankind	humankind, people, humanity, humans
manly	self-confident, courageous, straightforward
manmade	handmade, human-made, constructed
middleman	intermediary, go-between

mothering	parenting
mother tongue	native language
negro	black, African American
niggardly	stingy

(Note: The word *niggardly* has no etymological connection with *nigger*. Since the one suggests the other to many minds, however, it is safer to avoid using it.)

Oriental	Asian, Middle Eastern
policeman	police officer
postman	letter carrier, mail carrier
salesman, saleslady	salesperson, sales clerk, sales representative
snowman	snowbody (rhymes with *nobody*)
spokesman	representative, spokesperson, agent
sportsman	sportsperson
stewardess	flight attendant
thinking man	intellectual, thinking person
unsportsmanlike	unsporting
waitress	server
weatherman	weather forecaster
womanly	warm, tender, nurturing, sympathetic
workman	worker, labourer, wage earner

⦿ ACADEMIC WRITING

⦿ Writing about Literature / Writing about Texts

[Students may also find it helpful to consult the first section of this book ("The Writing Process") and the sub-section "English Studies" in Across the Disciplines (below).]

○ *The Meanings of Texts*

In some respects the practice of writing about a text in the context of literary studies has a good deal in common with the practice of writing about a text in the context of other disciplines in which ideas are sometimes discussed in similar ways—philosophy, or intellectual history, or political theory, or interdisciplinary programs such as Humanities and Liberal Studies. In all these contexts, the primary focus of discussion is very frequently on what meaning(s) we draw from the text at hand. Often this is no easy task; very frequently texts have no single, clear, surface meaning, and may suggest quite different meanings to different readers.

Even many texts that convey a powerful sense of being meaningful are often resistant to efforts to pin that meaning down to anything precise and straightforward. The experience of reading *The Adventures of Huckleberry Finn* is exciting, amusing, and emotionally engaging—and the book gives us a strong sense of saying something meaningful. But what is that meaning? Specifically, what does the book say to us about slavery, race, and racism? Does it, in effect, constitute a powerful argument against racism, as many have claimed? Or does it equivocate—sit on the fence, as it were, as some others have claimed, allowing or even encouraging privileged readers to feel good about themselves and their attitudes towards the injustices of the past without asking them to engage significantly with ongoing injustices?

Shakespeare's *The Merchant of Venice* is an enormously powerful story. But is it a story of a cruel and grasping moneylender receiving his comeuppance (as was presumed by Christian audiences for many centuries)? Should we read it rather as a story of anti-Semitism—of systemic cruelty against the moneylender? Or should we pay attention to those who remind us that Shylock the moneylender does not even appear in the play's final act, and read the play more for what it says about gender and about love—the love of one man for another as well as the love between a man and a woman?

W.H. Auden's poem "September 1, 1939," written just as World War II was breaking out in Europe (and now widely acknowledged to be among the most important poems in English of the twentieth century), appeals powerfully to readers in a variety of ways. Several of its lines ("a low, dishonest decade"; "those to whom evil is done / Do evil in return"; "We must love one another or die") have taken a permanent place in public discourse. But what should we take the poem to mean? Does it rate the sins of complacent democracies as poorly as the evils of psychopathic dictators such as Adolf Hitler, as some have suggested? Or is it a complex call to remain true to ideals of love as we struggle against evil?

Alongside all these questions may be questions of historical and biographical context. To what extent does it matter that *The Adventures of Huckleberry Finn* is a historical novel? (When Twain wrote the book, slavery was already in the past—though many African Americans were being forced to live in conditions that approximated slavery.) To what extent does it matter that Shakespeare wrote *The Merchant of Venice* soon after lending money for interest had finally become legal in England—and in the middle of a period of more than three centuries during which Jews were banished from English soil? To what extent does it matter to the politics of "September 1, 1939" that Auden had left (some said "abandoned") Britain for America earlier in 1939?

We may often ask very similar questions about meaning, and also about historical and biographical context, when we are studying texts such as Plato's *Republic*, or Thomas More's *Utopia* or Niccolo Machiavelli's *The Prince* (texts that are more commonly taught as history or political theory than they are as literature). Are we to take the advice given to Machiavelli's Prince in a straightforward fashion? Are we to take More's Utopia to be the sort of society we should truly strive for? Or is it more appropriate to read such texts as being in whole or in part ironic?

The evidence as to how Machiavelli intended *The Prince* to be read or More intended *Utopia* to be read in the sixteenth century is no more conclusive than is the evidence as to how Twain intended *Huckleberry Finn* to be read in the nineteenth century. And there is no evidence whatsoever as to how Shakespeare intended *The Merchant of Venice* to be read or performed. We do have considerable evidence as to the effect W.H. Auden felt "September 1, 1939" would have or should have on readers—but he changed his mind on these questions repeatedly, significantly altering the poem more than once after its initial publication, and then for a period of many years not even allowing it to be reprinted. To sort out one clear view that the author had of the poem's meaning is, in the circumstances, quite impossible—and, even if we could, this would not preclude the possibility that the meanings best supported by the poem itself are not what Auden intended them to be.

Much as context may be important, then, we must also learn to look at the text of a literary work as something independent of its author—and as something open to interpretation. Moreover, we must often accept that there can never be any single interpretation of a text that can clearly be proven to be correct, and that will be accepted as correct by future eras as well as by our own.

Does that mean that any interpretation is equally valid? By no means. It would be absurd to suggest, for example, that *The Adventures of Huckleberry Finn* constitutes a powerful argument for the United States to reinstitute slavery, or that "September 1, 1939" was written in support of Hitler and the Nazis. There are in every case limits to the range of reasonable arguments than can be made as to possible or plausible interpretations of a text.

Developing reasonable arguments as to how texts can or should be interpreted, then, is a central activity of literary studies. A related activity is to develop reasonable arguments as to how a text was interpreted when it was first published or performed—and to draw comparisons between the impact it had in its own time and the ways in which it is received today. Such arguments may be vitally relevant to our own situation. One might compare, for example, the reception to *Huckleberry Finn* in America of the 1880s with the reaction to it in the same country in the twenty-first century; an essay exploring that issue might well reach the controversial conclusion that reading the novel as an anti-racist text today requires a level of historical knowledge and an understanding of the workings of irony that are beyond the reach of most teenagers—and that for those reasons the novel should not be taught at the high school level. One might argue for or against the decision of some recent editors to replace the offensive word "nigger" in Twain's novel with the word "slave." Similarly, one might compare the way "September 1, 1939" was read during World War II with the way it was read in the early twenty-first century; the poem was widely reprinted in newspapers across North America following the September 11, 2001 attacks on New York and Washington. To what extent is the poem a meaningful reference point when it comes to discussing the struggle against twenty-first century terrorism?

Another activity within literary studies is developing arguments as to what should or should not be considered relevant to the interpretation of a literary text. If details about the author are known, when (if ever) should it be acceptable to take them into account in interpreting a text? Should it be considered relevant to how we interpret *Huckleberry Finn* that Twain as a young man briefly enlisted on the Confederate side in the Civil War, and then deserted? Should it be considered relevant that, later in life, he described the Civil War as "a blot on our history, but not as great a blot as the buying and selling of negro souls"? Should the fact that W.H. Auden was gay make a difference to how we read a line such as "We must love one another or die"?

Those questions may be interesting, but they will always be less important to how we interpret a text than the evidence within the text itself. To make a successful argument about a literary text you will need to be able to draw on evidence from within that text—which is something not a few students have difficulty figuring out how to do. Told to *refer to* the story of a work of fiction as they develop an argument in an essay, students all too easily find themselves *re-telling* the story of that work of fiction—summarizing it in their own words, while quoting selected phrases along the way. Summarizing is a useful and sometimes a necessary art, but summary can never take the place of argument. In the boxed insert below are three examples that should help to make clear the difference between summarizing part of the story of a work of literature and formulating an argument about that work of literature. All three examples are responses to the same assignment.

Framing Arguments about
The Adventures of Huckleberry Finn

Assignment: Develop an argument concerning the treatment of racial issues in *The Adventures of Huckleberry Finn*,
and write a short essay putting forward your views. Pay
particular attention to the ending of the novel (from Chapter XXXI onwards).

A) In Mark Twain's novel *The Adventures of Huckleberry Finn* racial
prejudice is expressed by many of the characters, among them Huck
himself. After the dauphin manages to dupe Huck and sell Jim to a
farmer named Silas Phelps, Huck reflects on what he should do and
at first decides he should let Jim's "rightful owner" know where her
runaway slave is now. Huck feels guilty for "stealing an old woman's
nigger that hadn't ever done me no harm," and resolves to tell Miss
Watson where she can find Jim. He drafts a letter to Miss Watson
telling her of Jim's whereabouts, and feels "all washed clean of sin
for the first time." But then he tears up the note and decides against
betraying Jim. Huck recalls the good times he and Jim have shared
together and thinks of how he is "the best friend old Jim ever had in
the world, and the *only* one he's got now." Huck decides that he will
go against what his conscience has told him, even if this means he
will "go to hell." Instead, he walks to the Phelps plantation, where
he meets a woman who, by coincidence, turns out to be the aunt of
Huck's friend Tom Sawyer. The two have a conversation in which
Tom's Aunt Sally makes it clear that she doesn't think of "a nigger" as
a person. Pretending to be Tom, Huck is explaining why a trip on a
Mississippi river steamer took longer than expected:

> "...We blowed out a cylinder-head."
> "Good gracious! anybody hurt?"
> "No'm. Killed a nigger."
> "Well, it's lucky; because sometimes people do get hurt...." (Ch. 32)

Comedy ensues when Aunt Sally goes off on a tangent, and before
long the comedy becomes more complicated when Tom Sawyer
appears on the scene and forms a plan to "steal" Jim; Huck is shocked
that the seemingly righteous Tom could become "a *nigger stealer*." In
the end the complicated plan goes wrong, but proves to have been

unnecessary; Jim is freed anyway. Not much is said about the issue of race in the book's last chapter.

B) Much has been made of the frequent appearance of the word "nigger" in *The Adventures of Huckleberry Finn*—and of other expressions of racism, including by sympathetically portrayed characters such as Aunt Sally, who speaks with a complete lack of feeling as she directly implies that "niggers" are not to be classed as "people":

> "…We blowed out a cylinder-head."
> "Good gracious! anybody hurt?"
> "No'm. Killed a nigger."
> "Well, it's lucky; because sometimes people do get hurt…." (Ch. 32)

How is the reader to take such passages? To the enlightened twenty-first century reader it may seem obvious that Aunt Sally's views are here being satirized. But is there anything in the text itself to support that reading? Is there any evidence in this case to suggest that the reader should fully reject Aunt Sally's view, and take black people and white people simply as people? Let us look at the passage immediately preceding that quoted. Before Huck catches a glimpse of Tom's Aunt Sally with her two children he sees a black woman with her two children. The two are presented in parallel fashion:

> A nigger woman come tearing out of the kitchen with a rolling-pin in her hand…. And behind the woman comes a little nigger girl and two little nigger boys, without anything on but tow-linen shirts, and they hung onto their mother's gown, and peeped out from behind her at me, bashful, the way they always do. And here comes the white woman running from the house, about forty-five or fifty year old, bareheaded, and her spinning-stick in her hand; and behind her comes her little white children, acting the same way the little niggers was doing. (Ch. 32)

The parallel is plain, and the implication should be clear; we should indeed see humans, whether black or white, simply as humans. The character of Huckleberry Finn may use the derogatory word that was universally used in his time—*niggers*—to describe African Americans. But the sensibility behind Huck's words (and Twain's) is one that strongly encourages the reader to reject race prejudice.

C) Twain's novel *The Adventures of Huckleberry Finn* is infected with racism at almost every turn. It's not only the much discussed matter of the word "nigger," which occurs over 220 times in the novel. Just as significant are conversations such as that between Huck and Tom's Aunt Sally, which make it explicit that African Americans are considered to be less than human, even by those white characters who are portrayed sympathetically in the novel. The context here is that Huck, pretending to be Tom, is explaining why a trip on a Mississippi river steamer took longer than expected:

> "…We blowed out a cylinder-head."
> "Good gracious! anybody hurt?"
> "No'm. Killed a nigger."
> "Well, it's lucky; because sometimes people do get hurt…." (Ch. 32)

Aunt Sally clearly does not regard "niggers" as equals—and there are no direct indications that we as readers should do any different. Even when Huck himself—the most sympathetically portrayed character of all—is praising Jim, he does so in racist terms; if Jim is good, he must to that extent be "white." So it is that when Tom has been wounded on the raft and Jim has said that he will refuse to leave him until a doctor is found, Huck comments approvingly of Jim: "I knowed he was white inside, and I reckoned he'd say what he did say" (Ch. 40).

No one could reasonably argue that *The Adventures of Huckleberry Finn* wholeheartedly endorses all the racist views expressed by the novel's characters; it is clearly a novel of considerable complexity, and considerable irony. Indeed, various critics have argued that the text's ironic layering should lead us to read the novel as entirely discrediting the racist sentiments expressed by the novel's characters, and that the novel deserves to be read as a text that subverts racist attitudes. But such arguments presume an audience of enlightened and sophisticated readers sensitive to irony and to context. The fact is that Twain's novel has been read most frequently not by enlightened and sophisticated adults but by young children; it remains a staple of the school curriculum across North America. If we keep in mind that fact about the novel's audience, it is not unreasonable to suggest that *The Adventures of Huckleberry Finn* may have done more to reinforce racist stereotypes than it has to undermine them.

The first of these is written competently enough so far as grammar and syntax are concerned. But it merely offers a recounting of various episodes from the book; it does not take a position, or develop an argument, as the assignment requires. The second and third passages, on the other hand, both put forward clear arguments relating to the novel and how it deals with the issue of race. The arguments point in very different directions, but both are well structured, and both are supported with evidence from the novel. Notice that the same quotation is used in all three passages. In the first, however, it is recounted as an incident in the story, not presented as evidence in an argument.

As was touched on above, the same sorts of textual material can in many cases count as evidence for the points you are making regardless of whether you are arguing for a particular interpretation of a novel or for a particular interpretation of a classic work of political theory. But there are also significant differences. For one thing, disciplines such as philosophy and history look to glean different sorts of meanings from classic texts. Most obviously, literary works do not always have to be discussed in the context of broad political and ethical issues in the sorts of ways we have discussed *Huckleberry Finn* (or, indeed, *The Merchant of Venice*, or "September 1, 1939"). We can read works of fiction, drama, and poetry with regard to poverty, social class, war, racial oppression, religious conflict—or any of the great ethical or social-political issues. But we can also consider what they have to say about the nature of love, or the experience of childhood, or the nuances of friendship, or the fear of death. In some cases those meanings may be quite plain to the reader—as they often are, for example, in the poems of Philip Larkin:

> They fuck you up, your mum and dad.
> They may not mean to, but they do. ("This Be the Verse")

> Life is first boredom, then fear.
> Whether or not we use it, it goes,
> And leaves what something hidden from us chose,
> And age, and then the only end of age. ("Dockery and Son")

More often than not, though, works of literature do not state meanings anything like so plainly as this. They deal very largely with those parts of our minds that we often find it difficult or impossible to neatly package meaning in this way. The meanings we experience may be hard to describe; we may experience time in ways that may have nothing to do with the clock or the calendar; our thoughts may flow one to the next in something of a jumble. Literature has the means to capture something of this experience, and to say something about it. But what it says to us in such circumstances will often be a matter of nuance: of conveying a sense of different sorts of meaning rather than of defining them; of suggesting rather than of explaining.

O *Meaning and Form in Literature*

Literature is of course also capable of conveying various feelings that may have little or nothing to do with what we think of as "meaning." To experience literature may be to experience excitement, or joy, or fear, or amusement, or suspense, or sadness, or relief. And literature may also inspire feelings that—much as they may be connected to our experience of various emotions—are at a remove from the emotions. A sense of pleasure at how well the sounds of a poem seem to fit the sense; a pleasurable recognition of how skilfully a story has been constructed or at how vividly the characters in a play or a novel have been "brought to life." These are feelings that we refer to as aesthetic in nature. They may be closely connected to our emotional response; we may be brought to tears by a literary work while at the same time being struck by the aesthetic qualities that have helped to shape that emotional response (and to shape our sense of the work's meaning). But we nevertheless recognize the aesthetic as a distinct realm.

Can we form arguments about the more nuanced meanings of literature, or about the emotional and the aesthetic responses that literature may prompt, in the same way as we can form arguments about *The Adventures of Huckleberry Finn* and race, or *The Merchant of Venice* and religion? Absolutely—and, in fact, you may find meaning and form so inextricable that you need to discuss the formal or stylistic qualities of a work such as *Huckleberry Finn* in order to make your point about its treatment of race. But some arguments about literature may focus on form more directly than others; literary studies is very much about being able to frame arguments on such topics as *how the juxtaposition of incidental detail helps to suggest ironic meaning in* The Adventures of Huckleberry Finn, or *how the narrative structure of* Heart of Darkness *affects the reader's response*, or *how the alternation of poetry and prose in* The Merchant of Venice *is a means both of reflecting and of resolving various tensions in the play*, or *how the rhythm of "September 1, 1939" (three stressed syllables per line, but no fixed pattern to the stresses, and no fixed number to the syllables) works in concert with the poem's themes.*

Let us look at some other examples, and let us look at love. If we are to explore the ways in which the meanings of a literary work and the emotions it may arouse connect to its aesthetic qualities, it is hard to think of a better place to start than Alice Oswald's 1996 poem "Wedding":

> From time to time our love is like a sail
> and when the sail begins to alternate
> from tack to tack, it's like a swallowtail
> and when the swallow flies it's like a coat;
> and if the coat is yours, it has a tear
> like a wide mouth and when the mouth begins
> to draw the wind, it's like a trumpeter
> and when the trumpet blows, it blows like millions...
> and this, my love, when millions come and go
> beyond the need of us, is like a trick;
> and when the trick begins, it's like a toe
> tip-toeing on a rope, which is like luck;
> and when the luck begins, it's like a wedding,
> which is like love, which is like everything.

Is the essence of the poem to give expression to the feeling of pure joy that is so much a part of the human feeling of romantic love? Does the poem also offer an implicit endorsement of traditional marriage? Or does the poem, in its insistence that the joy of love is "like a trick," "like luck," imply a more melancholy undercurrent—that love of this sort is a matter of chance and illusion and will always be transitory? Is there perhaps a hint in the poem that the rushing whirlwind of love is inherently thoughtless, even self-centred and lover-centred to the point of irresponsibility; "millions come and go / beyond the need of us," the lover says, thereby setting to one side a whole world of hardship and need, in the self-centred way humans tend to do when consumed by romantic love. But does the poem's ending suggest a widening of love, an expansive exuber-ance that might include within itself all the different sorts of love, in addition to the romantic joy of two humans? It would be possible to devote an entire essay to arguing any one of these positions.

It would be possible too to devote an entire essay to arguing any one of a large number of things about the poem's form, and the ways in which form relates to content. How do the poem's rhythm and syntax work to suggest a rush of feeling? How do its images work to suggest a sense of spontaneity? The poem is a sonnet with more half-rhymes and "off-rhymes" than traditional full rhymes; in what ways is that structure of rhyme appropriate to the poem's meaning(s)? Those are just a few of the questions about this poem that might inspire essay-length answers.

Oswald's "Wedding" is an extraordinary example of a love poem; let us look briefly at an equally extraordinary poem that, on the face of it, could hardly be more different—Eavan Boland's "Against Love Poetry":

> We were married in summer, thirty years ago. I have loved you
> deeply from that moment to this. I have loved other things as well.
> Among them the idea of women's freedom. Why do I put these
> words side by side? Because I am a woman. Because marriage is not
> freedom. Therefore, every word here is written against love poetry.
> Love poetry can do no justice to this. Here, instead, is a remembered
> story from a faraway history: A great king lost a war and was paraded
> in chains through the city of his enemy. They taunted him. They
> brought his wife and children to him—he showed no emotion. They
> brought his former courtiers—he showed no emotion. They brought
> his old servant—only then did he break down and weep. I did not
> find my womanhood in the servitudes of custom. But I saw my
> humanity look back at me there. It is to mark the contradictions of
> a daily love that I have written this. Against love poetry.

Is the essence of the poem merely to reject the sorts of feelings that underlie love poetry? Does it implicitly reject the ideals of romantic love itself? To what extent and in what ways does it differentiate between romantic love and other forms of love—or between love at the moment of getting married and the love that is able to survive through a long marriage? What does the poem suggest about the struggle between love and freedom—and how does the "remembered story from a faraway history" connect to the poem's themes of love and freedom? What contradictions does the poem mark? What if anything does it suggest as to how they may be resolved in the living of our lives? The poem uses verbal structures of argument ("because…", "therefore…"); does it in fact make sense in terms of the conventions of logical argument? The poem starts off addressing another person ("We were married…. I have loved you…") but by the end seems to be addressed to a more general audience; why would this be? Again, it would be possible to devote an entire essay to answering any one of these questions.

It would be possible too to devote an entire essay to any one of a number of arguments concerning the form of the poem. Is it intrinsically a poem at all—or only a poem by extension, as it were, in that conventional love poetry is its necessary reference point? Why is it significant that the work is published as exactly fourteen lines of prose? Does the rhythm of the poem—if we may call it that—reflect in any way the content of what is being said? Does the syntax? (It is noteworthy, for example, that the piece includes numerous incomplete sentences.) The poem was originally published in a book that was also entitled *Against Love Poetry*, but within the book it was the second in a series entitled "Marriage"; what significance might there be in such nested titles? Those are just a few of the questions about this poem that might inspire essay-length answers. And we might add one more set of questions, if it were to be a long essay; to what extent are the meaning(s) suggested by Alice Oswald's "Wedding" and Eavan Boland's "Against Love Poetry" in conflict with each other? Might the ideas suggested by the two poems be to some extent complementary? How do the two poems mirror each other in their formal qualities?

Students often find it even more difficult to frame written arguments dealing with aesthetic questions—with *how* the meanings of a literary work are presented—than they do framing arguments about the meanings themselves. One fundamental question that it is always helpful to have in the back of one's mind is this: "How do the formal qualities of the work—the ways in which its meanings are expressed—harmonize with the meanings themselves?" In most literary works that reward study there will be interesting connections between the two—and these connections can often provide the subject matter for successful student essays. As in the two examples above, the ways in which the words of a poem are arranged on the page may be highly suggestive of what the poem is saying. Similarly in a work of drama or prose fiction: a layered plot or a complex narrative structure may mirror complexities of meaning in the text. The reliability or unreliability of a narrator or a shift in viewpoint may signal the underlying approach of the work towards reality itself. The style of narration may convey to us something of the nature of human consciousness. The ways in which different characters are presented may create a wide range of different reactions. In any genre, patterns of imagery or metaphor may be suggestive of broader ideas or themes—or of traits of the characters, or of character traits.

Sometimes the style of presentation may seem to go against the nature of the material being presented, or its apparent meaning; a poem about death may be written with a lively rhythm, or a character entering eagerly into a new relationship may be described in a flat and unemotional style. In a work of little literary merit dissonance of that sort between style and meaning may simply be a case of poor writing. But instances of dissonance of that sort can also occur in extraordinarily accomplished literary work; there may be tensions between form and content that lend complexity as well as vitality to literary works—and that themselves become key parts of the work's aesthetic.

In order to formulate arguments that connect the meanings of a literary work to its form and style—that show how the way it is written connects to what it says—it is important to pay attention to things such as narrative viewpoints, ways of organizing or plotting stories, imagery and metaphor, rhythm and rhyme. One straightforward and often fruitful way to shape the "argument" of an essay about literature is simply to explain how some aspect of the form of a work expresses something of its meanings. Explain how the layered narrative structure of Mary Shelley's *Frankenstein* works to support the layers of meaning in the text. Explain how the half-rhymes and off rhymes of "Wedding" act in concert with the meanings suggested by the text. Explain what the use of verse and prose dialogue suggests about class and race dynamics in *The Merchant of Venice*. And so on. Beyond that, it may be helpful to run through the eight sets of questions that Ian Johnston provides as a prompt. (see below).

Essay Ideas: How to Think about Literary Works

To organize an argumentative essay about a literary work, it's usually best to select something very particular about the work and focus your attention exclusively on that. Here is a partial list of possible choices:

1. What is the significance of a particular character or a particular moment in the career of a single character? Why is that moment important? What human possibility does that part of the fiction hold up to us? What does that moment reveal about something significant in the story? What would be missing if that moment or that character were not in the story? Often you can organize a useful interpretative essay around the contribution of an apparently minor character or event.

2. Does a particular character learn or fail to learn something important in the story? If the resolution of a narrative depends upon the education of a main character, then a major interpretative point in the story will undoubtedly be what that character has learned (or failed to learn). This question is often very fruitful if a major part of the narrative is a journey of some kind, as in *Huckleberry Finn* or *Gulliver's Travels* or *Heart of Darkness* or the *Odyssey*. Is the main character the same person at the end of the journey as at the start? If not, what has happened? Why is that significant? How does the character behave when he returns? Why?

3. What is the importance of the setting (the physical environment) or some aspect of it? How does this help to define for the readers the sense of nature presented in the text—or the sense of how the world operates, of the values of human life?

4. Is there an interesting recurring pattern in the fiction (e.g., in the treatment of women, the significance of food, the nature of work, the depiction of the gods, the images of nature, the attitude to money, the style of the clothes, and so on)? Is there one object in the story that is particularly significant?

5. Why does the story end the way it does? How does the conclusion affect our understanding of what has gone on? Is there any irony in the ending (i.e., any unresolved ambiguities)? Does that raise any questions and invite us to think about them?

6. Does the story call attention to any important ideas or themes? In what sense is there a conflict of ideas or attitudes being explored in the fiction?

7. What role does the narrator play in our response to the story? Is that voice reliable, playful, ironic? Does the narrator understand the significance of the story? How does that affect the interpretation?

8. Often a particular remark in a fiction (or the title itself) can make a useful focus for an essay (once again, a popular form of exam question or essay topic), as in, for example, one of the following:

   - What does Catherine in Brontë's *Wuthering Heights* mean by her famous remark, "Nelly, I am Heathcliff"? How does that help us to understand anything significant in the novel?
   - Discuss the significance of Conrad's title "Heart of Darkness."
   - What is significant, if anything, about Lily Briscoe's comment to herself in Woolf's *To the Lighthouse*: "Yes, she thought, laying down her brush in extreme fatigue, I have had my vision"?

And so on. Remember that in a relatively short essay you can deal only with one very particular aspect of the fiction, so select carefully, and confine the argument to the significance of that one feature you have selected. And make sure that you do not just describe what you have selected. Instead create an argumentative opinion about its significance. That will be your thesis, a statement or series of statements which says, in effect, "If we look closely at this single aspect of the fiction we can see ways in which it contributes something important to our understanding of the total story."

—excerpted from Ian Johnston, *Essays and Arguments: A Handbook for Writing Essays* (Broadview Press, 2015)

Learning how to formulate arguments about texts can be challenging; so too can learning how to phrase arguments about literature in ways that will be clear and persuasive to readers. The following section discusses some common problems that arise in writing about literature at the level of sentence structure—and how to solve those problems.

O *Writing about Texts: Particular Problems*

D55. **verb tenses when writing about literary and other texts**: As is discussed in the next chapter, all academic subject areas have specialized vocabulary and conventions. One sort of convention that can take some getting used to is the way in which verb tenses are used. The past tense is, of course, normally used to name actions that happened in the past. But when one is writing about what happens in a work of literature (or, in some cases, about what is said in other sorts of texts), convention decrees that we use the simple present tense.

needs checking Romeo fell in love with Juliet as soon as he saw her.

revised Romeo falls in love with Juliet as soon as he sees her.

needs checking In her short stories, Alice Munro explored both the outer and the inner worlds of small town life.

revised In her short stories, Alice Munro explores both the outer and the inner worlds of small town life.

If literature in its historical context is being discussed, however, the simple past tense is usually the best choice:

needs checking Shakespeare writes *Romeo and Juliet* when he was about thirty years of age.

revised Shakespeare wrote *Romeo and Juliet* when he was about thirty years of age.

needs checking Alice Munro wins the Governor General's Award for the first time in 1968, for her collection *Dance of the Happy Shades*.

revised Alice Munro won the Governor General's Award for the first time in 1968, for her collection *Dance of the Happy Shades*.

In some circumstances either the past or the present tense may be possible in a sentence, depending on the context:

correct In her early work Munro often explored themes relating to adolescence.

[This phrasing is appropriate if the focus is on historical developments relating to the author.]

also correct In her early work Munro often explores themes relating to adolescence.

[This phrasing is appropriate if the focus is on the work itself.]

Notice that if the subject of a sentence is the work itself, the present tense is normally required:

needs checking Munro's early work often explored themes relating to adolescence.

revised Munro's early work often explores themes relating to adolescence.

Often in an essay about literature the context may require shifting back and forth between past and present tenses. In the following passage, for example, the present tense is used except for the sentence that recounts the historical fact of Eliot refusing permission:

T.S. Eliot's most notorious expression of anti-Semitism is the opinion he expresses in *After Strange Gods* that in "the society that we desire," "any large number of free-thinking Jews" would be "undesirable" (64). Tellingly, Eliot never allowed *After Strange Gods* to be reprinted. But his anti-Semitism emerges repeatedly in his poetry as well. In "Gerontion," for example, he describes....

In such cases even experienced writers have to think carefully during the revision process about the most appropriate tense for each verb. Note in the following example the change in verb tense from *was* to *is*:

needs checking In *The Two Gentlemen of Verona* Shakespeare exhibited a degree and a variety of technical accomplishment unprecedented in the English drama. He still had much to learn as a dramatist and as a poet; in its wit or its power to move us emotionally *The Two Gentlemen of Verona* was at an enormous remove from the great works of a few years later. But already, in 1592, Shakespeare had mastered all the basic techniques of plot construction that were to sustain the structures of the great plays.

revised   In *The Two Gentlemen of Verona* Shakespeare exhibits a degree and a variety of technical accomplishment unprecedented in the English drama. He still had much to learn as a dramatist and as a poet; in its wit or its power to move us emotionally *The Two Gentlemen of Verona* is at an enormous remove from the great works of a few years later. But already, in 1592, Shakespeare had mastered all the basic techniques of plot construction that were to sustain the structures of the great plays.

The same principles that are used in writing about literature apply too in many other disciplines.[1] Indeed, in these disciplines, if you are treating the ideas you are discussing as "live" ideas, it is wrong to use the past tense:

needs checking   In an important recent book, Nelly Ferguson surveyed the history of the decline of empires, and predicted that during the course of the twenty-first century China will replace the United States as the world's leading power.

revised   In an important recent book, Nelly Ferguson surveys the history of the decline of empires, and predicts that during the course of the twenty-first century China will replace the United States as the world's leading power.

needs checking   In their 2009 paper Smith and Johnson suggested that parental influence is more important than that of peers, even for adolescents. This essay will examine these claims and assess their validity.

revised   In their 2009 paper Smith and Johnson suggest that parental influence is more important than that of peers, even for adolescents. This essay will examine these claims and assess their validity.

---

1   In disciplines that follow APA style, however, the past tense or the present perfect tense are preferred in such situations.

In many disciplines, particularly in the sciences, it is also common to use the present perfect tense when discussing relevant recent research:

> Although research has often found the attitude-to-behavior connection to be quite weak, the behavior-to-attitude link has been shown to be quite strong. As Festinger (2008) and Kiesler, Nisbet, and Zanna (2006) have demonstrated, an asymmetry exists between the two possible directions. As Acheson (2009) has put it, "we are ... very good at finding reasons for what we do, but not very good at doing what we find reasons for" (25).

It is important to remember that the use of the present tense in such contexts is not dependent on how recently the ideas being discussed were first put forward; the key thing is whether or not you are discussing them as live ideas today. You may use the present tense when discussing a paper written six months ago—but you may also use the present tense when discussing a text dating from twenty-four centuries ago. Just as you may say when writing about literature that Shakespeare *explores* the potentially corrosive effects of ambition, so too you may say that Aristotle *approaches* ethical questions with an emphasis on individual virtue, and that Marx *values* highly the economic contribution of labour—even though Shakespeare and Aristotle and Marx are themselves long dead. As with the text of a story or poem, the writings of dead thinkers may be discussed as embodying live thoughts—ideas that may retain interest and relevance.

Conversely, if the ideas you are discussing are being considered historically, rather than as of current relevance, you should not use the present tense.

needs checking   In several articles the renowned astronomer Fred Hoyle advances arguments against the big bang theory of the origin of the universe. Hoyle suggests that the universe perpetually regenerates itself.

[Hoyle's arguments have now been refuted.]

revised   In several articles the renowned astronomer Fred Hoyle advanced arguments against the big bang theory of the origin of the universe. Hoyle suggested that the universe perpetually regenerates itself.

As is the case with writing about literature, academic writing in disciplines such as history or philosophy or political science may often look at a text *both* from a historical perspective *and* from the perspective of the live ideas that are put forward within it. In such circumstances the writer needs to be prepared to shift verb tenses depending on the context.

needs checking   In *An Introduction to the Principles of Morals and Legislation*, Jeremy Bentham asked what question should be foremost in our minds as we considered how to treat non-human animals: "The question is not, Can they reason?, nor Can they talk? but, Can they suffer? Why should the law refuse its protection to any sensitive being?"

revised   In *An Introduction to the Principles of Morals and Legislation*, Jeremy Bentham asks what question should be foremost in our minds as we consider how to treat non-human animals: "The question is not, Can they reason?, nor Can they talk? but, Can they suffer? Why should the law refuse its protection to any sensitive being?"

D56. consistency in verb tense when integrating quotations: If one is writing about literature the writing will usually be in the *present* tense, but the quotations one wishes to use are likely to be in the *past* tense. Often it is thus necessary, if you are incorporating a quotation into a sentence, to rephrase and/or adjust the length of the quotation in order to preserve grammatical consistency. If a quotation is set apart from the body of your own writing, on the other hand, you do not need to (and should not) rephrase.

needs checking   Emma Bovary lives largely through memory and fantasy. She daydreams frequently, and, as she reads, "the memory of the Vicomte kept her happy" (244).

[The past tense *kept* is inconsistent with the present tense *reads* and *daydreams*.]

revised   Emma Bovary lives largely through memory and fantasy. She daydreams frequently, and, as she reads, the "memory of the Vicomte [keeps] her happy" (244).

or   Emma Bovary lives largely through memory and fantasy. She daydreams frequently, and blends fact and fiction in her imaginings: "Always, as she read, the memory of the Vicomte kept her happy. She established a connection between him and the characters of her favorite fiction" (244).

Additional Material Online

Exercises on choosing the correct tense when writing about literature and about other academic subjects may be found at **sites.broadviewpress.com/writing**. Click on **Exercises** and go to **"Verbs."**

D57. attributing authorship / letting the text speak for itself: A tangle of issues surrounding authorship can make it difficult to phrase sentences having to do with what an author says, or what a text says. Views expressed by a character or narrator must not be confused with those of the author, and—for works of drama, poetry, and fiction—it is important to use phrasing that focuses on what the text does rather than making assumptions about what the author might have intended. But we must also be careful of phrases such as "the book says ..." that seem to grant authorial status to the text itself. Over time writers have developed a wide variety of strategies to deal with these sorts of awkwardness—to enable us to speak without obvious absurdity about the ways in which texts convey meanings. This is one area in which the passive voice often proves helpful.

needs checking   In the book it says that Victor Frankenstein becomes "capable of bestowing animation upon lifeless matter" (Ch. 3).

revised   Victor Frankenstein tells Robert Walton the story of how he became "capable of bestowing animation upon lifeless matter" (Ch. 3).

or   In Shelley's novel the lead character, Victor Frankenstein, recounts his great scientific discovery: "I succeeded in discovering the cause of generation and life; [and] more, I became myself capable of bestowing animation upon lifeless matter" (Ch. 3).

needs checking   In Genesis they give two quite different versions of the creation of Eve.

> [The use of "they" when assigning responsibility where the actual people are unknown ("they should fix the potholes on this street," "they never used to do it this way," etc.) is colloquial and should be avoided in formal written work.]

revised   Genesis offers us two quite different versions of the creation of Eve.

or   Two quite different versions of the creation of Eve are given in Genesis.

> [Notice how the passive voice ("are given") is used here.]

needs checking   The poem says that the 1930s were "a low dishonest decade."

also needs checking   In the poem it says that the 1930s were "a low dishonest decade."

revised   In the poem's first stanza the 1930s are described as "a low dishonest decade."

> [This construction, using the passive voice, can be used whether or not it is a character speaking, or the author speaking to us directly.]

or   The speaker refers to the 1930s as "a low dishonest decade."

When referencing text that is not attributed to a specific character, it is conventional to use phrases such as *the speaker* (in the case of a poem) or *the narrator* (in the case of a novel) instead of saying *the poet* or *the author*. For some poems where the author does not seem to have adopted a persona—such as, arguably, "September 1, 1939"—it can be acceptable to refer to the author directly:

- Auden refers to the 1930s as "a low dishonest decade."

If you are at all in doubt it is safest to use a phrase such as "the speaker."

The next example shows the danger of equating statements in a book with the author's opinions:

needs checking   In More's *Utopia* he says that landowners are "no longer content with leading an idle life and doing no harm to the country." In his view, they have now chosen to do real harm: "they leave no ground to be tilled, enclose every bit of land for pasture, pull down houses, and destroy towns."

[There are several problems here. The first is grammatical: *he* is a pronoun, and pronouns need to refer to nouns, whereas *More's* is a possessive adjective.]

still needs   In his *Utopia* More declares that English landowners are
checking   "no longer content with leading an idle life and doing no harm to the country." In his view, they have now chosen to do real harm: "they leave no ground to be tilled, enclose every bit of land for pasture, pull down houses, and destroy towns."

[Thomas More's *Utopia* is a work of fiction in which various characters give their views; it cannot be assumed that any of the views put forward by the characters were also those of the author.]

revised   In More's *Utopia* Raphael Hythloday declares that landowners are "no longer content with leading an idle life and doing no harm to the country." In Raphael's view, they have now chosen to do real harm: "they leave no ground to be tilled, enclose every bit of land for pasture, pull down houses, and destroy towns." Can we take this as More's own view? That question cannot be answered readily.

needs checking   The novel *The Jungle* tells us that the meatpacking industry is cruel to the workers in a wide variety of ways.

[We are not told this in so many words by the novel, as a non-fiction book or magazine article might tell us such things; rather we are shown the cruelties of the industry.]

revised   The novel *The Jungle* depicts the cruel treatment of workers in the early twentieth-century meatpacking industry.

> [where the emphasis is on the novel as a work
> that may still speak to us today—as literature
> rather than a historical artifact.]

or Upton Sinclair's 1906 novel *The Jungle* depicted the
cruel treatment of workers in the meatpacking industry;
it had a powerful effect on public opinion.

> [where the emphasis is on the historical impact
> of the novel.]

Here are some other approaches to wording that may be useful as
you write about texts—and try to negotiate the many issues involving what the characters have said, what the text has said, and what
the author has said:

> In the poem we are led to believe that ...
>
> Throughout the story we are led to sympathize with ...
>
> These lines in the poem suggest that ...
>
> The way this sentence is phrased implies that ...
>
> The fact that these deeds go unpunished at the end of the story
> suggests that ...
>
> The imagery in this stanza suggests that ...
>
> Characters who make us laugh tend to be easy to relate to, and
> Falstaff ... [*not* Characters who make us laugh tend to be easily
> relateable, ...]

⊙ Writing about Science

[Students may also find it helpful to consult the various sub-sections on scientific disciplines in "Across the Disciplines" (below).]

The many academic forms of writing about science include the review article (in which a writer surveys and assesses evidence on a particular topic from various sources); the research or experimental report, usually in the form of an article (in which a researcher writes up the results of an experiment of specific scope—lab reports are good practice for articles of this kind); the conference presentation or a poster board (in which scientists report in a limited or abbreviated fashion about specific research); the abstract (in which scientists provide a brief summary of the findings of a report or research paper); and the funding application, generally intended for a national or commercial grant or funding body (which usually includes an abstract and a statement of the importance of the research, along with a costing breakdown for the research).

O *Structure of the Research Paper*

The research article is in many ways the paradigmatic type of scientific writing. Unlike articles in the humanities, research articles in the sciences are generally organized into specific sections that usually appear in a set order: Introduction, Methods, Results, and Discussion. The opening section of the article, the *Introduction,* tells the reader the purpose and nature of the study. How does it fit in with previous research? What has it been designed to show? What was the hypothesis? The norm is to keep the introduction fairly brief; normally, it explains a bit about the background to the paper and indicates why the research was undertaken. The paper's introduction may, in fact, include a background section or be called *Background.* While it is appropriate to position the paper in the larger context of previous research here, extended discussion of that larger picture is not normally included in the introduction.

The *Methods* section is often very detailed. An important principle is that the paper should provide enough information about how the research was set up and conducted that other researchers can replicate the results. The reader also needs enough information to be able to understand the rationale for each step in the process.

The Methods section in a scientific research paper is always written in the past tense. When you are conducting your own research, however, it can be helpful to set out the details of the process beforehand in the present and/or future tenses, and then read over your notes with a view to the larger picture. Is the research being set up in the most unbiased way possible? Can the proposed method truly be expected to provide evidence one way or the other as to whether the hypothesis is valid? Are the most useful statistical methods being used to assess the data?

The *Results* section, as its name suggests, details the results at length. It often includes tables, charts, and graphs as a way of visually presenting these results.[1] The *Discussion* section provides an analysis of the meaning of those results, both in terms of the particular experiment and in terms of past experiments in the same area. Do the results confirm or refute the original hypothesis? What questions are left unanswered? What significance does the data have in the context of other research in this area? In what ways is the research subject to drawbacks (e.g., small sample size, indeterminate findings, confounding elements, short timeframe)? Do the results prompt any recommendations for the future?

Finally, scientific papers are almost always accompanied by an abstract, which comes before the actual paper. The *Abstract* summarizes the entire paper in no more than one or two paragraphs (usually 250 words or less); it is meant to convey the essence of the research to those who may not have time to read the entire paper, or who may be trying to determine if the entire paper will be of interest to them. Abstracts are often included in searchable databases for this latter purpose.

O *Scientific Tone and Stylistic Choices*

Most contemporary natural sciences writers strive for objectivity of tone, while writers in the humanities and social sciences may foreground their own subject positions and sometimes adopt a less formal tone. Look, for example, at the way in which anthropologist Emily Martin opens her classic article on "The Egg and the Sperm":

---

1   *Results* and *Discussion* are usually treated as separate sections of a paper; some journals, however, will ask that they be combined into one section of the paper.

> As an anthropologist, I am intrigued by the possibility that culture shapes how biological scientists describe what they discover about the natural world.... In the course of my research I realized that the picture of egg and sperm drawn in popular as well as scientific accounts of reproductive biology relies on stereotypes central to our cultural definitions of male and female. The stereotypes imply not only that female biological processes are less worthy than their male counterparts but also that women are less worthy than men. Part of my goal in writing this article is to shine a bright light on the gender stereotypes hidden within the scientific language of biology. Exposed in such a light, I hope they will lose their power to harm us.

Martin acknowledges at the outset that she occupies a specific position in relation to her research, and she uses the first person frequently ("I am intrigued," "I realized," "my goal"). Moreover, she acknowledges that her motive for conducting and publishing her research is not merely to expand objective knowledge about the world; she aims not only to shine a bright light on gender stereotypes, but also to reduce "their power to harm us." And yet, at its core, Martin's article is an example of careful scientific inquiry: she conducted a thorough survey of relevant scientific literature, her assessment of it follows scientific standards of objectivity, and she makes a strong argument based on clear and well-documented evidence.

Academics writing in natural science disciplines such as biology, chemistry, and physics, as well as those writing in the behavioural sciences (e.g., psychology, anthropology, sociology), all value scientific standards of objectivity and strive to make strong arguments based on strong evidence. However, differences in style and tone can be very noticeable, with the natural science disciplines tending towards a more formal and impersonal style than Martin adopts. But tone varies widely within the behavioural sciences as well; compare Martin's discussion of egg and sperm representations with the following behavioural science abstract for a 2012 scientific article that received a great deal of attention in general-interest media, "Facebook Use Predicts Declines in Subjective Well-Being in Young Adults":

> Over 500 million people interact daily with Facebook. Yet, whether Facebook use influences subjective well-being over time is unknown. We addressed this issue using experience-sampling,

the most reliable method for measuring in-vivo behavior and psychological experience. We text-messaged people five times per day for two-weeks [sic] to examine how Facebook use influences the two components of subjective well-being: how people feel moment-to-moment and how satisfied they are with their lives. Our results indicate that Facebook use predicts negative shifts on both of these variables over time. The more people used Facebook at one time point, the worse they felt the next time we text-messaged them; the more they used Facebook over two-weeks, the more their life satisfaction levels declined over time. Interacting with other people "directly" did not predict these negative outcomes. They were also not moderated by the size of people's Facebook networks, their perceived supportiveness, motivation for using Facebook, gender, loneliness, self-esteem, or depression. On the surface, Facebook provides an invaluable resource for fulfilling the basic human need for social connection. Rather than enhancing well-being, however, these findings suggest that Facebook may undermine it.

There are obvious differences in tone between this passage and that by Martin quoted above. Most obviously, the writers employ terminology specific to the academic discipline in which they are writing: "subjective well-being," "predicts," "moderated by," and "negative outcomes." More generally, the abstract is much more impersonal in tone than the first paragraph of Martin's paper; the reader is not told of any moment of realization which led to these researchers' work, or of what effects they hope their research will have. Instead, the passage provides a summary of the reasons for the study, the nature of the study, the main results, and some sense of their significance—all in reasonably direct and specific prose.

But what makes it clear to a reader in its discipline? Notice first that the abstract succinctly sketches in the background and the gap in the research that it aims to fill: "Over 500 million people interact daily with Facebook. Yet, whether Facebook use influences subjective well-being over time is unknown."

We may imagine how the topic might be introduced much less succinctly:

Facebook is used every day by people all round the world—overall, a total of more than 500 million people. There have been numerous studies that have examined Facebook use; a number of these have found correlations between high levels of Facebook use and low reported levels of subjective well-being. Those studies, however, have not tracked Facebook use and levels of subjective well-being together over time; doing so may provide a clearer picture of whether or not Facebook use does indeed negatively influence subjective well-being.

There is nothing grammatically wrong with these three sentences; they are simply long-winded, whereas in the abstract by Kross et al., everything except essential information is pared away.

Notice, too, the relative brevity of the sentences used as the abstract opens—the first is only eight words long. Long sentences are certainly sometimes appropriate (and indeed necessary)—but in scientific writing as in other sorts, varying sentence length is a good way to help maintain reader interest.

Expressing ideas concisely and varying sentence length are two ways of making your writing clear and readable. Using parallel or balanced sentence structures is another. Notice how the parallel grammatical structures in the following sentence (*the more ... the worse ...; the more ..., the more...*) emphasize the study's findings: "The more people used Facebook at one time point, the worse they felt the next time we text-messaged them; the more they used Facebook over two weeks, the more their life satisfaction levels declined over time."

Again, we may imagine how the same thoughts might be expressed in less readable fashion:

> Subjects who reported high levels of Facebook use at one time point also reported when we next text-messaged them that they felt worse, and this pattern was repeated over the full study, with subjects who used Facebook at high levels over the two-week period reporting declining levels of life satisfaction, a result that was strongest among those who reported the highest extended levels of Facebook use.

In this version the same ideas are expressed, but in far more words. Moreover, the sentence structure employed (successive subordinate clauses tacked onto a compound sentence) makes the reader work unnecessarily hard to understand what the writer is saying.

It is often imagined that complex and difficult-to-read sentence structures strike an appropriately academic tone—that direct sentences and rhetorical balance are for journalists or novelists, not students and scholars. If scientific research is important, however, then surely it's worthwhile to communicate that research in clear and readable prose.

O *The First Person and the Active Voice*

Students writing in disciplines such as biology, physics, psychology, or engineering are often advised to avoid grammatical structures associated with what might seem a subjective approach—most notably, the first person (*I* or *we*). Such advice is often also given to students writing English or history papers, and the reason is much the same: instructors want to discourage students from thinking of the writing of an academic paper as an exercise in expressing one's likes or dislikes. Unsubstantiated opinions are not appreciated in any of the academic disciplines. But how well one has supported one's argument bears no necessary relation to whether or not one has used the first person. In the Emily Martin example quoted above, Martin uses the first person extensively, but she doesn't just express an opinion; her study is supported using a lot of evidence, and the discussion itself is objective in nature.

Similarly, the abstract of the paper about Facebook by Ethan Kross et al. does not achieve its more formal and impersonal tone by avoiding the first person. Quite the contrary: Kross et al. use the first person twice in the first three sentences of the abstract: "We addressed," "We text-messaged."[1] Scientific objectivity, then, is not a matter of avoiding the first person; it is rather a matter of avoiding bias when framing one's research questions, of designing research projects intelligently and fairly, and of interpreting the results ethically.

Discussions of impersonality and objectivity in scientific writing have also often been framed in terms of the question of whether to use the active or the passive voice. For most of the twentieth century, many instructors in the natural sciences tried to train students

---

1   In the case of group authorship, which is very common in the sciences, the first person plural must, of course, be used.

to use the passive voice[1]—to write things like "*It **was decided** that the experiment **would be conducted** in three stages*" and "*These results **will be discussed** from several perspectives*" in order to convey a more impersonal and objective tone. However, statements in the active voice such as "*We **conducted** the experiment in three stages*" and "*We **will discuss** these results from several perspectives*" are not any more or less objective. The reader of an article knows the researchers did the experiment, so using the passive voice does not change the degree of objectivity—though it may add unnecessary words.

Indeed, while instructors in the natural sciences encouraged the passive voice, in the second half of the twentieth century many academics in English studies were reluctant to acknowledge that it had much of a part to play in academic writing—even scientific writing. In the 1990s, Andrea Lunsford and Robert Connors were playing something of a pioneering role in their discipline when they put forward the following advice in their influential handbook: "Much scientific and technical writing uses the passive voice effectively to highlight what is being studied rather than who is doing the studying." More than fifteen years later, a great many fellow writing studies scholars and composition teachers would give the same advice. Interestingly, just as handbook authors began to acknowledge that there could be a particular place for the passive voice in scientific writing, the scientific community began to swing around to the view that, much as the passive might sometimes have its place, the active voice should be the default writing choice. Here is Randy Moore, writing in *The American Biology Teacher* in 1991:

> The notion that passive voice ensures objectivity is ridiculous[;…] objectivity has nothing to do with one's writing style or with personal pronouns. Objectivity in science results from the choice of subjects, facts that you choose to include or omit, sampling techniques, and how you state your conclusions. Scientific objectivity is a personal trait unrelated to writing.

---

1 As Randy Moore and others have pointed out, nineteenth-century scientists used the active voice and the first person freely. The active voice and "first-person pronouns such as *I* and *we* began to disappear from scientific writing in the United States in the 1920s."

The 1990s saw heated debates in the pages of certain scientific journals on the matter of whether the active or the passive should be the default. But in the end the decision was clear: the active voice was the best choice. Nearly every major scientific journal[1] now recommends that its authors use the active voice in most situations—and that they use the first person where appropriate as well. The various *Nature* journals, the American Chemical Society Style Guide, and the American Society of Civil Engineers Style Guide are representative. The following instructions are from their respective websites:

> *Nature* journals prefer authors to write in the active voice ("we performed the experiment ...") as experience has shown that readers find concepts and results to be conveyed more clearly if written directly.

> Use the active voice when it is less wordy and more direct than the passive.... Use first person when it helps to keep your meaning clear and to express a purpose or a decision.

> Active Versus Passive Voice
> Wherever possible, use active verbs that demonstrate what is being done and who is doing it....
> > *Instead of:* Six possible causes of failure were identified in the forensic investigation.
> > *Use:* The forensic investigation identified six possible causes of failure.

Though the active voice is better as a default choice, in some circumstances it can still be better to use the passive. Especially in scientific writing, the passive voice is useful in many ways, including as a way of shifting attention away from the researcher to the experiment itself. Indeed, the following examples show clearly the types of statements that make effective use of the passive:

- The cooling process was completed in approximately two hours.
- This compound is made up of three elements.
- Phenomena of this sort may be seen only during an eclipse.

---

1   On his blog in 2012, Allen Downey conducted an informal survey and was able to identify only three exceptions: the *ICES Journal of Marine Science*, the *Journal of Animal Ecology*, and *Clinical Oncology and Cancer Research*.

Problems arise, however, when use of the passive reduces clarity or when the passive is used to disguise responsibility. Consider the following sentence in the passive voice, taken from the opening of a scientific article by Toby Knowles et al. from a 2007 PLoS ONE article entitled "Leg Disorders in Broiler Chickens": "Broiler chickens have been subjected to intense genetic selection." That is to say, they have been bred to grow so fast and become so heavy that they can barely walk. But this has not just happened; humans have done this to the birds, as part of a broad-based effort to generate more meat less expensively—too often, with little or no thought given to the birds themselves as sentient creatures. Here, the article's use of the passive voice de-emphasizes responsibility.

Yet the disguising or downplaying of agency—of just who is responsible for an action—is something that may be accomplished through a variety of verbal means. It need not be a matter of using the passive voice. Consider this example from another piece of scientific writing: Jeff Downing's "Non-invasive Assessment of Stress in Commercial Housing Systems": "hens need to deal with [challenges] in their environment.... In any flock there are likely to be some hens that perceive the challenges as more severe than others and have high corticosterone concentrations." In Downing's sentences, the hens are, in terms of grammatical voice, the active parties; they are the subjects of the verbs: "*hens **need** ... hens ... **perceive** the challenges*." But of course the controlling agents here in any sense other than a grammatical one are not the birds; it is humans who have subjected them to these "challenges"—if that euphemism is to be accepted. "Hardships," "privations," or "cruelties" are some of the other nouns that might be substituted for "challenges."

It would seem, then, that there is nothing pernicious in the passive voice itself. The passive voice is one means that *may* be used to disguise agency—and it is also a verbal construction that *may* involve unnecessary or inappropriate wordiness. If either is the case, if is often better to rephrase.

⊙ Across the Disciplines:
Different Subjects, Different Styles of Academic Writing

This section is designed to introduce the undergraduate student to some of the conventions of writing in a number of the main academic disciplines. The list of subjects covered is weighted towards those subjects that tend to place the greatest importance on writing (notably, the humanities and social sciences), though scientific writing is also covered.

Undergraduate students are often told that the conventions of writing vary between different disciplines, and that they should not expect that an approach to essay writing which works well in one discipline will work well in another. It is also the case that even *within* each discipline there can be more than one set of accepted practices when it comes to academic writing. What is entirely appropriate to an essay in the continental tradition of philosophy is not likely to suit the requirements of a course in epistemology taught entirely in the analytic tradition; an essay in the interpretivist tradition in sociology will be inappropriate for a course taught from a positivist perspective; and so on. This section attempts to give the student some sense of the divergent lines of approach in each discipline, and of the approach to academic writing in each case. Inevitably, the picture provided here in such a short space is a greatly simplified one. We hope that the information provided will nevertheless provide some guidance to those beginning the effort of reading and writing in a new academic subject.

Included with the discussions of writing practices of the disciplines are brief discipline-specific lists of useful websites and respected journals.

In the early years of this century a significant divide began to open up in the publishing of academic research. As the publishing of scholarly papers became more and more a digital enterprise, most journals went electronic, and made themselves available only through subscription, either to the journal directly or to one of the many aggregators that provide access to bundles of publications, primarily to university libraries. In the sciences and in some social sciences—most notably, Economics—many academics felt that these changes had resulted in a system that was too restrictive in the access it offered, too slow to publish new research, and too expensive. In response, scholars and scholarly associations began to found new open access journals and open access websites providing unrestricted free access to new research—including scholarly work in progress (drafts of journal articles, papers presented at conferences, etc.), as well as published academic papers that have already been peer-reviewed, edited, and so on. In Economics, most significant research now appears first in open access form through websites such as Research Papers in Economics and SSRN (the Social Science Research Network); in the sciences, PLoS (the Public Library of Science) and other open access publications are transforming the publishing landscape. The humanities have lagged behind the sciences and the social sciences in developing open access journals and websites—though SSRN now includes humanities networks in such subjects as Literature and Philosophy.

Students are also likely to benefit greatly from wide reading in general journals of news and opinion. Some of the most interesting, useful, and reliable of these are *The Atlantic Monthly, The Economist, Harper's Magazine, The New Yorker,* and *The New York Review of Books.* Some articles from these publications are available online, as are some materials from leading newspapers such as *The Australian, The Globe and Mail, The Guardian,* the *London Times,* the *Los Angeles Times, The New York Times, The Wall Street Journal,* and *The Washington Post.* As well, websites such as the Arts and Letters site (www.aldaily.com) provide access to a selection of the most interesting pieces from many of these and other sources.

Note: As this book is designed primarily for undergraduate use, some professional faculties (such as law) are not included in the following list. Business and commerce are included, however, as are engineering and health sciences, since at many institutions courses in these subjects are offered beginning at the first-year undergraduate level.

O *Anthropology*

Anthropology is unique among academic disciplines in the way it is configured. At many universities the department of anthropology includes four fields or subdivisions: cultural anthropology (the study of other cultures, or the study of one's own culture with a fresh eye); physical anthropology (the study of the physical evolution of humans, and connections to other primates); archeology (the study of the past through physical artifacts); and linguistics (the scientific study of human languages). In other universities archeology and linguistics may be separate departments on their own, with the anthropology department focusing on the study of physical and cultural anthropology. At still other institutions, the department of anthropology focuses exclusively on cultural anthropology— and in some cases, it is combined with sociology as one academic department. To complicate the picture further, what is known as "cultural anthropology" in the United States is referred to as "social anthropology" in Britain. (Both terms are understood and accepted in Canada and Australia, though the Canadians increasingly lean towards the American model.) Archeology, linguistics, and physical anthropology all tend towards a somewhat more scientific style of writing than does cultural anthropology. (For more on scientific styles of writing see below under "Biology" and "Psychology.") This section will focus on the most prevalent field within the discipline, cultural anthropology.

Until relatively recently the feature that most clearly distinguished cultural anthropology from sociology was that anthropology dealt with other cultures, sociology with our own culture. In the past generation, that distinction has very largely broken down, under both the pressure of a general realization among anthropologists of the degree to which perceptions of "otherness" were inherently problematic, and the practical pressures of greatly reduced funding for research in remote areas of the world. Cultural anthropologists are now at least as likely to focus on interesting and revealing aspects of cultures in the developed world as they are to focus on the kinship structures or belief systems of traditional societies in the Amazon basin or the forests of Papua New Guinea. But whereas the sociologist is likely to search for statistical information about aggregations of people, the anthropologist is far more likely to rely on observation and interviews to collect information on the basis of which are put forward "explanatory generalizations." (The early twentieth-century anthropologist Franz Boas, who was probably more influential than any other single figure in giving shape to the discipline, used this phrase to describe what anthropology, as a "human science," could offer; in contrast, he suggested that the natural sciences offer "particular descriptions.") Here are two passages of anthropological writing, one concerning the Yanomamo of southern Venezuela and northern Brazil, and the other discussing RVers in North America:

> The soul aspect of the *noreshi* [a sort of spirit or portion of the soul], however, can leave the human body at will and wander. Sickness results when the *noreshi* has left the body; unless it is brought back soon, the person will die.... When sickness is deemed to be the result of soul loss, the people who are closely related to the sick person hunt for his *noreshi*. I participated in one of these soul hunts. Kaobawa's group had set up a temporary camp across the river from its main village site, as they suspected raiders would attack them. While they were camped in their temporary village, one of the children became ill, and her malady was thought to be caused by soul loss.... (Napoleon Chagnon, *Yanomamo: The Fierce People*, New York, 1968, 49)

> The people whose lifestyle we describe here challenge the stereotype of old age as a time of decline into senility, poverty, and illness. Their descriptions of their experiences, and their depictions of themselves and their fellow RVers defy the myths about elderly North Americans. They do not think of themselves as suffering the 'plight' of the elderly. The stereotype of seniors being lonely, isolated, ill, dependent, and suffering from the trauma of the 'empty nest' or meaningless retirement does not apply to them. They see themselves and their peers as adventurous, self-reliant, flexible, friendly, and 'gutsy.'... One of our correspondents, Tonia Thornson, describes the difference between RVing seniors and those living in a home for the elderly. She left RVing in 1993 at the age of 81 because, she says, of the 'bunch of crooks' who repair RVs. She now regrets her decision. (Dorothy and David Counts, *Over the Next Hill: An Ethnography of RVing Seniors in North America*, Peterborough, 2/e 2001, 50)

Much as the subject matter of these two passages may differ, we may notice that both advance generalizations about a culture or a subculture; that both couch these generalizations in the present tense; and that both support the generalizations they are making with evidence gleaned from personal interaction with members of the group being studied.

Not all cultural anthropology is characterized by an emphasis on the personal and the particular. As with other social sciences, postmodernist theory has exerted considerable influence within the discipline of cultural anthropology—and with it has come a writing style featuring long sentences, complex syntax, extremely high levels of abstraction, and a vocabulary quite different from that of traditional anthropology. That style is discussed extensively elsewhere in these pages (in particular, under "Art History," "English Studies," "History," and "Sociology").

● Citation and Documentation

The American Anthropology Association publishes its own brief Style Guide. In almost all particulars it follows the Chicago Style of parenthetical citation. It does, however, make some exceptions, most notably in using a colon (rather than a comma) to separate date and page number in a parenthetical citation:

> Evidence now suggests that the kinship system of the Pacaa Nova is extraordinarily complex (Von Graeve 2003: 24–35).

The AAA Style Guide may be downloaded from the AAA website.

● Some Useful Websites

- *American Anthropological Association*
  www.aaanet.org The official site of the AAA includes a range of useful information, as well as many useful links.
- *Anthropology Research on the Internet*
  www.archeodroit.net/anthro This site, with an emphasis on archeology, includes links to a great deal of useful information.
- *JSTOR*
  www.jstor.org Founded in 1995 as a not-for-profit organization, this site is a leader in providing electronic access to a wide variety of scholarly journals online.
- *SSRN (Social Science Research Network)*
  www.ssrn.com This respected open access site includes a research network on Anthropology and Archaeology

(AARN) that is affiliated with the American Anthropological Association.

● Some Respected Journals

American Anthropologist The flagship journal of the American Anthropology Association.

American Ethnologist A respected journal published by the American Anthropological Association.

Annual Review of Anthropology Provides helpful reviews and syntheses of recent literature in the discipline.

Anthropologica The official journal of the Canadian Anthropological Society.

Anthropology Today A bimonthly, aimed at the general public as well as at anthropologists and students.

Australian Journal of Anthropology This respected journal is published by the Australian Anthropological Society.

Cultural Anthropology A leading journal published by the American Anthropological Association; the journal became open access in 2014.

Journal of the Royal Anthropological Society (formerly *Man*) The most established British journal in the discipline.

O *Art History*

Scholarly writing in art history, like that in several other disciplines, alternates frequently between the past tense and the present tense, with the past tense used to discuss historical developments and the present tense employed when the appearance or present effect of a work is being discussed. Here is a sample:

> To trigger the process of elevation, many crucifixes were introduced as signposts to the pathway upwards. On the Copenhagen reliquary (Plate 6), for instance, the painting of Christ's death is transformed by the crystal and then exalted by the picture of Christ in heaven rendered on the reverse....
>
> Most often, medieval image makers deployed usual iconographic means to present Christ as both earthly and divine. For example, a manuscript in Stuttgart (Landesbibliothek, Brev. 128, fol. 9v) assimilates numerous texts and pictorial sources ... to

establish the Lord's majesty; it incorporates personifications of light and dark and winter and summer to position Him in relation to the world. (Herbert L. Kessler, *Seeing Medieval Art*, Peterborough, 2004, 74–75)

The style of the above passage (by a leading historian of medieval art, writing both for fellow scholars and for general readers and students) is somewhat challenging conceptually, but relatively straightforward in the structure of its sentences. It employs concrete nouns (*crucifixes, pathway, manuscript*) more frequently than it does abstract nouns, and the abstract nouns that are used (*majesty, personifications*) tend to be readily comprehensible.

If this passage represents one pole in art history writing, another, quite different style finds expression in the following passage:

> Thus perhaps at stake has always been the murderous capacity of images, murderers of the real, murderers of their own model, as the Byzantine icons could murder the divine identity. To this murderous capacity is opposed the dialectical capacity of representations as a visible and intelligible mediation of the Real. All of Western faith was engaged in this wager on representation: That a sign could refer to the depth of meaning, that a sign could exchange for meaning, and that something could guarantee this exchange—God, of course. But what if God himself can be simulated, that is to say, reduced to the signs which attest his existence? Then the whole system becomes weightless, it is no longer anything but a gigantic simulacrum—not unreal, but a simulacrum, never again exchanging for what is real, but exchanging in itself, in an uninterrupted circuit without reference or circumference. (Jean Baudrillard, "The Evil Demon of Images and the Precession of Simulacra," in Thomas Docherty, ed., *Postmodernism: A Reader*, New York, 1993, 194)

This quotation (a translation from the French of a key passage by a leading postmodern theorist) is unlike the first passage in almost every respect. It aims to challenge the reader from every angle—in its style of writing as well as in the concepts themselves. It is extraordinarily dense, filled with abstract nouns (many of them specific to contemporary cultural theory), and lacking in concrete examples. It is syntactically complex, using devices such as the placing of phrases in apposition (*from the utopia of ..., from the radical negation of ..., from the sign as reversion and death sentence of ...*), which have the effect of continually recasting the thoughts being presented—as well as of lengthening the sentences. Writing such as this, in the style of certain sorts of theoretical schools commonly styled "postmodernist," is frequently used in several of the humanities and social sciences; it is discussed more fully below under the sections on English studies and history in particular. This style is frequently encountered in writing about art theory—contemporary theory in particular. The sorts of conventions that are followed in the Kessler passage, however, remain far more common in art history departments.

● Citation and Documentation

Art history and other disciplines in the fine arts generally use MLA Style. For a sample essay in art history see pages 605–32.

● Some Useful Websites

- *Association of Art Historians*
  www.aah.org The largest British association in this discipline maintains a helpful website.
- *College Art Association*
  www.collegeart.org This is the main site for America's umbrella association of art historians, curators, and other art professionals. It includes many helpful links.
- *The History of Art Virtual Library*
  www.chart.ac.uk/vlib/ This site provides a wide range of links and images.
- *Art Source*
  www.ilpi.com/artsource/welcome.html Selective but very useful site maintained by Mary Molinar of the University of Kentucky.
- *Image Collections and Online Art*
  www.umich.edu/%7Ehartspc/histart/mother/images.html Possibly the most comprehensive and helpful of all the online compendia of images and information about art history, this site has been developed at the University of Michigan.

● Some Respected Journals

Art and Australia This broadly based magazine is the leading Australian publication on the visual arts.

Art in America A broad-ranging monthly magazine, aimed at the general public and art dealers as well as art historians.

Art History This respected scholarly journal, published by the Association of Art Historians in the UK, is issued quarterly.

Art Journal This scholarly journal, founded in 1941, is the flagship publication of the College Art Association.

Artforum This monthly magazine provides good coverage of much of the contemporary art world.

Canadian Art This broadly based magazine is the leading Canadian publication on the visual arts.

O Biology

Academic writing about scientific subjects tends to be of two main sorts. The less common of these is the review article, in which the writer surveys and assesses evidence on a particular topic from various sources. Here is a passage from an abstract of a review article:

> Senescence is a complex, highly regulated, developmental phase in the life of a leaf that results in the co-ordinated degradation of macromolecules and the subsequent mobilization of components to other parts of the plant. The application of molecular biology techniques to the study of leaf senescence has, in the last few years, enabled the isolation and characterization of a large range of DNA clones representing genes that show increased expression in senescing leaves.... The analysis of these genes and identification of the function of the encoded proteins will allow a picture of the complex processes that take place during senescence to be assembled. To date, genes encoding degradative enzymes such as proteases and nucleases, enzymes involved in lipid and carbohydrate metabolism, and enzymes involved in nitrogen mobilization, have all been identified as senescence-enhanced genes. A variety of other genes of no obvious senescence-related function have also been identified; their role in senescence may be less predictable and, possibly, more interesting. (V. Buchanan-Wollaston,

"The Molecular Biology of Leaf Senescence," *Journal of Experimental Biology*, 1997, vol. 48, 181)

Notice here the variety of verb tenses used. When research is summarized the present perfect tense ("... *has enabled* the isolation ...," "... enzymes involved ... *have all been identified*") is used. The simple present tense is used when established scientific facts or ongoing realities are recounted ("Senescence *is* ...," "... genes that *show* ..."). The future tense is sometimes employed as well, when speculation as to the future direction of research is engaged in ("... *will allow* a picture ..."). One other aspect of this passage worth noting is that it makes no reference to other research. Whereas abstracts in the social sciences (and in a behavioural science such as psychology) tend always to place an article in the context of previous research, the abstracts of many papers in the pure sciences make little or no reference to previous research. Even in the introduction to a paper in biology, chemistry, or physics, there tends to be less by way of direct reference to previous research than is common in scientific papers in the social sciences.

The more common sort of scientific writing is the research paper, in which the writer reports on original research. Such papers follow a standardized format, with a precise **title**; an **abstract** summarizing the paper; an **introduction** outlining the nature of, rationale for, and background to the research; a section describing the **method** or procedures followed; a section presenting the **results**; a section providing a **discussion** of the results, their significance, and their implications; and a list of **references**. Here is a typical passage from a section setting out the method followed in an experiment:

Sperm samples were collected from adult males by penile electrostimulation, and sperm capacitation and IVF were done as described previously [20], with a few minor modifications [17]. Briefly, 10×10^6 washed sperm/ml were resuspended in 2 ml TALP medium and incubated at $37°$ in 5% CO_2 in air for 1–10 h. Sperm were treated for 30–35 min with 1 mW each of dibutyryl cyclic AMP (dbcAMP) and caffeine to induce hyperactivation. Hyperactivated sperm (300,000/ml) were then coincubated with oocytes for 12–16 h in TALP medium containing 1mM each of dbcAMP and caffeine in microdrops under mineral oil at $37°$ in a humidified atmosphere of 5% CO_2 in air. Sperm and remaining cumulus cells were then removed manually by pipetting through a finely pulled glass pipette, and oocytes were examined for evidence of fertilization. (Ping Zheng et al., "The Primate Embryo Gene Expression Resource: A Novel Resource to Facilitate Rapid Analysis of Gene Expression in Non-Human Primate Oocytes and Preimplantation Stage Embryos," *Biology of Reproduction*, published online ahead of print 14 January 2004)

As this passage well illustrates, the convention generally followed when describing methods employed and results obtained is to present the information in as clear and concise a fashion as possible, using the simple past tense.

While the equivalent of the review article in a university course is typically a term paper or research paper, the equivalent of the research paper is the lab report, in which the student writes up the results of an experiment performed in class.

For a broader discussion of writing in the sciences, see pages 411–19.

● Citation and Documentation

The Council of Science Editors (CSE) style is followed in biology. See the CSE Citation Guidelines for an overview of CSE style. Note that fields related to biomedicine often use the citation styles described under "Medicine and Health Sciences."

● Some Useful Websites

- *Agricola*
  http://agricola.nal.usda.gov Provides a wide variety of materials relating to agriculture, animal science, and forestry.
- *Canada Institute for Scientific and Technical Information*
  www.cisti-icist.nrc-cnrc.gc.ca The library of the National Research Council of Canada collection includes technical reports and conference papers as well as journal articles.
- *National Center for Biotechnology Information Tools*
  www.ncbi.nlm.nih.gov/guide/all/#tools A collection of online tools that can be used for analyzing biomedical and genomic information.

- *Pubmed Central*
  www.ncbi.nlm.nih.gov/pmc/ The US National Institutes of
  Health (NIH) digital archive of biomedical and life sciences
  journal literature.
- *Tree of Life Web Project*
  www.tolweb.org/tree A website organising information on a
  wide variety of organisms, arranged cladistically according to
  proposed evolutionary relationships and common ancestry.
- *Virtual Library: Biosciences*
  http://vlib.org/Biosciences This section of the Virtual Library
  includes a wide range of useful information and links.

● *Some Respected Journals*

Cell This journal publishes on experimental biology with an emphasis on
publishing results that advance the conceptual understanding of or
raise questions relating to important research areas in biology.

Journal of Biological Chemistry Founded in 1905, this journal covers new
developments in many areas of biochemistry.

PLOS Biology First published in 2003, this was the first open-access journal of the Public Library of Science.

Proceedings of the Royal Society B: Biological Sciences Proceedings B publishes
on all biological sciences but is particularly strong in ecology and in
behavioural and evolutionary biology.

O *Business and Commerce*

It is important, first of all, to be clear on the distinction between
business writing—the writing of business letters, memos, and so on,
which is covered in a separate chapter in this book—and academic
writing about business and commerce (pages 344–50). Academic
styles of writing in departments or faculties of business or commerce
fall into two broad categories. Much writing about business is highly
technical, and resembles academic writing about economics (see
below). Here is a sample:

A security market where the relative incidence of informed and
uninformed trading determines liquidity may have more than one
equilibrium. Equilibrium with high liquidity has a low bid-ask
spread. This increases participation by traders who want to hedge

risk exposure, as opposed to trading on private information, and justifies the small price impact of trades. Equilibrium with low liquidity has a high bid-ask spread. This deters some hedgers, increasing the relative incidence of informed trading, which justifies the larger spread. This analysis casts doubt on the relevance of comparative results in the existing literature relying on exogenous liquidity traders. (James Dow, "Is Liquidity Self-Fulfilling?" *Journal of Business*, 2004, vol. 77, no. 4, 78)

Notice that the discussion is largely couched in the present tense; the object of the study is to explore what *happens* as a general rule, not what happened in one particular case.

The other main style of academic writing about business is much less technical, and is in some respects unique to the study of business; this is the case study approach. Popularized by the Harvard Business School, this approach eschews abstract theoretical formulations and focuses instead on studies of real-world cases. Here is a sample:

Early in its development Nestlé established production facilities outside of Switzerland. By 1986, Nestlé had plants in 60 countries. In determining whether to set up production facilities in a particular country, the company considered several factors, including the availability of raw materials, the overall economic climate, and consumer tastes and purchasing power. (W.D. Dobson and Andrew Wilcox, *How Leading International Dairy Companies Adjusted to Changes in World Markets*, Babcock Institute, University of Wisconsin, 2002, 7)

Notice here that the sentence structures are relatively simple, and that abstract language is avoided. Business case studies are often written with a view to being accessible to business people as well as to academics, and to that end often include such features as point-form "executive summaries." As one would expect, business case studies tend to be couched largely in the simple past tense—though the present perfect may be used if the writer refers to a business practice that is still current at a particular company.

● *Citation and Documentation*

Although there is no universally accepted style of citation and documentation for business and commerce, APA style is very widely used. See the section on "Documentation" for a full outline of APA style.

● *Some Useful Websites*

- *Business.gov*
  www.business.gov This US government site provides a wide range of statistics on business activity.
- *Global Edge*
  www.globaledge.msu.edu/ibrd/ibrd.asp Provides a useful collection of information on international business.
- *JSTOR*
  www.jstor.org Founded in 1995 as a not-for-profit organization, this site is a leader in providing electronic access to a wide variety of scholarly journals online.
- *SSRN (Social Science Research Network)*
  www.ssrn.com This site provides access to hundreds of thousands of working papers, as well as an abstract database.
- *Virtual Library: Business and Economics*
  www.vlib.org/BusinessEconomics The business and economics section of the Virtual Library provides a wide variety of information and links.

● *Some Respected Journals*

The Academy of Management Journal This journal is respected for cutting-edge research.

Business Week Founded in 1929, this popular weekly magazine provides accessible news and analysis.

Fortune Founded in 1930, this respected twice-weekly magazine focuses on business and the economy.

The Journal of Business Founded in 1928, this journal is published by the University of Chicago; it is perhaps the most prestigious academic journal in the discipline.

The Journal of Finance This widely cited journal is the official publication of the American Finance Association.

O *Chemistry*

The conventions of writing followed in the pure sciences are broadly similar; they are discussed above under "Biology" and on pages 411–19.

● *Citation Style*

Coghill, Anne M., and Lorrin R. Garson, eds. *The ACS Style Guide: Effective Communication of Scientific Information.* 3rd ed. Washington: Amer. Chemical Soc., 2006. Print.

● *Some Useful Websites*

• *American Chemical Society*
   www.chemistry.org The website of the American Chemical Society includes a wide variety of information, as well as links to other sites.
• *IUPAC Compendium of Chemical Terminology*
   http://goldbook.iupac.org Also known as the Gold Book, this resource provides definitions for a variety of terms relating to · chemical science.
• *Links for Chemists*
   www.liv.ac.uk/chemistry/Links/links.html Run by the University of Liverpool chemistry department, this site is the chemistry section of the WWW Virtual Library.
• *Wolfram Alpha*
   www.wolframalpha.com A computational knowledge engine that can provide information and perform calculations based on an extensive database of facts and statistics.

● *Some Respected Journals*

Accounts of Chemical Research Published by the American Chemical Society, this journal uses "Conspectus" summaries instead of traditional abstracts. These are intended to provide the reader with greater detail on the contents, context, and significance of the articles.

Chemical Reviews Published by the American Chemical Society, Chemical Reviews provides comprehensive reviews of important recent research in organic, inorganic, physical, analytical, theoretical, and biological chemistry.

Chemical Society Reviews The flagship review journal of the Royal Society of Chemistry with a particular focus on interdisciplinary research.

Journal of the American Chemical Society Founded in 1879, this is the flagship journal of the American Chemical Society.

Nature Chemistry This publication focuses on high-impact research in analytical, organic, inorganic, and physical chemistry and in interdisciplinary research where the central theme falls within the discipline of chemistry.

O *Economics*

Writing on economics has its roots in the long but elegantly balanced sentences of Adam Smith in the eighteenth century. There was no such thing as a "discipline" of economics when Smith was writing, and it would be very much an anachronism to describe him as an economist. As passages such as the following illustrate, Smith came to the topic of "the wealth of nations" as a moral philosopher rather than as a social scientist:

> People of the same trade seldom meet together, even for merriment and diversion, [without] the conversation end[ing] in a conspiracy against the public, or in some contrivance to raise prices. It is impossible indeed to prevent such meetings, by any law which either could be executed, or would be consistent with liberty and justice. But though the law cannot hinder people of the same trade from sometimes assembling together, it ought to do nothing to facilitate such assemblies, much less to render them necessary. (Adam Smith, *The Wealth of Nations*, Book One, Chapter 10)

Ties with the traditions of philosophical and historical writing were not abandoned as the academic discipline of economics developed in the late nineteenth and earlier twentieth centuries, and even into the 1930s the arguments of economists were put forward more frequently with words than with numbers or equations. In 1933 the journal *Econometrica* was founded, with the intent of countering an anti-mathematical bias in the discipline.

No such bias against numbers and equations exists in the discipline of economics today. Most economists now rely very largely on mathematics and statistics, and largely as well on very specialized vocabulary. Even aside from obviously technical terms (*Pareto-neu-*

436 | ACADEMIC WRITING

tral, Phillips curve, and so on) a number of everyday English words
(e.g., *optimal, equilibrium*) are also used by economists with precise
technical meanings particular to the discipline. The following passage, taken from the introduction to a paper on measuring the well-
being of populations, gives something of the flavour:

> The dominance criteria of Atkins (1970) and Shorrocks (1983)
> have become well-known, and are now widely used for making
> welfare comparisons on the basis of income distribution data.
> These approaches, though, do not take into account the sort of
> non-income information—such as family size, age, type of hous-
> ing—which is these days available in plenty in micro datasets, and
> may be of welfare relevance. Hence the old results have begun to
> be viewed as of limited usefulness. One could not, for example,
> use the generalized Lorenz dominance approach to recommend
> as welfare-improving the transfer of income from single persons
> to families with children, or to those with special needs such as
> old age or infirmity.
>
> In response to this perceived shortcoming, Atkinson and Bour-
> guignon (1987) developed their sequential generalized Lorenz
> dominance criterion, for the comparison of joint distributions
> of income and needs, the latter assumed to be an ordinal vari-
> able, and this criterion has been found broad enough for some
> operational purposes. There is now a flourishing literature on
> the sequential approach. One thinks for example of Atkinson's
> (1990) illustrative account, Jenkins's and Lambert's (1993) exten-
> sion to allow for demographic change ... and the exploration of
> welfare fundamentals by Ok and Lambert (1999). (Peter J. Lam-
> bert and Xavi Ramos, "Welfare Comparisons: Sequential Procedures for
> Heterogeneous Populations," *Economica* Volume 69, No. 276, Novem-
> ber 2002, 549–62)

The above is typical not only in its highly technical vocabulary,
but also in the way it positions itself in the context of an extensive
literature. Here, as in most economic writing, the verb tenses are
quite straightforward, with the simple present tense and the present
perfect tense the most widely used.

Economics, as it is practised today, is probably more homoge-
nous in its approach than any of the other social science disciplines.
It is far from being all of a piece, however; writing in sub-disciplines

such as economic history is often quite non-technical. The following passage, for example, could as easily have been written by a historian as an economist:

> Students of southern agriculture in the United States after the Civil War discovered a similar phenomenon. As the average size of farms began to shrink, small farmers had no choice but to grow cotton instead of corn. Although cotton production entailed much more risk, farmers could hope to survive only by adopting a strategy of buying corn in order to have more resources to devote to their cash crop (C. Wright 1978, 169). Consequently, higher corn prices would tend to work to the disadvantage of those farms that were too small to market grain. (Michael Perelman, *The Invention of Capitalism: Classical Political Economy and the Secret History of Primitive Accumulation,* Durham, NC, 2000, 298)

When one is dealing with economic history, of course, the past tense is the norm.

● Citation and Documentation

Although there is no universally accepted style of documentation for economics, APA (American Psychological Association) style is very widely used. See the section elsewhere in this book on "Documentation" for a full outline of APA style.

● Some Useful Websites

- *History of Economic Thought*
  www.cepa.newschool.edu/net This site provides a range of reliable summaries of key ideas and movements in the history of economics.
- *EconLit*
  www.econlit.org This site, run through the American Economic Association, contains abstracts, indices, and links to articles in most major economic journals. It is available at libraries and on university websites throughout the world.
- *WebEc*
  www.helsinki.fi/webec WebEc (Worldwide Web Resources in Economics) provides links to a vast amount of free information in economics.

● Some Respected Journals

American Economic Review Founded in 1911, this is the flagship journal of the American Economic Association.

Econometrica An international journal of mathematical economics founded in 1933.

Economic Journal This British journal was founded in 1891, and remains influential.

Journal of Economic History Founded in 1941, this journal has maintained a high reputation.

Journal of Economic Literature This journal was created in 1969 by the American Economic Association in order to provide an annotated bibliography of publications in the discipline. It offers summaries of books and journal articles, and useful surveys of recent publications on particular topics within economics.

Journal of Political Economy Founded in 1892 at the University of Chicago, this journal has in the past generation been a leading venue for the expression of neoclassical and monetarist views.

Research Papers in Economics. Sponsored by a division of the American Federal Reserve Bank, this site provides a vast database of open access journal articles, working papers, and other material.

SSRN (the Social Science Research Network). This respected open access site is particularly strong in Economics; its Economics Research Network includes close to 350,000 research papers.

O Engineering

● Citation and Documentation

Institute of Electrical and Electronics Engineers. *IEEE Editorial Style Manual.* IEEE, n.d. Web. 9 Sept. 2009.

● Some Useful Websites

- *eFunda*
  http.//www.efunda.com A repository of fundamental information for review by engineering professionals.
- *Electrical Engineering Portal*
  http://electrical-engineering-portal.com A collection of tools, articles and resources for electrical engineers.

- *Engineering Toolbox*
  http://www.engineeringtoolbox.com A collection of tools and basic information for a variety of engineering disciplines, sorted by field.
- *Wolfram Alpha*
  www.wolframalpha.com A computational knowledge engine that can provide information and perform calculations based on an extensive database of facts and statistics.

● Some Respected Journals

Applied Energy In addition to articles on energy conservation and use of energy resources, this journal publishes on the environmental, social, and economic impacts of energy policies and usage.

IEEE journals The Institute of Electrical and Electronics Engineers publishes over one hundred peer-reviewed journals, many of which are highly prestigious in their fields. Examples include *Proceedings of the IEEE, IEEE Transactions on Industrial Electronics, IEEE Transactions on Power Electronics* and *IEEE Transactions on Antennas and Propagation.*

Journal of Fluid Mechanics This leading journal in its field publishes on the fundamental aspects of fluid mechanics as well as their application in other fields

Nature Biotechnology This journal focuses on new concepts in technology and methodology that impact the science and business of biotechnology.

Nature Materials This multidisciplinary journal focuses on fundamental and applied research that has the potential to impact research in classical sciences such as biology, chemistry, and physics.

O English Studies

In no academic discipline has the question of writing style been so vexed in the past generation as it has in English studies. For that reason—and because new styles of discourse that first took root in English studies have recently been spreading much more widely through other disciplines—more space will be devoted here to the writing conventions of this academic subject than to those of any other.

The study of English literature had by the late nineteenth century developed into a recognized academic subject, and for most of the twentieth century the discipline followed a broadly similar approach to writing about literature. While popular literary critics focused on evaluative judgements, academic critics moved substantially beyond the evaluative; the work of the scholar entailed pointing out aspects of a literary work that might not be obvious to the casual reader—whether they be points of style, of theme, of characterization, or of literary history—and clarifying those points for the reader. Irony, paradox, or contradiction were considered particularly fertile ground for the literary critic. Here is a sample:

> The prevailing literary mode in Nature poetry in the late eighteenth century (as derived from Edmund Burke) was the cult of the sublime and the picturesque, featuring views and inspirational scenery. In the first half of the nineteenth century this shifted to Wordsworthian Romanticism ... in which Nature was "good" and cities were "evil."...
>
> In *Roughing It in the Bush* [Susanna] Moodie's determination to preserve her Wordsworthian faith collides with the difficulty she has in doing so when Nature fails time and again to come through for her. The result is a markedly double-minded attitude towards Canada:
>
>> ... The aspect of Nature ever did, and I hope ever will, continue: "To shoot marvellous strength into my heart." As long as we remain true to the Divine Mother, so long will she remain faithful to her suffering children.
>>
>> All that period my love for Canada was a feeling very nearly allied to that which the condemned criminal entertains for his cell—his only hope of escape being through the portals of the grave.
>
> These two emotions—faith in the Divine Mother and a feeling of hopeless imprisonment—follow each other on the page without break or explanation.... Moodie copes with the contradiction by dividing Nature herself in two, reserving the splendid adjectives and the Divine Mother attributes for the half that she approves of and failing to account for the hostile activities of the other half. (Margaret Atwood, *Survival: A Thematic Guide to Canadian Literature*, Toronto, 1972, 49–51)[1]

---

1   Now long established as a core text in Canadian literature, *Survival* is an interesting case study in terms of audience and writing conventions. The book was

Notice here how the literary critic combines a discussion of historical change, for which the past tense is used, with a reading of a particular text—for which the present tense is used. Notice too the focus on an interesting paradox or contradiction.

The advent in the 1970s of several movements in literary theory that have come to be broadly termed postmodernist theory—structuralism, post-structuralism, deconstruction, and so on—called into question many of the fixed points of English studies' compass. Each of these approaches may be clearly distinguished from the others, but they have certain things in common, and together they brought an entirely fresh approach to the discipline in the 1980s and 1990s. They brought to it a more widespread awareness of the importance of the connections between politics and literature (the politics of gender, of race, and of sexual orientation in particular). They shared a deep-seated skepticism of claims concerning any supposedly essential or immutable truths. They entirely distrusted the tenets of old-style evaluative criticism. And they challenged the vocabulary, the writing style, and the argumentative strategy of the discipline as a whole. The old approaches to the marshalling of evidence and the old striving for clarity of thought and expression came to be widely mistrusted, and indeed actively resisted. Too often, it came to be believed, such striving for clarity had contributed to overconfidence or naïve judgements. In what may be very loosely characterized as the postmodernist view, texts required problematizing more often than they required clarifying. Moreover, the use of difficult language and complicated syntax could in itself aid in what was an inherently valuable process of subversion. Here is how the noted

---

written while Atwood was teaching Canadian literature at York University, and drew substantially on the academic research she had done as a graduate student in the English department at Harvard in the 1960s; given that background, it is not surprising that much of the book follows the conventions of academic writing within the discipline of English studies, very much in the manner of the passage quoted. But *Survival* was motivated less by a desire to communicate with scholars than by a desire on the part of Atwood to broaden awareness of certain traditions of Canadian literature and culture among the educated general public. In accordance with this aim (and with Atwood's range of talents as a writer), much of the book has a breeziness to its style that is rare in books of an academic nature.

theorist Judith Butler made the connection between writing style and social protest:

> Why are some of the most trenchant social criticisms often expressed through difficult and demanding language? No doubt scholars in the humanities should be able to clarify how their work informs and illuminates everyday life. Equally, however, such scholars are obliged to question common sense, interrogate its tacit presumptions, and provoke new ways of looking at a familiar world.... If common sense sometimes preserves the status quo, and that status quo sometimes treats unjust social hierarchies as natural, it makes good sense on such occasions to find ways of challenging common sense. Language that takes up this challenge can help point the way to a more socially just world. (Judith Butler, "A 'Bad Writer' Bites Back," *The New York Times*, 20 March 1999, A15)

Thus motivated, literary theorists evolved a new style of writing in English. The postmodern style, which drew on the often-labyrinthine texts of French philosophers such as Jacques Derrida and Julia Kristeva, is complex syntactically (often employing multiple phrases lined up in apposition), with challenging diction and a preponderance of abstract nouns. Free-flowing and given to bold assertions, at the same time it often embraces contradiction, and is resistant to absolute precision. Whereas the older tradition of writing in English studies had been to try to point out and analyze complexities, contradictions, or ironies in literary texts, postmodernist literary theory came to see itself in part as a vehicle for *embodying* complexities and even contradictions. Its role was less to argue towards any fixed conclusion or straightforward conclusion than to problematize, to lead the reader to see difficulty where before all had seemed clear. In its own way, indeed, theoretical and critical writing could also be a form of creative writing.

At its extreme the style approaches a purity of abstraction that presents enormous challenges to comprehension. The flavour of such writing may come as quite an eye-opener to the beginning student at university:

> To claim that this is what I *am* is to suggest a provisional totalization of this "I." But if the "I" can so determine itself, then that which it excludes in order to make that determination remains

constitutive of the determination itself. In other words, such a statement presupposes that the "I" exceeds its determination, and even produces that very excess in and by the act which seeks to exhaust the semantic field of that "I." In the act which would disclose the full content of that "I," a certain radical *concealment* is thereby produced. (Judith Butler, "Imitation and Gender Insubordination," in *inside/out: Lesbian Theories, Gay Theories*, edited by Diana Fuss, London, 1991, 15)

In order to pass as material or empirical reality, the historical or social process must pass through an aesthetic alienation or privatization of its public visibility. The discourse of "the social" then finds its means of representation in a kind of *unconsciousness* that obscures the immediacy of meaning, darkens the public event with an unhomely glow. There is, I want to hazard, an incommunicability that shapes the public moment, a psychic obscurity that is formative for public memory.... (Homi K. Bhabha, "The World and the Home," in *Dangerous Liaisons: Gender, Nation, and Postcolonial Perspectives*, edited by Anne McClintock et al., Minneapolis, 1997, 447)

It is worth pointing out here that the first of these two passages is by Judith Butler—the author of the very clearly worded defense of "difficult and demanding language" quoted above. The difference? In the first case Butler is addressing a broad audience (the readers of the op-ed pages of *The New York Times*), while in "Imitation and Gender Insubordination" she is addressing only her scholarly peers—and putting into practice her beliefs about difficult and demanding language.

The postmodernist approach does not always tend quite so overwhelmingly towards abstraction and opacity as do the above examples. Much as "pure" theory may be at the core of postmodernism, English studies has never ceased to look directly at literary texts. But when scholars with a strong background in deconstruction, for example, or in postcolonial theory, deal directly with textual evidence, they tend not to rely on a structure of "proof" buttressed by extensive quotation. The tendency is rather to focus on small, suggestive details—to work elliptically, as it were. Here is an example:

The resonant details of the scene in which Brontë has Jane acquire her fortune mark Jane's financial and literary implication in colonialism as well. St. John announces Jane's accession to fortune by pulling the letter out of a "morocco pocket-book" (483), and he is able to identify Jane as the heiress because she has written her name, on a white sheet of paper, in "Indian ink" (486).

In this way the novel implicates in colonialism not only Jane's finances (the leather of the wallet has a colonial provenance) but the act of writing itself, for the pigment in which Jane has absently traced her name, with its startlingly colonial appellation, has such a provenance as well.... Like imperialist trade itself, bringing home the spoils of other countries to become commodities in England, such as Indian ink, the use of the racial "other" as a metaphor for class and gender struggles in England commodifies the dark-skinned people of the British empire as they exist in historical actuality and transforms them into East or West Indian ink with which to write a novel about ending injustices within England.

The eruption of the words "Indian ink" into the novel at this telling moment hints at Brontë's uneasiness about the East Indian ventures to which England was turning in 1848, as well as about the West Indian colonies that were by then clearly becoming unprofitable after the abolition of slavery.... (Susan Meyer, *Imperialism at Home: Race and Victorian Women's Fiction*, Ithaca, 1996, 93–94)

In some respects this passage may be likened to the passage by Margaret Atwood that we looked at initially above; comment about the text is couched in the present tense, and the writer is clearly interested in drawing connections among the text, the author, and the wide sweep of historical and literary developments. But where the one passage relies on extended quotation and carefully limits the conclusions drawn, in the other passage quotation is minimal and one small detail—the "Indian ink"—is made to serve a variety of purposes, suggest a range of connections.

That such a free-flowing approach to scholarly argument can forge interesting connections is now beyond doubt; scholars working through this sort of method have exerted an enduring impact on the discipline in the past generation. But in recent years many within the discipline have begun to feel that this more free-flowing approach to building arguments may bring its own set of difficulties—that it too often may run the risk of resting its conclusions on flimsy or unreliable foundations.

If some have raised questions as to the soundness of certain argumentative strategies associated with postmodernism, a much louder chorus has criticized the opacity that is often said to be characteristic of the postmodern style. Attacks on the alleged impenetrability of theoretical discourse in English departments were launched frequently through the 1980s and 1990s—but launched almost exclusively by political conservatives in departments outside English studies. Given that most practitioners of such theory were politically left-of-centre academics within English departments, it is not surprising that a mild form of trench warfare for some time became the norm at many universities. By the turn of the century, however, many politically progressive scholars within the discipline of English studies (Terry Eagleton, who had done more than any other individual to promote postmodernist theory in the 1970s and 1980s, being the most prominent among them) began to reject what they saw as the inherent elitism of a style of communication so opaque as to impede communication more often than it facilitated it.

In fairness, it should be noted that the trend towards an opaque style of discourse was never so overwhelming in English departments as either its critics or its proponents suggested at the time. Throughout the last quarter of the twentieth century many of the leading figures of English studies—Stephen Greenblatt, Jerome McGann, Edward Said, and Elaine Showalter among them—continued to make extended connections with individual literary texts, and to write in styles accessible to the student and to the educated general reader as much as to their fellow scholars. They may not have enjoyed quite so large a public as did T.S. Eliot and Lionel Trilling in an earlier generation, but it is simply not the case that English studies became entirely a rarified scholarly pursuit in the 1980s and 1990s.

In any event, the locus of academic conflict over styles of discourse has now very largely shifted. Much as English academics are still widely derided for the supposed impenetrability of their prose styles, the irony as the twenty-first century moves forward is that the style that may be loosely characterized as postmodern is now to be found with greater frequency in disciplines such as history or anthropology than it is in English studies. There remains a variety of styles of writing practised in English studies, but on the whole the tide of postmodernism has receded in English departments throughout the world. Above and beyond a permanently stretched vocabulary, it has left behind two tendencies that seem likely to remain fixtures in the landscape of the discipline for many years to come: a deep-seated skepticism when it comes to truth-claims, and a heightened awareness of the strength of the connections between politics and literature. In terms of writing style, however, the discipline as a whole now again embraces the idea of clear and comprehensible expression, and advocates building arguments by marshalling a body of textual evidence, including extensive direct quotation.

A dominant activity of English Studies nowadays is contextualizing; today's literary scholarship often involves placing literary works in the context of literary, cultural, and socio-economic developments, in order to show how literary works reflect the values (and contradictions) of the era from which they emerge. Here is an example, from an article discussing "eighteenth-century tragedy's peculiar yoking of a serious play to a lighthearted epilogue":

> *The Gamester: A Tragedy* animates these contradictions between the fear of tragic consequences and the pleasure of risk-taking.... The domestic prose tragedy literally wore down the actors with its wildly effusive emotion: it "demanded so much of the actors that after ten successive evenings they cried respite before continuing" (Van Lennep et al. 317). ...
>
> At tragedy's end Mrs. Beverley cleaves to an unshakable belief in poetic justice: "Yet Heav'n the guiltless Sufferer regards, / And whom it most afflicts, it most rewards" (246; act 3, sc. 7).... Beverley is ... transformed into a hysterical female: "At last he started up, look'd wild, and trembled; and like a Woman, seiz'd with her Sex's Fits, laugh'd out aloud, while the Tears trickled down his Face" (248; act 4, sc. 3). Misplaced reliance on speculation turns men into women, but not the sort of women represented by Mrs. Beverley.
>
> While the play attempts to mobilize the audience's passions toward creating national stability and prosperity, the epilogue disrupts that impulse. [The actress Hannah] Pritchard, like the actresses who later played Mrs. Beverley, leaves the stage dumbstruck with grief at the end of the fifth act, only to reappear promptly to deliver the comic epilogue "written by a friend."

Speaking in her own person, she blithely asserts that gaming is the national addiction. Unlike the "Oriental" men with whom they are compared, Englishmen will not be swayed to abandon gambling.... (272). The epilogue caps off the tragedy by seeming to license the very vices the play warns against. (Felicity Nussbaum, "The Unaccountable Pleasure of Eighteenth-Century Tragedy," *PMLA*, October 2014, 698–700)

As was the case with the 1972 passage we began with, we may notice here a transition between discussions of historical developments (in the past tense), and discussions of the text as a living literary entity, for which the present tense is used. The argument is built using extensive direct quotation from the text. Clarity of argument and clarity of expression are the central goals of academic discourse.

For further discussion of writing about literature, see pages 387–410.

● *Citation and Documentation*

MLA style is standard in the discipline. See the section elsewhere in this book on "Documentation" for a full outline of MLA style, followed by a sample essay that makes use of the MLA system.

● *Some Useful Websites*

- *JSTOR*
  www.jstor.org Founded in 1995 as a not-for-profit organization, this site is a leader in providing electronic access to a wide variety of scholarly journals online.
- *Literary Resources on the Net*
  www.andromeda.rutgers.edu/~lynch/Lit Maintained by Jack Lynch of Rutgers University, this site provides access to a wide variety of reliable information.
- *Project Gutenberg*
  www.gutenberg.org This site provides an extraordinarily wide-ranging collection of online texts in the public domain. Not all are reliably transcribed, but the site is nevertheless an invaluable resource.

- *Project Muse*
  www.muse.jhu.edu This site, founded in 1995 by the Johns
  Hopkins University Press, provides access to a wide range of
  scholarly journals, with a strong emphasis on literature and
  culture.
- *Representative Poetry Online*
  www.rpo.library.utoronto.ca Run out of the University of
  Toronto, this site provides reliable texts and excellent notes for
  many English poems.

● Some Respected Journals

American Literature Founded in 1929, this journal is the most established
of those specializing in American literature.

Canadian Literature Founded in 1960, this journal is the leader among
academic publications specializing in Canadian literature.

PMLA Founded in 1844, this is the flagship journal of the Modern Languages Association (the leading association in North America for academics specializing in English studies).

Review of English Studies Published by Oxford University Press, this leading journal emphasizes historical scholarship rather than interpretive
criticism.

Studies in English Literature Published by Johns Hopkins University Press,
this leading journal focuses on four fields of British literature: English
Renaissance, Tudor and Stuart drama, Restoration and eighteenth
century, and nineteenth century.

O History

Of the several styles of writing frequently practised by historians, the
most established is much as one would expect—writing that tells a
story. Even if one wished to question the prevailing academic ortho-
doxy, until relatively recently the accepted way of doing so was to
tell the story again, from a different angle or with a different emphasis. One might pause periodically to analyze developments, discuss
their causes, or address issues concerning the historical evidence, but
the main mode of discussion would inevitably be narrative, using
the simple past tense (or the past perfect tense when making reference in the course of a discussion of one set of historical events to
something previous). Here is an example:

The crisis of August 1939 which led to the Second World War was, ostensibly at any rate, a dispute over Danzig. This dispute was formulated in the last days of March, when Germany made demands concerning Danzig and the Corridor, and the Poles rejected them. From that moment, everyone expected Danzig to be the next great topic of international conflict. Yet, in strange contrast to earlier crises, there were no negotiations over Danzig, no attempts to discover a solution, not even attempts to screw up the tension....

Both Hitler and the Poles held rigid positions in the war of nerves. After 26 March, Hitler did not again formulate demands concerning Danzig until the day before war broke out. This was not surprising; it was his usual method. So he had waited for offers from Schuschnigg over Austria; so he had waited for offers from Benes, from Chamberlain, finally from the conference at Munich over Czechoslovakia. Then he did not wait in vain. Did he appreciate that this time no offer would come from the Poles? It seemed so from the record. On 3 April he issued instructions that preparations for an attack on Poland "must be made in such a way that the operation can be carried out at any time as from 1 September 1939." [1] (A.J.P. Taylor, *The Origins of the Second World War*, London, 1961, 302–03)

---

1   Directive by Keitel, 3 April 1939. *German Foreign Policy*, Series D, VI, No. 149.

Though the narrative style is the most established approach to the writing of history, it is by no means the most widely practised by academic historians today. For much of the twentieth century, the trend in the academic discipline of history was toward a more scientific approach that emphasized social and economic forces rather than narratives involving individuals. This sort of historical writing, which remains widespread, is more likely to focus on numbers than on historical incidents. Again, the writing is typically in the past tense, but the tone is very different from that of a traditional historical narrative. Here is an example:

Was there any special character to these neighbourhoods? Were they red-light districts or merely poor quarters? The most striking feature of these streets is how different they were from one another. Simnell Street contained common lodging houses inhabited by single dock labourers and families of hawkers. Koss Street, Southampton, while a "low" street and the scene of frequent drunken brawls, was the residence of skilled artisans living in nuclear families. 45 out of 70 households were nuclear (64.3 per cent); including subfamilies, 57 out of 77 (74.0 per cent) families were two-parent headed. Yet both Simnell and Koss streets had one or two houses characterized as brothels, where single women resided apart from their families. On the other hand, Plymouth's Granby and Central streets, which opened into the Octagon, the pub and entertainment center of Plymouth, had nuclear families living in single tenement rooms, yet almost two of every three adults were women.[37]

(J.R. Walkowitz and D.J. Walkowitz, "'We are not the beasts of the field': Prostitution and the Poor in Plymouth and Southampton under the Contagious Diseases Acts," in *Clio's Consciousness Raised: New Perspectives on the History of Women*, edited by M.S. Hartman and L. Banner, New York, 1974, 192–225, 199)

---

37 Census (1871), 1873, LXXI; part 1. Statistical data for the five streets discussed are based on the manuscript 1871 Census schedules. PRO, RG10/2120, RG10/1193, and RG10/1194.

Such historical writing as this aims to provide demonstrable proof (most of it empirical) of a particular line of argument; it is on this sort of approach that the claims of history to be as much one of the social sciences as one of the humanities rests.

Another broad approach to historical writing has been developed over the past generation. Influenced substantially by French cultural historians and theorists, this approach focuses largely on culture. Rather than attempt to prove a historical argument by assembling empirical evidence, cultural historians of the past generation have tended to operate as much by suggestion as by efforts to provide proof. Often skeptical of truth claims, they rely on suggestive anecdotes or pieces of information to provide insight into particular themes or aspects of historical reality. Often they approach topics from new and surprising angles—so, for example, Paul Edward Dutton inquires into what Charlemagne's mustache can tell us about eighth- and ninth-century Carolingian history and Robert Darnton explores various aspects of eighteenth-century life by discussing an attack in the 1730s by a group of printing apprentices on their masters' cats. Here is a sample:

> Cats as symbols conjured up sex as well as violence, a combination perfectly suited for an attack on the mistress. The narrative identified her with *la grise,* her *chatte favorite.* In killing it, the boys struck at her: "It was a matter of consequence, a murder, which had to be hidden."[1] The mistress reacted as if she had been assaulted: "They ravished from her a cat without an equal, a cat that she loved to madness." The text described her as lascivious and "impassioned for cats" as if she were a she-cat in heat during a wild cat's Sabbath of howling, killing, and rape. An explicit reference to rape would violate the proprieties that were generally observed in eighteenth-century writing. Indeed, the symbolism would work only if it remained veiled.... It was metonymic insult, the eighteenth-century equivalent of the modern schoolboy's taunt. But it was stronger, and more obscene. By assaulting her pet, the workers ravished the mistress symbolically. At the same time, they delivered the supreme insults to their master. (Robert Darnton, "Workers Revolt: The Great Cat Massacre of the Rue Saint-Séverin," from *The Great Cat Massacre and Other Episodes in French Cultural History,* New York, 1984, 18)

---

1 This and the following quotations come from Nicolas Contat's account of the cat massacre, *Anecdotes typographiques,* pp. 48–56.

Those familiar with the styles of analysis and of writing that are common in English studies will note a number of similarities to the approach that Darnton takes here. Notice, though, that unlike literary scholars, cultural historians such as Darnton tend to use the past tense rather than the present tense when they are discussing texts.

Many historians in recent years have adopted far more of the style pioneered by continental theorists than has Darnton. The extreme here may be represented by the following passage from David Lloyd's *Ireland After History* on the need for a new approach to history:

> Constituted in simultaneity with, and different from, modern civil society, and representing in a certain sense the "constitutive other" of modernity, these spaces that are the objective of "new histories" are not, we have argued, to be conceived as alternative

continuities, parallel to dominant narratives and only awaiting, in Gramsci's sense, to attain hegemony in order to be completed. On the contrary, and at the risk of deliberate hypostatization, the apparent discontinuity of popular or non-elite history furnishes indications of alternative social formations, difficult as these may be to document and decipher for the disciplined historian; the same discontinuity as well as the formal grounds for the persistence in assimilability of non-elite formations to the state. (As quoted by David A. Wilson in *The Globe and Mail*, 28 December 2004, A–12)

These sentences—both nominated by Wilson as candidates for a Worst Sentence in the World Award—are not typical of twenty-first century historical writing, but this sort of style, with its contorted syntax, extraordinary density of abstraction, and verbal tics that resist precision (*in a certain sense*), is now not uncommon. Ironically, this has been happening just as this sort of dense, opaque style is going very much out of fashion in English studies.

For a broader discussion of writing in the humanities, see pages 387–410.

● Citation and Documentation

There is no universally accepted style of documentation for history. Many journals use some variety of Chicago Style; many use traditional footnotes or endnotes. For students the most important guideline is thus to follow whatever specifications each instructor may give you.

● Some Useful Websites

- *Historical Journals Online*
  www.tntech.edu/history/journals.html Provides links to a wide variety of historical journals.
- *JSTOR*
  www.jstor.org Founded in 1995 as a not-for-profit organization, this site is a leader in providing electronic access to a wide variety of scholarly journals online.
- *Labyrinth*
  www.georgetown.edu/labyrinth This site provides access to a

very wide range of materials on medieval history, including many primary sources.

* *Project Muse*
www.muse.jhu.edu This site, founded in 1995 by the Johns Hopkins University Press, provides access to a wide range of scholarly journals. The strongest emphasis is on literature and culture, but many historical journals are included as well.
* *Virtual Library: History*
www.vlib.org/History In this subject, as in others, the Virtual Library provides access to a great deal of useful information.

● *Some Respected Journals*

American Historical Review Founded in 1895, this is the flagship journal of the American Historical Association; it covers all historical fields, not just American history.

English Historical Review Founded in 1886, this journal is the oldest journal of historical scholarship in the English-speaking world, and it remains one of the most prestigious. Published by Oxford University Press, the journal covers world as well as British history.

History Founded in 1916, this journal remains the official journal of the Historical Association in Britain.

History and Theory Founded in 1960, this leading journal often features interdisciplinary articles.

Journal of World History Official journal of the World History association, this publication specializes in historical studies that cross cultural boundaries.

O *Medicine and Health Sciences*

● *Citation Style*

In biomedical publications, the two most common formats for preparing manuscripts are the American Medical Association (AMA) Manual of Style and Citing Medicine, and the NLM Style Guide for Authors, Editors, and Publishers. Citing Medicine uses Vancouver style referencing as set out by the International Committee of Medical Journal Editors in Uniform Requirements for Manuscripts Submitted to Biomedical Journals.

In both AMA and Vancouver styles, citations are numbered in the order that they appear in the text using parentheses(1), square brackets[1], superscript[1], or a combination thereof[1]. A small number of journals use other in-text reference systems described by the Council of Science Editors, found in this book under Biology citations and references.

- Iverson C, Christiansen S, Flanagin A, et al. *AMA Manual of Style: A Guide for Authors and Editors.* 10th ed. New York, NY: Oxford University Press; 2007.
- Patrias K. Citing medicine: the NLM style guide for authors, editors, and publishers [Internet]. 2nd ed. Wendling DL, technical editor. Bethesda (MD): National Library of Medicine (US); 2007 -   [updated 2011 Sep 15]. Available from: http://www.nlm.nih.gov/citingmedicine

● *Some Useful Websites*

- Medscape
  http://www.medscape.com This website for physicians and health professionals offers news, education resources and a customized version of the National Library of Medicine's MEDLINE database.
- National Center for Biotechnology Information Tools
  www.ncbi.nlm.nih.gov/guide.all.#tools A collection of online tools that can be used for analysing biomedical and genomic information.
- *Pubmed Central*
  www.ncbi.nlm.nih.gov/pmc/ The US National Institutes of Health (NIH) digital archive of biomedical and life sciences journal literature.

● *Some Respected Journals*

BMJ Formerly known as the British Medical Journal, this publication follows a "continuous publication" model to distribute news and information to healthcare works as quickly as possible.

Journal of the American Medical Association First published in 1883, JAMA is the most widely circulated medical journal in the world.

New England Journal of Medicine First published in 1812, NEJM is the oldest continuously published medical journal in the world.

PLOS Medicine The journal aims to provide open-access research with the highest priority given to diseases and risk factors with the greatest health burden worldwide.

The Lancet First published in 1823, this general medical journal publishes a broad range of content with the goal of advancing medical science or practice.

O *Philosophy*

The academic discipline of philosophy as it has been practised in the English-speaking world in recent generations divides into two broad streams. By far the dominant stream is that of analytic philosophy. Perhaps above all, the tradition of analytic philosophy values clarity, and devotes very considerable effort to making fine distinctions that may help to clarify lines of thought. In doing so, it often employs hypothetical examples. Arguments are typically couched in the present tense, though the past tense is used if reference is being made to an argument from the past that is not being discussed as a live philosophical issue today. Thus, one would write "Hume *argued* ..." if discussing an argument of the eighteenth-century philosopher David Hume in the context of intellectual history, but "Hume *argues* ..." if analyzing or discussing the argument itself. Analytic philosophers have a few verbal tics particular to their discipline (e.g., they tend to write "*on* Rawls's theory" where academics in other disciplines would write "*according to* Rawls's theory ..."), and they tend to employ a great many abstract nouns. Other than that, however, they prefer the clarity of sentences that are syntactically straightforward. Here is a sample:

> Deontological theories also capture our intuitions that certain things that have happened in the past are morally relevant. Consequentialist theories are strictly forward-looking moral theories. They look forward from the time of the decision at issue to see how we can bring about the best possible results in the future. Deontological theories allow that backward-looking considerations can have moral significance. To take Ross's example, suppose that you have made a promise to someone. It now happens that you could produce 1,001 units of happiness if you break the promise, but only 1,000 units of happiness if you keep the

promise. A strict consequentialist will look only at the number of units of happiness you can achieve in the future, all things considered, and may therefore tell you to break the promise. Intuitively, it seems seriously wrong to break a promise for such a frivolous reason. The fact that you have made a promise in the past cannot simply be dismissed because you want to bring about slightly better results you could achieve in the future by breaking it. Ross's theory holds that we have a prima facie duty to keep the promises we have made, and that this duty can be overridden only for serious reasons. Kant also holds that deceiving persons or making false promises to them constitutes using them as mere means to our own ends, and is therefore wrong. Likewise, deontological theories will not allow us to punish innocent persons even if we can promote general welfare in the future by doing so. Backward-looking considerations of desert are morally significant to the deontologist. It is simply wrong to punish someone who does not deserve the punishment, even if we could produce good consequences in the future by doing so. (Heimir Geirsson and Margaret Holmgren, *Ethical Theory*, Peterborough, 2000, 110–11)

The other stream of academic philosophy is commonly referred to as "continental philosophy." As the name suggests, it is heavily influenced by the writings of philosophers from continental Europe, from Nietzsche and Habermas to Heidegger and Foucault. Like analytic philosophers, those in the continental tradition tend to use a great many abstract nouns, but beyond that there are few similarities of style. Those in the continental tradition tend to be less interested in fine distinctions than in broad brushstrokes, and in many cases they embrace difficulty, even to the extent of cultivating a style that makes it difficult for the reader to decipher the meaning. Arguments are generally advanced in the present tense. Here is a sample:

> Notice that, unlike Barthes, Gadamer insists on the re-identification of one and the same text under plural, potentially infinite, interpretation and re-interpretation. The infinite openness of texts—in both an interpretive and historical sense (ultimately the same sense)—is ensured by the notion of reflexive application: the intentional import *of* a text essentially incorporates

into *its* developing, endlessly reconstituted meaning but its recovery for our own historical experience and prejudice can make it out to be. Its meaning is heuristically schematized in the intersection between *our* present power of reading and what, from that evolving perspective, we posit as *its* collected past. In this regard, our logical proposal about interpretable texts is closer to Gadamer's usage than to Barthes's. (Joseph Margolis, "Reinterpreting Interpretation," *Journal of Aesthetics and of Criticism* 43, Summer 1989: 249)

If the styles of philosophy may be broadly divided into the analytic and the continental, the content of philosophy is also divided into a variety of sub-disciplines, including aesthetics, ethics, epistemology, logic, and metaphysics. For the most part, conventions of writing do not vary widely among these; an analytic philosopher writing on a topic in aesthetics, for example, follows very much the same conventions of writing as an analytic philosopher writing on a topic in epistemology or ethics. The exception here is symbolic logic, which uses its own language—or rather, its own variety of symbolic languages.

For a broader discussion of writing in the humanities, see pages 387–410.

● *Citation and Documentation*

There is no universally accepted style of documentation for philosophy. Many journals use some variety of Chicago Style; many use traditional footnotes or endnotes. For students the most important guideline is thus to follow whatever specifications each instructor may give you.

● *Some Useful Websites*

- *JSTOR*
  www.jstor.org Founded in 1995 as a not-for-profit organization, this site is a leader in providing electronic access to a wide variety of scholarly journals.
- *Philosophy Pages*
  www.philosophypages.com A wide range of useful basic information in accessible form.

- *Project Muse*
  www.muse.jhu.edu This site, founded in 1995 by the Johns
  Hopkins University Press, provides access to a wide range of
  scholarly journals, with a strong emphasis on literature and culture, but a good representation of philosophy journals as well.
- *Stanford Encyclopedia of Philosophy*
  This open access reference work provides extended survey discussions of virtually every aspect of the discipline.
- *Virtual Library: Philosophy*
  www.vlib.org Click on Humanities and go to Philosophy. This
  section of the Virtual Library site is run through the University
  of Bristol.

● Some Respected Journals

Australian Journal of Philosophy A respected general journal.
Canadian Journal of Philosophy A respected general journal.
Ethics One of the leading journals for analytic articles on topics in ethics.
Journal of Ethics and Social Philosophy A highly respected open access jour-
   nal sponsored by the University of Southern California.
Journal of Philosophy The most prestigious general journal in the discipline.
Mind One of the leading journals for analytic articles on topics in the
   philosophy of mind.
Philosophy and Public Affairs This respected journal is aimed at the general
   reader as well as an academic audience.

O Physics

The conventions of writing followed in the pure sciences are broadly
similar; they are discussed above under "Biology" and more broadly
on pages 411–19.

● Citation and Documentation

Citation style: American Institute of Physics. *Style Manual: Instructions to Authors and Volume Editors for the Preparation of AIP Book
Manuscripts.* 5th ed. New York: AIP, 1995. Print.

● *Some Useful Websites*

- *Net Advance of Physics*
  web.mit.edu/redingtn/www/netadv/ This site, supported by MIT, offers a wide range of information in an encyclopedic format.
- *Physics News*
  www.het.brown.edu/news This site provides information and links on all aspects of the subject.
- *Physics Today Online*
  http://scitation.aip.org/content/aip/magazine/physicstoday This site, run by the American Institute of Physics, offers information on recent research and provides links to databases, societies, and a variety of electronic publications.
- *Wolfram Alpha*
  www.wolframalpha.com A computational knowledge engine that can provide information and perform calculations based on an extensive database of facts and statistics.

● *Some Respected Journals*

Applied Physics Letters This journal focuses on the prompt publication on the application of physics to all branches of science, engineering, and modern technology.

Nature Physics This journal publishes significant discoveries across the core physics disciplines and interdisciplinary research with an emphasis on experimental physics.

Physical Review Letters Originally the letters to the editors of Physical Review, this publication focuses on short reports of fundamental physics research.

Physical Review One of the most established journals in the discipline, this publication is divided into five sections on different sub-disciplines.

Reviews of Modern Physics This journal focuses on reviewing fundamental physics literature for students and established researchers.

O *Politics*

The discipline that is variously styled "politics," "political studies," and "political science" borders on a considerable number of other

academic disciplines. At one end, it looks at political theory historically (from Aristotle and Plato onwards), with interests not dissimi-
lar to those of philosophers. What is the nature of the state? How
may politics, morality, and the law best interact? And so on. The
study of politics also inevitably overlaps with the study of history.
And political science shares a border with sociology, too—not only
in the interest they share in social trends, but also in their shared
interest in ideology.

In most departments, the "science" in political science is a very
real presence, and frequent reference is made to empirical studies as
arguments are made concerning such things as the causes of elec-
toral victories and defeats, and of changes in public opinion. Following are two examples:

> These results for the presidency also make it possible to return to
> a parallel analysis for the Senate, in ways that now seem substan-
> tively interpretable rather than statistically idiosyncratic. Indeed,
> the difference between the fortunes of local versus cosmopolitan
> Democratic candidates for Senate seats appears to reside largely
> in the way that the locals were following the pattern typical of
> local candidates for the House of Representatives, whereas cos-
> mopolitans had already begun to follow the pattern of ... North-
> ern Democratic candidates for the presidency. Figure 5.11 offers
> this parallel comparison. (Byron E. Shafer and Richard Johnson, *The
> End of Southern Exceptionalism: Class, Race, and Partisan Change in the
> Postwar South* (Cambridge, MA, 2009, 158)

> The CBS News/*New York Times* poll of March 21 to 25 [1994]
> covers the four days after the Illinois primary, the days during
> which news was disseminated about Hart's campaign controver-
> sies. There are enough interviews in this survey to divide it in
> half and treat each half of the survey independently. During the
> first half of this poll, the two days after the Illinois primary, when
> the commercials fracas was getting some publicity, Hart still led
> Mondale, 41 per cent to 38 per cent. In the second half of the sur-
> vey, when the campaign news centered on Hart's embassy posi-
> tions and his campaign management, Mondale jumped ahead 49
> per cent to 29 per cent! This extraordinary turnaround is one
> more demonstration of how fragile the images and votes can be
> for candidates like Hart, or [George H.] Bush in 1980, or Carter

in 1976, when voters are projecting future performance from campaign behavior.[35] It reemphasizes the discussion in Chapter 3 of the logic of incumbents' attacking their challenger(s) instead of trying to change opinions about themselves. (Samuel L. Popkin, *The Reasoning Voter: Communication and Persuasion in Presidential Campaigns*, Chicago: 2/e 1994, 207)

35 Percentages from the March 5–8 CBS News/*New York Times* poll are based on 573 interviews: percentages from the second poll are based on 411 interviews, 235 on the first days and 176 on the last two days. Some of the interviews in the last two days are with people who were sampled but could not be reached on the first two days; eliminating these interviews makes no difference.

Notice in both of the above passages the shifts in verb tense. When Shafer and Johnston refer directly to events occurring in the past, the past verb tenses ("*were* following," "*had* already begun"), whereas when they comment on the meaning and relevance of the statistics they use the present tense ("These results *make* it possible" "the difference … *appears* to reside"). Popkin also uses different verb tenses. When discussing the changes that occurred during the 1984 campaign, he uses the past tense ("Hart still *led*," "Mondale *jumped* ahead"), whereas when he comments on the ongoing relevance of these developments, he too switches to the present tense.

There are also interesting differences between the two passages. Shafer and Johnston use far more of the jargon that has been developed by the academic discipline of political science—including such phrases as *parallel analysis* and *substantively interpretable*. In contrast, Popkin adopts a less scholarly style, and for the most part relies on the vocabulary of everyday English. Notice too that Popkin employs the footnoting method that is traditional in history and several disciplines in the humanities. (Unlike many other disciplines, the study of politics has not developed its own documentation style; APA style and the Chicago Style of footnoting are the two most common approaches.)

Much as the "science" is a frequent presence in political science, there remains a good deal of writing within the discipline that analyzes political realities and political trends with little or no reference to empirical data. Again, here is a sample:

These aims require an appreciation of tolerance as not only protean in meaning but also historically and politically discursive in character. They require surrendering an understanding of tolerance as a transcendent or universal concept, principle, doctrine, or virtue so that it can be considered instead as a political discourse and practice of governmentality that is historically and geographically variable in purpose, content, agents, and objects. As a consortium of para-legal and para-statist practices in modern constitutional liberalism—practices that are associated with the liberal state and liberal legalism but are not precisely codified by it—tolerance is exemplary of Foucault's account of governmentality as that with organizes "the conduct of conduct" at a variety of sites and through rationalities not formally countenanced as political. (Wendy Brown, *Regulating Aversion: Tolerance in the Age of Identity and Empire*, Princeton, 2008, 4)

● Citation and Documentation

There is no universally accepted citation and documentation system in this discipline, but the *Chicago Manual of Style* is probably the most widely used.

● Some Useful Websites

- *Canadian Supreme Court Decisions*
  www.scc-csc.lexum.com/scc-csc/en/nav.do   Canadian
  Supreme Court decisions may be accessed through this site.
- *Election Resources*
  www.electionresources.org This site provides a wealth of information on election results from nations around the world.
- *JSTOR*
  www.jstor.org Founded in 1995 as a not-for-profit organization, this site is a leader in providing electronic access to a wide variety of scholarly journals.
- *US Supreme Court*
  www.supremecourtus.gov US Supreme Court opinions may be accessed through the site.
- *Virtual Library: International Affairs*
  www.vlib.org/internationalaffairs A wide range of useful information and links.

● *Some Respected Journals*

Canadian Journal of Political Science The most respected political science journal in Canada.

Congressional Quarterly Focuses on American national politics.

The Economist The world's most authoritative weekly news magazine.

Foreign Affairs This quarterly journal publishes a wide range of articles on international affairs. Aimed at the general reader as well as the scholar.

Political Science Quarterly Founded in 1886, this journal remains one of the most respected.

Washington Monthly A magazine that appeals to the general public as well as to scholars.

O *Psychology*

Like others of the sciences and social sciences, psychology has many of its roots in philosophy; philosophers from Aristotle to John Locke and David Hume spent a good deal of time attempting to draw conclusions as to the workings of the human mind. It was not until the late nineteenth century that psychology began to be established as a scientific discipline—and even then writing on psychology tended more to resemble philosophical writing than the sort of writing we now associate with the academic discipline of psychology. William James, for example, whose classic work *The Principles of Psychology* helped to establish the discipline as a behavioural science, appeals in his writing to common experience in much the same way as had Locke or Hume in earlier centuries:

> When we have been exposed to an unusual stimulus for many minutes or hours, a nervous process is set up which results in the haunting of consciousness by the impression for a long time afterwards. The tactile and the muscular feelings of a day of skating or riding, after long disuse of the exercise, will come back to us all through the night. Images of the field of view of the microscope will annoy the observer for hours after an unusually long sitting at the instrument. (William James, *The Principles of Psychology*, 1890, Chapter 25)

At the same time as James was laying the foundations for the empirical study of psychology, another tradition of psychology was also beginning to take shape—psychoanalysis. Even more than had James, this tradition adopted a writing style that had little in common with scientific writing as we know it today. The writings of Freud, Jung, and English-speaking followers such as Havelock Ellis and Ernest Jones, while often elegant, relied on personal observation, anecdote, and often bold assertion, rather than empirical measurements.

By the middle of the twentieth century, however, the influence of the psychoanalytic tradition was starting to wane, while the growth of psychology as a scientific discipline was quickening. The vast majority of writing in psychology came to rely on experimental evidence gathered according to standardized research methods. The typical article in psychology reports on an experiment, first summarizing the background of research against which the experiment has been conceived, then presenting method and results, before moving to a discussion of the results and a conclusion:

> Research on complex relational processes within families has revealed that parents' differential treatment of siblings is consistently linked with negative outcomes, such as children's poorer socio-emotional well-being (McGuire, Dunn, and Plomin, 1995; Stocker, 1995) and less positive sibling relationships (Brodie, Stoneman, and McCoy, 1992). However, what is not yet fully understood is how differential treatment relates to the quality of parent-child relationships. For example, do children or adolescents who feel they receive less-favoured treatment than a sibling develop feelings of resentment toward this parent, setting the stage for poorer parent-child relationships? Or do children understand and perhaps "forgive" unequal treatment as warranted for particular reasons? ...
>
> Method.
>
> The sample included mothers, fathers, and two adolescents from 74 maritally intact families. Participating families lived in one of two small adjoining Mid-western cities (combined population 120,000) or a suburban or rural area proximal to the two cities. Participating families were recruited using newspaper ads and through flyers distributed at local schools. Families were offered $15 for their participation. Families selected for inclusion in the

study had a younger sibling between the ages of 11 and 13 years (M = 12.45, SD = 1.58) and an older sibling who was two to four years older (M = 15.58, SD = 1.87).... (Amanda K. Kowal, Jennifer L. Krull, and Laurie Kramer, "How the differential treatments of siblings is linked with parent-child relationship quality," *Journal of Family Psychology*, Volume 18, No. 4, 2004, 658–59)

Not all psychological writing is devoted to presenting the results of experiments, of course. But when writing for their fellow academics, psychologists tend to maintain the same vocabulary and writing style that characterizes reports on experiments. It may be interesting in this connection to compare the following two passages. In the first, psychologist Judith Rich Harris is writing for other psychologists in an academic journal; in the second, she is expressing very much the same idea in a book aimed at the general reader as well as the psychologist:

When group identity is not salient, differentiation is likely to predominate over assimilation. If siblings see themselves as separate individuals rather than as part of the family group, status hierarchies and social comparisons may increase the differences among them. Dominance hierarchies would tend to make older siblings dominant over younger ones, which happens as a matter of course in most societies and which North American parents try very hard, and not very successfully, to prevent (Whiting and Edwards, 1988). However, there is little or no resemblance between children's relationships with their siblings and their relationships with their peers (Abramovitch et al., 1986), which is consistent with the finding that birth order has no reliable effects on personality (Ernst and Angst, 1983; Reiss et al., 1994). (Judith Rich Harris, "Where is the child's environment? A group socialization theory of development," *Psychological Review*, Volume 102, No. 3, 1995, 332)

Inevitably, children's relationships with their siblings are unequal. In most cases, the elder is the leader; the younger is the follower. The elder attempts to dominate, the younger to avoid domination. Peer relationships are different; peers are more equal, and often more compatible, than siblings. Among American children, conflict and hostility erupt far more frequently among siblings than among peers. (Judith Rich Harris, *The Nurture Assumption: Why Children Turn Out the Way They Do*, New York, 1998, 61)

Not only are the parenthetical references to scholarship absent from the second passage above; the vocabulary is also far less abstract, and the syntax is much simpler. Like all disciplines, psychology has developed a special vocabulary involving not only terms specific to the discipline (e.g., *dominance hierarchies*) but also habits of using particular words with great frequency (*salience* is a word that psychologists and social scientists generally find very useful, for example). Psychologists also often use variants of common English words in ways peculiar to the discipline; they tend, for example, to use the plural form *behaviours*, whereas people outside the discipline of psychology tend to use *behaviour* only in its singular form.

Psychologists tend to use the past tense when reporting on the methods they have followed and the results they have obtained in an experiment. They use the present tense, however, when discussing what the evidence shows about human behaviour. They also often use the present perfect tense when reporting on the findings of other research (e.g., *Barclay and Jones have found that ...*).

For a broader discussion of writing in the sciences, see pages 411–19.

● Citation and Documentation

Citation style: APA Style. See the APA section elsewhere in this book for a full discussion of this citation style.

● Some Useful Websites

- *American Psychological Association*
  www.apa.org The APA site provides access to a wide range of useful information.
- *Classics in the History of Psychology*
  www.psycclassicsals.yorku A useful archive of many key texts in the history of psychology.
- *Encyclopedia of Psychology*
  www.psychology.org A helpful and wide-ranging site.
- *PsychWeb*
  www.psywww.com An informal site with a range of useful links.

- *Social Psychology Network*
  www.socialpsychology.org Including a wide range of useful
  information, this site bills itself as "the largest social psychology database on the Internet."

● *Some Respected Journals*

Annual Review of Psychology A leader in the discipline.

American Journal of Psychology Founded in 1887, AJP was the first English-language journal to focus primarily on experimental psychology.

Psychological Bulletin This journal publishes quantitative (meta-analytic)
and qualitative (narrative) reviews and interpretation of issues in scientific psychology. There is a goal of summarizing past research by
drawing overall conclusions from similar studies.

Psychological Review A quarterly journal with an emphasis on psychology
theory, founded in 1894.

Trends in Cognitive Sciences This journal aims to provide concise updates
and discussion on the most exciting current topics in cognition, the
mind, and the brain.

O *Sociology*

The discipline of sociology is often said to divide into two broad
streams. One of these, the positivist tradition (with roots going back
to the classic work of Emile Durkheim) emphasizes empirical studies and employs methods that have much in common with those of
the natural sciences. The writing style favoured by most sociologists
writing in this tradition tends to be purposefully dry in tone (no
matter how striking or provocative the information presented may
be), and to be written in syntactically straightforward sentences.
Such writing employs the present tense where an ongoing social
situation or structure is being described, but shifts to the past tense
frequently when referring to how specific studies were conducted.
Here is a sample:

> The surveys also show important differences in terms of the par-
> ticipation in paid and unpaid work on a given day. In 1986, 85
> per cent of women and 52 per cent of men participated in domes-
> tic activities (excluding childcare and shopping). Conversely, 54
> per cent and 34 per cent of men and women participated in paid

work activities on a given day (Harvey, Marshall, and Frederick 1991: 43, 50; Marshall 1990). Among married employed parents in 1986, the participation rate in household work was 63 per cent for men and 95.3 per cent for women (Haddad, 1996: 153).

In 1992, for parents with children under 19, with both spouses employed full-time, 95.9 per cent of women and 77.4 per cent of men participated in housework on a given day. In addition, for those who have children under 19, 63.7 per cent of women and 43.9 per cent of men participated in childcare (McFarlane, 1997: 73–77). Not only do employed men spend slightly less time in total productive activity than do employed women, but men's participation in unpaid work shows greater flexibility; they can more easily work around their paid work. This is probably a key factor underlying the higher stress experienced by women. (Rod Beaujot, *Earning and Caring*, Peterborough, 2000, 213)

The language of sociologists writing in this tradition is similar to that of those who employ empirical studies extensively in other social science disciplines; they often write of *controlling for various factors*, and of the *salience* of certain sorts of information. Particular to sociology is a frequent use of the noun *outcome*, including in the plural (e.g., *the study found several outcomes*).

In contrast, the interpretivist tradition of sociology, stemming largely from the classic works of Max Weber, tends to rely much less on empirical evidence—and, indeed, often to be skeptical of such evidence. It tends towards more free-flowing analyses, and makes reference far more frequently to theories and to broadly perceived social and cultural forces. In their writing style, interpretivist sociologists of the past generation have tended towards long sentences that are syntactically fairly complex, and towards abstract words that foreground their theoretical orientation. Here is a sample:

Social theory, and more specifically post-colonial social theory, must be able to make sense of such events, which testify among other things to the cultural dynamism of peoples living in oppressive conditions. To make sense of this, it is necessary to get past a blanket notion of incommensurability between cultures. An imbalance in social power, favouring the white stream, was integral to the traditions that produced the merging of previously foreign cultural elements. The fact remains that the merging happened, creating new cultural practices, in the Coast Salish case, practices strongly associated with aboriginality as a cultural and emancipatory project.

Should we conclude from this that *difference* loses its theoretic importance? Not exactly. What we see in the inter-cultural recognition portrayed here is not the kind of "unbiased communication" (as Habermas would say) that could found a renewed universalism. Communication between the two cultures is not easy; their codes are far from transparent to each other, and the power imbalances are enormous. Thus, there is a large gap between a belief in absolute incommensurability and a renewed universalism. (Claude Denis, *We Are Not You*, Peterborough, 1997, 157)

The author quoted above, like many (though by no means all) interpretivist sociologists of recent years, employs much of the vocabulary that theoretically oriented academic circles in the English speaking world imported from France in the 1970s and 1980s—the style that may be loosely characterized as postmodern.

● Citation and Documentation

The most widely accepted style of citation and documentation is that of the American Sociological Association (ASA style). This is in many ways similar to other styles of parenthetical citation. Note, however, that page numbers may be given in the citation, and that in that case they are preceded by a colon:

- What Wright terms "idealized capitalism" (2000: 959) relates to the neoclassical economic model.

References are provided at the end of an essay, alphabetically by author:

Pakulski, Jan and Malcolm Waters
  1996 *The Death of Class*. London: Sage.

Wright, Erik Olin
  2000 "Working-class power, capitalist class interests, and class compromise." *American Journal of Sociology* 105: 957–1002.

● *Some Useful Websites*

- *Auraria Library*
  www.library.auraria.edu   Established as a shared library for
  three universities in Denver, Colorado, the Auraria Library
  includes useful subject guides that provide access to a wealth
  of information.
- *American Sociological Association*
  www.asanet.org This site provides a wide range of information
  about the discipline, together with useful links to other sites.
- *JSTOR*
  www.jstor.org Founded in 1995 as a not-for-profit organization,
  this site is a leader in providing electronic access to a wide
  variety of scholarly journals.

● *Some Respected Journals*

American Journal of Sociology This highly respected journal is published by
the University of Chicago Press; it was founded in 1895. Issues from
recent years are available online at www.journals.uchicago.edu.

American Sociological Review This wide-ranging and prestigious journal
is published six times yearly; it is the flagship journal of the American
Sociological Association. Available online through JSTOR.

Canadian Journal of Sociology Published by the University of Toronto
Press, this is the most highly respected of Canadian journals in the
discipline.

Criminology Probably the most highly respected journal in this important
branch of sociology.

Journal of Marriage and the Family The leading North American journal
in the area of the sociology of the family.

Social Forces An influential interdisciplinary journal published by the
University of North Carolina Press (also available through JSTOR).

Sociology The flagship journal of the British Sociological Association.

◎ SEEING AND MEANING
How to Read (and Write about) Visual Images

What does it mean to "read" a visual image? What is "visual literacy"? What should we be aware of when images interact with words?

Visual literacy is, at one level, a matter of not allowing oneself to be factually misled by what one sees. How dramatically has the stock of the Butterine Corporation risen? A cursory glance at the graph below seems to show pretty clearly that the value of Butterine shares has soared in recent months:

Look again, though, and we see the numbers on the left: the y axis begins not at 0 but at 39. From $41 to $56 within a few months is doing pretty well—but it's a far less dramatic increase than the immediate visual impression left by the graph suggests.

Another way to alter the visual impression conveyed by graphs is to increase or decrease the distance between the coordinates. Change the layout, and the very same facts convey a very different impression. Look at the graph below, for example—presenting Butterine's share price for the same four months, October through January:

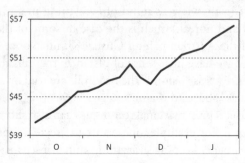

471

This graph presents exactly the same information for these months as does the one above it. Yet the impression it conveys is of a much more gradual increase; change the spacing between each point on the x axis makes a considerable difference to the visual impression.

There is nothing inherently sinister in the existence of options such as these for presenting information. In many respected financial publications the accepted convention is, as a space-saving measure, to include only that portion of the full graph that shows the information; if the shares have fluctuated only between $40 and $60 over a given period, then there is no need to show the values below $40 or above $60. But it's important to be aware that the existence of a range of options for presenting information visually creates opportunities for the unscrupulous. As shady stock promoters and unprincipled advertisers have long known, a graph quickly flashed before our eyes can very easily create a misleading impression.

Once you are on the lookout, understanding visual conventions of this sort (and their potential to be misused) is a relatively straightforward matter. Understanding the visual language of paintings or photographs or other sorts of images can often be a good deal more challenging.

Focus: When our eyes focus on something, we remain aware of the surrounding area, but as a blurred presence; nothing except what we are focusing on is sharply defined. The representational techniques of photography and painting can mimic that visual experience by showing one part of an image in much sharper detail than the rest of the image. They can also create two or more focal points in an image. A further possibility is to present everything in the image (even objects in the far distance) in sharp focus. (The latter can create an effect in the viewer's mind of everything in an image being at once real and unreal.) Such is the case in some of the landscape paintings of the Austrian painter Gustav Klimt. Notice how, in the image below, we have little sense of distance: the hills that one part of our brains reads as "behind" the near hills are read by another part of our brain as "above" those hills.

Of course, representational techniques can also show everything out of focus; if, for example, one wants to create a sense of movement in an image, keeping everything out of focus is one way of

Gustav Klimt, *Litzlberg am Attersee* (c. 1915)

doing so—as we see in the image on the next page, taken on the New York subway.

Perspective: Blurred though it may be, the photograph below gives a clear sense of three dimensions; the converging lines of the subway riders to the left and the right (as well as their diminished size as they become more distant from the viewer) create the illusion of spatial depth. Whether in a painting, a drawing, a photograph, or a computer-generated image, objects represented according to the "laws of perspective" will appear smaller as they are more distant—just as they do when the human eye perceives them. Lines that would be parallel in three dimensions will converge towards a far-away "vanishing point"—again, as they seem to do as perceived by the human eye. (At the same time, of course, more distant objects will appear less distinct and fainter in colour.)

"Shake, Rattle, and Roll": New York Subway, February 2, 2015

An image such as the Illinois Central travel poster (below) may not be entirely true-to-life in presenting Chicago in 1933, but it does appeal strongly to our sense of perspective—and thereby draws the viewer into the image. The Ghirlandaio painting (on the same page) has a less obvious vanishing point, but nevertheless makes strong use of perspective in representing the distant world as a backdrop to the event that is the painting's primary focus, the birth of Christ.

Each of these images have a single vanishing point. A vanishing point may, as in these cases, be in the far distance of an image; alternatively, it may be beyond or "behind" what we are shown in the image, and need to be inferred from the information provided. There may also be more than one vanishing point in a single image. In Gustave Caillebotte's vast Paris street scene, for example (see below), there is one vanishing point up the street to the left, another up the street behind the couple underneath the umbrella.[1]

---

1   It should perhaps also be noted here that many images in which objects are presented in perspective do not provide the viewer with any vanishing point. More distant objects are smaller in proportion to the degree they are more distant, but the viewer is given no sets of converging lines from which to infer one or more vanishing points.

Illinois Central travel poster (1933)

Ghirlandaio, *Adoration of the Magi* (1488)

Gustave Caillebotte, *Paris: Rainy Day* (1877)

On the following page is one more example of an image in which perspective plays a prominent part—this time a very different skyscraper picture, the historic Wainwright Building in St. Louis. The Wainwright Building is far less tall than the skyscrapers in the "Chicago: Vacation City" image above—but the use of perspective in the photograph makes the Wainwright building *feel* taller than the buildings in the Chicago poster. Here, perspective operates primarily in terms of height; we are given little or no other sense of distance.

Viewpoint and Distance: Looking up at something, of course, will make it seem more imposing, whereas looking down on it will make it seem less so. If a business wants its 70-storey headquarters to seem more impressive, it is likely to feature photographs from ground level, looking up; if a city filled with skyscrapers wants to make its canyon-like streets seem more friendly, one way is to make the viewer feel above it all.[1]

---

1 Interestingly, advertisements for luxury condominiums in tall buildings nowadays will often feature views looking straight out towards surrounding towers from a window on one of the highest floors.

Viewpoint makes a tremendous difference in shaping our visual perceptions of humans and other animals too; metaphors such as "I really look up to her" and "It felt like he was looking down on me" reflect an unfortunate reality about human perception. (Some studies have suggested that height is a greater predictor of future "earnings power" than level of education, or level of sociability, or anything else.)

When an image places the viewer on the same level as the subject of the image, any sense of superiority or inferiority tends to be minimized. Here again, we may sense how a frequently used metaphor—putting one person "on the same level" as someone else—reflects a powerful reality in our perceptual habits. Where the viewer is thus brought into direct visual connection with the eyes of the subject, particularly strong effects may be created; you may notice that in

Wainwright Building, St Louis (2010)

advertisements that seem designed to convey sensual allure, the subject is often looking directly at the viewer. So too with appeals for funds from relief agencies; such appeals are often accompanied by visual images of children looking directly towards the viewer, shot either at eye level or looking slightly up. Direct eye contact can create a very direct appeal—even, according to the influential scholars Gunther Kress and Theo Van Leeuwen, a *visual demand*.

In the Manet painting below, the barmaid is depicted at the same level as the viewer; she is not quite looking directly at the viewer, however. What effect is created in this instance?

The barmaid is also separated from the viewer by the bar in the foreground. Visual distance (quite aside from the matter of perspective) is another key element in the construction of visual images. If the viewer is brought close to the subject, that facilitates the creation of a broader sense of closeness, or intimacy. Such closeness may be of a sort to encourage warmly sympathetic feelings in the viewer—but close-ups may also be powerful conveyors of other emotions.

Edouard Manet, *Un Bar aux Folies-Bergère* (1881–82)

Below is an example of an image—a nineteenth-century icon[1]—in which two sets of eyes are directed towards the viewer. In this case the invitation (or, perhaps it may be said, the demand) concerns religious belief. Images such as this, common throughout much of

Nineteenth-century icon of the Madonna and baby Jesus. ("TIKHVINSKI" is written on the back.) The original is painted on a piece of wood measuring 7.6 x 10 inches.

---

1   Used in this context, *icon* refers to a sacred painting of Jesus, a saint, or another holy figure. In modern English, by contrast, the word *icon* and the phrase *iconic image* are not typically used to imply that viewers will use the image in question to engage in prayer; the terms may refer to any easily recognized image that serves as a symbol for something larger—or they may simply refer to any image that is widely recognized.

Christian history,[1] were created as an aid to prayer and contemplation; the spiritual attachment of a believer to the holy figures was felt to be made more powerful if an image of those figures could always be viewed—and the direct gaze common to religious icons reflects this emphasis on the viewer's personal connection.

Even when the gaze of the subject(s) of an image is not turned towards the viewer, the sight lines within an image can be vitally important to the impression the image conveys. Look, for example, at the direction of gazes in the Giotto fresco below (another Christian image, this time depicting those mourning the death of Jesus Christ).

In every way the head of Christ is the focus of this image. Sight lines run towards it not only from the humans but also from the angels above. And interestingly, greater emotion is displayed on the faces of those closest to that centre than on the faces of those farthest away. (Giotto is thought to have been the first painter to use degrees of emotion in the expressions of the subjects in this way, to help create an emotional focus for a representational work.)

Let's look at a painting in which there are only two sight lines within the image—a late nineteenth-century work by the American painter Mary Cassatt (below). Cassatt has often been accused of sentimentalizing the connection between mother and child. Is that the case here? What emotions may we read into the mother's sidelong gaze? What might be implied here about parenting? Is the child or the mother the primary focus of the painting for the viewer?

---

1   In the medieval period, it was believed that icons were not created by an artist in the way that we think of an artist today painting an image on wood or paper or canvas; it was rather the Holy Spirit who created the image, acting through a human hand. The point was not that the icon would portray the figures in any naturalistically convincing way; what made them real was not verisimilitude but the direct contact of the Holy Spirit in their creation.

Icons have continued to feature prominently in the Eastern Orthodox Church through to the modern era. Such images have been highly controversial, however. Various branches of Christianity have denounced their use as sinful (calling it "idolatry"), on the grounds that humans may too easily worship the image itself rather than that which it represents. Similarly, in Judaism it is forbidden to create or display a physical representation of Yahweh, and in Islam physical images of Allah and Muhammad are forbidden (and depictions of any people and animals are discouraged).

Giotto, *Lamentation*, c. 1305 (Scrovegni Chapel, Padua)

Mary Cassatt, *Breakfast in Bed* (1896)

Structural lines: Most representational images have a structure of lines formed by (or suggested by) the elements within them. In the Giotto fresco above, for example, the line of the wall forms a structural line in the image that provides further support to the "focusing" of the painting on the face of the dead Christ. In the Caillebotte painting above, the lamppost in the centre forms a very strong structural line that boldly separates the painting into two halves. How are the halves connected? In part by the sight lines of the couple; both are looking to the "other half" of the painting. In part as well the two halves are connected by the diagonals leading towards the two vanishing points. And in part they are connected by other lines suggested by the elements of the painting—the line, for example, running across the painting from left to right from the couple on the extreme left along the cobblestones to the man in front of them, and on beyond to the right side of the painting.

What is the effect of the line of the lamppost being "broken" by the man's umbrella? By the collaboration between the man's coat and the shadow of the lamppost in continuing the central line through the lower part of the image?

Where do the structural lines run in the "Chicago: Vacation City" poster above? Or in the Cassatt painting above? How do they affect our interpretation of each work?

Relative scale of objects: One other thing we may notice as we read the Cassatt painting is the relative size of child and mother. With the mother reclining and below the covers, it is the sitting child who takes up more of the painting. It would be too much to say that the mother is crowded out, but it is striking that the baby occupies more space. (The Russian icon above is in several respects an interesting point of comparison.)

A frequently cited image in discussions of relative scale is the painting below (a detail from which is reproduced on the cover of this book), depicting the classical story of hubris and disobedience in which Icarus, flying with wings his father made him from feathers and wax, ignores his father's instructions and flies too close to the sun; the wax melts and he falls to his death in the sea.

In the original tale, Icarus is a heroic, tragic figure. How does Bruegel's picture provide a commentary on that tale? Why might the farmer be placed in the centre of the picture, and Icarus's legs on the lower right hand side? What are the sightlines in the image? What are the structural lines in the image? To what extent does the picture follow the "laws of perspective"? Is there a vanishing point? If so, how is it created? What part does the ox play in the image?

The legs of Icarus are a strikingly small part of the image as a whole, and yet, in relation to nearby objects (notably, the ship), they are depicted as substantially larger than life. How should that irony be interpreted?

What (if anything) is implied about life in the distant city on the shore to the left? In the 1560s Holland was beginning to develop into a great commercial and trading power; it was also becoming heavily urbanized, such that by the end of the century almost half the population was living in cities (the highest percentage in the world at the time). How and to what extent might this broader historical context be relevant to a reading of this image?

Pieter Bruegel, *Landscape with the Fall of Icarus* (c. 1560s)

Colour, contrast, tone, symbol, etc.: A short overview such as this chapter attempts to provide can do no more than scratch the surface when it comes to covering the ways in which humans read visual images. The role of colour (bright colours / dull colours, level of saturation of colour, colour symbolism and suggestiveness, association of similarly coloured objects) is often of vital importance to the effect an image may have on viewers. So too is the role played by tone; sharp lines and high definition images create one sort of tone; soft lines and slightly blurred images a very different tone. And so too is the degree of contrast in an image; if bright, high definition areas abut very dark or low definition areas in an image, the impression created will be very different from that of an image featuring little contrast.

In addition, images may have powerful symbolic as well as literal value. A picture of a red maple leaf in a Canadian publication or of a bald eagle in an American publication will inevitably not simply be a leaf or a bird to viewers in those countries. A line or a wall or a shore may often function symbolically as well as literally in an image. Particular sorts of images may convey strongly gendered associations, or associations with youth or old age, or associations with a particular social status. The ways in which images may be read are numerous and varied; the point of this introduction is not to provide a full catalogue but rather to give some sense of where to start when trying to understand what a given image means—and how it conveys that meaning.

Words and Images: W.H. Auden's 1938 poem "Musée des Beaux Arts" famously captures the central idea behind *Landscape with the Fall of Icarus*:

> In Breughel's *Icarus*, for instance: how everything turns away
> Quite leisurely from the disaster; the ploughman may
> Have heard the splash, the forsaken cry,
> But for him it was not an important failure ...

The painting, though, is not called *Icarus*. Precisely the point that Auden makes and that the painting itself makes visually is also made in the painting's title, *Landscape with the Fall of Icarus*—

a title that foregrounds landscape in much the same way as the painting does. The words offer one clue to the painting's meaning, or at least to one of its most important meanings.[1]

A similar function is performed by the titles of many other images. Think, for example, of the associations that come to mind with the phrase "breakfast in bed." The phrase suggests leisure: typically, an adult relaxing contentedly in bed while a servant or a family member brings breakfast. Look again at the Cassatt painting above and consider its title: *Breakfast in Bed*.

Below is another example of the difference a title can make. The picture is in each case the same, but the impression created is very different. The title *House on Cameron Blvd., New Orleans* is very specific; it suggests little or nothing about the world outside the picture. The title *New Orleans, 2011*, on the other hand, could easily be taken to suggest that this derelict house is representative of the city as a whole in 2011. (That would be a false impression; by 2011 the city was well on the way to cleaning up the horrendous damage from Katrina, the August 2005 storm in which over 1,000 died and much of the city was submerged for many days.) Finally, the title *Everything Must Go* suggests that the image may be taken as representative of the transience of all things in this world; such a title extends the image's meaning beyond the context of any particular place.

---

1   Here again it is interesting to consider historical context. The sort of painting and drawing that has come to be known as *landscape art*—that is to say, art that portrays the land "by itself, for its own sake" (as the English writer Henry Peacham wrote in 1612, commenting on the development of *landtskip* in Dutch art), and not merely as ornament in images dominated by human subjects—developed in late sixteenth- and early seventeenth-century Holland. For the first time in human history, it was becoming common for paintings to bear titles beginning "Landscape with…."

Everything Must Go

New Orleans, 2011

House on Cameron Blvd., New Orleans

In many images, of course, words are included within an image itself. A famous example of the powerful effect words in an image can have is the photograph below, by Margaret Bourke-White.

Margaret Bourke-White, *World's Highest Standard of Living* (1937)

Bourke-White, a well-known American photographer, was one of several photographers commissioned by the Farm Security Administration to document the lives of Americans during the 1930s. This particular image was taken in Louisville, Kentucky; it shows people who had been badly affected by a 1937 flood of the Ohio River waiting in line for relief. The image soon came to be taken as expressive of a much broader set of problems, though—the hardships suffered across the country during the Great Depression.[1]

What can be said of the contrast between the people portrayed in the poster and the people in the line-up beneath? To

---

1   Indeed, it is not uncommon to see this picture referred to as depicting people
     suffering the effects of drought rather than of flooding, as a result of the degree
     to which the "Dust Bowl" drought of the 1930s is associated with the eco-
     nomic hardship of the era.

what extent does the line-up's spatial position below the poster help to make the photograph memorable? What does the contrast between the implied movement of the automobile and the evident stasis of those in line contribute to the effect of the photograph? Does the photograph implicitly comment on contrasts in American life other than that between prosperity and economic hardship? Would the photograph be as memorable if it were in colour?

Let's look at how words interact with an image in a very different sort of context: the poster below, which has been called the most influential political advertisement of the twentieth century. In the 1970s, Britain's Labour Party, which (as its name suggests) maintained close ties to organized labour, was becoming highly unpopular—in large part because of high unemployment, together with a series of labour disruptions that the government seemed powerless to control. The poster preyed on voters' concerns about both those topics; one can read "not working" as "unemployed" (as the unemployment line on the poster suggests) but also as "on strike." More broadly, of course, the advertisement plays on the meanings of "not working"—the powerful suggestion being that the solutions to the nation's problems that were being

Advertisement (1978), designed for the Conservative Party of Britain by Martyn Walsh of Saatchi and Saatchi. A follow-up, "Labour Still Isn't Working," was used in the 1979 British election campaign. The original ad was voted poster of the century in 1999 by a British advertising industry magazine.

tried by the Labour government weren't working. Finally, there is the implication that the Labour government hadn't been working hard enough—that it had been lazy in searching for solutions to Britain's problems.

Notice, too, how the advertisement presents the alternative; what do the words "better off" suggest? What does the relative size and position of words and images on the poster add to its meaning?

In 2012 the presidential campaign of Mitt Romney in the United States for a time employed a similar campaign, using the slogan "Obama isn't working"—sometimes in signs using text alone, sometimes with the slogan placed beside a picture of a smiling Barack Obama. Why do you think that combination of image and words turned out to be quite ineffective compared to the 1978–79 "Labour Isn't Working" campaign?

Think for a moment of Canadian politics. Which Canadian political party do you think would benefit most from a campaign that featured its leader's face in advertisements, accompanied by this slogan: NOT JUST A PRETTY FACE. A LEADER? What party or parties would benefit least from advertisements featuring its leader in this way? Why? If you were creating such an advertising campaign, what other words (if any) would you include with the image? From what angle would you show the face in question? Would you use an image that showed the leader looking directly at the viewer? Why?

Let's look at another advertisement, and try to bring together some of the perspectives discussed so far in this chapter. The advertisement below is one of a series; the Vancouver Humane Society has campaigned for years to ban rodeo competitions in calf-roping (often referred to by the rodeos themselves as "tie-down roping"). The subject is a controversial one, though there is surprisingly little argument over the central issue of whether or not calf-roping does involve cruelty; a clear majority of humane societies, veterinarians, and other authorities seem agreed that, at a minimum, it causes considerable fear and discomfort for the animal. (The Calgary Stampede itself does not argue directly that there is no suffering involved; they claim rather that they "care passionately" for the safety of the animals, and that serious injury is very rare.) A great deal could be said about the issues in the background[1]—but let's look at the advertisement itself.

Vancouver Humane Society advertisement, 2013

---

1   The controversy has been largely over side issues. Arguments against the VHS campaign often suggest that those living elsewhere should not be putting forward their views on what happens in Calgary, and that the Vancouver Humane Society should pay attention to what happens in Vancouver, period. Further controversy has sometimes erupted over the refusal of some Calgary newspapers to publish the advertisements.

For its part, the Calgary Humane Society has tried to stake out a middle ground. The statement on its website reads as follows: "the CHS fundamentally opposes high risk rodeo events like chuckwagon racing, calf-roping, and steer wrestling. While other organizations may wish to intervene to change rodeo and the Stampede through protest or other advocacy means, the CHS has found it can best protect the interests of the animals involved by working with organizations that put on such events."

Earlier advertisements in the campaign made explicit reference to the comparison between a human baby and a calf. The 2009 advertisement shows a picture of a cowboy roping the calf, seen from above, with the words *Bully* and *Baby* included and with lines connecting each word to the one it referred to. The 2010 advertisement shows a picture of a human baby beside a picture of a calf, made to look about the same size; both stare directly at the viewer. Underneath is this tag line: "Just three months old. Would you abuse a baby to entertain a crowd?"

The 2013 advertisement is considerably less forceful in its approach. It cannot be interpreted by the viewer as suggesting that a human baby and a baby cow are in some way equivalent. Nor does it use the word "baby" to name the calf. Rather the image shows a young human expressing affection towards a young non-human animal. Visually, though, it does suggest a parallel and a connection between the two. One is on the left, one on the right, with each occupying about the same amount of space in the frame. We can see the child's eyes directed towards the calf, and we can see the calf's eyes too—looking in her direction with evident contentment.

In the "Stampede blindness" image we see the eyes of a calf too—but clearly the animal is anything but contented. So far as the human figure is concerned, we see only his lower half, and his eyes are not shown—and we don't see any part of his body associated with either thought or emotion. The loosely implied suggestion is of a human who is unseeing, unfeeling. (Here we may notice the tie-in with the sentence below: "have a heart for animals.")

The two images are visually linked: the child, like the calf-roper, is wearing denim, and both images show a white fence in the background. There is, however, a considerable contrast in colour between the images: the dull grey and grey/blue background of the rodeo image contrasts with the brightness of the white fence and green grass (suggestive of growth, and of life) in the image of the child and calf together. We may notice too that, although the frame of the top image is largely filled with a close-up of child and calf, the perspective of the receding fence lends a feeling of depth and spaciousness to the image; in an environment such as this, the image seems to suggest, non-human animals are given the space they need. The horizontal fence that blocks the top half of the second image, crowded by denim-clad legs, contributes to a very different atmosphere.

Notice the camera-angle in both images: low down, at almost the same level as the calf. Through the use of this viewpoint, the photographer is able to lend the image a more vivid sense of the experience as it is being lived by the calf.

The 2013 advertisement is a good deal more subtle than some of its predecessors, but it still targets viewers' emotions. Some would say that emotional appeals of this sort are inherently "manipulative"—that they are based on sentimentality and should have no part in advocacy advertisements concerning public issues (whether advertisements such as this one or equally "sentimentalized" appeals to help the victims of a drought or a tsunami). Others argue that it is entirely legitimate to appeal to our emotions as well as our intellect—indeed, that one important way in which advertisements should try to engage the viewer is through appeals to emotion.

What do you think? Try to analyze your own reaction to the advertisement; how persuasive do you find it? Is your response emotional, rational, or some of both? Where is the dividing line between legitimate appeals to emotion and efforts to "manipulate" the emotions? Or does any "difference" just boil down to choosing different words to describe the same thing?

The VHS has also run controversial advertisements on other subjects—this one perhaps the most memorable among them:

Vancouver Humane Society, transit advertisement (2013)

How would you compare this ad to the "Human kindness" Stampede advertisement? Which is more impactful or persuasive? What comments do you have about the way the image conveys its message?

One other point of comparison may be of interest here: a two-page "Meet the Faces of Farming and Ranching" advertisement that was published December 28, 2014 in *The New York Times Magazine*. The advertisement is not readable when reduced in size to fit the format of this book, but may be viewed online on *The Broadview Guide to Writing* website (where it is accompanied by questions and suggestions for discussion).[1]

Additional Material Online

Additional images and discussion
questions may be found at
sites.broadviewpress.com/writing.
Click on **"Seeing and Meaning."**

Images to Read, Consider, and Discuss: To end the chapter and provide some opportunity to practise reading images, we will present below three images accompanied by questions but no direct commentary.

---

[1] The Vancouver Humane Society Images are copyright © Vancouver Humane Society. The VHS made them available without restriction on their use in the book, and with no permission fee charged. (Similarly, the US Farmers & Ranchers Alliance made their "Meet the Faces of Farming and Ranching" advertisement available without restriction on its use for this project, and with no permission fee charged.)

The photograph below shows an observer considering two of the figures that comprise American sculptor George Segal's *Gay Liberation* (1980), one of the world's first pieces of public art created in honour of the struggle for LGBT rights. The park in which this copy of the sculpture has been on display since 1992 is adjacent to the Stonewall Inn, site of the events that set off the modern movement for gay rights in 1969. The history of those events rewards study—as does the history of Segal's sculpture. The questions below, however, relate primarily to the image itself and what we can read there.

Looking at *Gay Liberation*, the Sculpture, Christopher Park, 2011 (2011)

Questions to consider:
- What can be read into the attitudes of the individuals who form the two couples? What may we infer about the connections between them?
- What are the sightlines of the figures in the sculpture? What can you say about their body language?
- What does the sculpture suggest about sexual orientation? About human relationships generally?
- Segal's sculptures are always coloured chalk white like this one. Comment on the effect this has on the viewer. Does the colour (or the absence thereof) have any racial connotations?
- Thirty-one years separate the making of this sculpture and the taking of the photograph above. Comment on the attitudes of both the people in the photograph above. What may we infer from the photograph about the changes that occurred in those thirty-one years—or about anything that has *not* changed between the 1980s and the 2010s?
- What message do you think the sculpture might have conveyed in 1980 about stereotypes of gays and lesbians? To what extent (if at all) does it address stereotypes held today?
- What do you think the man on the bench in the centre of the photograph might be thinking? To what degree is the viewer led to share those thoughts? Is the view invited to adopt any particular point of view?
- What effect is created by the position of the bench on an angle within the photograph? How would the effect be different if the bench formed a straight line across the photograph?
- Until the second half of the twentieth century almost all sculptures of human figures were placed on pedestals that brought the figures off the ground. What effect is created when that is done? What effect is created by Segal's style of placing sculpted human figures directly on the ground?
- Comment on the viewpoint from which the photograph is taken. Does this viewpoint work against what you take to be the message of the sculpture, or in harmony with it? Why?

William Brymner, *A Wreath of Flowers* (1884)

William Brymner, a Canadian painter who worked for some years in Paris in the 1880s, donated this large painting to the Royal Academy of Arts when he was elected a fellow of the academy in 1886. It now hangs in the National Gallery of Canada. The subject of the painting is a group of girls on a hillside, near a town on the coast of Yorkshire, England.

Questions to consider:

- What draws the viewer into this painting? Is there more than one area of the painting to which the viewer's eyes are particularly drawn by the structural lines of the image?

- How do you read the expressions of the girls? Does the painting suggest a thread of narrative? The girl to the right is knitting rather than participating in the making of the daisy chain. What comments might be made about the contrast between the two activities?

- What effect does the size of the central figures have in comparison to the size of the distant town? What effect does the presence of the sea have?

- What effect does the placement of the sea within the overall composition have on the viewer's perception? Comment on the workings of perspective in the painting, and how they may connect to the meanings we may read into it.

- What (if anything) does the painting say about exclusion? About the ways in which children relate to one another? About jealousy and envy? About hierarchy? About social class? About the social construction of gender roles in nineteenth-century England?

- How would the impression given us by the painting be different if the viewpoint were from slightly above the children rather than slightly below them?

- What effect do the painting's bright but soft hues have on the viewer? How do they connect to the meaning(s) suggested by the image?

- What comment might you make about the placing of the path (a) in terms of the composition of the painting; and (b) in terms of the symbolism involved?

- How does the background scenery in the painting reinforce—or contrast with—the emotional content of the painting's narrative?

Restoring *Oppression Breeds Resistance*, Belfast (2010)

From the 1960s through to the signing of the "Good Friday Agreement" in 1998, the history of Northern Ireland was one of sectarian
religious violence. That violence was part of a centuries-long conflict
between Protestant and Catholic, English and Irish, and—for many
of those centuries—rich and poor. From the 1970s onwards, murals
were an important part of the struggle, for both the Catholic and
the Protestant militants (the Irish Republican Army and the Ulster
Volunteer Force, respectively). The twenty-first century has seen
efforts both to create new murals (primarily on themes of peace and
reconciliation) and to restore the historic ones from the 1970s and
1980s; both sorts of murals have become the subject of sightseeing
tours.

• Comment on as many aspects of this image as you can.

◎ "EAL": *For Those Whose Native Language Is Not English*

The fact that different languages have different grammatical and syntactical conventions creates particular problems for anyone learning a new language. That is a point that may seem obvious, but a large percentage of the population of North America, Britain, and Australia (a majority of whom are unilingual) remain unaware of it as a felt reality. It is a measure of the degree to which English-speaking North Americans are unaccustomed to learning other languages that ESL—English as a Second Language—remains a widely-used umbrella term. We prefer EAL—English as an Additional Language—a term that allows for the possibility that someone learning English may already know several other languages.

This section of *The Broadview Guide to Writing* focuses on some of the peculiarities of English that are most likely to present difficulties to those learning the language. More often than not, multilingual students who are not yet fully fluent in English have at least as good a grasp of the formal grammatical principles of the language as do those for whom English is their first language. If you are not familiar with these principles, however, the section "Basic Grammar: An Outline" (pages 95–112) may be helpful.

Because of the differences in the ways that the structure of a student's own language may compare with English, students from different linguistic backgrounds are likely to want to focus on different aspects of English; what is particularly challenging for someone whose first language is Vietnamese may seem straightforward to someone whose first language is Spanish, and vice versa. For that reason the following guide may be helpful:

> Many speakers of languages such as Chinese (in its various forms), Japanese, and Vietnamese are likely, as a result of the ways in which those languages differ structurally from English, to have particular difficulty with topics treated under the following headings in this book: articles (E1–2); plurals (E5); infinitives (E12); conjugation of verbs, especially in the simple present tense (A2); word order (B1–10, E17–18).

Many speakers of languages such as Russian, Polish, and Bulgarian are likely, as a result of the ways in which those languages differ structurally from English, to have particular difficulty with topics treated under the following headings in this book: articles (E1–2); omission of the predicate (E3); double negatives (E9); the present perfect tense (A7); word order (B1–10, E17–18); possessives (E7); relative pronouns such as *who* and *which* (E6); countable and uncountable nouns and words such as *much, many, little,* and *few* (Please check index, E1).

Many speakers of languages such as French, Spanish, and Italian are likely, as a result of the ways in which those languages differ structurally from English, to have particular difficulty with topics treated under the following headings in this book: relative pronouns such as *who* and *which* (E6); double negatives (E9); comparatives and superlatives (E10); progressive (or continuous) verb tenses (A4, E14); word order (E17–18).

E1. **articles**: Articles are words used to introduce nouns. Unlike many other languages, English often requires the use of articles:

needs checking   We are interested in house with garage.
   revised   We are interested in a house with a garage.

There are only three articles—*a, an,* and *the.* Articles show whether or not one is drawing attention to a particular person or thing. For example, we would say *I stood beside a house* if we did not want to draw attention to that particular house, but *I stood beside the house that the Taylors used to live in* if we wanted to draw attention to the particular house.

A (or *an* if the noun following begins with a vowel sound) is an indefinite article—used with singular nouns when you do not want to be definite or specific about which thing or person you are referring to. *The* is a definite article, used with singular or plural nouns when you *do* want to be definite or specific. Remember that, if you use *the,* you are suggesting that there can be only one or one group of what you are referring to.

In order to use articles properly in English it is important to understand the distinction English makes between nouns naming things that are countable (*houses, books, trees,* etc.) and nouns naming things that are not countable (*milk, confusion,* etc). *A* can be used with singular count nouns (*a radio*), *the* with singular and plural count nouns (*the carpet, the horses*). *The* should be used with a non-count noun when it is followed by a specifying phrase (*the furniture in my house*). Some non-count nouns name things that it does seem possible to count: *sugar, grass, furniture*, etc. In such cases counting must in English be done indirectly: *a grain of sugar, two grains of sugar, three blades of grass, four pieces of furniture*, and so on.

Distinguishing between count and non-count nouns is inevitably a challenge for those whose first language is not English. A dictionary such as *The Oxford Advanced Learner's Dictionary* can be very helpful; unlike most dictionaries it indicates whether or not each noun is a count noun.

> *needs checking* They bought a nice furniture.
> *revised* They bought a nice piece of furniture.

● *Frequently Used Non-count Nouns*

abstractions: advice, anger, beauty, confidence, courage, fun, happiness, hate, health, honesty, information, knowledge, love, poverty, truth, wealth, wisdom.

to eat and drink: bacon, beef, beer, bread, broccoli, butter, cabbage, candy, cauliflower, celery, cereal, cheese, chicken, chocolate, coffee, corn, cream, fish, flour, fruit, ice, ice cream, lettuce, margarine, meat, milk, oil, pasta, pepper, rice, salt, spinach, sugar, tea, water, wine, yogurt.

other substances: air, cement, clothing, coal, dirt, equipment, furniture, gas, gasoline, gold, grass, homework, jewellery, luggage, lumber, machinery, metal, mail, money, music, paper, petroleum, plastic, poetry, pollution, research, scenery, silver, snow, soap, steel, timber, traffic, transportation, violence, weather, wood, wool, work.

Note: The plural of many of these non-count nouns may be employed when you want to denote more than one type of the substance. *Breads*, for example, refers to different sorts of bread; *coffees* refers to different types of coffee, *grasses* to different types of grass, and so on.

E2. **dropping the article:** Articles are not used in English to the same extent that they are used in some other languages; nouns can frequently stand alone without their article, particularly when they are being used in a general, non-specific sense. When used in this way, non-count and plural-count nouns need no article.

needs checking	If the English is to be spoken correctly, the good grammar is important.
revised	If English is to be spoken correctly, good grammar is important.
needs checking	The freedom is something everyone values.
revised	Freedom is something everyone values.

In most cases no article is necessary before a noun that is capitalized:

needs checking	They were strolling through the Stanley Park.
revised	They were strolling through Stanley Park.

Unfortunately, there are many exceptions to this rule (e.g., *the Hebrides, the Netherlands, the Dominican Republic, the United Kingdom, the Soviet Union, the United States*). A dictionary such as *The Oxford Advanced Learner's Dictionary* should be consulted in any case where you are uncertain if an article is needed.

E3. **omission of the subject or predicate:** Many languages allow the subject or the predicate to be assumed in certain situations, whereas (with the exception of imperative formations such as [*you*] *come here this instant!*) English requires that sentences include explicit subjects and predicates.

needs checking	Is very hot this afternoon.
revised	It is very hot this afternoon.
needs checking	She doctor and her husband carpenter. They both like their jobs.
revised	She is a doctor and her husband is a carpenter. They both like their jobs.
needs checking	Is not possible to finish the job this week.
revised	It is not possible to finish the job this week.

needs checking	Most authorities agree that malaria is a disease that could be targeted for eradication because would be feasible and relatively inexpensive to develop and distribute effective vaccines.
revised	Most authorities agree that malaria is a disease that could be targeted for eradication because it would be feasible and relatively inexpensive to develop and distribute effective vaccines.
needs checking	By the end of the century, were almost one million more people in Houston than there had been in 1980.
revised	By the end of the century, there were almost one million more people in Houston than there had been in 1980.

Note: In this sort of sentence construction English requires a "dummy" subject (such as *it* or *there*) before the verb *to be*; by contrast, languages such as Spanish allow the subject to be assumed in similar circumstances.

E4. repetition of the subject: Unlike many other languages, English does not permit the repetition of either the subject or the object within a single clause.

needs checking	The body of water outside the hotel it is called Chesapeake Bay.
revised	The body of water outside the hotel is called Chesapeake Bay.
needs checking	The members of the cast loved the play that they were acting in it.
revised	The members of the cast loved the play that they were acting in.

E5: plurals: Since many languages do not form plural nouns differently from nouns in the singular, it is easy if your background is in one of those languages to omit the *s* in plural formations in English.

needs checking	Many team play here every weekend.
revised	Many teams play here every weekend.

E6. gendered words/neutered words: In Romance languages such as French all nouns are masculine or feminine; for that reason many speakers of these languages use a masculine or feminine pronoun in English where the neuter pronoun is required.

needs checking   When I first saw the lake he was as smooth as glass.

      revised   When I first saw the lake it was as smooth as glass.

Most Romance languages and Slavic languages do not differentiate things from people in their relative pronouns. For that reason it is easy to forget to use *who* or *whom* rather than *that* or *which* in English.

needs checking   I spent the weekend visiting my grandparents, which are both in their eighties.

      revised   I spent the weekend visiting my grandparents, who are both in their eighties.

E7. **possessives**: Some languages make no distinction between possessive pronouns and possessive adjectives; in others possessive adjectives agree with what is possessed, not the possessor. In both cases English's different approach can cause difficulty.

needs checking   I told him that the book was my.

      revised   I told him that the book was mine.

         or   I told him that it was my book.

needs checking   As he sat in his office he looked out of her window at the moon.

      revised   As he sat in his office he looked out of his window at the moon.

Additional Material Online

Exercises specially designed for those whose native language is not English may be found at **sites.broadviewpress.com/writing**. Click on **Exercises** and go to **"EAL."**

E8. **negatives**: Whereas English uses auxiliaries to form standard negatives, many languages use particles. As a result of this difference, the correct formation of negatives in English can present difficulties.

needs checking   In later life he not wanted to see his old friends.

> *revised*   In later life he did not want to see his old friends.
> *or*   In later life he never wanted to see his old friends.

E9. **double negatives:** Languages in both the Slavic and Romance groups permit double negatives, thus making it difficult for those whose first language is from one of those groups to become habituated to the English prohibition against double negatives—and to grasp that words such as *without* can function as negatives.

> *needs checking*   I never not like to be away from home very long.
> *revised*   I never like to be away from home for long.
> *or*   I do not like to be away from home for long.

> *needs checking*   No one can survive in this society without no money.
> *revised*   No one can survive in this society without money.
> *or*   No one can survive in this society with no money.
> *or*   No one can survive in this society without any money.

E10. **comparatives and superlatives:** In many languages comparatives and superlatives must always include a word equivalent to *more* or *most*; there are no parallels for English formations such as *better*, *best* or *larger*, *largest*. Not surprisingly, many whose first language is not English find it difficult to get used to the English system of alternative forms of the comparative and superlative.

> *needs checking*   I wanted to buy the more larger size.
> *revised*   I wanted to buy the larger size.

E11. **compound verb formations:** English has many verb tenses, and many compound verb forms, including compound negative forms; these cause particular difficulty for those who are used to a less heavily conjugated system of verb tenses.

> *needs checking*   I waited for some time, but he not come.
> *revised*   I waited for some time, but he did not come.

> *needs checking*   She always working hard to help her family.
> *revised*   She is always working hard to help her family.

E12. **infinitives:** The infinitive form (*to go, to be, to do*, etc.) is not native to many languages, particularly many Far Eastern languages. For that reason it is sometimes given tense or person markers. In English the infinitive must always keep the same form.

> *needs checking*   When she first met him she found it difficult to felt any sympathy for him.
> *revised*   When she first met him she found it difficult to feel any sympathy for him.

E13. **phrasal verbs:** A phrasal verb occurs when a word that would normally function as a preposition instead becomes part of a two-word verb. *Break in, take off, put on, pick up, give up*—these are all examples of phrasal verbs. In such combinations an adverb cannot intercede between the two.

> *needs checking*   He put hurriedly on his clothes.
> *revised*   He put on his clothes hurriedly.

E14. **continuous verb tenses** (see also under "Verbs and Verb Tense Difficulties" in "Writing Grammatically"): In English the continuous tenses are not normally used with many verbs having to do with feelings, emotions, or senses. Some of these verbs are *to see, to hear, to understand, to believe, to hope, to know, to think* (meaning *believe*), *to trust, to comprehend, to mean, to doubt, to suppose, to wish, to want, to love, to desire, to prefer, to dislike, to hate.*

> *needs checking*   He is not understanding what I mean.
> *revised*   He does not understand what I mean.

> *needs checking*   At that time he was believing that everything on Earth was created within one week.
> *revised*   At that time he believed that everything on Earth was created within one week.

E15. **infinitives and gerunds:** As discussed in the chapter on this topic earlier, there are no rules in English as to why some verbs must be followed by an infinitive and others by a gerund, while still others may take either. Some combinations are particularly odd from the point of view of anyone whose first language is not English. For example, *start to go* and *start going* may be used interchangeably in most circumstances, whereas *stop going* is the opposite of both; *stop to go* has a quite different meaning. Unfortunately, these combinations must be learned one by one. One helpful rule, however, is that an infinitive can never follow a preposition.

needs checking	They were planning for to go to New York for the holidays.
revised	They were planning to go to New York for the holidays.
or	They were planning on going to New York for the holidays.
or	They were planning a trip to New York for the holidays.

E16. **prepositions:** As discussed in the chapter on preposition problems earlier, there are no overarching logical principles governing the use of prepositions in English. We say *angry with someone* rather than *angry to someone* or *angry against someone* purely as a matter of convention. In some cases general guidelines may be offered, however. For example, where place and time are concerned, *in* is used for larger expanses of space and larger durations of time; *at* is used for specific times and specific addresses; and *on* is used for street names (without precise addresses) and days of the week or the month (without precise times). *She lives in England, she lives on Downing St., she lives at 10 Downing St; she will meet you at 1 p.m.; she will see you some time in December; she will see you on December 15.*

needs checking	I live in 316 7th St. NW.
revised	I live at 316 7th St. NW.
or	I live on 7th St. NW.
or	I live in the house at 316 7th St. NW.

E17. **word order (subject/verb/object):** The rules governing word order in English are much more rigid than those of many other languages. For one thing, the subject, verb, and object normally appear in that order. Many other languages permit far more freedom in the ordering of subject, object, and verb, and for that reason this basic structural element of English can be difficult to grasp.

| *needs checking* | Yoshiki opportunities always welcomes. |
| *revised* | Yoshiki always welcomes opportunities. |

(Note: Speakers of languages such as Japanese and Korean, in which the verb must always come last in a sentence, are particularly likely to experience this sort of difficulty with English.)

| *needs checking* | Opportunities welcomes Yevgeny always. |
| *revised* | Yevgeny always welcomes opportunities. |

(Note: Speakers of languages such as Russian, in which the object may appear before the subject, are particularly likely to experience this sort of difficulty with English.)

In most Romance languages object pronouns come before the verb. This often creates difficulties for native speakers of those languages with the word order required in English, where object pronouns normally follow the verb.

needs checking   When we these give him, he will be very grateful.
revised   When we give him these, he will be very grateful.

E18. **word order (adjectives and adverbs)**: In English, adjectives generally precede the noun to which they refer, while adverbs generally follow the verb to which they refer. Moreover, there are rules governing the order of adjectives and adverbs—rules which native English speakers have absorbed unconsciously, but which otherwise must be learnt. Since it is common to use two or more adjectives to describe something, problems often arise.

The proper order of adjectives: determiners (*my, his, this, that,* etc.); adjectives concerning number or quantity (*first, many, some,* etc.); adjectives expressing a subjective opinion (*beautiful, sad, fascinating,* etc.); adjectives concerning size or shape (*large, small, straight, flat,* etc.); adjectives describing age or condition (*old, clean, sharp, wet,* etc.); adjectives describing colour (*red, mauve, blue,* etc.); adjectives naming substances and adjectives that may also be used as nouns (*metal, woollen, English,* etc.); the noun.

needs checking   They lived in a white lovely house near the sea.
revised   They lived in a lovely white house near the sea.

◎ PUNCTUATION, FORMAT, AND SPELLING

⊙ Punctuation

● *The Period* .

The most important mark of punctuation is the full stop (or period), which is used to separate one complete sentence from another. But what constitutes a complete sentence? What constitutes a run-on sentence, or a sentence fragment? These questions are complex ones, involving the structures of English grammar (pages 106–112) and the conventions governing the use of various joining words (pages 276–301), as well as the rules governing the use of periods, commas, and semicolons that are treated in this section of the book. For a full understanding, we recommend you read all these sections.

F1. **run-on sentence**: A run-on sentence is a sentence that continues running on and on when, as a matter of grammatical correctness, it should be broken up into two or more sentences. Sometimes people use the expression *run-on sentence* loosely to refer to a sentence that is simply very long, regardless of whether or not it is grammatically correct. A well-constructed long sentence, though, can be an excellent means of expressing complex ideas; for the sake of clarity, then, it's important not to confuse the idea of a long sentence with the idea of a run-on sentence. The term *run-on sentence* should be used only when issues of grammatical correctness are involved.

One variety of run-on sentence (a **fused sentence**) occurs when independent clauses are not separated by any punctuation.

> *needs checking*   Early last Thursday we were walking in the woods it was a lovely morning.
> *revised*   Early last Thursday we were walking in the woods. It was a lovely morning.

A second (and more common) variety of run-on sentence occurs when a comma (rather than a period or a semi-colon) is used between independent clauses, without the addition of any coordinating conjunction. This type of run-on sentence is called a **comma-splice**.

needs checking It was a lovely morning, we were walking in the woods.
revised It was a lovely morning. We were walking in the woods.
or It was a lovely morning, and we were walking in the woods.

In simple examples such as those above the matter may seem straightforward. Sometimes, though, it is not so simple. The conventions of English dictate that only certain words may be used to join two independent clauses into one sentence; the seven coordinating conjunctions (*and, but, or, for, nor, so,* and *yet*) may be used to join independent clauses.

needs checking The temperature stayed below freezing, therefore the ice did not melt.
revised The temperature stayed below freezing. Therefore, the ice did not melt.
or The temperature stayed below freezing, so the ice did not melt.

> [The word *therefore* is not a coordinating conjunction, and thus may not be used to join independent clauses. The word *so* is a coordinating conjunction, and may thus be used to join independent clauses—provided that a comma is used as well.]

needs checking The pilot checked the speedometer and the altimeter, then she knew what to do.
revised The pilot checked the speedometer and the altimeter. Then she knew what to do.
or The pilot checked the speedometer and the altimeter; then she knew what to do.
or The pilot checked the speedometer and the altimeter, and then she knew what to do.

> [The word *then* is not a coordinating conjunction, and thus may not be used to join independent clauses. The word *and* is a coordinating conjunction, and may thus be used to join independent clauses—provided that a comma is used as well.]

Another class of joining word is the conjunctive adverb. Some of the words most commonly used as conjunctive adverbs are *also, hence, however, moreover, nevertheless, otherwise,* and *therefore.* When used as conjunctive adverbs, these words typically indicate how the main idea in one sentence relates to the main idea of a previous sentence. In such cases a period (or semicolon) should separate the ideas from each other. They should not be "spliced" together with a comma:

needs checking	With the exception of identical twins no two people have exactly the same genetic makeup, hence it is impossible for two people to look exactly the same.
revised	With the exception of identical twins no two people have exactly the same genetic makeup. Hence, it is impossible for two people to look exactly the same.
needs checking	During the rainy season more water flows over Victoria Falls than over any other falls in the world however several other falls are higher than Victoria.
revised	During the rainy season more water flows over Victoria Falls than over any other falls in the world. However, several other falls are higher than Victoria.
or	During the rainy season more water flows over Victoria Falls than over any other falls in the world; several other falls, however, are higher than Victoria.
needs checking	Money was tight and jobs were scarce, therefore she decided to stay in a job she did not like.
revised	Money was tight and jobs were scarce; therefore, she decided to stay in a job she did not like.

Notice in the above cases one good way to correct a comma splice is often to use a semicolon. Unlike a comma, a semicolon may be used as a connector between clauses. (The discussion of the semicolon below may be helpful in this connection.)

F2. **then:** An even more common cause of run-on sentences than any of the above is the word *then.* Unlike *when, then* should not be used to join two clauses together into one sentence. *And then* may be used, or a semicolon, or a new sentence may be begun.

needs checking   We applied the solution to the surface of the leaves then we made observations at half-hour intervals over the next twelve hours.

revised   We applied the solution to the surface of the leaves. Then we made observations at half-hour intervals over the next twelve hours.

or   We applied the solution to the surface of the leaves; then we made observations at half-hour intervals over the next twelve hours.

or   We applied the solution to the surface of the leaves, and then we made observations at half-hour intervals over the next twelve hours.

needs checking   On June 10, 1999, Yugoslav troops began withdrawing, then the NATO bombing was suspended and the war in Kosovo ended.

revised   On June 10, 1999, Yugoslav troops began withdrawing. Then the NATO bombing was suspended and the war in Kosovo ended.

F3. sentence fragments (incomplete sentences): An incomplete sentence (or sentence fragment) is a group of words that has been written as if it were a complete sentence, but that, as a matter of grammatical correctness, needs something else to make it complete.

A grammatically complete sentence must of course include both a subject and a verb. The group of words *in a minute*, for example, cannot be a complete sentence; it's a phrase, lacking both a subject and a verb. But including a subject and a verb is not enough; all clauses include both a subject and a verb, but only independent clauses can form sentences. The group of words *When the meeting ends tomorrow*, for example, cannot form a complete sentence on its own; it begins with a coordinating conjunction and is thus structured grammatically as a subordinate (or "dependent") clause. To form a complete sentence, one can either transform it into an independent clause (*The meeting will end tomorrow*) or attach it as a subordinate clause to a separate, independent clause (*When the meeting ends tomorrow, we should have a comprehensive agreement*).

Focusing on the word fragment, some people imagine incomplete sentences to be always very short. That's not the case. Whether a sentence is complete or not complete is a matter of grammar, not of sentence length. For example, the short group of words Marina walked to the sea can form a complete sentence, but this much longer group of words is a sentence fragment:

needs checking	While Marina was walking to the sea and thinking of her father and the sound of a woodthrush.
revised	While Marina was walking to the sea she heard the sound of a woodthrush and thought of her father.

needs checking	Unemployment was a serious problem in Britain in the early 1990s. In fact, throughout the world.
revised	Unemployment was a serious problem in the early 1990s, not just in Britain but throughout the world.

needs checking	So long as you have a place to live and enough to eat.
revised	So long as you have a place to live and enough to eat, you have some reason to be thankful.

The three words which most frequently lead students to write incomplete sentences are *and*, *because*, and *so*; each is discussed below.

acceptable sentence fragments: For a discussion of contexts in which sentence fragments may be considered acceptable, see the companion website to this book. Click on **Exercises** and **Punctuation**, and then go to **Run-on Sentences and Sentence Fragments 4 (acceptable sentence fragments)**.

F4. **and**: Although there are certain cases in which it is possible to begin a sentence with *and*, these are extremely difficult to sense. It is usually better for all except professional writers not to begin sentences with *and* if they wish to avoid incomplete sentences.

worth checking	To make this crop grow well you should add Compound 'D' fertilizer to the soil. And you should add top dressing a few months later.
revised	To make this crop grow well you should add Compound 'D' fertilizer to the soil, and top dressing a few months later.

F5. **because**: In order to prevent young children who have difficulty in writing long sentences from writing incomplete sentences, many elementary school teachers wisely tell their pupils not to begin sentences with *because*. In fact it is not incorrect to begin with *because*, so long as the sentence is complete. The rule to remember is that any sentence with *because* in it must mention both the cause and the result. Whether the word *because* comes at the beginning or in the middle of the sentence does not matter; what is important is that the sentence has two parts.

needs checking	In the early 1980s Sandinista leaders told their people to be ready for war. Because the United States had been trying to destabilize Nicaragua.
revised	In the early 1980s Sandinista leaders told their people to be ready for war, because the United States had been trying to destabilize Nicaragua.

F6. so: This word is probably the biggest single cause of incomplete sentences. As is the case with *and*, there are certain situations in which professional writers manage to get away with beginning sentences with *so*, but normally this should not be attempted. *So* should be used to join ideas together into one sentence, not to separate them by starting a new sentence.

needs checking	I did not know what was happening. So my friends explained the procedure to me.
revised	I did not know what was happening, so my friends explained the procedure to me.
needs checking	The meat was too heavily spiced. So most of it had to be thrown away.
revised	The meat was too heavily spiced, so most of it had to be thrown away.

F7. abbreviations: The period is also used to form abbreviations. If in any doubt about whether or not to use a period in an abbreviation, or where to put it, think of (or look up) the full form of what is being abbreviated.

needs checking	Jones, Smithers et. al. will be there in person.
revised	Jones, Smithers et al. will be there in person.
	(*Et al.* is short for the Latin *et alia*, meaning *and others*.)

● *The Ellipsis*　．．．

Three dots are used to indicate the omission of one or more words needed to complete a sentence or other grammatical construction.

F8. **ellipsis:** Note that when used in quotation an ellipsis comes inside the quotation marks, and that when an ellipsis precedes a period the sentence should end with four dots (essentially the three-dot ellipsis followed by the period).

   needs checking   Harris shows more than a trace of paranoia in her book; she speaks, for example, of "the elements trying to subvert the essence of liberal society, of tolerance, of goodwill ... They are all around us."

   revised   Harris shows more than a trace of paranoia in her book; she speaks, for example, of "the elements trying to subvert the essence of liberal society, of tolerance, of goodwill.... They are all around us."

Ellipses may also be used to indicate the trailing off of speech: *Violet struggled for breath. "All my money," she gasped, "goes to...." Those were her last words.*

● *The Comma*　　,

(See also pages 509–12 for comma splices.)

Perhaps the most important function of the comma in modern English usage is to help the reader recognize the grammatical structure of a sentence. As a side benefit, commas also help those reading aloud to pause at places in a sentence where there are natural breaks in the grammatical structure. But commas should not be used simply to create pauses at any point in a long sentence where the writer thinks the reader might run out of breath.

It was not always thus. When commas began to appear in English prose (in the late sixteenth century), they were used simply as a way of suggesting pauses in speech. Given the extent to which people's natural speech patterns differ, it is no wonder that the placing of commas in seventeenth- and eighteenth-century usage seems to us haphazard. (In this respect eighteenth-century habits of punctuation resemble eighteenth-century habits of capitalization—see page 536.) A striking example is the Second Amendment to the American Constitution:

> A well regulated Militia, being necessary to the security of a free State, the right of the people to keep and bear Arms, shall not be infringed.

This is a sentence comprising two clauses, with a subordinate clause at the beginning providing context for the declaration made in the main clause. Though it is a long sentence, there is according to grammatical principles no good reason to include a comma anywhere except at the break between the two clauses:

> A well regulated Militia being necessary to the security of a free State, the right of the people to keep and bear Arms shall not be infringed.

In saying this sentence aloud some readers will undoubtedly pause slightly at points other than at the one marked by the comma. But it is at that point alone that there should be a comma (at least according to the conventions of modern English). The additional commas in early texts are in this case far more than a historical curiosity; they have fuelled endless debate and more than one court case over the constitutionality of twentieth- and twenty-first-century gun control measures in America.

The above should not be taken to imply that there is no room for individuality when it comes to the inclusion of "structural" commas; far from it. Many writers, for example, like to use a comma to set off an opening phrase from the sentence that follows. And that is perfectly acceptable; both the versions below of the sentence that opened the previous paragraph are correct, as are both versions of the other sample sentence below:

> In saying this sentence aloud some readers will undoubtedly pause slightly at points other than at the one marked by the comma.

> In saying this sentence aloud, some readers will undoubtedly pause slightly at points other than at the one marked by the comma.

In the spring of 2008 she left her family and moved to Rome.

In the spring of 2008, she left her family and moved to Rome.

Again, the key point is that if structural commas are to be included, they must come at points in the sentence where there are natural breaks in the grammatical structure.

Although the omission or wrong use of a comma sounds like a small mistake, it can be very important. The following group of words, for example, forms a sentence only if a comma is included:

needs checking	Because of the work that we had done before we were ready to hand in the assignment.
revised	Because of the work that we had done before, we were ready to hand in the assignment.

Restrictive and non-restrictive modifiers: The omission or addition of commas can also completely alter the meaning of a sentence—as it did in the Queen's University Alumni letter that spoke of the warm emotions still felt by alumni for *our friends, who are dead* (rather than *our friends who are dead*). The second would have been merely a polite remembrance of those alumni who have died; the first suggests that all the friends are dead.

Such differences in meaning are not usually matters of life and death. In the following two sentences, the difference is a matter of how many stroganoffs are on the menu.

The stroganoff, made with mushrooms and cashew cream, is the most popular item on our menu.

The stroganoff made with mushrooms and cashew cream is the most popular item on our menu.

In the first sentence the implication is that there is only one stroganoff available; the one and only stroganoff is the most popular item on the menu, and in mentioning the mushrooms and cashew cream the server is simply providing some additional, incidental information. In the second sentence the omission of commas leaves open the possibility that there may be several stroganoffs on the menu; it's the one with the mushrooms and cashew cream that's the most popular. (Hint from the server: *don't order the beef stroganoff.*)

The grammatical distinction involved here is between restrictive and non-restrictive modifiers. Restrictive modifiers are essential to the full meaning of the word being modified; they restrict or limit the meaning of that word within the sentence. To indicate that they are essential to the meaning of the noun, they are not separated from it by commas. (The meaning of the second sentence is restricted to *the stroganoff made with mushrooms and cashew cream.*)

Non-restrictive modifiers, on the other hand, provide additional information that is not essential to the core meaning of the word being modified. As a way of indicating that the information provided by non-restrictive modifiers is incidental rather than essential to the word being modified, non-restrictive modifiers should be set off with commas. (In the first stroganoff sentence, in which the information about the mushrooms and the cashew cream is not essential to the meaning of *stroganoff* within the sentence, *made with mushrooms and cashew cream* is set off by commas.)

needs checking   Shoppers, who spend $100 or more, are eligible for the prize.
[The modifying clause who spend $100 or more is in this case essential to the meaning of *shoppers* in the context of this sentence; the group of people eligible is restricted to those who spend $100 or more.]

revised   Shoppers who spend $100 or more are eligible for the prize.

The distinction between restrictive and non-restrictive modifiers may apply to adjective clauses (such as those above), adjective phrases, and also to appositives—nouns or noun phrases in apposition to another noun. Mistakes with appositives are common.

needs checking   In Shakespeare's play, *The Tempest,* Gonzalo uses the same words that appear in Florio's translation of Montaigne's "Of Cannibals."
[This could be taken to imply that Shakespeare wrote only one play.]

revised   In Shakespeare's play *The Tempest* Gonzalo echoes the language of John Florio's translation of Montaigne's "Of Cannibals."

(For more on restrictive and non-restrictive modifiers, see the discussion of *that* and *which* on pages 298–300.)

F9. **omission of commas**: Commas very commonly come in pairs, and it is wrong to omit the second comma in a pair. Be particularly careful when putting commas around a name, or around an adjectival subordinate clause.

needs checking	My sister Caroline, has done very well this year in her studies.
revised	My sister, Caroline, has done very well this year in her studies.
needs checking	The snake which had been killed the day before, was already half-eaten by ants.
revised	The snake, which had been killed the day before, was already half-eaten by ants.

F10. **extra comma**: Writers often add a comma when they feel a sentence is getting long, regardless of whether one is needed or is appropriate.

needs checking	The ever-increasing gravitational pull of the global economy, is drawing almost every area of the earth into its orbit.
revised	The ever-increasing gravitational pull of the global economy is drawing almost every area of the earth into its orbit.

F11. **serial comma**: An important use of commas is to separate the entries in lists. Many authorities feel that a comma need not appear between the last and second-last entries in a list, since these are usually separated already by the word *and*. Omitting the last comma in a series will occasionally lead to ambiguity, though; when in doubt, include the serial comma. And when the list includes items that have commas within them, use a semicolon to separate the items in the list.

needs checking   This book is dedicated to my parents, Ayn Rand and God.

revised   This book is dedicated to my parents, Ayn Rand, and God.

needs checking   The three firms involved were McCarthy and Walters, Harris, Jones, and Engleby, and Cassells and Wirtz.

revised   The three firms involved were McCarthy and Walters; Harris, Jones, and Engleby; and Cassells and Wirtz.

Additional Material Online

Exercises on comma splices, sentence fragments, and how to use punctuation may be found at **sites.broadviewpress.com/writing**. Click on **Exercises** and go to **"Punctuation."**

● *The Question Mark*   **?**

F12. **question mark:** Everyone knows that a question should be followed by a question mark, but it is easy to forget, particularly if one is writing quickly or if the question mark should appear within other punctuation.

needs checking   Would Britain benefit from closer ties with Europe. More than 30 years after the UK joined the EC, the question continues to bedevil British political life.

revised   Would Britain benefit from closer ties with Europe? More than 30 years after the UK joined the EC, the question continues to bedevil British political life.

It is easy to forget that sentences beginning with combinations such as *He asked if...* or *She wondered whether...* are statements, not questions. They may report a question in indirect speech, but they are not themselves questions, and should thus not end with a question mark.

needs checking	Many scholars have asked whether Truman was justified in dropping the atomic bomb on Japan, or whether he should have relied on conventional weapons?
revised	Many scholars have asked whether Truman was justified in dropping the atomic bomb on Japan, or whether he should have relied on conventional weapons.
or	Many scholars have asked the following question: was Truman justified in dropping the atomic bomb on Japan, or should he have relied on conventional weapons?

● *The Exclamation Mark* !

This mark is used to give extremely strong emphasis to a statement. It should be used very sparingly, if at all, in formal written work; most good writers avoid it completely, since they realize that it does not lend any additional impact to what they are saying.

● *The Semicolon* ;

F13. This mark is used to separate independent clauses where the ideas are closely related to each other. In most cases a period could be used instead; the semicolon simply signals to the reader the close relationship between the two ideas. In the following example the second sentence reinforces the statement of the first; a semicolon is thus appropriate, although a period is also correct:

- This book is both exciting and profound. It is one of the best books I have read.
- This book is both exciting and profound; it is one of the best books I have read.

Similarly in the following example the second sentence gives evidence supporting the statement made in the first sentence. Again, a semicolon is appropriate:

- The team is not as good as it used to be. It has lost four of its past five games.
- The team is not as good as it used to be; it has lost four of its last five games.

The semicolon is also used occasionally to divide items in a series that includes other punctuation:

- The following were told to report to the coach after practice: Jackson, a sophomore; Marshall, a junior; Nicola, a senior.

A common notion is that the central distinction among punctuation marks such as the comma, semicolon, colon, and period is rooted simply in the length of the pause they ask the reader to make. Such indeed was the norm several centuries ago, when punctuation was designed less to indicate grammatical relationships than to mark pauses as an aid to the listener's understanding when the text was read aloud. Under that system, a period counted as four beats, a colon as three, a semicolon as two, and a comma as one. Ian Coutts, in an interesting article in *Quill and Quire* ("All About the Pause," February 2005, 7), uses a passage from the 1549 *Book of Common Prayer* as an example of how strangely such a system strikes the modern sensibility:

Easter Day. The Collect.
Almighty God, who through thine only begotten Son Jesus Christ hast overcome death, and opened unto us the gate of everlasting life; We humbly beseech thee, that, as by thy special grace preventing us thou dost put into our minds good desires, so by thy continual help we may bring the same to good effect; through Jesus Christ our Lord, who liveth and reigneth with thee and the Holy Ghost, ever one God, world without end.

Perhaps even stranger to modern eyes is the fashion in which the reading that follows is punctuated in sixteenth-century style:

Mortify therefore your members which are upon the earth; fornication, uncleanness, inordinate affection, evil concupiscence, and covetousness, which is idolatry: For which things, sake the wrath of God cometh on the children of disobedience. In the which ye also walked some time, when ye lived in them.

It is not only the practice of punctuation here that is at odds with today's practice; so too are the principles of capitalization and of grammar considerably different. Here are the two passages again, set down according to modern practice:

Almighty God, who through thine only begotten Son Jesus Christ hast overcome death, and opened unto us the gate of everlasting life, we humbly beseech thee that, as by thy special grace preventing us thou dost put into our minds good desires, so by thy continual help we may bring the same to good effect; through Jesus Christ our Lord, who liveth and reigneth with thee and the Holy Ghost, ever one God, world without end.

Mortify therefore your members which are upon the earth: fornication; uncleanness; inordinate affection; evil concupiscence; and covetousness, which is idolatry. For these things' sake the wrath of God cometh on the children of disobedience, in the which ye also walked some time, when ye lived in them.

Echoes of the ancient principles of punctuation are still to be found in surprising places. The section on punctuation in the fifteenth edition of *The Chicago Manual of Style* advises at one point that "the semicolon, stronger than a comma but weaker than a period, can assume either role." As Louis Menand fairly commented in discussing this passage in his review of the fifteenth edition, "What could the authors possibly have been thinking?" ("The End Matter," *The New Yorker*, 6 October 2003, 125). To retain elements of the old system of "pause punctuation" in the context of modern academic practice is simply to sow the seeds of confusion. In such a context, the semicolon has a set of precise grammatical functions; it is not to be used simply to indicate a longer-than-usual pause, any more than the comma is to be used to join independent clauses.

needs checking The threat to the planet is constant and growing, it is to be found in the factories of Ohio; in the shrinking rain forests of Brazil; in the massive growth and massive pollution of China's cities; and in the coal-fired generation stations that still produce much of the world's electricity.

revised The threat to the planet is constant and growing. It is to be found in the factories of Ohio, in the shrinking rain forests of Brazil, in the massive growth and massive pollution of China's cities, and in the coal-fired generation stations that still produce much of the world's electricity.

or   The threat to the planet is constant and growing; it is to be found in the factories of Ohio, in the shrinking rain forests of Brazil, in the massive growth and massive pollution of China's cities, and in the coal-fired generation stations that still produce much of the world's electricity.

● *The Colon*   **:**

F14. **colon:** This mark is often believed to be virtually the same as the semicolon in the way it is used. In fact, there are some important differences. The most common uses of the colon are as follows:

- in headings, to announce that more is to follow, or that the writer is about to list a series of things.
- to introduce a quotation.
- between two clauses, to indicate that the second one provides an explanation of what was stated in the first.

This last (the least common way in which the colon is used) is very similar to the main use of the semicolon. The subtle differences are that the semicolon can be used in such situations when the ideas are not quite so closely related, and the colon asks the reader to pause for a slightly longer period. Some authorities, it should be noted, feel it is inappropriate to use a colon in this way; if in any doubt as to the appropriateness of using a colon to separate two independent clauses, the student is well advised to use a semicolon instead.

- Unquiet Union: A Study of the Federation of Rhodesia and Nyasaland.
- In the last four weeks he has visited five countries: Mexico, Venezuela, Panama, Haiti, and Belize.
- The theory of the Communists may be summed up in a single phrase: abolition of private property.

Be sure to use a colon (rather than a comma or a semicolon) to introduce a list.

needs checking The operation in Toronto has supplied Mr. Bomersbach
with four luxury cars, two Cadillacs, a Mercedes, and a
Jaguar.

revised The operation in Toronto has supplied Mr. Bomersbach
with four luxury cars: two Cadillacs, a Mercedes, and a
Jaguar.

● *The Hyphen*

F15. **hyphen**: This mark may be used to separate two parts of a
compound word (e.g., *tax-free*, *hand-operated*). Notice that many
such word combinations are hyphenated only if the combination
acts as an adjective:

- No change is planned for the short term.
  (*Term* acts here as a noun, with the adjective *short* modifying it.)
- This is only a short-term plan.
  (Here the compound *short-term* acts as a single adjective, modifying
  the noun *plan*.)
- George Eliot is one of the major figures in the literature of the
  nineteenth century.
  (*Century* acts here as a noun, with the adjective *nineteenth* modifying
  it.)
- George Eliot is one of the major figures of nineteenth-century
  literature.
  (Here the compound *nineteenth-century* acts as a single adjective,
  modifying the noun *literature*.)

Hyphens are also used to break a word at the end of a line if
there is not enough space. A hyphen should never be used to break
up proper nouns, and should be used to break up other words only
when it is placed between syllables. Any noun beginning with a
capital letter (e.g., *Halifax, Blair, January, Harriet*) is a proper noun.

Whenever one is uncertain about whether or not to use a
hyphen, the easy solution is to put the entire word on the next line.

● *The Dash*

F16. **dash:** Dashes are often used in much the same way as parentheses, to set off an idea within a sentence. Dashes, however, call attention to the set-off idea in a way that parentheses do not:

- Peterborough (home of Broadview Press's distribution facility) is a pleasant city of 80,000.
- Peterborough—home of Broadview Press's distribution facility—is a pleasant city of 80,000.

A dash may also be used in place of a colon to set off a word or phrase at the end of a sentence:

- He fainted when he heard how much he had won: one million dollars.
- He fainted when he heard how much he had won—one million dollars.

Em dashes and en dashes: The above applies to what is known as the em dash—so-called because in most typefaces it is about the same length as the letter *m*. There is also a slightly shortened form of dash—known as the en dash—which fulfills a different function. Whereas an em dash is used to separate groups of words, an en dash is used to separate numbers, as in these examples:

- Paul Newman (1925–2008) was both a philanthropist and a noted actor.
- The street numbers are as follows: in the first block west of Main Street, 1–100; in the second block, 100–200; and so on.

Although it is standard to use the en dash in such circumstances in published work, the en dash does not appear on most keyboards, and the hyphen is usually used in its stead in everyday work. In most word processing programs an em dash may be formed by typing two hyphens (--). Note that no spaces should be left either before or after the dash. In some word processing programs a dash may be chosen from the menu symbols.

needs checking   Taipei 101-at the time the tallest building in the world-was completed in 2004. Towers in Shanghai and Dubai have since surpassed it.

revised   Taipei 101—at the time the tallest building in the world—was completed in 2004. Towers in Shanghai and Dubai have since surpassed it.

● *Parentheses*   ( )

F17. **parentheses**: Parentheses are used to set off an interruption in the middle of a sentence, or to make a point which is not part of the main flow of the sentence. They are frequently used to give examples, or to express something in other words using the abbreviation i.e. Example:

- Several world leaders of the 1980s (Deng in China, Reagan in the US, etc.) were very old men.

● *Square Brackets*   [ ]

F18. **square brackets**: Square brackets are used for parentheses within parentheses, or to show that the words within the parentheses are added by another person.

- Lentricchia claims that "in reading James's Preface [to *What Maisie Knew*] one is struck as much by what is omitted as by what is revealed."
- Smith writes that as the end of the trial approached, "Sacco and Vanzetti had a good idea of what there [sic] fate would be."
  (Here the Latin *sic*, meaning *thus*, is used to indicate that the error is reproduced just as it appears in the original quotation.)

● *The Apostrophe*   '

apostrophe: The two main uses of the apostrophe are to show possession (e.g., *Peter's book*) and to shorten certain common word combinations. The shortened forms (e.g., *can't, shouldn't, he's*) are known as contractions.

F19. **contractions:** Contractions are used frequently in this book, which is relatively informal in its style. Contractions, however, should not be used in more formal written work. Use *cannot*, not *can't*; *do not*, not *don't*; and so on.

> *informal*   The experiment wasn't a success because we'd heated the
>   solution to too high a temperature.
> *more formal*   The experiment was not a success because we had heated
>   the solution to too high a temperature.

F20. **possession:** The correct placing of the apostrophe to show possession can be a tricky matter. When the noun is singular and does not already end with an *s*, an *s* at the end of the word, preceded by an apostrophe, shows possession (e.g., *Peter's, George's, Canada's*). When the noun is plural and ends in an *s* already, the apostrophe should be added after the *s*.

> *needs checking*   We have been asked to dinner by Harriets mother.
> *revised*   We have been asked to dinner by Harriet's mother.
> *needs checking*   His parent's house is filled with antiques.
> *revised*   His parents' house is filled with antiques.
> *needs checking*   All three groups of parents attended their infant's one-
>   month pediatric checkup, and observations were made
>   of father's interactions with their infants.
> *revised*   All three groups of parents attended their infants' one-
>   month pediatric checkup, and observations were made
>   of fathers' interactions with their infants.

Authorities differ on how one should show possession with singular nouns that already end in *s*. The MLA recommends that an *s* always be added at the end of such nouns, even where they are multi-syllabic and pronunciation with an additional *s* is ungainly:

- Dickens's next novel was *Bleak House*.
- The riding was a stronghold for Duplessis's Union Nationale party.
- Ulysses's voyage was a long one.
- Socrates's method of communicating his ideas has been as influential as the ideas themselves.

The Chicago Manual of Style, on the other hand, recommends adding just the apostrophe (with no additional *s*) where a singular noun ending in *s* is already more than one syllable. This approach has the great advantage of avoiding amusing but distracting tongue twisters:

- Dickens' next novel was *Bleak House*.
- The riding was a stronghold for Duplessis' Union Nationale party.
- Ulysses' voyage was a long one.
- Socrates' method of communicating his ideas has been as influential as the ideas themselves.

Whichever convention a writer chooses, he should be consistent. And be sure in such cases not to put an apostrophe before the first *s* in a noun ending with *s*.

needs checking	Shield's novel is finely, yet delicately constructed.
	(concerning novelist Carol Shields)
revised	Shields's novel is finely, yet delicately constructed.

Where possession is joint, an *s* should be added to the last mentioned noun:

- Bob and Carol's view is that this can be settled amicably.
- Woodward and Bernstein's persistence eventually paid off.

One important exception to the convention of using an apostrophe to show possession is the possessive *its*. In that case the form *it's* is used as a contraction of *it is*, and no apostrophe is included in the possessive *its*. If you are ever uncertain as to whether or not you are making the correct choice between *it's* and *its*, ask yourself if the sentence would make sense if you substituted *it is*. If it would, *it's* is the one you want; if not, you should be using *its*.

Apostrophes are used by some writers to form the plurals of letters and numbers:

- That sort of music was popular in the 1990's.
- She received straight A's in high school.

Since apostrophes are not otherwise used to show plurality, most authorities now prefer to omit the apostrophe:

- That sort of music was popular in the 1990s.
- She received straight As in high school.

● *Quotation Marks* " "

The main use of quotation marks is to show that the words are repeated exactly as they were originally spoken or written. For a discussion of difficulties associated with this use see the chapter on direct and indirect speech immediately following.

According to different conventions, words that are being mentioned in a grammatical sense, rather than used to convey meaning, may be set off by quotation marks, single quotation marks, or italics:

- The words "except" and "accept" are sometimes confused.
- The words 'except' and 'accept' are sometimes confused.
- The words *except* and *accept* are sometimes confused.

Quotation marks (or single quotation marks) are sometimes used to indicate that the writer does not endorse the quoted statement, claim, or description. Quotation marks are usually used in this way only with a word or a brief phrase. When they are so used they have the connotation of *supposed* or *so-called*; they suggest that the quoted word or phrase is either euphemistic or downright false:

- After a violent workout the weightlifters would each consume a "snack" of a steak sandwich, a half-dozen eggs, several pieces of bread and butter, and a quart of tomato juice.

In the following two versions of the same report, the more sparing use of quotation marks in the second version signals clearly to the reader the writer's skepticism as to the honesty of the quoted claim, and may be taken to imply that the former Russian president indulged his legendary fondness for alcohol during the flight.

- President Yeltsin appeared to stagger as he left the plane. "The president is feeling tired and emotional," his press secretary later reported.
- A "tired and emotional" President Yeltsin appeared to stagger as he left the plane.

F21. **misuse of quotation marks to indicate emphasis**: Quotation marks (unlike italics, bold letters, capital letters, or underlining) should never be used to try to lend emphasis to a particular word or phrase. Because quotation marks may be used to convey the sense *supposed* or *so-called* (see above), the common misuse of quotation marks to try to lend emphasis often creates ludicrous effects.

needs checking	All our bagels are served "fresh" daily.
	(The unintended suggestion here is that the claim of freshness is a dubious one.)
revised	All our bagels are served fresh daily.
or	All our bagels are served *fresh* daily.
	(if emphasis is required in an advertisement)
needs checking	Dogs must be "leashed." (BC ferries sign)
revised	Dogs must be leashed.

● *Single Quotation Marks* ‘ ’

In North America the main use of single quotation marks is to mark quotations within quotations:

- According to Obama's press secretary, "When the president said, 'I will bring change to Washington,' he meant it."

Depending on convention, single quotation marks may also be used to show that a word or phrase is being mentioned rather than used (see above).

In the United Kingdom and some other countries, quotation marks and single quotation marks are used for direct speech in precisely the opposite way that North Americans use them; single quotation marks (or inverted commas, as they are sometimes called) are used for direct speech, and double quotation marks are used for quotations within quotations. Here is the correct British version of the above sentence:

- According to Obama's press secretary, 'When the president said, "I will bring change to Washington", he meant it.'

Note here that UK usage also places the comma outside the quotation mark.

⊙ Direct and Indirect Speech

O *Direct Speech*

Direct speech is a written record of the exact words used by the person speaking. The main rules for writing direct speech in English are as follows:

- The exact words spoken—and no other words—must be surrounded by quotation marks.
- A comma should precede a quotation, but according to American convention other punctuation should be placed inside the quotation marks. Examples:

  - He said, "I think I can help you."
    (The period after *you* comes before the quotation marks.)
  - "Drive slowly," she said, "and be very careful."
    (The comma after *slowly* and period after *careful* both come inside the quotation marks.)

Additional Material Online
Exercises on direct and indirect speech may be found at **sites.broadviewpress.com/writing**. Click on **Exercises** and go to **"Punctuation."**

With each change in speaker a new paragraph should begin. Example:

"Let's go fishing this weekend," Mary suggested. "It should be nice and cool by the water."

"Good idea," agreed Faith. "I'll meet you by the store early Saturday morning."

British convention, however, places the punctuation outside the quotation marks:

- 'An iron curtain is descending across Europe', declared Winston Churchill in 1946.

Canadian usage demands that all punctuation go inside the quotation marks in quotations that are stand-alone sentences. At the same time, it allows writers either to follow the American convention or to make an exception when the punctuation clearly pertains only to the structure of the surrounding sentence and not to the quoted word or phrase:

- "An iron curtain is descending across Europe," declared Winston Churchill in 1946.
- Was it Churchill who described the post-war divide between newly Communist Eastern Europe and the West as "an iron curtain"?

The most common difficulties experienced when recording direct speech are as follows:

F22. omission of quotation marks: This happens particularly frequently at the end of a quotation.

needs checking	She said, "I will try to come to see you tomorrow. Then she left.
revised	She said, "I will try to come to see you tomorrow." Then she left.

F23. placing punctuation outside the quotation marks:

needs checking	He shouted, "The house is on fire"!
revised	He shouted, "The house is on fire!"

F24. including the word *that* before direct speech: *That* is used before passages of indirect speech, not before passages of direct speech.

needs checking	My brother said that, "I think I have acted stupidly."
revised	My brother said, "I think I have acted stupidly."
or	My brother said that he thought he had acted stupidly.
needs checking	The official indicated that, "we are not prepared to allow galloping inflation."
revised	The official said, "We are not prepared to allow galloping inflation."
or	The official indicated that his government was not prepared to allow galloping inflation.

F25. when to indent: In a formal essay, any quotation longer than four lines[1] should normally be single-spaced and indented to set it

---

1   This is what the MLA recommends; *The Chicago Manual of Style* specifies forty words.

off from the body of the text. Any quotation of more than three lines from a poem should also be single-spaced and indented. Quotations set off from the body of the text in this way should not be preceded or followed by quotation marks.

> *needs checking*   Larkin's "Days" opens with childlike simplicity: "What are days for? / Days are where we live. / They come, they wake us / Time and time over." But with Larkin, the shadow of mortality is never far distant.

> *revised*   Larkin's "Days" opens with childlike simplicity:
> What are days for?
> Days are where we live.
> They come, they wake us
> Time and time over.
> But with Larkin, the shadow of mortality is never far distant.

O *Indirect Speech*

Indirect speech reports what was said without using the same words that were used by the speaker. The rules for writing indirect speech are as follows:

- Do not use quotation marks.
- Introduce statements with the word *that*, and do not put a comma after *that*. Questions should be introduced with the appropriate question word (*what, why, whether, if, how, when,* etc.).
- First-person pronouns and adjectives (e.g., *I, me, we, us, my, our*) must often be changed to third person (*he, she, they, him, her, them,* etc.) if the subject of the main clause is in third person.

> *correct*   "I am not happy with our team's performance," said Paul.

> *also correct*   Paul said that he was not happy with his team's performance.

> *correct*   I said, "I want my money back."

> *also correct*   I said that I wanted my money back.

> (Here the subject, *I*, is first person.)

- Second-person pronouns must also sometimes be changed.

- Change the tenses of the verbs to agree with the main verb of the sentence. Usually this involves moving the verbs one step back into the past from the tenses used by the speaker in direct speech. Notice in the first example above, for instance, that the present tense *am* has been changed to the past tense *was* in indirect speech. Here are other examples:

  correct "We will do everything we can," he assured me.
  correct He assured me that they would do everything they could.
  (*Will* and *can* change to *would* and *could*.)
  correct "You went to school near Brandon, didn't you?" he asked me.
  correct He asked me if I had gone to school near Brandon.
  (*Went* changes to *had gone*.)

- Change expressions having to do with time. This is made necessary by the changes in verbs discussed above. For example, *today* in direct speech normally becomes *on that day* in indirect speech, *yesterday* becomes *on the day before*, *tomorrow* becomes *the next day*, and so on.

The most common problems experienced when indirect speech is being used are as follows:

F26. confusion of pronouns: Many writers do not remember to change all the necessary pronouns when shifting from direct to indirect speech.

- When I met him he said, "You have cheated me." (direct)

  needs checking When I met him he said that you had cheated me.
  revised When I met him he said that I had cheated him.

- He will probably say to you, "I am poor. I need money."

  needs checking He will probably tell you that he is poor and that I need money.
  revised He will probably tell you that he is poor and that he needs money.

F27. verb tenses: Remember to shift the tenses of the verbs one step back into the past when changing something into indirect speech.

- She said, "I will check my tires tomorrow."

needs checking She said that she will check her tires the next day.
revised She said that she would check her tires the next day.

- "Can I go with you later this afternoon?" he asked.

needs checking He asked if he can go with us later that afternoon.
revised He asked if he could go with us later that afternoon.

⊙ Format and Spelling

O *Capitalization*

F28. **capitalization**: Conventions concerning capitalization have been anything but fixed in the history of the English language. It was not until the late medieval period that capital letters began to be used consistently to begin sentences and proper names. From there the use of capitals became more and more common, until, during the eighteenth century, a great many common nouns were often capitalized. In particular, common nouns naming abstract qualities were capitalized frequently, but many writers would also capitalize without any great degree of consistency any noun or pronoun that they felt to be important. Here is a sample: *... you may be Mine in the manner you now are for a much longer time, yet I at last may lose you, and one unlucky Moment destroy the Constancy of Ages.*

In the past ten years there has been a substantial resurgence of this eighteenth-century practice. Students and other writers—many of whom have not been taught at school the difference between a proper and a common noun—are reverting more and more frequently to the eighteenth-century practice of simply making a stab at what words should begin with a capital letter, without much sense of any rules governing the practice. The basis of those rules is very simple, but there are also a good many subtleties and grey areas.

needs checking In this Company we want to hire Managers who convey a strong sense of Authority.
revised In this company we want to hire managers who convey a strong sense of authority.

In English the fundamental principle on which the rules of capitalization are based is that proper nouns (naming specific persons, places, or things) should always be capitalized. Proper adjectives (adjectives formed from these proper nouns) are also always capitalized. Common nouns, however, are not normally capitalized. *Marx*, *California*, and *Spain*, are all proper nouns. *Marxist*, *Californian*, and *Spanish* are all proper adjectives. The nouns *sinker*, *state*, and *nation*, on the other hand, are all common nouns; they do not name *specific* persons, places, or things. Here are a number of other examples of proper and common nouns:

Proper	Common
June	summer
Parliament of Canada	in parliament
Mother (used as a name)	my mother
Remembrance Day	in remembrance
Memorial Day	as a memorial
National Gallery	a gallery
Director	a director
Professor	a professor
the Enlightenment	the eighteenth century
the Restoration	the restoration
(historical period in England)	(other uses of the word)
the Renaissance	renaissance
(historical period)	(a revival)
God	a god
Catholic	catholic
(belonging to that particular church)	(meaning *wide-ranging* or *universal*)
a Liberal	a liberal
(belonging to the Liberal Party)	(holding liberal ideas)
a Democrat	a democrat
(belonging to the Democratic Party)	(believing in democratic ideals)

Some categories frequently cause difficulty over the issue of capitalization. When should one write *professor* and when *Professor*, for example? Following are some more detailed guidelines.

Names of People
Margaret Atwood, Professor Smith, Samantha.

Names of Places
Cleveland, Asia, the North Pole, the White House, Parliament Hill. Note here that all nouns in a name should be capitalized (*Central Park, the Statue of Liberty*).

Names of Days of the Week, Months, and Holidays
Monday, January, Boxing Day, Yom Kippur. Note that the names of seasons are not capitalized.

F29. **Academic names:** All nouns in a formal name should be capitalized: *the University of Chicago, Camosun College, Philosophy 150, Economics 205.* Note that, when not describing a specific course, the names of academic subjects are not capitalized unless they are names of languages. In formal use, capitalize *the Physics Department, the Department of History,* etc.

needs checking	Most offices in the Philosophy department are located in the Arts Tower.
revised	Most offices in the Philosophy Department are located in the Arts Tower.
needs checking	She is studying Philosophy at the University of Michigan.
revised	She is studying philosophy at the University of Michigan.

Additional Material Online
Exercises on capitalization may be found at **sites.broadviewpress.com/writing**.
Click on **Exercises** and go to **"Punctuation."**

F30. **institutional names:** All nouns in these names should be capitalized (*the University of San Diego, the Audit Committee, the Board of Directors, the Golden Financial Corporation, the Department of Jus-*

tice). Note that where a specific body is not being named, capitals should not be used.

needs checking	Every large company must have an Audit Committee.
revised	Every large company must have an audit committee.

F31. occupational names: When a title is used before a person's name, it must be capitalized: *Reverend Philips*; *President Carter*; *Professor Said*; *Claude Johnson, minister of justice*, or *Justice Minister Claude Johnson*. When the title appears as a substitute for the name, capitalizing the title is optional. As always in such cases, be sure to be consistent.

worth checking	The Prime Minister will deliver a speech this afternoon, and the president of Shell Oil will be speaking this evening.
revised	The Prime Minister will deliver a speech this afternoon, and the President of Shell Oil will be speaking this evening.
or	The prime minister will deliver a speech this afternoon, and the president of Shell Oil will be speaking this evening.

When titles follow a name, capitalization of the title is optional.

	Sandra Mbeki, professor of German
or	Sandra Mbeki, Professor of German
	Frank Gibbs, president of Acme Tools
or	Frank Gibbs, President of Acme Tools

Names of Major Historical Events, Movements, or Periods
It is not surprising that students and other writers often become confused over whether or not to capitalize historical references of this sort, since the names of centuries, decades, and so on are not normally capitalized. It is thus correct to refer to *the eighteenth century* in lower case, but *the Enlightenment* with a capital; to *the medieval period*, but to *the Middle Ages* with capitals; *the thirties*, to refer to the 1930s, but *the Depression* to refer to the economic condition that dominated the period. If we speak of the study of *Romantic literature* we are speaking of the study of the Romantic

period (i.e., the late eighteenth and early nineteenth centuries), whereas if we speak of studying romantic literature we are referring to the study of any literary works with romantic themes. Here are a few more examples of major historical events, movements, or periods that are normally capitalized: *the Thirty Years War, the Great Fire of London, World War II, the Big Bang, the Impressionists.*

Names of Religions, Deities, Religious Persons, Terms, or Texts
Nouns or adjectives of this sort are normally capitalized: *Buddhism, a Buddhist, Islam, a Muslim, Christian, Jewish, Holy Ghost, the Bible, the Koran.*

Names of Races, Groups, Nationalities, and Their Languages
Nouns or adjectives of this sort should be capitalized: *Mexican, Hispanic, the Yoruba, Nova Scotians, a Native American, First Nations, a European professor, Chinese, students learning Mandarin or French.* Note that capitalization when referring to colour is optional. It is more common to use lower case, however (e.g., *In South Africa blacks and whites are on far better terms than was the case twenty years ago*).

Names of Geographical Areas
Depending on context, certain geographical words may denote either a direction or an area—or, indeed, more than one area. If, for example, we say *keep travelling west, and you will reach the sea,* the word *west* is a direction and should not be capitalized. If, however, we write that *in the West, American voters tend to be fiscally conservative,* when referring to the western portion of the United States, it is normal to capitalize *West.* In a different context we might write *in the West, capitalism took root in the seventeenth and eighteenth centuries.* In that context *the West* is a synonym for *the Western World.* Similar multiple meanings may attach to the words *south, north,* and *east* and *South, North,* and *East.*

F32. **literary titles:** Major words in titles should be capitalized. Articles, short prepositions, and conjunctions are normally not capitalized in titles.

needs checking Robert Boardman discusses *The Bridge On The River Kwai* extensively in his book.

revised Robert Boardman discusses *The Bridge on the River Kwai* extensively in his book.

Names of Teams or Clubs
Where a specific name is given it should be capitalized (*the Toronto Maple Leafs, Team USA, Manchester United*). Where a specific team or club is mentioned but not given its formal name, no capitals should be used (*the national team, our bridge club*).

Names of Abstract Qualities
As in the eighteenth century, writers today are often inclined to capitalize the names of abstract qualities in order to signal their importance. These are common nouns, however, and should in almost all cases not be capitalized. An exception occurs if in the context the abstract quality is personified; in that case the noun may be regarded as a proper name (*if Chance is often blind, it is also often a powerful friend*).

needs checking Keats shared with writers of the Romantic period a strong interest in notions of Truth and Beauty.

revised Keats shared with writers of the Romantic period a strong interest in notions of truth and beauty.

Capitalization Following a Colon
Some style guides recommend capitalizing independent clauses that begin after a colon. Somewhat oddly, they do not similarly recommend capitalizing independent clauses that begin after a semicolon. In view of this inconsistency—and in view as well of the fact that the colon is often used for purposes other than separating independent clauses—it is probably wisest for students to refrain from any use of capitals following a colon.

O *Abbreviations*

Abbreviations are a convenient way of presenting information in a smaller amount of space. This section discusses conventions for using abbreviations in formal writing.

Titles

Titles are normally abbreviated when used immediately before or after a person's full name.

Mr. Isaiah Thomas	*Dr. Jane Phelps*
Sammy Davis Jr.	*Marcia Gibbs, MD*

When using a title together with the last name only, the full title should be written out.

Prof. Marc Ereshefsky	*Professor Ereshefsky*
Sen. Keith Davey	*Senator Davey*

Academic and Business Terms

Common abbreviations are acceptable in formal writing so long as they are likely to be readily understood. Otherwise, the full name should be written out when first used and the abbreviation given in parentheses. Thereafter, the abbreviation may be used on its own, as shown in these examples:

- The Atomic Energy Commission (AEC) has broad-ranging regulatory authority.
- The American Philosophical Association (APA) holds three large regional meetings annually.

Latin abbreviations

Several abbreviations of Latin terms are common in formal academic writing:

cf.	*compare* (Latin *confer*)
e.g.	*for example* (Latin *exempli gratia*)
et al.	*and others* (Latin *et alia*)
etc.	*and so on* (Latin *et cetera: and the rest*)
ibid.	*in the same book or passage* (Latin *ibidem: in the same place*)

i.e.   *that is to say* (Latin *id est*)
NB   *note well* (Latin *nota bene*)

F33. numbers: Numbers of one or two words should be written out. Use figures for all other numbers.

needs checking   The building is 72 storeys tall.
revised   The building is seventy-two storeys tall.

The same principle applies for dollar figures (or figures in other currencies).

needs checking   She lent her brother 10 dollars.
revised   She lent her brother ten dollars.

It is acceptable to combine figures and words for very large numbers:

- The government is projecting a $200 billion deficit.

In general, figures should be used in addresses, in dates, to give percentages, and to report scores or statistics.

needs checking   In the third game of the tournament, Canada and the Czech Republic tied three three.
revised   In the third game of the tournament, Canada and the Czech Republic tied 3–3.

F34. italics: Italics serve several different functions. While short stories, poems, and other works are set off by quotation marks, longer works and the names of newspapers, magazines, and so on should appear in italics:

"The Dead"   *Dubliners*
"Burnt Norton"   *Four Quartets*
"Budget Controversy Continues" *The Economist*
"Smells Like Teen Spirit"   *Nevermind*

Italics are also used for the names of paintings and sculptures, television series, and software. In addition, italics are used for words or phrases from other languages in written English.

needs checking   The play ends with an appearance of a deus ex machina.
revised   The play ends with an appearance of a *deus ex machina*.

Either italics or quotation marks may be used to indicate that words are mentioned rather than used (see above, under "Quotation Marks"). Finally, italics are often used to provide special emphasis that is not otherwise clear from the context or the structure of the sentence.

⊙ Spelling

○ *Spelling and Sound*

The wittiest example of the illogic of English spelling remains Bernard Shaw's famous spelling of *fish* as *ghoti*. The *gh* sounds like the *gh* in *enough*; the *o* sounds like the *o* in *women* (once spelled *wimmen*, incidentally); and the *ti* sounds like the *ti* in *nation* or *station*. Shaw passionately advocated a rationalization of English spelling; it still has not happened, and probably never will. Perhaps the best way to learn correct spelling is to be tested by someone else, or to test yourself every week or so on a different group of words. For example, you might learn the words from the list below beginning with *a* and *b* one week, the words beginning with *c* and *d* the next week, and so on.

spell-check: No computer can be a substitute for careful proofreading. Spell-check is wonderful, but it cannot tell if it is your friend or your fiend, or if you have signed off a letter with best wishes or beast wishes.

F35. spelling and sound—a/an: Authorities agree that an *n* should be added to the indefinite article when the following word begins with a vowel sound. This is a "rule," it should be noted, that is based entirely on euphony; the reason that *a egg* is not "good English" is simply that it is awkward to say. Thus it is that we use *an* not only before words that begin with a vowel, but also before words that are pronounced as if they began with a vowel (*an hour, an f-word*).

Something of a grey area exists with a small group of words that have a *his-* sound at the beginning, and in which the second syllable is stressed. No one would think of writing *an hiccup* or *an hellish day*, and nor are most people ever tempted to write *an history* or *an hysterectomy*. Many people, though, think that *an hysterical outburst* sounds better than *a hysterical outburst*, and that *an historical introduction* sounds better than *a historical introduction*. As the first sound in an unstressed syllable, the *h* in such words is softer than the *h* in such words as *history*, where a strong stress is placed on the first syllable. Some authorities ridicule this common practice; we sound the *h* in such words, goes the argument, and therefore we should use *a* rather than *an*. But what is the rationale for this "rule" in the first place? Again, purely what sounds better. And the fact is that many people find it easier to say *an historical introduction* than *a historical introduction*. So why the fuss? We may reasonably disagree as to which sounds better, but there is surely no justification for terming one correct and the other incorrect.

F36. **spelling and sound**: Many spelling mistakes result from similarities in the pronunciation of words with very different meanings. These are covered in the list below. Other words that cause spelling difficulties are listed separately.

absent (adjective)	absence (noun)
absorb	absorption
accept	except
access (*entry*)	excess (*too much*)
advice (noun)	advise (verb)
affect (verb)	effect (noun)
allowed (*permitted*)	aloud
alter (*change*)	altar (*in a church*)
appraise (*value*)	apprise (*inform*)
base (*foundation*)	bass (*in music*)
bath (noun)	bathe (verb)
berry (*fruit*)	bury (*the dead*)
beside (*by the side of*)	besides (*as well as*)
birth	berth (*bed*)
bitten	beaten
bizarre (*strange*)	bazaar (*market*)
bloc (political grouping)	block
breath (noun)	breathe (verb)
buoy (*in the water*)	boy
buy (*purchase*)	by
cash	cache (*hiding place*)
casual (*informal*)	causal (*to do with causes*)
cause	case
ceased (*stopped*)	seized (*grabbed*)

ceiling (*above you*) — sealing

chick — cheek/chic (*stylish*; pronounced *sheek*)

chose (*past tense*) — choose (*present tense*)

cite (*make reference to*) — sight/site

climatic (*climate*) — climactic (*climax*)

cloths (*fabric*) — clothes

colonel (*officer*) — colonial (*of colonies*)

coma (*unconscious*) — comma (*punctuation*)

compliment (*praise*) — complement (*make complete*)

conscious (*aware*) — conscience (*sense of right*)

contract — construct

conventional (*usual*) — convectional (*transfer of heat*)

conversation — conservation/concentration

convinced — convicted (*of a crime*)

cord (*rope*) — chord (*music*)

council (*group*) — counsel (*advice*)

course — coarse (*rough*)

credible (*believable*) — creditable (*deserving credit*)

critic (*one who criticizes*) — critique (*piece of criticism*)

defer (*show respect*) — differ

deference (*respect*) — difference

deprecate (*criticize*) — depreciate (*reduce in value*)

desert (*dry place*; also *what is deserved*) — dessert (*sweet*)

device (*thing*) — devise (*to plan*)

died/had died — dead/was dead/dyed (*coloured*)

dissent (*protest*) — descent (*downward motion*)

distant (adjective) — distance (noun)

edition (*of a book*, etc.) — addition (*something added*)

emigrant — immigrant

entomology (*study of insects*) — etymology (*study of words*)

envelop (verb) — envelope (noun)

except — expect

exercise — exorcise (*remove*)

fear — fair/fare (*payment*)

feeling — filling

fell — feel/fill

flaunt (*display*) — flout (*disobey*)

formally — formerly (*previously*)

forth (*forward*) — fourth (*after third*)

forward — foreword (*in a book*)

foul — fowl (*birds*)

future — feature

genus (*biological type*) — genius (*creative intelligence*)

greet — great/grate (*scrape*)

guerrillas — gorillas

guided (*led*) — guarded (*protected*)

had — heard/head

heat	heart/hate
heir (*inheritor*)	air
human	humane (*kind*)
illicit (*not permitted*)	elicit (*bring forth*)
illusion (*unreal image*)	allusion (*reference*)
immigrate	emigrate
independent (adjective)	independence (noun)
inhabit (*live in*)	inhibit (*retard*)
instance (*occurrence*)	instants (*moments*)
intense (*concentrating*)	intents (*purposes*)
isle (*island*)	aisle (*to walk in*)
know	no/now
kernel	colonel
lack	lake
later	latter/letter
lath (*piece of wood*)	lathe (*machine*)
lead (*heavy element*)	led (*guided*)
leave	leaf
leave	live
leaving	living
lessen (*reduce*)	lesson
let	late
lightning (*from clouds*)	lightening (*becoming lighter*)
lose (*be unable to find*)	loose (*not tight*)
mad (*insane*)	maid (*servant*)
man	men
martial (*to do with fighting*)	marshal
mental	metal
merry	marry
met	meet/mate
minor (*underage*, or *lesser*)	miner (*underground*)
mist (*light fog*)	missed
moral (*ethical*)	morale (*spirit*)
mourning (*after death*)	morning
new	knew
of	off
on	own
ones	once
ordinance (*decree*)	ordnance (*guns*)
pain	pane (*of glass*)
patients (*sick people*)	patience (*ability to wait*)
peer (*look closely*)	pier (*wharf*)
perpetrate (*be guilty of*)	perpetuate (*cause to continue*)
perquisite (*privilege*)	prerequisite (*requirement*)
personal (*private*)	personnel (*employees*)
perspective (*vision*)	prospective (*anticipated*)
peruse (*study*)	pursue (*follow*)
poor	pour (*liquid*)/pore

precede (*go before*)	proceed (*continue*)
precedent	president
price (*cost*)	prize (*reward*)
prostate (*gland*)	prostrate (*lying down*)
quay (*wharf*; pronounced *key*)	key
quite	quiet (*not noisy*)
rein (*to control animals*)	rain/reign
release (*let go*)	realize (*discover*)
relieve (verb)	relief (noun)
residence (*place*)	residents (*people*)
response (noun)	responds (verb)
rid	ride
ridden	written
rise	rice
rite (*ritual*)	right/write
rod	rode/reared
rote (*repetition*)	wrote
saved	served
saw	seen
saw	so/sew
scene (*location*)	seen
seam (*in clothes*)	seem (*appear*)
secret	sacred (*holy*)
sell (verb)	sail (*boat*)/sale
senses	census (*population count*)
shed	shade
shone	shown
shot	short
sit	sat/set
smell	smile
snake	snack (*small meal*)
soar	sore (*hurt*)
sole (*single, a fish,* or *an undersurface*)	soul (*spirit*)
sort (*type or kind*)	sought (*looked for*)
steal (present tense)	stole (past tense)
straight (*not crooked*)	strait (*of water*)
striped (e.g., *a zebra*)	stripped (*uncovered*)
suite (*rooms* or *music*)	suit/sweet
super	supper (*meal*)
suppose	supposed to
sympathies (noun)	sympathize (verb)
tale (*story*)	tail
talk	took
tap	tape
than	then
they	there/their

thing	think
this	these
throw	threw (past tense)
tied	tired
urban (*in cities*)	urbane (*sophisticated*)
vanish (*disappear*)	varnish
vein (*to carry blood*)	vain
vicious (*brutal*)	viscous (*sticky*)
waist (*your middle*)	waste
wait	weight (*heaviness*)
waive (*give up*)	wave
wants	once
weak (*not strong*)	week
weather (*sunny, wet*, etc.)	whether (*or not*)
wedding	weeding
were	where
whole (*complete*)	hole (*empty space*)
wholly (*completely*)	holy (*sacred*)/holly
woman	women
won	worn
yoke (*for animals*)	yolk (*of an egg*)

F37. English language spelling variations: A number of words that cause spelling difficulties are spelled differently in different countries. In most cases Australians prefer British spellings. Either British or American is correct in Canada, so long as the writer is consistent.

American	British
behavior	behaviour
center	centre
color	colour
defense	defence
favor	favour
favorite	favourite
fiber	fibre
fulfill	fulfil
gray	grey
humor	humour
likable	likeable
maneuver	manoeuvre
marvelous	marvellous
meter (*measurement*)	metre
neighbor	neighbour
omelet	omelette
program	programme
Shakespearian	Shakespearean

skillful	skilful
skeptical	sceptical
theater	theatre
traveling	travelling

Additional Material Online
Exercises on spelling may be found at
sites.broadviewpress.com/writing.
Click on **Exercises** and go to
"Punctuation, format, and spelling."

F38. commonly misspelled words: Following is a list of some other commonly misspelled words:

abbreviation	ameba (also	approach	boast
absence	*amoeba*)	architect	boastful
accelerator	among	arguable	bouillon
accident	ammonia	argument	breakfast
accidentally	amortize	arsonist	bulletin
accommodation	amount	arteriosclerosis	burglar
achieve	anachronism	artillery	burial
acknowledge	analogous	asinine	buried
acquire	analysis	atheist	business
acquisition	anchor	author	candidate
acquit	androgynous	auxiliary	capillary
acre	annihilate	awful	cappuccino
across	antecedent	awesome	Caribbean
address	anti-Semitic	bacteria	carpentry
adjacent	anxious	basically	cautious
advertisement	apocalypse	battery	ceiling
affidavit	apparatus	beautiful	chaise longue (or
aficionado	apparently	beginning	*chaise lounge*)
ambulance	appreciate	believe	changeable

character
chilblain
chlorophyll
choir
cholesterol
chrome
chromosome
chronological
chrysalis
chrysanthemum
coincidence
colleague
colonel
colossal
column
commitment
committee
comparative
competition
competitor
complexion
conceive
condemn
conjunction
connoisseur
consensus
consistent
controller
convenience
cooperation
cooperative
courteous
courtesy
creator
creature
criticism
cyst
decisive
definite
delicious
description
desirable
despair
despise
destroy
develop
diesel
different

dilemma
dining
disappear
disappoint
disastrous
discrimination
disease
disintegrate
dissatisfied
dominate
dormitory
double
doubtful
drunkard
drunkenness
duchess
due
dyeing
dying
eclipse
eczema
effective
efficient
eighth
embarrass
employee
encourage
enemy
enmity
enormous
entertain
enthusiasm
entitle
entrepreneur
environment
enzyme
epidermis
epididymis
erroneous
esophagus
especially
espresso
essential
exaggerate
excessive
excite
exercise
exhilaration

existence
existent
experience
extraordinary
Fahrenheit
faithful
faithfully
farinaceous
fault
February
financial
foreigner
foretell
forty
fourth
gauge
gamete
germination
government
grammar
grateful
gruesome
guarantee
guerrillas
guilty
happened
happiest
harass
hatred
hectare
helpful
hyena
hypothesis
ichthyology
idiosyncratic
imaginary
imagine
immigration
immersible
impeccable
importance
impresario
inchoate
incomprehensible
indigenous
independent
indestructible
indispensable

ineffable
infinitesimal
inoculate
insufferable
intention
intentional
interrupt
irrelevant
irresponsible
isosceles
isthmus
itinerary
jealous
jeopardy
journalist
junction
kneel
knowledge
knowledgeable
laboratories
laboratory
language
lazy, laziness
ledger
leisure
liaise
liberation
library
license
lieutenant
liquid, liquefy
literature
lying
medicine
medieval
membrane
memento
merciful
mermaid
millennia
millennium
millionaire
mischief
mischievous
modern
naked
naughty
necessary

necessity	psychiatric	seize	surprised
noticeable	psychological	sense	surreptitious
nuclear	punctuation	separate	surrounded
nucleus	pursue	shining	survive
obscene	questionnaire	shotgun	synthesis
obsolescent	really	sigh	symbol
obsolete	receipt	significant	talkative
occasion	recommend	simultaneous	tarred
occasional	referee	sincerely	television
occupy	reference	ski, skis, skied,	temperature
occur	regret	skiing	tendency
occurred	repeat	slippery	theoretical
occurrence	repetition	slogan	theory
omit	replies	smart	title
ophthalmology	reply	solemn	tough
ourselves	residence (*place*)	spaghetti	tragedy
paid	residents (*people*)	speech	trophy
parallel	restaurant	spongy	truly
parliament	restaurateur	sponsor	unique
parliamentary	revolutionary	stale	until
party	rheumatism	stingy	vacancy
permissible	rhododendron	stomach	vacillate
permission	rhombus	stubborn	valuable
perpendicular	rhubarb	studious	vegetable
perseverance	rhyme	studying	vehicle
photosynthesis	rhythm	stupefy	vicious
playful	saddest	stupid	visitor
possess	sandals	subordinate	volume
possession	scene	subpoena	voluntary
poultry	schedule	substitute	Wednesday
predictable	schizophrenic	subtle, subtlety	welcome
pregnancy	science	suburbs	whisper
pregnant	scintillate	succeed	writer
prerogative	scissors	success, successful	writing
prescription	scream	sue, suing	written
privilege	scrumptious	summary	yield
properly	search	supersede	zucchini

◎ DOCUMENTATION AND RESEARCH

Writers have a variety of reasons for including the results of research in their essays. Outside sources can help support or clarify authors' points, or can provide opposing arguments against which authors can make their own case. Sources are also useful in showing where a paper can be located in the wider conversation among writers engaged by the same subject. At the very least, including source material is one way writers can show that they are acquainted with the latest thinking on their topics.

Whatever the reasons for incorporating research into their essays, good writers are careful in how they do so, making sure to document their sources accurately and completely. This is, first of all, a service to readers who would like to embark on a fuller investigation into the topic of a paper by looking up its sources themselves; every academic citation system gives readers all the information they need to access original source material. But it is also critical that there be complete clarity about which parts of an essay are the author's and which parts come from elsewhere. To allow any blurriness on this question is to be dishonest, to engage in a kind of cheating, in fact—known as plagiarism.

⊙ Avoiding Plagiarism—and Choosing When and What to Quote

Most people understand that taking someone else's writing and passing it off as one's own is intellectual thievery. But it is important to be aware that you may commit plagiarism even if you do not use precisely the same words another person wrote in precisely the same order. For instance, here is an actual example of plagiarism. *Globe and Mail* newspaper columnist Margaret Wente borrowed material for one of her columns from a number of works, including an article by Dan Gardner that had appeared the previous year in another newspaper (the *Ottawa Citizen*) and a book by Robert Paarlberg called *Starved for Science* (which was the subject of Gardner's article). The similarities were brought to light by media commentator Carol Wainio, who presented a series of parallel passages, including the following, on her blog *Media Culpa* (the fonts are Wainio's—simple bold is for direct copying; the bold + italics is for "near copying"):

> Gardner: **_Many NGOs working in Africa in the area of development and the environment have been advocating against the modernization of traditional farming practices_**, Paarlberg says. **"They believe that traditional farming in Africa incorporates indigenous knowledge that shouldn't be replaced by science-based knowledge introduced from the outside.** They encourage Africa to stay away from fertilizers, and be certified as organic instead. And in the case of genetic engineering, they warn African governments against making these technologies available to farmers."

> Wente: **_Yet, many NGOs working in Africa have tenaciously fought the modernization of traditional farming practices._** **They believe traditional farming in Africa incorporates indigenous knowledge that shouldn't be replaced by science-based knowledge introduced from the outside.** As Prof. Paarlberg writes, "They encourage African farmers to stay away from fertilizers and be certified organic instead. And they warn African governments to stay away from genetic engineering."

Wente does not always use exactly the same words as her sources, but no one reading the passages can doubt that one writer is appropriating the phrasings of the others. Additionally, where Wente *does* quote Paarlberg directly, the quotation is lifted from Gardner's article and should be identified as such.

The penalties for such practices are not trivial; Wente was publicly reprimanded by her employer, and the CBC radio program *Q* removed her from its media panel. Other reporters have been, justifiably, fired under similar circumstances. At most colleges and universities, students are likely to receive a zero if they are caught plagiarizing—and they may be expelled from the institution. It's important to be aware, too, that penalties for plagiarism make no allowance for intent; it is no defense that a writer took someone else's words "by mistake" rather than intentionally.

How, then, can you be sure to avoid plagiarism? First of all, be extremely careful in your note-taking, so as to make it impossible to imagine, a few days later, that words you have jotted down from somewhere else are your own. This is why notes need to be in a separate file or book from your own ideas. (In her *Globe and Mail* column responding to the plagiarism charges, Wente, in fact, claimed that she had accidentally mixed a quotation into her own ideas.) If your note-taking is reliable, then you will know which words need to be credited. One way to rewrite the passage above would simply be to remove the material taken from Gardner and to credit Paarlberg by quoting him directly, if you were able to access his book and could do so: "As Robert Paarlberg has argued in his book *Starved for Science*, many NGOs 'believe that traditional farming in Africa incorporates indigenous knowledge that shouldn't be replaced by science-based knowledge introduced from the outside.'" You would, of course, look up and provide the page number as well.

You may notice that the quoted material is a statement of opinion rather than fact—controversial views are being given, but without any evidence provided to back them up—so a careful reader would wonder whether NGOs are really as anti-science as the quotation suggests, or whether the writer hasn't done enough research on the debate. If you were to make an assertion like this in a paper of your own it would not be enough just to quote Paarlberg; you would need to do much more research and find information to support or deny your claim. If you are including quotations in an essay, the best sources to quote are not necessarily those which express opinions that mirror the ones you are putting forward. In a case such as this, for example, the argument would have been much more persuasive if Wente had quoted an official statement from one of the NGOs she was attacking. If her article had quoted a source making this specific case against "science-based knowledge" and then argued directly against that source's argument, Wente's own position would have been strengthened. Quoting many such sources would provide proof that the article's characterization of the position of NGOs was factually accurate.

Whenever you do quote someone else, it's important to cite the source. But do you need a citation for everything that did not come from your own knowledge? Not necessarily. Citations are usually unnecessary when you are touching on common knowledge (provided it is, in fact, common knowledge, and provided your instructor has not asked you to do otherwise). If you refer to the chemical composition of water, or the date when penicillin was discovered, you are unlikely to need to provide any citation, even if you used a source to find the information, since such facts are generally available and uncontroversial. (Make sure, however, to check any "common knowledge" with several reputable sources; if your information is incorrect, it reflects poorly on you, especially if you have not cited your source.) If you have any doubts about whether something is common knowledge or not, cite it; over-cautiousness is not a serious problem, but plagiarism always is.

⊙ Citation and Documentation

Citing sources is fundamental to writing a good research paper, but no matter how diligent you are in making your acknowledgements, your paper will not be taken seriously unless its documentation is formatted according to an appropriate and accepted referencing style. For the sake of consistency, each academic discipline has adopted a particular system of referencing as its standard, which those writing in that discipline are expected to follow. *The Broadview Pocket Guide to Citation and Documentation* outlines the four most common of these systems. Almost all of the humanities use the documentation guidelines developed by the Modern Language Association (MLA), a notable exception being history, which tends to prefer those of the *Chicago Manual of Style* (Chicago Style). The social and some health sciences typically follow the style rules of the American Psychological Association (APA), while the basic sciences most commonly use the referencing systems of the Council of Science Editors (CSE). Each of these styles is exacting and comprehensive in its formatting rules; following with precision the one recommended for a given paper's discipline is one of a responsible research writer's duties. Details of these systems are in the pages that follow.

As important as documentation is to a well-written paper, by itself it is not always enough. Writers must also be attentive to the ways in which they integrate borrowed material into their essays.

○ *Incorporating Sources*

There are three main ways of working source material into a paper: summarizing, paraphrasing, and quoting directly. In order to avoid plagiarism, care must be taken with all three kinds of borrowing, both in the way they are handled and in their referencing. In what follows, a passage from page 102 of a book by Terrence W. Deacon (*The Symbolic Species: The Co-Evolution of Language and the Brain*, New York: Norton, 1997) serves as the source for a sample summary, paraphrase, and quotation. The examples feature the MLA style of in-text parenthetical citations, but the requirements for presenting the source material are the same for all academic referencing systems. For a similar discussion with a focus on APA style, see Incorporating Sources in APA Style (starting on page 633).

original source   Over the last few decades language researchers seem to have reached a consensus that language is an innate ability, and that only a significant contribution from innate knowledge can explain our ability to learn such a complex communication system. Without question, children enter the world predisposed to learn human languages. All normal children, raised in normal social environments, inevitably learn their local language, whereas other species, even when raised and taught in this same environment, do not. This demonstrates that human brains come into the world specially equipped for this function.

O *Summarizing*

An honest and competent summary, whether of a passage or an entire book, must not only represent the source accurately but also use original wording and include a citation. It is a common misconception that only quotations need to be acknowledged as borrowings in the body of an essay. In fact, without a citation, even a fairly worded summary or paraphrase is an act of plagiarism. The first example below is faulty on two counts: it borrows wording (underlined) from the source, and it has no parenthetical reference.

needs checking   Researchers agree that language learning is innate, and that only innate knowledge can explain how we are able to learn a system of communication that is so complex. Normal children raised in normal ways will always learn

> their local language, whereas other species do not, even when taught human language and exposed to the same environment.

The next example correctly avoids the wording of the source passage, and a signal phrase and parenthetical citation note the author and page number.

> *revised* As Terrence W. Deacon notes, there is now wide agreement among linguists that the ease with which human children acquire their native tongues, under the conditions of a normal childhood, demonstrates an inborn capacity for language that is not shared by any other animals, not even those who are reared in comparable ways and given human language training (102).

○ *Paraphrasing*

Whereas a summary is a shorter version of its original, a paraphrase tends to be about the same length. However, paraphrases, just like summaries, must reflect their sources accurately, must use original wording, and must include a citation. Even though it is properly cited, the paraphrase of the first sentence of the Deacon passage, below, falls short by being too close to the wording of the original (underlined).

> *needs checking* Researchers in language have come to a consensus in the past few decades that the acquisition of language is innate; such contributions from knowledge contribute significantly to our ability to master such a complex system of communication (Deacon 102).

Simply substituting synonyms for the words and phrases of the source, however, is not enough to avoid plagiarism. Despite its original wording, the next example also fails but for a very different reason: it follows the original's sentence structure too closely, as illustrated in the interpolated copy below it.

> *needs checking* Recently, linguists appear to have come to an agreement that speaking is an inborn skill, and that nothing but

a substantial input from inborn cognition can account for the human capacity to acquire such a complicated means of expression (Deacon 102).

Recently (*over the last few decades*), linguists (*language researchers*) appear to have come to an agreement (*seem to have reached a consensus*) that speaking is an inborn skill (*that language is an innate ability*), and that nothing but a substantial input (*and that only a significant contribution*) from inborn cognition (*from innate knowledge*) can account for the human capacity (*can explain our ability*) to acquire such a complicated means of expression (*to learn such a complex communication system*) (Deacon 102).

What follows is a good paraphrase of the passage's opening sentence; this paraphrase captures the sense of the original without echoing the details and shape of its language.

> *revised*   Linguists now broadly agree that children are born with the ability to learn language; in fact, the human capacity to acquire such a difficult skill cannot easily be accounted for in any other way (Deacon 102).

○ *Quoting Directly*

Unlike paraphrases and summaries, direct quotations must use the exact wording of the original. Because they involve importing outside words, quotations pose unique challenges. Quote too frequently, and you risk making your readers wonder why they are not reading your sources instead of your paper. Your essay should present something you want to say—informed and supported by properly documented sources, but forming a contribution that is yours alone. To that end, use secondary material to help you build a strong framework for your work, not to replace it. Quote sparingly, therefore; use your sources' exact wording only when it is important or particularly memorable.

To avoid misrepresenting your sources, be sure to quote accurately, and to avoid plagiarism, take care to indicate quotations as quotations, and cite them properly. Below are two problematic quotations. The first does not show which words come directly from the source.

> *needs checking*   Terrence W. Deacon maintains that children enter the world predisposed to learn human languages (102).

The second quotation fails to identify the source at all.

> *needs checking*   Linguists believe that "children enter the world predisposed to learn human languages."

The next example corrects both problems by naming the source and indicating clearly which words come directly from it.

> *revised*   Terrence W. Deacon maintains that "children enter the world predisposed to learn human languages" (102).

○ *Formatting Quotations*

There are two ways to signal an exact borrowing: by enclosing it in double quotation marks and by indenting it as a block of text. Which you should choose depends on the length and genre of the quotation and the style guide you are following.

⊙ Short Prose Quotations

What counts as a short prose quotation differs among the various reference guides. In MLA style, "short" means up to four lines; in APA, up to forty words; and in Chicago Style, up to one hundred words. All the guides agree, however, that short quotations must be enclosed in double quotation marks, as in the examples below.

> *Short quotation, full sentence:*
> According to Terrence W. Deacon, linguists agree that a human child's capacity to acquire language is inborn: "Without question, children enter the world predisposed to learn human languages" (102).

> *Short quotation, partial sentence:*
> According to Terrence W. Deacon, linguists agree that human "children enter the world predisposed to learn human languages" (102).

⊙ Long Prose Quotations

Longer prose quotations should be double-spaced and indented, as a block, one tab space from the left margin. Do not include quotation marks; the indentation indicates that the words come exactly from the source. Note that indented quotations are often introduced with a full sentence followed by a colon.

> Terrence W. Deacon, like most other linguists, believes that human beings are born with a unique cognitive capacity:
>
> > Without question, children enter the world predisposed to learn human languages. All normal children, raised in normal social environments, inevitably learn their local language, whereas other species, even when raised and taught in this same environment, do not. This demonstrates that human brains come into the world specially equipped for this function. (102)

⊙ Verse Quotations

Quoting from verse is a special case. Poetry quotations of three or fewer lines (MLA) may be integrated into your paragraph and enclosed in double quotation marks, with lines separated by a forward slash with a space on either side of it, as in the example below.

> Pope's "Epistle II. To a Lady," in its vivid portrayal of wasted lives, sharply criticizes the social values that render older women superfluous objects of contempt: "Still round and round the Ghosts of Beauty glide, / And haunt the places where their Honor dy'd" (lines 241–42).

If your quotation of three or fewer lines includes a stanza break, MLA style requires you to mark the break by inserting two forward slashes (//), with spaces on either side of them.

> The speaker in "Ode to a Nightingale" seeks, in various ways, to free himself from human consciousness, leaving suffering behind. Keats uses alliteration and repetition to mimic the gradual dissolution of self, the process of intoxication or death: "That I might drink, and leave the world unseen, / And with thee fade away

into the forest dim: // Fade far away, dissolve, and quite forget"
(lines 19–21).

Poetry quotations of more than three lines in MLA, or two or
more lines in Chicago Style, should be, like long prose quotations,
indented and set off in a block from your main text. Arrange the
lines just as they appear in the original.

> The ending of Margaret Avison's "September Street" moves from
> the decaying, discordant city toward a glimpse of an outer/inner
> infinitude:
>
> > On the yellow porch
> > one sits, not reading headlines; the old eyes
> > read far out into the mild
> > air, runes.
> > See. There: a stray sea-gull. (lines 20–24)

⊙ Quotations within Quotations

You may sometimes find, within the original passage you wish to
quote, words already enclosed in double quotation marks. If your
quotation is short, enclose it all in double quotation marks, and use
single quotation marks for the embedded quotation.

> Terrence W. Deacon is firm in maintaining that human language
> differs from other communication systems in kind rather than
> degree: "Of no other natural form of communication is it legiti-
> mate to say that 'language is a more complicated version of that'"
> (44).

If your quotation is long, keep the double quotation marks of the
original.

> Terrence W. Deacon is firm in maintaining that human language
> differs from other communication systems in kind rather than
> degree:
>
> > Of no other natural form of communication is it legitimate
> > to say that "language is a more complicated version of that."
> > It is just as misleading to call other species' communication
> > systems *simple* languages as it is to call them languages. In

addition to asserting that a Procrustean mapping of one to the other is possible, the analogy ignores the sophistication and power of animals' non-linguistic communication, whose capabilities may also be without language parallels. (44)

○ *Adding to or Deleting from a Quotation*

While it is important to use the original's exact wording in a quotation, it is allowable to modify a quotation somewhat, as long as the changes are clearly indicated and do not distort the meaning of the original.

○ *Using square brackets to add to a quotation*

You may want to add to a quotation in order to clarify what would otherwise be puzzling or ambiguous to someone who does not know its context; in that case, put whatever you add in square brackets.

> Terrence W. Deacon writes that children are born "specially equipped for this [language] function" (102).

○ *Using an ellipsis to delete from a quotation*

If you would like to streamline a quotation by omitting anything unnecessary to your point, insert an ellipsis (three spaced dots) to show that you've left material out.

When the quotation looks like a complete sentence but is actually part of a longer sentence, you should provide an ellipsis to show that there is more to the original than you are using.

> Terrence W. Deacon says that ". . . children enter the world predisposed to learn human languages" (102).

Note that if the quotation is clearly a partial sentence, ellipses aren't necessary.

> Terrence W. Deacon writes that children are born "specially equipped" to learn human language (102).

When the omitted material runs over a sentence boundary or constitutes a whole sentence or more, insert a period plus an ellipsis.

Terrence W. Deacon, like most other linguists, believes that human children are born with a unique ability to acquire their native language: "Without question, children enter the world predisposed to learn human languages. . . . [H]uman brains come into the world specially equipped for this function" (102).

Be sparing in modifying quotations; it is all right to have one or two altered quotations in a paper, but if you find yourself changing quotations often, or adding to and omitting from one quotation more than once, reconsider quoting at all. A paraphrase or summary is very often a more effective choice.

⊙ Integrating Quotations

Quotations must be worked smoothly and grammatically into your sentences and paragraphs. Always, of course, mark quotations as such, but for the purpose of integrating them into your writing, treat them as if they were your own words. The boundary between what you say and what your source says should be grammatically seamless.

needs checking   Terrence W. Deacon points out, "whereas other species, even when raised and taught in this same environment, do not" (102).

revised   According to Terrence W. Deacon, while human children brought up under normal conditions acquire the language they are exposed to, "other species, even when raised and taught in this same environment, do not" (102).

○ *Avoiding "dumped" quotations*

Integrating quotations well also means providing a context for them. Don't merely drop them into your paper or string them together like beads on a necklace; make sure to introduce them by noting where the material comes from and how it connects to whatever point you are making.

needs checking   For many years, linguists have studied how human children acquire language. "Without question, children

       enter the world predisposed to learn human language"
       (Deacon 102).

revised Most linguists studying how human children acquire
       language have come to share the conclusion articulated
       here by Terrence W. Deacon: "Without question, chil-
       dren enter the world predisposed to learn human lan-
       guage" (102).

needs checking "Without question, children enter the world predis-
       posed to learn human language" (Deacon 102). "There
       is . . . something special about human brains that ena-
       bles us to do with ease what no other species can do
       even minimally without intense effort and remarkably
       insightful training" (Deacon 103).

revised Terrence W. Deacon bases his claim that we "enter the
       world predisposed to learn human language" on the
       fact that very young humans can "do with ease what
       no other species can do even minimally without intense
       effort and remarkably insightful training" (102–03).

○ *Signal Phrases*

To leave no doubt in your readers' minds about which parts of your
essay are yours and which come from elsewhere, identify the sources
of your summaries, paraphrases, and quotations with signal phrases,
as in the following examples.

- As Carter and Rosenthal have demonstrated, . . .
- In the words of one researcher, . . .
- In his most recent book McGann advances the view that, as he
  puts it, . . .
- As Nussbaum observes, . . .
- Kendal suggests that . . .
- Freschi and other scholars have rejected these claims, arguing
  that . . .
- Morgan has emphasized this point in her recent research: . . .
- As Sacks puts it, . . .
- To be sure, Mtele allows that . . .
- In his later novels Hardy takes a bleaker view, frequently sug-
  gesting that . . .

In order to help establish your paper's credibility, you may also find it useful at times to include in a signal phrase information that shows why readers should take the source seriously, as in the following example:

> In her landmark work, biologist and conservationist Rachel Carson warns that . . .

Here, the signal phrase mentions the author's professional credentials; it also points out the importance of her book, which is appropriate to do in the case of a work as famous as Carson's *Silent Spring*.

Below is a fuller list of words and expressions that may be useful in the crafting of signal phrases:

according to _____,	confirms	intimates
acknowledges	contends	notes
adds	declares	observes
admits	demonstrates	points out
advances	denies	puts it
agrees	disputes	reasons
allows	emphasizes	refutes
argues	endorses	rejects
asserts	finds	reports
attests	grants	responds
believes	illustrates	suggests
claims	implies	takes issue with
comments	in the view of _____,	thinks
compares	in the words of _____,	writes
concludes	insists	

Additional Material
The discussions above of "Your Arguments,
Others' Arguments" (pages 43–46) and
of "Collaboration and Research"
(pages 78–92) may also be helpful.

◎ MLA Style

"MLA style" refers to the referencing guidelines of the Modern Language Association, which are favoured by many disciplines in the humanities. The main components of the MLA system are in-text author-page number citations for the body of an essay, and a bibliography giving publication details—the list of "Works Cited"—at the end of it.

This section outlines the key points of MLA style. A full-length sample essay appears at the end of this book, and additional sample essays can be found on the Broadview website; go to sites.broadviewpress.com/writing. Consult the *MLA Handbook* (8th edition, 2016) if you have questions not answered here; you may also find answers at the website of the MLA, www.mla.org, where updates and answers to frequently asked questions are posted.

O *About In-Text Citations*

1. **in-text citations**: Under the MLA system a quotation or specific reference to another work is followed by a parenthetical page reference:

- Bonnycastle refers to "the true and lively spirit of opposition" with which Marxist literary criticism invigorates the discipline (204).

The work is then listed under "Works Cited" at the end of the essay:

- Bonnycastle, Stephen. *In Search of Authority: An Introductory Guide to Literary Theory*. 3rd ed., Broadview Press, 2007.

(See below for information about the "Works Cited" list.)

2. **no signal phrase** (or author not named in signal phrase): If the context does not make it clear who the author is, that information must be added to the in-text citation. Note that no comma separates the name of the author from the page number.

- Even in recent years some have continued to believe that Marxist literary criticism invigorates the discipline with a "true and lively spirit of opposition" (Bonnycastle 204).

3. placing of in-text citations: Place in-text citations at the ends of clauses or sentences in order to keep disruption of your writing to a minimum. The citation comes before the period or comma in the surrounding sentence. (If the quotation ends with punctuation other than a period or comma, then this should precede the end of the quotation, and a period or comma should still follow the in-text citation.)

- Ricks refuted this point early on (16), but the claim has continued to be made in recent years.
- In "The Windhover," on the other hand, Hopkins bubbles over; "the mastery of the thing!" (8), he enthuses when he thinks of a bird, exclaiming shortly thereafter, "O my chevalier!" (10).

When a cited quotation is set off from the text, however, the in-text citation should be placed after the concluding punctuation.

- Muriel Jaeger draws on the following anecdote in discussing the resistance of many wealthy Victorians to the idea of widespread education for the poor:

  > In a mischievous mood, Henry Brougham once told [some well-off acquaintances who were] showing perturbation about the likely results of educating the "lower orders" that they could maintain their superiority by working harder themselves. (105)

4. in-text citation when text is in parentheses: If an in-text citation occurs within text in parentheses, square brackets are used for the reference.

- The development of a mass literary culture (or a "print culture," to use Williams's expression [88]) took several hundred years in Britain.

5. page number unavailable: Many Web sources lack page numbers. If your source has no page or section numbers, no number should be given in your citation. Do not count paragraphs yourself, as the version you are using may differ from others.

- In a recent Web posting a leading critic has clearly implied that he finds such an approach objectionable (Bhabha).

If the source gives explicit paragraph or section numbers, as many Websites do, cite the appropriate abbreviation, followed by the number.

- Early in the novel, Austen makes it clear that the "business" of Mrs. Bennet's life is "to get her daughters married" (ch. 1).

- In "The American Scholar" Emerson asserts that America's "long apprenticeship to the learning of other lands" is drawing to a close (par. 7).

Note that (as is not the case with page numbers), MLA style requires a comma between author and paragraph or section numbers in a citation.

- Early in the novel, Mrs. Bennet makes it clear that her sole business in life is "to get her daughters married" (Austen, ch. 1).

6. one page or less: If a source is one page long or less, it is advisable to still provide the page number (though MLA does not require this).

- In his *Chicago Tribune* review, Bosley calls the novel's prose "excruciating" (1).

7. multiple authors: If there are two authors, both authors should be named either in the signal phrase or in the in-text citation, connected by *and*.

- Chambliss and Best argue that the importance of this novel is primarily historical (233).

- Two distinguished scholars have recently argued that the importance of this novel is primarily historical (Chambliss and Best 233).

If there are three or more authors, include only the first author's name in the in-text citation, followed by *et al.*, short for the Latin *et alia*, meaning *and others*.

- Meaning is not simply there in the text, but in the complex relationships between the text, the reader, and the Medieval world (Black et al. xxxvi).

8. corporate author: The relevant organization or the title of the piece should be included in the in-text citation if neither is included in the body of your text; make sure enough information is provided for readers to find the correct entry in your Works Cited list. Shorten a long title to avoid awkwardness, but take care that the shortened version begins with the same word as the corresponding entry in "Works Cited" so that readers can move easily from the citation to the bibliographic information. For example, *Comparative Indo-European Linguistics: An Introduction* should be shortened to *Comparative Indo-European* rather than *Indo-European Linguistics*. The first two examples below cite unsigned newspaper or encyclopedia articles; the last is a corporate author in-text citation.

- As *The New York Times* reported in one of its several December 2 articles on the Florida recount, Vice-President Gore looked tired and strained as he answered questions ("Gore Press Conference" A16).

- In the 1990s Sao Paulo began to rapidly overtake Mexico City as the world's most polluted city ("Air Pollution" 21).

- There are a number of organizations mandated "to foster the production and enjoyment of the arts in Canada" (Canada Council for the Arts 2).

9. more than one work by the same author cited: If you include more than one work by the same author in your list of Works Cited, you must make clear which work is being cited each time. This may be done either by mentioning the work in a signal phrase or by including in the citation a short version of the title.

- In *The House of Mirth*, for example, Wharton writes of love as keeping Lily and Selden "from atrophy and extinction" (282).

- Wharton sees love as possessing the power to keep humans "from atrophy and extinction" (*House of Mirth* 282).

- Love, as we learn from the experience of Lily and Selden, possesses the power to keep humans "from atrophy and extinction" (Wharton, *House of Mirth* 282).

10. **multi-volume works:** Note, by number, the volume you are referring to, followed by a colon and a space, before noting the page number. Use the abbreviation "vol." when citing an entire volume.

- Towards the end of *In Darkest Africa* Stanley refers to the Victoria Falls (2: 387).

- In contrast with those of the medieval period, Renaissance artworks show an increasing concern with depicting the material world and less and less of an interest in metaphysical symbolism (Hauser, vol. 2).

11. **two or more authors with the same last name:** If the Works Cited list includes two or more authors with the same last name, the in-text citation should supply both first initials and last names, or, if the first initials are also the same, the full first and last names:

- One of the leading economists of the time advocated wage and price controls (Harry Johnston 197).

- One of the leading economists of the time advocated wage and price controls (H. Johnston 197).

12. **indirect quotations:** When an original source is not available but is referred to by another source, the in-text citation includes *qtd. in* (an abbreviation of *quoted in*) and a reference to the second source. In the example below, Casewell is quoted by Bouvier; the in-text citation directs readers to an entry in Works Cited for the Bouvier work.

- Casewell considers Lambert's position to be "outrageously arrogant" (qtd. in Bouvier 59).

13. **short poems:** For short poems, cite line numbers rather than page numbers.

- In "Dover Beach" Arnold hears the pebbles in the waves bring the "eternal note of sadness in" (line 14).

If you are citing the same poem repeatedly, use just the numbers for subsequent references.

- The world, in Arnold's view, has "really neither joy, nor love, nor light" (33).

14. longer poems: For longer poems with parts, cite the part (or section, or "book") as well as the line (where available). Use Arabic numerals, and use a period for separation.

- In "Ode: Intimations of Immortality" Wordsworth calls human birth "but a sleep and a forgetting" (5.1).

15. novels or short stories: When a work of prose fiction has chapters or numbered divisions the citation should include first the page number, and then book, chapter, and section numbers as applicable. (These can be very useful in helping readers of a different edition to locate the passage you are citing.) Arabic numerals should be used. A semicolon should be used to separate the page number from the other information.

- When Joseph and Fanny are by themselves, they immediately express their affection for each other, or, as Fielding puts it, "solace themselves" with "amorous discourse" (151; ch. 26).

- In *Tender Is the Night* Dick's ambition does not quite crowd out the desire for love: "He wanted to be loved too, if he could fit it in" (133; bk. 2, ch. 4).

16. plays: Almost all plays are divided into acts and/or scenes. For plays that do not include line numbering throughout, cite the page number in the edition you have been using, followed by act and/or scene numbers as applicable:

- As Angie and Joyce begin drinking together Angie pronounces the occasion "better than Christmas" (72; act 3).

- Near the conclusion of Inchbald's *Wives as They Were* Bronzely declares that he has been "made to think with reverence on the matrimonial compact" (62; act 5, sc. 4).

For plays written entirely or largely in verse, where line numbers are typically provided throughout, you should omit the reference to page number in the citation. Instead, cite the act, scene, and line numbers, using Arabic numerals. For a Shakespeare play, if the title isn't clear from the introduction to a quotation, an abbreviation of the title may also be used. The in-text citation below is for Shakespeare's *The Merchant of Venice*, Act 2, Scene 3, lines 2–4:

- Jessica clearly has some fondness for Launcelot: "Our house is hell, and thou, a merry devil, / Dost rob it of some taste of tediousness. / But fare thee well; there is a ducat for thee" (*MV* 2.3.2–4).

17. works without page numbers: If you are citing literary texts where you have consulted editions from other sources (on the Web or in an ebook, for instance), the principles are exactly the same, except that you need not cite page numbers. For example, if the online Gutenberg edition of Fielding's *Joseph Andrews* were being cited, the citation would be as follows:

- When Joseph and Fanny are by themselves, they immediately express their affection for each other, or, as Fielding puts it, "solace themselves" with "amorous discourse" (ch. 26).

Students should be cautioned that online editions of literary texts are often unreliable. Typically there are far more typos and other errors in online versions of literary texts than there are in print versions, and such things as the layout of poems are also frequently incorrect. It is often possible to exercise judgement about such matters, however. If, for example, you are not required to base your essay on a particular copy of a Thomas Hardy poem but may find your own, you will be far better off using the text you will find on the Representative Poetry Online site run out of the University of Toronto than you will using a text you might find on a "World's Finest Love Poems" site.

18. sacred texts: The Bible and other sacred texts that are available in many editions should be cited in a way that enables the reader to check the reference in any edition. For the Bible, book, chapter, and verse should all be cited, using periods for separation. The reference below is to Genesis, chapter 2, verse 1.

- According to the Judeo-Christian story of creation, at the end of the sixth day "the heavens and the earth were finished" (Gen. 2.1).

19. works in an anthology or book of readings: In the in-text citation for a work in an anthology, use the name of the author of the work, not that of the editor of the anthology. The page number, however, should be that found in the anthology. The following citation refers to an article by Frederic W. Gleach in an anthology edited by Jennifer Brown and Elizabeth Vibert.

- One of the essays in Brown and Vibert's collection argues that we should rethink the Pocahontas myth (Gleach 48).

In your list of Works Cited, this work should be alphabetized under Gleach, the author of the piece you have consulted, not under Brown. If you cite another work by a different author from the same anthology or book of readings, that should appear as a separate entry in your list of Works Cited—again, alphabetized under the author's name.

20. tweets: Cite tweets by giving the author's name in your text rather than in an in-text citation.

- Jack Welch quickly lost credibility when he tweeted that the US Bureau of Labor had manipulated monthly unemployment rate statistics in order to boost the post-debate Obama campaign: "Unbelievable job numbers..these Chicago guys will do anything..can't debate so change numbers."

O *About Works Cited; MLA Core Elements*

The Works Cited list in MLA style is an alphabetized list at the end of the essay (or article or book). The entire list, like the main part of the essay, should be double-spaced throughout, and each entry should be given a hanging indent: the first line is flush with the left-hand margin, and each subsequent line is indented one tab space.

The Works Cited list should include information about all the sources you have cited. Do not include works that you consulted but did not cite in the body of your text.

MLA style provides a set of citation guidelines that the writer follows and adapts, regardless of whether the source being cited is print, digital, audio, visual, or any other form of media. All sources share what the MLA call "Core Elements," and these, listed in order, create the citation for all your entries: Author, Title of Source, Title of Container (larger whole), Other Contributors, Version, Number, Publisher, Publication Date, and Location. Each element is followed by the punctuation marks shown in the table below, unless it is the last element, which should always close with a period. (There are a few exceptions to this rule, which are outlined below.) Most sources don't have all the elements (some don't have an author, for example, or a version, or a location); if you find that this is the case, omit the element and move on to the next.

The table can function as a guide when creating citations. Once you have found all the publication details for your source, place them in order and punctuate according to the table, leaving out any elements for which you don't have information.

1. Author.
2. Title of source.
3. Title of container,
4. Other contributors,
5. Version,
6. Number,
7. Publisher,
8. Publication Date,
9. Location.

In the sections below, you will discover how to identify the core elements of MLA style and how to use them across media. For a list of examples, please see pages 592–604.

Author

This element begins your citation. For a **single author**, list the author's last name first, followed by a comma, and then the author's first name or initials (use whatever appears on the work's title page or copyright page), followed by a period.

Graham, Jorie. *From the New World*. Ecco, 2015.

McKerlie, Dennis. *Justice between the Young and the Old*. Oxford UP, 2013.

If a source has **two authors**, the first author's name should appear with the last name first, followed by a comma and *and*. Note also that the authors' names should appear in the order they are listed; sometimes this is not alphabetical.

> Rectenwald, Michael, and Lisa Carl. *Academic Writing, Real World Topics*. Broadview Press, 2015.

If there are **three or more authors**, include only the first author's name, reversed, followed by a comma and *et al.* (the abbreviation of the Latin *et alii*, meaning *and others*).

> Blais, Andre, et al. *Anatomy of a Liberal Victory*. Broadview Press, 2002.

Sources that are **edited** rather than authored are usually cited in a similar way; add "editor" or "editors" after the name(s) and before the title.

> Renker, Elizabeth, editor. *Poems: A Concise Anthology*. Broadview Press, 2016.

When referring to an edited version of a work written by another author or authors, list the editor(s) after the title, in the Other Contributors element.

> Trollope, Anthony. *The Eustace Diamonds*. 1873. Edited by Stephen Gill and John Sutherland, Penguin, 1986.

Authors can be organizations, institutions, associations, or government agencies ("corporate authors"). If a work has been issued by a **corporate author** and no author is identified, the entry should be listed by the name of the organization that produced it.

> Ontario, Ministry of Natural Resources. *Achieving Balance: Ontario's Long-Term Energy Plan*. Queen's Printer for Ontario, 2016, www.energy.gov.on.ca/en/ltep/achieving-balance-ontarios-long-term-energy-plan. Accessed 10 May 2016.

If the work is published by the same organization that is the corporate author, skip the author element and list only the publisher. The citation will begin with the source title.

> *2014 Annual Report*. Broadview Press, 2015.

> "History of the Arms and Great Seal of the Commonwealth of Massachusetts." Commonwealth of Massachusetts, www.sec/ state.ma.us/pre/presea/sealhis/htm. Accessed 9 May 2016.

"Our Mandate." Art Gallery of Ontario, www.ago.net/mandate.
　　Accessed 10 May 2016.

Works with an **anonymous author** should be alphabetized by title,
omitting the author element.

Sir Gawain and the Green Knight. Edited by Paul Battles, Broad-
　　view Press, 2012.

Works under a **pseudonym** should appear with the pseudonym in
place of the author's name. Online usernames are copied out exactly
as they appear on the screen.

@newyorker. "With the resignation of Turkey's Prime Minister,
　　the country's President now stands alone and unchallenged."
　　Twitter, 6 May 2016, twitter.com/NewYorker/status/
　　728676985254379520.

Note that the author element is flexible. If you are discussing the
work of a film director, for example, the director's name should be
placed in the author element, with a descriptor.

Hitchcock, Alfred, director. *The Lady Vanishes*. United Artists,
　　1938.

If, on the other hand, you are discussing film editing, you would
place the film editor in the author element. In this case, you might
also include Hitchcock's name in the "Other Contributors" element.

Dearing, R.E., film editor. *The Lady Vanishes*, directed by Alfred
　　Hitchcock, United Artists, 1938.

If no single contributor's work is of particular importance in your
discussion of a film or television source, omit the author element
altogether.

"The Buys." *The Wire*, created by David Simon and Ed Burns,
　　directed by Peter Medak, season 1, episode 3, HBO, 16 June
　　2002, disc 1.

If you are citing a **translated source** and the translation itself is the
focus of your work, the translator or translators can be placed in the
author element.

> Lodge, Kirsten, translator. *Notes from the Underground.* By Fyo-
> dor Dostoevsky, edited by Kirsten Lodge, Broadview Press,
> 2014.

When the work itself is the focus, as is usually the case, the author should remain in the author element, and the translator moved to the "other contributors" element:

> Dostoevsky, Fyodor. *Notes from the Underground.* Translated and
> edited by Kirsten Lodge, Broadview Press, 2014.

This principle holds true across media and elements. Adapt the MLA structure to create citations that are clear, most relevant to your work, and most useful to your reader.

● Title of Source

The title of your source follows the author element. Copy the title as you find it in the source, but with MLA-standard capitalization and punctuation. Capitalize the first word, the last word, and all key words, but not articles, prepositions, coordinating conjunctions, or the *to* in infinitives.

> Carson, Anne. *The Albertine Workout.* New Directions, 2014.

If there is a **subtitle**, include it after the main title, following a colon.

> Bök, Christian. *The Xenotext: Book 1.* Coach House Books, 2015.

Your title gives the reader information about the source. Italicized titles indicate that the source is a complete, independent whole. A title enclosed in quotation marks tells the reader that the source is part of a larger work.

A **book** is an independent whole, so the title is italicized.

> Wordsworth, William. *Poems, in Two Volumes.* Edited by Richard
> Matlak, Broadview Press, 2016.

Other examples include **long poems** (*In Memoriam*), **magazines** (*The New Yorker*), **newspapers** (*The Guardian*), **journals** (*The American Poetry Review*), **websites** (*The Camelot Project*), **films** (*Memento*), **television shows** (*The X-Files*), and **compact discs** or **record albums** (*Dark Side of the Moon*).

A **poem**, **short story**, or **essay** within a larger collection is placed in quotation marks.

> Wordsworth, William. "The Solitary Reaper." *Poems, in Two Volumes*, edited by Richard Matlak, Broadview Press, 2016, p. 153.

Other examples include **chapters in books** ("The Autist Artist" in *The Man Who Mistook His Wife for a Hat and Other Clinical Tales*), **encyclopedia articles** ("Existentialism"), **essays in books or journals** ("Salvation in the Garden: Daoism and Ecology" in *Daoism and Ecology: Ways within a Cosmic Landscape*), **short stories** ("Young Goodman Brown"), **short poems** ("Daddy"), **pages on websites** ("The Fisher King" from *The Camelot Project*), **episodes of television shows** ("Small Potatoes" from *The X-Files*), and **songs** ("Eclipse" from *Dark Side of the Moon*). Put the titles of **public lectures** in double quotation marks as well ("Walls in *The Epic of Gilgamesh*").

These formatting rules apply across media forms. A website is placed in italics; a posting on the website is placed in quotation marks.

> Stein, Sadie. "Casting the Runes." *The Daily: The Paris Review Blog*, 9 Oct. 2015, www.theparisreview.org/blog/2015/10/09/casting-the-runes/.

If the title of a stand-alone work contains the title of a work that is not independent, the latter is put in double quotation marks, and the entire title is put in italics (*"Self-Reliance" and Other Essays*). If the title of a stand-alone work appears within the title of another independent work, MLA recommends that the latter be put in italics and the former not (*Chaucer's House of Fame: The Poetics of Skeptical Fideism*). If the title of a non-independent work is embedded in another title of the same kind, put the inner title into single quotation marks and the outer title in double quotation marks ("The Drama of Donne's 'The Indifferent'").

When a stand-alone work appears in a **collection**, the work's title remains in italics.

> James, Henry. *The American. Henry James: Novels 1871-1880*, edited by William T. Stafford, Library of America, 1983.

● Title of Container

Very often your source is found within a larger context, such as an **anthology, periodical, newspaper, digital platform,** or **website.** When this is the case, the larger whole is called the "container." For an article in a newspaper, for example, the article is the "source" and the newspaper is the "container." For a song in an **album,** the song is the "source" and the album is the "container."

The title of the container is usually italicized and followed by a comma.

> Gladwell, Malcolm. "The Art of Failure: Why Some People Choke and Others Panic." *The New Yorker*, 21 Aug. 2000, www.newyorker.com/magazine/2000/08/21/the-art-of-failure. Accessed 18 Feb. 2013.

The container can be a website; a book that is a collection of stories, poems, plays, or essays; a magazine; a journal; an album; or a database.

When doing research, particularly online, one often comes across nested containers, in which, for example, an article is found in a collection of essays, which is itself found on a database. All containers are recorded in the citation, so your reader knows exactly how to find your source. Add more Container elements as needed. Additional containers should follow the period at the end of the information given for the preceding container (usually after the date or location element).

It can be helpful to see this process charted out. Notice that the publication information for the container follows that of the source.

Here is an example of an **article from a periodical,** accessed from an online database.

1. Author.	Sohmer, Steve.
2. Title of source.	"12 June 1599: Opening Day at Shakespeare's Globe."
CONTAINER 1:	
3. Title of container,	*Early Modern Literary Studies: A Journal of Sixteenth- and Seventeenth-Century English Literature,*
4. Other contributors,	
5. Version,	
6. Number,	vol. 3, no.1,
7. Publisher,	
8. Publication Date,	1997.
9. Location.	
CONTAINER 2:	
3. Title of container,	*ProQuest,*
4. Other contributors,	
5. Version,	
6. Number,	
7. Publisher,	
8. Publication Date,	
9. Location.	www.extra.shu.ac.uk/emls/ emlshome.html.

Citation as It Would Appear in Works Cited List:

Sohmer, Steve. "12 June 1599: Opening Day at Shakespeare's Globe." *Early Modern Literary Studies: A Journal of Sixteenth- and Seventeenth-Century English Literature*, vol. 3, no.1, 1997. *ProQuest*, www.extra.shu.ac.uk/emls/emlshome.html.

The next example is an **e-book version** of Jane Austen's *Emma*, accessed from a publisher's website. The novel is self-contained, so no title of a container is given until the digital platform information is recorded in the second container.

1. Author.	Austen, Jane.
2. Title of source.	*Emma*.
CONTAINER 1:	
3. Title of container,	
4. Other contributors,	Edited by Kristen Flieger Samuelian,
5. Version,	
6. Number,	
7. Publisher,	
8. Publication Date,	2004.
9. Location.	
CONTAINER 2:	
3. Title of container,	*Broadview Press,*
4. Other contributors,	
5. Version,	
6. Number,	
7. Publisher,	
8. Publication Date,	
9. Location.	www.broadviewpress.com/ product/emma /#tab-description.

Citation as It Would Appear in Works Cited List:

> Austen, Jane. *Emma*. Edited by Kristen Flieger Samuelian, 2004. *Broadview Press*, www.broadviewpress.com/product/ emma/#tab-description. Accessed 5 Feb. 2016.

The elements are recorded sequentially to create your citation. Notice that any elements that don't apply to this source are left out. Any element that is the same for both containers (in this case, the publisher) is recorded in the last (here the second) container; however, the location of this e-book (the website) contains the name of the publisher, so in this case the publisher field is left empty. This removes the need to repeat information in the citation.

Here is an example citation of a **performance in a television series**, accessed on Netflix.

1. Author.	Spacey, Kevin, performer.
2. Title of source.	"Chapter 5."
CONTAINER 1:	
3. Title of container,	*House of Cards*,
4. Other contributors,	directed by Joel Schumacher,
5. Version,	
6. Number,	season 1, episode 5,
7. Publisher,	
8. Publication Date,	2013.
9. Location.	
CONTAINER 2:	
3. Title of container,	Netflix,
4. Other contributors,	
5. Version,	
6. Number,	
7. Publisher,	
8. Publication Date,	
9. Location.	www.netflix.com/search/house?jbv=70178217&jbp=0.

Citation as It Would Appear in Works Cited List:

Spacey, Kevin, performer. "Chapter 5." *House of Cards*, directed by Joel Schumacher, season 1, episode 5, 2013. *Netflix*, www.netflix.com/search/house?jbv=70178217&jbp=0.

Notice that in this case Netflix produced the show, so the publisher field is left empty in both containers. If the source had been an episode from a series produced by, for example, the BBC, you would include the BBC as publisher.

> Tennant, David, performer. "Gridlock." *Dr. Who*, directed by Richard Clark, series 3, episode 3, BBC, 2007. *Netflix*, www.netflix.com/search/dr%20who?jbv=70142441&jbp=0.

● Other Contributors

There may be other key people who should be credited in your citation as contributors. This element follows the title of the source and the container (if there is one). The MLA recommends that you include the names of contributors who are important to your research, or if they help your reader to identify the source. Before each name, place a description of the role (do not abbreviate):

> adapted by
> directed by
> edited by
> illustrated by
> introduction by
> narrated by
> performance by
> translated by

If your listing of a contributor follows the source title, it is capitalized (following a period). If the contributor follows a container, it will be lower-case (following a comma).

> Lao Tzu. *Tao Te Ching: A Book about the Way and the Power of the Way*. Translated by Ursula K. Le Guin. Shambhala, 1997.

> James, Henry. *The American. Henry James: Novels 1871-1880*, edited by William T. Stafford, Library of America, 1983.

In the Other Contributors element, include the most relevant contributors not already mentioned in the author element. If you are writing about a television episode and a certain performance is one of the elements you discuss, for example, include the performer's name in the Other Contributors element, along with any other contributors you wish to include.

Medak, Peter, director. "The Buys." *The Wire*, created by David
Simon and Ed Burns, performance by Dominic West, season
1, episode 3, HBO, 16 June 2002.

Note that the MLA guidelines are flexible; for this part of the citation especially, consider what your readers most need to know about
your source and include that information. Note also that there is
some flexibility in the author element; if a particular performance or
other contribution is the major focus in your discussion of source, it
can be cited in the author element instead.

● Version

If your source is **one of several editions**, or if it is a **revised version**,
record those details in this element of your citation, followed by a
comma. The word "edition" is abbreviated in your citation (ed.).

Fowles, John. *The Magus*. Rev. ed., Jonathan Cape, 1977.

Shelley, Mary. *Frankenstein*. Edited by D.L. Macdonald and
Kathleen Sherf, 3rd ed., Broadview Press, 2012.

You may also come across **expanded editions**, **revised editions**,
and **updated editions**, all of which can be noted in this element
of your citation. Different media might use different terminology.
For example in film you may find a **director's cut**, or in music an
abridged version of a concerto: use the same principles as above,
providing the relevant information in the Version element of your
citation.

Coen, Ethan, and Joel Coen, directors. *Blood Simple*. Director's
cut, Universal, 2001.

● Number

If your source is part of a **multi-volumed work**, or if it is part of a
journal that is issued in numbers and/or volumes, include the volume information in this Number element of your citation.

If you are citing **two or more volumes** of a multi-volume work, the
entry should note the total number of volumes. If you cite only one
of the volumes, list it after the title.

Jeeves, Julie, editor. *A Reference Guide to Spanish Architecture.* 3 vols, Hackett, 2005.

Mercer, Bobby, editor. *A Reference Guide to French Architecture.* Vol. 1, Hackett, 2002.

Include the **volume and issue numbers** for journals. Use the abbreviations *vol.* for volume and *no.* for issue number.

Gregory, Elizabeth. "Marianne Moore's 'Blue Bug': A Dialogic Ode on Celebrity, Race, Gender, and Age." *Modernism/Modernity,* vol. 22, no. 4, 2015, pp. 759–86.

Some journals do not use volume numbers and give only an issue number.

Sanger, Richard. "Goodbye, Seamus." *Brick,* no. 93, Summer 2014, pp. 153–57.

The Number element is also where you record issue numbers for comic books, or the season and episode numbers for a television series.

Spacey, Kevin, performer. "Chapter 5." *House of Cards,* directed by Joel Schumacher, season 1, episode 5, 2013. *Netflix,* www.netflix.com/search/ house?jbv=70178217&jbp=0.

● Publisher

In this element of your citation, record the organization that produced the source, whether it be the publisher of a book, the organization running a website, or the studio producing a film. (In the case of a secondary container, include the organization that produced the container.) Do not abbreviate, except in the case of university presses, which may be abbreviated as *UP.*

To find the publisher of a **book**, look on the title page or on the copyright page.

Dickens, Charles. *The Uncommercial Traveller.* Edited by Daniel Tyler, Oxford UP, 2015.

Rush, Rebecca. *Kelroy.* Edited by Betsy Klimasmith, Broadview Press, 2016.

For a **film** or **television series**, the studio or company that produced the show is recorded in the information on the back of a DVD or in the opening and closing credits.

> Simon, David, creator. *The Wire*. HBO, 2002–2008.

For **websites**, the publisher's information can often be found in the copyright notice at the bottom of the page.

> Bogan, Louise. "Women." 1922. *Representative Poetry Online*, edited by Ian Lancashire, University of Toronto, 2000.

A **blog network** may be cited as the publisher of the blogs it hosts.

> Cairney, Paul, and Kathryn Oliver. "If scientists want to influence policymaking, they need to understand it." *Political Science*, The Guardian Science Blog Network, 27 Apr. 2016.

You may omit a publisher's name in the following kinds of publications:

- A periodical (journal, magazine, newspaper).
- A work published by its author or editor.
- A website whose title is essentially the same as the name of the publisher.
- A website not involved in producing the works it is making available (YouTube, JSTOR, ProQuest). These are listed as containers, but not as publishers.

If **two or more publishers** are listed for your source, cite them both and separate them with a forward slash (/).

> Banting, Keith G., editor. *Thinking Outside the Box: Innovation in Policy Ideas*. School of Policy Studies, Queen's University / McGill–Queen's University Press, 2015.

● Publication Date

In this element of your citation, record the date of publication for your source. For **books**, this date is found on the copyright page (and sometimes on the title page). If several editions are listed, use the date for the edition you have consulted.

Stevenson, Robert Louis. *Strange Case of Dr. Jekyll and Mr. Hyde.*
Edited by Martin A. Danahay, 3rd ed., Broadview Press,
2015.

Online sources almost always have a date posted, and this is the date
you should record in this element.

Heller, Nathan. "The Big Uneasy: What's Roiling the Liberal-
Arts Campus?" *The New Yorker*, 30 May 2016,
www.newyorker.com/magazine/2016/05/30/the-new-
activism-of-liberal-arts-colleges.

A source may be associated with **more than one publication date.**
An article online may have been previously published in print, or
an article printed in a book may have been published previously in
a periodical. In this case, the MLA recommends that you record the
date that is most relevant to your use of the source. If you consulted
the online version of an article, for example, ignore the date of print
publication and cite the online publication date.

For books, we record the year of publication. For other sources,
whether to include a year, month, and day depends on your source
and the context in which you are using it. If you are citing an **episode from a television series**, for example, it is usually enough to
record the year it aired.

Medak, Peter, director. "The Buys." *The Wire*, created by David
Simon and Ed Burns, season 1, episode 3, HBO, 2002.

If, however, the context surrounding the episode is being discussed
in your work, you should be more specific about the date:

Medak, Peter, director. "The Buys." *The Wire*, created by David
Simon and Ed Burns, season 1, episode 3, HBO, 16 June
2002.

For a **video posted on a website**, include the date on which the
video was posted. In the example below, the posting date should be
included in the second container, which records the details for the
digital platform. The date the video was released is included in the
publication details for the source.

Gleeson, Thomas, director. *Home*. Screen Innovation Production, 2012. *Vimeo*, uploaded by Thomas Gleeson, 31 Jan. 2013, www.vimeo.com/58630796.

If you are citing a **comment posted on a Web page**, and the time the content was posted is indicated, include the time in your entry.

Evan. Comment on "Another Impasse on Gun Bills, Another Win for Hyperpolitics." *The New York Times*, 21 June 2016, 9:02 a.m., www.nytimes.com/2016/06/22/us/politics/washington-congress-gun-control.html.

Larger projects are created over a longer span of time. If you are documenting a Web project as a whole, include the full range of years during which it was developed.

Secord, James A. et al., editors. *Darwin Correspondence Project*. 1974–2016, www.darwinproject.ac.uk/.

The dates of publication for **periodicals** vary. Include in full the information provided by the copyright page, whether it be indicated by season, year, month, week, or day.

Sanger, Richard. "Goodbye, Seamus." *Brick*, no. 93, Summer 2014, pp. 153–57.

Trousdale, Rachel. "'Humor Saves Steps': Laughter and Humanity in Marianne Moore." *Journal of Modern Literature*, vol. 35, no. 3, 2012, pp.121–38. *JSTOR*, www.jstor.org/stable/10.2979/jmodelite.35.3.121.

● Location

The content of the Location element varies considerably between print, digital, and other sources.

For **print sources** within a periodical or anthology, record a page number (preceded by p.) or a range of page numbers (preceded by pp.).

Gregory, Elizabeth. "Marianne Moore's 'Blue Bug': A Dialogic Ode on Celebrity, Race, Gender, and Age." *Modernism/Modernity*, vol. 22, no. 4, 2015, pp. 759–86.

Walcott, Derek. "The Sea Is History." *The Broadview Anthology of Poetry*, edited by Herbert Rosengarten and Amanda Goldrick Jones, Broadview Press, 1992, p. 757.

Wills, Garry. "A Masterpiece on the Rise of Christianity." Review of *Through the Eye of a Needle: Wealth, the Fall of Rome, and the Making of Christianity in the West, 350–550 AD*, by Peter Brown. *New York Review of Books*, 11 Oct. 2012, pp. 43–45.

An **online work** is located by its URL, or Web address. When copying the URL into your citation, remove the *http://*; this means that usually the URL will begin with *www*. If you need to break a URL over two or more lines, do not insert any hyphens at the break point; instead, when possible, break after a colon or slash or before other marks of punctuation.

Trousdale, Rachel. "'Humor Saves Steps': Laughter and Humanity in Marianne Moore." *Journal of Modern Literature* vol. 35, no. 3, 2012, pp. 121–38. *JSTOR*, www.jstor.org/stable/10.2979/jmodelite.35.3.121.

Some publishers assign DOIs (Digital Object Identifiers) to their online publications, and these, when available, are preferable to URLs, as they do not change when the source moves (whereas URLs do). If your source has no DOI but offers a "stable" URL, choose that one to include in your citation. The publisher in this case has agreed not to change the URL.

Yearling, R. "*Hamlet* and the Limits of Narrative." *Essays in Criticism: A Quarterly Journal of Literary Criticism*, vol. 65, no. 4, 2015, pp. 368–82. *ProQuest*, doi:dx.doi.org/10.1093/escrit/cgv022.

We find a **television episode** on a DVD by its disc number. Place the disc number in the Location element.

"The Buys." *The Wire*, created by David Simon and Ed Burns, directed by Peter Medak, season 1, episode 3, HBO, 2002, disc 1.

For a **work of art** that you have seen in person, cite the name of the institution and city where you saw it in the Location element. Leave out the name of the city if the city name is part of the institution name (e.g., The Art Institute of Chicago).

Sargent, John Singer. *Henry James.* 1913, National Portrait Gallery, London.

Some **archived sources** have a different system for locating objects in the archive. Where this is the case, include the code or number in the Location element.

Blake, William. *The Marriage of Heaven and Hell.* 1790–1793. The Fitzwilliam Museum, Cambridge, 123-1950. Illuminated printed book.

If you are citing a **live performance** or **lecture**, name the location and the city. Omit the city name if it is part of the location name.

Royal Winnipeg Ballet. *The Princess and the Goblin.* Directed and choreographed by Twyla Tharp, performances by Paloma Herrera and Dmitri Dovgoselets, 17 Oct. 2012, Centennial Concert Hall, Winnipeg.

● Optional Elements

You may include any of the following elements in your citation if you think they are helpful to your reader.

Date of Original Publication

If your source has been republished, it may give your reader some important context if you include the date of original publication. If you do so, place the date immediately after the source title and close with a period.

Trollope, Anthony. *The Eustace Diamonds.* 1873. Edited by Stephen Gill and John Sutherland, Penguin, 1986.

City of Publication

Including the city of publication is not very useful these days, so the MLA has decided to remove this element from citations. There are two situations, however, where you may wish to include the city. If the book was published before 1900, the city of publication is associated more closely with the source than the publisher. For these books, you may substitute the city of publication for the publisher.

Dickens, Charles. *Our Mutual Friend.* Vol. 1, New York, 1800.

Some publishers release more than one version of a text in different countries (a British and an American edition, for example). In you are reading an unexpected version of a text, or the version you are reading has historical significance, place the name of the city in front of the publisher.

> Lawrence, D.H. *Lady Chatterley's Lover.* London, Penguin, 1960.

Books in a Series
If your source is a book in a series, you may add the series name in roman (i.e., without italics) at the end of your citation, preceded by a period.

> Shakespeare, William. *As You Like It.* Edited by David Bevington, Broadview Press, 2012. Broadview Internet Shakespeare Editions.

Unexpected Type of Work
If your source needs further explanation, place a descriptive term (e-mail, transcript, broadcast, street performance, talk, address) at the end of the citation, preceded by a period.

> Rosenheim, Jeff. "Diane Arbus." Art Gallery of Ontario, 6 May 2016, Toronto. Lecture.

Date of Access
It is optional to include a date of access for your online citations, but it can be a good idea, particularly if the source does not have a date of publication.

> Crawford, Isabella Valancy. "The Canoe." *Representative Poetry Online*, edited by Ian Lancashire, Web Development Group, Information Technology Services, University of Toronto Libraries, www.tspace.library.utoronto.ca/html/1807/4350/poem596.html. Accessed November 24 2015.

O *Examples*
The following are examples of MLA-style citations for sources across various media. While these examples can offer useful guidance, remember that the MLA guidelines may be adapted to suit the details of the sources you are documenting, as well as the context in which you are using them.

21. single author:

Graham, Jorie. *From the New World*. Ecco, 2015.

Malory, Thomas. *Le Morte D'Arthur: Selections*. Edited by Maureen Okun, Broadview Press, 2014.

22. two authors:

Auden, W.H. and Louis MacNiece. *Letters from Iceland*. Faber & Faber, 2002.

Rectenwald, Michael, and Lisa Carl. *Academic Writing, Real World Topics*. Broadview Press, 2015.

23. three or more authors:

Blais, Andre, et al. *Anatomy of a Liberal Victory*. Broadview Press, 2002.

Fromkin, Victoria, et al. *An Introduction to Language*. 4th Canadian ed., Nelson, 2010.

24. corporate author:

2014 Annual Report. Broadview Press, 2015.

"History of the Arms and Great Seal of the Commonwealth of Massachusetts." Commonwealth of Massachusetts, www.sec/state.ma.us/pre/presea/sealhis/htm. Accessed 9 May 2016.

Ontario, Ministry of Natural Resources. *Achieving Balance: Ontario's Long-Term Energy Plan*. Queen's Printer for Ontario, 2016, www.energy.gov.on.ca/en/ltep/achieving-balance-ontarios-long-term-energy-plan. Accessed 10 May 2016.

25. works with an anonymous author: Works with an anonymous author should be alphabetized by title.

Beowulf. Edited and translated by R.M. Liuzza. 2nd ed., Broadview Press, 2012.

26. two or more works by the same author: The author's name should appear for the first entry only; for subsequent entries substitute three hyphens for the name of the author.

Menand, Louis. "Bad Comma: Lynne Truss's Strange Grammar." Review of *Eats, Shoots and Leaves*, by Lynne Truss.

The New Yorker, 28 June 2004, www.newyorker.com/
magazine/2004/06/28/bad-comma. Accessed 18 Feb. 2013.

---. *The Metaphysical Club: A Story of Ideas in America.* Farrar,
Straus and Giroux, 2001.

27. works under a pseudonym: These are given using the same
formatting as author's names. Online usernames are given as they
appear.

@newyorker. "With the resignation of Turkey's Prime Minister, the country's President now stands alone and unchallenged." *Twitter,* 6 May 2016, twitter.com/NewYorker/
status/728676985254379520.

28. edited works:

Renker, Elizabeth, editor. *Poems: A Concise Anthology.* Broadview
Press, 2016.

When referring to an edited version of a work written by another
author or authors, list the editor(s) after the title.

Trollope, Anthony. *The Eustace Diamonds.* 1873. Edited by Stephen Gill and John Sutherland, Penguin, 1986.

29. works in translation:
The translator is normally listed in the Other Contributors element
of the citation.

Bolaño, Roberto. *By Night in Chile.* Translated by Chris Andrews,
New Directions, 2003.

If your work focuses on the translation itself, you may list the translator in the author element, moving the author to the Other Contributors element.

Andrews, Chris, translator. *By Night in Chile.* By Roberto Bolaño,
New Directions, 2003.

30. selections from anthologies or collections of readings: A selection from a collection of readings or an anthology should begin with
the name of the author of the selection. If they are available, be sure
to add the selection's inclusive page numbers after the anthology's
publication date.

Crawford, Isabella Valancy. "The Canoe." *Representative Poetry Online*, edited by Ian Lancashire, U of Toronto, 1997, www.rpo.library.utoronto.ca/poems/canoe. Accessed 20 Apr. 2015.

Gleach, Frederic W. "Controlled Speculation: Interpreting the Saga of Pocahontas and Captain John Smith." *Reading Beyond Words: Contexts for Native History*, edited by Jennifer S. H. Brown and Elizabeth Vibert, Broadview Press, 1996, pp. 21–42.

Mahfouz, Naguib. "Half a Day." *The Picador Book of African Stories*, edited by Stephen Gray, Picador, 2001, pp. 3–6.

31. cross-references for works from the same collection or anthology: It can be more efficient to create a full entry for the collection or anthology, and then to list each cited item in its own entry. Position the entries in the Works Cited list alphabetically, as you normally would, and use a short form for the collection or anthology, as in the following example:

Brown, Jennifer S.H., and Elizabeth Vibert, editors. *Reading Beyond Words: Contexts for Native History*. Broadview Press, 1996.

Cruikshank, Julie. "Discovery of Gold on the Klondike: Perspectives from Oral Tradition." Brown and Vibert, pp. 433–59.

Gleach, Frederic W. "Controlled Speculation: Interpreting the Saga of Pocahontas and Captain John Smith." Brown and Vibert, pp. 21–42.

32. multi-volume works: If you are citing one or more of the volumes, list them after the title. The entry may note the total number of volumes at the end of the citation (this is optional).

Mercer, Bobby, editor. *A Reference Guide to French Architecture.* Vol. 1, Hackett, 2002. 3 vols.

Jeeves, Julie, editor. *A Reference Guide to Spanish Architecture.* 3 vols., Hackett, 2005.

33. different editions: The edition should be specified whenever it is not the first edition. Include whatever the title page indicates about the particular edition, and use abbreviations (e.g., *rev. ed.* for *revised edition*, *2nd ed.* for *second edition*, and so on).

Fowles, John. *The Magus*. Rev. ed. by Jonathan Cape, 1977.

Shelley, Mary. *Frankenstein*. 1818. Edited by Lorne Macdonald and Kathleen Scherf, 2nd ed., Broadview Press, 1999.

The Bible. Authorized King James Version, Oxford UP, 2008.

34. republished sources: When a source was previously published in a different form, you may include information about the prior publication. This is an optional element; include this information at your discretion, if you feel it would give your reader important context for the source.

MacMillan, Margaret. "Hubris." *History's People: Personalities and the Past, Massey Lectures*, CBC Radio, 3 Nov. 2015, www.cbc.ca/radio/ideas/history-s-people-personalities-the-past-lecture-2-1.3301571. Podcast. Originally delivered at the Arts and Culture Centre, St. John's, NL, 25 Sept. 2015, 7:00 p.m. Lecture.

35. reference work entries: List by the author of the entry, if known; otherwise, list by the entry itself. The citation of a well-known reference work (because such works are frequently updated) should not have full publication details; provide the edition number, date, and location only. Don't include page numbers for works that arrange their entries alphabetically.

"Artificial." *Oxford English Dictionary*. 2nd ed., 1989.

Fowler, H.W. "Unique." *The King's English*, 2nd ed., 1908. *Bartleby.com*, bartleby.com/116/108.html#2. Accessed 5 Mar. 2016.

Marsh, James. "Canoe, Birchbark." *The Canadian Encyclopedia*, 2000 ed., McClelland & Stewart, 1999.

36. works with a title in the title: A title that is usually italicized should remain italicized when it appears within quotation marks:

Yearling, R. "*Hamlet* and the Limits of Narrative." *Essays in Criticism: A Quarterly Journal of Literary Criticism*, vol. 65, no. 4, 2015, pp. 368–82. *ProQuest*, doi:dx.doi.org/10.1093/escrit/cgv022

Titles that are in quotation marks that appear within other titles in quotation marks are enclosed by single quotation marks:

Bettelheim, Bruno. "'The Goose Girl': Achieving Autonomy." *The Uses of Enchantment: The Meaning and Importance of Fairy Tales*, Vintage-Random House, 1989, pp. 136–43.

An italicized title that is included within another italicized title is neither italicized nor placed in quotation marks. It appears in roman:

Morelli, Stefan. *Stoppard's* Arcadia *and Modern Drama*. Ashgate, 2004.

If a title normally enclosed in quotation marks appears in an italicized title, keep the quotation marks:

Wimsatt, C.W. *"Fern Hill" and British Poetry in the 1950s*. ECW, 2004.

37. material from prefaces, introductions, etc.: If you refer to something from a work's preface, introduction, or foreword, the reference under Works Cited should begin with the name of the author of that preface, introduction, or foreword. Add inclusive page numbers after the date of publication.

Warkentin, Germaine. Introduction. *Set in Authority*, by Sara Jeannette Duncan, Broadview Press, 1996, pp. 9–51.

38. magazine articles: The title of the article should appear in quotation marks, the title of the magazine in italics. If no author is identified, the title of the article should appear first. If the magazine is published monthly or every two months, give the date as month and year. For magazines published weekly or every two weeks, give the date as day, month, and year. Abbreviate the names of months (except for *May*, *June*, and *July*).

MacRitchie, Lynn. "Ofili's Glittering Icons." *Art in America,* Jan. 2000, pp. 44–56.

"Greens in Pinstriped Suits." *The Economist*. 21 May 2016, www.economist.com/news/business/21699141-climate-conscious-shareholders-are-putting-big-oil-spot-greens-pin-striped-suits.

If you accessed the article online yourself, you may include the date of access, though it is an optional element. If the website is hosted by a body other than the magazine itself, include it as a second container with its accompanying publication details.

> Gladwell, Malcolm. "The Art of Failure: Why Some People Choke and Others Panic." *The New Yorker,* 21 Aug. 2000, www.newyorker.com/magazine/2000/08/21/the-art-of-failure. Accessed 18 Feb. 2013.
>
> Kreimer, Julian. "Mernet Larsen." *Art in America,* vol. 104, no. 4, 2016, pp. 115–16. *Academic Search Complete,* www.search.ebscohost.com/login.aspx?direct=true&db=114088897&site=ehost-live. Accessed 4 Nov. 2015.

39. newspaper articles: The basic principles to follow with newspaper articles or editorials are the same as with magazine articles (see above). Note, however, that when the newspaper's sections are paginated separately, section as well as page numbers are often required. If an article is not printed on consecutive pages, include only the first page number followed by a plus sign. In the following reference the article begins on page 3 of the first section:

> Yakabuski, Konrad. "Many Looking for Meaning in Vice-Presidential Debate." *The Globe and Mail,* 12 Oct. 2012, p. A3+.

If you are citing an online version of a newspaper article you should include the date you accessed the site. The site name, if it is different from the container title, should also be included.

> Kaplan, Thomas. "Bernie Sanders Wins Oregon; Hillary Clinton Declares Victory in Kentucky." *The New York Times,* 17 May 2016, www.nytimes.com/2016/05/18/us/politics/bernie-sanders-oregon-results.html. Accessed 17 May 2016.

40. journal articles: The basic principles are the same as with magazine articles, but entries for journal articles include the volume and issue numbers.

> Roy, Indrani. "Irony and Derision in Congreve's *The Way of the World.*" *PMLA,* vol. 120, no.6, 2005, pp. 60–72.

If you are citing an online version of a journal article you should include the date you accessed the site, as well as any additional containers and their publication details (databases, for example).

Sohmer, Steve. "12 June 1599: Opening Day at Shakespeare's Globe." *Early Modern Literary Studies: A Journal of Sixteenth- and Seventeenth-Century English Literature*, vol. 3, no.1, 1997. *ProQuest*, www.extra.shu.ac.uk/emls/emlshome.html. Accessed 18 May 2016.

41. book reviews: The name of the reviewer (if it has been provided) should come first, followed by the title of the review (if there is one), and the information on the book itself.

Leiter, Brian, and Michael Weisberg. "Do You Only Have a Brain? On Thomas Nagel." Review of *Why the Materialist Neo-Darwinian Conception of Nature Is Almost Certainly False*, by Thomas Nagel, *The Nation*, 22 Oct. 2012, www.thenation.com/article/do-you-only-have-brain-thomas-nagel/. Accessed 22 Oct. 2012.

Wills, Garry. "A Masterpiece on the Rise of Christianity." Review of *Through the Eye of a Needle: Wealth, The Fall of Rome, and the Making of Christianity in the West, 350–550 AD*, by Peter Brown, *New York Review of Books*, 11 Oct. 2012, pp. 43–45.

42. periodical publications in online databases:

Hill, Katherine C. "Virginia Woolf and Leslie Stephen: History and Literary Revolution." *PMLA*, vol. 96, no.3, 1981, pp. 351–62. *JSTOR*, www.jstor.org/stable/461911. Accessed 6 Oct. 2012.

43. illustrated books: Include the illustrator's name as well as the author's name.

Juster, Norman. *The Phantom Tollbooth*. Illustrated by Jules Feiffer, Yearling-Random House, 1961.

44. graphic narratives: In many graphic narratives, both the illustrations and the text are created by one person; these kinds of works should be documented as in the first example below. Use the second example's format for works whose text is by one person and illustrations by another.

Leavitt, Sarah. *Tangles: A Story about Alzheimer's, My Mother, and Me*. Freehand Books, 2010.

Pekar, Harvey. *Ego and Hubris: The Michael Malice Story*. Art by Gary Dumm, Ballantine-Random House, 2006.

45. films or television episodes: These entries may be tailored to the context in which you are citing the work. If you are discussing the work of a director, for example, place the director's name in the Author element:

> Zeitlin, Behn, director. *Beasts of the Southern Wild.* Performances by Quvenzhané Wallis and Dwight Henry, Fox Searchlight, 2012.
>
> Medak, Peter, director. "The Buys." *The Wire*, created by David Simon and Ed Burns, season 1, episode 3, HBO, 16 June 2002.

If you are discussing a particular performance, place the actor's name in the Author element.

> Moss, Elizabeth, performer. "A Little Kiss." *Mad Men*, directed by Jennifer Getzinger, AMC, 25 Mar. 2012.
>
> Spacey, Kevin, performer. "Chapter 5." *House of Cards*, directed by Joel Schumacher, season 1, episode 5. *Netflix*, www.netflix.com/search/house?jbv=70178217&jbp=0.

46. online videos: If your source is a video on a website, cite, if you can, who uploaded the video, and the date on which the video was posted.

> Gleeson, Thomas, director. "Home." Screen Innovation Production Fund, 2012. *Vimeo*, uploaded by Thomas Gleeson, 31 Jan. 2013, www.vimeo.com/58630796.

47. radio broadcasts:

> "Glenn Gould Special." *The Sunday Edition*, narrated by Robert Harris and Michael Enright, CBC Radio One, 23 Sept. 2012.

48. podcasts:

> "Too Old to Be Governable Too Young to Die Edition." *Slate's Culture Gabfest*, narrated by Stephen Metcalf, Julia Turner, and Laura Miller, 18 May 2016, www.slate.com/articles/podcasts/culturegabfest/2016/05/. Accessed 18 May 2016.

49. recorded music:

> Williams, Lucinda. "Real Love." *Little Honey*, Lost Highway, 2008.

50. live performances: If you are citing a live performance or lecture, include the physical location and the city where the performance or lecture was delivered, as well as the date. Omit the city name if it is part of the location name. Include other information about the performance—the names of the director, the conductor, and/or lead performers, for instance—where such information is relevant. If your work focuses on the contribution of a performance's director, for example, cite that person in the Author element. Other important contributors follow the title in the Other Contributors element.

> Bedford, Brian, director. *The Importance of Being Earnest*, by Oscar Wilde. Performances by Brian Bedford, Santino Fontana, David Furr, Charlotte Parry, and Sarah Topham, Roundabout Theatre Company, American Airlines Theatre, New York. 3 July 2011.
>
> MacMillan, Margaret. "Hubris." *History's People: Personalities and the Past*, Arts and Culture Centre, St. John's NL, 25 Sept. 2015, 7:00 p.m. Massey Lecture.

51. works of visual art: When citing a physical object you have experienced, such as a work of art, provide in the Location element the name of the institution and city where you experienced it. Leave out the name of the city if the city name is part of the institution name (e.g., Art Institute of Chicago).

> Housser, Yvonne McKague. *Cobalt*. 1931. National Gallery of Canada, Ottawa.
>
> Sargent, John Singer. *Henry James*. 1913. National Portrait Gallery, London.

If you access a work of art online or in a book, you should include full information about the website or volume you consulted.

> Colquhoun, Ithell. *Scylla*. 1938. Tate Gallery, London. *Tate Women Artists*, by Alicia Foster, Tate, 2004, p. 85.
>
> Giotto di Bondone. *Lamentation*. 1304–06. Capella Scrovegni, Padua, *Web Gallery of Art*, www.wga.hu/frames-e.html?/html/g/giotto/. Accessed 29 Jan. 2013.

52. interviews: Begin all entries for interviews with the name of the person being interviewed, and if there is a title for the interview, include it (in quotation marks if it is part of another work, or in italics if it has been published by itself). If there is no title, or if the title does not make clear that the work is an interview, write *Interview*, and give the name of the interviewer, if known. Finish with whatever publication information is appropriate. If you conducted the interview yourself, give the name of the person you interviewed, the medium (*Personal interview, Telephone interview*), and the date.

> Erdrich, Louise. Interview by Bill Moyers, *Bill Moyers Journal*, PBS, 9 Apr. 2010, www.pbs.org/moyers/journal/04092010/watch2.html. Accessed 16 Jan. 2013.
>
> Nelson, Willie. "The Silver-Headed Stranger." Interview by Andrew Goldman, *New York Times Magazine,* 16 Dec. 2012, p. 12.
>
> Rosengarten, Herbert. Personal interview, 21 Jan. 2013.

53. online projects: In the case of large projects, cite the full range of years during which the project has been developed:

> Secord, James A., et al., editors. *Darwin Correspondence Project.* 1974–2016, www.darwinproject.ac.uk/.
>
> Willett, Perry, editor. *Victorian Women Writers Project.* Indiana University Digital Library Program, 1995–2016, webapp1/dlib.indiana.edu/vwwp/welcome.do. Accessed 26 Nov. 2012.

54. e-books: E-books should be documented according to the same principles as other digital media. Make sure to add a Container element citing the digital platform from which the e-book has been accessed or downloaded.

> Austen, Jane. *Pride and Prejudice.* 1813. *Project Gutenberg,* 2008, www.gutenberg.org/files/1342/1342-h/1342-h.htm. Accessed 20 Feb. 2016.
>
> Emerson, Ralph Waldo. *The American Scholar.* 1837. *American Transcendentalism Web*, ed. Ann Woodlief, Virginia Commonwealth U, 1999, www.transcendentalism-legacy.edu/authors/emerson/essays/amscholar.html. Accessed 16 Mar. 2013.

Herman, Jonathan R. *I and Tao: Martin Buber's Encounter with Chuang Tzu.* State U of New York P, 1996. *Google Books*, books.google.ca/books?id=l1U10Ei8ob0C. Downloaded 30 May 2015.

Shakespeare, William. *As You Like It.* Edited by David Bevington, Broadview Press, 2012. *Broadview Press*, www.broadview-press.com/product/as-you-like-it/#tab-description. Downloaded 3 Mar. 2016.

55. information databases:

Gaston, Craig. "Consumption-related greenhouse gas emissions in Canada, the United States and China." *Statistics Canada*, 8 Dec. 2011, www.statcan.gc.ca/pub/16-002-x/2011004/part-partie4-eng.htm. Accessed 17 Apr. 2016.

56. entry in a wiki: Wikis are online sites that can be added to and edited by any site user; as such, they may be subject to frequent changes made by any number of authors and editors. Do not, therefore, provide any authors' names. Start with the entry's title; then give the name of the wiki, the site publisher, the date of the entry's last update, the medium, and the date you accessed the site.

"William Caxton." *Wikipedia.* Wikimedia Foundation, 20 Oct. 2012, www.en.wikipedia.org/wiki/William_Caxton. Accessed 26 Oct. 2012.

57. blog post: Include the title of the posting as your source title, the blog title as the first container, and the name of the blog host as a publisher.

LePan, Don. "Reading and Writing and Work." *Animals, Rising Stories, Etc.*, Blogspot, 21 May 2016, www.donlepan.blogspot.ca. Accessed 24 May 2016.

58. e-mail message: Use the subject as the title and place it within quotation marks.

Milton, Frank. "Thoughts on Animal Rights." Received by the author, 15 Jan. 2013.

If it is not clear from the context of your work that the source being cited is an e-mail, you may wish to add an optional element to the end of your citation that indicates the type of work.

> Stuart, Jennifer. "My Experience of the Attack." Received by the author, 17 May 2016. E-mail.

59. tweet: Copy the full, unchanged text of the tweet in the title element and enclose it in quotation marks. The username is included as the Author element.

> @newyorker. "With the resignation of Turkey's Prime Minister, the country's President now stands alone and unchallenged." *Twitter*, 6 May 2016, twitter.com/NewYorker/status/728676985254379520.

60. comment posted on a web page: Usernames are given in full, unchanged. If the comment is anonymous, skip the author element. If the comment does not have its own title, provide instead a description of the comment that includes the title of the work being commented on (e.g., Comment on "Clinton Aims for Decisive Victory"). If it is available, include the exact time of posting in the Publication Date element.

> Evan. Comment on "Another Impasse on Gun Bills, Another Win for Hyperpolitics." *The New York Times*, 21 June 2016, 9:02 a.m., www.nytimes.com/2016/06/22/us/politics/washington-congress-gun-control.html.

O MLA Style Sample Essay

Following is a sample essay written in MLA style. Note that further sample essays, some of which also employ MLA style, are available on the companion website associated with this book.

What Limits to Freedom?

Freedom of Expression and the Brooklyn Museum's

"Sensation" Exhibit

by Melissa Davis

Prof. K. D. Smith

Humanities 205

16 June 2015

cover page (not required in MLA style, but may be required by some instructors)

all text centred

Melissa Davis

Professor Smith

Humanities 205

16 June 2015

name
and page
number in
top right
corner

What Limits to Freedom?

Freedom of Expression and the Brooklyn Museum's

"Sensation" Exhibit

first line
of all
paragraphs
indented

    For over a century public galleries in Western democracies have

been forums not only for displaying works by "old Masters" but also

for presenting art that is new, as well as ideas that are sometimes

radical and controversial. In the United States that tradition has

been under wide attack in the past generation. Various political and

religious leaders have criticized exhibits of works of art that they claim

offend against notions of public decency, and have crusaded against

text left-
justified
and
ragged
right

providing public funding for the creation or display of such works.

The largest such controversy of the past generation was sparked by

the display of a painting entitled "The Holy Virgin Mary," by the

British artist Chris Ofili at the Brooklyn Museum in 1999. Though

the image appears inoffensive at a distance, the artist has affixed

to the painting cutouts of body parts from magazines, and has

text
double-
spaced
through-
out

incorporated clumps of elephant dung into the piece, both below

the main body of the work as if supporting it and as part of the

collage. The uproar that surrounded the painting's exhibition led

Davis 2

both to a widely publicized court case and to an ongoing campaign to support "decency" in artistic expression. Should such art be banned? Should it be exhibited at public expense? In the course of the Ofili controversy cultural conservatives raised legitimate concerns about the obligation of any society to provide funding for activities of which it disapproves. This essay will argue, however, that the greater concern is in the other direction; a free society must continue to provide opportunities for the free expression both of artistic vision and of controversial thought.

The Ofili piece was part of a much-hyped exhibit entitled "Sensation: Young British Artists from the Saatchi Collection." As the title indicated, the show was made up entirely of works from one collection, that of the wealthy British advertising executive Charles Saatchi.[1] The exhibition had been shown first at the Royal Academy of Arts in London and then at a major gallery in Berlin. (In London what sparked controversy was not Ofili's work but rather a realistic painting by Marcus Harvey of child-murderer Myra Hindley that incorporated hundreds of children's handprints into the image.) Bringing the show to Brooklyn cost one million dollars—a cost covered in part by Christie's, a London auctioneer—and from the outset it could be argued that the museum was courting controversy. It claimed in its advertising that the exhibition "may cause shock,

first paragraph ends with a statement of the essay's thesis

2

numbered note for additional information provided as an aside

Davis 3

paren-
thetical
reference;
Internet
source
has no
page
number

vomiting, confusion, panic, euphoria, and anxiety. If you suffer from high blood pressure, a nervous disorder, or palpitations, you should consult your doctor" (qtd. in Barry and Vogel).

No doubt that warning was tongue-in-cheek, but there was nothing ironic about the angry reactions provoked by the show in general and directed toward the Ofili piece in particular. On one side

italics
used for
titles of
books,
news-
papers,
journals,
etc.

art critics and civil libertarians were full of praise; in *The New York Times* the work was praised as "colourful and glowing" (Kimmelman). On the other side John Cardinal O'Connor called it "an attack on religion," and the president of the Catholic League for Religious and Civil Rights called on citizens to picket the exhibition (Vogel). The United States Senate and the House of Representatives both passed

3

resolutions condemning the exhibit. Even more vehement was the response of New York Mayor Rudy Giuliani; he declared himself "offended" and the work itself "disgusting" (Barry and Vogel). As Peter Cramer has detailed, Giuliani's comments received widespread attention in the press—especially the informal remark "I mean, this

paren-
thetical
references
at end
of short
quotations
followed
by punc-
tuation

is like, sick stuff," from which the phrase "sick stuff" was extracted for repeated circulation. But Giuliani and Deputy Mayor Joseph J. Lhota, the city administration's "enforcer in the case" (Barbaro 2), did much more than comment. They ordered that ongoing city funding of the museum be withheld until the offensive work was

Davis 4

removed, and launched eviction proceedings against the museum. Other conservative politicians—then-Texas Governor George W. Bush prominent among them—spoke out in support of Giuliani's stand ("Bush Backs Giuliani").

What was the substance of Mayor Giuliani's case? Here is how he explained his stance to the press:

> You don't have a right to a government subsidy to desecrate someone else's religion. And therefore we will do everything that we can to remove funding from the [museum] until the director comes to his senses and realizes that if you are a government subsidized enterprise then you can't do things that desecrate the most personal and deeply held views of people in society. (Brooklyn Institute of Arts and Sciences v. City of New York 7)

In Giuliani's view, the constitution's guarantee of freedom of speech was not the central issue:

> "If somebody wants to do that privately and pay for that privately . . . that's what the First Amendment is all about," he said. "You can be offended by it and upset by it, and you don't have to go see it, if somebody else is paying for it. But to have the government subsidize something like that is outrageous."
> (qtd. in Vogel)

The issue for Giuliani, then, is not one of censorship per se. He is

4

long quotations indented—no quotation marks used except for quotation within a quotation

Davis 5

not arguing that works of art should be banned for causing offense to
a significant segment of the public; it is merely the provision of any
government funding for such activity that he finds "outrageous."

5   But is it in fact outrageous? Let us examine the implications of
Giuliani's argument. According to him, government should never
provide funding for activities that some people may find deeply
offensive. But governments have long funded much artistic and
intellectual activity in advance on the grounds that such activity
in general represents a social good, without knowing precisely
what sort of artistic work will be created or exhibited, what results
academic research may come up with, and so on. If such funding
were to be always contingent on no one ever being deeply offended
by the results of the artistic or intellectual activity, the effect would
be to severely damage freedom of speech and expression. (Here it is
important to note that the actions Giuliani took were retroactive; the
annual funding for the museum had not been provided with strings
attached.[2])

6   Social conservatives are often characterized as favouring
censorship of any material they find offensive; to be fair, that is
clearly not the position Giuliani takes here. Nor is the issue whether
or not the material is offensive; Hillary Clinton, for example, agreed
that works such as that by Ofili were "objectionable" and "offensive"

Davis 6

(qtd. in Nagourney), while opposing any punitive actions against the museum. Rather, the issue at stake is under what conditions government has an obligation to fund controversial artistic or intellectual activity. At issue here are both a quite narrow and specific question, and a much broader one. The narrow question is this: to what degree must public officials be held to prior commitments of the sort that were involved in this case?

To this question at least, it does not seem difficult to find an answer: a continuing obligation surely does indeed exist where a prior commitment has been made. As Judge Nina Gershon put it in her eventual ruling on the case,

> the issue is . . . whether the museum, having been allocated a general operating subsidy, can now be penalized with the loss of that subsidy, and ejectment from a City-owned building, because of the perceived viewpoint of the works in that exhibit. The answer to that question is no. (Brooklyn Institute v. City of New York 17)

Where such a commitment has been made, it can only be fairly broken if the activity has in some way contravened previously agreed-on guidelines or if it has broken the law. If, for example, a work of art or of literature is thought to violate laws against obscenity, laws concerning hate crimes, laws concerning libel and slander—or,

7

sentence structured so that it flows grammatically into quotation

indeed, laws concerning cruelty to animals, as in the cases of certain "works of art" in recent years[3]—then legal recourse is available. But not even the most vociferous of the opponents of the "Sensation" exhibit suggested that Ofili, the curators, or anyone else had broken the law. Moreover, the ongoing funding for the Museum had never been made contingent on the institution's exhibits never offending anyone. There were therefore no just grounds for taking punitive action as Giuliani did.

8   But how much further than this should the obligation of government to fund controversial artistic or intellectual activity extend? Here we come to the broader issue: do governments have a general obligation to support and to fund such activity? The tradition of government support for artistic and intellectual activity in Western democracies has for many generations been one in which support was provided at "arm's length" from the political process; if judgements based on the merit of individual works need be made, they are typically made by bodies independent of government. That approach has stemmed from a number of sensible general principles. One such principle has been a recognition of the inherent value of intellectual and artistic activity. Another has been a recognition that such activity will sometimes be challenging, disturbing, even offensive or disgusting.[4] And a third has been that if politicians are involved

no citation needed for information that is common knowledge

Davis 8

in judging individual artistic or intellectual works, the judgements will tend to be made more on political and religious grounds than on intellectual and aesthetic ones. We value a society in which a wide range of free expression is supported, and we have come to expect that governments will provide a good deal of that support.

Despite the general support for these principles that exists in our society, we should not assume an unlimited obligation on the part of government. In particular, liberals and civil libertarians are unwise if they suggest that the obligation of the government to support artistic or intellectual endeavour is always a strong and compelling one, or that any failure of a government to provide financial support for such endeavour somehow constitutes censorship.[5] There is no clear agreement as to what constitutes art; it follows that there can be no legal or moral obligation to fund everything that may be classified as art. And to decide in advance not to subsidize an activity is not the same as censoring that activity; civil libertarians do not advance their case by equating the two. Indeed, as philosopher Peter Levine has pointed out, attempts to remove all restrictions on government support can easily backfire, since the law

cannot compel governments to subsidize art in the first place. When the Supreme Court ruled in 1998 that individual artists may not be denied federal grants because of the content of

9

Davis 9

their work, Congress simply cancelled all support for individual artists. (20)

It is never wise, then, for the artistic and intellectual communities to press too hard for unrestricted government support.

10   It is perhaps an even greater mistake, however, for cultural conservatives to seek to restrict government support to work that conforms to their definition of "decency." The moral obligation of government to support a broad range of artistic and intellectual expression may be a relatively weak one, but if we cast it aside we are choosing to narrow ourselves, to discourage rather than encourage the sorts of challenge from new ideas and new artistic expressions that continually replenish the red blood cells of democratic society.

11   In approaching such questions we should ask ourselves what really constitutes freedom of thought, speech, and expression. One defining pillar is legal: constitutional guarantees of freedom and the case law that has helped to define them.[6] But is that all there is to it? A moment's reflection should make it clear that a great deal else is involved. Regardless of what is allowed or prohibited, if there exists a scarcity of art galleries—or of book publishers, or of academic journals, or of newspapers, or of radio and television stations—that are willing to put forward original and controversial works of art, or works of scholarly research, or political treatises, then freedom of

Davis 10

speech and expression is *in practice* severely limited.⁷ And economic

reality dictates that a number of valued activities, including academic

research as well as many of the arts, would be severely curtailed

without some degree of public funding. If we choose as a society

not to fund such activities we will inevitably be erecting real barriers

against freedom of speech and expression, even if we have passed no

laws restricting such freedoms. That is the reality at the heart of the

"Sensation" controversy.

It is interesting that in the midst of the controversy Ofili's work

itself became oddly invisible, lost in the clamour of arguments from

principle on both sides of the debate. Photographic representations

of "Holy Virgin Mary" are widely available on the Web,⁸ and viewers

coming to these after sampling the heat of the arguments surrounding

the piece are likely to be surprised by how calm and pleasant an image

is presented to them. Ofili himself was the recipient of the prestigious

Turner Prize in 1998 and was already becoming widely recognized

as one of the most important of his generation of British artists.

Fairly typical are the comments of a writer in *Art in America*, one of

the most authoritative journals of contemporary art criticism: "his

paintings are a joy to behold. . . . His technique, as it becomes ever

richer and more complex, is developing an emotional range to match

its decorative facility" (MacRitchie 97). The painter, who was born in

Davis 11

Britain to parents of Nigerian background, was raised a church-going Catholic—and remained so at the time he painted the controversial work. (Clearly critics' claims that "The Holy Virgin Mary" is offensive to Catholics cannot be true of all Catholics!)

13   Ofili has spoken interestingly of how in his art of that period he drew connections between the subjects of his work and the materials he used, including shiny varnish to make it seem that the subject of a painting is "in some ways more imagined than real" (Vogel), and, of course, the notorious balls of elephant dung that adorn the work and on which it rests.[9] Significantly, during that stage of his career Ofili incorporated dung into many of his works, including those portraying slaves and other African subjects. As Arthur C. Danto has pointed out, "since it is unlikely that as a black Anglo-African Ofili would have used dung to besmirch the slaves [in the picture "Afrobluff"], there is no reason to suppose he was bent on besmirching the Holy Virgin through its presence there either" (2). From one angle, Ofili clearly saw the use of dung as a way of connecting his paintings to his African heritage and of giving the paintings "a feeling that they've come from the earth" (Vogel). But his art of that period was also drawing connections between the superficially appealing nature of his images and the inherent unpleasantness of some of the materials he has used to create them:

quotation with author named in signal phrase; page number in parentheses

Davis 12

"The paintings themselves are very delicate abstractions, and
I wanted to bring their beauty and decorativeness together
with the ugliness of shit[10] and make them exist in a twilight
zone—you know they're together, but you can't really ever feel
comfortable about it." (qtd. in "Sensation")

title cited
when work
has no
attributed
author

Ofili's intention, in short, was to create a disturbing tension in the
mind of the viewer.

One does not need to endorse all of Ofili's theorizing about what
he does, or agree fully with the favourable assessments of the critics,
in order to conclude that it would be unreasonable not to classify his
work as art. Even the narrowest and most conservative definitions
of art allow the term to be applied to work that many people find
pleasing to the eye and that many agree demonstrates creative skill.
Ofili's work unquestionably fulfills those criteria. More than that,
there is evidently a good deal of subtlety and nuance to both the
work and the ideas of this painter, far more than the polarized debate
swirling around the painting might suggest. Even if some find this
art offensive, it is hard not to think that on its merits Ofili's work
deserves to be widely exhibited.

14

In a narrow sense the controversy of the Ofili work and the
"Sensation" exhibit ended with a clear victory for the Brooklyn
Museum. Federal Judge Nina Gershon ruled that in these

15

circumstances the City of New York's attempt to shut down the exhibit constituted a violation of the First Amendment—the Constitutional guarantee of freedom of expression—and in March of 2000 the City and the museum reached an agreement under the terms of which all further lawsuits were dropped and the City agreed to contribute 5.8 million dollars towards a museum restoration project. (The museum re-opened in 2004 after the completion of restorations.)

16   In a wider sense, however, the outcome is far less certain. In 2001 Mayor Giuliani attempted to develop "decency standards" intended to restrict these sorts of works from being shown in future in publicly funded exhibitions, and such initiatives received strong support from the administration of George W. Bush. Among certain commentators the crusade against Ofili continued unabated long after the exhibit itself had ended. Phyllis Schlafly is one such crusader (2004); Tammy Bruce is another. In her best-selling book *The Death of Right and Wrong*, for example, Bruce used the case as an example in urging us to "make no mistake: the degrading of symbols important to Christianity is . . . propaganda meant to change your view of Christianity as a whole" (52).

17   Given the virulence of attacks of this sort, it would have been extraordinary had major museums and galleries not begun to back away from mounting exhibitions of work that they considered

Davis 14

likely to be controversial. Tellingly, the "Sensation" exhibit was never
seen after it closed in Brooklyn; the National Gallery of Australia
cancelled its plans to show the exhibit, and a Tokyo museum that had
expressed interest in exhibiting it thereafter did not in the end make
any commitment (Rosenbaum 41). In 2008, the San Francisco Art
Institute closed Adel Abdessemed's controversial "Don't Trust Me"
show after only a few days "for safety reasons" (DeBare B1) in the face
of protests by animals' rights groups and some artists, though there
had been no suggestion that any law had been broken, and though
condemnation of the show had been far from universal.[11]

    Since 2008 controversies of this sort have been less common
in North America at public galleries and museums.[12] In the United
States, at least, that may have to do in part with a change in tone from
the federal government under the Obama administration. No doubt
in part it may also have to do with changes in tone in the world of
contemporary art; the urge to shock seems less widespread among
artists now than it was in the last decades of the twentieth century.
But it may well be that public galleries in North America have become
reluctant to risk being attacked in the way the Brooklyn Museum was
attacked over "Sensation."[13] It is striking that the most controversial
exhibit in any public gallery in recent years was not in any of the
great museums and galleries of the western democracies that have

page
number
follows
author's
name in
paren-
thetical
reference

18

Davis 15

long prided themselves on their openness. It was the historically staid Hermitage Museum in St Petersburg, Russia, that risked the wrath of the socially conservative citizenry by mounting the Chapman brothers' "End of Fun" exhibition in 2012.[14]

19   In theory at least, public institutions in the United States, Canada and Britain—universities and colleges[15] as well as museums and galleries—have far more legal room than do those in partially free countries such as Russia to risk controversy. But freedom of expression is never only a matter of what is or is not legal. The preservation of a truly open society requires, on the part of those who wish to allow and to encourage freedom of expression, a moral determination that is at least as strong as the moral determination of those who wish to roll back its frontiers. Much as constitutional guarantees of freedom of expression are important, even more so is whether we wish as a society to narrow the range of what citizens may readily see or hear, or instead to encourage the wide dissemination of information, opinion, and artistic expression—even opinions and artistic expressions that some may find offensive. In the years following the September 11, 2001 attack, it was understandable that many both within the United States and around the world were prepared to accept some extraordinary new restrictions on freedom—and many, of course, argue that the need for such restrictions remains. But whatever security justifications there

final paragraph restates and broadens the essay's main argument

Davis 16

may be for such restrictions do not extend to the sphere of intellectual and artistic activity. If we wish to retain a robustly democratic society we should continue to choose the path of openness.

Davis 17

Notes

1. Saatchi contributed $100,000 to mounting the show, the
economics of which became another subject for controversy when it
was shown in Brooklyn. As well as complaining about the content of
the works in the exhibit, Mayor Rudy Giuliani and others suggested
that the show had been intended in large part to raise the value of
works in the Saatchi collection, and on those grounds, too, argued
that the exhibit should not be receiving a subsidy from taxpayers.

2. Because its content was recognized as controversial, city
officials had been provided in advance of the "Sensation" show with
photographs and full descriptions of all pieces to be included in the
exhibit, including the information that Ofili's works incorporated
elephant dung into the images they portrayed. The mayor insisted
that he personally had not been alerted to the content of the show
beforehand, however.

3. Animal rights activists have protested against works by the
renowned British artist Damien Hirst, which present, among other
things, a sectioned cow and a bisected pig in formaldehyde cases.
(Several such works by Hirst were included in the "Sensation" show.)
In Toronto, art student Jesse Power and two friends pleaded guilty in
2001 to charges of animal cruelty and public mischief after making

*notes
numbered
as in text*

*each note
indented*

Davis 18

what they called an art video recording their torturing and killing a cat; the case again aroused controversy in 2004 following the release of a documentary film about the incident, *Casuistry: The Art of Killing a Cat*, directed by Noah Cowan and Piers Handling. See also the articles by Christie Blatchford and by Gayle MacDonald, Note 11 below on the 2008 "Don't Trust Me" exhibition in San Francisco, and Note 15 below on the 2013 ACAD controversy in Calgary.

4. There are many defenses of the principle that an open society must make a place even for controversial or disgusting material. The case for the other side is put by John Kekes in *A Case for Conservatism*; he argues for what he terms "the moral importance of disgust" (100–109).

5. To be fair, although some individuals make assertions as extreme as this one, responsible civil liberties organizations such as the ACLU stop short of any such all-embracing claim.

6. The First Amendment to the American Constitution specifies that Congress "shall make no law . . . abridging the freedom of speech, or of the press; or the right of the people to assemble. . . ." In American legal practice it has long been established that "freedom of speech" should also cover other forms of expression—such as artistic works. Other, more recent constitutions tend to make such protections explicit; the Charter of Rights and Freedoms that forms a central part of the Canadian Constitution, for example, protects

Davis 19

"freedom of thought, belief, opinion, and expression, including
freedom of the press and other media of communication."

7. A good example of how such freedoms may be constrained
is the March 2003 case in which Natalie Maines of the Dixie Chicks
criticized George W. Bush—and promptly found that two media
conglomerates controlling over 1,300 radio stations refused to play
Dixie Chicks music. That case is discussed by Robert B. Reich in
Reason: Why Liberals Will Win the Battle for America.

8. Among the many Web addresses at which photographs of the
work may be found are www.artsjournal.com/issues/Brooklyn.htm
and www.postmedia.net/999/ofili.htm and www.brooklynmuseum.org/
opencollection/exhibitions/683.

9. Many who have attacked the piece have chosen to describe
the dung as being "*smeared* on a Christian icon" (Bruce 39, my
italics), which is substantially to misrepresent the nature of the work.

10. It is interesting to contemplate the impact diction may
have on arguments such as this; it is difficult not to respond slightly
differently depending on whether the material is referred to using the
noun Ofili uses here or referred to less provocatively as "dung."

11. The show included video clips of the killing of animals in
rural Mexico. The artist had evidently not arranged for the killings;
he was merely recording local practice. For more on this and other

Davis 20

recent controversies, see the articles by Kenneth Baker and Phoebe
Hoban.

12. Such controversies have been more common at private
galleries, which do not run the risk of losing public funding, and
which may even gain desired publicity from them. Notable private
gallery controversies have occurred, for example, in 2010, when a
protestor attacked a work associating Christianity with cannibalism
at the Loveland Museum/Gallery in Colorado; and in 2012, when
the Catholic League deplored the showing of Andres Serrano's 1980s
work "Piss Christ" at a private gallery in New York.

13. It is noteworthy that, when Ofili's "The Holy Virgin Mary"
was again exhibited in the New York area in 2014–15, it was at the
New Museum—a privately owned gallery, not a public institution.
The exhibition was greeted by rave reviews (see Smith and Tomkins),
and little or no controversy. Perhaps in large part because Ofili's
reputation as an artist of the first rank has continued to grow, "The
Holy Virgin Mary" no longer seems to elicit such a vitriolic response.
That much, at least, has changed over time. What has not changed
since the close of the "Sensation" exhibit, though, is the reluctance
of North American public institutions to mount shows that court
controversy. In fact, the painting has been exhibited only once in a
major public institution since the "Sensation" controversy—as part

of an Ofili retrospective at the Tate Modern in London in 2010. (The
painting now belongs to David Walsh, owner of a private gallery in
Hobart, Australia, where it is frequently on display.)

14. Among the objects included in the exhibition were a
crucified image of Ronald McDonald and human figures forming
swastika shapes. Hundreds of complaints regarding alleged blasphemy
were made to the authorities. Legally, the issue was whether the
exhibit violated a law against the incitement of hatred; two members
of the group Pussy Riot were jailed under the provisions of the same
law in 2012. For accounts and discussion see Brooks, and Elder.

15. The twenty-first century reluctance in much of the western
world to risk controversy over works of art has not been confined
to galleries and museums; it has also become common in other
areas of the art world. Art education is an important case in point.
In theory, art educators have a great deal of freedom to share and
discuss controversial work with their students. In practice, as David
Darts has shown, in many jurisdictions "the threat of termination or
worse [is] a very real possibility for art teachers who stray from ultra-
conservative curricula, or who engage in the production of potentially
controversial artwork" (115).

One highly controversial incident that received considerable
coverage in Canada occurred in Calgary, Alberta, in 2013. A student

Davis 22

at the Alberta College of Art and Design brought a live chicken into the college cafeteria and proceeded to cut off her head, drain the blood, and wash and pluck the bird, all as part of a performance art project intended by the artist to draw attention to "the connection between animals and the food we eat" (qtd. in Schmidt). The project had been approved in advance by an ACAD faculty member; police interviewed the student and the faculty member and declined to press charges under animal cruelty legislation. Three weeks after the incident occurred, however, the college fired the professor who had given his student the go-ahead on the project. For more on the controversy see the articles by Samantha Escobar, Manisha Krishnan, Colleen Schmidt, and Sherri Zickenfoose.

Davis 23

Works Cited

Associated Press. "Bush Backs Giuliani on Museum Flap." *Washington Post,* 4 Oct. 1999, www.washingtonpost.com/wp-srv/aponline/19991004/aponline163720_000.htm. Accessed 20 May 2015.

Baker, Kenneth. "Show's Cancellation a Rare Case of Artists Advocating Censorship." *San Francisco Chronicle,* 1 Apr. 2008, p. E1.

Barbaro, Michael. "For Mayoral Hopeful Who Lost Fight to Remove Art, No Regrets." *New York Times,* 27 March 2013, www.nytimes.com/2013/03/28/nyregion/for-lhota-mayoral-hopeful-who-lost-fight-to-remove-art-no-regrets.html?_r=0. Accessed 14 May 2015.

Barry, Dan, and Carol Vogel. "Giuliani Vows to Cut Subsidy over Art He Calls Offensive." *New York Times,* 23 Sept. 1999, partners.nytimes.com/library/arts/092399brooklyn-museum-funds.html. Accessed 20 May 2015.

Blatchford, Christie. "Face to Face with Cruelty." *Globe and Mail,* 4 Sept. 2004, p. A13.

Brooklyn Institute of Arts and Sciences v. City of New York 99CV 6071. *National Coalition Against Censorship,* 1 Nov. 1999, ncac.org/resource/brooklyn-institute-of-arts-and-sciences-v-city-of-new-york. Accessed 2 May 2015.

Brooks, Katherine. "Russia's Hermitage Museum Under Investiga-

each entry begins at left margin; subsequent lines are indented

works cited are listed alphabetically

Davis 24

tion For 'Blasphemous' Jake and Dinos Chapman Exhibit."

Huffington Post, 11 Dec. 2012, www.huffingtonpost.com/2012/

12/11/hermitage-museum-blasphemy-investigation-jake-and-

dinos-chapman_n_2272987.html. Accessed 3 May 2015.

Bruce, Tammy. *The Death of Right and Wrong.* Three Rivers Press,

2003.

Catholic League. "Piss-Christ Coming to New York." *Catholic*

League for Civil and Religious Rights, 21 Sept. 2012,

www.catholicleague.org/piss-christ-coming-to-nyc/. Accessed

19 May 2015.

Cramer, Peter. "Sick Stuff: A Case Study of Controversy in a

Constitutive Attitude." *Rhetoric Society Quarterly,* vol. 43,

no. 2, 2013, pp. 177–201. Taylor & Francis Online, DOI:

10.1080/02773945.2013.768352. Accessed 21 May 2015.

Danto, Arthur C. "'Sensation' in Brooklyn." *The Nation,* 1 Nov.

1999, www.thenation.com/article/sensation-brooklyn/. Accessed

4 May 2015.

Darts, David. "The Art of Culture War: (Un)Popular Culture, Free-

dom of Expression, and Art Education." *Studies in Art Educa-*

tion, vol. 49, no. 2, Winter 2008, pp. 103–21. JSTOR,

www.jstor.org/stable/25475862. Accessed 3 May 2015.

DeBare, Ilana. "Art Institute Halts Exhibition Showing Killing of

Animals. " *San Francisco Chronicle,* 30 Mar. 2008, p. B1.

Elder, Miriam. "Russian Museum Could Be Prosecuted over Chap-

double
spacing
used
through-
out

italics
used for
titles of
books,
journals,
magazines,
etc.

Davis 25

man Brothers Exhibit." *The Guardian,* 7 Dec. 2012, www.the-
guardian.com/ world/2012/dec/07/russian-museum-chapman-
brothers. Accessed 3 May 2013.

Escobar, Samantha. "Professor Fired after Student Kills Chicken in
School Cafeteria as 'Performance Art.'" *Blisstree,* 18 Apr. 2013,
www.blisstree.com/2013/05/14/food/professor-fired-after-
student-kills-chicken-at-school-as-art/. Accessed 19 May 2015.

Hoban, Phoebe. "How Far Is Too Far?" *ArtNews,* Summer 2008, pp.
145–49.

Kekes, John. *A Case for Conservatism.* Ithaca, Cornell UP, 1988.

Kimmelman, Michael. "A Madonna's Many Meanings in the Art
World." *New York Times,* 5 Oct. 1999, www.nytimes.com/
1999/10/05/arts/critic-s-notebook-a-madonna-s-many-mean-
ings-in-the-art-world.html. Accessed 20 May 2015.

Krishnan, Manisha. "Calgary Art Student Kills Chicken in College
Cafeteria." *Macleans,* 19 April 2013, www.macleans.ca/educa-
tion/uniandcollege/calgary-art-student-kills-chicken-in-college-
cafeteria/. Accessed 21 May 2015.

Levine, Peter. "Lessons from the Brooklyn Museum Controversy."
Philosophy and Public Policy Quarterly, vol. 20, no. 2/3, Summer,
2000, pp. 19–27.

MacDonald, Gayle. "TIFF Contacts Police over Death Threat: Caller
Threatens Programmer over Cat-Killer Documentary." *Globe and
Mail,* 1 Sept. 2004, p. R1.

Davis 26

MacRitchie, Lynn. "Ofili's Glittering Icons." *Art in America,* Jan. 2000,
pp. 96–101.

Mincheva, Svetlana. "Symbols into Soldiers: Art, Censorship, and
Religion." *Artsfreedom,* 19 Oct. 2012, artsfreedom.org/?p=3358.
Accessed 2 May 2015.

Nagourney, Adam. "First Lady Assails Mayor over Threat to
Museum." *New York Times,* 28 Sept. 1999, www.nytimes.com/
1999 /09/28/nyregion/first-lady-assails-mayor-over-threat-to-
museum.html. Accessed 20 May 2015.

Reich, Robert B. *Reason: Why Liberals Will Win the Battle for America.*
Knopf, 2004.

Rosenbaum, Lee. "The Battle of Brooklyn Ends, the Controversy
Continues." *Art in America,* June 2000, pp. 39–43.

Rosenberg, Lela Capri. "The Meaning of Sensation: Young British Art
in the Nineties." Duke University, 2008. ProQuest,
search.proquest.com/docview/304639236?accountid=9838.
Accessed 20 Feb. 2015. Dissertation.

Schlafly, Phyllis. "Time to Abolish Federally Financed 'Hate Art.'"
Eagle Forum, 13 Oct. 1999, www.eagleforum.org/column/1999/
oct99/99-10-13.html. Accessed May 2015.

Schmidt, Colleen. "No Charges in Chicken Killing at ACAD." CTV
Calgary News, 19 April 2013, calgary.ctvnews.ca/no-charges-in-
chicken-killing-at-acad-1.1245321. Accessed 10 Jan. 2015.

"Sensation: Young British Artists from the Saatchi Collection."

Davis 27

Brooklyn Museum, 2 October 1999 to 9 January 2000, www.brooklynmuseum.org/opencollection/exhibitions/683. Exhibition.

Smith, Roberta. "Medium and Message, Both Unsettling." Rev. of *Chris Ofili: Night and Day*. New Museum, New York. *New York Times*, 30 Oct. 2014, www.nytimes.com/2014/10/31/arts/design/chris-ofili-night-and-day-a-survey-at-the-new-museum.html. Accessed 29 May 2015.

Tomkins, Calvin. "Into the Unknown: Chris Ofili Returns to New York with a Major Retrospective." *New Yorker*, 6 Oct. 2014, www.newyorker.com/magazine/2014/10/06/unknown-.

"Turner Prize: Year By Year." *Tate Britain*. www.tate.org.uk/visit/tate-britain/turner-prize/year-by-year. Accessed 12 May 2015.

Vogel, Carol. "Chris Ofili: British Artist Holds Fast to His Inspiration." *New York Times*, 28 Sept. 1999, partners.nytimes.com/library/arts/092899ofili-brooklyn-museum.html. Accessed 20 May 2015.

Zickenfoose, Sherri. "Public Slaughter of Chicken Defended as Art." *Calgary Herald*, 18 April 2013, www.calgaryherald.com/public+slaughter+chicken+defended/8263036/story.html. Accessed 10 May 2015.

◎ APA Style

The American Psychological Association (APA) style is used in many behavioural and social sciences. Like MLA style, APA style calls for parenthetical references in the body of a paper, although the main components in these are author and date rather than author and page number. APA also requires that full bibliographical information about the sources be provided in a list called "References" at the end of the essay.

This section outlines the key features of APA style and includes, at the end, a full sample essay using APA citation. Additional full sample essays in APA style are available on the Broadview website. Go to <http://sites.broadviewpress.com/writing/>. If you have more detailed questions, consult *Concise Rules of APA Style* (6th edition, 2010). You may also find answers at www.apastyle.org.

◉ Incorporating Sources in APA Style

The following material should be read in conjunction with the introductory discussion of citation, documentation, and plagiarism (see pages 553–56).

There are three main ways of working source material into a paper: summaries, paraphrases, and direct quotations. In order to avoid plagiarism, care must be taken with all three kinds of borrowing, both in the way they are handled and in their referencing. In what follows, a passage from page 102 of a book by Terrence W. Deacon (*The Symbolic Species: The Co-Evolution of Language and the Brain*, published in New York City by Norton in 1997) serves as the source for a sample summary, paraphrase, and quotation. The examples feature the APA style of in-text parenthetical citations, but the requirements for presenting the source material are the same for all academic referencing systems.

> *original source* Over the last few decades language researchers seem to have reached a consensus that language is an innate ability, and that only a significant contribution from innate knowledge can explain our ability to learn such a complex communication system. Without question,

children enter the world predisposed to learn human languages. All normal children, raised in normal social environments, inevitably learn their local language, whereas other species, even when raised and taught in this same environment, do not. This demonstrates that human brains come into the world specially equipped for this function.

O *Summarizing*

An honest and competent summary, whether of a passage or an entire book, must not only represent the source accurately but also use original wording and include a citation. It is a common misconception that only quotations need to be acknowledged as borrowings in the body of an essay, but without a citation, even a fairly worded summary or paraphrase is an act of plagiarism. The first example below is faulty on two counts: it borrows wording (underlined) from the source, and it has no parenthetical reference.

> *needs checking* Researchers agree that language learning is innate, and that only innate knowledge can explain how we are able to learn a system of communication that is so complex. Normal children raised in normal ways will always learn their local language, whereas other species do not, even when taught human language and exposed to the same environment.

The next example avoids the wording of the source passage, and a parenthetical citation notes the author and date (but note that no page number is provided, as APA does not require these in citations of summarized material).

> *revised* There is now wide agreement among linguists that the ease with which human children acquire their native tongues, under the conditions of a normal childhood, demonstrates an inborn capacity for language that is not shared by any other animals, not even those who are reared in comparable ways and given human language training (Deacon, 1997).

O *Paraphrasing*

Whereas a summary is a shorter version of its original, a paraphrase tends to be about the same length. However, paraphrases, like summaries, must reflect their sources accurately while using original wording, and must include a citation. The original material's page number (or paragraph number for a nonpaginated online source) is not absolutely essential for a paraphrase, but APA suggests it be added as an aid to any reader who would like to refer to the original text. What follows is a paraphrase of the first sentence of the Deacon passage, which despite having a proper citation, falls short by being too close to the wording of the original (underlined).

> *needs checking* Researchers in language have come to a consensus in the past few decades that the acquisition of language is innate; such contributions from knowledge contribute significantly to our ability to master such a complex system of communication (Deacon, 1997, p. 102).

Simply substituting synonyms for the words and phrases of the source, however, is not enough to avoid plagiarism. Even with its original wording, the next example also fails but for a very different reason: it follows the original's sentence structure, as illustrated in the interpolated copy below it.

> *needs checking* Recently, linguists appear to have come to an agreement that speaking is an in-born skill, and that nothing but a substantial input from in-born cognition can account for the human capacity to acquire such a complicated means of expression (Deacon, 1997, p. 102).

> Recently (*over the last few decades*), linguists (*language researchers*) appear to have come to an agreement (*seem to have reached a consensus*) that speaking is an in-born skill (*that language is an innate ability*), and that nothing but a substantial input (*and that only a significant contribution*) from in-born cognition (*from innate knowledge*) can account for the human capacity (*can explain our ability*) to acquire such a complicated means of expression (*to learn such a complex communication system*) (Deacon, 1997, p. 102).

What follows is a good paraphrase of the passage's opening sentence; this paraphrase captures the sense of the original without echoing the details and shape of its language.

> *revised* Linguists now broadly agree that children are born with the ability to learn language; in fact, the human capacity to acquire such a difficult skill cannot easily be accounted for in any other way (Deacon, 1997, p. 102).

O Quoting Directly

Unlike paraphrases and summaries, direct quotations must use the exact wording of the original. Because they involve importing outside words, quotations pose unique challenges. Quote too frequently, and you risk making your readers wonder why they are not reading your sources instead of your paper. Your essay should present something you want to say—informed and supported by properly documented sources, but forming a contribution that is yours alone. To that end, use secondary material to help you build a strong framework for your work, not to replace it. Quote sparingly, therefore; use your sources' exact wording only when it is important or particularly memorable.

To avoid misrepresenting your sources, be sure to quote accurately, and to avoid plagiarism, take care to indicate quotations as quotations, and cite them properly. If you use the author's name in a signal phrase, follow it with the date in parentheses, and be sure the verb of the phrase is in the past tense (*demonstrated*) or present perfect tense (*has demonstrated*). For all direct quotations, you must also include the page number (or paragraph number for a nonpaginated online source) of the original in your citation, as in the following examples.

Below are two problematic quotations. The first does not show which words come directly from the source.

> *needs checking* Deacon (1997) maintained that children enter the world predisposed to learn human languages (p. 102).

The second quotation fails to identify the source at all.

> *needs checking* Many linguists have argued that "children enter the world predisposed to learn human languages."

The next example corrects both problems by naming the source and indicating clearly which words come directly from it.

> *revised* Deacon (1997) maintained that "children enter the world predisposed to learn human languages" (p. 102).

○ *Formatting Quotations*

There are two ways to signal an exact borrowing: by enclosing it in double quotation marks and by indenting it as a block of text. Which you should choose depends on the length and genre of the quotation and the style guide you are following.

⊙ Short Quotations

What counts as a short quotation differs among the various reference guides. In MLA style, "short" means up to four lines; in APA, up to forty words; and in Chicago Style, up to one hundred words. All the guides agree, however, that short quotations must be enclosed in double quotation marks, as in the examples below.

> *Short quotation,* According to Deacon (1997), linguists agree that a
> *full sentence:* human child's capacity to acquire language is inborn: "Without question, children enter the world predisposed to learn human languages" (p. 102).

> *Short quotation,* According to Deacon (1997), linguists agree that
> *partial sentence:* human "children enter the world predisposed to learn human languages" (p. 102).

⊙ Long Quotations

In APA style, longer quotations of forty words or more should be double-spaced and indented, as a block, about one-half inch from the left margin. Do not include quotation marks; the indentation indicates that the words come exactly from the source. Note that indented quotations are often introduced with a full sentence followed by a colon.

> Deacon (1997) maintained that human beings are born with a unique cognitive capacity:
>> Without question, children enter the world predisposed to learn human languages. All normal children, raised in

normal social environments, inevitably learn their local language, whereas other species, even when raised and taught in this same environment, do not. This demonstrates that human brains come into the world specially equipped for this function. (p. 102)

⊙ Quotations within Quotations

You may sometimes find, within the original passage you wish to quote, words already enclosed in double quotation marks. If your quotation is short, enclose it all in double quotation marks, and use single quotation marks for the embedded quotation.

> Deacon (1997) was firm in maintaining that human language differs from other communication systems in kind rather than degree: "Of no other natural form of communication is it legitimate to say that 'language is a more complicated version of that'" (p. 44).

If your quotation is long, keep the double quotation marks of the original. Note as well that in the example below, the source's use of italics (*simple*) is also faithfully reproduced.

> Deacon (1997) was firm in maintaining that human language differs from other communication systems in kind rather than degree:
>
> > Of no other natural form of communication is it legitimate to say that "language is a more complicated version of that." It is just as misleading to call other species' communication systems *simple* languages as it is to call them languages. In addition to asserting that a Procrustean mapping of one to the other is possible, the analogy ignores the sophistication and power of animals' non-linguistic communication, whose capabilities may also be without language parallels. (p. 44)

○ *Adding to or Deleting from a Quotation*

While it is important to use the original's exact wording in a quotation, it is allowable to modify a quotation somewhat, as long as the changes are clearly indicated and do not distort the meaning of the original. You may want to add to a quotation in order to clarify what would otherwise be puzzling or ambiguous to someone who does not know its context; put whatever you add in square brackets.

    ○ *Using square brackets to add to a quotation*

    Deacon (1997) concluded that children are born "specially equipped for this [language] function" (p. 102).

If you would like to streamline a quotation by omitting anything unnecessary to your point, insert an ellipsis (three spaced dots) to show that you've left material out.

    ○ *Using an ellipsis to delete from a quotation*

When the quotation looks like a complete sentence but is actually part of a longer sentence, you should provide an ellipsis to show that there is more to the original than you are using.

    Deacon (1997) concluded that "… children enter the world predisposed to learn human languages" (p. 102).

Note the square brackets example above; if the quotation is clearly a partial sentence, ellipses aren't necessary.

When the omitted material runs over a sentence boundary or constitutes a whole sentence or more, insert a period plus an ellipsis.

    Deacon (1997) claimed that human children are born with a unique ability to acquire their native language: "Without question, children enter the world predisposed to learn human languages.… [H]uman brains come into the world specially equipped for this function" (p. 102).

Be sparing in modifying quotations; it is all right to have one or two altered quotations in a paper, but if you find yourself changing quotations often, or adding to and omitting from one quotation more than once, reconsider quoting at all. A paraphrase or summary is very often a more effective choice.

⊙ Integrating Quotations

Quotations must be worked smoothly and grammatically into your sentences and paragraphs. Always, of course, mark quotations as such, but for the purpose of integrating them into your writing, treat them otherwise as if they were your own words. The boundary between what you say and what your source says should be grammatically seamless.

needs checking   Deacon (1997) pointed out, "whereas other species, even when raised and taught in this same environment, do not" (p. 102).

revised   According to Deacon (1997), while human children brought up under normal conditions acquire the language they are exposed to, "other species, even when raised and taught in this same environment, do not" (p. 102).

○ *Avoiding "dumped" quotations*

Integrating quotations well also means providing a context for them. Don't merely drop them into your paper or string them together like beads on a necklace; make sure to introduce them by noting where the material comes from and how it connects to whatever point you are making.

needs checking   For many years, linguists have studied how human children acquire language. "Without question, children enter the world predisposed to learn human language" (Deacon, 1997, p. 102).

revised   Most linguists studying how human children acquire language have come to share the conclusion articulated by Deacon (1997): "Without question, children enter the world predisposed to learn human language" (p. 102).

needs checking   "Without question, children enter the world predisposed to learn human language" (Deacon, 1997, p. 102). "There is ... something special about human brains that enables us to do with ease what no other species can do even minimally without intense effort and remarkably insightful training" (Deacon, 1997, p. 103).

revised   Deacon (1997) based his claim that we "enter the world predisposed to learn human language" on the fact that very young humans can "do with ease what no other species can do even minimally without intense effort and remarkably insightful training" (pp. 102–103).

O *Signal Phrases*

To leave no doubt in your readers' minds about which parts of your essay are yours and which come from elsewhere, identify the sources of your summaries, paraphrases, and quotations with signal phrases, as in the following examples.

- As Carter and Rosenthal (2011) demonstrated that, …
- According to Ming, Bartlett, and Koch (2014), …
- In his latest article McGann (2015) advanced the view that, …
- As Beyerstein (2000) observed, …
- Kendal and Ahmadi (1998) have suggested that …
- Freschi (2004) was not alone in rejecting these claims, arguing that …
- Cabral, Chernovsky, and Morgan (2015) emphasized this point in their recent research: …
- Sayeed (2003) has maintained that …
- In a landmark study, Mtele (1992) concluded that …
- In her later work, however, Hardy (2005) overturned previous results, suggesting that …

In order to help establish your paper's credibility, you may also find it useful at times to include in a signal phrase information that shows why readers should take the source seriously, as in the following example:

In this insightful and compassionate work, clinical neurologist Oliver Sacks (1985) described …

Here, the signal phrase mentions the author's professional credentials; it also points out the importance of his book, which is appropriate to do in the case of a work as famous as Sacks' *The Man Who Mistook His Wife for a Hat*.

Below is a fuller list of words and expressions that may be useful in the crafting of signal phrases:

according to _____	endorsed
acknowledged	found
added	granted
admitted	illustrated
advanced	implied
agreed	in the view of _____,
allowed	in the words of _____,
argued	insisted
asserted	intimated
attested	noted
believed	observed
claimed	pointed out
commented	put it
compared	reasoned
concluded	refuted
confirmed	rejected
contended	reported
declared	responded
demonstrated	suggested
denied	took issue with
disputed	thought
emphasized	wrote

O *About In-text Citations*

1. **in-text citation:** The APA system emphasizes the date of publication, which must appear within an in-text citation. Whenever a quotation is given, the page number, preceded by the abbreviation *p.*, must also be provided:

- Bonnycastle (2007) refers to "the true and lively spirit of opposition" (p. 204) with which Marxist literary criticism invigorates the discipline.

It is common to mention in the body of your text the surnames of authors that you are citing, as is done in the example above. If author names are not mentioned in the body of the text, however, they must be provided within the in-text citation. In the example below, note the comma between the name and date of publication.

- One overview of literary theory (Bonnycastle, 2007) has praised "the true and lively spirit of opposition" (p. 204) with which Marxist literary criticism invigorates the discipline.

If the reference does not involve a quotation (as it commonly does not in social science papers), only the date need be given as an in-text citation, provided that the author's name appears in the signal phrase. For paraphrases, APA encourages, though does not require, a page number reference as well. The in-text citation in this case must immediately follow the author's name:

- Bonnycastle (2007) argues that the oppositional tone of Marxist literary criticism invigorates the discipline.

A citation such as this connects to a list of references at the end of the paper. In this case the entry under "References" at the end of the paper would be as follows:

- Bonnycastle, S. (2007). *In search of authority: A guide to literary theory* (3rd ed.). Peterborough, ON: Broadview Press.

Notice here that the date of publication is again foregrounded, appearing immediately after the author's name. Notice too that the formatting of titles differs from that of MLA style; the details are in sections three and four, below.

2. **no signal phrase (or author not named in signal phrase)**: If the context does not make it clear who the author is, that information must be added to the in-text citation. Note that commas separate the name of the author, the date, and the page number (where this is given):

- Even in recent years some have continued to believe that Marxist literary criticism invigorates the discipline with a "true and lively spirit of opposition" (Bonnycastle, 2005, p. 4).

3. **titles of stand-alone works**: Stand-alone works are those that are published on their own rather than as part of another work. The titles of stand-alone works (e.g., journals, magazines, newspapers,

books, and reports) should be in italics. Writers in the social and behavioural sciences do not normally put the titles of works in the bodies of their papers, but if you do include the title of a stand-alone work, all major words and all words of four letters or more should be capitalized. For book and report titles in the References list, however, capitalize only the first word of the title and subtitle (if any), plus any proper nouns. Journal, magazine, and newspaper titles in the list of References are exceptions; for these, capitalize all major words.

4. **titles of articles and chapters of books**: The titles of these works, and anything else that is published as part of another work, are also not usually mentioned in the body of an essay, though if they are, they should be put in quotation marks, with all major words capitalized. In the References, however, titles of these works should *not* be put in quotation marks or italicized, and no words should be capitalized, with the exception of any proper nouns, and the first word in the title and the first in the subtitle, if any.

5. **placing of in-text citations**: When the author's name appears in a signal phrase, the in-text citation comes directly after the name. Otherwise, the citation follows the paraphrased or quoted material. If a quotation ends with punctuation other than a period or comma, then this should precede the end of the quotation, and a period or comma should still follow the parenthetical reference, if this is grammatically appropriate.

- The claim has been convincingly refuted by Ricks (2010), but it nevertheless continues to be put forward (Dendel, 2013).
- One of Berra's favourite coaching tips was that "ninety per cent of the game is half mental" (Adelman, 2007, p. 98).
- Berra at one point said to his players, "You can observe a lot by watching!" (Adelman, 2007, p. 98).
- Garner (2011) associates statistics and pleasure.

6. **citations when text is in parentheses**: If a parenthetical reference occurs within text in parentheses, commas are used to set off elements of the reference.

- (See Figure 6.1 of Harrison, 2012, for data on transplant waiting lists.)

7. electronic source—page number unavailable: If a Web document cited is in PDF format, the page numbers are stable and may be cited as one would the pages of a printed source. The page numbers of many Web sources are unstable, however, and many more lack page numbers altogether. In such cases you should provide a section or paragraph number if a reference is needed. For paragraphs, use the abbreviation "para."

- In a recent Web posting a leading theorist has clearly stated that he finds such an approach "thoroughly objectionable" (Bhabha, 2012, para. 7).
- Bhabha (2012) has clearly stated his opposition to this approach.
- Carter and Zhaba (2009) describe this approach as "more reliable than that adopted by Perkins" (Method section, para. 2).

If you are citing longer texts from electronic versions, chapter references may be more appropriate. For example, if the online Gutenberg edition of Darwin's *On the Origin of Species* were being cited, the citation would be as follows:

- Darwin refers to the core of his theory as an "ineluctable principle" (1856, Chapter 26).

Notice that *chapter* is capitalized and not abbreviated.

Students should be cautioned that online editions of older or classic works are often unreliable; typically there are far more typos and other errors in such versions than there are in print versions. It is often possible to exercise judgement about such matters, however. If, for example, you are not required to base your essay on a particular edition of Darwin's *Origin of Species* but may find your own, you will be far better off using the text you will find on the reputable Project Gutenberg site than you will using a text you might find on a site such as "Manybooks.com."

8. two or more dates for a work: If you have consulted a re-issue of a work (whether in printed or electronic form), you should provide both the original date of publication and the date of the re-issue (the date of the version you are using).

- Emerson (1837/1909) asserted that America's "long apprenticeship to the learning of other lands" was "drawing to a close" (para. 1).

The relevant entry in the list of references would look like this:

- Emerson, R. W. (1909). *Essays and English traits.* New York, NY: P. F. Collier & Son. (Original work published 1837)

If you are citing work in a form that has been revised by the author, however, you should cite the date of the revised publication, not the original.

- In a preface to the latest edition of his classic work (2004), Watson discusses its genesis.

9. **multiple authors**: If there are two or three authors, all authors should be named either in the signal phrase or in the in-text citation. Use *and* in the signal phrase but *&* in parentheses.

- Chambliss and Best (2010) have argued that the nature of this research is practical as well as theoretical.
- Two distinguished scholars have argued that the nature of this research is practical as well as theoretical (Chambliss & Best, 2010).

three to five authors: In the body of the text list the names of all authors the first time the work is referred to; for subsequent references use only the first author's name, followed by *et al.* (short for the Latin *et alia*: *and others*).

- Chambliss, Best, Didby, and Jones (2011) have argued that the nature of this research is practical as well as theoretical.
- Four distinguished scholars have argued that the nature of this research is practical as well as theoretical (Chambliss, Best, Didby, & Jones, 2011).

more than five authors: Use only the first author's name, followed by *et al.* (short for the Latin *et alia*: *and others*).

- Chambliss et al. (2011) have argued that the nature of this research is practical as well as theoretical.
- Six distinguished scholars have argued that the nature of this research is practical as well as theoretical (Chambliss et al., 2011).

10. **corporate author**: As you would with an individual human author, provide the name of a corporate author either in the body

of your text or in a parenthetical citation. Recommended practice is to provide the full name of an organization on the first occasion, followed by an abbreviation, and then to use the abbreviation for subsequent references:

- Blindness has decreased markedly but at an uneven pace since the late 1800s (National Institute for the Blind [NIB], 2002).

11. **author not given:** If the author of the source is not given, it may be identified in the parenthetical reference by a short form of the title.

- Confusion over voting reform is widespread ("Results of National Study," 2012).

12. **date not given:** Some sources, particularly electronic ones, do not provide a date of publication. Where this is the case, use the abbreviation *n.d.* for *no date*.

- Some still claim that evidence of global climate change is difficult to come by (Sanders, n.d.; Zimmerman, 2012).

13. **two or more works in the same citation:** In this case, the works should appear in in-text citations in the same order they do in the list of references. If the works are by different authors, arrange the sources alphabetically by author's last name and separate the citations with a semicolon. If the works are by the same authors, arrange the sources by publication date. Add *a*, *b*, *c*, etc. after the year to distinguish works written by the same authors in the same year.

- Various studies have established a psychological link between fear and sexual arousal (Aikens, Cox, & Bartlett, 1998; Looby & Cairns, 2008).
- Various studies appear to have established a psychological link between fear and sexual arousal (Looby & Cairns, 1999, 2002, 2005).
- Looby and Cairns (1999a, 1999b, 2002, 2005a, 2005b) have investigated extensively the link between fear and sexual arousal.

14. **two or more authors with the same last name:** If the References list includes two or more authors with the same last name, the in-text citation should supply an initial:

- One of the leading economists of the time advocated wage and price controls (H. Johnston, 1977).

15. **works in a collection of readings or anthology:** In the in-text citation for a work in an anthology or collection of readings, use the name of the author of the work, not that of the editor of the anthology. If the work was first published in the collection you have consulted, there is only the one date to cite. But if the work is reprinted in that collection after having first been published elsewhere, cite the date of the original publication and the date of the collection you have consulted, separating these dates with a slash. The following citation refers to an article by Frederic W. Gleach that was first published in a collection of readings edited by Jennifer Brown and Elizabeth Vibert.

- One of the essays in Brown and Vibert's collection argues that we should rethink the Pocahontas myth (Gleach, 1996).

In your list of references, this work should be alphabetized under Gleach, the author of the piece you have consulted, not under Brown.

The next example is a lecture by Georg Simmel first published in 1903, which a student consulted in an edited collection by Roberta Garner that was published in 2001.

- Simmel (1903/2001) argues that the "deepest problems of modern life derive from the claim of the individual to preserve the autonomy and individuality of his existence" (p. 141).

The reference list entry would look like this:

Simmel, G. (2001). The metropolis and mental life. In R. Garner (Ed.), *Social theory–Continuity and confrontation: A reader* (pp. 141–153). Peterborough, ON: Broadview Press. (Original work published in 1903)

As you can see, in your reference list these works are listed under the authors of the pieces (Gleach or Simmel), not under the compilers, editors, or translators of the collection (Brown & Vibert or Garner). If you cite another work by a different author from the same anthology or book of readings, that should appear as a separate entry in your list of references—again, alphabetized under the author's name.

16. **indirect source:** If you are citing a source from a reference other than the source itself, you should use the phrase "as cited in" in your in-text citation.

- In de Beauvoir's famous phrase, "one is not born a woman, one becomes one" (as cited in Levey, 2001, para. 3).

In this case, the entry in your reference list would be for Levey, not de Beauvoir.

17. **private and personal communications:** Since the list of references should include only sources that your readers can access themselves, it should not include personal, private, and undocumented or unarchived communications, whether these are by telephone, written letter, e-mail, or other means. Cite these communications only in your text. Provide the initials and surname of the person you communicated with as well as the date of communication.

- K. Montegna (personal communication, January 21, 2013) has expressed skepticism over this method's usefulness.

O *About References*

The list of references in APA style is an alphabetized listing of sources that appears at the end of an essay, article, or book. Usually, it includes all the information necessary to identify and retrieve each of the sources you have cited, and only the works you have cited. In this case the list is entitled *References*. If the list includes all works you have consulted, regardless of whether or not you have cited them, it should be entitled *Bibliography*. The list of references should include only sources that can be accessed by your readers, and so it should not include private communication, such as private letters, memos, e-mail messages, and telephone or personal conversations. Those should be cited only in your text (see the section above).

Entries should be ordered alphabetically by author surname, or, if there is no known author, by title. The first line of each entry should be flush with the left-hand margin, with all subsequent lines indented about one half inch. Double-space throughout the list of references.

The basic format for all entries is author (if available), date (give *n.d.* if there is no date), title, and publication information. Remember that one function of the list of references is to provide the information your readers need if they wish to locate your sources for themselves; APA allows any "non-routine" information that could assist in identifying the sources to be added in square brackets to any entry (e.g., [Sunday business section], [Motion picture], [Interview with O. Sacks]).

In the References examples that follow, information about entries for electronic sources has been presented in an integrated fashion alongside information about referencing sources in other media, such as print, film, and so on. Whenever you are required to give a website URL that does not all fit on one line, do not insert a hyphen; break the URL before a slash or period (with the exception of the slashes in *http://*).

18. **book with single author**: For a work with one author the entry should begin with the last name, followed by a comma, and then the author's initials as applicable, followed by the date of publication in parentheses. Note that initials are generally used rather than first names, even when authors are identified by first name in the work itself. For publishers in North America, give the city and an abbreviation of the state or province of publication; give the city and country for works published elsewhere. Leave out abbreviations such as *Inc.* and *Co.* in publisher's names but keep *Press* and *Books*.

> Gee, J. P. (2012). *Social linguistics and literacies: Ideology in discourses* (4th ed.). London, England: Routledge.

19. **two to seven authors**: Last names should in all cases come first, followed by initials. Use commas to separate the authors' names, and use an ampersand rather than *and* before the last author. Note that the authors' names should appear in the order they are listed; sometimes this is not alphabetical.

> Eagles, M., Bickerton, J. P., & Gagnon, A. (1991). *The almanac of Canadian politics*. Peterborough, ON: Broadview Press.

20. **more than seven authors**: List the names of the first six authors, add an ellipsis, and then give the last author's name.

> Newsome, M. R., Scheibel, R. S., Hanten, G., Chu, Z., Steinberg, J. L., Hunter, J. V. ... Levin, H. S. (2010). Brain activation while thinking about the self from another person's perspective after

traumatic brain injury in adolescents. *Neuropsychology, 24*(2), 139–147.

21. **corporate author:** If a work has been issued by a government body, a corporation, or some other organization and no author is identified, the entry should be listed by the name of the group. If this group is also the work's publisher, write *Author* where the publisher's name would normally go.

> Broadview Press. (2005). *Annual report.* Calgary, AB: Author.
>
> Broadview Press. (n.d.). Questions and answers about book pricing. Broadview Press Web Site. Retrieved from www .broadviewpress.com/bookpricing.asp?inc=bookpricing
>
> City of Toronto, City Planning Division. (2000, June). *Toronto at the crossroads: Shaping our future.* Toronto, ON: Author.

22. **works with unknown author:** Works with an unknown author should be alphabetized by title.

> *Columbia encyclopedia* (6th ed.). (2001). New York, NY: Columbia University Press.

If you have referred to only one entry in an encyclopedia or dictionary, however, the entry in your list of references should be by the title of that entry (see below).

23. **two or more works by the same author:** The author's name should appear for all entries. Entries should be ordered by year of publication.

> Menand, L. (2002). *The metaphysical club: A story of ideas in America.* New York, NY: Knopf.
>
> Menand, L. (2004, June 28). Bad comma: Lynne Truss's strange grammar [Review of the book *Eats, shoots & leaves*]. *The New Yorker.* Retrieved from http://www.newyorker.com

If two or more cited works by the same author have been published in the same year, arrange these alphabetically and use letters to distinguish among them: (2011a), (2011b), and so on.

24. **edited works:** Entries for edited works include the abbreviation *Ed.* or *Eds.* The second example below is for a book with both an author and an editor; since the original work in this entry was

published earlier than the present edition, that information is given in parentheses at the end.

> Gross, B., Field, D., & Pinker, L. (Eds.). (2002). *New approaches to the history of psychoanalysis.* New York, NY: Duckworth.
>
> Sapir, E. (1981). *Selected writings in language, culture, and personality.* D. G. Mandelbaum (Ed.). Berkeley, CA: University of California Press. (Original work published 1949)

25. works with an author and a translator: The translator's name, along with the designation *Trans.*, is included in parentheses after the title; the original publication date is given in parentheses following the present edition's publication information.

> Jung, C. G. (2006). *The undiscovered self* (R. F. C. Hull, Trans.). New York, NY: Signet. (Original work published 1959)

26. selections from anthologies or collections of readings: A selection from a collection of readings or an anthology should be listed as follows:

> Gleach, F. W. (1996). Controlled speculation: Interpreting the saga of Pocahontas and Captain John Smith. In J. Brown & E. Vibert (Eds.), *Reading beyond words: Contexts for Native history* (pp. 21–42). Peterborough, ON: Broadview.
>
> Rosengarten, H. (2002). Fleiss's nose and Freud's mind: A new perspective. In B. Gross, D. Field, & L. Pinker (Eds.), *New approaches to the history of psychoanalysis* (pp. 232–243). New York, NY: Duckworth.
>
> Taylor, E. (1992). Biological consciousness and the experience of the transcendent: William James and American functional psychology. In R. H. Wozniak (Ed.), *Mind and body: René Descartes to William James.* Retrieved from http://serendip.brynmawr.edu/Mind/James.html

27. electronic version of a print book: Give the site's URL in the place where publication information would normally go.

> Bailey, K. D. (1994). *Sociology and the new systems theory: Toward a theoretical synthesis.* Retrieved from https://play.google.com/

28. journal articles: Notice that article titles are not enclosed in quotation marks, and that both the journal title and the volume number are in italics. If all issues of a given volume of a journal begin with page 1, include the issue number as well, directly after the volume number, in parentheses and not italicized. For online journal articles, you should also include the digital object identifier (DOI): a string of numbers, letters, and punctuation, beginning with *10*, usually located on the first or copyright page. If no DOI is available, you should include the URL for the journal's homepage.

> Barker, P. (2004). The impact of class size on the classroom behaviour of special needs students: A longitudinal study. *Educational Quarterly, 25*(4), 87–99.
>
> Best, R. K. (2012). Disease politics and medical research funding: Three ways advocacy shapes policy. *American Sociological Review, 77*, 780–803. Retrieved from http://asr.sagepub.com/
>
> Laughlin, C. D., & Tiberia, V. A. (2012). Archetypes: Toward a Jungian anthropology of consciousness. *Anthropology of Consciousness, 23*, 127–157. doi:10.1111/j.1556-3537.2012.01063.x
>
> Surtees, P. (2008). The psychology of the children's crusade of 1212. *Studies in Medieval History and Society, 3*(4), 279–325. doi:10.1008/smhs.2008.0581

29. abstract of a journal article: Cite as you would the journal article itself, adding *Abstract* in square brackets.

> Laughlin, C. D., & Tiberia, V. A. (2012). Archetypes: Toward a Jungian anthropology of consciousness [Abstract]. *Anthropology of Consciousness, 23*, 127–157. doi:10.1111/j.1556-3537.2012.01063.x

30. magazine articles: The basic principles are the same as for journal articles. Note that neither quotation marks nor italics are used for the titles of articles. If no author is identified, the title of the article should appear first. For monthly magazines, provide the month as well as the year; for magazines issued more frequently, give the day, month, and year. Include the homepage URL for magazine articles online.

> Dyer, A. (2012, November/December). The end of the world … again. *SkyNews, 18*(4), 38–39.
>
> The rise of the yuan: Turning from green to red. (2012, October 20). *The Economist, 405*(42), 67–68.

Steavenson, W. (2012, November 12). Two revolutions: Women in the new Egypt. *The New Yorker, 88*(35), 32–38. Retrieved from http://www.newyorker.com

31. newspaper articles: The basic principles to follow with newspaper articles or editorials are the same as with magazine articles (see above), but volume and issue numbers are not included, and page numbers are preceded by *p.* or *pp.* APA requires that all page numbers for print versions be provided when articles do not continue on consecutive pages. Notice that if there is no letter assigned to a newspaper section, you should give the section's title in square brackets.

Bennett, J. (2012, December 16). How to attack the gender pay gap? *The New York Times* [Sunday business section], pp. 1, 6.

Gray, J. (2012, December 20). Stepping into the proxy frays. *The Globe and Mail,* p. B6.

If you are citing an online version of a newspaper article you have retrieved through a search of its website, you should provide the URL for the site, not for the exact location of the article. Since the online version of the article in the example below does not have page numbers, none are included in the References entry.

Gray, J. (2012, December 20). Stepping into the proxy frays. *The Globe and Mail.* Retrieved from http://www.globeandmail.com

32. book reviews: The name of the reviewer (if it has been provided) should come first, followed by the date and title of the review, and the information on the book itself, as follows:

Tavris, C. (2012, April 25). Psychology and its discontents. [Review of the book *Psychology's ghosts: The crisis in the profession and the way back,* by J. Kagan]. *Wall Street Journal.* Retrieved from http://online.wsj.com/article/SB10001424052702304537904577277760260276148.html

33. reference work entries: List by the author of the entry, if known; otherwise, list by the entry itself.

Lister, M. (1999). Consumers' Association of Canada. *The Canadian encyclopedia* (Year 2000 ed.). Toronto, ON: McClelland & Stewart.

Saint Lawrence Seaway. (2001). *The Columbia encyclopedia* (6th ed.). Retrieved from http://www.bartleby.com/65/st/STLawrSwy.html

34. films and video recordings: Begin entries for motion pictures with the names of the producers and director, followed by the date of release, the film's title, the medium in square brackets, the location of origin, and the name of the studio.

Ball, C. J., Ryder, A., Tyrer, W., Dysinger, E., Todd, J., Todd, S., Thomas, E. (Producers), & Nolan, C. (Director). (2000). *Memento* [Blu-ray disc]. United States: Newmarket Films.

Egoyan, A., Weiss, J., Vroll, S., Iron, D. (Producers), & Polley, S. (Director). (2006). *Away from her* [Motion picture]. Canada: Lionsgate Films.

35. episodes from television series: Entries for television show episodes should begin with the names of the writer and director, followed by the date, episode title, medium, producer's name, series title, location, and production company's name. Identify the role, in parentheses, of each person listed.

Weiner, M. (Writer), & Getzinger, J. (Director). (2012). A little kiss [Television series episode]. In M. Weiner (Executive producer), *Mad men*. Santa Monica, CA: Lionsgate Television.

36. podcasts: Use the entry for a television series episode as a model, giving the type of podcast as the medium, and adding the website's URL. Give the full date of the original broadcast.

Eisen, J. (Writer). (2010, May 17–31). Have your meat and eat it too! Parts 1–3. [Audio podcast]. In L. Noth (Producer), *CBC ideas*. Retrieved from http://www.cbc.ca/ideas/episodes/2010/05/17/have-your-meat-and-eat-it-too-part-1-2-listen/

37. music recordings: Arrange an entry for a music recording as follows: give the writer's name, the copyright date of the piece of music, its title, the album title, the medium in square brackets, the place of origin, and the label name. If the piece is recorded by someone other than the writer, note that in square brackets after the piece's title. Add the recording date at the end of the entry if it differs from the copyright date.

Berlin, I. (1935). Cheek to cheek [Recorded by J. Pass]. On *Blues for Fred* [CD]. Berkeley, CA: Pablo Records. (1988, February 3).

Waits, T. (1999). Eyeball kid. On *Mule Variations* [CD]. Los Angeles, CA: Anti.

38. **interviews**: How you format an entry for an interview will depend on where it is located. If you watched or listened to a recording of the interview, use the format appropriate to the medium. The second example below is for an interview of Jane Goodall on the television program *Bill Moyers Journal*, which was accessed online as a video webcast. Notice that the interviewee's name comes first, and that the entry is formatted in the same way as an entry for a television series episode that is available online. The first example is for an interview with Willie Nelson printed in a periodical. Here, the entry follows the format for a newspaper article, with the interviewer in the author position, and information about the interviewee in square brackets. Notice as well that, although the periodical is called a magazine, this publication goes by date only, not volume and issue number, and so the newspaper article format is the appropriate choice. These guidelines apply only to published interviews; unpublished interviews you have conducted yourself are considered private correspondence and should not be included in your References list.

Goldman, A. (2012, December 16). The silver-headed stranger [Interview with W. Nelson]. *New York Times Magazine*, p. 12.

Goodall, J. (2009, November 27). Interview by B. Moyers. In G. Ablow, W. Brangham, P. Meryash, B. Rate, & C. White (Producers), *Bill Moyers journal* [Video webcast]. Retrieved from http://www.pbs.org/moyers/journal/11272009/watch1.html

39. **documents on a website**: Give the author's name and date, if available (use *n.d.* for no date), the work's title, and the retrieval information.

LePan, D. (n.d.) The psychology of skyscrapers. Retrieved from http://donlepan.com

40. **blog posts**: Start with the writer's name; then give the full date, entry title, blog title, and retrieval information.

Gautam, S. (2012, July 22). Structure of childhood temperaments. *The mouse trap*. Retrieved from http://the-mouse-trap.com/2012/07/22/structure-of-childhood-temperaments/#comment-6470

41. **entries in a wiki**: Because wikis can be revised by anyone, their content tends to change over time. It is important, therefore, to include your date of access in the References entry. Wiki entries often have no single date of publication; if that's the case, use *n.d.*

> Code-switching. (n.d.). In *Wikipedia*. Retrieved January 17, 2013, from http://en.wikipedia.org/wiki/Code_switching

42. **tweets**: If the author's real name is known, provide it first, followed by the author's screen name in square brackets. If the author's real name cannot be determined, provide only the screen name, without the square brackets. Include only the date, not the time, of posting, and add *Twitter post* in square brackets. Include the entire tweet.

> Welch, J. [jack_welch]. (2012, October 5). Unbelievable jobs numbers..these Chicago guys will do anything..can't debate so change numbers [Twitter post]. Retrieved from http://twitter.com /jack_welch

43. **other Web references**: In the case of online sources not covered by the above, the same basic principles apply. Where an author or editor is indicated, list by author; otherwise, list by title. If the source is undated or its content likely to change, you should include the date on which you accessed the material. Use square brackets to include information that will help identify the source.

> Brown University. (2006, May). Brown University. Women writers project. Retrieved February 28, 2013, from http://www.brown .edu/

44. **maps or charts**: Include the medium in square brackets.

> Profile of book publishing and exclusive agency, for English language firms [Chart]. (2012). Statistics Canada. Retrieved from http:// www.statcan.ca/english/pgdb/arts02.htm

---

○ *APA Style Sample Essay*

Following is a full sample of text with citations in APA style. Note that full additional sample essays in APA style appear on the adjunct website associated with this book.

Among the details to notice in this reference system:

- Where two or more works by the same author are included in References, they are ordered by date of publication.

- APA style prefers author initials rather than first names.

- Only the first words of titles and subtitles are capitalized, except for proper nouns.

- The date appears in parentheses near the beginning of each entry in References.

- The in-text citation comes directly after the name of the author or after the end quotation mark. Often, these citations fall just before the period or comma in the surrounding sentence.

- If an in-text citation occurs within text in parentheses, commas are used to set off elements of the reference.

- When a work has appeared in an edited collection, information on the editors must be included in the reference.

- Authors' first and last names are reversed; note the use of the ampersand (&) in place of *and* between author names.

- Translators should be included where appropriate in the References list.

- Publisher as well as city of publication, including abbreviations for all states and provinces, should be given in References entries for print works.

- Months and publisher names are not abbreviated; the day of the month follows the name of the month.

- Online references include the date of publication or of last revision in parentheses immediately after the author's name. Note that, if a URL ends a reference entry, there is no period at the end of the entry.

Running head: RESISTANCE TO VACCINATION   I

top
right-hand
corner
pagination
begins with
title page

Resistance to Vaccination:

A Review of the Literature

Jeremy Yap

Vancouver Island University

author's
name may
appear
either just
below the
title (as
shown) or
at the bot-
tom of the
page with
course and
instructor
information

Author note

This paper was prepared for Psychology 230,

taught by Professor J.B. Martin.

Abstract

separate page for the abstract

In the past generation concern over the safety of vaccination against a variety of diseases has become common in North America, as well as in Britain and some other European countries. This paper reviews findings as to the safety of vaccines, as well as of their effectiveness in preventing the diseases they are designed to combat. It also explores the reasons for the now-widespread mistrust of vaccination, looking at the role played by the media, by health care professionals—and looking too at the findings of social psychologists. Finally, it asks what approaches may be most effective in increasing rates of vaccination; in all likelihood, the paper suggests, no single approach is likely to be enough.

Resistance to Vaccination:

A Review of the Literature

title should
be centred

Since the late 1990s, vaccination has become highly

controversial. This paper will review the literature on the subject,

with a particular focus on the vaccination of children, by posing and

responding to three key questions:

1.   How effective is the practice of vaccination—and how safe?

2.   Why have vaccination rates declined?

3.   What are the best ways to increase rates of vaccination?

This is an area in which medical science must engage with the

research findings of social psychologists; there is an urgent need

to find effective solutions. The problems are sufficiently complex,

however, that it seems unlikely that any single approach will be

sufficient to resolve them.

How Effective Is the Practice of Vaccination—and How Safe?

There is overwhelming evidence on a variety of fronts that

vaccination is one of the great triumphs of modern medical science.

Thanks to the spread of vaccination, smallpox and polio have been

eliminated in most of the world. The Centers for Disease Control

and Prevention (2014) reports that diseases such as measles, mumps,

and rubella, for which a combined vaccine has for generations been

routinely given to children, are almost unknown in areas where vaccination is near-universal. The example of measles is an instructive

one. Before the practice of vaccination was introduced, measles

infected several million children every year in the United States

alone, and killed more than 500 annually. After vaccination became

common practice, measles almost entirely disappeared in North

America—until recently. Now it is a threat once again in the United

States and Canada—and not a threat to be taken lightly. According

to the World Health Organization (2015), measles still kills over

100,000 worldwide each year; for 2012 the figure was 122,000.

Evidence for the effectiveness of vaccination is very strong

in the case of polio and smallpox, and in the case of "childhood

diseases" such as measles and rubella. There is also strong evidence

that vaccination against influenza has been successful in bringing

about significantly reduced rates of infection (Brewer et al., 2007).

Importantly, though, the success of vaccination depends in large

part on so-called "herd immunity." So long as approximately 95%

or thereabouts of a population have been vaccinated, the incidence

of a disease catching on in that population are negligible. When

vaccination rates dip below that level, however, the risk for those

who have not been vaccinated increases dramatically. Despite this,

some communities where vaccination is readily available nonetheless

have vaccination rates dramatically below the percentage required for

for
citation
of work
with six
or more
authors
use "et
al."

herd immunity. In California, for example, where a 2015 outbreak of measles has received wide attention, Maimuna et al. (2015) have estimated that in the relevant population clusters vaccination rates have dropped below 50%.

What about the other side of the ledger? Have there been cases of patients suffering adverse effects after taking a vaccine? And if so, do the benefits of vaccination outweigh the risks? Here too the answers seem clear. Yes, there have been cases of adverse effects (notably, fever and allergic reactions for some individuals). But as Bonhoeffer (2007) and others have concluded, these are rare, and on balance vastly outweighed by the benefits of mass vaccination. Perhaps the broadest study of vaccines, their effectiveness, and their occasional side effects was that conducted by the Institute of Medicine (2011), which reviewed vaccines used against chickenpox, influenza, hepatitis B, human papillomavirus, measles, mumps, rubella, meningitis, and tetanus. Their conclusion was clear:

> Vaccines offer the promise of protection against a variety of infectious diseases ... [and] remain one of the greatest tools in the public health arsenal. Certainly, some vaccines result in adverse effects that must be acknowledged. But the latest evidence shows that few adverse effects are caused by the vaccines reviewed in this report. (p. 4)

square brackets used for a word not in the original quotation

Except in rare cases, then (as with certain individuals susceptible to severe allergic reactions), the benefits of vaccines clearly far outweigh the risks.

centred
head-
ings for
sections

Why Have Vaccination Rates Declined?

Near the end of the last century, British medical researcher Andrew Wakefield and his colleagues (1998) published a study linking the vaccination of children against diseases such as measles, mumps, and rubella to increased incidence of gastrointestinal disease, and also to increased incidence of "developmental regression"— notably, autism. The study appeared in *The Lancet*, one of the world's leading medical journals, and had a major impact—but an entirely unfortunate one. News of the study's findings spread widely, with thousands of articles in the popular press in 2001 and 2002 questioning the safety of vaccination. Parents whose children suffered from autism started to blame vaccination, and many of them launched lawsuits.

It was not until six years later that serious doubts were publicly raised. Investigative journalist Brian Deer (2004) revealed that Wakefield's study was compromised by a serious conflict of interest; he had received financial compensation from parties intending to sue vaccine manufacturers before he embarked on the research. And, as was gradually discovered, the research itself had been fabricated.

RESISTANCE TO VACCINATION   7   running
                                                                    head may
                                                                    either be
                                                                    in caps (as
In 2010 *The Lancet* finally retracted the 1998 article, and Wakefield   shown) or
                                                                    upper and
himself was censured. By that time, a very great deal of damage had   lower case

been done; public confidence in vaccines had dropped precipitously.

Fabricated research results are not the sole cause of the lack of

confidence in vaccination that many continue to express. To some

extent, confidence in vaccination among the general public has always

been shaky. The very nature of vaccination—giving the patient a

very small, modified dose of an illness in order to prevent further

harm—seems counterintuitive to many. As Brendan Nyhan observed

in an interview with Julia Belluz (2015), "people have always been

suspicious of vaccines. There has always been an instinctive response

to the idea of using a disease to protect yourself against the disease. It

gives people the heebie jeebies" (para. 8). In a meta-analysis, Brewer

et al. (2007) report that humans are far more likely to get vaccinated

when they believe the disease in question to pose a serious threat—a

finding which should not come as surprising, and which explains

why doubts about vaccines have found fertile ground in places

where the vaccines themselves have largely or entirely succeeded. As

Jerome Groopman (2015) has observed, "we no longer see children

stricken with polio in wheelchairs, or hear of those suffocating from

diphtheria, of babies born to mothers with rubella whose eyes are

clouded by cataracts and hearts deformed" (p. 30). If one continually sees people suffering from such diseases, one is likely to be far more aware of their dangers than is the case in nations where vaccination has succeeded in reducing their incidence to zero or near-zero.

When doubts have been raised and scandals have arisen, the media have too often not been as responsible as one would wish. On the one hand, as discussed by Nelson (2014), Mooney (2011) and others, some media outlets have tacitly encouraged scientifically irresponsible statements by taking an "impartial" approach to the facts, reporting the claims of anti-vaccination activists with no scientific credentials and of reputable scientific authorities as if they had equal authority. Other media outlets, however, have sometimes swung too far in the other direction, adopting a supercilious or contemptuous tone towards those who have doubts about vaccination. Much as it is important to spread factual information as to the dangers of allowing one's children to remain unvaccinated, it is counterproductive to present information in a tone that is disrespectful of the audience one is hoping to persuade. As Angelina Chapin (2015) has pointed out, when

accept-
able to
include
first
name in
a signal
phrase

> people's beliefs contradict science, there's an obvious temp-
> tation to cut them down. But we should be more careful
> with how we deliver our arguments. On a policy level, mes-
> saging should come from people that communities trust,

such as doctors or religious leaders. At the dinner table or

on Facebook, try a little empathy. It will help the medicine

go down and the immunization rates go up. (para. 12)

The attitudes with which we approach these discussions, in short, can

make a world of difference.

Interestingly, studies such as that of Maimuna et al. (2015)

suggest that those with high levels of education are at least as likely

as those with less education to be anti-vaccination. One important

factor in the social psychology of attitudes towards vaccination that

does seem to have had an impact (albeit a negative one), has been

the degree to which the issue has become charged with ideological

content. Those who are generally suspicious of government and/

or of modern science have been slow to accept the overwhelming

weight of evidence in support of vaccination. That should perhaps

not be surprising; as Kraft, Lodge, and Taber (2015) and others

have reported, to the extent that beliefs about factual matters are

intertwined with ideology, our minds become immunized against

information in the other direction, even when that information is of a

purely factual nature. Moreover, this is a "tendency that appears to be

evident among liberals and conservatives alike" (p. 121). When they

are coloured by ideology—and by emotion—our beliefs as to the facts

of the matter are highly resistant to change.

in signal phrase, "and" used to link author names

What Are the Best Ways to Increase the Rates of Vaccination?

Clearly it is important for health care workers, educators, and those in the media to inform themselves of the facts and to spread this information. But simply informing the public of the facts is evidently insufficient to change behaviour. Several studies have found that parents who have been fully informed of the scientific background are no more likely to vaccinate their children—and in some cases are *less* likely (Nyhan, Reifler, Richey, & Freed, 2014; Mills, Jadadc, Ross, & Wilson, 2005).

in parenthetical citation, ampersand (not "and") used to link author names

Just as important as the facts themselves, it seems, is the way they are reported to patients. The attitudes expressed by health care workers to patients play a key role. Though the vast majority of health care workers accept the evidence regarding vaccination, they have become aware that it is a hot-button issue and—not wanting to be insensitive to patients' concerns—have sometimes not been clear and emphatic about the dangers of not vaccinating. If health care workers ask parents if they "believe in" vaccinating their children, their phrasing is likely to provide support to the views of those patients who think the science about vaccinations to be uncertain. Conversely, an attitude that remains friendly while taking the facts as a given may be more helpful. There have been numerous studies on the degree to which it may help to frame information positively to patients (Marsh, Malik, Shapiro, & Omer, 2014; Wegwartha, Kurzenhäuser-Carstens, & Gigerenzera, 2014; and O'Keefea & Xiaoli, 2012). Though these have not been entirely conclusive, it is hard to imagine that it is not preferable to present facts in a tone that will encourage others to appreciate them, and to act accordingly. Angelina Chapin's common-sense advice on this point (quoted above) rings true.

It may well be, however, that adopting the right tone with patients and in media reports will not be enough; regulatory and/or legislative changes may be required as well in some jurisdictions. It is important to note that the United States as a whole has not suffered any steep decline in vaccination rates; to a large extent the problem is associated with jurisdictions that make it easy for parents to opt out of vaccinations for their children. In contrast, where vaccination is the strong "default position"—mandatory for children with few possible exemptions—vaccination rates in recent years have tended to remain at well over 90%. As Margaret Talbot (2015) has observed of the United States,

> the highest vaccination rate in the country is in
> Mississippi, a state with an otherwise dismal set of
> health statistics. It allows people to opt out of vaccines
> only for medical reasons—not for religious or personal

quotation of more than 40 words is indented

ones. States that make it easier not to vaccinate have
higher rates of infectious diseases. (pp. 19–20)

Is the answer, then, simply to pass stricter laws in jurisdictions that
currently have loose ones? Much as such action may be desirable,
given current levels of resistance to vaccination of children, it is
questionable whether efforts to make the practice mandatory would
be successful in many areas—and they would be sure to inflame
passions on all sides.

The experience of the European Union suggests that it may not
always be necessary to make vaccination mandatory. Vaccination rates
are high throughout Europe, even though only 14 of the 29 countries
in the EU have any mandatory vaccinations (Haverkate et al., 2012).
In the remainder, vaccination is recommended rather than required.
There is some evidence that in North America, too, non-compulsory
strategies can in certain circumstances be as effective as compulsion
in raising vaccination rates (El-Amin et al., 2012). Again, the strength
with which a recommendation is put forward can make a world of
difference to the degree to which that recommendation is followed.
If parents are simply informed that vaccination is recommended and
that they may vaccinate their children against measles if they wish at
such and such a time and place, the uptake rate is likely to be low. If
parents are informed that a medical ordinance specifies that children

should be vaccinated against measles, and that low vaccination rates put all children at risk, the uptake rate will surely be much higher.

There is a widespread tendency to presume that Americans will be more likely to resist government "intrusions" into citizens' lives than will Canadians. In the case of attitudes towards vaccination, however, it is not at all clear that the presumption is correct. Whereas every American state has at least some requirement (albeit often weakened by "personal belief" exemptions) that children be vaccinated before attending school, only a minority of Canadian provinces have such regulations (Walkinshaw, 2011).

Whatever approaches are taken in each jurisdiction, it will be essential that attention be paid not only to the medical and biological facts, but also to laws and regulations—and to social psychology.

list of
references
begins on a
new page

References

list of
references
alphabet-
ized by
author's
last name

Belluz, J. (2015, February 7). Debunking vaccine junk science won't

    change people's minds. Here's what will. [Interview

    with B. Nyhan]. *Vox.* Retrieved from http://www.vox

    .com/2015/2/7/7993289/vaccine-beliefs

Bonhoeffer, J., & Heininger, U. (2007). Adverse events following

    immunization: perception and evidence. *Current Opinion in*

    Infectious Diseases, 20(3), 237–246. doi:10.1097

    /QCO.0b013e32811ebfb0

author
initials
used—not
first names

Brewer, N. T., Chapman, G. B., Gibbons, F. X., Gerrard, M.,

    McCaul, K. D., & Weinstein, N. D. (2007). Meta-analysis of

    the relationship between risk perception and health behaviour:

    The example of vaccination. *Health Psychology, 26*(2), 136–145.

    doi:10.1037/0278-6133.26.2.136

Chapin, A. (2015, February 13). How to talk to anti-vaxxers. *Ottawa*

    Citizen. Retrieved from http://ottawacitizen.com/opinion

    /columnists/how-to-talk-to-anti-vaxxers

Deer, B. (2004, February 22). Revealed: MMR research scandal.

    The Sunday Times (London). Retrieved from http://www

    .thesundaytimes.co.uk/sto/

El-Amin, A. N., Parra, M. T., Kim-Farley, R., & Fielding, J. E.

    (2012). Ethical issues concerning vaccination requirements.

Public Health Reviews, 34(1), 1–20. Retrieved from http://www

.publichealthreviews.eu/upload/pdf_files/11/00_El_Amin.pdf

Groopman, J. (2015, March 5). There's no way out of it. [Review of

the book *On immunity: An introduction*]. *The New York Review of

Books*, 29–31.

Haverkate, M., D'Ancona, F., Giambi, C., Johansen, K., Lopalco,

P. L., Cozza, V., & Appelgren, E. (2012, May). Mandatory

and recommended vaccination in the EU, Iceland and

Norway: results of the VENICE 2010 survey on the

ways of implementing national vaccination programmes.

Eurosurveillance, 17(22), 31. Retrieved from http://www

.eurosurveillance.org/ViewArticle.aspx?ArticleId=20183

Institute of Medicine. (2011, August 25). Adverse effects of vaccines:

Evidence and causality. Report brief. Retrieved from http://www

.iom.edu/Reports/2011/Adverse-Effects-of-Vaccines-Evidence

-and-Causality.aspx

Kraft, P. W., Lodge, M., & Taber, C. S. (2015, March). Why people

"don't trust the evidence": Motivated reasoning and scientific

beliefs. *Annals of the American Academy of Political and Social

Science, 658*(1), 121–133. doi:10.1177/0002716214554758

Maimuna, S., Majumder, M. P. H., Cohn, E. L., Sumiko, R.,

Mekaru, D. V. M., Huston, J. E., & Brownstein, J. S. (2015,

for web-
accessed
material
provide
DOI
whenever
available

RESISTANCE TO VACCINATION   16

March 16). Substandard vaccination compliance and the 2015

measles outbreak. *JAMA Pediatrics*. doi:10.1001

/jamapediatrics.2015.0384

Marsh, H. A., Malik, F., Shapiro, E., & Omer, S. B. (2014,

September). Message framing strategies to increase influenza

immunization uptake among pregnant African American

women. *Maternal and Child Health Journal, 18*(7), 1639–1647.

doi:10.1007/s10995-013-1404-9

Measles History. (2014, November 3). Center for Disease Control

and Prevention website. Retrieved from http://www.cdc.gov

/measles/about/history.html

Mills, E., Jadadc, A. R., Ross, C., & Wilson, K. (2005, November).

Systematic review of qualitative studies exploring parental beliefs

and attitudes toward childhood vaccination identifies common

barriers to vaccination. *Journal of Clinical Epidemiology,*

58(11), 1081–1088. doi:http://dx.doi.org/10.1016/j

.jclinepi.2005.09.002

Mooney, C. (2011, May/June). The science of why we don't believe

science. *Mother Jones*. Retrieved from http://www.motherjones

.com/politics/2011/03/denial-science-chris-mooney

Nelson, R. (2014, October). The reporting of health information

in the media. *American Journal of Nursing, 114*(10), 19–20.

doi:10.1097/01.NAJ.0000454842.04985.c6

Nyhan, B. (2013, July 16). When "he said, she said" is dangerous.
Columbia Journalism Review. Retrieved from http://www.cjr.org
/united_states_project/media_errs_giving_balanced_coverage
_to_jenny_mccarthys_discredited_views.php

Nyhan, B., Reifler, J., Richey, S., & Freed, G.L. (2014, April 1).
Effective messages in vaccine promotion: A randomized trial.
Pediatrics, 133(4), e835-e842. doi:10.1542/peds.2013-2365

O'Keefea, D. J., & Xiaoli, N. (2012). The relative persuasiveness of
gain- and loss-framed messages for promoting vaccination: A
meta-analytic review. *Health Communication, 27*(8), 776–783.
doi:10.1080/10410236.2011.640974

Talbot, M. (2015, February 16). Not immune. *The New Yorker, 91*(1),
19–20.

Wakefield, A. J., Murch, S. H., Anthony, A., Linnel, J., Casson, D.
M., Malik, M., … Walker-Smith, J. A. (1998). Ileal-lymphoid-
nodular hyperplasia, non-specific colitis, and pervasive
developmental disorder in children. *Lancet, 351,* 637–41.
(Retraction published 2010, *Lancet, 375,* p. 445)

Walkinshaw, E. (2011, November 8). Mandatory vaccinations: The
international landscape. *Canadian Medical Association Journal,
183*(16), e1167–e1168. doi:10.1503/cmaj.109-3993

provide URL for web-sourced material when DOI not available

Wegwartha, O., Kurzenhäuser-Carstens, S., & Gigerenzera, G.

(2014, March 10). Overcoming the knowledge–behaviour

gap: The effect of evidence-based HPV vaccination leaflets

on understanding, intention, and actual vaccination decision.

Science Direct: Vaccine, 32(12), 1388–1393. doi:10.1016/j

.vaccine.2013.12.038

World Health Organization (n.d.). Measles (Immunization, Vaccines

and Biologicals). World Health Organization website.

Retrieved from http://www.who.int/immunization

/monitoring_surveillance/burden/vpd/surveillance_type/active

/measles/en/

◎ Chicago Style

○ *About Chicago Style*

The University of Chicago's massively comprehensive *Chicago Manual of Style* (17th edition, 2017) provides full information on two documentation systems: an author-date system of citation that is similar to APA style, and a traditional foot- or endnoting system. The latter, which this book refers to as Chicago Style, and which is often used in the history and philosophy disciplines, is outlined below. This chapter also includes, at the end, a short essay excerpt using Chicago Style documentation. Full sample essays in Chicago Style are available on the Broadview website. Go to sites.www. broadviewpress.com/writing/. You can also find additional information at Chicago Style's online site (www.chicagomanualofstyle. org).

In the pages that follow, information about electronic sources has been presented in an integrated fashion, with information about referencing hard copies of print sources presented alongside information about referencing online versions. General guidelines covering entries for online sources are as follows. Begin each note and bibliography entry for an electronic source as you would for a non-electronic source, including all relevant publication information that the source makes available. Then provide either the website's URL, followed by the usual end punctuation for the note or entry, or, if available, the source's digital object identifier (DOI): a string of numbers, letters, and punctuation, beginning with *10*, usually located on the first or copyright page. If both a URL and DOI are available, provide only the latter; DOIs are preferred because they are stable links to sources, whereas URLs are often not permanent. If you need to break a URL or DOI over two or more lines, do not insert any hyphens at the break point; instead, break after a colon or double slash or before other marks of punctuation. Note that Chicago Style does not put angle brackets around URLs. Except when there is no publication or modification date available, Chicago Style does not require the addition of access dates for online material, but your instructors may wish you to include them. If so, put them after the URL or DOI, after the word *accessed*.

1. **notes:** The basic principle of Chicago Style is to create a note each time one cites a source. The note can appear at the foot of the page on which the citation is made, or it can be part of a separate list, titled *Notes*, situated at the end of the essay and before the bibliography. For both foot- and endnotes, a superscript number at the end of the clause in which the reference appears points to the relevant note:

- Bonnycastle refers to "the true and lively spirit of opposition" with which Marxist literary criticism invigorates the discipline.[1]

The superscript number [1] here is linked to the information provided where the same number appears at either the foot of the page or in the list of notes at the end of the main text of the paper:

1. Stephen Bonnycastle, *In Search of Authority: An Introductory Guide to Literary Theory*, 3rd ed. (Peterborough, ON: Broadview Press, 2007), 204.

Notice that the author's name is in the normal order, elements of the note are separated by commas, publication information is in parentheses, and the first line of the note is indented. The note ends with a page number for the citation.

In addition, all works cited, as well as works that have been consulted but are not cited in the body of your essay, must be included in an alphabetically arranged list, titled *Bibliography*, that appears at the end of the essay. The entry there would in this case be as follows:

Bonnycastle, Stephen. *In Search of Authority: An Introductory Guide to Literary Theory.* 3rd ed. Peterborough, ON: Broadview Press, 2007.

In the entry in the bibliography, notice that the author's name is inverted, elements of the entry are separated by periods, and no parentheses are placed around the publication information. Also, the entry is given a hanging indent: the first line is flush with the left-hand margin, and subsequent lines are indented. Notice as well that the province or state of publication is included in both notes and bibliography entries if the city of publication is not widely known.

In the various examples that follow, note formats and bibliography entry formats for each kind of source are shown together.

2. titles: italics/quotation marks: Notice in the above example that both the title and the subtitle are in italics. Titles of short works (such as articles, poems, and short stories) should be put in quotation marks. In all titles key words should be capitalized. For more details, see the Source Title section in the chapter on MLA documentation above.

3. multiple references to the same work: For later notes referencing an already-cited source, use the author's last name, title (in shortened form if it is over four words long), and page number only.

> 1. Bonnycastle, *In Search of Authority*, 28.

If successive references are to the same work, you may omit the title of the work just cited, in order to avoid repetition.[1]

> 1. Sean Carver, "The Economic Foundations for Unrest in East Timor, 1970–1995," *Journal of Economic History* 21, no. 2 (2011): 103.
>
> 2. Carver, 109.
>
> 3. Carver, 111.
>
> 4. Jennifer Riley, "East Timor in the Pre-Independence Years," *Asian History Online* 11, no. 4 (2012): par. 18, http://www.aho.ubc.edu/prs/text-only/issue.45/16.3jr.txt.
>
> 5. Riley, par. 24.

Carver, Sean. "The Economic Foundations for Unrest in East Timor, 1970–1995." *Journal of Economic History* 21, no. 2 (2011): 100–121.

Riley, Jennifer. "East Timor in the Pre-Independence Years." *Asian History Online* 11, no. 4 (2012). http://www.aho.ubc.edu/prs/text-only/issue.45/16.3jr.txt.

4. page number or date unavailable: If an Internet document cited is in PDF format, the page numbers are stable and may be cited in the same way that one would the pages of a printed book or journal article. Many Internet page numbers are unstable, however, and many more lack page numbers. Instead, provide a section number, paragraph number, or other identifier if available.

> 2. Hanif Bhabha, "Family Life in 1840s Virginia," *Southern History Web Archives* 45, no. 3 (2013): par. 14. http://shweb.ut.edu/history/american.nineteenthc/bhabha.html (accessed March 3, 2009).

---

1 This recommendation represents a change from previous editions, which had recommended using *ibid.* (an abbreviation of the Latin *ibidem*, meaning *in the same place*) for successive references. The 17th edition discourages the use of *ibid.*

Bhabha, Hanif. "Family Life in 1840s Virginia." *Southern History Web Archives* 45, no. 3 (2013). http://shweb.ut.edu/history /american.nineteenthc/bhabha.html.

If you are citing longer texts from electronic versions, and counting paragraph numbers is impracticable, chapter references may be more appropriate. For example, if the online Gutenberg edition of Darwin's *On the Origin of Species* were being cited, the citation would be as follows:

- Darwin refers to the core of his theory as an "ineluctable principle."[1]

1. Charles Darwin, *On the Origin of Species* (1856; Project Gutenberg, 2001), chap. 26, http://www.gutenberg.darwin .origin.frrp.ch26.html.

Darwin, Charles. *On the Origin of Species*. 1856. Project Gutenberg, 2001. http://www.gutenberg.darwin.origin.frrp.ch26.html.

Students should be cautioned that online editions of older or classic works are often unreliable; typically there are far more typos and other errors in online versions of literary texts than there are in print versions. It is often possible to exercise judgement about such matters, however. If, for example, you are not required to base your essay on a particular edition of Darwin's *Origin of Species* but may find your own, you will be far better off using the text you will find on the reputable Project Gutenberg site than you will using a text you might find on a site such as "Manybooks.com."

When there is no date for a source, include *n. d.*, as in the first example below. When there is no date for an online source, include your access date.

1. Thomas Gray, *Gray's Letters*, vol. 1 (London: John Sharpe, n. d.), 60.

2. Don LePan, *Skyscraper Art*, http://www.donlepan.com /Skyscraper_Art.html (accessed February 10, 2013).

Gray, Thomas. *Gray's Letters*. Vol. 1. London: John Sharpe, n. d.
LePan, Don. *Skyscraper Art*. http://www.donlepan.com/Skyscraper _Art.html (accessed February 10, 2013).

5. **two or more dates for a work**: Note that in the Darwin example above both the date of the original publication and the date of the

modern edition are provided. If you are citing work in a form that has been revised by the author, however, you should cite the date of the revised publication, not the original, and use the abbreviation *rev. ed.* to indicate that the work has been revised.

> 1. Eric Foner, *Free Soil, Free Labor, Free Men: A Study of Antebellum America*, rev. ed. (New York: Oxford University Press, 1999), 178.

> Foner, Eric. *Free Soil, Free Labor, Free Men: A Study of Antebellum America*. Rev. ed. New York: Oxford University Press, 1999.

6. two or three authors: If there are two or three authors, they should be identified as follows in the footnote and in the bibliography. Pay attention to where commas do and do not appear, and note that in the bibliography entry, only the first author's name is inverted. Put the names of the authors in the order in which they appear in the work itself.

> 4. Eric Alderman and Mark Green, *Tony Blair and the Rise of New Labour* (London: Cassell, 2002), 180.

> Alderman, Eric, and Mark Green. *Tony Blair and the Rise of New Labour*. London: Cassell, 2002.

7. four or more authors: In the footnote name only the first author, and use the phrase *et al.*, an abbreviation of the Latin *et alia*, meaning *and others*. In the bibliography name all authors, as below:

> 11. Victoria Fromkin et al., *An Introduction to Language*, 4th Canadian ed. (Toronto: Nelson, 2010), 113.

> Fromkin, Victoria, Robert Rodman, Nina Hyams, and Kirsten M. Hummel. *An Introduction to Language*. 4th Canadian ed. Toronto: Nelson, 2010.

8. author unknown/corporate author/government document: Identify by the corporate author if known, and otherwise by the title of the work. Unsigned newspaper articles or dictionary and encyclopedia entries are usually not listed in the bibliography. In notes, unsigned dictionary or encyclopedia entries are identified by the title of the reference work, e.g., *Columbia Encyclopedia*, and unsigned newspaper articles are listed by the title of the article in footnotes but by the title of the newspaper in the bibliography.

Ignore initial articles (the, a, an) when alphabetizing.

>   6. *National Hockey League Guide, 1966–67* (Toronto: National Hockey League, 1966), 77.
>
>   7. "Argentina's President Calls on UK Prime Minister to Relinquish Control of Falkland Islands," *Vancouver Sun*, January 3, 2013, A9.
>
>   8. Broadview Press, "Questions and Answers about Book Pricing," Broadview Press, http://www.broadviewpress.com/bookpricing .asp?inc=bookpricing (accessed January 18, 2013).
>
>   9. Commonwealth of Massachusetts, *Records of the Transportation Inquiry, 2004* (Boston: Massachusetts Publishing Office, 2005), 488.
>
>   10. *Columbia Encyclopedia*, "Ecuador," http://bartleby.com .columbia.txt.acc.html (accessed February 4, 2013).
>
>   11. U.S. Congress. House Committee on Ways and Means, Subcommittee on Trade, *Free Trade Area of the Americas: Hearings*, 105th Cong., 1st sess., July 22, 1997, Hearing Print 105–32, 160, http:// www.waysandmeans.house.gov/hearings.asp (accessed January 22, 2013).

Following are the bibliography entries for the preceding notes (notice that, because unsigned newspaper articles and articles from well-known reference works are not usually included in Chicago Style bibliographies, the *Vancouver Sun* and *Columbia Encyclopedia* articles are not included):

> Broadview Press. "Questions and Answers about Book Pricing." Broadview Press. http://www.broadviewpress.com/bookpricing .asp?inc=bookpricing (accessed January 18, 2013).
>
> Commonwealth of Massachusetts. *Records of the Transportation Inquiry, 2004.* Boston: Massachusetts Publishing Office, 2005.
>
> *National Hockey League Guide, 1966–67.* Toronto: National Hockey League, 1966.
>
> U.S. Congress. House Committee on Ways and Means. Subcommittee on Trade. *Free Trade Area of the Americas: Hearing before the Subcommittee on Trade.* 105th Cong., 1st sess., July 22, 1997. Hearing Print 105–32. http://www.waysandmeans.house.gov /hearings.asp (accessed January 22, 2013).

9. works from a collection of readings or anthology: In the citation for a work in an anthology or collection of essays, use the name of the author of the work you are citing. If the work is reprinted in one source but was first published elsewhere, include the details of the original publication in the bibliography.

> 6. Eric Hobsbawm, "Peasant Land Occupations," in *Uncommon People: Resistance and Rebellion* (London: Weidenfeld & Nicolson, 1998), 167.
>
> 7. Frederic W. Gleach, "Controlled Speculation: Interpreting the Saga of Pocahontas and Captain John Smith," in *Reading Beyond Words: Contexts for Native History*, 2nd ed., ed. Jennifer Brown and Elizabeth Vibert (Peterborough, ON: Broadview Press, 2003), 43.

> Gleach, Frederic W. "Controlled Speculation: Interpreting the Saga of Pocahontas and Captain John Smith." In *Reading Beyond Words: Contexts for Native History*, 2nd ed., edited by Jennifer Brown and Elizabeth Vibert, 39–74. Peterborough, ON: Broadview Press, 2003.
>
> Hobsbawm, Eric. "Peasant Land Occupations." In *Uncommon People: Resistance and Rebellion*, 166–90. London: Weidenfeld & Nicolson, 1998. Originally published in *Past and Present* 62 (1974): 120–52.

10. **indirect source:** If you are citing a source from a reference other than the source itself, you should include information about both sources, supplying as much information as you are able to about the original source.

> • In de Beauvoir's famous phrase, "one is not born a woman, one becomes one."[1]

> 1. Simone de Beauvoir, *The Second Sex* (London: Heinemann, 1966), 44, quoted in Ann Levey, "Feminist Philosophy Today," *Philosophy Now*, par. 8, http://www.ucalgary.ca.philosophy.nowsite675 .html (accessed February 4, 2013).

> de Beauvoir, Simone. *The Second Sex*. London: Heinemann, 1966. Quoted in Ann Levey, "Feminist Philosophy Today," *Philosophy Now*, http://www.ucalgary.ca.philosophy.nowsite675.html (accessed February 4, 2013).

11. **two or more works by the same author:** After the first entry in the bibliography, use three hyphens to begin subsequent entries of works by the same author (rather than repeat the author's name). Entries for multiple works by the same author are normally arranged alphabetically by title.

Menand, Louis. "Bad Comma: Lynne Truss's Strange Grammar." *The New Yorker,* June 28, 2004. http://www.newyorker.com/critics /books/?040628crbo_books1.

———. *The Metaphysical Club: A Story of Ideas in America.* New York: Knopf, 2002.

12. **edited works:** Entries for edited works include the abbreviation *ed.* or *eds.* Note that when *ed.* appears after a title, it means "edited by."

> 5. Brian Gross, ed., *New Approaches to Environmental Politics: A Survey* (New York: Duckworth, 2004), 177.
> 6. Mary Shelley, *Frankenstein,* 2nd ed., ed. Lorne Macdonald and Kathleen Scherf, Broadview Editions (1818; Peterborough, ON: Broadview Press, 2001), 89.

Gross, Brian, ed. *New Approaches to Environmental Politics: A Survey.* New York: Duckworth, 2004.

Shelley, Mary. *Frankenstein.* 2nd ed. Edited by Lorne Macdonald and Kathleen Scherf. Broadview Editions. Peterborough, ON: Broadview, 2001. First published in 1818.

13. **translated works:** The name of the translator follows the work's title. Notice that, in the first example below, the work's author is unknown; begin with the author's name if it is known.

> 1. *Beowulf,* trans. R. M. Liuzza, 2nd ed. (Peterborough, ON: Broadview, 2012), 91.
> 2. Franz Kafka, "A Hunger Artist," *The Metamorphosis and Other Stories,* trans. Ian Johnston (Peterborough, ON: Broadview, 2015), 112.

Beowulf. Translated by R. M. Liuzza. 2nd ed. Peterborough, ON: Broadview, 2012.

Kafka, Franz. "A Hunger Artist." *The Metamorphosis and Other Stories.* Translated by Ian Johnston. Peterborough, ON: Broadview, 2015.

14. **e-books:** Electronic books come in several formats. The first of the two sample citations below is for a book found online; the second is for a book downloaded onto an e-reader.

4. Mary Roberts Rinehart, *Tish* (1916; Project Gutenberg, 2005), chap. 2, http://www.gutenberg.org/catalog/world/readfile?fk_files=1452441.

5. Lao Tzu, *Tao Te Ching: A Book about the Way and the Power of the Way*, trans. Ursula K. Le Guin (Boston: Shambhala, 2011), iBook Reader e-book, verse 12.

Lao Tzu. *Tao Te Ching: A Book about the Way and the Power of the Way*. Translated by Ursula K. Le Guin. Boston: Shambhala, 2011. iBook Reader e-book.

Rinehart, Mary Roberts. *Tish*. 1916. Project Gutenberg, 2005. http://www.gutenberg.org/catalog/world/readfile?fk_files=1452441.

15. **magazine articles**: The titles of articles appear in quotation marks. The page range should appear in the bibliography if it is known. (This will not always be possible if the source is an electronic version.) If no authorship is attributed, list the title of the article as the "author" in the footnote, and the magazine title as the "author" in the bibliography. Do not include page numbers for online articles.

2. Alan Dyer, "The End of the World … Again," *SkyNews*, November/December 2012, 38.

3. "The Rise of the Yuan: Turning from Green to Red," *Economist*, October 20, 2012, 68.

4. Wendell Steavenson, "Two Revolutions: Women in the New Egypt," *The New Yorker*, November 12, 2012, http://www.newyorker.com/reporting/2012/11/12/121112fa_fact_steavenson.

Dyer, Alan. "The End of the World … Again." *SkyNews*, November/December 2012, 38–39.

Economist. "The Rise of the Yuan: Turning from Green to Red." October 20, 2012, 67–68.

Steavenson, Wendell. "Two Revolutions: Women in the New Egypt." *The New Yorker*, November 12, 2012. http://www.newyorker.com/reporting/2012/11/12/121112fa_fact_steavenson.

16. **newspaper articles**: The basic principles to follow with newspaper articles or editorials are the same as with magazine articles (see above). Give page numbers in the note if your source is a hard copy rather than an electronic version, but indicate section designation alone in the bibliography entry.

1. Konrad Yakabuski, "Many Looking for Meaning in Vice-Presidential Debate," *The Globe and Mail*, October 12, 2012, A3.

2. Claudia La Rocco, "Where Chekhov Meets Christopher Walken," *New York Times*, January 2, 2013, http://theater.nytimes.com /2013/01/03/theater/reviews/there-there-by-kristen-kosmas-at -the-chocolate-factory.html?ref=theater&_r=0.

La Rocco, Claudia. "Where Chekhov Meets Christopher Walken." *New York Times*, January 2, 2013, http://theater.nytimes.com /2013/01/03/theater/reviews/there-there-by-kristen-kosmas-at -the-chocolate-factory.html?ref=theater&_r=0.

Yakabuski, Konrad. "Many Looking for Meaning in Vice-Presidential Debate." *The Globe and Mail*, October 12, 2012, sec. A.

17. **journal articles**: The basic principles are the same as with magazine articles, but volume number, and issue number after *no.* (if the journal is published more than once a year), should be included as well as the date. Give page numbers where available. For online journal articles, provide the DOI, if available, rather than the URL.

1. Paul Barker, "The Impact of Class Size on the Classroom Behaviour of Special Needs Students: A Longitudinal Study," *Educational Quarterly* 25, no. 4 (2004): 88.

2. Maciel Santos and Ana Guedes, "The Profitability of Slave Labour and the 'Time' Effect," *African Economic History* 36 (2008): 23.

3. Thomas Hurka, "Virtuous Act, Virtuous Dispositions," *Analysis* 66, no. 1 (2006): 72.

4. Ruth Groenhout, "The 'Brain Drain' Problem: Migrating Medical Professionals and Global Health Care," *International Journal of Feminist Approaches to Bioethics* 5, no. 1 (2012): 17, doi: 10.2979 /intjfemappbio.5.1.1.

Barker, Paul. "The Impact of Class Size on the Classroom Behaviour of Special Needs Students: A Longitudinal Study." *Educational Quarterly* 25, no. 4 (2004): 87–99.

Groenhout, Ruth. "The 'Brain Drain' Problem: Migrating Medical Professionals and Global Health Care." *International Journal of Feminist Approaches to Bioethics* 5, no. 1 (2012): 1–24, doi: 10.2979/intjfemappbio.5.1.1.

Hurka, Thomas. "Virtuous Act, Virtuous Dispositions." *Analysis* 66, no. 1 (2006): 69–76.

Santos, Maciel, and Ana Guedes. "The Profitability of Slave Labour and the 'Time' Effect." *African Economic History* 36 (2008): 1–26.

18. **films and video recordings:** Include the director's name, the city of production, the production company, and date. Add the medium of publication if the film is recorded on DVD or videocassette.

5. *Memento*, directed by Christopher Nolan (Universal City, CA: Summit Entertainment, 2000), DVD.

6. *Beasts of the Southern Wild*, directed by Behn Zeitlin (Los Angeles: Fox Searchlight Pictures, 2012).

Beasts of the Southern Wild. Directed by Behn Zeitlin. Los Angeles: Fox Searchlight Pictures, 2012.

Memento. Directed by Christopher Nolan. Universal City, CA: Summit Entertainment, 2000. DVD.

19. **television broadcasts:** Start with the title of the show; then give the episode number, broadcast date, and network. Include the names of the director and writer.

1. *Mad Men*, episodes no. 53–54, first broadcast March 25, 2012, by AMC, directed by Jennifer Getzinger and written by Matthew Weiner.

Mad Men. Episodes no. 53–54, first broadcast March 25, 2012, by AMC. Directed by Jennifer Getzinger and written by Matthew Weiner.

20. **sound recordings:** Include the original date of recording if it is different from the recording release date, as well as the recording number and medium.

1. Glenn Gould, performance of *Goldberg Variations*, by Johann Sebastian Bach, recorded 1981, CBS MK 37779, 1982, compact disc.

Gould, Glenn. Performance of *Goldberg Variations*. By Johann Sebastian Bach. Recorded 1981. CBS MK 37779, 1982, compact disc.

21. **interviews and personal communications:** Notes and bibliography entries begin with the name of the person interviewed. Only interviews that are broadcast, published, or available online appear in the bibliography.

7. Louise Erdrich, interview by Bill Moyers, *Bill Moyers Journal*, PBS, April 9, 2010.

8. Ursula K. Le Guin, "Beyond Elvish," interview by Patrick Cox, *The World*, podcast audio, December 13, 2012, http://www.theworld .org/2012/12/beyond-elvish/.

9. Willie Nelson, "The Silver-Headed Stranger," interview by Andrew Goldman, *New York Times Magazine*, December 16, 2012, 12.

10. Herbert Rosengarten, telephone interview by author, January 17, 2013.

Erdrich, Louise. Interview by Bill Moyers. *Bill Moyers Journal*. PBS, April 9, 2010.

Le Guin, Ursula K. "Beyond Elvish." Interview by Patrick Cox. *The World*. Podcast audio. December 13, 2012. http://www.theworld .org/2012/12/beyond-elvish/.

Nelson, Willie. "The Silver-Headed Stranger." Interview by Andrew Goldman. *New York Times Magazine*, December, 2012, 12.

22. **book reviews**: The name of the reviewer (if it has been provided) should come first, as shown below:

1. Brian Leiter and Michael Weisberg, "Do You Only Have a Brain? On Thomas Nagel," review of *Why the Materialist Neo-Darwinian Conception of Nature Is Almost Certainly False*, by Thomas Nagel, *The Nation*, October 22, 2012, http://www.thenation.com/article/170334 /do-you-only-have-brain-thomas-nagel.

Leiter, Brian, and Michael Weisberg. "Do You Only Have a Brain? On Thomas Nagel." Review of *Why the Materialist Neo-Darwinian Conception of Nature Is Almost Certainly False*, by Thomas Nagel. *The Nation*, October 22, 2012. http://www.thenation.com/article /170334/do-you-only-have-brain-thomas-nagel.

23. **blog posts**: Begin with the author's name, if there is one.

1. Karen Ho, "What Will Gioni's Biennale Look Like?," *The Art History Newsletter*, July 20, 2012, http://arthistorynewsletter.com/.

Ho, Karen. "What Will Gioni's Biennale Look Like?" *The Art History Newsletter*. July 20, 2012. http://arthistorynewsletter.com/.

24. **websites**: Unless the website title is also that of a book or periodical, do not put the site's title in italics. If possible, indicate when the site was last updated; otherwise, include your date of access.

1. The Camelot Project. University of Rochester, last modified December 21, 2012, http://www.lib.rochester.edu/camelot/cphome .stm.

The Camelot Project. University of Rochester. Last modified December 21, 2012. http://www.lib.rochester.edu/camelot/cphome .stm.

25. online videos: Include the author or principal performer, length of the video, and date of posting, if available, as well as the medium and its source.

1. Great Ape Trust, "Kanzi and Novel Sentences," YouTube video, 1:43, January 9, 2009, http://www.youtube.com /watch?v=2Dhc2zePJFE.

Great Ape Trust. "Kanzi and Novel Sentences." YouTube video, 1:43. January 9, 2009. http://www.youtube.com /watch?v=2Dhc2zePJFE.

26. tweets: As of this book's press time, Chicago Style recommends that a tweet be described fully in the essay's text, as in the first example below. Following that is, as an alternative, Chicago Style's suggested format for a Twitter feed note citation. There is as yet no guidance for formatting a bibliography entry for a tweet, but one would not go far wrong in following Chicago Style's general guidelines for Web source entries; a suggested example is given in what follows.

- Jack Welch (@jack_welch) quickly lost credibility when, on October 5, 2012 at 5:35 a.m., he tweeted that the U. S. Bureau of Labor had manipulated monthly unemployment rate statistics in order to boost the post-debate Obama campaign: "Unbelievable jobs numbers..these Chicago guys will do anything..can't debate so change numbers."[1]

1. Jack Welch, Twitter post, October 5, 2012, 5:35 a.m., http:// twitter.com/jack_welch.

Welch, Jack. Twitter post. October 5, 2012, 5:35 a.m. http://twitter .com/jack_welch.

O *Chicago Style Sample*

A sample of text with citations in Chicago style appears below. Note that a full sample essay in Chicago style appears on the adjunct website associated with this book.

> Urban renewal is as much a matter of psychology as it is of bricks and mortar. As Paul Goldberger has described, there have been many plans to revitalize Havana.[1] But both that city and the community of Cuban exiles in Florida remain haunted by a sense of absence and separation. As Lourdes Casal reminds us,
>
> > Exile
> > is living where there is no house whatever in
> > which we were ever children ...[2]
>
> The psychology of outsiders also makes a difference. Part of the reason Americans have not much noticed the dire plight of their fifth-largest city is that it does not "stir the national imagination."[3] Conversely, there has been far more concern over the state of cities such as New Orleans and Quebec City, whose history and architecture excite the romantic imagination. As Nora Phelps has discussed, the past is in itself a key trigger for romantic notions, and it is no doubt inevitable that cities whose history is particularly visible will engender passionate attachments.[4] And as Stephanie Wright and Carole King have detailed
>
> ---
>
> 1. Paul Goldberger, "Annals of Preservation: Bringing Back Havana," *The New Republic*, January 2005, 54.
> 2. Lourdes Casal, "Definition," trans. Elizabeth Macklin, *The New Yorker*, January 26, 1998, 79.
> 3. Witold Rybczynski, "The Fifth City," review of *A Prayer for the City*, by Buzz Bissinger, *New York Review of Books*, February 5, 1998, 13.
> 4. Nora Phelps, "Pastness and the Foundations of Romanticism," *Romanticism on the Net* 11 (May 2001): par. 14, http://users .ox.ac.uk/~scato385/phelpsmws.htm (accessed March 4, 2009).

in an important case study,[1] almost all French-speaking Quebecers feel their heritage to be bound up with that of Quebec City. (Richard Ford's character Frank Bascombe has suggested that "New Orleans defeats itself" by longing "for a mystery it doesn't have and never will, if it ever did,"[2] but this remains a minority view.)

Georgiana Gibson[3] is also among those who have investigated the interplay between urban psychology and urban reality. Gibson's personal website now includes the first of a set of working models she is developing in an attempt to represent the effects of psychological schemata on the landscape.[4]

1. Stephanie Wright and Carole King, *Quebec: A History*, 2 vols. (Montreal: McGill-Queen's University Press, 2003).

2. Richard Ford, *The Sportswriter*, 2nd ed. (New York: Random House, 1995), 48.

3. Georgiana Gibson, *Cities in the Twentieth Century* (Boston: Beacon, 2004).

4. Gibson, Homepage, accessed March 4, 2014, http://www.geography .by/u.edu/GIBSON/personal.htm.

The bibliography relating to the above text would be as follows:

Bibliography

Casal, Lourdes. "Definition." Translated by Elizabeth Macklin. *The New Yorker*, January 26, 1998, 79.

Ford, Richard. *The Sportswriter*. 2nd ed. New York: Random House, 1995.

Gibson, Georgiana. *Cities in the Twentieth Century*. Boston: Beacon, 2012.

---. Homepage. http://www.geography.by/u.edu/GIBSON/personal .htm (accessed March 4, 2013).

Goldberger, Paul. "Annals of Preservation: Bringing Back Havana." *The New Yorker*, January 26, 2005, 50–62. http://www .findarticles.com.goldberg.p65.jn.htm (accessed March 4, 2009).

Phelps, Nora. "Pastness and the Foundations of Romanticism." *Romanticism on the Net* 11 (May 2001). http://users.ox.ac .uk/~scato385/phelpsmws.htm (accessed March 4, 2009).

Rybczynski, Witold. "The Fifth City." Review of *A Prayer for the City*, by Buzz Bissinger. *New York Review of Books*, February 5, 1998, 12–14.

Wright, Stephanie, and Carole King. *Quebec: A History*. 2 vols. Montreal: McGill-Queen's University Press, 2012.

Among the details to notice in this reference system:

- Where two or more works by the same author are included in the bibliography, they are normally arranged alphabetically by title.

- All major words in titles and subtitles are capitalized.

- Date of publication must appear, where known. Provision of your date of access to electronic materials may be helpful, but is not required.

- Commas are used to separate elements within a footnote, and, in many circumstances, periods separate these same elements in the bibliographic entry.

- When a work has appeared in an edited collection, information on the editors must be included in both the first note and the bibliographic reference.

- First authors' first and last names are reversed in the bibliography.

- Translators must be noted both in footnotes and in the bibliography.

- Publisher as well as city of publication should be given.

- Months and publisher names are not abbreviated.

- The day of the month comes after the name of the month.

- Online references should *not* include the revision date but may include the date on which you visited the site (access date).

⊚ CSE Style

The Council of Science Editors (CSE) style of documentation is commonly used in the natural sciences and the physical sciences. Guidelines are set out in *Scientific Style and Format: The CSE Manual for Authors, Editors, and Publishers,* 7th ed. (2006). The key features of CSE style are outlined below, and short sample essays using the three formats of the CSE documentation system follow at the end of this section.

In-text Citation: Citations in CSE style may follow three alternative formats: a **citation-name** format, a **citation-sequence** format, or a **name-year** format.

In the **citation-name** format, a reference list is compiled and arranged alphabetically by author. Each reference is then assigned a number in sequence, with the first alphabetical entry receiving the number 1, the second the number 2, and so on. Whenever you refer in your text to the reference labelled with number 3, for example, you use either a superscript number 3 (in one variation) or the same number in parentheses (in another).

- The difficulties first encountered in this experiment have been accounted for, according to Zelinsky[3]. However, the variables still have not been sufficiently well controlled for this type of experiment, argues Gibson[1].
- The difficulties first encountered in this experiment have been accounted for, according to Zelinsky (3). However, the variables still have not been sufficiently well controlled for this type of experiment, argues Gibson (1).

In the **citation-sequence** format, superscript numbers (or numbers in parentheses) are inserted after the mention of any source. The first source mentioned receives number 1, the second number 2, and so on.

- The difficulties first encountered in this experiment have been accounted for, according to Zelinsky[1]. However, the variables still have not been sufficiently well controlled for this type of experiment, argues Gibson[2].
- The difficulties first encountered in this experiment have been accounted for, according to Zelinsky (1). However, the varia-

bles still have not been sufficiently well controlled for this type of experiment, argues Gibson (2).

Reuse the number you first assign to a source whenever you refer to it again.

In the **name-year** format, you cite the author name and year of publication in parentheses:

- The key contributions to the study of variables in the 2000s (Gibson et al. 2008; Soames 2009; Zelinsky 2007) have been strongly challenged in recent years.

For two authors, list both, separated by *and* only; for more than two authors, give the first author's surname, followed by *et al.*

List of References: Citations in CSE style must correspond to items in a list of References.

In the **citation-name** format, entries are arranged alphabetically and assigned a number.

1. Gibson DL, Lampman GM, Kriz FR, Taylor DM. Introduction to statistical techniques in the sciences. 2nd ed. New York: MacQuarrie Learning; 2008. 1254 p.
2. Soames G. Variables in large database experiments. J Nat Hist. 2009; 82: 1811–41.
3. Zelinsky KL. The study of variables: an overview. New York: Academic; 2007. 216 p.

In the **citation-sequence** format, the references are listed in the sequence in which they have been cited in the text.

1. Zelinsky KL. The study of variables: an overview. New York: Academic; 2007. 216 p.
2. Gibson DL, Lampman GM, Kriz FR, Taylor DM. Introduction to statistical techniques in the sciences. 2nd ed. New York: MacQuarrie Learning; 2008. 1254 p.
3. Soames G. Variables in large database experiments. J Nat Hist. 2009; 82: 1811–41.

In the **name-year** format, the references are listed alphabetically, and the year of publication is given prominence.

Gibson DL, Lampman GM, Kriz FR, Taylor DM. 2008. Introduction to statistical techniques in the sciences. 2nd ed. New York: MacQuarrie Learning. 1254 p.

Soames G. 2009. Variables in large database experiments. J Nat Hist. 82: 1811–41.

Zelinsky KL. 2007. The study of variables: an overview. New York: Academic. 216 p.

The basic principles of the system are the same regardless of whether one is citing a book, an article in a journal or magazine, a newspaper article, or an electronic document. Here are the main details.

Author names in the References list are all inverted, with initials given instead of full first names. Initials have no periods after them, and no commas separate them from surnames. If a source in the References list has two to ten authors, include all of them; do not include *and* at any point in the list. For more than ten authors, give the names of the first ten, with *and others* following the last one listed.

Capitalize all major words in the titles of periodicals (journals, magazines, and newspapers). For books and articles, capitalize only the first words of the title, as well as any proper nouns. Abbreviate journal titles according to standardized guidelines. You can find the accepted abbreviation of a journal title at the Genamics JournalSeek site online (http://journalseek.net/); enter the journal's full title into the *Search Title* field.

Entries for books include the city of publication, the publisher, and the date of publication.

Entries for periodical articles should include the date: for journal articles, give the year; for magazine articles, give the year and month (abbreviated); for newspaper articles, give the year, the month (abbreviated), and the day.

For online sources, include all of the publication information that you would for print sources. Add *[Internet]* after the book or periodical title. The position of the date of access (e.g., *cited 2013 Feb 13*) varies according to which format you use. Give the URL after *Available from:*, and then, if there is one, the DOI (digital object identifier—a string of numbers, letters, and punctuation, beginning with *10*, usually located on the first or copyright page). Do not put a period at the end of a DOI or a URL (unless it ends with a slash).

O *CSE Style Sample*

The following is written using the citation-sequence format.

Over the centuries scientific study has evolved into several distinct disciplines. Physics, chemistry, and biology were established early on; in the nineteenth and twentieth centuries they were joined by others, such as geology and ecology. Much as the disciplines have their separate spheres, the sphere of each overlaps those of others. This may be most obvious in the case of ecology, which some have claimed to be a discipline that makes a holistic approach to science respectable[1]. In the case of geology, as soon as it became clear in the nineteenth century that the fossil record of geological life would be central to the future of geology, the importance of connecting with the work of biologists became recognized[2]. Nowadays it is not surprising to have geological research conducted jointly by biologists and geologists (e.g., the work of Newton, Trewman, and Elser[3]). And, with the acceptance of "continental drift" theories in the 1960s and 1970s, physics came to be increasingly relied on for input into discussions of such topics as collision tectonics (e.g., Pfiffton, Earn, and Brome[4]).

The growth of the subdiscipline of biochemistry at the point of overlap between biology and chemistry is well known, but many are unaware that the scope of biological physics is almost as broad; Frauenfrommer[5] provides a helpful survey. Today it is not uncommon, indeed, to see research such as the recent study by Corel, Marks, and Hutner[6], or that by Balmberg, Passano, and Proule[7], both of which draw on biology, chemistry, and physics simultaneously.

Interdisciplinary scientific exploration has also been spurred by the growth of connections between the pure and applied sciences such as meteorology, as even a glance in the direction of recent research into such topics as precipitation[8] or cratonising[9] confirms. But to the extent that science is driven by the applied, will it inextricably become more and more driven by commercial concerns? Christopher Haupt-Lehmann[10] thinks not.

The citations above would connect to References as follows:

References

1. Branmer A. Ecology in the twentieth century: a history. New Haven: Yale UP; 2004. 320 p.

2. Lyell C. Principles of geology. London: John Murray; 1830. 588 p.

3. Newton MJ, Trewman NH, Elser S. A new jawless invertebrate from the Middle Devonian. Paleontology [Internet]. 2011 [cited 2013 Mar 5]; 44(1): 43–52. Available from: http://www.onlinejournals .paleontology.44/html doi:10.1136/p.330.6500.442

4. Pfiffton QA, Earn PK, Brome C. Collision tectonics and dynamic modelling. Tectonics 2012; 19(6): 1065–94.

5. Frauenfrommer H. Introduction. In: Frauenfrommer H, Hum G, Glazer RG, editors. Biological physics third international symposium; 1998 Mar 8–9; Santa Fe, NM [Melville, NY]: American Institute of Physics. 386 p.

6. Corel B, Marks VJ, Hutner H. The modelling effect of Elpasolites. Chem Sci 2013; 55(10): 935–38.

7. Balmberg NJ, Passano C, Proule AB. The Lorenz-Fermi-Pasta-Ulam experiment. Physica D [Internet]. 2005 [cited 2013 Mar 7]; 138(1): 1–47. Available from: http://www.elseviere.com/locate/phys

8. Caine JS, Gross SM, Baldwin G. Melting effect as a factor in precipitation-type forecasting. Weather Forecast 2010; 15(6): 700–14.

9. Pendleton AJ. Gawler craton. Reg Geo 2001; 11: 999–1016.

10. Haupt-Lehmann C. Money and science: the latest word. New York Times 2001 Mar 23; Sect. D:22 (col 1).

Among the details to notice in the citation-sequence format of the CSE style:

- The entries in References are listed in the order they first appear in the text.
- Unpunctuated initials rather than first names are used in References.
- The date appears near the end of the reference, before any page reference.
- Only the first words of titles are capitalized (except for proper nouns and the abbreviated titles of journals).
- When a work has appeared in an edited collection the names of the editor(s) as well as the author(s) must appear in the reference.
- Publisher as well as city of publication should be given.
- Months and journal names are generally abbreviated.
- References to electronic publications include the date of access as well as date of publication or latest revision.
- Names of articles appear with no surrounding quotation marks; names of books and journal titles appear with no italics.

Here is the same passage with the CSE name-year format used:

Over the centuries scientific study has evolved into several distinct disciplines. Physics, chemistry, and biology were established early on; in the nineteenth and twentieth centuries, they were joined by others, such as geology and ecology. Much as the disciplines have their separate spheres, the sphere of each overlaps those of others. This may be most obvious in the case of ecology, which some have claimed to be a discipline that makes a holistic approach to science respectable (Branmer 2004). In the case of geology, as soon as it became clear in the nineteenth century that the fossil record of geological life would be central to the future of geology, the importance of connecting with the work of biologists became recognized (Lyell 1830). Nowadays it is not surprising to have geological research conducted jointly by biologists and geologists (e.g., Newton, Trewman, and Elser 2011). And, with the acceptance of "continental drift" theories in the 1960s and 1970s, physics came to be increasingly relied on for input into discussions of such topics as collision tectonics (e.g., Pfiffton, Earn, and Brome 2012).

The growth of the subdiscipline of biochemistry at the point of over-lap between biology and chemistry is well known, but many are unaware that the scope of biological physics is almost as broad; Frauenfrommer (1998) provides a helpful survey. Today it is not uncommon, indeed, to see research such as the recent study by Corel, Marks, and Hutner (2013) or that by Balmberg, Passano, and Proule (2005), both of which draw on biology, chemistry, and physics simultaneously.

Interdisciplinary scientific exploration has also been spurred by the growth of connections between the pure and applied sciences such as meteorology, as even a glance in the direction of recent research into such topics as precipitation (Caine, Gross, and Baldwin 2010) or cratonising (Pendleton 2001) confirms. But to the extent that science is driven by the applied, will it inextricably become more and more driven by commercial concerns? Christopher Haupt-Lehmann (2001) thinks not.

The citations above would connect to References as follows:

References

Balmberg NJ, Passano C, Proule AB. 2005. The Lorenz-Fermi-Pasta-Ulam experiment. Physica D [Internet] [cited 2013 Mar 7]; 138(1): 1–47. Available from: http://www.elseviere.com/locate/phys

Branmer A. 2004. Ecology in the twentieth century: a history. New Haven: Yale UP. 320 p.

Caine JS, Gross SM, Baldwin G. 2010. Melting effect as a factor in precipitation-type forecasting. Weather Forecast. 15(6): 700–14.

Corel B, Marks VJ, Hutner H. 2013. The modelling effect of Elpasolites. Chem Sci. 55(10): 935–38.

Frauenfrommer H. Introduction. In Frauenfrommer H, Hum G, Glazer RG, editors. 1998 Mar 8–9. Biological physics third international symposium. Santa Fe, NM [Melville, NY]: American Institute of Physics. 386 p.

Haupt-Lehmann C. 2001 Mar 23. Money and science: the latest word. New York Times; Sect D:22 (col 1).

Lyell C. 1830. Principles of geology. London: John Murray. 588 p.

Newton MJ, Trewman NH, Elser S. 2011. A new jawless invertebrate from the Middle Devonian. Paleontology [Internet] [cited 2013 Mar 5]; 44(1): 43–52. Available from: http://www.onlinejournals .paleontology.44/html doi:10.1136/p.330.6500.442

Pendleton AJ. 2001. Gawler craton. Reg Geol; 11: 999–1016.

Pfiffton QA, Earn PK, Brome C. 2012. Collision tectonics and dynamic modelling. Tectonics. 19(6): 1065–94.

Among the details to notice in the name-year reference system:

- The entries in References are listed in alphabetical order by author.

- Unpunctuated initials rather than first names are used in References.

- The date appears immediately after the author name(s) at the beginning of the reference.

- The in-text citation comes before the period or comma in the surrounding sentence.

- Only the first words of titles are capitalized (except for proper nouns and the abbreviated titles of journals).

- When a work has appeared in an edited collection the names of the editor(s) as well as the author(s) must appear in the reference.

- The word *and* is used for in-text citations of works with more than one author—but not in the corresponding reference list entry.

- Publisher as well as city of publication should be given.

- Months and journal names are generally abbreviated.

- References to electronic publications include the date of access as well as the date of publication or latest revision.

- Names of articles appear with no surrounding quotation marks; names of books, journals, etc. appear with no italics.

Here is the same passage again, this time using the CSE citation-name format:

Over the centuries scientific study has evolved into several distinct disciplines. Physics, chemistry, and biology were established early on; in the nineteenth and twentieth centuries they were joined by others, such as geology and ecology. Much as the disciplines have their separate spheres, the sphere of each overlaps those of others. This may be most obvious in the case of ecology, which some have claimed to be a discipline that makes a holistic approach to science respectable[2]. In the case of geology, as soon as it became clear in the nineteenth century that the fossil record of geological life would be central to the future of geology, the importance of connecting with the work of biologists became recognized[7]. Nowadays it is not surprising to have geological research conducted jointly by biologists and geologists (e.g., Newton, Trewman, and Elser[8]). And, with the acceptance of "continental drift" theories in the 1960s and 1970s, physics came to be increasingly relied on for input into discussions of such topics as collision tectonics (e.g., Pfiffton, Earn, and Brome[10]).

The growth of the subdiscipline of biochemistry at the point of overlap between biology and chemistry is well known, but many are unaware that the scope of biological physics is almost as broad; Frauenfrommer[5] provides a helpful survey. Today it is not uncommon, indeed, to see research such as the recent study by Corel, Marks, and Hutner[4] or that by Balmberg, Passano, and Proule[1], both of which draw on biology, chemistry, and physics simultaneously.

Interdisciplinary scientific exploration has also been spurred by the growth of connections between the pure and applied sciences such as meteorology, as even a glance in the direction of recent research into such topics as precipitation[3] or cratonising[9] confirms. But to the extent that science is driven by the applied, will it inextricably become more and more driven by commercial concerns? Christopher Haupt-Lehmann[6] thinks not.

The citations above would connect to References as follows:

References

1. Balmberg NJ, Passano C, Proule AB. The Lorenz-Fermi-Pasta-Ulam experiment. Physica D [Internet]. 2005 [cited 2013 Mar 7]; 138(1): 1–47. Available from: http://www.elseviere.com/locate/phys

2. Branmer A. Ecology in the twentieth century: a history. New Haven: Yale UP; 2004. 320 p.

3. Caine, JS, Gross SM, Baldwin G. Melting effect as a factor in precipitation-type forecasting. Weather Forecast 2010; 15(6): 700–14.

4. Corel B, Marks VJ, Hutner H. The modelling effect of Elpasolites. Chem Sci 2013; 55(10): 935–38.

5. Frauenfrommer H. Introduction. Frauenfrommer H, Hum G, Glazer RG, editors. Biological physics third international symposium; 1998 Mar 8–9; Santa Fe, NM [Melville, NY]: American Institute of Physics. 386 p.

6. Haupt-Lehmann C. Money and science: the latest word. New York Times 2001 Mar 23; Sect. D:22 (col 1).

7. Lyell C. Principles of geology. London: John Murray; 1830. 588 p.

8. Newton MJ, Trewman NH, Elser S. A new jawless invertebrate from the Middle Devonian. Paleontology [Internet]. 2011 [cited 2013 Mar 5]; 44(1): 43–52. Available from: http://www.onlinejournals. paleontology.44/html doi:10.1136/p.330.6500.442

9. Pendleton AJ. Gawler cration. Reg Geo 2001; 11: 999–1016.

10. Pfiffton QA, Earn PK, Brome C. Collision tectonics and dynamic modelling. Tectonics 2012; 19(6): 1065–94.

Among the details to notice in the citation-name format of the CSE style:

- The entries in References are numbered and listed in alphabetical order according to author.

- Unpunctuated initials rather than first names are used in References.

- The date appears near the end of the reference, before any page reference.

- Only the first words of titles are capitalized (except for proper nouns and the abbreviated titles of journals).

- When a work has appeared in an edited collection the names of the editor(s) as well as the author(s) must appear in the reference.

- Publisher as well as city of publication should be given.

- Months and journal names are generally abbreviated.

- References to electronic publications include the date of access as well as date of publication or latest revision.

- Names of articles appear with no surrounding quotation marks; names of books and journal titles appear with no italics.

◎ APPENDIX 1: *Correction Key*

Ab	Faulty abbreviation
Adj	Improper use of adjective
Adv	Improper use of adverb
Agr	Faulty agreement
Amb	Ambiguous
Awk	Awkward expression or construction
Cap	Faulty capitalization
D	Faulty diction
Dgl	Dangling construction
Frag	Fragment
lc	Use lowercase
Num	Error in use of numbers
‖	Lack of parallelism
P	Faulty punctuation
Ref	Unclear pronoun reference
Rep	Unnecessary repetition
R-O	Run-on
sp	Error in spelling
SS	Faulty sentence structure
T	Wrong tense of verb
~	Transpose elements
∨	Wrong verb form
Wdy	Wordy
∨	Add apostrophe or single quotation mark
⌣	Close up
⌃	Add comma
ℓ	Delete
∧	Insert
¶	Begin a new paragraph
No ¶	Do not begin a new paragraph
⊙	Add a period
⌣⌣	Double quotation marks
#	Add space

⊚ APPENDIX 2: *Some National Variations*

The following list of variants from some nations in which English is a primary first language does not include slang or idioms.

Australia	Canada
announcer/host/presenter	announcer/host
attic/loft	attic
autumn	fall/autumn
award rate	minimum wage
baby carriage/pram	baby carriage
backyard	backyard/garden
back bacon	back bacon
baked potato/jacket potato	baked potato
bangs (hair)	bangs
bank note	bill
bathers/cozzy	bathing suit/swimsuit
beanie	toque
billion	billion
biscuit	cookie
bitumen road	paved road
block of land	plot of land
bowser	gas pump
brew (tea)	steep
bus/coach (inter-city)	bus
cake (layer)	cake (layer)
can/tin (of food)	can/tin
car (rail passenger)	car
chemist	drugstore/pharmacy
chips (potato)/crisps	chips
Cludo	Clue (board game)
coloured pencil	pencil crayon
concrete block	concrete block
constituency	riding/constituency
(House of Representatives)	(House of Commons)
contraceptive	condom/safe/rubber
cornstarch/corn flour	cornstarch
dam (human-made)	pond/lake/dugout
dessert/pudding	dessert
diaper/nappy	diaper
different from/to	different from
drapes	curtains/drapes
dumpster	dumpster
eggplant/aubergine	eggplant
electrical cord/flex	electrical cord
elevator/lift	elevator
engaged (phone)	busy
eraser	rubber/eraser
escalator/moving staircase	escalator

England	United States
presenter/host	host/announcer
loft	attic
autumn	fall/autumn
minimum wage	minimum wage
pram	baby carriage
back garden	backyard
back bacon	Canadian bacon
jacket potato	baked potato
fringe	bangs
bank note	bill
swimming costume	swimsuit
woolly hat	wool hat
thousand million	billion
biscuit	cookie
metalled road	paved road
plot of land	plot of land
petrol pump	gas pump
brew	steep
coach	bus
gateau	cake (layer)
tin	can
carriage	car
chemist	drugstore
crisps	chips
Cludo	Clue
pencil crayon	colored pencil
breeze block/concrete block	concrete block
constituency	district
(House of Commons)	(House of Representatives)
condom/rubber	condom/safe
corn flour	cornstarch
pond/lake	pond/lake
sweet/pudding	dessert
nappy	diaper
different from/to	different from/than
curtains	drapes/curtains
rubbish skip	dumpster
aubergine	eggplant
flex	electrical cord
lift	elevator
engaged	busy
eraser	rubber
moving staircase	escalator

Australia	Canada
extension cord/lead	extension cord
fire plug	fire hydrant
first-year student	first-year student
fish fingers	fish sticks
fizzy drink	soft drink/pop
flashlight/torch	flashlight
frankfurt	hotdog/wiener
freeway/motorway	expressway/freeway
gas/petrol (for a car)	gas
general store	grocery store
generator/dynamo	generator
get a rise (in pay)	get a raise
give (someone) a bell	a call/ring
globe (light)	bulb
grazier	farmer
green beans	green beans
gum boots	rubber boots
half-mast (flag)	half-mast
hamburger (prepared)/mince	hamburger/ground beef
hang up/ring off	hang up
hood/bonnet (of a car)	hood
hot-water service	hot water heater
house for let	house for rent
house for sale	house for sale
icing (cake)	icing
in the post	in the mail/by post
intersection	intersection
invigilate (exam)	invigilate
kerosene/paraffin	kerosene
latex paint/emulsion	latex paint
lima beans/broad beans	lima beans
locked/shut tight	locked/shut tight
lollies	candies
match/game	game
Mother's Day	Mother's Day
(Father's Day is the same in all cases)	
moving company	movers
muffler/silencer (of a car)	muffler
nature strip	shoulder
odometer/milometer	odometer
outbuildings (at a farm)	outbuildings
outside toilet	outhouse
oval/sports field	sports field
pacifier	pacifier/soother
paddock	field
parka	rain jacket/windbreaker/raincoat/parka
pie/flan	pie
post box	post box/mailbox
prawns	shrimps

England	United States
lead	extension cord
fire hydrant	fire hydrant
first-year student	freshman
fish fingers	fish sticks
fizzy drink	soda
torch	flashlight
frankfurter	frank/wiener/hotdog
dual carriageway/motorway	freeway/thruway
petrol	gas
grocer	grocery store
dynamo	generator
get a rise	get a raise
a ring	a call
bulb	bulb
farmer	farmer
runner beans	green beans
wellingtons	rubber boots/rainboots
half-mast	half-staff
beefburger/mince	hamburger
ring off	hang up
bonnet	hood
immersion heater	hot water heater
house for let	house for rent
house under offer	house for sale
frosting	icing
in the post/by the post	in the mail/by mail
junction	intersection
proctor	invigilate
paraffin	kerosene
emulsion paint	latex paint
broad beans	lima beans
made fast/locked	locked/shut tight
sweets	candies
fixture/match	game
Mothering Sunday	Mother's Day
removals	van line
silencer	muffler
verge	shoulder
milometer/trip meter	odometer
outhouses	outbuildings
outdoor privy	outhouse
pitch/sports field	sports field
dummy	pacifier/soother
field	field
anorak/mac	windbreaker/rainjacket
flan	pie
pillar box	mailbox
prawns	shrimps

Australia	Canada
prospectus (university)	calendar
public holiday	public holiday
car hire/rental	car rental
ring off (phone)	hang up
rowboat	rowboat
rubbish tin	wastebasket/garbage can
rubbish tip/tip	garbage dump
runners	track shoes/runners/sneakers
sailboat/sailing boat	sailboat
sand shoes	running shoes/canvas shoes
scrapyard/car breaker	scrapyard (car)
second floor	second floor
semi-(trailer)	semi-/transport trailer
(road train—more than one trailer)	
shallots	green onions/spring onions/scallions
skirting board	baseboard
skivvy	turtleneck
sleepers (railway)	ties
standings (sports)	standings
station (sheep or cattle)	ranch/farm
sticky tape	scotch tape
stockyard	stockyard
stretcher	cot
stroller	stroller
study/revise (for a test)	study
subway/underground	subway
sun bake	sunbathe
surgery	doctor's office
sweater/jumper	sweater
take away (food)	take-out
taxi-truck	rent-a-truck
traffic circle	traffic circle
trailer/caravan	trailer/camper
trousers	pants/trousers/slacks
truck/lorry	truck
ute (utility vehicle)	pick-up truck
trucks (railway)	freight cars
trunk/boot (of a car)	trunk
turf/sods	turf
underground walkway	underground walkway
vacuum/hoover	vacuum
vest	vest/waistcoat
wait on	wait for
wake up (someone else)	wake up
washcloth/flannel	washcloth
washing-up liquid	dish detergent
winery	vineyard
woolgrower	sheepfarmer

England	United States
prospectus	catalog
bank holiday	public holiday
car hire	car rental
ring off	hang up
rowing boat	rowboat
wastepaper basket	wastebasket
rubbish tip/refuse tip/tip	garbage dump
trainers	track shoes
sailing boat	sailboat
plimsolls	sneakers/tennis shoes
car breaker	scrapyard
third floor	second floor
articulated lorry	eighteen-wheeler
spring onions	green onions
skirting board	baseboard
polo-neck top	turtleneck shirt
sleepers	ties
tables	standings
farm	ranch
sellotape	scotch tape
cattle pen	stockyard
camp bed	cot
push chair/pusher	stroller
revise (for a test)	study
underground/tube	subway
sunbathe	sunbathe
surgery	doctor's office
jumper	sweater
take away	take out
van hire service	rent-a-truck
roundabout	traffic circle
caravan	trailer
trousers	slacks/pants
lorry	truck
pick-up	truck
trucks	freight cars
boot	trunk
sods	turf
subway/underpass	underground walkway
hoover	vacuum
waistcoat	vest
wait for	wait for
knock up/wake up	wake up
flannel	washcloth
washing-up liquid	dish detergent
vineyard	vineyard
sheepfarmer	sheepfarmer

◎ APPENDIX 3: *Essay Checklist*

_____ Does this piece of writing have a clear purpose? Have I made that purpose clear to the reader?

_____ What audience is this written for? Is the tone suited to the intended audience?

_____ Of what am I trying to persuade my audience? Is this made completely clear near the beginning (whether in a formal thesis statement or otherwise)? Is it again made clear near the conclusion?

_____ Does the essay follow a clear path? Are there too many digressions? Is there extraneous material that should be cut, or transferred out of the body of the text and into a note?

_____ Is the structure of the argument signalled by the paragraphing? Does the paragraph remain the unit of composition throughout?

_____ Does the point I am making remain clear in every paragraph? In every sentence?

_____ Is there some variety in sentence structure? Have I avoided awkward sentence constructions? And run-on sentences?

_____ Are most verbs in the active voice?

_____ Do the verbs always agree with the subjects?

_____ Do I use concrete and specific language wherever possible?

_____ Do I avoid excessive use of jargon or unnecessarily obscure language?

_____ Am I careful in my use of qualifiers, avoiding statements that are too bald or extreme, but not qualifying all the strength or interest out of my argument?

_____ Is my writing ever wordy? Where could I still trim? Did I revise (from hard copy) and rewrite the essay thoroughly? Did I proofread after I revised?

_____ Have I checked the punctuation carefully throughout?

_____ Have I proofread as well as used a computer spell-check?

_____ Have I used the correct system of documentation? Do the references follow this system consistently throughout?

_____ Have I given appropriate acknowledgement to all the sources I used? Is there any point at which I might have been guilty of plagiarism by paraphrasing without acknowledgement?

_____ Does the format (spacing, margins, etc.) follow specifications?

_____ Have I answered all the above questions honestly?

⊚ PERMISSIONS ACKNOWLEDGEMENTS

◎ INDEX

Entries in **bold** are to words, not topics.

From the Publisher

A name never says it all, but the word "Broadview" expresses a good deal of
the philosophy behind our company. We are open to a broad range of academic
approaches and political viewpoints. We pay attention to the broad impact book
publishing and book printing has in the wider world; we began using
recycled stock more than a decade ago, and for some years now we have used
100% recycled paper for most titles. Our publishing program is
internationally oriented and broad-ranging. Our individual titles often
appeal to a broad readership too; many are of interest as much
to general readers as to academics and students.

Founded in 1985, Broadview remains a fully independent company owned by
its shareholders—not an imprint or subsidiary of a larger multinational.

For the most accurate information on our books (including information on
pricing, editions, and formats) please visit our website at www.broadviewpress.
com. Our print books and ebooks are also available for sale on our site.

broadview press
www.broadviewpress.com

MIX
Paper from
responsible sources
FSC® C103567

The interior of this book is printed on 30% recycled paper.

PERMANENT

BIO GAS
ENERGY

30%